THE ENTRY
OF THE SLAVS INTO
CHRISTENDOM

AN INTRODUCTION
TO THE MEDIEVAL HISTORY
OF THE SLAVS

The Entry
of the Slavs into
Christendom

AN INTRODUCTION
TO THE MEDIEVAL HISTORY
OF THE SLAVS

A. P. VLASTO

Lecturer in Slavonic Studies in the
University of Cambridge

CAMBRIDGE
At the University Press
1970

Published by the Syndics of the Cambridge University Press
Bentley House, 200 Euston Road, London N.W.1
American Branch: 32 East 57th Street, New York, N.Y.10022

© Cambridge University Press 1970

Library of Congress Catalogue Card Number: 70-98699

Standard Book Number: 521 07459 2

Printed in Great Britain
at the University Printing House, Cambridge
(Brooke Crutchley, University Printer)

The saints who from generation to generation
follow by the practice of God's commandments
in the steps of those saints who went before...
make as it were a golden chain, each of them
being one link, each joined to the preceding in
faith, works and love, so as to form in the One
God a single line which cannot easily be broken.

—St Symeon the New Theologian
(κεφάλαια πρακτικὰ καὶ θεολογικά, ρ̄)

CONTENTS

PREFACE

The survey of early Slav history which I have attempted in this book covers roughly the period A.D. 500–1200. It is primarily a narrative describing how the various Slav peoples entered Christendom, moved by the currents reaching each of them from outside and guided by the great men who most furthered the transformation.

No one embarking on such a narrative could have the temerity to assert with Ranke's crude optimism that he would tell the story *wie es eigentlich gewesen*. This would be impossible even if our sources were many times more voluminous and more evenly distributed than they are. There are 'probablys' and 'possiblys' at every turn; there should be more. I have tried to avoid being tedious without being unscrupulous. The reader must always bear in mind that many passages are little better than construction laced with surmise. The few books in English which treat this period of Slav history often impart a spurious air of precision.

In a general survey of this kind discussion of every variant hypothesis at every step is ruled out in advance, but I hold it necessary to make clear to the reader what is relatively certain and what is not, and to give some account of rival theories at points of special importance. Even this required strict selection. Some parts of the story are better documented, some of wider historical interest, some of more particular interest to me personally. Therefore the degree of detail will be found to vary considerably, but not, I trust, to the detriment of the story as a whole.

In this connection I have taken the risk, at a few especially important points, of interrupting the narrative in order to present in some detail the documentary evidence from which the pages which follow have to be pieced together. These portions are printed in smaller type and may easily be omitted by those who have not the need or the leisure to enter into the minutiae of the historical sources.

Many things which we should particularly like to know are ignored in contemporary writings. This is of course the common false perspective of history. Men are not prone to dissect the mechanism of their life as long as it is working well nor the axioms of their thought as long as they are deemed secure. We cannot therefore expect the many planes of intellectual and practical life to receive equal illumination at all times and in all places. A historian must build on what is given, sometimes on one plane, sometimes on another. Moreover I have had to ignore certain fields with which I am not properly equipped to deal and have intruded into others, more angelically than foolishly, where it could not be avoided.

I regret the lack of figures in the text, which would in particular have made some passages involving architectural developments easier to follow. There are instead full references to the most accessible works on this subject.

NOTES

1. One uniform system of transliteration for all Slav personal and place names is neither possible nor desirable. For those Slav Languages which use the Latin alphabet (Czech, Polish) the standard modern spelling is normally used (a few exceptions in the case of Czech are specially noted). Serbian names, normally in Cyrillic, are given according to their equivalent transcription in the Croat form of the Latin alphabet, the languages themselves being no more than regional variants of 'Serbo-Croat'. The languages which use forms of the Cyrillic alphabet (see pp. 38 ff.)—Russian, Bulgarian, Old Church Slavonic (OCS)—appear in Latin transcription, with the exception of occasional Russian words and phrases. The conventions for OCS and Old Russian are generally the same as for Czech or Croat, with the addition of ĭ, ŭ for the two *jers* or ultra-short vowels (Cyrillic ь, ъ). In Russian and Bulgarian ж, х, ц, ч, ш are rendered *zh*, *h*,* *ts*, *ch*, *sh*. Bulgarian ъ appears as ŭ. In Russian *y* represents the vowel ы only and *ë* is to be read *yo*; final -ый, -ий are simplified to -*y*, -*i*. Further, the palatalisation of a consonant is not always noted: Russian scholars will supply it where it would appear fussy in transcription; those who are not will lose very little. Palatalisations are also built into Polish spelling; this is not the place to explain their acoustic effect. Finally, the sign *j* invariably represents the same sound in all transcriptions, viz. the English consonantal *y* approximately, and the sign *ě* should be read as a long open *e*. The table below gives the equivalents for the more troublesome sounds.

In general I have retained Greek quotations in the Greek alphabet. Names in the text are transcribed in a form rather nearer to the actual Byzantine pronunciation than is usual: I do not see any good reason for retaining the fiction that Greek words look better in Latin dress.

* *Kh* is retained in personal names in the bibliography since this corresponds to the transcription in most catalogues.

Czech, Serbo-Croat, Old Russian and OCS	Polish	Russian and Bulgarian
c	*c*	*ts*
č	*cz*	*ch* ($\pm$ as in *church*)
h (Czech *ch*)	*ch*	*h*
j	*j*	*j* ($\pm$ as in *yes*)
š	*sz*	*sh*
ž (Czech *ř* is also close to this)	*ż* (also *rz*)	*zh* ($\pm$ as in *measure*)

I have taken the liberty of indicating the position of the stress on many names, on their first appearance, since English speech-habits are liable to introduce an unnecessary deformation. This is not necessary in Czech and Polish: in Czech the stress is always on the initial syllable, in Polish always on the penultimate. At the risk of offending philologists I have used the usual symbol of stress (') on Serbo-Croat names also, despite the fact that this has a more restricted significance in an exact transcription of that language (namely stress plus long rising tone); but this is irrelevant for the present purpose. No indication is necessary in a disyllable since final syllables cannot take stress.

Place names which have a generally accepted English form are so given, e.g. Cracow, Prague (not Kraków, Praha). If a place name has widely differing forms in different languages, I give both, at least on its first appearance, since maps are not always fully informative. This is particularly common in Dalmatia, e.g. Serbo-Croat *Zadar* but Italian *Zara*, etc. Further, to obviate confusion between very similar Slav forms certain names are retained in a medieval Latin shape, e.g. Boleslas for Czech Boleslav (Polish Bolesław).

2. Many of the dates given must be treated as unreliable: the evidence of the sources is often insufficient or contradictory. Only at certain important points is it appropriate—since sequence of events bears on our interpretation of them—to enter into a discussion of the chronology. Otherwise I have adopted what seems in the present state of our knowledge to be the most probable date or alluded in a note to alternative opinions.

Throughout the period covered by the narrative several concurrent systems of time-reckoning were in use, especially in the East. It must suffice to remind the reader that the 'Constantinopolitan' system reckoned from the Creation of the World in 5508 B.C., but the 'New Alexandrian' or 'Antiochene'—the more ancient and apparently the more common till the tenth century—from 5500 B.C.* The latter was used by several prominent Byzantine historians. The widespread practice of excerpting led to portions of the one chronology becoming embedded in the other. The reckoning from the Birth of Christ, which early became general in Western Europe, was rare or unknown in Orthodox lands.

In the Byzantine Empire the Constantinopolitan New Year started on 1 September (Russian сентябрский год). The old Roman civil year began, as ours still does, on 1 January. But years starting in March were widely current; rarely on 1 March, usually (as in the Alexandrian system) on the Feast of the Annunciation or Lady Day, 25 March (Latin *annus ab annuntiatione*; Russian благовещенский год)—hence called the Marian Year. Moreover there were two variants of this—one beginning some six months *later* (мартовский год) and one beginning some six months *earlier* (ультрамартовский год) than the corresponding September year. In early Russian annals the Marian year appears to have been frequently coupled with the Constantinopolitan era. It will be readily seen that, other uncertainties apart, many dates will be subject to an error of ± 1 if the exact month of the event is not ascertainable from other circumstantial evidence.†

Numerical errors have crept into Slav texts as a result of transcription from the Glagolitic into the Cyrillic alphabet. The correction is usually but not invariably obvious. For further details see pp. 38–9 and A. Vaillant, *Manuel du vieux slave*, tome 1, pp. 23–4.

3. The superior arabic *figures* in the text refer to the main body of notes (quotations, references to authorities, and the like), which will be found together towards the end of the book, pp. 320–406. The superior *letters* in the text refer to notes appearing at the foot of the page, and are reserved for cross-references and certain biographical, geographical and linguistic information which, I believe, the reader will find more convenient to have directly under his eye.

Selwyn College, Cambridge   A.P.V.
September 1969

* The 'Old Alexandrian' reckoning (not needed here) was from 5493 B.C., so that the 'New' is the mean between this and the 'Constantinopolitan'.

† Consult: E. I. Kamentseva, Русская хронология (Moscow, 1960); N. G. Berezhkov, Хронология русского летописания (Moscow, 1963).

INTRODUCTION

'Beginnings', wrote Teilhard de Chardin, 'have an irritating but essential fragility.'[1] Only rarely can we put our finger on that precise moment and place which marks a fundamental change, whether material or spiritual. The very nature of human tradition is unfavourable to such precision. Long after the event those who look back may attempt to recover and put on record the point which separates the old from the new. But their record is bound to be a gross approximation. In tracing in the following pages such a momentous new departure among the various Slav peoples we shall be obliged to admit again and again that the true beginning is beyond our ken.

No sooner did the recurrent disasters which overtook the Roman Empire at the hands of migrating Germanic peoples seem to be coming to an end than it was realised that other peoples were ready and waiting to follow in their wake. The Slavs, from their homelands north of the Carpathian chain, had been expanding not only eastwards and westwards across the North European plain but also southwards, following the lowlands of the Black Sea coast and filtering through the mountain chain into the Central European basin. The Danube was still accounted the frontier of the civilised world. In the fifth century A.D. the main power beyond that frontier had been the Huns. Attila held sway over many Germanic tribes in the Danube basin and no doubt over some Slavs also, but the latter did not yet stand out prominently.[2] Only after his death in 453 and the rapid decline of Hunnish power did the Slavs become a dominant factor in Byzantine frontier affairs under their own names. Theoderic and his Goths moved out of the Balkans into Italy in 488; by the year 500 Slavs were already massed on the left bank of the lower Danube. Their most widespread ethnic designation—Slověne—was taken over into both Greek and Latin, more or less contemporaneously, on the Danube frontier.[3]

In the West the stable frontier lay along the Rhine. But the right bank was still solidly Germanic; there was consequently no direct Slav pressure on the settled lands until the Frankish world had itself found its feet and integrated these remaining barbarian cousins into their own adopted civilisation.

It will be appropriate, therefore, to consider first the Byzantine

I

reaction to direct Slav pressure, then the history of the Slavs on the fringes of the Germanic world and finally to return to examine the later history of the Balkans and of the Slavs who lived furthest east in Russia.

1

THE SLAVS IN THE
BYZANTINE EMPIRE[1]

The Slav invasion and settlement of the Balkans can be divided into three
phases. During the first, covering the first half of the sixth century, the
Slavs were still based north of the Danube but kept up a constant
pressure of raids across the river, which yielded them plunder, slaves,
and bribes to remove themselves. They were behaving much as other
barbarian peoples before them and the Byzantine authorities reacted
predictably. There were as yet few attempts to make permanent lodge-
ments south of the Danube. The events of this half-century are treated
in Prokopios's *Gothic War*.[2] A few landmarks must suffice here. The
wide-ranging movements of the Getae in the North Balkans from 517
may have brought Slavs in as contingents in their armies. Prokopios
alludes to a large-scale Slav raid on Thrace about 527.[3] In the 530s there
were further substantial incursions and in the 540s massive raids, which
at one moment menaced Constantinople itself. In 547–8 a great offensive
reached the Adriatic coast and devastated Dyrrachium (Durazzo). In the
550s the Imperial City was again menaced; this time the Slavs were
strengthened by Kutrigur Turks.

As usual, the Empire made some attempt to tame the barbarians by
attracting them as mercenary contingents into its armies and employing
them on other war fronts: as early as 536–7 we find a record of such
Slav mercenaries fighting against the Ostrogoths in Italy.[4] This was an
important method of rapid if superficial civilisation,[a] and though the
barbarian military units might remain pagan as long as they preserved
their unity, they saw the civilised world and gained some inkling of
Christianity, while some of their officers were soon converted as a
necessary step in their careers. Germanic barbarians had done exactly
the same.

Such acts of ambitious individuals had naturally no effect on the main
mass of the Slavs still outside the Empire. The first steps towards general

[a] It is probable that some of the earliest Latin loanwords in Slav are due to these
mercenaries since Latin was the language of the Byzantine army down to and including
Justinian's time. *Cěsarǐ* is an obvious example, perhaps also such military words as
cęta (< *quinta, *centa=target) and *dǔska* (< discus). The usually suggested Gothic
intermediate step is not necessary.

I-2

conversion may only be expected to follow a favourable political and military situation when the barbarians realise that the adoption of the civilised way of life is the best way to hold on to and expand the advantages which they have already wrested from their opponents; and the regulator of civilised life, as of their own, is religion.

The earliest records of such Slav officers accepted into Byzantine military service come at the beginning of the second phase, which covers the second half of the sixth century. By then permanent settlements south of the Danube had been made and enough was known by the Slavs about the Empire to make the capture of a great port such as Thessaloniki (Saloniki) a definite, if as yet remote, aim. The historian Agathias records three undoubtedly Slav names of officers employed, presumably with their own contingents, on the Persian front: Vsegord, Svarun and Dobrojezda.[5] This was in 555. It is evident that Dobrojezda's son, Leontios, was a Christian.[6] They were Slavs from the north-west shores of the Black Sea, known to the Greeks as *Antai*.[a]

Before the death of Justinian in 565 a new factor was added. The Avars, incited by the Byzantine government to attack the Slavs in the rear, established themselves in their turn in the former Hunnic lands. They were a Turkic people, more warlike than the Slavs.[b] Their military might was based, as always among nomads, on cavalry and they succeeded in imposing their rule, at least transitorily, on many of the more peaceable Slavs. Under their leadership, and notably from the reign of Justin II (565–78) under their great military commander Bajan, the severity of the invasions increased. Sometimes the Slav penetrations were attempts to escape the clutches of the Avars, sometimes Slavs formed the mass of troops under Avar command. A large-scale invasion of Greece led by a Slav[7] in 577/8 seems to have been of the former kind. The Byzantine provinces immediately south of the Danube must be assumed permanently lost by about this time, their sees abandoned and their population subject to the new pagan overlords. Justinian, who prided himself on his alliance with the Antes against other Slavs by adopting the by-name *Antikos*, did his best to protect Macedonia, the centre of Balkan communications, by strong new defences along the

[a] To what extent the Antai ("Ἄνται) or Antes were predominantly Slav or (more probably) mixed with other peoples such as Iranians cannot be entered into here. The name *Antai* is attested in Byzantine use from *c.* 550 to *c.* 630, after which it disappears, evidently with the loose federation which it denoted.

[b] The Avars who settled in Europe probably had no right to that name. There may have been a Mongol element in their blood but their language was apparently Altaic. See pp. 18–20.

4

Danube, but in vain; he had to move the civil capital of Illyricum back from Sirmium in Pannonia to Saloniki. Sirmium was destroyed by the Avars in 582. It could be seen in retrospect that to allow the militaristic and less adaptable Avars to manipulate the Slavs, who were potentially sedentary settlers and valuable as such, was an irreparable mistake. Thereby the Slavs' adoption of Orthodox civilisation was certainly delayed.

The last two decades of the sixth century show a rapid decline in Byzantine resistance. On the one hand the barbarian pressure continued to increase, especially as the Avars were now always enemies. On the other, the Empire was increasingly endangered from the 580s by the recrudescence of Persian power. Constantinople's position at the hub of communications, equally accessible from all points of the compass, though an overwhelming economic advantage, was a recurrent military weakness. The heart of the Byzantine Empire—Asia Minor—had to be defended at all costs from eastern enemies. But equally the approaches to the capital and to Saloniki, the second city of the Empire, from the north and west had to be guarded. The Slavs owe their permanent lodgement in the Balkans at least partly to the fatal division of Byzantine power between two fronts. By the 580s they reached the point of being able to lay siege to the city of Saloniki, sometimes with Avar help. The most serious of many such attempts to take the city came in the early seventh century: a siege in 612 is recorded in an inscription in the church of St Demetrios, the patron saint of the city; and others followed in 614–16 and about 618. The *Miracles of St Demetrios* show that by this time the most favourably placed Slavs had already adopted much of the Byzantine art of war.[8] Slavs are reported in the Peloponnese in the 580s. It is evident that by 600 all the country north of Saloniki was virtually lost to the Empire and that the penetration of peninsular Greece followed at once.

The third phase therefore runs from the beginning of the seventh century. The Emperor Maurice's last half-hearted attempt at maintaining the Danube as the frontier of the Empire was abandoned by his successor Phokas. Slav settlement reached its peak in the North Balkans.[9] Heraklios had to abandon Greece in order to save Asia Minor from the Persians; the major part of his Balkan troops had been withdrawn in 602/3 and transferred to the Eastern Front. In 617 a combined Avar and Slav attack on the Imperial City was beaten off; in August 626 it was threatened by Persians from the one side and Slavs from the other.

5

Further Slav attempts to reduce Saloniki continued to be made till the end of the seventh century but in the main it was now a question of how much territory the Slavs could occupy permanently in face of only local and inferior Byzantine resistance. Peninsular Greece and the Peloponnese gradually filled up. The islands were not beyond Slav attention: a large expedition to Crete took place in 623. This implies considerable occupation of the Peloponnese already.

Justinian's proud new metropolitan see, Justiniana Prima, which he had erected at his alleged birthplace,[a] can scarcely have continued to exist except in shreds and patches. To create it he had detached from the Vicariate of Saloniki all the lands to the north and west of the new town, from the Sirmium district of Pannonia to the South Dalmatian province of Prevalitana. It is thought that the towns of Justiniana Prima, Ulpiana (modern Lipljan) and Nissa (Niš) must have been abandoned by the end of Heraklios's reign.[10] They fell to ruin since the Slavs were not yet interested in urban life. Like the Germanic peoples faced with Roman towns, they saw them as 'walled tombs'. Justiniana Prima is last mentioned in 602.

Once again the Byzantine Empire received an unexpected and dangerous blow. No sooner had Heraklios got the better of the Persians than the armies of Islam suddenly erupted out of the Arabian peninsula. The Persian Empire was rapidly overwhelmed. Syria was lost to the Byzantine Empire first (from 634); attacks on Asia Minor began in 647, on Cyprus in 649. By the 660s Constans II despaired even of defending the capital. But control of the sea just tipped the scales in Byzantine favour, as neither the Slavs nor the bedouin Arabs were maritime peoples, though the latter early appreciated the value of Syrian and Egyptian skill at sea. The first great Arab blockade of Constantinople took place in 674–8; the Slavs immediately made further ineffectual attacks on Saloniki. The last Arab attempt to win the Imperial City came in 717–18. From that date the Byzantine Empire regained confidence that it could hold its own against Islam and a certain stability in the East was slowly re-established.[b]

Small wonder that little attention could be given to Greece in the

---

[a] It is now identified with the ruins at Caričin Grad, some 6 km. from Lebane (S.W. of Leskovac in Serbian Macedonia).

[b] So also in the West. After the Moslem conquest of the Iberian peninsula from 711, Charles Martel's victory over the Saracens in France in 732 marks the limit of their attempts at expansion into Western Europe. The Carolingians shortly afterwards went over to the counter-attack but the Byzantine Empire's offensive against Islam scarcely got under way before the second half of the tenth century.

seventh century. Byzantine historians provide little information on the extent and organisation of the new Slav areas of settlement, or σκλαβηνίαι.[11] Throughout the seventh and eighth centuries effective Byzantine rule, secular and ecclesiastical, scarcely reached beyond the seaports to which the Greeks tenaciously clung, except in a limited part of Central Greece. Saloniki, Patras, Nauplia, Monemvasía, Corinth (with the great fortress of Acrocorinth) remained Greek; the interior was left to the barbarians. As farmers the Slavs wanted land but they were often prepared to use land which had been less attractive to the resident population—marsh and forest.[a] The fact that the Byzantine writ hardly ran outside the maritime towns does not imply that the interior of Greece was emptied of Greeks. In the Peloponnese it is probable that the Greek peasant population still outnumbered the infiltrating Slavs at least till the middle of the eighth century. When the Emperor Constantine Porphyrogennetos wrote, in the middle of the tenth century, that all Greece 'became Slav and was lost to civilisation', he was not thinking of proportions of blood.[12]

Here and there Byzantine institutions survived even in the interior of the Balkans. It is known for example that the garrison and population of Serdica (modern Sofia) held out for a long time in the middle of a Slav sea—possibly until its capture by the Bulgarians in 809—but the town gradually dwindled till it was no more than a village round the church of the Holy Wisdom; hence the modern name. Even such small Greek centres may have exerted an influence on the surrounding Slavs quite out of proportion to their size; but the silence of history does not allow us to follow the process.

The social organisation of the Slavs during the centuries of immigration appears to have been still largely tribal *sensu lato*. To them would still apply Prokopios's term δημοκρατία, implying the communal responsibility vested in the tribal council or *veche*. But the sixth and seventh centuries must have given rise here and there to a more powerful military aristocracy. Fluctuating supra-tribal combinations came into temporary being when a capable war-leader could impose himself. Thus five tribes concerted in the siege of Saloniki in 614–16 under a common

---

[a] Some of these bad lands must in fact have been created by the ravages of the Slavs themselves and their Avar partners. Pillage and enslavement on top of sheer destruction produced at least in parts of the Balkans those depopulated wastes such as are frequently bewailed in Western sources after the passage of various Germanic peoples, especially in the fifth century (*loca invia, solitudines*). The Vandals were among the worst devastators.

commander. But there is little sign that the process of settlement led to larger units stable enough to become a new stage in social development. The 'great family', no doubt similar to the institution preserved almost to our own times in the *zádruga* of Serbia and Montenegro, was the social unit. This system allowed the Slavs to intermingle with existing populations, taking advantage of less favourable parcels of land.[13] Thus in contradistinction to many other areas colonised by Slavs, no strong political organisations arose in Greece such as could in due course become foci of resistance to hellenization.

The density of Slav settlements in Greece was also far from even; study of Slav place names suggests that the western parts both of peninsular Greece and of the Peloponnese received or retained a denser Slav population than the eastern. Over 500 Slav place names are still identifiable in the area Epirus–Acarnania–Aetolia, only some 300 in the larger area Thessaly–Attica. Similarly in the Peloponnese there are about three times as many Slav place names in the western as in the eastern half (Argolis, Laconia). As is to be expected, the absolute figure for Macedonia is very high indeed.[14]

Byzantine hold on Greece reached its lowest ebb about the year 700. The Empire became resigned to the disaster. Its own political instability and the armies and fleets of Islam were capable of destroying it; the Slavs did not seem such a formidable menace. They were on a par with the Goths and might in fact, if a little tamed, provide that extra military manpower as mercenaries which was so urgently needed. As with the Goths, their loyalty would no doubt be precarious, but it was better than nothing. The Byzantine government was thus now quite glad to accept Slav colonisation of certain areas where they might act as buffers against further barbarian incursions. Moreover it early practised deliberate transportation of Slavs to depopulated regions where they could be peacefully hellenized and drawn on for manpower—for instance the transfer of considerable numbers under their own chiefs to Bithynia in 658 and 688/9. Perhaps Constantinople had similar hopes of the Bulgars who were admitted into the Dobrudja in about 679 and soon dominated all the Slavs of that region.[a] But in the event Bulgar rule over Slavs was to be a greater menace to the Byzantine Empire than that of the Avars.

Slav Greece may be said to cover the period 600–860.[15] It is difficult to say what the Byzantine Empire considered its effective northern frontier to be in the seventh–eighth centuries. Macedonia was certainly

<hr />

[a] See p. 155.

8

lost. Kastoria (in present-day Greek Macedonia) apparently remained in Byzantine hands but probably little to the north of it. Thrace up to the Balkan range had to be held at all costs.

Full of Slavs though Greece might be Constantinople never considered it irretrievably lost. So gradual was the process of recovery that few events were recorded before the end of the eighth century. The creation of a *Theme* is the sign of the effective reimposition of Byzantine administration. The *Theme* of Thrace, on the doorstep of the City, was organised as early as the reign of Justinian II (658–95), soon after the settlement of the Bulgar horde, that of Macedonia (Western Thrace, centred on Adrianople) not till the end of the eighth century, following the successful pacificatory campaigns of Stavrakios (783) under Empress Irene.[16] A *Theme* of Saloniki became practicable not later than 836.

The Slavs of northern Greece were, for strategic and economic reasons, of more immediate concern: any spread of Bulgarian power had to be countered. The campaign of 783 repeated the work of Constantine V in 758, who also resettled in Bithynia a large number of Slavs restive under Bulgarian aggression. The policy of protecting and encouraging the loyalty of the Slav peasantry can be observed also in some clauses of the *Farmers' Law* (Νόμος γεωργικός) which probably took form as early as the end of the seventh century.[17] But peace was always precarious. The habit of raiding, two centuries old, was always liable to break out afresh: a typical case is noted in 768 when Constantine V had to ransom Christian prisoners taken by the Slavs on various North Aegean islands.[18]

Yet in an empire where hellenization counted far above racial origin an Imperial career was now open to any enterprising Slav. By the eighth century—and patently in the ninth—this process must have gone far. It is even asserted that the insignificant Iconoclast Patriarch Niketas (*fungebatur* 766–80) was a Slav, but the details of his career are unknown.[a] Thomas, a Slav of Asia Minor, became a prominent officer under the Emperor Leo (813–20). He attempted to avenge the murder of his patron by the usurping Michael II by a general revolt in which he himself was acclaimed as rival emperor.[19] He is said to have drawn support from the as yet relatively uncivilised Slavs of the Peloponnese. The seriousness of the revolt was indirectly responsible for the occupation of undefended Crete by the Moslems in 827.

[a] It is quite plausible to accept a Slav derivation for the name of the prominent Byzantine family Rangavis ('Ραγκαβῆς), which provided an emperor in Michael (*regnabat* 811–13), though it is more probably Armenian.

The Peloponnese was still largely outside Imperial control. In about 807 a dangerous Slav attack on the city of Patras was heavily defeated[20]— particularly dangerous in that Saracen ships were prepared to combine with the Slav land army in this enterprise. The Byzantine authorities were very sensitive to the danger of such an alliance. The 'battle of Patras' was probably decisive in making the Peloponnese thenceforward accessible to rapid rehellenization; it was reorganised as a *Theme* not later than the reign of Michael I Rangavís.

By the middle of the ninth century further *Themes* of Strymon and Epirus had been set up, perhaps expansions or conflations of what had earlier been called ἀρχοντία,[a] that is, a province predominantly inhabited by Slavs under special administration. The *Theme* of Strymon, centred on Serres, now linked those of Saloniki and Macedonia into a solid Byzantine reacquisition.[21] The increase in tempo and urgency of Byzantine measures of rehellenization at this time was obviously motivated by the ever more formidable menace of the virtually Slav state of the Bulgars, whose ruler Krum had just defeated and slain the Christian Emperor himself (811).[b] Slav tribes not under his direct rule were still liable to join his armies on campaign. The *Life of St Gregory the Decapolite*[22], who died in Saloniki in 842, provides a few sidelights. We learn that in the early decades of the ninth century—that is, when SS Cyril and Methodios[c] were born in Saloniki—the Slavs living on the lower reaches of the Strymon were very active as pirates and no doubt still pagan. But the tide was now about to turn. Only a small area of agricultural hinterland remained in control of the city and therefore particular attention was paid to those Slavs who were a danger to its communications and food supplies. By 879 the evangelisation of these Slavs was well in hand; for Paul, Bishop of the Strymonians, a tribe which stood across the Bulgarian trade-route, and Peter, Bishop of the Druguvitai who, with the Sagudatai, occupied part of the rich plains to the west of the city, were signatories to the acts of the Council of Constantinople in that year. The Ezerites and Serbs of Macedonia also had bishops by 879.[23]

Evangelisation necessarily started from the coastal cities which the Greeks held. We must suppose that the main source of missionaries was

[a] This is clearly what is meant by *knjaženije* in *VM* 2–3, which Methodios was sent to govern at an early age: see p. 33.

[b] See p. 157.

[c] Cyril and Methodios were the monastic names of Constantine and Michael (?): see pp. 32 and 56 below.

Saloniki itself, together with such monasteries as may have survived here and there inland. Peoples admitted to permanent settlement 'within the Empire'—an elastic expression—were of course expected to show their gratitude by conversion and provision of manpower.[24] As the Slavs everywhere formed only small compact bodies or were already intermingled with existing populations, there was nothing spectacular for a historian to record. We hear of missionaries (περιοδευτής) working among the Balkan Slavs in the seventh, perhaps even in the sixth century. An individual mission which evidently had some local success is suggested by the so-called *Legend of Saloniki* which has become attached to St Cyril-Constantine.[25] It refers with a high degree of probability to the work of St Cyril of Cappadocia among the Macedonian Slavs in the valley of the River Bregalnica (a tributary of the Vardar) in the seventh century. The natural base for such work would have been Stobi, on the Vardar route between Saloniki and Skopje, which had not yet been reduced to ruins.[26]

The rapid Christianisation of the Slavs in Greece from the middle of the ninth century is part of the great work set in train by Basil I and Patriarch Photios, which achieved the conversion of Bulgaria itself in 864/5 and was already reaching out to the Serbs north of Macedonia.[a] Moreover, as much of the Balkan peninsula as possible was to be reclaimed for the Greek language. In most areas hellenization went *pari passu* with conversion. Only here and there can we detect a bilingual period: Slav-speaking Christians are indicated by such place names as Γιαννάκοβο in Macedonia, Ἀναστάσοβα and Νίκοβο in the Peloponnese. By the end of the century the Slav language was almost everywhere extinct.

In the Peloponnese also Byzantine administration had been reinstated by and large by the middle of the ninth century; Byzantine money began to circulate again after long absence. The pattern of recovery was the same as in the north. The only known bishopric at the worst period (*c.* 680) was Corinth but even this may then have been an empty title. A probably recent see of Monemvasia is recorded in 787. In the ninth century Patras took the lead, being raised to a metropolis about 805. The metropolis of Corinth followed shortly after. Several saintly bishops are recorded in this century: Athanasios of Methone, Vasilaios of Lacedaimon, and in the tenth century Peter of Argos and an Armenian, St Nikon, who died in the Peloponnese about 998 after much work in Crete and among the Maniots.[27]

[a] See pp. 158 ff. and 208.

11

Only gradually were new inland dioceses re-established all over Greece. It has been calculated that there were not above twenty-five all told down to the reign of Leo VI (886–912). Of these about ten were in the Peloponnese.[28] By then only a few pockets of unabsorbed and probably still pagan Slavs remained in the less accessible mountains, for example the Ezeritai and Milingi of the Taýgetos range.[29] As late as the 920s Romanós I revised the taxes, or tribute, which they were paying.[30] These and no doubt some other small clans were not absorbed into the Greek population for a long time. Their alien character was still obvious to the Frankish masters of the Morea in the thirteenth century, when William Villehardouin built castles to control them.[31] Some were still distinct in the fifteenth century.

By the time that the work of SS Cyril and Methodios laid the foundation of Slav Orthodox culture among Slavs outside the Byzantine Empire, the population of the Empire itself had taken in a considerable proportion of Slav blood, whether in Thrace, Anatolia or Greece. This admixture, as in the case of the Armenians, cannot be exactly estimated but had its effect on the course of Byzantine history. But above all success in reimposing Byzantine rule virtually coincided with success in hellenization. Those regions were lost to Greek (or Latin) speech which had not returned to the Empire by the end of the ninth century—Bulgaria, Serbia and much of Macedonia. Later vicissitudes have not greatly altered down to the present day the new frontier then established betwen Greek and Slav speech. Peninsular Greece was one of the few areas where a large immigrant population of Slavs failed to impose itself. Little enough is known of their evangelisation; nothing suggests that Byzantine policy could favour the raising of their barbarous tongue to civilised use.

2

THE SLAVS IN
CENTRAL EUROPE

The case of Greece was exceptional in Slav history. Following as they did in most parts of Europe more closely on the heels of Germanic peoples, the Slavs remained largely unaffected by the civilised world until the Germans themselves had been absorbed and converted. Few, if any, Germans were evangelised by missions sent for the purpose beyond the frontiers of civilisation.[a] But once they had settled within these frontiers they were brought comparatively rapidly into the Christian fold. No one in those times had thoughts for the further geographical extension of Christendom: all energies were required for redeeming former civilised provinces from barbarisation.

There is a superficial similarity, therefore, but no more, between the hellenization of the Slavs in Greece and the romanization of the Franks in Gaul. In contrast, most approaches to the Slavs in Central Europe came to be made in the first place by Germanic peoples and in the event by Germanic peoples themselves relatively recently made Christian, particularly the Bavarians and the Saxons.

BAVARIA, CARANTANIA AND AVARIA

The Bavarians settled in the territories which they still occupy today in the early decades of the sixth century, at the same time as the Lombards (Langobards) entered Pannonia. Both movements may have been partly due to Slav pressure on their eastern flank. The arrival of the Avars, a Turkic or Mongoloid horde,[b] in the Central European steppes in the middle of the sixth century added strength to the Slav pressure, both westwards and southwards, and caused the Langobards to move on into north Italy (568). By the beginning of the seventh century the tide of Slavs, avoiding the Avar-dominated lowlands, had washed up against

[a] The work of Ulfilas among the Danubian Goths is scarcely an exception: the Goths from whom he sprang already felt themselves as Imperial clients and lived partly within the recognised frontier and there were still a few Imperial establishments north of the Danube.

[b] The name Avar will be used, though they may have had no right to it, in preference to 'pseudo-Avar'. The civilised world frequently called them Huns in virtue of their similarity to the horde which had dominated the same area a century earlier.

the eastern slopes of the mountains bounding Bavaria and had pushed up the valleys into the eastern Alps, reaching the head-waters of the Rivers Drava, Mura and Enns, and as far as the River Tagliamento in northeast Italy. All those Slavs who settled in the lands between the right bank of the Danube and the head of the Adriatic were probably closely related in blood and dialect and can be referred to proleptically as Slovenes.

The Bavarians were still wholly or largely pagan at the time of their settlement. They had never been Arians. Their conversion was slow:[1] it was not till after about 700, when the Avars had destroyed Lorch[a] and the Bavarians had consequently moved their capital up-river to Regensburg (Ratisbon), that the decisive steps were taken. At about this date St Emmeram (Haimhramm) baptised Duke Theodo (*c*. 695–*c*. 718) and many other Bavarians.[2] St Rupert, wrongly called 'of Worms', worked in Salzburg in the first decades of the eighth century where he acted *more scottorum* as bishop (St Martin's Church) and abbot (St Peter's monastery).[b] He died about 718. St Corbinian worked from Freising *c*. 715–25. These three great missionaries are thought to have been wholly or partly Irish in blood. Their status was the typically Irish one of unattached missionary bishop (German *Wanderbischof*). But by this time it is difficult to separate Irish enterprise from Frankish enterprise in the Irish manner.

The first attempt at founding a Bavarian church dates from 716 when Duke Theodo applied to Pope Gregory II for a bishop of his own in order to avoid incorporation in the Frankish church; the Dukedom was jealous of its independence. This came to nothing as Charles Martel feared a possible alliance of the Bavarians with the Lombards, which would have aggravated his difficulties in dealing with the latter. It fell to St Boniface in 739 to organise the Bavarian church as part of his general reforms, approved and directed by the Papacy to a degree greatly resented by the Franks. He formally constituted the sees of Regensburg, Salzburg, Freising and Passau. None of these was as yet made a metropolitan see. Throughout the eighth century the pious Bavarian dukes maintained good relations with Rome in their desire not to be dominated by the Frankish church, but Charlemagne's incorporation of Bavaria in the Frankish Empire in 788 put an end to these hopes of political and ecclesiastical independence.

[a] Lorch, at the confluence of Enns and Danube, was once the Roman frontier post of Lauriacum. The see of Lorch was reinstated at Passau.

[b] Those who exercise such a dual office are referred to as abbot-bishops or claustral bishops.

By 800 Salzburg was a well organised diocese with numerous parish churches.[3] Bavarian Christianity was already mature enough to initiate evangelical work on its own account. Up to this time missionary work along the barbarian frontier from the Danube to Istria had been limited to local and individual enterprise. St Columban at one time planned to evangelise certain Slavs, perhaps on the upper Danube, perhaps in Carantania; but a vision dissuaded him on the grounds that the time had not yet come.[4] St Amandus, who had worked among the Frisians and Basques, followed this lead about 630 but again apparently without success.[5] St Rupert of Salzburg may have made contact with Carantanian Slavs.[6] St Boniface, whose great energies were devoted to the reorganisation of the Frankish church and to missions among the Germanic peoples, had little to spare for Slavs and other even more remote and barbarous races. Most of his references to the Slavs are contemptuous.[7] At most he took some notice of those who were already mixed with Germans within the recognised Western frontiers.[8] But whatever the prejudices of individual churchmen and even popes, men were not lacking, above all Irish monks, who were not deterred by any distances or difficulties from following the Divine command *docete omnes gentes* and believed that all men were capable of and none too barbarous for salvation.[9]

Of the ecclesiastical centres best placed to develop this work in due course Salzburg proved considerably more active than Passau in the north or Aquileia in the south. At Salzburg Rupert had been followed by a fellow-Celt, Virgil,[a] sent by Pippin to Duke Odilo in 745—a man of great learning and energy.[10] He found the Slavs of Carantania (Carinthia and Styria),[11] who had been living in relative independence of Avars and Bavarians alike for about a century, ripe for evangelisation. Virgil's activities were supported by the Bavarian duke. Political relations between Bavaria and Carantania were already close: the Carantanian chieftains had more than once had to seek Bavarian help against the Avars and Lombards. It proved easy for Tassilo III to establish a protectorate over these lands. As Bavaria itself came more and more under Frankish control from the middle of the eighth century Frankish interest was superimposed on purely Bavarian. Carantania thus became, together with Bavaria, a province of the Carolingian empire in 788.

About the year 743 Boruta of Carantania sent his son Gorazd[b] and his

---

[a] The Latinised *Virgilius* represents Irish Fergil. He was born *c.* 710.

[b] The *Cacatius* of *Conversio* (see p. 32 below) must be a corruption of *Carastus* or the like (Slav *Garazdŭ?*). Boruta is a familiar form of Borislav or a similar compound.

nephew Hotimir (Chetmarus, Cheitmar) to be educated as Christians at the recently founded monastery of Chiemsee.[a] Boruta himself probably remained a pagan but baptism was a condition made by most Christian rulers in return for their military aid or protection, which Boruta fulfilled in this way. Hotimir brought back a priest, Maioranus, with him from Bavaria. During his reign (*c.* 750–*c.* 770) Christianity evidently made considerable advances. It was to him that Virgil of Salzburg sent an assistant bishop,[12] Modestus, based on the church of Maria Saal (S. Maria in Solio) near Klagenfurt, where he died and was buried.[b] Priests, if not bishops, continued to be sent from Salzburg in face of recurrent opposition from the pagan majority.[13] Among the other early churches of Carantania, S. Peter im Holz at Lurnfeld near Spittal (formerly the Roman city of Tiburnia or Teurnia) and 'ad Undrimas', perhaps at Ingering in Styria, are thought to be Modestus's foundations. The churches were naturally as much or more for the local German population as for the Slavs. But to the second half of the eighth century, we must suppose, belong the first versions, however crude, of Christian texts in Slav, to be learnt by heart by converts before baptism. Carolingian documents make it quite clear that candidates were expected to memorise the Creed and the Lord's Prayer both in their own language and in Latin.[14]

In 769 Duke Tassilo founded a monastery near Innichen (Roman *Aguntum*) at the source of the River Drava, on one of the important Alpine routes, specifically for missionary work among the neighbouring Slavs.[15] Evangelisation went forward hand in hand with German settlement on new cultivable land and as much by the employment of Slav labourers on the monastic estates as by other means. There were many setbacks, local revolts of recalcitrant Slavs, which may account for further campaigns of pacification which Tassilo carried out in Carantania between 769 and 772. The foundation of the monastery of Kremsmünster followed in 777. The bishops of Salzburg, Passau and Regensburg were all associated in this and again stressed its double duties as centre of economic penetration and of evangelisation. The lands which it was granted in the following decades show largely Slav place names. About 799 Theoderic (Deodoricus) became bishop in Carantania, sent by Arno of Salzburg, the equally active successor of Virgil. From this

---

[a] Chiemsee = *in insulam chemingi lacus* (*Conversio* 4).

[b] Maria Saal, known to the Slovenes as *Gospá Sveta* (the Holy Lady), is not far from the fortress of Karnburg (*Krnski grad*). The dates of Modestus's arrival and death are quite uncertain.

time Freising, of which Innichen was a daughter house, began to acquire extensive lands in Carinthia, Styria and Carniola, the basis of further evangelical work by its monks as well as of German colonisation.[16] Among Theoderic's successors were Otto and Oswald (d. 873)—both presumably sent from Salzburg.[17]

Carantania owed its early evangelisation mainly to the work of one diocese—Salzburg—and notably to the vision and enterprise of one man—Virgil. Aquileia, however, had not abandoned all work in these parts. After the disasters of the great Slav invasions this Lombard city found itself particularly well placed to take the initiative in salvaging Christian remnants.[a] It was natural for Aquileia (that is, old Aquileia)[b] to reach out again into the areas lost to Avars and Slavs as soon as conditions were favourable and Frankish policy demanded it. Theoretically Aquileia could claim an interest in all the lands up to the Danube. However *Noricum ripense* had apparently been allotted to Passau by the dispositions of 739. The Bavarian Duke Odilo may have persuaded Pope Zacharias to give Salzburg more or less exclusive rights in northern Carantania in the 740s.[18] Certainly Aquileia lost the diocese of Säben (later Brixen) to Salzburg about 770. The work of Aquileia and Salzburg tended to overlap on the River Drava; it thus became advisable to re-define their spheres of influence. In 796/7 and again in June 811 Charlemagne made the Drava the dividing-line. Aquileia was thereby again the loser but Paulinus II of Aquileia (*fungebatur c.* 786–803), a good friend of Alcuin and of Arno of Salzburg, made no difficulties.[19] It seems unlikely that Aquileian missionaries were in practice prevented from penetrating north—and a long way north—of the Drava by this administrative ruling. For it was in the time of Ursus and Maxentius, the successors of Paulinus, that Aquileian missionary activity notably gathered strength. By then a new situation had arisen on the eastern frontiers of the Frankish empire.

Charlemagne created a series of marches from Saxony through Thuringia to Ostmark (the germ of later Austria), covering the most natural frontiers. To the west of this line there were relatively few Slavs. His first task had been the conquest and forcible conversion of the Germanic Saxons (772–97), a constant menace to the heartlands of the

---

[a] It is difficult to estimate how far Christian communities survived as islands in the Slav sea. Bishops of Emona (modern Ljubljana) and Poetovio (Ptuj), and even of towns further north, attended synods at Grado at the end of the sixth century but records then cease and a long continuance of such sees is highly improbable. See pp. 206–7

[b] On the two Aquileias see p. 189 note d.

Franks. There was no question yet of carrying the work of civilisation to the Slavs beyond the Elbe.[20] Further south there were Slavs settled on the upper Main, about Bamberg, who were reached by Christian missionaries from Würzburg, perhaps mainly Irish, in the last decades of the eighth century. When the see of Würzburg was constituted in 741 it received all churches 'in confiniis Francorum et Saxonum atque Sclavorum'.[21] Little was probably achieved before Charlemagne's time, when these Slavs became subject to strong germanisation. Over a dozen churches seem to have been built principally for Slavs in the diocese of Würzburg, in the first half of the ninth century.[22] Bavaria too had many scattered Slav settlements of which nothing further is heard.[23]

But along the south-eastern frontiers the Avars created a special problem. They were aggressive barbarians lying across the most attractive direction for Frankish expansion. Once the Saxons had been subdued Charlemagne turned his attention to the conquest of Avaria—the central Danubian steppes. Many Slavs had come under Avar rule; in some regions the mixture was certainly more intimate than in others. Contemporary references to Avars must be held normally to include a greater or less proportion of Slavs. The conquest of Avaria meant the addition of a large new Slav population to the Empire. Not only conquest but conversion was particularly in Charlemagne's mind. He was intensely conscious of his position as *sanctae fidei defensor* in this quarter no less than towards the Saxons and on the Spanish march. In this he was assuming the same role as the Emperor of the East. The year 795 is a turning-point. In that year Charlemagne and Pope Leo III together drew up a general plan—*defensio romanae ecclesiae*—by which the King undertook to defend Christian lands against pagan aggression and to propagate the faith, the Pope on his part to exert his spiritual powers in support.[24] A series of campaigns, commanded in part by Charles's son Pippin, brought about the collapse of Avar military might, already on the wane, in the years 793–6. In summer 796 Pippin summoned a synod to his camp on the Danube to plan the requisite missions.[25] In all this the plans were largely the work of the Frankish church, not of the Pope. Alcuin, Charles's chief ecclesiastical adviser, was a prime mover; it was for this new missionary area that he caused to be circulated St Augustine's *Handbook for Missionaries—Ratio de catechizandis rudibus*—and himself wrote an *Ordo de baptizandis rudibus* for local use. Alcuin stressed one vital principle: no forcible conversion was to be attempted. The Slavs and Avars were not to be treated as the Saxons had been. 'Fides ex voluntate fit non ex necessitate',[26] he wrote, and therefore 'ipsa vero praedicantium doctrina non debet esse violenta... sed benigna, suadebilis...' With this policy Paulinus of Aquileia fully concurred. His directions for baptism have survived: the candidate must apply for baptism of his own free will and no force is to be used; he must recite the Creed correctly after a preparation of not less than a week (preferably forty days); if candidates are many and workers few, baptism need not be restricted to the periods of Easter and Pentecost—any Sunday is allowable.

Alcuin was well aware of the human weaknesses which frontier situations brought to the fore. He stressed that missionaries must be 'praedicatores, non praedatores'[27] and that it would be advisable to avoid imposing the tithe in new areas too soon. Possibly also Charles was not himself happy about the 'baptism or death' which had finally been offered to the Saxons not many years earlier, when military necessity had no doubt been allowed to override better judgment. In 797 he repealed the over-severe ordinances made about 782 at Paderborn for the Saxons. Yet, however admirable these principles, the secular interest, entirely lacking in the Irish missions, had now a stake in all missionary enterprise. Not only were Charlemagne's bishops an integral part of his administration; he also brought the monasteries, through their abbots, under his personal control. However, he showed little interest in new foundations, though frontier monasteries were often better placed than bishoprics for missionary work.[28] The ideal economic and cultural role of a monastery at this time can be gauged from the St Gall plan of *c.* 820.[29]

A further step in the plan was the Pope's agreement to raise Salzburg to an archbishopric (798)[a]—not perhaps without protests from Regensburg as the Bavarian capital and Passau as the self-styled heir to Lorch[b] —with a view to even greater missionary activity.[30] Charles appointed Arno, a pupil of the learned Arbeo of Freising, first archbishop and instructed him to go 'in partes sclavorum...praedicare verbum dei.' Arno's *Instructio pastoralis* (798) deals with the training of missionaries along the lines of the great educational programme initiated for the whole Frankish church by Charles and Alcuin.[31] Salzburg thus assumed a position similar to that later allotted to Magdeburg for the Slavs in the North.[c]

[a] The bishoprics then set under it were Regensburg (*reganensis*), Passau (*patavensis*), Freising (*frisingensis*), Brixen (*sabionensis*) and Staffelsee (*stafnensis*).
[b] See p. 14 above. [c] See pp. 118 and 146.

Of the remnants of the Avars little need be said. They were allowed to settle between the Danube and the Raab under their chieftain Theodore, who appears to have accepted baptism immediately after the military defeat. His successor Abraham was also baptised in 805.[32] After that the Avars as a separate people disappear from history.

The effects on the Slav world were immense. Not only was the southeast opened up to Frankish penetration but Moravia, and to a lesser extent Bohemia, became at once more accessible to the currents of civilisation. After the death of Charlemagne, Louis the Pious made a division of the Empire and allotted to Louis 'the German' in 817 'Bavaria and Carantania and Bohemia and the Avars and the Slavs', with his capital at Regensburg.[33] Even modern Slovakia was not considered beyond Frankish reach. It is to Moravia that attention must now be turned.

MORAVIA

A glance at the map will show that Moravia is a vital point in Central European communications. It commands the age-old North–South route through the Moravian Gate and abuts on the East–West route up and down the Danube. The name of Moravia and the Moravians (from the River Morava, *germanice* March) begins to appear in documents of the early ninth century. The *Geographus Bavarensis*[34] divides these Slavs into *Marharii* and *Merehani* (perhaps the more easterly branch in Slovakia)—the former a more German, the latter a more Slav form of the name. A Slav dynast, Mojmir, arose in Moravia in the 820s. Whether he was the first to unite the local Slav tribes into a larger political unit or merely came into prominence as a result of the rapidly changing political situation, is uncertain. According to a Bavarian source he had 'predecessors'.[35] It has been suggested that some continuity of statehood should be posited here from as far back as the seventh century when a certain Samo for a short time (*c.* 625–*c.* 659) brought diverse Slav tribes from Bohemia to Carantania under his personal rule and called a temporary halt to their domination by the Avars. The whole episode is obscure and only recorded by Fredegar,[36] from whom we learn that Samo, a subject of the Merovingian King Dagobert, cast in his lot with the Slavs to whom he had been sent and defeated Dagobert's attempts to recall him to obedience. However this may be, Samo's 'reign' was short, his unification ephemeral; Moravia remained a backwater which received no attention in the annals of the next 200 years. There is no reason to suppose that Samo was so zealous a Christian that he put in hand the evangelisation of his subjects.[37]

The Slavs of Moravia, who had been settling these lands since about the year 500, could have had little contact with Christianity until the eighth century. There is no sign in later history of a tincture of Arianism such as might have been acquired from a mixing with Langobards or other Germanic peoples. It is more probable that they came sufficiently under Avar influence to acquire some of their religious practices. The style of many Moravian burials and grave-goods of the seventh–eighth centuries, for example at Devinska Nová Ves, is distinctly Avar, and this remains true till *c.* 800.[38] After that date Avar customs would linger on here and there.

It would seem that the prosperity of Moravia increased rapidly on the removal of Avar control, however tenuous. It was able to progress independently since Frankish interests had not yet expanded north of the Danube. The rapid growth in the early ninth century of quasi-urban settlements round the *grad* (*germanice* burg) of ruler or magnate can be traced at a number of sites. The profits of the transit trade were probably added to a normal agricultural economy of the time. That there was anything in Central Europe since the great migrations and down to the ninth century which could properly be called international trade has often been doubted. But recent evidence supports the view that Mediterranean links with the Danubian region were never wholly broken.[39] Indeed barbarians such as the Avars coveted much from the sedentary peoples and certainly employed Byzantine craftsmen. The real volume of trade may have been small, especially in the eighth century when Byzantium only just surmounted all her own external and internal dangers, but it was steady. In the Moravian sites jewellery of Byzantine style is especially prominent: this was, according to date, either imported or made locally by Byzantine craftsmen, or imitated by Moravian craftsmen.[40] Coloured glass beads were another undoubted import from the Byzantine Empire. Moravia under Mojmir shows the typical signs of a society in transition: the old tribal structure and the religion associated with it had long been breaking down; therefore these Slavs were receptive to ideas from outside. This may be contrasted with the situation among the Slavs in north Germany where, at the same period, traditional society and religion were still relatively intact and therefore resistant.[a]

While Salzburg was active principally in Carantania *sensu lato*, Passau

[a] See chapter 3, pp. 142 ff..

also began to reach out into the Slav lands. Monasteries deliberately placed on the frontiers of this diocese had been active since the 770s, in particular Kremsmünster, though little is known of individual achievements.[a] The kernel of Mojmir's Moravian state—the middle Morava valley—was most easily accessible from the direction of Passau. When the Imperial frontier was advanced from the Enns to the Raab in 791 it would be natural for the diocese of Passau to become responsible for the new area. Regensburg in due course also acquired interests in this direction mainly through large grants of land made to the see by Louis the German in the 850s. A grant dated 18 January 853 assigns land on the left bank of the Danube opposite Linz and thence northwards indefinitely (*sine terminorum conclusione*).[41] Such a grant was not unusual and in this case brought Regensburg's potential interests within striking distance of Moravia.

It has been claimed that one of the earliest Christian churches in Moravia is of distinctly Irish style—the small church at Modrá, near Staré Město, the date of which was originally estimated at about 800.[42] There was still at this time a considerable Irish element in some of the Bavarian monasteries, notably Niederaltaich, but it is improbable that their monks would have continued to follow Irish ways as emissaries of a Bavarian house. Charlemagne's capitularies of 787–9 laid the foundation for uniformity of religious practice throughout the Frankish Empire and local variations were in process of elimination.[b] Virgil of Salzburg (d. 784) seems to have been one of the last great Irish churchmen who propagated Irish peculiarities on the Continent: as abbot of St Peter's, Salzburg, he refused until 767 to be made bishop, which in Irish eyes was the lesser charge.[43] The Irish missionary methods which he had applied in Carantania cannot anywhere have long survived the Frankish incorporation of Bavaria in 788 and the consequent reorganisation of the Bavarian monasteries on the Benedictine model. Modrá has something in common with certain Irish foundations in the Rhineland and with a

[a] Niederaltaich (founded 741) is perhaps the next most conspicuous, from which Kremsmünster (founded 777) drew monks. Niederaltaich was itself affiliated to Frankish Reichenau (founded 724).

[b] Suspicion of unorthodox Irish ways was voiced as early as the Council of Soissons (744), their continuance banned by the Council of Châlons (813). Carolingian standardisation (within the limits of its modest success) bore notably on the use of the uniform Gregorian sacramentary, of a single newly-corrected text of the Latin Bible, and of one collection of Canon Law; and of the Rule of St Benedict in all monasteries. Similarly, in the East, the re-establishment of Orthodoxy (843) led to much standardisation in liturgy (based finally on the practice of the Studios monastery) and consequently in the internal design of churches.

small church near Salzburg probably built by Virgil. But the weight of the evidence is against its Irishness. Its date is more likely to be about 830. The internal features apart, which have been shown to have nothing to do with the exterior walls, similar ground-plans are known from Dalmatia[44] and there are features in common with several churches at Mikulčice[a] (*germanice* Mikulschitz), in particular no. 1, ascribed to the first quarter of the ninth century, no. 2 of about 840–60 and no. 8 of rather later date.[45] In none of these is there any reason to suppose an Irish connection or influence. Even if Modrá's rectangular apse were an undoubted Western feature it would not connect it incontrovertibly with Irish missionary activity.

In contrast, a rotunda known as Mikulčice no. 6, estimated to date from the second quarter of the ninth century (though the stratigraphy is still far from clear), is plausibly Dalmatian–Istrian in style. Its dimensions are based on the Lombard foot; its form suggests a princely chapel. But others see Carolingian features. 'Na Valách' at Staré Město also strongly suggests southern connections.[46]

We must certainly reckon with a tide of Christian influence reaching Moravia from the diocese of Aquileia in the early and middle ninth century, despite the ruling of 811. That both Moravia and Pannonia exhibit a considerable southern, that is, essentially Lombard, element in their earliest Christian architecture is scarcely surprising when we consider that the first cathedral at Salzburg itself, built by Virgil in the years 767–74, was a large basilica of typically Lombard design.[47] Politically and culturally, Bavaria looked as much south to Lombardy as west to the Franks. Lombard culture was the superior and Lombard craftsmen were in demand over a very large area, since more skilful than those from further west.[b]

The main centres of Moravian life, Mikulčice among them, lay in the middle Morava valley.[c] Though not without Lombard traits in its culture Mikulčice would appear to have been the main centre of Frankish ecclesiastical influence from Passau.[48] Its greatest development falls in the second quarter of the ninth century.

Thus at the moment when Moravia, or Great Moravia,[49] emerges as a

---

[a] See pp. 70–1 below.

[b] Anglo-Saxon craftsmen were also to be found as far east as Bavaria but do not seem to have left any architectural traces. Lombard traits also naturally spread to the Carolingian lands after the downfall of Lombard independence (774). The direction is therefore not always sure as regards Bavaria.

[c] The more southerly sites, siuch as Devín (near Bratislava) and Pohansko on the River Dyje, were principally fortresses against Frankish attack.

factor in European politics, we find that Christian influences have already penetrated there from several directions and in several forms. And the partly stone churches revealed by archaeology surely imply a greater number of wholly wooden ones of which there is now no trace. The estimated date of Mikulčice nos. 1 and 6 is precisely that put forward for Mojmir's conversion. The evidence for his baptism is indirect but it must have taken place between 818 and 825, most probably about 822 when both Moravian and Bohemian representatives were present, apparently on both a friendly and an independent footing, at the Diet of Frankfurt.[50] According to Dittrich his baptism will have been performed by Bishop Reginhar of Passau (*fungebatur* 818–38).[a] A mass baptism of Moravians is recorded for 831, again by Reginhar.[51] Moravia was then set on the way to becoming a Christian state.

Meanwhile, despite geographical difficulties, Salzburg was laying claim to Slovakia as a mission field. Within a few years of 830 Bishop Adalram of Salzburg (*fungebatur* 821–36) consecrated a church at Nitra for the local Slav ruler Pribina,[b] or for his Bavarian wife and other Franks. It is uncertain whether it was dedicated to St Emmeram of Regensburg (hence a tradition carried over to the present cathedral of Nitra) or to St Martin, as the location on St Martin's Hill, where foundations of a ninth century church have recently been identified, suggests. More probably the latter since Pribina's later history connects him with St Martin's church at Traismauer.[c]

Pribina's relations with Salzburg may well be the result of Mojmir's conversion. He was probably a member of Mojmir's house and held Nitra as his lieutenant. Aspiring to independence, he had to avoid Mojmir's attachment to Passau. About the year 833 Mojmir took the field against his rebellious subordinate, defeated him and took his territory under his own rule. After fruitless appeals to the rulers of Bulgaria, Croatia and Carinthia, Pribina preferred to throw himself on the mercy of the Franks, with a view, no doubt, to dislodging Mojmir in due course. His possible usefulness to Frankish policy was eventually recompensed by a fief in Lower Pannonia, where he built himself a new

---

[a] Those who consider the evidence for Mojmir's baptism insufficient must make Rastislav the first Christian ruler (for Mojmir's predecessors were certainly pagan), baptised no doubt in 846 as part of the conditions for his support by Louis (see p. 25).

[b] So usually spelt. Some favour Privina and a derivation from prv- (*first*), but much more likely is Pribyna, a hypocoristic of Pribyslav or the like.

[c] Traismauer (contemporary *Treisma*) corresponds to present-day Sankt Pölten rather than Traismauer further downstream.

residence, Mosaburg, at the southern end of Lake Balaton (Plattensee).[a] The prerequisite for this grant was of course baptism. The ceremony took place, under the auspices of the Salzburg see, in St Martin's church at Traismauer in 836/7.[52] Mosaburg remained ecclesiastically under Salzburg. The earliest church of which there is mention was St Mary's, consecrated by Archbishop Liupramm (*fungebatur* 836–59) on 24 January 850.[53] Pribina's chaplain Dominic (perhaps from Regensburg, not Salzburg) was confirmed in his functions. From that date the priest in charge (later archpriest) was sent from Salzburg—Svarnagal, then Alfred (Altfrid) and Rihpald (Richbald). Pribina may also have maintained some contacts with Aquileia. He clearly became a zealous Christian under the influence of the energetic Liupramm. When the latter died in 859 there were more than a dozen churches in Pannonia.[54]

Christianity made considerable strides in Moravia in the second quarter of the ninth century. Missionary bishops were appointed from time to time. There were resident archpriests before the arrival of the Greek missionaries in 863.[55] It is no doubt chance that the historical records of Passau's work are inadequate, so that no mention of a church consecration in this period is extant. By the middle of the century the cemeteries of the *burgs* indicate that the Moravian upper class was already predominantly Christian; bronze and other crosses associated with the graves are identified as of Carolingian origin or style. The churches were all presumably private chapels belonging to the ruler or the owner of the *burg*;[56] this remained the normal state of affairs for some time to come. It is very probable that the words for church and priest, peculiar to the West Slavs, date from this stage of Christian development, since church is *kostelŭ* (Czech kostel, Polish kościół) from Latin *castellum = burg* (via OHG *kastel*), and priest is *kŭnędzĭ* (Czech kněz, Polish ksiądź), that is, *chieftain* or *prince*, influenced by Latin *dominus*.

On Mojmir's death a disputed succession gave Louis the German a pretext for intervention in Moravian affairs (August 846). He installed Rastislav, Mojmir's nephew, in the expectation that he would be a subservient client prince.[57] If Pribina expected to receive support for his candidature or had received any conditional promise, he was disappointed. Louis's quite exceptional grant to him of his lands in hereditary possession (October 847) with the rank of Markgraf (though he is

[a] High German Mosapurc is a calque of Slav *blat(en)ĭskŭ kostelŭ*—near modern (Hungarian) Zalavár.

25

still referred to as *dux* or *comes* in the annals) is perhaps to be interpreted as a consolation prize.[58] Rastislav did not prove to be the loyal vassal that Louis hoped. Though Moravia and Slovakia might be theoretically under Frankish suzerainty, he did not follow Pribina's way.

Towards the end of Mojmir's reign the work of Passau missionaries in Moravia appears to have slackened off somewhat. Hartwig of Passau (*fungebatur* 838–65) was lukewarm and finally more or less incapacitated.[59] No new priests were arriving. Rastislav's own position was by no means secure, either internally or *vis-à-vis* Louis. The Frankish priests already in the country may have served Frankish political ends too well and the church of Christ too ill. There was little likelihood that the Frankish church would grant either Rastislav or Pribina a bishop of his own, nor would Rastislav have welcomed this. There is some evidence that even Pribina, who was on good terms with Salzburg, applied to the Pope for a bishop, which would of course also imply a raising of his own status; but nothing came of it. On the contrary Louis's charter for the archbishopric of Salzburg, dated 20 November 860, which gives a very complete record of Salzburg's estates and interests in Carantania and Pannonia, must have been occasioned by a desire to strengthen Salzburg's control of these lands. Louis was strongly behind Salzburg and continued to grant further lands during the 860s.[60] Rastislav approached the Holy See about 860 in the same sense as Pribina but his request was turned down or ignored.[61] Pope Nicholas was preoccupied with Balkan problems. Louis as the friend of Bulgaria could be of great value to him; moreover he had to be persuaded to curb the insolence of the Frankish episcopate. But Rastislav had no intention of being subservient to the Franks. This led to a rapid deterioration of relations. With intermittent war from 849 Rastislav had all the more reason to dislike the presence of Frankish clergy in his lands. Louis's pressure on Moravia continued to increase though he was unable to prevent Rastislav helping his rebellious son Carloman, particularly in 863. As the Synod of Mainz (Canon XI) noted in 852, Moravian Christianity was still rudimentary;[62] in the following decade there may even have been some backsliding.[63] Rastislav urgently required a bishop of his own and the moment came when an approach to the Eastern church was no surprising or illogical move.

Rastislav, who could rightly be considered an independent ruler from at least 855, saw himself in danger of being crushed out of existence; the Frankish Empire hemmed him in on the west and south, the Bulgarian state on the east—for the incorporation of Pribina's lands gave

Moravia and Bulgaria a more clearly defined frontier along the River Tisza (Theiss).[64] Rastislav had to bear in mind possible Bulgarian aggression in the future. Moreover Salzburg, backed by the whole Frankish church, could still claim Slovakia, through Nitra, as legitimately within its interest. The imminence of a Franco–Bulgarian alliance must have decided him to send an embassy in 862 to the Emperor in Constantinople. One can see Rastislav's dilemma. His country was already partly Christian, but if it were absorbed into the Frankish Empire and its church into the Frankish church, no doubt as a mere extension of an existing diocese—Passau, there would no longer be any guarantee of managing his own affairs. The rapacity of the Germans, laymen and ecclesiastics alike, was well known. We must therefore give Rastislav the personal credit for conceiving the idea of seeking support from Constantinople, not so much to create a Christian community as to consolidate one and above all to organise a church— a church capable of resisting German encroachments. His letter to the Emperor is that of a fellow-Christian.[65] No doctrinal or ritual questions entered into his appeal; the subtle differences between East and West would scarcely weigh with him even if he understood them. Although he was clearly well informed about the Byzantine Empire how much could he have known about Eastern Christianity? Rather he was bewildered by the diversity of missionaries already present in his lands and concerned above all for the ecclesiastical affiliation of his realm. The *Life of Methodios* gives his own words as follows: 'many Christian missionaries have come to us from [North] Italy, the Byzantine lands and Western Europe, instructing us in different ways...'[66] Where traders and craftsmen (perhaps formerly in Avar employ) from the Byzantine Empire could penetrate, Greek missionaries could certainly follow. At this moment affiliation with the East would have one great advantage—the possibility of being granted a bishop of his own or conceivably even an autocephalous archbishop, and yet another which we cannot however be sure was present in his mind—the possibility of promoting the Christianisation of his country exclusively in the native tongue.[67] All missionaries are bound to use the local vernacular for elementary communication with the people. But any church which the Franks created had to be Latin in language.[a] This requirement was no doubt retarding a process which Rastislav was eager to expedite. Hence his embassy emphasised the need for a 'teacher' capable of working in

[a] See also discussion on pp. 44–6.

Slav. None was forthcoming from the West or from the Pope. But the Byzantine Empire included a large Slav population: Rastislav would have every reason to believe, if not to know, that the Emperor could supply what he needed. The Emperor Michael III acceded to his request by sending the brothers Constantine[68] and Methodios, who reached Moravia (probably taking the normal overland route through Bulgaria) in summer 863,[69] with a small following, among whom were their closest collaborators, Clement and Naum. The gifts which any such embassy or mission would bring in the name of their sovereign included in this case relics of exceptional value—those of St Clement (Pope Clement I), found by Constantine himself at Kherson in the Crimea.[a]

This was essentially a religious mission, but it had of course a diplomatic aspect, though this has sometimes been unduly stressed. The Byzantine government would welcome contacts with Moravia at a time when the Franks were making both political and ecclesiastical overtures to Bulgaria, with the full approval of the Papacy, but it can scarcely have expected any positive political or military advantages. The mission could at most have been exploratory in this respect.[b] No ecclesiastical acts were any longer entirely free from political overtones. The penetration of the civilised powers into barbarian lands always involved—and still involves—a measure of both.

The mission, it must be repeated, was exploratory. It was not in fact probable that the Emperor would at once send a bishop for Moravia, the essential desideratum from Rastislav's point of view. He may at this moment have held back in order to give no cause of annoyance to Pope Nicholas who was being slow to recognise Photios as Patriarch of Constantinople. Conversely a Byzantine bishop would not have had the status which Rastislav perhaps imagined. Both theory and practice were quite explicit on this: all newly evangelised areas automatically came under the jurisdiction of the Patriarch of Constantinople and through him under the Emperor as God's viceregent on earth, superior to the formal head of the church. Only an autocephalous church could be independent of one of the Orthodox patriarchates—and this status was bestowed very grudgingly. Therefore even if the Emperor had been

[a] See pp. 35–6. All churches were expected to have a relic, in the majority of cases naturally those of their patron saint. It was therefore necessary to take relics to provide for a new mission church. See p. 71 on a possible church of St Clement in Moravia.

[b] Franco–Bulgarian *rapprochement* ended in a formal alliance at Tulln (863). A corresponding Byzantine–Moravian formal treaty, concluded by the mission or others, has not been satisfactorily proved though some form of close alliance is clearly not to be excluded.

willing to send a bishop, the act would have had no less political significance than the attachment to the Frankish church and Empire that
Rastislav wished to avoid. Constantinople now and for a long time to
come thought in terms of the one universal Empire embracing an indefinitely extensible number of Christian peoples. Since the inception
of the Christian Empire the organisation of the church had been coupled
to that of the civil administration, that is to say, civil and ecclesiastical
boundaries and status normally coincided. Consequently, although
missionary bishops could be and were sent beyond the recognised
confines of the Empire, the permanent establishment of a new church
implied at least some degree of dependence on the Byzantine Empire.[a]
The Emperor considered himself head of a great family of rulers, whose
titles in diplomatic practice were carefully graded according to their
degree of 'relationship'.[b] In fact only the Pope, whose authority was not
territorially bound, could appoint, as far as Central Europe was con-
concerned, an unpolitical bishop.

At most the Byzantine authorities must have felt that a strong Byzantine influence in a Moravian church might have a favourable effect on
the matter of real moment to Constantinople—Bulgaria. It would be the
task of the mission to report on the real state of affairs in Moravia.

The arrival of two men, however highly qualified for the second
desideratum of 'teachers', who could have no authority over the
Frankish clergy in Moravia, must therefore have been something of a
disappointment to Rastislav. If his letter to the Emperor Michael is
correctly reported, he had had in mind far more ambitious plans: 'that,
seeing this, other lands may follow our example'.[70]

Constantine (Cyril) and Methodios

Primary sources and associated texts

For the lives of these saints we have the following primary sources in Old
Church Slavonic,[c] of which the first two are by far the most valuable (and
unusually reliable, as was proved beyond a shadow of doubt by F. Dvornik).[71]

---

[a] See also pp. 283 ff.

[b] The *De Cerimoniis* of Constantine Porphyrogennetos is the best reflection of this
system. See also p. 373 n. 78.

[c] Old Church Slavonic is the most usual term for the Slav written language elaborated
by Constantine for ecclesiastical purposes. It is true that some early texts are not
strictly ecclesiastical and that OCS soon became a literary language in the wider sense,
but the term is clearer than such alternatives as 'Old Bulgarian'. See also p. 64 note b
(abbreviations).

1. The *Life of St Cyril*[72] (usually referred to as *Vita Constantini*, abbreviation *VC*). Of the many extant manuscripts of this *Life* none is earlier than the mid-fifteenth century (a Serbian version preserved in Russia). The original text can scarcely have been composed later than 882, for Gauderich of Velletri, whose cathedral was dedicated to St Clement of Rome, clearly used *VC* or a closely related source for his *Life of St Clement* and he dedicated the work to Pope John VIII who died on 15 December of that year.[73] Further, the Slav text was perhaps not made before Methodios's consecration as archbishop in 870.[74] Some scholars, notably Vaillant, posit the existence of a lost *Life* in Greek prior to or contemporary with the Slav version as a source for the Latin versions, which cannot be derived directly from the Slav as we have it. If so it was made in Rome very soon after Constantine's death and the Slav version was perfected a few years later in Moravia under Methodios's personal direction. A pointer to Methodios's authorship or editorship is seen in the inclusion (*VC* 5) of the episode of the saint's dispute with the last iconoclast patriarch, John the Grammarian (*fungebatur* 837–43), if this is accepted as historical and not a purely literary embellishment: the matter would only have seemed important by then to one closely in touch with Byzantine ecclesiastical affairs of those years. On the other hand, the mistake over 'Alexander' could scarcely have been made by Methodios.[75] Assuming the above hypothesis, the two versions must have been partly independent of one another, having different readers in view: Methodios would have intended the OCS *Life* for Moravia and the Greek *Life* for Constantinople.

2. The *Life of St Methodios* (*Vita Methodii*—*VM*).[76] About a dozen Slav manuscripts; the earliest, of the twelfth or early thirteenth century, formed part of a collection in the Cathedral of the Dormition (*Uspenski sobor*) in Moscow, of Bohemian provenance.[a] The *Life* was composed very shortly after Methodios's death in 885, probably before the expulsion of his followers from Moravia. The obvious choice for author is St Clement, his lifelong disciple.[77] In this case also no parallel Greek version has survived, if there was one. Vaillant believes in a Greek original for at least the opening chapter, the syntactical complexity of which is distinctly Greek. He is perhaps right in suggesting that this part is of different origin from the rest, conceivably a profession of faith presented by St Constantine in Rome in 868 or by Methodios in Rome or Constantinople in the 880s.[b]

VC and *VM* are complementary; *VM* rarely repeats what has already been adequately told in *VC* and there are few discrepancies.[c] They are too different to be attributed to the same author but both authors clearly belonged to the immediate company of the saints. Both, for example, refer to the Pope regnant as *apostolikŭ* (from Latin *apostolicus*), a Western usage presumably current also in Moravia but unknown in Byzantium. Though the authors are proficient in Byzantine literature neither slavishly follows the standard

---

[a] See pp. 109–10.   [b] See pp. 73 and 77.
[c] Notably that the Slav service books were deposited in S. Maria *ad praesepe* (*VC*), but in St Peter's (*VM*). But *VM* is not concerned with this phase of the Roman events and also fails to note that Hadrian II had already succeeded Nicholas I.

Byzantine hagiographical model. Their intention is, especially as regards *VM*, as much historical as hagiographical. *VC* is nearer to a typical saint's *Life*; *VM* contains an element of apologia for Methodios's policy and the quotation of Papal letters further marks it as a document of international affairs. The apologetic element led Vaillant to propose a rather later date for *VM*—nearer 893 than 885—supposing it a defence of Methodios's work written in Bulgaria when the extension of his work to that country was already a fact.[78] It cannot be later than the *Office* (no. 7 below). But on the whole it fits the situation in Moravia in 885/6 better, and the use of the word *miša*, probably also of *vŭsǫdŭ*,[a] increases the likelihood that it was not written outside Moravia. The author also appears to assume that his readers will understand the geography of Central Europe without his being too precise. Thus it was designed to enlist the support of influential Moravian Christians in the crisis which followed Methodios's death. One might say that its main purpose is not to prove that anyone was right but that the Franks were always wrong and a pernicious influence in Moravia.[79]

3. The *Encomium* or *Panegyric of St Cyril*.[80] There are seven Slav manuscripts of the thirteenth–fourteenth centuries, two of which give St Clement as author. Since an *Encomium* is the normal concomitant of a *Life* and an *Office* this increases the likelihood that Clement had a hand in writing *VC* too. It contains no new material.

4. The *Encomium of SS Cyril and Methodios*,[81] probably written in Bulgaria in association with nos. 7 and 8. Over a dozen Slav manuscripts, one of which is in the same collection as *VM*. Contains a few valuable facts about Methodios.

5. The *Prolog Combined Lives of Cyril and Methodios*.[82] Two Balkan Slav manuscripts, one in the Hilandar *Prolog* of *c*. 1300, the other in a fourteenth-century *Prolog* from Lesnovo monastery. Short but valuable and possibly written wholly or partly in Moravia.

The separate Synaxarion *Lives* of Cyril and Methodios[83] are late Bulgarian works of little value, already containing the fiction that the saints evangelised Bulgaria in person.

6. The *Office of St Cyril*[84] (14 February): three early Slav manuscripts (not later than the twelfth century). This is the third text required (with nos. 1 and 3) for veneration as a saint and therefore should be of similar date—all three composed under Methodios's own eye.

7. The *Office of St Methodios*[85] (6 April): two thirteenth-century Slav manuscripts from Zográphou Monastery (Athos). The acrostic in the Canon shows that it was composed by a certain Constantine—very probably the Bulgarian Constantine 'the Priest';[b] this suggests a date of *c*. 893.

Nos. 6 and 7 are *Offices* of the Byzantine type and based generally on the *Lives* (nos. 1 and 2).

8. The combined *Office*[86] exists in one manuscript of the thirteenth century preserved in Russia. The acrostic in the Canon reads: КОУРИЛА ѲИЛО-СОФА И БЛАЖЕНА МЕТОДИЮ ПОЮ. It may also be ascribed to Constantine the Priest (see no. 7).

[a] See p. 58 below.   [b] See pp. 177–8.

9. There are also Roman *Offices* from Croatia whose language still preserves here and there very antique traits, but no manuscripts survive older than the fourteenth century.

10. The most important Latin source is the so-called *Legenda italica—Vita cum translatione S. Clementis*—of which the earliest extant manuscript is *c.* 1182. The final revision was done by Leo, Bishop of Ostia and Velletri (d. 1115), formerly a monk at Monte Cassino, following Gauderich (see no. 1 above), to whom Anastasius the Papal Librarian had sent his personal information on the Brothers.[87] Gauderich probably completed his work *c.* 879–80; hence its value.

11. *De Conversione Bagoariorum et Carantanorum libellus* (referred to as *Conversio*).[88] A partisan tract attacking Methodios but extremely valuable both on Methodian affairs and on the previous history of Salzburg missions.

12. Papal correspondence is naturally of fundamental importance. Western chronicles and annals provide the general historical framework. It should be noted that there is nothing whatever about the Moravian mission in Byzantine historians.

Methodios (whose baptismal name appears to have been Michael)[a] was born about 815, Constantine in 826 or 827. They were sons of a military officer in the province of Thessaloniki (Saloniki, Slav *Solun*), of which town he was probably a native. In such a time and place it is impossible to be dogmatic about a man's race. To be Greek meant to speak Greek.[b] Saloniki was the second city of the Byzantine Empire and a melting-pot of peoples, who thronged it at the great trade fairs, especially in October. There were many resident Slavs, in particular Bulgarian merchants; Slav speech was commonly heard within the city. The hinterland had been largely inhabited by Slavs for more than two centuries. The trade route down the Vardar valley kept them in constant peaceful or hostile contact with the great port. The organisation of a new *Theme* based on Saloniki during the early years of the ninth century implies that the Slav population was by then amenable to the ways of civilisation. Hand in hand with the imposition of Byzantine administration (taxation, military service, etc.) would of course go their conversion to Christianity. Intermarriage of Greek and Slav must have been frequent. It is generally assumed that the father of the two saints was Greek; nothing is known of their mother except that her name was Maria.[c]

---

a So given in the Χιλανδαρικὴ Διήγησις (*Legend of Hilandar*).

b Comparatively few emperors of Byzantium were pure Greek. Basil I, who was born about 830 and made himself autocrat in 867, was probably half Armenian and half Slav, and his descendants, the euphemistically named 'Macedonian' dynasty, ruled for nearly two centuries.

c Only given in some of the later sources, e.g. the *Prolog Life* of St Cyril, but it may be correct.

There are of course partisans of their Slavness, that is, that they should be counted as Bulgarians, since the Slav tribes and speech of the region were more or less Bulgarian. Later texts of Bulgarian provenance often call Constantine 'the Bulgar' but they were naturally designed for Bulgarian readers. Whatever may have been the blood of their parents the brothers' proficiency in Slav suggests a bilingual home, in which case the mother was probably the Slav speaker and therefore more Slav than Greek.

Methodios first entered the civil service. At an early age he was appointed governor of some district in Macedonia with a predominantly Slav population, where he may have served for some ten years.[a]

Constantine felt the call of learning and went in 843 to Constantinople to complete his education. His adolescence in the capital thus coincided with the final reinstatement of Orthodoxy in 843 after the death of the Emperor Theophilos. Theodora and the moderate party were doing their best to calm tempers once and for all, neither dealing severely with relegated iconoclasts nor allowing partisans of the opposite extreme to take their places. The new patriarch, Methodios I (843–7), was eminently a moderate. The deposed patriarch, John, was merely sent to a monastery on the Bosphorus. The iconoclast archbishop of Saloniki, Leo the Mathematician, was even brought to Constantinople to teach. It may well be that Constantine's decision to seek higher education in the capital was due to the encouragement of this learned prelate. In Constantinople the young man enjoyed the patronage of the Logothete (minister) Theóktistos, from 843 the influential tutor of Michael III,[89] and the friendship of Photios, the most learned man of his generation. Photios was the typical 'Humanist' of the ninth-century Byzantine 'Renaissance', widely read in pagan Greek literature. Under him Constantine mastered both profane and Christian knowledge. He thus received the broadest education which the time offered, and the time was one when pent-up intellectual energies could be vigorously released after the difficult passage of the seventh and eighth centuries. The re-founding by the Caesar Várdas of the university at the Magnaura Palace, where Leo the Mathematician, Photios and later Constantine himself taught, was one manifestation of this rapid upsurge. The promising young scholar was given the post of Private Secretary to the Patriarch[90]—a recognised stepping-stone to high ecclesiastical office. Such clerks were normally deacons. He soon, however, resigned this

[a] The geography and the figures are quite unreliable.

post, partly no doubt since it left him no leisure for private study and partly owing to personal differences with the Patriarch Ignatios (elected July 847). For a short time he appears to have been in retreat in a Bosphoran monastery but by early 851 he had returned to the capital to succeed Photios as professor at the university. He taught secular subjects (ἡ ἔξω or κοσμικὴ σοφία). His devotion to these may have been a reason for the monastically rigid Ignatios's disapproval of him, for monastic education excluded virtually all the secular Hellenism affected by the Byzantine layman; nor did monks teach in secular schools. Constantine had a great gift for languages; his teaching kept him in contact with many young foreigners seeking the prestige of a Greek education in the multilingual Empire.

Meanwhile Methodios abandoned his worldly career, his wife and family and entered one of the monasteries on the Bithynian Olympos, the greatest centre of Byzantine monasticism during the fifth to eighth centuries.[a] In 855/6 Constantine was a member of an official mission to the Caliph Mutawákkil (847–61) at Samarra.[91] The mission was principally diplomatic—to arrange an exchange of prisoners—but religious matters also entered in since the unusually intolerant Caliph had recently excluded Christians from his Civil Service and ordered other repressive measures against resident Christians. *Vita Constantini* records a disputation between Constantine and Moslem doctors on the Trinity, the great stumbling-block to Moslem theologians. The disputation as given is similar to many Moslem–Christian debates known from this period, a type of literature with which Constantine was surely familiar. He certainly studied Semitic languages at an early age, especially Hebrew.[b] There is no specific mention of Arabic but his knowledge of Islam and quotation from the *Koran* need occasion no surprise:[92] the Moslems were equally familiar with the New Testament.

Shortly after his return from this mission he retired to join his brother in his monastery. Presumably the *coup d'état* in Constantinople, in which his patron Theoktistos was assassinated (November 855), prompted this step. There is no evidence that he took monastic vows at this time.

The next task was a diplomatic and religious mission to Khazaria

---

[a] The limits seem to be c. 845–55, most probably the early 850s. If he was born c. 815 he can scarcely have retired to a monastery c. 840 (as some state) *after* ten years' public service.

[b] The *Prolog Life* states that he studied them in Constantinople, *VC* 8 (surely wrongly) that he learnt Hebrew and 'Samaritan' only in Kherson (860). Samaritan might have been a new acquisition then, or Syriac, useful since the Khazars used a form of Syriac script. See pp. 43, 245–6.

(autumn 860–1). Photios was now Patriarch (December 858) and able to resume his patronage of Constantine. The brothers[a] travelled by way of Kherson, the great Greek outpost in the Crimea, to the Caspian Sea.[b] Islamic and Jewish cultural influences were paramount in Khazaria; once again Constantine's semitic scholarship determined the choice. He was also expected to be a learned Christian apologist; his debate with the Jews of Khazaria is given at considerable length in his *Life*.[93]

The diplomatic was, however, surely more important than the religious aspect of this mission. The interpretation of it has given rise to much controversy since Constantine's report has not survived and we have only the abbreviated form included in his *Life* with all its obscurities. As this is essentially a saint's Life the real diplomatic work of the mission is hardly touched on. Khazaria was at this time, and had been since the seventh century, an ally of Byzantium. Relations were particularly close since *c.* 830. It was generally in their common interest to curb the plundering instincts of the nomadic peoples of the steppes.[c] The initiative in this exchange appears to have come from the Khazars. Constantine is presented in the account as leader of the mission. On the religious side there was no question of trying to convert the Khazar ruling class from Judaism to Christianity but merely to safeguard the practice of Christianity and the persons of Christians in the Khazar Empire, where the normally prevailing tolerance had apparently been temporarily broken.

Several incidents on their journey call for special mention. First, the miraculous discovery by Constantine of the relics of St Clement of Rome near Kherson. According to legend Clement, probably the third successor of St Peter in the Roman see, was exiled to the Crimea, where he was martyred by being thrown into the sea tied to an anchor.[d] Constantine,

---

[a] The inclusion of Methodios in the mission has been considered suspect. But clearly if *VC* was written before 885 substantially in its present form—which seems certain—the mentions of Methodios, however incidental, must be genuine. Methodios preferred to keep his participation in the background. Moreover some of the more picturesque details read like the account of an eye-witness and would very improbably have been included in Constantine's own official report.

[b] The site of the Greek city of Khersónnesos (Slav *Korsun*) is a short distance west of modern Sevastópol. Derbent (or Semender on the lower Terek) was the winter capital, Itil (near Astrakhan on the Volga) the summer capital of Khazaria. See also p. 238. [c] Cf. pp. 237 ff.

[d] There seems to be no historical foundation for this. He died *c.* A.D. 96. He was never in the Crimea. The story of his martyrdom there is not developed before *c.* A.D. 400. On the other hand true cases of exile thither are known from at least the fifth century, among them the Patriarch Timothy of Alexandria (*c.* 457) and Pope Martin I, who died there in 655. The Crimea then received many exiles and refugees during the Iconoclast troubles.

with the enthusiastic help of clergy and people, recovered the relics. They were borne in triumphal procession by easy stages to the cathedral. It may well be for a service to celebrate this that he wrote (and delivered?) a sermon.[a] Part of the relics was presented to the cathedral of Kherson; the remainder was eventually brought back by him to Constantinople and then formed the most valuable gift taken to Moravia in 863. Secondly, Constantine exercised his gift of tongues on certain books which he came across in Kherson. This will be discussed below.[b] In the third place, on the way back Constantine succeeded in converting some pagans, or rather improving the Christianity of some semi-Christians, in the district of Phullae.[94] This is one of the rare glimpses which we are given of Constantine as evangelist. His learned address to them is no doubt a literary fiction but by one means or another he persuaded them to cut down and burn their sacred tree. Lastly, on the diplomatic side we note that the customary present to ambassadors at the conclusion of a mission took the form, at Constantine's special request, of the liberation of Greek prisoners in Khazaria. This is curious since Khazaria was an ally of Byzantium. No doubt one of the peoples loosely subject to the Khazar Khagan had taken them in some local affray in the Caucasus and the Khagan had done nothing about righting this technical breach of faith. The incident would be hardly worth mentioning had it not given rise to completely different interpretations of the whole mission. Kartashëv,[95] for example, supposes that the mission was never sent to the Khazar Khagan at his capital, but to some pagan Slav Khagan under Khazar suzerainty (it is true that the Slavs did adopt the title Khagan),[c] not far from the Crimea. There is little substance in these doubts.[96]

After this successful mission Methodios became abbot of the important Polychron monastery on the Bithynian Olympos and Constantine resumed his learned studies. When Rastislav's request for teachers reached the Emperor in 862 it was natural for him to send these two. They were no doubt the men best qualified for the task: 'You are both natives of Saloniki, and all of you speak Slav perfectly', the Emperor is reported to have said when giving them their commission.[97] But perhaps there is more to it than that: it may have been well known to the authorities that the brothers were interested specifically in missionary work among the Slavs. It must be borne in mind that both *Vita Constantini* and *Vita Methodii* are principally concerned with the Moravian mission. Neither attempts a complete account of the saints' earlier

<hr/>

[a] See p. 57.   [b] See pp. 40 and 245.   [c] See p. 282 note b.

activities. Methodios had governed Slavs, at most imperfect Christians, for ten years.[a] It is at least possible, indeed probable, that when Constantine joined his brother in his monastery about 855 they discussed missions to Slavs, in particular Balkan Slavs, and the prerequisites for their successful prosecution. It is often suggested, though not open to proof, that Constantine visited his brother when governor of his Slav province. Surely Methodios, if not Constantine, was thereby stimulated early in his career to consider the practical problems of such missions.[98] But there was material nearer to hand. There was a large Slav population in Bithynia, still unassimilated in the ninth century, which was in need of enlightenment. Monks of various Olympian monasteries are known to have been active missionaries as far afield as Armenia and would scarcely have neglected peoples within easier reach. Methodios had at least one devoted pupil on Olympos—Clement. The main problem was not language but writing. Once past the preliminaries a new Christian community could not continue to thrive without the provision of a literate clergy. The surest method was naturally the education of natives in the reading and writing of Christian religious texts. As with the Mosaic Law, the immutable written text is the foundation of the new dispensation. No pagan Slav people had as yet created an alphabet for itself.[99] Constantine came to the conclusion that the Slav tongue needed a special alphabet designed for it. In the mid-ninth century Slav speech over a very large area was not yet widely differentiated and he will have estimated that an alphabet which fitted the phonetic pattern of the dialect which he spoke[b] would serve for all Slavs. Only given an adequate system of writing could progress be made. A passage in *Vita Methodii* may be held to suggest that Methodios and Clement agreed.[100]

The author of *Vita Constantini* presents the invention of such an alphabet by Constantine as a miracle following directly on the Emperor Michael's declaration of his intention to send them to Moravia. Constantine had expressed his willingness to go but stressed that without an alphabet the effort would be vain.[101] By dint of prayer he was enabled at once to design a satisfactory one and forthwith began to write his first Slav version of a Christian text—the beginning of St John's Gospel.[c]

[a] See also pp. 10 ff. Less than fifty years later Slavs of similar provinces to his own (not certainly identified) had received bishops, if only missionary bishops.

[b] The dialects spoken in the hinterland of Saloniki in the ninth century could be described as Macedonian or south-west Bulgarian, and seem to have some affiliation with some modern dialects in the Rhodope area. Macedonian is here a geographical, not a linguistic, term.

[c] See also p. 65.

It is rather more likely that Constantine, in association with Methodios and others (for one adept was not enough) had been elaborating an alphabet since about 855. The *Life* understandably preferred to suggest that it was now presented to the Emperor as a divine inspiration. A date 855 is in fact given by one source—the monk Hrabr—but the computation gives rise to some doubts.[102] In any case the designing of an alphabet must have taken considerable time and experiment. We can reconcile the possibilities best by assuming that Constantine perfected in 862/3, when an immediate practical need arose, an alphabet which he had been planning for some years previously.[103] He must also have been experimenting in the creation of a Slav literary language and teaching it to his circle; this too does not spring ready-made to the pen.[104] Consequently the summons to Moravia was a heaven-sent opportunity to give practical shape to a scholarly pursuit.

The Slav alphabets and written language

The question now arises, what alphabet did Constantine invent? That he did invent one—giving the word the widest possible interpretation—can scarcely be doubted if only because in 880 Pope John VIII was well aware that the alphabet used in the service-books submitted to the Pope in 868 was new.[105]

The Orthodox Slavs use to this day the alphabet which they call after St Cyril (Constantine)—Cyrillic (Russian кири́ллица). The make-up of Cyrillic is quite plain. It preserved the Greek letters for all sounds more or less common to Greek and Slav, maintained unnecessarily the two *i*'s and two *o*'s embedded in Greek orthography but no longer by the ninth century distinguished in pronunciation, and also the representation of *u* as a digraph.[a] It followed as closely as possible the Greek numerical system even to the point of including several otherwise unwanted Greek letters purely for their numerical value.[b] The earliest Cyrillic letters known are based on the formal Greek uncials of the ninth–tenth centuries. There remain the additional signs for special Slav sounds to be accounted for.

On the other hand Glagolitic,[c] the only other early specifically Slav

---

[a] И$=\eta$, I$=\iota$; o, ω; oy$=ov$ (*v* by itself was evolving from [ü] to [i]).

[b] E.g. $\Theta=9$, $\overset{\vee}{\mathsf{Z}}=60$, $\Psi=700$.

[c] The name is comparatively recent, being borrowed from its continued use in parts of Croatia (see p. 196), where a priest who celebrated in Slav was known as *glagoljaš* (from *glagolati*=speak, talk) in contrast to the *latinjaš* who celebrated in Latin.

alphabet, is patently an artificial script. This is clear from three things: that no certain filiation for it has yet been found; that the earliest surviving forms do not show a general principle of symmetry such as a much-used alphabet inevitably acquires;[106] and that the numerical values of the letters follow exactly the order of the alphabet, with its special additions, and thus get out of step with the Greek and the Cyrillic. We have therefore to determine which alphabet was the earlier and where and by whom each was invented.

Early scholars who worked on the palaeography of Glagolitic, accepting it as Constantine's invention, thought that they had found prototypes for at least a large proportion of the letters in Greek minuscules of the ninth century.[107] With the increasing use of cursive at this time even for sacred texts and the corresponding obsolescence of uncials, there is perhaps no objection to be made, though one might have expected an inventor to choose a more hieratic style on which to model a new sacred alphabet.[108] Other theories among an abundant crop of more recent speculations may be shortly reviewed, divisible into Western and Eastern.

Western

The Glagolitic alphabet took shape in the eighth century in north-east Italy, that is, in the Aquileian province, or possibly even at Salzburg, on the basis of Carolingian minuscules—with which of course similarities can be found—or otherwise, in connection with the earliest missions to the local Slavs.[109] Some have seen its earliest forms in an alphabet appended by Virgil of Salzburg to his *Edicta Aethici Philosophi Cosmographi*, written between about 768 and 774.[110] He attributed the alphabet out of prudence to St Jerome. This gives a specious link with the later Croat tradition, probably not earlier than the late eleventh century and first mentioned in 1248, that St Jerome was the inventor of Glagolitic; he was supposed to have been a native of Dalmatia or Bosnia. If this were true Constantine either did not miraculously invent an alphabet in Constantinople or else abandoned it in favour of adopting and adapting an alphabet already familiar to some Moravian Slavs. But Virgil's alphabet is either some form of North Italian Gothic script or a learned joke.

A variation on this theme proposes that Constantine first composed the Cyrillic alphabet, therefore rightly called after him, but later he or others invented the Glagolitic in Moravia as a script that could be kept secret from the Franks, Cyrillic being too close to Greek.[111]

Eastern

The first Slav alphabet arose not in Europe proper but in the Black Sea region. Hypotheses of this kind are particularly aimed at accounting for a passage in *Vita Constantini* which states that Constantine came across an enigmatic Psalter and Gospel Book in Kherson on his way to Khazaria (winter 861), found a man who spoke the language in which they were written and was thus enabled rapidly to familiarise himself with the system of writing.[112] The language is called that of the *Rus* or *Ros*. It is certain that *Rus* here refers neither to Goths nor to Scandinavians (Swedes). Although Constantine might well have met with Gothic scriptures in the Crimea[a] the Goths were never called Rus and moreover appear under their own name in *VC* 16. The Scandinavians had long had runes but they used them only for epigraphic and certain magical purposes—the book was still foreign to them.[113] Moreover, as far as we know, Constantine knew no Germanic language.

If *Rus* means Slavs, the orthographic system must have been either some local adaptation of Greek or Semitic type[114] or else an entirely unfamiliar system. Had then the Slavs of South Russia already invented for themselves an alphabet by the middle of the ninth century? There is as yet no tangible evidence of writing among them at that time. Nor is there any firm support for the assumption of a sufficiently advanced level of Christianity to warrant Christian texts in the native tongue.[b]

The text therefore is probably corrupt.[115] Worse still, such hypotheses ask us to believe that Constantine deliberately deceived the Emperor, passing off as his own invention an alphabet which he had at most improved. It cannot be said that either Western or Eastern theories command the minimum of factual support for serious consideration. Setting aside the remote possibility that Constantine composed *both* alphabets, we are bound to conclude that he invented the Glagolitic if we can show its priority over the Cyrillic. This fortunately can now be done with a fair measure of certainty. The argument converges from two directions:

[a] The Crimean Goths remained a distinct people in the mountain fastnesses after the Gothic Empire on the steppes had dissolved (late fourth century A.D.). They were converted early (probably third century) to Orthodox Christianity and had their own hierarchy. Thus their religious affairs were quite separate from those of the Danubian Goths evangelised by Wulfila (fourth century) and provided by him with a translation of the Bible. The Gothic language only became extinct in the Crimea about the fourteenth century.

[b] Cf. pp. 245–6.

1. There are strong reasons to accept the premiss that the Cyrillic alphabet was either drawn up or finally codified at the great Bulgarian assembly in 893,[a] which made it the official alphabet both for ecclesiastical and secular use.[116] The maximum identity with Greek script and with the Greek numerical system was an obvious convenience in Bulgaria where Greek was the second language, carrying all the cultural prestige, and already had a considerable tradition of administrative use behind it.

Much will therefore depend on the analysis of the extra signs in both Glagolitic and Cyrillic required for Slav sounds not represented in Greek. Two of the simplest signs, those for *š* and *ž*, are nearly identical in both alphabets and therefore equivocal. As for the rest, to derive the more complicated (Glagolitic) from the simpler is in itself somewhat improbable, except if secrecy is seriously held to be the object. Goshev's recent study of all available inscriptions,[117] in particular the *graffiti* in the Round Church at Preslav[b] the Bulgarian capital, now reveals exactly the situation that we should expect if the codification of the Cyrillic alphabet was ordered in 893. The Round Church was built in the years immediately following. Here we find Greek letters supplemented by Glagolitic letters precisely for those sounds and for those sounds only which had no equivalent in the Greek alphabet. Glagolitic *b*, *ž*, *dz*, *c* (=ts), *č*, *š* and the two *jers* (ultra-short vowels) are all represented; the two Slav nasals by chance are absent. The reverse has not been found anywhere—occasional Cyrillic (that is, Greek) letters in Glagolitic words.

The transition from the Glagolitic to the Cyrillic forms of the special letters meets few insuperable difficulties since intermediate stages of evolution are in most cases there to be seen.[c] The forms of the Cyrillic alphabet were substantially stabilised by 943 at the latest, the date of the 'Dobrudja' inscription.[118] One of the Preslav inscriptions is dated, according to the best possible reading, 6401 = 893, and the date is expressed according to the Cyrillic (Greek) numeration, thus showing once again that there was no intention of employing the confusing Glagolitic numeration in a country where the Greek system was long familiar.

To this may be added that so far no trace has been found in the

[a] See pp. 174–5.   [b] On Preslav see pp. 170–2.
[c] Epigraphic evidence now points to the new Cyrillic letter ѣ being not a modification of Cyrillic ь but a new combination of Glagolitic *i*+*a*—a close approximation to its sound—and is therefore further support for Glagolitic's contribution to Cyrillic and not *vice versa*.

Bulgarian lands—or indeed anywhere else—of the use of two alphabets before 893.

2. The essay 'On the alphabet' by the monk Hrabr[a] is the defence of *a* Slav alphabet against Greek. He argues that the Slavs have as much right to an alphabet of their own as the Greeks and that St Cyril's invention was the greater achievement in that it was the work of one genius, not the mere result of improving the work of others (the Phoenician alphabet). Hrabr wrote his essay in Church Slavonic, not in Greek; therefore it was not Greeks whom he wished to influence but Bulgarians. Consequently the Greek alphabet which he opposes is not that used for writing Greek but for writing Slav—that is to say the uncodified or unsystematic use of the Greek alphabet in Bulgaria before 893.[119]

It follows that the Glagolitic alphabet was then known in Bulgaria and can only be the alphabet brought from Moravia by St Clement and other exiles in 885/6.[b] The question of the following decade was whether Bulgaria should adopt this more perfect but strange medium for recording the Slav language or whether it should continue to use the convenient Greek alphabet without any special adaptations (in Hrabr's term—*bez ustrojenija*).

It is understandable that the scholars of Preslav, including Tsar Symeon himself, a product of Constantinopolitan higher education, showed no enthusiasm for Glagolitic. Moreover, Hrabr speaks throughout of one Slav alphabet only and that as a complete new invention of thirty-eight letters, not as the addition of some fourteen supplementary signs to usable Greek ones. The inescapable conclusion is that only the Glagolitic existed at the time: there was nothing that he recognised as a 'Cyrillic alphabet' which, if it had existed, would have made all his arguments nugatory.[c]

This, with the epigraphic evidence, allows virtual certainty that the solution of 893 was, on this occasion, a fruitful compromise: Glagolitic was to be allowed to contribute the extra precision which the Greek alphabet by itself could not easily provide.[d] In this way the principle of

[a] See p. 177.   [b] See pp. 163 ff.
[c] Though the extant manuscripts are all in Cyrillic it is clear from internal evidence that he wrote originally in Glagolitic.
[d] It is unlikely (and not borne out by the epigraphic material) that the incorporated Glagolitic signs were simplified in one operation by one man. The compromise may have been suggested by Naum or Constantine the Priest (see pp. 177–8). Of the two perhaps the latter has more claim to be considered the 'inventor' of Cyrillic, specifically of new signs such as ѣ, not taken over from Glagolitic. Did the identity of the name Constantine lead to the confusion over the name 'Cyrillic' for the alphabet in later years?

St Cyril's achievement was saved though the fortunes of the Glagolitic alphabet thereafter declined. For, given that there was no codified Cyrillic alphabet before 893, it follows automatically that St Cyril's invention was the Glagolitic.

3. Finally, the philological evidence is also in favour of this conclusion. Though preservation has of course been haphazard, the oldest texts in Glagolitic record not merely different variants but also a more antique state of the Slav language than those in Cyrillic. It is naturally not possible to interpret with complete certainty the original phonetic values of a system of conventional signs (such as the Glagolitic alphabet) but the best analysis points to the conclusion that Glagolitic was originally constructed to fit a Bulgarian–Macedonian dialect. Certain modifications were then introduced to suit a West Slav dialect[120] and later still various Balkan dialects. In the same way Cyrillic, after its first codification, was subjected to local modification in every country where it was adopted.

Nothing in the make-up of the Glagolitic alphabet contradicts Constantine's authorship. All is in favour of it: the fine phonetic analysis of Slav speech, dependence on the Greek model no less than Cyrillic,[a] and the adoption of at least one manifestly Semitic sign for a non-Greek sound.[b] The geographical distribution of manuscripts in Glagolitic—Bohemia, Croatia, Macedonia—itself points to a focus of expansion in Central Europe, and their language connects them, more or less remotely according to date, with the Cyrillomethodian mission to Moravia and Pannonia.

Yet many problems remain. Why did Constantine opt for such elaborate signs in the first place? It is true, as Kiparski has recently stressed,[121] that the Glagolitic letters are for the most part made up of the three sacred symbols—the circle (eternity), triangle (Trinity) and cross. Nevertheless they are complicated to write. Was it merely to be as different as possible from both Latin and Greek, as the *Encomium* of the two saints perhaps suggests?[122] Again, why, when variants of the same sign were used for different sounds, did Constantine allot them in such an apparently arbitrary fashion?[c] The difficulties over Constantine's

---

[a] Principally: two types of *i* and *o*; the diphthongal representation of *u*, as also of the purely Slav vowel *y*. It would be true to say that the departures of Glagolitic from an exact phonetic rendering of the Slav language are just those which Greek habits of mind would produce, certainly not Latin habits of mind. Its inventor therefore had a Greek education.

[b] *š* is represented by Semitic **ѡ**. Several other signs may have Semitic prototypes but are more open to dispute.

[c] E.g. **Ѵ** = v, **Ꙗ** = d; **Ꙁ** = i, **Ꙋ** = s. In the latter case it has been suggested that the common abbreviation for *Jesus* was in mind: $\overline{\text{Ꙁ Ꙋ}}$ = Greek $\overline{\text{ΗΣ}}$. But this does not get us much further.

Glagolitic are comparable to those over the Armenian alphabet, perfected by St Mesrop Mashtots' in the early years of the fifth century. He had as fine an ear as Constantine; he likewise designed signs for the most part not clearly referable to standard Greek or Semitic scripts; but Greek in particular stands behind the vowel system, where once again the digraph *ou* appears.[123]

In the troubled centuries which followed the formation of the two Slav alphabets attribution of them was made at hazard since the tradition was lost.[124] The sole pointer to a reversal of names is the statement of a Russian monk, Upýr Lihój, in the second half of the eleventh century, that he was transcribing a text 'from the Cyrillic' (из коурилицѣ). As his transcription is Cyrillic in the modern sense, evidently he believed that Glagolitic was Constantine's alphabet.

Would the Byzantine authorities have approved in 862/3 such a 'fancy' alphabet as the Glagolitic, submitted to them by Constantine, even if miraculously revealed? One can suppose that they would have preferred something more obviously Greek. The most that we can assume is that some unofficial or conditional approval was given in Constantinople to Constantine's alphabet before the missionaries left for Moravia.

The precise instructions given to them can only be guessed in default of sources. Rastislav had asked for a bishop and Slav instructors. The Emperor was gladly sending the Slav instructors. Given the insistence of Constantine on the necessity for an alphabet, the Emperor must also have approved some measure of translation of Christian texts into Slav. But this falls far short of an unconditional approval of a Slav version of the liturgy—the most sacred text of all. Opinion on liturgical languages differed by this time in East and West, though the differences were mainly of emphasis and have been exaggerated. In the East the Byzantine Empire had always been a multilingual body. Since Justinian's time Latin had rapidly lost its position as the language of the army, the law and government generally. Greek was supreme in the church. Latin, Greek and Hebrew were widely held to be the only three truly sacred tongues. Supporters of this view were known as 'trilinguists'.[125] But a number of Christian peoples in the East had adopted their own languages on conversion for all ecclesiastical purposes, including the text of the liturgy—as far afield as the Georgians and Armenians, converted in the fourth–fifth centuries A.D. Nearly all these churches were, however, now heterodox churches (mostly Monophysites) and their withdrawal from Orthodoxy may well have helped to preserve their national liturgies.[126] Syria and Egypt, the great provinces lost to Islam, were likewise the home of a multiplicity of liturgical languages. Within Orthodoxy, local variations were expected and tolerated but a proposal for any new sacred language would have now met grave doubts. There had been no recent case; the problem had to be examined afresh. For Greeks Greek was the only civilised language no less than Latin for a Westerner. Moreover the manifest Byzantine policy of the most rapid hellenization possible of the vast number of Slavs who had squatted within the Imperial frontiers, especially in northern and peninsular Greece,[a] was not apt to lead, and apparently had not in fact led over the previous two centuries or more, to any great interest in the Slav tongue or to any desire to perpetuate it in any form or for any purpose. However, Moravia was outside the Empire; in this respect Constantine could be allowed considerable freedom. When it came to the possibility of a Slav language church in Bulgaria, much nearer home, the Byzantine authorities appear to have hesitated at first, then accepted it, then repudiated it again in favour of hellenization when they conquered the country.[b] The doctrine of the Orthodox church on this matter was finally formulated by Theodore Balsamon (Patriarch of Antioch, 1185–95): 'Those who are Orthodox in all respects but who are altogether ignorant of the Greek tongue may celebrate in their own language, provided that they have unaltered versions of the customary prayers exactly as transcribed from well-written Greek texts.'[127]

In the West the narrow 'trilingual' view was commoner in the peripheral churches than at the centre in Rome. The Holy See maintained (and has until our own times continued to maintain) the greatest reserve towards proposals for translation of the Latin Mass. The Papacy was the supreme symbol of religious unity in the West and the Mass was the supreme manifestation of the church's unity, overriding all local differences. Charlemagne had succeeded with considerable difficulty in imposing some semblance of Latin unity on the church within his Empire. The West now took its stand on this principle. This attitude had been partly bred by the long struggle against Arianism among the Germanic peoples; not until the middle of the seventh century did the

---

[a] See pp. 5–12.

[b] The Byzantine authorities surely did not envisage anything but a Greek church in Bulgaria at the time of Boris's baptism. Nor does Photios mention the Moravian mission in his letter to Boris (865—see p. 160). The hellenization of Bulgaria, as for Slavs within the Empire, still seemed the safest policy. See also pp. 181 ff.

last recalcitrants, the Lombards, finally enter the Catholic church. The use of the vernacular had been widespread in the Arian churches, beginning with Wulfila's great Gothic translation of the Bible. As a result the Church was chary of allowing the people at large too easy access to the sacred texts. Just as important was the practical difficulty of ensuring that new translations which might be made in wild and distant mission fields were in fact accurate and free from heresy.[128]

On the other hand, no Western authority (and of course no Eastern) objected to the use of the local vernacular in the mission field; this was a *sine qua non* for communicating the elementary stages of the Christian faith. The earliest steps of written Germanic were taken almost exclusively in the service of the church. Charlemagne insisted that the Lord's Prayer and the Creed must be learnt by heart by converts in their own tongue before baptism.[a] The Germanic peoples did not apparently have on their part any reservations about using their own vernaculars, uncouth though they might still be called.[129] There is much in favour of the view that Charlemagne's personal enthusiasm for Latin culture and imposition of Latin uniformity in the Frankish church put an abrupt end to its further Germanisation; no German dialect was accepted as a liturgical language. However that may be, Carolingian councils continued to reiterate the need to use local languages (*sermo rusticus*) except in the central mysteries of the Church. Thus the Synod of Frankfurt (794) proclaimed: 'Ut nullus credat quod nonnisi in tribus linguis Deus orandus sit, quia in omni lingua Deus adoratur et homo exauditur si iusta petierit.'[130] Similar statements were made throughout the first half of the ninth century.[b]

Constantine makes the principle of his own missionary work abundantly clear: all peoples should be able to praise God in their native tongue; only thus can they become perfect in the understanding and practice of the faith. It is in this sense that Isaiah is quoted in chapter 15 of his *Life*[131] and the arguments of the trilinguists answered in Venice in chapter 16. The verse Preface to the Gospels[c] (possibly by Constantine) reiterates it.[132] His last appeal to his brother on his death-bed was not to abandon the Slav church which they were still struggling to establish. Personally then he may have taken this principle to its logical conclusion

---

[a] See p. 16 above, and p. 323, n. 14.

[b] Catholic opinion did not harden till a very late date; even the Council of Trent did not formally exclude the use of all vernaculars. Their exclusion followed the Protestant secessions since the Protestant churches made a point of abandoning Latin in favour of the language of the country.   [c] Below, p. 57 no. 5.

and envisaged from the start a Moravian church with a Slav liturgy. It was from this that all the troubles were to arise.

There is some doubt about the ecclesiastical orders which the brothers had received by the time of their arrival in Moravia. One at least must have been a priest. Methodios, as abbot of an important monastery, may have become a *hieromonakh* (monk in priest's orders).[a] Constantine might have been ordained before the Khazar or the Moravian mission but in any case not before the canonical age of thirty, i.e. before 856/7.[b] On the whole it seems more probable that Constantine was only a deacon.[133]

Their task in Moravia was to teach (that is, to train young Slavs for the church), to convert and baptise the unconverted as opportunity offered, to study the ecclesiastical situation and report thereon to the Byzantine government.[c] We cannot assume that they were welcomed unreservedly by the Moravians. Rastislav's strategy had not been signally successful. This was little more than the arrival of yet another party of missionaries in an already complicated situation. However, they brought with them the highly venerated relics of St Clement and were able to pursue their work under his patronage. The training of Moravians in the new alphabet and sacred language was certainly the main task. It is surely likely that they interfered with existing religious practices and institutions as little as possible, Moravian Christianity being perhaps further advanced than they had been led to believe. Though they objected to some Western customs[d] they respected existing tradition. They could not pretend to any exclusive rights; they could not count on the Moravians unhesitatingly adopting their conception of a Slav church. Friction with the Frankish clergy there must have been, but at first as intruders (perhaps as political agents) rather than on any doctrinal or ritual grounds. Most of the Frankish clergy cannot but have appeared uncouth and untrained to these highly educated Byzantines, perhaps even hardly competent to develop such a mission field; for this was a time of high achievement in the Eastern, but relative decadence in

[a] It was preferred, but not obligatory, that an abbot should be a priest; he could be a deacon or even a layman.

[b] Justinian had decreed (*Novel* 123 of 546): priests must be thirty, deacons twenty-five and readers eighteen. These canonical ages tended to be lowered with passage of time.

[c] We do not know whether diplomatic envoys accompanied them as in the case of the previous missions. If any formal treaty between the Byzantine Empire and Moravia was in view, as some think, this becomes more probable.

[d] In particular the prerequisites for baptism were much stricter in the East.

the Western church.[134] The provision of trained natives for the priesthood, the matter of supreme importance, would tend to exacerbate Frankish resentment. For the Franks were relatively little interested in this, a shortcoming which partly arose from their system of 'proprietary churches' (German *Eigenkirchen*), by which the owner of the land had the right to build a church on it and appoint the incumbent.[a] That the Franks introduced this practice in Pannonia is clear from *Conversio* (chapter 13), where churches are described in such terms as *in proprietate Wittimaris* ('on Witmar's estate'). The same was surely true in Moravia.

The methods of the brothers and their difficulties are not described in the *Lives*; we have none of the documentation such as allows us a clear picture of St Augustine's *familia* and missionary practice in England. Presumably they were maintained entirely at Rastislav's charges and followed a more or less monastic régime. We know only that it took three years[b] before they considered that their pupils were ready and worthy to receive their first orders. In those three years they must have seen sufficient progress in the Christian life of the Moravians to believe that their withdrawal (for they did not expect to return) would not prejudice what had already been achieved. They were not so much pioneers as consolidators of the second stage of Moravian Christianity.

From Moravia to Rome

The decision now had to be taken: who was to ordain the newly trained Slavs? The question of ordination is so obvious that it must have been considered in advance, whether or not a time-limit was originally set for the mission. Three years sounds a likely limit. But at the end of three years, we may be sure, the actual situation no longer fitted the provisional instructions. The decision on what was best to be done was not straightforward. One thing could be ruled out as a practical possibility:

a In the early ninth century Frankish bishops were still voicing disapproval of the proprietary system, since the logical outcome was that all members of the clerical estate needed a protector (feudal superior) in the secular estate, and the parish priest, usually of humble birth, became a minor, if the only educated, servant of the lord of the manor. But such protests were without effect. The Western reformers of the eleventh century again attacked this feudalisation of the clergy. The practice was rare in the East, where Justinian's ruling obtained (*Novel* 57 of 537), that those who build churches are not to have the right to appoint whom they like as clergy. See also p. 72.

b Three years according to *VM*, three years and four months according to *VC*; the difference is easily accounted for by inclusion or not of part of the subsequent journey. But four and a half years according to the *Italian Legend*. This longer period has been defended but the shorter raises less difficulties in the chronology as a whole.

the offices of a Frankish bishop. In 864 Louis once more dominated Rastislav and we may conjecture a new ascendancy of Frankish clergy unwelcome to Rastislav, who was still hankering after a bishop of his own.[a]

Communications with Constantinople may have been difficult or impossible. No correspondence survives between any of the three points Constantinople–Rome–Moravia relating to the missionary work of the years 863–6. This makes the interpretation of the brothers' actions very delicate. The simplest assumption is that most consonant with common sense: the brothers expected to return to Constantinople in due course (as they had on completing previous official missions) to report fully on the Moravian situation, to see whether they could personally be spared for further work in Moravia or whether the Byzantine Government had other plans for them. They were prominent men, sent on a mission with important diplomatic and ecclesiastical implications. Constantinople could not remain indifferent if no reports were received or if they did not return at the agreed time. Nor would the Imperial authorities wash their hands of them for any trivial reason.[135] Two points tend to confirm the assumption that they were now proposing to return home, whether directly or indirectly: that they *both* left Moravia and that they brought away with them such parts of the relics of St Clement of Rome as had not been deposited in Moravian churches.[136] So far in conformity with original instructions. But as to *ordinations* they now had to consider these points:

1. They found Latin Christianity far more firmly entrenched in Moravia than anyone in Constantinople had supposed. Ought they not then to have their pupils ordained by some Western ecclesiastical authority?

2. They knew that Moravia had no historical and only tenuous geographical claims to be considered a Byzantine mission-field. This did not exclude the possibility of establishing there an Eastern church but the claims of the Frankish church geographically and of the Papacy as to missions were manifestly better. It cannot be said that Rome had shown much interest in Central European missions since the elevation of Salzburg (798) but it would be known to them that the Pope had reserved for Rome a general interest in the new areas. Rastislav too would realise

---

[a] We do not know whether Hermanrich of Passau, appointed to succeed the incapacitated Hartwig in 866, immediately made clear to the brothers that they were *personae non gratae* in Moravia.

that sooner or later Rome must be consulted, if only on the question of liturgical language.

3. We must assume that the brothers had at least some information about the undignified quarrel between Pope and Patriarch which had reached a critical stage just after they left Constantinople. When Michael III assumed power in 856 with the help of his uncle Vardas, he soon fell out with Patriarch Ignatios and replaced him in December 858 by Photios, a layman. Despite the formal confirmation of Photios's appointment by the Council of 861 the Pope was swayed by the arguments of Ignatian partisans and felt obliged to deny the validity of Photios's ordination and elevation. At a Lateran Synod about August 863 he finally declared Photios's election null and void. In doing so he exceeded the powers which Constantinople was prepared to acknowledge in the supreme hierarch.[137] Coolness between the Byzantine authorities and Rome on the one hand and a change of personalities in Constantinople itself might influence the brothers in their decision as to the next step. At all events, they did not proceed far on the direct overland route to Constantinople. We next hear of them at Mosaburg where Kotsel had succeeded his father Pribina[a] in 860/1. He had presumably been baptised as a child and was a zealous Christian, attached, as we have seen, to Salzburg; he already had at least five churches in or near his residence.[138] It is possible that Kotsel himself invited them, learning of their original work in Moravia and disturbed at the heavy hand which Salzburg had recently been using in his church affairs: *Conversio* records an exceptional visitation of Pannonia by Archbishop Adalwin of Salzburg during the Christmas period 864/5.[139] Frankish suzerainty and the domination of Salzburg irked the new ruler of Pannonia.

The brothers remained some considerable time at Kotsel's court— approximately the first half of 867—finding here perhaps a greater appreciation of the advantages of a Slav church than Rastislav had shown. Kotsel at once put fifty young people under them for training. Some of these apparently attained the requisite proficiency in a very short time and joined the number of ordinands.[140] This success at Mosaburg might have caused some further modification in the decision over ordinations, for Pannonia had always had close contacts with north-east Italy (Aquileia), which Kotsel presumably valued though a Frankish vassal.

The brothers went on to Venice. This was now the obvious route to

[a] See p. 24.

Constantinople, once Bulgaria had been rejected.[a] Conceivably, at the instance of Kotsel if not of Rastislav, they now wished to explore the possibility of procuring ordinations by Aquileia. There is much to suggest that Moravia had had to depend more on Aquileian (Lombard rather than Byzantine) clergy between Rastislav's break with the Franks (849) and the arrival of the Greek missionaries (863).[b] The brothers reached Italy some time in the second half of 867.

The *Life of Constantine* gives an inadequate account of the next episode for our purposes. It records only a dispute between Constantine and Venetian trilinguists, in which, relying principally on 1 Cor. 14, he argues that for the untutored Slavs religious truth presented in a foreign tongue has no power to reach their hearts and minds.[141] It is permissible to suppose that, if application was in fact made to Patriarch Lupus of Aquileia for ordinations and for approval of a Slav version of the liturgy, the prelate, being indeed himself a Frank, felt that this unusual situation was beyond his competence and referred the whole matter to Rome. We cannot, unfortunately, estimate precisely how many months these discussions in Aquileia and then in Venice took. The final decision of the brothers to proceed to Rome may have been made then. This would be all the more certain if we could be sure that in Venice they were accurately informed of recent events in the East.[c] For two important things had happened. In September 867 Basil had assumed power after assassinating Michael III and had at once deposed Photios and reinstated Ignatios. Though Photios had been Constantine's patron there are yet no grounds for considering Constantine such a devoted Photian that he would refuse to enter into relations with Ignatios.[142] As missionaries neither Constantine nor Methodios was particularly concerned with the internal quarrels of their church. Indeed the two *Lives* correctly present the Emperor rather than the Patriarch as their patron, since in the East the church was not, as in the West, a separate corporate body; the Patriarch is nowhere referred to by name in either text. The Emperor himself directed the affairs of the church, presided over councils, created sees and altered dioceses, and chose (theoretically) the Patriarch of

---

[a] It does not seem likely that internal changes in Bulgaria during these years (see pp. 161–2) would in themselves have dissuaded the brothers from travelling to Constantinople that way. This increases the likelihood that a westerly route, eventually joining the *Via Egnatia* at Dyrrachium was envisaged from the first.

[b] See the architectural considerations on p. 23 above.

[c] Western annals of the early Middle Ages show very clearly how haphazard was the transmission of information, even of important events. But communications between Constantinople and Venice are known to have been particularly regular and good.

Constantinople from a list of three names submitted to him by the assembled Metropolitans. None of the brothers' actions up to now or later in Rome shows a partisan spirit. A change of Emperor would be more likely to influence them than a change of Patriarch.

More important, in 866 Boris of Bulgaria had made approaches to Rome and to the Frankish church, being dissatisfied with the attitude of the Eastern church into which he had just been baptised.[a] If the brothers learnt in Venice that the Pope now had a mission working in Bulgaria, they would realise even more clearly that their own problems had better be discussed in Rome also. They went to Rome: the decision may have been entirely their own or finally determined by a summons from Pope Nicholas I (on receiving a report from Venice) towards the end of the year 867.[b]

Nicholas I (858–67) was an outstanding occupant of the Holy See in the ninth century. In him the conception of the Papacy as the supreme authority in the West and the final court of appeal for all Christians reached a notable peak. Though in no sense a sacred personage,[c] Charlemagne considered himself and acted fully as head of his church— the Frankish church; it was as such that he planned his eastward expansion and missionary policy—with or without the Pope's help. The administration of the Frankish church was entirely in his hands through the bishops whom he appointed. For the short time after his death that the Carolingian Empire remained united Imperial and ecclesiastical policy still went hand in hand. But after 843 the unity was broken and the three separate realms shared out between Charlemagne's sons attempted to go their own ways. The archbishoprics created by him grew in power after his control was removed. Many prelates felt more loyal to their prince than to the distant Pope.[143] In West Francia and Lotharingia territorial churches (German *Landeskirchen*) were fairly established; in East Francia, that is the predominantly missionary area,

a See pp. 159 ff.

b It is impossible to consider in detail all the other possibilities. Briefly, it seems less probable: (1) that *Constantinople* had instructed them, while still in Moravia, either to seek ordinations at Aquileia (to avoid a longer journey?) or to proceed to Rome; (2) that the Pope had instructed Rastislav to send them to Rome; (3) that the brothers were seeking, on their own initiative, Aquileian ordinations. It must have been as clear to them as to their patron Rastislav that only the Pope could provide a bishop for Moravia (and Pannonia) with authority over both Slav and Latin clergy, and moreover settle the language question with the Frankish church.

c That is to say, he was a layman but, as contemporary comparisons show, conceived his royal office in the spirit of King David: he was *a Deo coronatus*, entrusted with the spiritual no less than the material well-being of all his peoples. In this he was not far from the Byzantine conception.

less firmly. Thus by the 860s the time had come when the Papacy could again come forward as the upholder of a unity superior to increasing political fragmentation. Pope Nicholas is the first notable exponent of this Papal role. His independence of action was further assured by the fact that by this time neither the Greeks nor the Franks had the military strength to dominate Italy. Moreover, while resisting Frankish particularism in the settled realms, Nicholas had the best chance of preventing its further extension precisely in East Francia, which included, notionally or actually, Moravia and Pannonia.

Papal policy on missionary work also involved certain principles. The Holy See claimed a general direction of the church in newly converted areas until the obedience of that area was definitely decided. England had been a case in point. The most notorious instance had concerned the Scandinavian missions of St Ansgar of Corbie.[144] His status was regularised by his appointment as first archbishop of Hamburg in 831. When the town was destroyed by the Norsemen in 845 the Pope transferred the see to Bremen, till then a diocese subordinate to Cologne. The Archbishop of Cologne at once protested at being deprived of this bishopric and its missionary dependencies. The situation in Bavaria had been similar: though Charlemagne had appointed Arno to Salzburg, the Pope reserved his interest in the missionary areas. As recently as 860–3 Nicholas had quarrelled violently with the Frankish rulers and bishops over episcopal powers in general. Though Nicholas had won his point, the Frankish church had climbed down very reluctantly.[145] There was constant friction between the ambitions of the territorial hierarchy who initiated or followed Frankish expansion and the general control which the Papacy desired to exercise over missionary enterprise and over the results of missionary enterprise. Nicholas wrote to the Christian community of Nin in Dalmatia: 'If, according to the sacred ordinances, new churches may not be built without the sanction of the Pope, how can a [territorial] church...be established without the approval of the Apostolic See'?[146] Such control might be more or less actual under individual Popes but the principle remained. Further, in 867 the Frankish church had again suffered a setback, having had to retire from Bulgaria in favour of the Papal mission.[a]

Again, Nicholas had a firm policy towards the Eastern Empire. Early in his pontificate he had openly demanded the return of Illyricum to Rome.[147] His manoeuvres in the Balkans, including the mission to

[a] See p. 161.

Bulgaria, were all relevant to this demand. He was himself smarting under the rebuff suffered when his legates had been denied entry into Byzantine territory owing to Greek fury at his 'interference' in Bulgaria.

Thus when Nicholas was perhaps for the first time fully informed in the last months of his life of the work of Byzantine missionaries in Moravia he would wish to know if they were a danger to or could be turned to the advantage of his plans. He summoned them to Rome.[148] Such a summons would be obeyed without question.

To sum up: the available evidence is best explained on the hypothesis that the brothers intended from the first to return to Constantinople via Rome; the situation required it, whether or not they had received instructions from Constantinople to do so. This coincided with Nicholas's wish to see them. Their intentions about ordinations must remain obscure.

By the time they reached Rome Nicholas was dead (13 November 867). It is thought that they took up their residence in one of the Greek monasteries in Rome, most probably St Praxedis, near S. Maria Maggiore, founded not long before by Paschal I (817–24). As bearers of the relics of St Clement of Rome they were assured of a warm welcome.[149] The good offices of several prominent men could be expected—above all Anastasius, the Papal Librarian, a notable Greek scholar in a Rome that now knew little Greek; in the second place his uncle Arsenius, Bishop of Orta. But this connection was not without danger as Anastasius had been antipope in 855 and only returned to favour at the Curia in 862. On the other hand Formosus of Porto, who had just been recalled from Bulgaria,[a] was not likely to have much to say in favour of any form of Slav ecclesiastical particularism.[150] As Greeks the reception of the brothers might thus depend on the momentary ascendancy of pro-Greek and anti-Greek political factions at the Curia.

The new Pope, Hadrian II, was a wholehearted follower of Nicholas's policy. On this particular matter his attitude was still unknown. He appears to have made up his mind quickly. The decision did not rest primarily on any question of dogma or ritual but on ecclesiastical politics. The immediate need was clearly to consecrate a bishop or bishops for Moravia (Rastislav) and Pannonia (Kotsel) and to curb the pretensions of Passau and Salzburg.

In terms of the past Moravia was a no-man's land. Pannonia, however, had had a chequered history. In the fourth century *Illyricum*

[a] See p. 161.

occidentale (which was part of the Prefecture of Italy) comprised seven provinces from *Pannonia superior* in the North, through *Pannonia inferior* (with administrative capital at Sirmium), *Savia* (modern Slovenia) to *Dalmatia* (capital Salona). Its eastern boundary was roughly a line from Belgrade to Kotor. The separate Prefecture of *Illyricum orientale* was from 397 part of the government of the East. Between 424 and 437 a number of provinces, certainly including both Pannonias and Savia, were transferred from *Illyricum occidentale* to *Illyricum orientale*. From the eighth century the provinces were abandoned in favour of the new military *Themes*; but the ecclesiastical map, insofar as it was still intact, was not basically altered. However, about 732[151] Leo III transferred the rest of *Illyricum occidentale* as an ecclesiastical province to the Patriarchate of Constantinople, thus bringing it into line with the civil administration. The transference was part of Leo's actions directed against Popes Gregory II and III who firmly resisted his iconoclast policy, refused to recognise the new iconoclast patriarch Anastasios (730) and dared to excommunicate him. The Emperor had taken South Italy away at the same time, hoping to control it better under the Patriarchate of Constantinople. In any case, Pannonia was then largely in Avar hands; only after 796, with Charlemagne's subjection of the Avars, did the attachment of Pannonia and neighbouring provinces become again of practical importance. The Holy See had never acquiesced in Leo's 'robbery'.[152] Now in 868 Hadrian (no doubt following Nicholas) judged that the time had come to make a formal claim to Pannonia again. It also suited the strong desire of Rome to curb the Frankish church. The missions may have been Frankish work but the organisation of the church in this disputed area was to be settled by Rome, and Constantinople might well have to accept a *fait accompli*. Indeed the ecclesiastical allegiance of all the developing Slav peoples in Central Europe and the north Balkans was in the balance; it was a moment of great opportunity. It would be well to forget the old administrative groupings and start afresh.

It will be seen, then, that Papal control of the brothers' missionary areas, if it could be made actual, would be of great strategic advantage and a new Slav church, with a liturgy in Slav, as strange to Rome as to Constantinople, could act as a buffer, equally distinct from the Latin church of the Franks and from the Byzantine church, over which the Holy See could exercise direct control. At the same time Hadrian's attitude towards Constantinople was broadly conciliatory; it was important to treat this Byzantine mission with every mark of respect. It was in this sense that Hadrian consented to accept the 'Slav books' brought by the brothers and to ordain their pupils.[153] The books were consecrated in the church of S. Maria *ad praesepe*.[154] The Pope then had four Slav priests and two readers (lectors) ordained by Bishops Formosus and Gauderich. These certainly included Clement, Gorazd and Naum as priests. The Slav liturgy was forthwith celebrated by them in St Peter's and on the succeeding days in St Petronilla's and St Andrew's[a] and in the church of St Paul *extra muros*. It must be particularly noted that no source considers it worth while to mention what form the Slav liturgy took. The Pope would no more disapprove a Slav liturgy on a Byzantine model than the brothers would disapprove a Roman form of ordination. Next the relics of St Clement were ceremonially deposited in his own church. All this was done before 10 March 868, since Arsenius and Anastasius assisted at the services in St Paul's; on that date Arsenius left Rome again hurriedly and Anastasius fell into disgrace for more than a year. It is noteworthy that Formosus, to whom the Pope's policy must have been repugnant, was obliged by him to officiate at the ordinations.

The final act was to be the appointment of a bishop for the new Slav church. It remains an assumption, but one that does no violence to the facts, that Hadrian proposed to send Constantine, probably against the latter's desire and better judgment. He was a teacher and scholar who had never aspired to high ecclesiastical office. But later in this year (868) Constantine fell mortally ill and the Pope deferred further decision. On 14 February 869 Constantine died in Rome, having taken monastic vows and assumed the monastic name of Cyril. On his death-bed he reiterated his faith in a Slav church and exhorted his brother Methodios not to abandon the great enterprise: for he knew his devotion to the monastic life and neither had envisaged returning to Moravia once they had established a competent succession.[155] He was buried at Methodios's wish (after removal to Constantinople had been judged impracticable) in the church of St Clement; the Pope had proposed St Peter's. His tomb has long been lost.

That Cyril died a monk is certain.[156] It is improbable that he was ever consecrated bishop, if that was the Pope's intention. The *Life of Constantine*, written, we believe, under Methodios's eye, is silent on the

[a] These were virtually parts of St Peter's, having been joined to it by covered passages by Pope Paul I for the convenience of pilgrims.

matter. Late sources often couple him with his brother as a bishop,[157] which is a natural error with lapse of time. Indeed it soon became almost a convention to depict both as bishops.[a]

St Cyril's works

St Cyril's outstanding achievements were the creation of a Slav alphabet and a Slav liturgical, and thence literary, language. He was no mere philologist but also an original author, at least in Greek. He was accorded the rare title of 'philosopher', which may be compared to 'doctor' in the West.[158]

The following Greek works of his are more or less reliably deduced:

1. An account of his mission to Khazaria and his Christian apologetics there. Lost, but *VC* 9–11 give the substance in OCS translation, made by Methodios or one of the companions.

2. An account of the *Invention of the Relics of St Clement*, probably a part of 1.

3. A sermon on the *Translation of the Relics of St Clement*, probably delivered in Kherson.

The Greek originals of 2 and 3 are also lost and they have no doubt been partly conflated in the existing OCS text (sometimes referred to as the *Kherson Legend*).[159]

4. A hymn to St Clement. The original Greek is said to have been very popular but is not preserved, except perhaps in part in the *troparion* of the Office of SS Clement and Peter.[160] Anastasius confessed to Gauderich that he could not make a Latin version adequate to its poetic merits.[161] No OCS version is known.

5. A prose Preface to the translation of the *Aprakos* (see pp. 64–5 below). Vaillant identified the so-called 'Macedonian fragment' (Hilferding's) as part of this and assumes a Greek original but it is difficult to see for whom it was intended, if so.[162] A verse Preface to the *Tetrevangel*, surviving in a corrupt state in four manuscripts (three Balkan of the thirteenth–fourteenth centuries and one Russian of the sixteenth century)[163] is also ascribed to Constantine, but opinion differs on which Constantine is meant. Vaillant favours Constantine the Priest of Preslav (denying Cyril any original OCS works, still less one of the only two poems, the other of which is more certainly by Constantine of Preslav);[164] Georgiev advocates Cyril's authorship on internal grounds.[165]

A tract, *Napisanije o pravěj věrě*, is often attributed to St Cyril. It only survives in a fourteenth-century Bulgarian manuscript and in a Russian one of the seventeenth century. It would have been written by him shortly before his death as an *Apologia pro vita sua*. Georgiev[166] considers that the words 'izuštenoje Konstantinomŭ blaženymŭ' (dictated by the late Constantine) could well be an accurate tradition. But the content, especially the attack on *filioque*, is not characteristic of him. The tract is best relegated to the end of the twelfth century.[167]

---

[a] E.g. on one of the frescoes in Old St Clement's, Rome, probably dating from the last quarter of the eleventh century.

In the sphere of liturgical translation Constantine appears as the leading partner but *VM* 15 makes it clear that Methodios, and no doubt also their most devoted companion, Clement, did not take a negligible part. Constantine, however, must be considered as the chief creator of the Slav liturgical language. No manuscript of the ninth century has survived, that is, a text as Constantine or his immediate companions wrote it; the earliest is ascribed to the second half of the tenth century. We do not know how much translation Constantine had completed before leaving Constantinople.[168] It is an assumption, but a reasonable one, that the basis of his language was at first the phonetics and vocabulary of the Macedonian dialect which he had known from childhood. Greek liturgical language provided the style, particularly in syntax, and the model for the creation of the elaborate new abstract vocabulary required to raise this hitherto barbarian vernacular to sacred dignity.[a] The years spent in Moravia introduced two factors: some phonetic modifications to bring the language nearer the local dialect and the adoption of a considerable Christian vocabulary of other than Greek origin which the mission already found established in Moravian usage. As in other matters, the brothers showed their readiness to pursue that spirit of 'economy' which marked Byzantine diplomacy, whether secular or ecclesiastical—a bending to practical necessities without sacrificing essentials. Thus the following words all came into the Slav language as loans from or modelled on the Germanic vocabulary current in Moravia (some in their turn ultimately from Latin), though not all were retained later: *ciruky*,[169] church; *mǐša*, mass; *nepriězni*, Satan (calque of Ger. *unholda*); *oplatǔ*,[170] communion elements; *papeži*, Pope; *popǔ*, priest (ultimately from Greek); *postǔ*, fast; *pogan(isk)ǔ*, pagan;[b] *milosrǔdǔ*, merciful (cf. Ger. *barmherzig*); *mǐnihǔ*, monk; *sǔlǔ*, apostle (Ger. *boto*, lacking the prefix of Gk. ἀπόστολος); *vǔsǫdǔ*, communion (Ger. *wizzôd*);[171]

[a] A few OCS words are demonstrably from spoken, not literary, Greek. They were no doubt already normal in the vernacular of Slavs within the Empire, e.g. *sǫbota* < pl. σάμβατα, not σάββατον (cf. the West Slav and occasional OCS form *sobota*, presumably based on familiar Latin neut. pl. *sa(b)bata*), *krevato* < κρέββατα, not κράββατος (cf. Modern Greek κρεββάτι), and titles such as *stratigǔ* (στρατηγός) and *ikonomǔ* (οἰκονόμος), occurring at e.g. Luke 22, 52 and 16, 1.

[b] Latin *paganus*, originally 'country-dweller, peasant', in military jargon a 'civilian'. By the end of the fourth century *paganus* had taken on the modern sense of 'pagan' since the earlier term *gentilis* had been transferred to the new important class of barbarian mercenaries who were by then for the most part Christians. It is now accepted that the synonym 'heathen' and its congeners in other Germanic languages is not a calque of *paganus* in the old sense 'country-dweller' but a loan from Gothic *haiþnô*, which is no more than Ulfila's transliteration of Greek ἔθνος = *gentilis*.

zakonĭnikŭ, priest (calque of Ger. *êuuart*). Such words were part of the very earliest Slav Christian vocabulary in Central Europe, especially Carantania, where, as we have seen, translations of the Lord's Prayer, the Creed and some penitential texts must have been made not later than *c.* 800.[a] Some were made from Germanic, some no doubt direct from Latin.

Constantine's written language was from the outset an artificial mixture. The proportion of Moravian (or at least West, as opposed to South, Slav) vocabulary introduced by him into his texts in the interests of intelligibility is still not fully worked out, but it must have been considerable.[172] As the 'standard' Church Slavonic of its golden age in Bulgaria reverts closer to the type which it is assumed Constantine originally used, texts of Moravian type are often thought of as aberrant. This is unfair. A considerable part, if not the bulk, of the early translations was done in Moravia and their language must have been more Moravian than is now evident.[173]

The texts translated in Moravia, solemnly placed upon the altars of the Roman churches and approved as accurate and orthodox by the Pope, were some or all of the following: Liturgy, Daily Offices, Psalter, New Testament. These must now be examined in turn.

The Liturgy

The liturgical practice of Constantine and Methodios in Moravia is not stated anywhere in unequivocal terms. The circumstantial evidence is provided by two texts—the *Kiev Folia* and the *Euchologium Sinaiticum*—both of which set problems of interpretation.

The *Euchologium* (*Euch. Sin.*), a Glagolitic manuscript of the late eleventh century, as preserved today, is only a fragment of a very large service-book which normally contains both the Missal (book of liturgies; Russian служебник) and the Ritual (a collection of other sacraments, occasional offices and prayers; Russian требник). It is the latter portion that survives. But the *Sinai Glagolitic fragments*, now separated from it, which are part of a Slav translation of the Liturgy of St Chrysostom (the most widely used Eastern liturgy), are now generally held to belong to the *Euchologium*.[174] Among the occasional offices appears also a confessional sequence[175] having no parallel in any Greek *Euchologium* but

---

[a] To be included here are also such loans from Latin as *oltarĭ* (unknown in Greek), *kŭmă* (commatre), *komŭkati* (communicare). The *Penitentiale Columbani*, in Latin and probably also in Irish, circulated on the Continent *pari passu* with the spread of the Irish custom of private penance.

manifestly preserving a Slav version of Old High German pre-baptismal texts such as the widely used Prayer of St Emmeram.[176] The Latin and German versions must have been current in Moravia. The inference is that the earliest portions of *Euch. Sin.* are texts of Cyrillomethodian date; the younger portions are additions made in the next generation in Macedonia. The translation of the Liturgy could well be Constantine's own; the penitential texts may be revisions of existing oral versions. Thus useful Western texts were not rejected as a matter of principle by the Eastern mission.

The *Kiev folia* tend to confirm this hypothesis. This is not only the oldest surviving Glagolitic manuscript[177]—mid to late tenth century— but also the most markedly Moravian, strictly speaking West Slav, in language. The extant portion contains ten mass formularies: masses of St Clement of Rome and of St Felicity (23 November), six weekday masses (*cotidianae*), *Missa de martyribus* and *Missa de omnibus virtutibus caelestibus*. It is judged to be the final pages of a sacramentary beginning, as was very usual, with Advent and having as the last feast 23 November rather than 30 November (St Andrew), the latter being frequently included in the main festival cycle. It may be incomplete in this respect also that only the Propers (*pars variabilis*) are given and not the Canon (*pars invariabilis*). Mohlberg was the first to show[178] that the Slav text is close to a manuscript of *c.* 840 (*Cod. Pad.* D 47) which is a sacramentary of Aquileian type revised to bring it nearer to the increasingly dominant Gregorian standard. Padua, with all Venetia, was in the province of Aquileia. A still closer parallel has now been found in the *Salzburg fragments*,[179] dating from shortly after 800, into which less Gregorian elements had yet penetrated. It is evident that such sacramentaries will have been taken north by Aquileian missionaries from the time of Patriarch Paulinus and the Avar missions[a] and thereafter remained in local use in outlying parts after more uniform practice had been imposed in the more civilised centres and new types introduced in North Italy by the mid-ninth century. Unusual diversity of texts is demonstrable for the period 750–850 in the Aquileian province. Thus, whatever their original intentions and instructions may have been, the brothers may have used *inter alia* mass formularies already current in Moravia, emanating from divers points to the south. It cannot be assumed, however, that the translation as we have it is substantially Constantine's own. The Latin has been not infrequently misunderstood. That it was

[a] See pp. 17 ff.

translated from Latin and by a Greek speaker is beyond question.[a] The difficult point to decide is whether this liturgical book was translated in Moravia, in Rome, or at some other place and date.

The copy is variously judged to have been made in Bohemia or the Balkans, but the original would be out of place in either. The closer we put the date of the original translation to the date of the extant copy the less probable does the translation and use of such an antiquated sacramentary become. The vocabulary points strongly to an early Moravian type of Church Slavonic.[b] The quality of the translation is against the years 863–7. There is nothing convincing to connect this text with the years spent in Rome (868–70). Would the Pope have approved such an obsolescent text if he had seriously examined the 'Slav books'? It is improbable that preparation or perpetuation of such a text would have been permitted.[180] A date before Methodios's death (885), or at least before the extinction of Moravia (906), but after Constantine's death (869), is therefore perhaps the safest assumption. The deeply buried Western elements in the Croat Glagolitic tradition,[c] clearly linked to such texts as the *Kiev folia*, are sufficient indication that the *Kiev folia* themselves were not an isolated and aberrant production. We thus have a high probability that a Slav translation of a Latin mass was employed in Moravia. But attempts to prove its priority over a Slav translation of an Eastern liturgy are not conclusive.

Another factor in our estimate of the situation concerns the liturgy known as the *Liturgy of St Peter*, to which the formularies mentioned above are affiliated.[181] Broadly, the *Liturgy of St Peter* was an Eastern adaptation of the Roman Mass according to the sacramentary of St Gregory. Its early history is still obscure. The original adaptation has been ascribed to the first quarter of the ninth century for use especially in Byzantine South Italy, which received a considerable influx of Greek refugee monks as a consequence of the second iconoclast persecution and the Arab invasion of Sicily. It is also held to have been used in Illyricum (North Balkans), the meeting-ground of East and West. The

---

[a] It is nowhere specifically stated that either Constantine or Methodios knew Latin (or mastered it in Moravia). Constantine's knowledge of the language is a reasonable presumption though it appears to be an established fact that his teacher Photios knew none.

[b] The *Kiev folia* may be taken to represent the average adaptation, not only in vocabulary but also in phonetics to West Slav conditions. Thus while the reflexes of *tj, dj* are consistently given in West Slav form, other South Slav traits are not effaced: we have *moliti* not *modliti*, *viṡi* not *viṡi*. Pannonia cannot be formally excluded as place of origin but there is nothing specifically Pannonian in the language on the best assumption that this was then a South Slav dialect ancestral to modern Slovene.

[c] See pp. 196 ff.

name points to its being considered by Greeks as a modified Roman liturgy. The Canon was essentially Roman, Byzantine elements more prominent in the other portions. There exist nine Greek manuscripts, several in a mixture of Greek and Latin, two Georgian, and one Cyrillic manuscript in Church Slavonic.[a] Some of these were perhaps only experiments never put to use. But there seems little doubt that this liturgy was used, if only unofficially, in some Greek monasteries in Italy and in the province of Saloniki, whose archbishop had been since the beginning of the fifth century *ex officio* Papal vicar (exarch) for those parts of Illyricum transferred to the jurisdiction of Constantinople in 421.

If the *Kiev folia* depend upon the Latin formularies suggested above, the missing Canon could have been of a type that could properly be called a Liturgy of St Peter; and this usage may conceivably have been known to Constantine and Methodios from their youth in Saloniki and met by them again in Rome in the Greek monasteries which they frequented.[182] Such a compromise text, partaking both of East and West, could have appeared to them particularly suitable for use in Moravia and Pannonia, and likewise to the Holy See in giving its *nihil obstat* to a Slav liturgy. A passage in *Vita Methodii* has been held to prove that Methodios, on his return to Moravia, did use the Liturgy of St Peter. But the words are more probably to be interpreted as a celebration on St Peter's day.[183]

The brothers certainly celebrated on occasion in Greek in Moravia; indeed the Pope specifically approved it subsequently, side by side with Latin (879).[b] We cannot tell whether they would have felt it incumbent on them to seek approval in Rome for a Slav version of a Byzantine liturgy as well as of a Latin mass. The daily offices (see below) and the *Euchologium sinaiticum* both imply the early translation of some Greek eucharistic text.[184] On the other hand continued Papal approval, especially during the pontificate of John VIII (872–82), would be more likely to be predicated on a Latin Mass. A mixture of practices prevailed in Moravia, and a mixture of languages—Latin, Greek and Slav. Though a knowledge of Latin was essential, as Methodios himself stressed,[c] it must remain doubtful whether any attempt was made to teach Greek.[185] The brothers themselves would not of course shed their Byzantine customs. The *Lives* occasionally illuminate this. Thus

---

a The Georgian manuscripts come from their monastery on Athos (Ivéron) and may date *c.* 1000; the OCS manuscript is also Athonite (from Hilandar) and very late eighteenth century, but shows signs of long tradition in the archaic language of the Canon.

b See p. 342 n. 232.   c See p. 81.

Methodios celebrated the feast of St Demetrios on the Eastern date, 26 October, not on the Western, 8 October;[186] his Lenten regulations followed Eastern practice. The mixture of languages remained right down to Methodios's death; his funeral service was held in Latin, Greek and Slav.[187]

The question of priority of Latin Mass or Greek Liturgy in Slav is likely to be insoluble. It is not of real significance: both were surely translated and used before Methodios's death.[188]

The Daily Offices

Vita Constantini 15 specifically records that Constantine translated the Offices or Hours,[a] viz. vespers, compline, night office,[b] the little hours (prime, terce, sext and none). The Slav names are translations from the Greek, in particular *pavečerĭnica* = ἀπόδειπνον, not Latin *completorium* (compline). The daily offices were thus early translated and with a high degree of certainty from the Greek. This clearly implies that an Eastern liturgy was concurrently in use. The evidence of the *Euchologium sinaiticum* tends in the same direction: the early translation of the second part (Ritual) implies that all the most vital texts of the first part—the daily order of service for Vespers, Matins and the Liturgy—had already been translated. In sum, it was the intention of Constantine and Methodios to provide a Slav translation of the *complete set* of Eastern service books (about a dozen). This intention was however not carried out before Constantine's death, that is, during the first period of the Moravian mission, since *Vita Methodii* 15 stresses that the brothers had only succeeded in translating together 'selected offices'.[c]

The Psalter

This central book in Christian worship was needed from the outset and translated in its entirety. In addition to the set psalms in other daily offices, in the Eastern church the whole Psalter was sung in twenty

[a] *Vĭsĭ cĭrkovĭnyi činŭ* = ἡ ἐκκλησιαστικὴ ἀκολουθία, Latin *cursus* or *ordo ecclesiasticus*. While these terms can apply to the whole cycle of *annual* offices (i.e. the complete set of normal service-books) the context appears to refer only to the *daily* cycle. Attendance at all the canonical hours was in theory compulsory for all clergy, *a fortiori* for all monks, from the time of Justinian.

[b] The various terms *nocturn, vigils, mat(t)ins, lauds* have had different connotations at different times and in different places. Greek practice normally recognised three parts of the Night Office—μεσονυκτικόν, ὄρθρος (=Matins), αἶνοι (=Lauds), counting together as one canonical hour. The Slav *utrĭnica* of *VC* 15 corresponds to Matins; no term is given corresponding to Lauds.

[c] See also p. 65 below (various sacraments).

καθίσματα (whence the Slav term *sĕdilĭna*[a]) of about eight psalms each, day by day at Vespers. Vajs estimated that the original Slav translation was made from the Lucianic text, but at some date it was retouched with the help of Latin versions.[189] The earliest extant manuscripts are the Glagolitic *Sinai Psalter* (Ps. 1–137 only) and the Cyrillic Chúdovo Psalter (also incomplete, but with commentary), both of the eleventh century. The latter is clearly already a Bulgarian revision. The *Sinai Psalter* is certainly Macedonian and probably represents the translation accepted as canonical by Clement and his school, though not untouched by later hands.[190]

The Daily Offices and the Psalter together (the common practice) form the *Horologion* or *Breviary* (Russian часослов).

The New Testament

Vita Methodii 15 tells us that the brothers together translated from the Greek *evangelije sŭ apostolomĭ*. The term *evangelije* is ambiguous. It may cover either a complete translation of the four Gospels, or an *Áprakos* (book of pericopes or evangelistary), that is, a book containing only those excerpts appointed to be read as lessons. Moreover there are several types of *Aprakos*:[191]

1. The 'full' type, giving the lessons for each day, of which again there are several variants according to the selection of lessons;

2. the 'short' type, typically giving the lessons for all days in the period Easter–Pentecost but only those for Saturdays and Sundays for the rest of the year;

3. an uncommon type giving the Saturday and Sunday lessons only (Russian воскресное евангелие).

Of the extant early Old Church Slavonic manuscripts[b] *Ass.*, *Savv.* and *Ostr.* are of type 2, while *Zogr.* and *Mar.* are *Tetrevangels* (the full text

---

[a] Also *sĕdalĭna*, *sĕdĕlĭna*.

[b] The following abbreviations are conventional for the earliest surviving manuscripts of the OCS 'canon', limited to those earlier than *c.* 1100 (after which time local variations in language make it necessary to speak of Russian Church Slavonic, Serbian Church Slavonic, etc.):

Ass.	*Codex Assemanianus*
Cloz.	*Codex Clozianus*
Euch. Sin.	*Euchologium sinaiticum* (see p. 59)
Mar.	*Codex Marianus*
Ostr.	*Ostromir's Gospel Book* (1056–7)
Ps. Sin.	*Psalterium sinaiticum* (*Sinai Psalter*)
Savv.	*Savvina Kniga*
Supr.	*Codex suprasliensis*
Zogr.	*Codex zographensis.*

of all four gospels). It is likely that Constantine would choose to start with type 2 as the most immediately useful, and as *Ass.* and *Ostr.* go back to a common prototype, this is plausibly Constantine's own translation. Moreover *Ass.*, based on a very conservative Macedonian tradition, and *Ostr.*, a Russian copy of an early East Bulgarian copy, both open with *John* 1, 1—the first words which Constantine recorded in Slav writing.[192] The *Aprakos* was later expanded into a *Tetrevangel*, certainly in Moravia and most probably after Constantine's death.[a] *Ass.* would seem to be the most faithful to Constantine's version. As far as can be judged, the latter cannot be precisely referred to any now extant Greek text.

The *Apóstol* (the Acts and Epistles) is an equally fundamental requirement and is vouched for above. In this case too the prescribed extracts (Greek *Praxapóstolon*) were probably translated first, concurrently with the *Aprakos*.[b]

There can be little doubt that we should also include the following among the Constantinian translations:

Various sacraments

These, such as the orders of baptism, marriage and burial, are included under the *izbĭranymi služĭbami crĭkŭvĭnymi* of *VM* 15. Some of this presumably is preserved in *Euch. Sin.*

Legal texts

The Law Code now commonly known as *Zakon sudnyj ljudem* is based on Leo III's Ἐκλογὴ τῶν νόμων. The earliest manuscript is thirteenth century.[193] The translator was fully conversant with Eastern ecclesiastical matters but the modifications in the direction of Frankish practice, e.g. on mixed ecclesiastical courts, show that the translation is of Cyrillomethodian date, not Bulgarian. The language too contains a number of the Westernisms characteristic of the *Kiev folia*.[194]

---

[a] See also p. 78 below. Certainly not *vice versa*. The portions missing in the *Aprakos* are not so well translated, following the Greek more slavishly than Constantine was wont to do. It is not known when an *Aprakos* of type 1 was extracted from the *Tetrevangel*. There is also the possibility of Constantine's having translated an *Aprakos-Synaxarion*—a common combination—that is, including also the Proper of Time and Proper of Saints (to use the Western terms).

[b] The best manuscripts are Bulgarian of the twelfth century. An imperfect eleventh century manuscript (Praxapostolon) has recently been discovered at Enina, of which no full examination is yet available. See K. Mirchev in *Slavjanska filologija* 3 (Sofia, 1963) and N. Demircheva-Khafuzova in *Bŭlgarski ezik* 14 (1964).

There is much in favour of the view that a Law Code was one of Rastislav's original requests from Constantinople and consequently that this was one of Constantine's early translations.[195] To possess such a code was not only an important step in passing from barbarism to civilisation but also in gaining independence from the Franks.[196] The word *ljudi* here probably envisages more or less exclusively the Christian Moravians, just as *populus* in *Conversio* means 'Christian flock, parishioners'.[197]

We should bear in mind that Constantine was proficient in church music and that the Slav versions of most liturgical texts had to fit already existing musical settings. Music and words were indissoluble and were learnt together. Thus the training given in Moravia must have included church music. In particular the Psalter demanded a metrically suitable translation. We know that the new Slav liturgy was sung in Rome: phrases such as 'missas canere', 'in sclavonica lingua canonicas horas et missas...decantare' and 'horarum officia omnia psallere', which appear in subsequent Papal correspondence, are no mere figures of speech but normal practice.[198] Of Constantine's and Methodios's own practice in this respect nothing precise can be said.

Archbishop Methodios

The premature death of Cyril left Methodios as the natural choice for the proposed bishopric. Cyril had charged him on his death-bed not to abandon the mission at this delicate moment since it was now clear that their task could not be considered finished. Methodios was entirely loyal to his admired brother's work. Yet his first reaction had been to ask permission to take his body back to Constantinople—their intended destination—and to return to monastic life on Olympos was no doubt his private wish.[199]

Shortly after Cyril's death a delegation arrived in Rome from Kotsel to request that the appointment of a bishop might not be unduly delayed. Archbishop Adalwin of Salzburg had been making quite plain his determination to control the church in Pannonia. Pope Hadrian sent a letter addressed to all three Slav rulers—Rastislav, his nephew Svatopluk[a] and Kotsel—both expressly approving the use of the Slav liturgy and preparing the ground for the appointment of Methodios as bishop of the Central European Slavs.[200] In the summer or autumn of 869 Methodios travelled to Pannonia (Moravia being already inaccessible owing to

[a] I adopt this conventional spelling (Russian Svjatopólk, Slovak Svätopluk, etc.).

warlike operations) to arrange with Kotsel the necessary formalities for his consecration. On his return he was consecrated archbishop by Pope Hadrian with the added dignity of Legate. He appears to have made his formal entry into Pannonia about February 870, being received with great honour.

There is no question of Methodios 'betraying' Constantinople by this step. The Byzantine authorities must by now have been fully apprised of the recent history of Constantine and Methodios. That Constantine should have spent a whole year in Rome without reporting on his mission and the Roman ordinations has only to be stated to be seen to be absurd. Similarly Methodios would immediately have reported Constantine's death and his own subsequent actions. Once again no correspondence on the situation survives between any parties in Rome and Constantinople.[a] It would be an imputation of disloyalty and bad manners to suggest that either brother did not still attempt to receive instructions from Constantinople and to reconcile them as far as possible with what they themselves had been urging as the best policy for Moravia and Pannonia and with what the Pope had in mind for them. If the Byzantine government did not initiate or approve Methodios's consecration it must at least have acquiesced in it.

Methodios's appointment was hardly what Kotsel had requested: a bishop of his own, not one for the Slavs in general. But the Pope continued to favour a large Slav diocese of elastic limits, between East and West, controlled by his own legate, and allotted Methodios the titular see of Sirmium, far to the south-east of the then political centres. Sirmium,[b] destroyed by the Huns in 448 and again by the Avars in 582, had been the administrative and ecclesiastical capital of all *Illyricum occidentale* from Dalmatia to the Danube. This title thus continued Nicholas's policy of restaking the Papal claim to the West Balkans.[c] Pannonia was the real centre of gravity of Methodios's charge since of the old Sirmian lands the two Noricums and Carantania were too strongly attached to Bavaria and too germanised, and the Pope was making other arrangements for Dalmatia. But Methodios would be well

[a] The Greeks—spokesmen of the Photian and Ignatian parties—who had been arriving in Rome since early 869 for the Council held in St Peter's about June, at which the Photian affair was again deliberated, could have been a channel of communication with Constantinople.

[b] Srěm, now Sremska Mitrovica, on the River Sava.

[c] See pp. 54–5. It was the see of St Andronicus (as *Vita Methodii*, chapter 8, notes), reputed the first Bishop of Pannonia and near relation of the Apostle Paul. It seems unlikely that Kotsel knew this ecclesiastical history.

placed for contacts with all the old provinces and, above all, with Bulgaria and Serbia.[a] Indeed, the district of Srěm was actually in Bulgarian hands and had been so more or less continuously since about 827. A direct challenge to Constantinople over Bulgaria has therefore often been read into this Papal act. But this cannot be so. The VIIIth Œcumenical Council sat in Constantinople from October 869 to March 870, at the conclusion of which Bulgaria officially reverted to the obedience of the Patriarchate of Constantinople. But the news of the Bulgarian 'defection' did not reach Rome before 871. It was not the decisions of the Council which prompted the Pope's act; *a fortiori* it was not a countermove to the appointment of a Byzantine prelate to Bulgaria, which had followed without delay (March 870).[b] If the chronology is correct, Methodios was already in Pannonia. Moreover, at the time when Hadrian first contemplated consecrating Constantine (summer 868), Bulgaria was still nominally Roman.[201] Nor could he count on Methodios's giving active support to a policy designed to win back Bulgaria for Rome. The Pope may also have calculated (wrongly in the event) that such a titular see would also be least offensive to Bavarian susceptibilities, for he was practically if not theoretically encroaching on the rights of Salzburg while allowing Methodios a free hand to proceed as circumstances dictated. Methodios's appointment as archbishop may also strike as a little curious in that no other bishops were appointed to serve under him.[c] This was, however, not unusual in what was considered still a missionary or semi-missionary field. It was after all precisely the status of that great organizer of the Western Church, St Boniface—an archbishop without fixed see.[202] The Pope's intentions are clear.

Salzburg interpreted Methodios's new position as an infringement of its long-standing rights. It is to the year 870 that we must attribute the tract *Conversio Bagoariorum et Carantanorum*, certainly written by one of the Salzburg clergy.[203] It recapitulates Salzburg's claims to have been the only considerable missionary organisation in Pannonia and that its rights thereto were clearly defined by Charlemagne.[204] Moreover, the Papal patronage of Slavs was unfair in areas which contained an increasing proportion of German settlers. One of Methodios's first acts

---

[a] See pp. 163–4, 208.   [b] See p. 162.

[c] It would be rash to assume that there were (Aquileian) bishops at such old sees as Emona (Ljubljana), who would have come under him, about whom the available records are totally silent since about the year 600. Again the hypothesis that the Pope from the beginning envisaged an independent ecclesiastical province with three bishoprics—one for each Slav ruler (see p. 66)—runs counter to what he did in the immediately succeeding years.

was no doubt to ordain some of the Slavs given to the brothers for training by Kotsel, as Kotsel had undoubtedly depended hitherto on Salzburg for his clergy.[a] Methodios, presumably imperfectly informed of the situation, then went on to Moravia about May 870 to make contact with Rastislav and Svatopluk. But the Franks were in command, Svatopluk being in league with Carloman to oust Rastislav. Methodios was arrested and tried before an *ad hoc* court in Regensburg.[b] It was easy for the Bavarian prelates to bring charges of interference, intrigue and even irregularities in doctrine against him, though the last were not made into an important issue. The main charge was trespassing on their preserves,[205] by which they meant Pannonia, not Moravia. They claimed that Salzburg had had exclusive and indeed unchallenged rights in Pannonia for well over half a century: 'usque in praesens tempus sunt anni lxxxv quod nullus episcopus *alicubi veniens* potestatem habuit ecclesiasticam in illo confinio nisi salzburgenses rectores, nec presbyter *aliunde veniens* plus tribus mensibus ibi suum ausus est colere officium priusquam suam dimissoriam episcopo praesentavit epistolam'.[206] Methodios claimed overriding authority received direct from the Pope— from St Peter. On the contrary, it was the Frankish bishops who had encroached illegally on ancient Papal territories.[207]

Conversio was the case of the Frankish prosecution presented to Louis. It is entirely directed against Methodios personally and by implication against the Pope; Constantine is not mentioned. In all this the Bishops of Salzburg and Freising appear to have been less aggressive than the Bishop of Passau, whose path Methodios may have already crossed in 866.[c] Methodios was imprisoned in a monastery in Swabia, probably Ellwangen.[208] The court was certainly uncanonical.

Kotsel and the Pope appear to have remained ignorant of what had happened for a long time. Not until Svatopluk regained power in Moravia (872)[d] did Kotsel feel that he was in a strong enough position to promote an investigation. Pope John VIII (elected December 872) was aware of the suspicion aroused at the Curia by the fact that Bishop Anno of Freising, who had recently been in Rome, denied any know-

---

[a] We do not know where the companions ordained in Rome were at this time. They could have been sent straight back to Moravia in 868.

[b] No doubt in November 870 when Louis the German was holding a diet there. It was in this month also that Rastislav was finally deposed in favour of Svatopluk.

[c] See pp. 49 note a and 161.

[d] In 871 the Franks held Svatopluk captive for a time but a priest, Slavomir, perhaps one of the Cyrillomethodian pupils, organised a revolt and Svatopluk was able to return.

ledge of an Archbishop Methodios. The Pope sent Bishop Paul of Ancona to enquire into the matter. He castigated the presumption of the Franks in so treating a Papal Legate[209] and confirmed Methodios's defence by describing him as *episcopus noster*.[210] It was made abundantly clear to Louis that Illyricum was a Papal preserve. Methodios was released about May 873 after three years' restraint and fully reinstated.[211] The contumacious bishops, or at least Hermanrich of Passau, were suspended and excommunicated.[a] However, as a pacificatory gesture, John VIII imposed restrictions on the use of the Slav liturgy in Pannonia, the main bone of contention.[212]

But the cause of the Slav church was lost in Pannonia. Checked in Moravia by Svatopluk's crushing victory over them in 872, the Franks brought more and more pressure to bear on Pannonia. Svatopluk was also attempting to take it for himself. But when Kotsel was killed in 874 the Franks were able to incorporate his province in the Empire and attach it firmly to Salzburg.[213] Conversely, by the settlement of Forchheim (874) Svatopluk accepted Frankish suzerainty in return for a guarantee of internal independence. Moreover Methodios had come to Moravia on his release in 873 (presumably on Papal instructions)[214] and was now useful to him. The title of Archbishop of Sirmium was tacitly dropped by all concerned: Methodios is Archbishop of Moravia,[215] of a well-defined ecclesiastical province. Although Svatopluk usually resided at Nitra in Slovakia, a better centre for his campaigns of conquest,[216] it is probable that Methodios returned to his original headquarters in Moravia. As missionary archbishop without as yet any subordinate bishops he did not have a fixed see tied to a capital city.[217]

Training for the Slav church was resumed on a considerable scale. Svatopluk's conquests now also provided new directions for missionary enterprise—Bohemia and South Poland.[218] The years 874–85 saw the first real consolidation and expansion of the Slav church. The archaeological evidence does not yet allow any precise picture of expansion even within Moravia. Nearly all the churches so far discovered are in the Morava valley. This was evidently the most populous area and for a considerable time the most important politically. Guesses have been made that the churches known as *Na valách* at Staré Město and no. 3 at Mikulčice were the centres of mission work in the 860s or at least of

---

[a] The fact that all three prelates died within the next two years was regarded by some as a Divine judgment (see *VM* 10). Hermanrich died on 26 December 874, Anno on 9 October 875. Adalwin of Salzburg died on 14 May 873, so perhaps never received the Pope's letter.

Methodios's work. Both may have been built before 863; both were clearly added to thereafter.[219] A coin of the Emperor Michael III was recovered from this church at Mikulčice, which may be held to connect it closely with the Cyrillomethodian mission: its mint condition could imply that it was brought by them as part of their gifts for distribution.[220] Further, the church *Na špitálkách* at Staré Město (with Byzantine-style narthex) and nos. 4, 5, 7 and 8 at Mikulčice certainly belong to the period 860–900.[221] Indeed few, if any, churches are likely to have been built after Methodios's death in 885.[a] To these must be added churches at Sady (otherwise Derfle, between Staré Město and Uherské Hradište[b])[222] and Pohansko (near Břeclav). The church at Sady is particularly interesting on a number of counts: the ground plan had originally a square apse, similar to that at Modrá, and must be of similar date (*c*. 830).[c] The extensions—a large narthex with a Byzantine round apse at the West end, in which a school can be held and catechumens, according to Eastern custom, can be present at the liturgy without actually entering the sacred building proper—will be additions of after 863. Moreover, there are indications of monastic buildings associated with this church, which greatly strengthens its identification as a residential centre of Cyrillomethodian missionary work. Sady might even be the 'capital' Velegrad. The Pohansko church also had a narthex added at the West end.[223]

Pošmourný has tried to show that the majority of these churches are so markedly Byzantine in their structural features, particularly in the modulus of their proportions, that they must be ascribed to the Cyrillomethodian mission.[224] But these calculations cannot be accepted in all cases without reserve.[225] At Osvětimany (about 20 km. west of Staré Město) tradition has preserved the name 'Hill of St Clement'. It is possible that the church here was the mission's own church of St Clement where his relics were kept. At Nitra little is yet known. Svatopluk's capital has been tentatively identified on a different hill from the present town (St Martin's hill) but the cathedral remains unidentified. A monastery on nearby Mt Zobor, dedicated to the popular Bavarian saint Hippolytus, is generally ascribed to the Great Moravian period.[226] Only further archaeological investigation can fill in the ecclesiastical map of Moravia.

Svatopluk, however, never gave Methodios his unqualified support:

---

[a] We must allow for a possible increase in Christian activity after 898 (see pp. 83 ff. below) but whether this was sufficient to require new buildings cannot be estimated.

[b] German *Ungarisch Hradisch*.

[c] See pp. 22–3 above.

he was no Kotsel. In ecclesiastical matters, insofar as political and military expediency did not come first, Svatopluk leaned to the Frankish and Latin church. He and his magnates no doubt preferred the Frankish system of proprietary churches, foreign to the East.[a] In any case he had to tread circumspectly with Frankish interests.

The fate of Kotsel's Slav-trained clergy during the Frankish occupation of Pannonia (874–84) can only be surmised. Some may have made their way South to Carniola (Slovenia) and other lands within the orbit of Aquileia, others perhaps even to Carantania. Savia (North Croatia) is an important link. The Pope may even have conceived this area as part of Methodios's archdiocese of Sirmium, since it was dominated, if not actually ruled, by Kotsel. Thus the Cyrillomethodian Glagolitic tradition may have survived there until Savia became a part of the Croatian state in the early tenth century, when it would have joined hands with the Dalmatian Glagolitic church. But little is known of the intervening history.[b] The so-called *Freising texts*[227] lend some support to this line of thought. They comprise three texts written down towards the end of the tenth century in the Latin alphabet and in a language with a notably Slovene tincture. To judge by its orthography no. 2 (conventionally known as *Adhortatio ad poenitentiam*) must have been dictated by a Slav to a German who had little conception of how to record the Slav sounds in the Latin alphabet. Yet the text appears to be a Cyrillomethodian homily or more probably a Western text reworked by one of the Moravian missionaries, as a closely related homily attributed to St Clement suggests.[c] Thus we should expect the dictation to have been done from a Glagolitic original. Nos. 1 and 3 are texts based on *St Emmeram's Prayer*, taught to converts before baptism (as laid down by Alcuin) and must be accounted pre-Cyrillomethodian translations from Latin and OHG, later improved and recorded.[228] That these too were used in the Cyrillomethodian years, and therefore were at some stage recorded in Glagolitic, is made very probable by the evidence of the *Euchologium sinaiticum*.[d] The connection of these texts with Freising, either directly or through its daughter-houses (Innichen?) or estates, is assured by the fact that nos. 2 and 3 are in the same hand as a deed issued by Bishop

---

[a] There were in fact in the Byzantine Empire too private churches, built by a great landowner for his tenants, which remained his property and whose priest he appointed (subject to the bishop's confirmation), but such churches did not loom large in the structure of the church as a whole.

[b] See pp. 206–7. [c] Cf. n. 55 p. 371.

[d] See pp. 59–60.

Abraham of Freising about 980 concerning properties near Spittal in Carinthia.[229]

Methodios developed his work in relatively peaceful conditions for some years. But intrigues at the court, led by a Frankish priest Wiching, gathered strength.[a] Methodios's propagation of the Slav church to new areas, especially Bohemia,[b] was apt further to inflame Frankish tempers. In 879 Svatopluk sent John of Venice, probably his go-between with the Frankish authorities and a known opponent of the Slav church, to Rome to try and achieve some settlement of ecclesiastical differences. The Frankish clergy were now bent again on discrediting Methodios. In 870 the gravamen of the charge had been interference. Such a charge could not now be preferred in Rome. The ground was now shifted to language and its presumptive companion, heresy. Methodios was accused of not including *filioque* in the Creed—a matter upon which the Frankish church felt strongly.[c] In raising this issue however the Franks were evidently not very conversant with opinion in Rome, for as recently as 810 Leo III had still disapproved of it as an uncanonical addition to the Creed,[230] though he raised no theological objections. The Eastern church firmly rejected it as theologically unsound[231] and it did not gain official acceptance in the West until the early eleventh century under new German pressure. The Pope however summoned Methodios to Rome, to answer charges of disobedience in the matter of language.[232] Svatopluk also requested that Wiching be consecrated Bishop of Nitra.

Methodios's orthodoxy was of course easily confirmed in Rome. The Pope was concerned primarily with preserving Methodios's authority since his importance to Papal policy was in fact increasing. Events in Croatia[d] and Bulgaria[e] suggested again the feasibility of a great Slav area

[a] It is perhaps an oversimplification to suggest a Latin court at Nitra and a Slav church in Moravia, but clearly a certain geographical (not class) dichotomy was developing. Methodios had also to take a stricter attitude to irregularities in Christian life: *VM* 11 gives a momentary glimpse of this kind of friction—his objection to the marriage of a Frankish magnate as being against the Byzantine rules (though acceptable in Western eyes).

[b] See pp. 86 ff.

[c] The addition had originated in Spain in the sixth century to combat Arianism and had spread to many parts of the West by the eighth century. Charlemagne's insistence in 790, against Papal advice, on retaining *filioque* and on rejecting the *per filium* of the Œcumenical Council of 787 was one small factor in the early stages of estrangement between East and West. But the intervention of the Eastern Emperor in matters of dogma had been and continued for long to be a much more serious danger, especially in the eyes of Rome, than the few feeble steps taken in this direction by Western monarchs.

[d] See pp. 194 ff.

[e] Following Ignatios's death on 23 October 877; see pp. 162 ff.

under Roman jurisdiction, provided at least that the general use of the Slav liturgical language was conceded.

In only one respect did John VIII satisfy Svatopluk: he promoted Wiching Bishop of Nitra, no doubt against Methodios's advice. The theoretical advantage was greater independence of the Moravian church, now recognised as 'under the protection of St Peter' and possessing two bishops of its own, with the prospect of a third held out by the Pope if there were a suitable candidate. That Methodios argued against Wiching's appointment is suggested by the Bull *Industriae tuae* (June 880), the only source, which makes a point of stressing the requirement of obedience to his archbishop.[233] The complaint that Methodios had disregarded the Pope's interdiction on the Slav liturgy was also not taken seriously. The Pope repeated that the Latin Mass was to be sung whenever requested (that is, for Svatopluk and the court). He turned down the arguments of the trilinguists and reaffirmed what was later called the *Privilegium moraviensis ecclesiae*.[234] It is surmised that Methodios personally supervised the composition of this letter since the Slav names are unusually well spelt (e.g. Sfentopulk for earlier Pentepelch, Zventapu *et al.*). The essential part of *Industriae tuae* runs as follows:

Nec sane fidei vel doctrine aliquid obstat sive missas in eadem sclavinisca lingua canere, sive sacrum evangelium vel lectiones divinas novi et veteris testamenti bene translatas et interpretatas legere, aut alia horarum officia omnia psallere; quoniam qui fecit tres linguas principales...ipse creavit et alias omnes ad laudam et gloriam suam. Jubemus tamen ut in omnibus ecclesiis terrae vestrae propter maiorem honorificentiam evangelium latine legatur et postmodum sclavinisca lingua translatum in auribus populi latina verba non intelligentis adnuncietur, sicut in quibusdam ecclesiis fieri videtur...et si tibi [Svatopluk] et judicibus tuis placet missas latina lingua magis audire praecepimus ut latine missarum tibi sollemnia celebrentur.

These prescriptions hardly indicate a personal enthusiasm of the Pope for the Slav liturgy, which he may well have assumed to be normally a translation of the Byzantine office, but a permissive attitude fully safeguarding the use of Latin rites. Nevertheless Papal support at this moment, if only as a matter of policy, must have contributed much to the survival of the Slav liturgical language.

From summer 880, when Methodios returned vindicated to Moravia with *Industriae tuae*, there was however no lessening of the tension. Wiching's position had been greatly strengthened. He had not balked at hurrying back to Moravia with spurious documents purporting to appoint him archbishop in Methodios's stead and to forbid the use of the Slav liturgical language. Svatopluk did not know where he stood. Wiching was always at his ear to persuade him that Methodios was not orthodox in some detail or other. Methodios's vindication was valueless. Indeed one independent Latin bishop, Wiching, was all that Svatopluk had wanted; he had no further call to support the eccentric structure headed by Methodios. A further Papal letter to Methodios (*Pastoralis sollicitudinis*, 23 March 881),[235] which must be an answer to further complaints by Methodios that the Pope's orders were being disregarded by Svatopluk, is no more than a restatement of the Pope's admiration for Methodios's ministry. Should we conclude from this that thenceforward Methodios began to feel that he could no longer be certain of Papal support for his brother's lifework and that, in disillusionment both with Rome and Svatopluk, he began to have thoughts of closer contact with Constantinople again?—a thing which he must have long desired.[236] There is no trace, once again, of correspondence with Constantinople in these years but it is difficult to suppose that he never communicated with his home. So about autumn 881 he made the journey to the City. The details given in his *Life* are not sufficient to decide whether the approach came first from Methodios or whether the Imperial government summoned him, as there implied: 'I [the Emperor] greatly desire to see you, so do your best to come here'.[237] These words are perfectly friendly as is all the following account of his stay in Constantinople. They conflict only with the preceding taunts of his Moravian ill-wishers, which must not be taken too seriously.[238] If Photios, Patriarch again from October 877, sent Methodios an invitation as early as 879, the whole situation could have been discussed by Methodios in Rome in 880. But such a pressing need to consult with Methodios would more logically follow the decisions of the Council in Constantinople (March 880),[a] whereby the Pope finally recognised Photios as Patriarch in return for Papal jurisdiction over Bulgaria, with the proviso that the Greek clergy there should not be removed nor the use of *filioque* imposed.[239] With Bulgaria *de jure*, if not *de facto*, out of Byzantine hands again, Methodios was in a strong position not merely to defend but to urge the desirability of his Slav church.[240] His position between Bulgaria and Rome and the Slav texts of which he was now the repository both became for the first time of immediate practical significance to Constantinople in attempting to minimise Papal authority in the Balkans, in particular in Bulgaria. And

[a] See also pp. 162–3.

whereas the Byzantine authorities could have had no great objection to his archiepiscopal title in the 870s, when they were sure of Bulgaria and the artificiality of the title itself was patent, it would now be expedient to ascertain exactly what Methodios had committed himself to. That he had latterly been no more than Archbishop of Moravia was neither here nor there. From the inception of the mission until Methodios's death the Byzantine attitude towards it was always regulated primarily by the Bulgarian situation.

It must not be supposed that there was nothing but strained relations between Rome and Constantinople after March 880. The work of the Council had in fact effected a *détente*.[241] Rome saw herself in more and more urgent need of Byzantine military help against Moslem aggression in South Italy; no power in the West could provide it. In this very year 880 Byzantine forces waged a successful campaign in Calabria and won a great victory at sea off Sicily.[a]

The Pope therefore had every reason to avail himself of Methodios's good offices. He was showing complaisance towards the use of the Slav liturgy in Dalmatia and perhaps would not oppose it in Bulgaria if this seemed advantageous. That he also sent Theodosius of Nin, who cannot have been an opponent of the Glagolitic tradition, to Boris of Bulgaria in 880 is clearly relevant; it is most unfortunate that no record survives of these discussions in Bulgaria and Rome.[b]

Constantinople on the other hand was privately of the opinion—and events proved it correct—that the transference of Bulgaria was an empty formality, provided that Bulgaria was handled rightly. Knowing all these moves and the general principles of the work of Cyril and Methodios, it is not improbable that Constantinople too should now reach the conclusion that Bulgaria could be more effectively held if the use of the Slav language were to be freely recognised and that the same policy might serve to maintain Byzantine influence in Dalmatia.

Methodios's journey to Constantinople in 881 therefore could be of decisive importance for the whole future of the Slav church. Moravia was the least part of the matter. The full weakness of Methodios's position there was no doubt not yet appreciated in Rome either. It goes

---

a Sicily came wholly under the rule of the Aghlabids of Tunisia (Ifriqiya) with the destruction of Syracuse in 878 and remained in Moslem hands till the coming of the Normans. But Moslem raids on Sicily had begun as early as 827 and on Central Italy as early as 840. A raid had threatened Rome in 877. The destructive attack on the monastery of Monte Cassino, not far south of Rome, was to come as soon as 882/3.

b See p. 194. The mission is no more than mentioned in a letter of John VIII (*PL* 126, Ep. 308).

against the grain to suppose that he set out for Constantinople without Papal approval, though whether he received instructions which would tie up with those given to Theodosius of Nin, we do not know. Two things only are clear: that the visit was no mere sentimental one, and that Methodios must have been fully aware that the moment was particularly favourable for the propagation of St Cyril's Slav liturgical language since this concession was now equally advantageous to East and West in their continuing bid for ecclesiastical control of the Balkans. Did Methodios believe that he could bring about some permanent settlement before it was too late? There could be no more impartial counsellor than a Greek bishop appointed by the Pope, fully conversant with the Slav world.

He was in Constantinople for about a year. We may adopt Dittrich's suggestion[242] that in that time, among other things, his orthodoxy was tested and reaffirmed on the Byzantine side, and that his Slav language and texts—the fruit of Cyril's genius—were now officially accepted. A deacon and perhaps other pupils were left behind there with Slav texts to serve as a nucleus for further expansion.[a] The reunion with Photios appears to have been cordial. The Emperor found nothing in Methodios's actions or proposals to condemn. We are justified in maintaining that he sent him back to Moravia with full Byzantine approval.[243]

After his return to Moravia in the course of 882 or the following year Methodios devoted his energies to achieving the translation of the whole Bible, feeling perhaps that his days were numbered. He had done all that he could in the sphere of ecclesiastical diplomacy.

New difficulties, too obscure to analyse, arose in 884 which led to Wiching and others incurring Methodios's ultimate sanction—excommunication.[244] The crisis is likely to have been political, perhaps connected with the peace made at Tulln in the autumn of 884 between Charles III the Fat and Svatopluk (there had been war during the journey to Constantinople), at which Methodios was present.[245]

Methodios died on Easter Sunday, 6 April 885. According to the *Prolog Combined Life*—which may enshrine a true tradition—he was buried in the Moravian Cathedral.[b] This has not yet been identified. Staré Město became more important than Mikulčice in the second half of the

---

[a] The deacon is credibly identified as Constantine 'the Priest', later Bishop of Preslav (see p. 177). On Byzantine reservations about the Glagolitic alphabet see also p. 164.

[b] See also n. 217 to this chapter.

ninth century, so perhaps the cathedral should be sought there. There is no trace of his relics in any country; one may presume that the Magyars destroyed all.

The work of translation which he carried on after Cyril's death includes the following:

1. The Bible. *VM* 15 states that he completed the translation of the whole Bible with the exception of Maccabees. This took eight months—from March to 26 October (884)[a]—with the help of two scribes or stenographers (*skoropisec*). This complete translation was soon lost, which is hardly surprising if there was only one or at most two copies, in the turmoil which followed Methodios's death. In assessing Methodios's task here, it must be remembered that all or the greater part of the New Testament had already been translated, except for Revelation, from which no lessons were drawn, and at least the Psalter out of the Old Testament. We must accept that the translation was made although scarcely a generation later John the Exarch, in East Bulgaria, did not know it for a fact.[b] The complete Bible was not in fact widely used in the Eastern church, the Old Testament being mainly required in excerpts.[c] Vajs has demonstrated, on the evidence of the Old Testament lessons in Croat Glagolitic service-books, that they posit a Cyrillomethodian translation from the Greek. Although the most archaic traits do in fact appear in passages which are included in the *Parimejnik*, we can scarcely take the liberty of doubting the explicit statement in *Vita Methodii*. Revisions will also have been made in the parts of the New Testament already translated. There are indications that the Vulgate was now used for comparison.

2. The *otičĭskyje kŭnigy* of *VM* 15—also lost. It was some form of *Paterikon* (Homiliary), conceivably the Greek compilation entitled Ἀνδρῶν ἁγίων βίβλος. *Cloz.* could partly derive from Methodios's work.

3. The *Nomokanon* of *VM* 15. This translation is best preserved in the thirteenth-century Russian *Ústjužnaja Kórmčaja*, showing as it does some very archaic vocabulary characteristic of the Moravian period. Linguistically its closest links are with *VM* itself, the *Zakon sudnyj* (which is included in it as ff. 55 a–61 b) and the Gospels. [246] Methodios based his compilation on the *Synagoge* of John Scholastikos (Patriarch of Constantinople 565–77) and on a Latin compilation which Vašica estimates might have originated in Ravenna *c.* 867 and been presented to Methodios by the Pope. Methodios omitted many articles which could have no relevance to Moravia and significantly also Canon XXVIII of Chalcedon, which put the Patriarchate of Constantinople next in seniority after Rome, a change which the Curia had then and later refused to accept. The conclusion is that Methodios made the translation in the 870s.[247]

[a] Six months in the text; a Glagolitic numeral has been misread.
[b] *Jakože slyšaahŭ* (as I have been told) in the Preface to his *Nebesa* (see p. 177).
[c] The book is called in Greek παροιμιάριον, in Russian *pariméjnik*. There was no complete translation of the Bible available in Russia (in OCS) until the version of 1499 made by order of Archbishop Gennadii of Novgorod.

4. Methodios also composed a Canon for the Office of St Demetrios of Saloniki. It contains allusions to the 'trilinguists'.[248] Most scholars also believe that he was the author of a homily in *Cloz.* (though Vaillant is again inclined to assume a lost Greek original). Its text is the proper conduct of princes and magnates and could therefore well relate to Methodios's difficulties in keeping the moral conduct of Svatopluk (probably still a polygamist) and others within strictly Christian bounds. If the identification is correct, the work must date to the second half of the 870s and gives a valuable chronological *point de repère.*

Evidence has recently been accumulating—all in favour of the predominantly Byzantine practice of Constantine and Methodios—that the greater part of the Eastern service-books containing the variable texts of the annual cycle (in particular the elaborate metrical hymns) must have been translated into Slav before Methodios's death in 885. Latin texts and translations of Latin texts were used by them when convenient but were in effect only a side-line. Thus the *Life of St Clement* credits the saint with completing the translation of the *Triodion* in Macedonia.[249] This was the *Pentekostarion* (Russian триодь цветная) covering the variable parts of the weekly cycle for the period Easter Sunday to the Sunday after Pentecost. Of the three service-books of this type embracing the whole ecclesiastical year the first part of the *Triodion* (триодь постная), covering the ten weeks preceding Easter, must therefore have been complete by 885, and the *Oktoikh* (ὀκτώηχος), with which musically speaking the cycle starts, is ascribed to Constantine and Methodios together in one source.[250]

Further, a *Hirmologion* was almost certainly available in Slav form by 885.[251] This book gives the chants to be used, with the *incipits* of the texts.[a] The need for the Byzantine chant-book guarantees that the Greek liturgy in Slav translation and generally the Greek cycle of offices represented the normal Cyrillomethodian practice, whatever else it may have seemed advisable to provide for Moravia from the services of the Latin church.

The multilingual character of the Moravian church is very evident. Celebrations must have taken place in Latin and Greek and Slav but also, in all probability, in various combinations of these languages.

---

[a] Greek εἱρμολόγιον from εἱρμός = the second stanza of a hymn (κοντάκιον) or first stanza of an ode (κανών), which sets the metre and melody for all the rest. The *Hirmologion* or chant-book gives the melodies, which can be used for other poems in the same metre.

The entry of the Slavs into Christendom

The extinction of Moravia

Dittrich is hardly exaggerating when he calls Methodios 'the last great figure of the universal church'. There had been schisms before; irrevocable schism was still more than two centuries ahead. Yet from the end of the ninth and particularly in the tenth century—the time when the Slav churches were being born and growing with young vigour—it was scarcely possible any longer to belong indifferently to both East and West. This was due not merely to the gradual estrangement between the churches on matters that touched their doctrine, ritual, customs, and all other aspects, but also, more obviously, to political factors in a Europe that was undergoing a rapid process of crystallisation.

Cyril and Methodios were still œcumenical in their outlook. During their mission in Central Europe they surely had more reservations about the pretensions of the Western Empire (though the Carolingian unity was already impaired) than about those of the Papacy: for them the Emperor of Byzantium was still the one universal vicegerent of God.[252]

But their missionary work, which still put a higher value on the enlargement of Christendom than on the attachment of the new Christians, inevitably fell a prey to the temper of the times. All the Slavs were forced to opt for either the Western (Latin) or the Eastern (Greek) church. Only the greater tolerance of the East towards liturgical languages other than Greek introduced an added contrast: Cyril's liturgical language prospered, extended itself and is still cultivated as a precious inheritance in the Slav Orthodox churches.

Their sainthood was generally acknowledged at an early date, no doubt already in the practice of Clement and the other disciples in Bulgaria. We have noted that their separate and combined Offices were written and propagated at that time.[a] The precise date of their canonisation is, however, not known but must fall in the tenth or eleventh century.

The Bulgarians passed on their cult to Serbia and Russia.[253] Their separate festivals remained (correctly) on 14 February and 6 April. The date of their joint festival, which was especially widespread, has varied: it was sometimes fixed as 25 August but from the early years of the thirteenth century in Bulgaria as 11 May.[254] In the Western church St Cyril, buried in Rome, was venerated in course of time principally as

---

[a] See p. 31 nos. 6–8.

the bringer of St Clement's relics thither. So for example in Jacopo de Voragine's *Golden Legend*.[a] St Methodios, as a Papal archbishop, was also not forgotten. In the Roman calendar their joint commemoration was fixed on 9 March.

In his last days Methodios had indicated Gorazd, one of his out-standing Moravian pupils, as most worthy to succeed him. He could not, of course, personally appoint his successor.[255] His choice fell on Gorazd, other qualities apart, for his excellent command of Greek and Latin, an essential qualification for the head of the Moravian church. Conceivably the matter had been discussed by Methodios in Constantinople. Subse-quent events suggest that the senior missionaries did not now intend to leave Moravia and that Gorazd considered himself as Methodios's successor-designate. On Methodios's death Gorazd did not or could not immediately submit his candidature for the ratification of Rome—the necessary step.[256] Wiching, the Frankish bishop of Nitra, also aspired to step into Methodios's shoes and hurried to Rome. By laying before the new Pope, Stephen V (VI) (May 885–91), who was evidently not yet *au fait* with the whole question, false documents purporting to have been written by his predecessors in St Peter's chair,[257] he persuaded him that Methodios had ignored John VIII's orders in the matter of the Slav liturgy and that his orthodoxy had not been satisfactorily proved. Stephen believed Wiching and formally prohibited the Slav liturgy in a letter (*Quia te zelo*) to Svatopluk.[258] The letter further exhorts Svatopluk to follow the policy which he probably favoured in any case—to make the Moravian church a normal Latin church. He urges him to accept the addition of *filioque* to the Creed and to give up such peculiar Byzantine practices as fasting on Saturdays. The letter was flattering, addressing Svatopluk as *rex* (a title occasionally found in Frankish annals also during the years of his greatest power), and highly conciliatory: he reassures Svatopluk that if the Holy See finds any grounds for repudiating Methodios's work, no blame will attach to Svatopluk himself.

At the same time he despatched a mission under Bishop Dominic to Moravia to study the situation. It arrived there in early 886. In his instructions to Dominic (*commonitorium*) the Pope makes it quite clear that he cannot yet accept Gorazd; he must come to Rome (as Methodios had) for all the necessary formalities.[259] The prohibition of the Slav

---

[a] *The Golden Legend or Lives of the Saints*, as englished by Caxton (1483): 'the blessed Cyrille, bysshop of Moryanne'. Voragine was no longer clear that Cyril and 'Philosophus', who recovered the relics in 'Tersona' (Kherson) is one and the same person. His source is the *Italian Legend* (see p. 32).

liturgy is repeated. John VIII's liberal gesture of only six years before now found no supporters in Rome. There is nothing in these documents to suggest that the Pope intended to promote Wiching to the archbishopric. All that the latter had achieved was the prohibition of the Slav tongue; but he could be certain that this would have Svatopluk's approval.

Wiching arrived back in Moravia shortly before the Papal Legate with what purported to be full Papal support. Svatopluk was preoccupied with military affairs. He would be glad to settle once and for all this ecclesiastical quarrel which was not of his making and was merely an annoyance beyond his understanding. His main concern was unity and tranquillity at home, that his foreign adventures might not be endangered. He at once summoned Gorazd, Clement and the other leaders to submit to the Papal directions in *Quia te zelo*. This they refused to do.[260] After that he gave Wiching a free hand to take action against them. He pointedly withdrew his support from the Methodians. Wiching resorted to force. The leaders were first thrown into prison, soon hurriedly expelled from the land when the arrival of the Papal Legate was known to be imminent.[a] Some were even sold as slaves to Jews and ended up in the Venice market—notably Naum, whom a local Byzantine official bought and restored to freedom.[b] Clement and Angelar made for the Bulgarian frontier at Belgrade, where they were received with joy by the Governor.[c] Others may have found refuge in Bohemia,[d] Dalmatia[e] and Cracow in South Poland.[f]

Thus was Methodios's flock dispersed by heretics, according to the phrase of one of his pupils, written not long after.[261] This does not imply that all the Slav clergy were removed from Moravia and Slovakia. Even in Slovakia, where Wiching's purge is likely to have been more intensive, some remnants of the Slav church seem to have lived on. In Moravia Wiching's work may have been less thorough. Gorazd himself, who certainly did not flee either to the Balkans or to Bohemia, perhaps merely went into hiding. So also others. If Rome assumed, after the Legate's visitation, that the Moravian church was wholly Latin, it was relying on the assertions of the mendacious Wiching.

Wiching had his own way until 892/3. But he can scarcely have had

---

[a] It is not known what the Legate Dominic reported to Rome.

[b] Apparently before August 886, since the *Life of Naum* implies that Basil I was still alive (d. 29 August 886).

[c] See p. 163.

[d] See pp. 86 ff.

[e] See p. 196.

[f] See pp. 135 ff.

the means to develop rapidly a strong Latin church even in Slovakia.[262] Meanwhile relations between the Franks and Svatopluk went from bad to worse, culminating in a new war. Wiching, never popular even in Slovakia, saw that Arnulf of Bavaria's star was rising and fled to him in 893. Arnulf made him his chancellor. He was eventually elevated to the see of Passau (899), with its nominal jurisdiction over Moravia, and died not many years later after having been deposed from his bishopric by the Archbishop of Salzburg.

Svatopluk died in 894—'diem ultimum clausit infeliciter'.[263] Mojmir II inherited an overgrown state which could not be held together. Bohemia seceded in 895. Mojmir was almost at once faced with a new crisis. The Magyars, called in by Constantinople to stab the Bulgars in the back (894-6), were themselves so treated by the Pechenegs under Bulgarian instigation, and moved westward to settle in the Central European steppe. They soon embarked on raids, in the normal nomad fashion, on the surrounding sedentary peoples. These pagans virtually wiped out Christianity again in Pannonia and reduced it to miserable remnants in Slovakia and Moravia.[264]

Mojmir had a few more years' grace. After Wiching's flight he was without a recognised bishop. From October 891 to April 896 the Pope was that Formosus who had always been (so far as we can tell) an opponent of the Slav church.[a] No approach to him by Mojmir is known. Only about 898/9 did the latter feel in a position to turn to ecclesiastical affairs. The Holy See received from him a delegation asking for the reinstatement of the archbishopric. The new Pope, John IX (898–900), agreed to consecrate an archbishop and three bishops for Moravia, thus making it at last an independent hierarchy. It is not wholly clear whether this intention was carried out. He sent three legates, Archbishop John and Bishops Benedict and Daniel, to Moravia, which would imply that the consecration of bishops was intended. A letter of Bishop Pilgrim of Lorch (i.e. Passau) to Pope Benedict VI (973) may be held to confirm that the sees were in fact duly constituted.[265] But this sheds no light on whether Mojmir hoped to reestablish the Slav church rather than merely a hierarchy separate from the Bavarians. Nothing in the documents points conclusively either way. If Wiching had indeed eradicated the Slav priesthood effectively it is most unlikely that Mojmir would have pressed for the rehabilitation of a Slav church without the men to make it. The *Life of Naum*[b] records, perhaps correctly, the arrival of further

[a] See p. 54   [b] See p. 165 no. 3.

6-2

Moravian refugees in Bulgaria in 907, after the Magyar invasion of Moravia. Were these other Slav clergy who had survived the persecution of 886? We do not know. The nature of Mojmir's church remains in doubt.

Dittrich has put forward the improbable suggestion that Gorazd was duly installed by the mission as Papal archbishop, following the Methodian pattern.[266] The Methodian pattern was at least followed in other respects: there was an immediate violent protest on the part of the Bavarian hierarchy.[267] But John IX died and by the Peace of Regensburg (January 901) Moravian independence was reaffirmed and the protest apparently went unheeded. No further incidents are known until the final collapse of the Moravian state at the hands of the Magyars (aided and abetted by Arnulf of Bavaria) in 906/7. The four sees may thus be supposed to have existed for about a decade. They must evidently be fitted to the territories then still held by Mojmir, to wit, Moravia (the archbishopric of Methodios), Slovakia (Nitra), and South Poland (Cracow?). The fourth is more difficult; though Mojmir controlled parts of Silesia and Galicia, it is perhaps most likely to have been at Olomouc (Olmütz) in North Moravia.[268]

The continued existence of these sees after 907 is problematical, still more so their increase to seven.[269] At most we can say that some sort of Christian community persisted at Nitra for the place was not wholly destroyed by the Magyars. Some churches survived, though the unbroken existence of any community with properly ordained priests throughout the century from the catastrophe to the time of St Stephen of Hungary is hardly susceptible of proof.[270] Survival is also claimed for a monastery on nearby Mt Zobor, a Benedictine house allegedly founded in the ninth century and dedicated to St Hippolytus. The story of St Andrew (the Pole Świerad), who came to the monastery about 1022 and died there in 1034, does not suggest a recent foundation, but cannot be taken as evidence of such antiquity.[271] The language of its rite is nowhere mentioned. The survival of the see of Nitra, in view of the new creation of Ladislas I and Koloman (perhaps as late as 1133), remains a mere hypothesis. Further, though a bishop of Moravia, residing at Olomouc, is not mentioned again till 976,[a] this area too may have retained a Christian population. Olomouc owed its growing importance to the destruction of the old centres by the Magyars.

Of the bishoprics the hypothetical Cracow had the best chance of

---

[a] See p. 108.

continuing an uninterrupted existence in an area unravaged by the Magyars, conceivably becoming an active centre of evangelisation and maintaining (perhaps not exclusively) the tradition of the Slav church. This will be discussed further under Poland.[a]

Elsewhere the Magyar destruction was thorough. There are signs of fire at the old centres of Staré Město and Mikulčice. Moravia became an eventless desert for half a century. But here and there, as in Hungary itself,[272] sedentary life and Christian ways must have remained, to exert an influence in due course on the last horde of barbarians in Central Europe.

[a] See pp. 135 ff.

3

THE WESTERN SLAVS

Between the beginning of the sixth century and the end of the seventh Bohemia had been occupied by a variety of Slav tribes, entering from the East and North. By the time of Charlemagne the Franks began to look on it as a dependency of the Empire, though the degree of Frankish control and level of Frankish interest was still small.[1]

No traces have so far been found in Bohemia of Christian objects or institutions that can be dated before about the middle of the ninth century. In 845 fourteen Bohemian chieftains (*duces*) came to Regensburg asking for Christian instruction.[2] Thus by the time when an embryonic Bohemian state was coming into existence—in the middle of the ninth century—we can assume some slight influence of Christianity during the preceding fifty years and some stirrings of interest on the Slav side in entering into closer relations with Christendom. The event of 845 must not be taken as a widespread, still less a general conversion of the country. Information is extremely scarce compared with contemporary Moravia and Pannonia. We gain the impression that Bohemia (where Prague appears to be the most active centre throughout the ninth century) was socially and politically less advanced than the Moravian lands. Its development was stimulated by the great Franko–Moravian rivalry. Thus in 858 the Bohemians were already prepared to give Moravia military help against the Franks and closer relations were surely maintained from that time. But only towards the end of the century do the names of Bohemian rulers enter the records.

Some of the early Czech legends relate that Borivoj of Prague was the first of his line to be converted; that he was baptised by Methodios himself at Svatopluk's court. But though the *Vita Methodii* connects Methodios with a mission in South Poland nothing is there said about Bohemia and Borivoj.[3] Cosmas of Prague places the alleged baptism in 894: 'anno dominice incarnationis 894 Borivoy baptizatus est primus dux sancte fidei catholicus'; and again: 'Borivoy qui primus dux baptizatus est a venerabili Metudio episcopo in Moravia...'[4] Taken together the statements are impossible: Methodios died in 885. But the choice of date is significant: it stands for a date no longer known accurately (if not wholly legendary), since 894 was the date of the death of Svatopluk of

Moravia, followed by the rapid collapse of the state and its conquest by the Magyars.[a] An author writing at the end of the tenth century—and such we must assume to be Cosmas's source at this point—would have some reason not only to connect the Christianisation of Bohemia with Moravia (which was a fact) but with the moment when Bohemia might be thereby held to have become the heir of Moravia in the political sense as well. He wrote at a time when the rulers of Prague were laying claim to Moravia in rivalry with Poland and when there was reason to stress the attachment of Bohemian Christianity to Moravia and its Slav church in order to counter the pretensions of the German church in Bohemia.[5]

The date of Borivoj's baptism, if true, must fall in Methodios's second Moravian period, more probably in the middle of the 870s than in the 88os. In all respects Bohemia was then coming more and more under Moravian domination—a process which led to a short period during which Svatopluk subjected Bohemia to his direct rule (890–4). It remains problematical whether we ought to assume a missionary undertaking by Methodios and his disciples in Bohemia or an unsolicited approach on the part of this Czech ruler during Methodios's lifetime.

The occasion of Borivoj's baptism gives us one of the few recorded glimpses of life on the frontiers of the Christian world. For Borivoj as a pagan found himself sitting like a slave on the floor of the hall with all his men while the great Christian ruler Svatopluk dined in a civilised manner surrounded by his court.[6] This practice of shaming the barbarians was evidently effective, even if not wholly Christian in spirit. Borivoj decided to be baptised forthwith, with thirty of his followers. A Moravian priest Kaich was at once sent to serve as chaplain at his castle of Levý Hradec, a short way north of Prague (modern Žalov). Whether he was a Slav or Latin priest is not stated; but the church was dedicated to St Clement, the patron of the Cyrillomethodian mission.[7] May we not also suppose that it received a relic of the saint from Methodios? That he visited Prague in person to consecrate this first church and at the same time to baptise Borivoj's wife Ljudmila[b] has a more legendary ring. But she appears in the tradition as an ardent Christian.

Be this as it may, it would be reasonable, whether we could prove any earlier mission or not, to assume that a certain number of the Slav

[a] See p. 83.
[b] Modern Czech *Lidmila* or *Ludmila*. She came of the neighbouring Czech tribe of the Pšované.

clergy who fled Moravia in 885–6 made their way to Bohemia with their Slav liturgical language and books. The presence of Slav clergy in Bohemia is thus conceivable any time after 870 and probable from 885–6, mainly from the old Cyrillomethodian centres in West Moravia where Wiching's persecution was likely to have been less violent and thorough. Many other small points go to show that Bohemia received her Christianity as much, if not more, in Cyrillomethodian form as in Latin. Thus early Czech forms of the names Clement and Demetrius, embedded in place names, point to a period when Greek forms were current there, which can only have come about through the propagation of Old Church Slavonic from Moravia to Bohemia. They are demonstrably older than the eventually dominant Latin forms.

Other sources, in their account of St Wenceslas and the beginnings of Christianity in Bohemia, have given the honour of first convert in the dynasty to his uncle Spytigněv, not to his grandfather Bořivoj. With Spytigněv we are on solid ground. After the death of Svatopluk Bohemia was left exposed to Frankish pressure. It became more and more expedient for Prague to recognise some closer tie with the German world. Moreover the Moravian church was disorganised and in no state to be useful to Bohemia. Regensburg became the natural source both of political support and of further Christian development. Indeed the next churches which can be dated with certainty are dedicated to patrons connected with Regensburg—SS Emmeram, Peter and George—in particular Spytigněv's church of St Peter at his castle of Budeč.[8] The *Fulda Annals* report in some detail how as early as 895 Spytigněv and another chieftan Vitěslav were received by Arnulf of Bavaria at Regensburg and formally professed their allegiance.[9] Vitěslav may have been the chieftain of Libice in East Bohemia, where a dynasty, apparently of White Croat origin,[a] was shortly to come into prominence in rivalry with Prague.[b] Thus by 895 Bohemia was recognised as a semi-Christian country within the Frankish political system.

The venue of Spytigněv's baptism is nowhere specified. Either he or Bořivoj built a wooden church dedicated to the Virgin Mary in the citadel of Prague, to be succeeded in due course by a better stone edifice. The original portions of this are closely similar in style to several of the more or less contemporary Moravian churches.[10]

[a] See p. 187. The White Croat tribes were mainly in Silesia.

[b] The Prague dynasty will be referred to conventionally as the Premyslids after the eponymous founder Premysl (modern Czech Přemysl), that of Libice as the Slavniks after its most prominent member Slavník.

Christianity continued to develop, certainly at Prague (with which almost all the scanty records are concerned) and perhaps in some other centres throughout the reigns of Borivoj's sons Spytignĕv (*c.* 893/4–*c.* 915) and Vratislav (*c.* 915–*c.* 920).[a]

Politically Bavaria had now become the dominant influence at Prague. This was no doubt the reason for glossing over Borivoj's Moravian connection in later texts. Those which retained Borivoj cherished the Moravian connection; they may be called 'Bohemian' versions. Those which ignore him—therefore in all probability falsely—are 'Bavarian' versions, more orientated towards the Western church. The Magyar danger, acute from the very first years after their settlement in the Danubian steppes in 896, at once made Bohemia an ally of Bavaria for common defence. But the Saxon dukedom, with its aspirations to political leadership of all Germans, was also vitally interested in Bohemia for strategic reasons, especially after the loss of the greater part of Moravia to the Magyars in 906/7.[b] Bohemia became a bone of contention between Saxony and Bavaria. This political rivalry was brought to a head by the election of Duke Henry of Saxony (the Fowler) as King of Germany in 919. Saxony was the less civilised province; it had as yet no cultural centre to rival Regensburg. Entry into Bohemia was easier from the north up the Elbe valley than from Bavaria with high mountain barriers intervening. But the Saxons did not have undisputed access up the Elbe until the middle of the tenth century. The Bavarian capital continued to provide the main line of entry of Latin Christian culture into Bohemia. It may even have been responsible for part of the Slav culture too. Over and above direct Moravian-Bohemian links we must also bear in mind that, after the *débâcle* of 885/6, even if no Slav clergy would be likely to make for Regensburg, confiscated Slav liturgical books certainly were sent or found their way there. It was a place where the Slav dialects were relatively well known and missions to the Slavs of North Europe a long-standing preoccupation. The prejudice about language, which had bedevilled the years of Methodios's mission, may well not have had such narrow partisans in Regensburg as it had had a generation earlier in Salzburg and Passau. We therefore must not exclude the possibility that the ecclesiastical influence of Regensburg, though preponderantly

[a] These dates are quite uncertain. Spytignĕv's death is variously reckoned within the period 905–15.

[b] The Franks took advantage of Moravian weakness after Svatopluk's death but the Magyars soon made Moravia too unsafe for them to reap any advantage. The Magyar hold on Moravia did not relax till after the great defeat of 955. See p. 108.

German-Latin, brought with it also some Slav elements in reinforcement. The text known as *Geographus Bavarensis*, of which the earliest portions date from *c.* 844–62, bears witness to this interest; it was probably compiled at St Emmeram in Regensburg.[a]

The rivalry of Saxony and Bavaria reached a critical point, profoundly affecting the internal affairs of Bohemia, in the reign of Vratislav's son, Wenceslas.[b] Vratislav died in 920 or 921. Though a Christian, he is no more than a shadowy figure in Czech tradition. It is only recorded that he built the church of St George at Prague.[c]

Native sources for the life of St Wenceslas and connected matters[11]

Bohemian sources for the history of the tenth century have raised much controversy on reliability and date. But since the wide acceptance of Pekař's argument that the author known as Christian wrote at the end of the tenth century and is worthy of confidence,[12] more certainty has been attained in constructing a coherent sequence. They fall into three main groups, in two languages—Latin and Old Church Slavonic.

I A   Works of the tenth century—Latin:

1. The *First Latin Legend of Wenceslas* (*Crescente fide*), later rewritten in various forms. The Bohemian recension is exemplified in the Stuttgart *Passionale* (first half of the twelfth century), the Bavarian (in Ludvíkovský's terminology) in an eleventh-century Munich manuscript (CLM 4605). The work has been variously dated. Most experts consider it a source for Christian and Laurence and assume that it was written either shortly after 973 (foundation of the see of Prague) or shortly after 983 (when Adalbert was the Bishop of Prague). But these are little better than guesses. A few consider Christian's narrative definitely the older.

2. The *Legend* by the monk Laurence (Czech *Vavřinek*) of Monte Cassino, compiled between 989 and 997 (mainly 996–7) from material provided by Bohemians who came to the monastery, in particular by St Adalbert.[13] This was unknown in Bohemia and therefore stands outside the general development.

3. Christian's *Legend—Vita et Passio sancti Wenceslai et sancte Ludmile avie*

---

a Regensburg's interest in Slav missions remained strong in the tenth century too, witness the work of Boso of St Emmeram (d. 970) who was a Slav speaker and had considerable success amongst the Sorbs. The centres of his activity were Merseburg, of which he was first bishop, and Memleben. See p. 147.

b Modern Czech Václav. The Latin form Wenceslas will be used as the most familiar.

c Recent excavation on the Citadel has not yet found traces of it though it is presumably under the later buildings. The extant St George is of late tenth century only and was largely destroyed again by fire in 1142.

eius. Written, if its antiquity is accepted, about the year 994,[a] in the reign of Boleslas II.[b] His version combined the various diverging texts into a new literary whole. Its main themes are the Cyrillomethodian origins of Bohemian Christianity and the martyrdoms of Borivoj's wife Ljudmila and her grandson Wenceslas. The oldest extant manuscript is of the first half of the fourteenth century but the Latin style is estimated by most scholars to be typical of the earlier period. Those who still consider 'Christian' a late pastiche characterise the style as 'deliberately archaic'.[c]

4. Gumpold's *Legend*, written not long before 1000,[14] embroidering freely on the above. It is supposed to have been commissioned by Otto II before his sudden death in 983 and therefore could be as early as 982/3. The most popular but not the best literary work.

From Christian are held to be derived such secondary thirteenth-century works as *Ut annuncietur* and *Oriente jam sole*, from Gumpold—*Oportet nos* (*c.* 1050).

I B Works of the tenth or very early eleventh century in OCS:

1. The original *Life of St Wenceslas*, surely a mid-tenth-century Glagolitic text, now only extant in Russian Church Slavonic (Cyrillic) manuscripts of the sixteenth–seventeenth centuries and Croat Glagolitic manuscripts of the fourteenth–fifteenth centuries. Begun *c.* 940, or perhaps as early as 932 at the time of the translation of his relics to the church of St Vitus in Prague, it was reshaped towards the end of the century with additions from *Crescente fide* and other sources. This is known as the *1st OCS Legend*. The author is unknown; certain misconceptions of Bohemian facts may point to a foreigner, therefore perhaps a Croat, brought to Prague by Bishop Adalbert from Italy.[15]

The *1st OCS Legend* was the source of further Russian developments, to wit, the *Life of St Wenceslas* as included in the *Prolog* (Synaxarion)—two variants under 28 September (martyrdom) and 4 March (translation of his relics); the version in Makari's *Minei*; and the so-called *Vostokov text*.[16]

2. The *2nd OCS Legend* (*Nikolski's Cyrillic manuscript* is the only surviving form), dating from *c.* 1000, largely independent of the *1st OCS Legend* but not of Gumpold.

No Bohemian Slav manuscripts of the tenth century survive to provide tangible evidence of these deductions.

II A group of texts plausibly connected with the Slav monastery of Sázava and composed therefore in the later eleventh century, principally two forms of the *Legend of St Ljudmila*:

[a] Partly based on the assumption that the Christian mentioned by St Bruno of Querfurt in his *Vita sancti Adalberti* (cap. 15) is our Christian. If so, he came of the highest blood in the land but whether he was the uncle of Vojtěch the Slavnik (as he himself claims), or a nephew of St Wenceslas, as others opine, is not resolved. Though the two dynasties were certainly linked it does not seem possible that he could be both simultaneously. As his whole historical outlook is bound up with Prague, Libice being not so much as mentioned, his Slavnik genealogy does not inspire confidence.

[b] Czech *Boleslav*. Here also the Latin form is adopted to avoid possible confusion with the Polish Bolesław. [c] See p. 346 n. 12.

1. The *OCS Legend of St Ljudmila*, based on Christian. This again only survives in certain Russian *Prologs* (16 September) but can safely be assumed.[17]

2. The Latin Legend referred to as *Fuit*, partly based on Christian or having a common source with him. Date very uncertain.

Christian did not separate the lives of Wenceslas and Ljudmila. Her cult was evidently not considerable until the late eleventh century (especially at Sázava), when separation became necessary. Her canonisation is thought to date from the middle of the twelfth century.

III Versions dating from the time of the revival of OCS culture in the fourteenth century (especially in the reign of Charles IV), though the following relevant ones are in Latin:

1. The *Bohemian Legend* (*Diffundente sole*) of St Ljudmila, based on Christian (first half of fourteenth century).

2. *Quemadmodum* (first half of fourteenth century).

3. The *Moravian Legend* (*Tempore Michaelis imperatoris*)[18] of c. 1350–70, dependent on these two and other earlier sources.

4. To this period belongs also the rhymed chronicle going under the name of Dalimil (*c.* 1310),[19] based mainly on Christian, and Charles IV's own *Life of St Wenceslas* (*Crescente religione christiana*).[20]

The still highly disputable dates of such texts as the *Legenda bodecensis* (Böddecke manuscript), considered by most a fifteenth-century rehash of Christian of no independent evidential value, and of *Beatus Cyrillus* (*Quirillus*), may be taken as typical of the difficulties in analysis. Some are prepared to see in the latter a source for Christian, thus placing it among the earliest texts;[21] others look upon it as derived from the *Moravian Legend* (whence the links with Christian) and therefore posterior to c. 1350.[22] Králík's suggestion that this text is the mysterious *Privilegium* [i.e. Papal Charter] *moraviensis ecclesiae* would naturally only make sense if it were in fact an early text at least not later than the second half of the eleventh century.[a]

The *Life of St Wenceslas*, as edited in the 1st *OCS Legend*, shows clear signs of being the work of one fully trained in the Cyrillomethodian tradition, most probably therefore of one of the Moravian emigrants. Both language and manner are typical. It is also certain that Christian had read *VC* and *VM* and the *Life of Naum*[b]—presumably all in OCS, with which he was quite familiar, using the *Life of St Wenceslas* for his own Latin version. Thus the Bohemian-Moravian link in language, alphabet and texts is assured. It remains to assess its scope and vitality after transplantation.

Born about 907, Wenceslas was some twelve years old when his father died.[23] He showed an inclination for pious studies from an early age and was sent to be educated at the school attached to the family foundation of St Peter's, Budeč. He learnt both Latin and Slav letters—

as significant a combination in early Bohemian Christianity as in Moravia.[24] Moreover, he had undergone the ceremony of having his hair cut (the *postřižiny*)—a form of commendation usually performed about the age of seven, well known among the Slavs and other Indo-European peoples, which easily passed, as here, into Christian use.[25] According to a rather late Croat text the ceremony was performed by a Bishop Notar who, it is suggested, must be one of the bishops appointed for Moravia in or after 898 at the request of Mojmir II.[a] If the alleged Bishop Notar left Moravia about 906 he could have done considerable evangelical work in Bohemia. But it is more probable that Notar is a misconception for 'notary' or a deformation of Notker and that the participants in the ceremony were Arnulf of Bavaria and a representative of Bishop Tuto of Regensburg. At all events the incident suggests that Wenceslas was intended for the service of the church.[26] Wenceslas's mother Dragomira (modern Czech *Drahomíra*) was a daughter of the Slav chieftain of the Havolané in Brandenburg (part of the Veletian confederation)[b] and was surely a Christian from the time of her marriage, if not before. On 16 September of 920 or 921, no doubt consequent on Vratislav's death, a palace revolution took place in which Wenceslas's grandmother Ljudmila was assassinated. The details are obscure but it is reasonable to suppose that Dragomira attempted to assume power, perhaps with Arnulf of Bavaria's support. It is unlikely that Dragomira had thrown in her lot with a still considerable pagan faction. A defeat by the Christian dynasty of the remaining diehard pagans may be called a conventional episode in early legends and cannot be accepted without some support in the historical records. The author Christian alludes to a 'pagan reaction' after the conversion of Borivoj; *Crescente* indicates one on Vratislav's death (the present incident); the *1st OCS Legend* makes his brother Boleslas lead one when Wenceslas is already ruling; Christian alludes to both the latter. All or none may be fact. Whatever the truth in this case, Dragomira's bid for power was frustrated and Wenceslas's rights upheld. The ultimate result was that the murdered Ljudmila was soon elevated to the dignity of a martyr for the faith.

Coming of age about 924, Wenceslas was apparently strong enough to pursue his own policy. He relegated Dragomira to confinement at Budeč and brought his grandmother Ljudmila's relics back to Prague from Tetín, where a repentant Dragomira had enshrined them in St

[a] See pp. 83–4.   [b] See p. 144.

Michael's church. In external affairs Wenceslas began to feel that Bavaria was becoming too oppressive a neighbour and that the overlordship of Saxony (the King of Germany) would be preferable. By 924 Henry the Fowler had on his part greatly strengthened his position. We may date the change of front in Bohemia to about 926. There were also religious considerations: the Saxons were plainly on the point of expanding Christendom to the north of Bohemia among the still largely pagan Slavs from whom Wenceslas's mother had sprung.[a] It might be advantageous to Bohemia to be a party to this long-term policy. Conversely, Bavarian separatism, though mainly political, might make attachment to the Bavarian church, for all its great services to Bohemia, awkward in the future. These considerations did not imply any sudden and complete break with Bavaria in 926. Regensburg continued for a long time to come to be the most important cultural centre for Bohemia, right down to the time when the bishopric of Prague was subordinated to Mainz, and beyond.[b] About 925 Wenceslas invited the Bishop of Regensburg to consecrate his father's church of St George.[27] More important, he intended to dedicate his own new church at Prague to St Emmeram of Regensburg, the patron saint of Bavaria. But it was eventually dedicated to the patron saint of Saxony and of the great Saxon abbey of Corvey, St Vitus (Guy, German *Veit*), no doubt because Prague received an arm of the saint as a diplomatic gift from Henry. While it is clear that Wenceslas was turning his face towards Saxony, it is not certain that the change in dedication was his personal decision. Even if, as the more reliable sources indicate, it was Wenceslas himself who submitted to Henry when he invaded Bohemia in spring 929, the new political relationship was scarcely formalised until after his assassination and then symbolised in the sending of the relic and in the dedication of the church to St Vitus, reliably dated to 22 September 930. Yet 22 September is St Emmeram's day.

Wenceslas had built the church in the years 925–9. It was a small stone rotunda, generally considered to be in the Carolingian style[28]. Charlemagne's octagonal Palatine Chapel at Aix (Aachen), modelled on San Vitale at Ravenna, stood out as one of the great prototypes in Western Europe for centrally organised buidings.[c] But the conchoidal type (trefoil, quatrefoil), to which St Vitus belongs, has no such obvious

---

[a] See pp. 143 ff.   [b] See p. 99.

[c] The octagonal form is characteristic of a baptistery, the number eight being symbolic of eternal life.

source. It is widely distributed but more characteristic of Byzantine lands. Though Wenceslas surely employed foreign craftsmen it is not established where they came from. The rotunda was a convenient form for small churches in a new Christian country with limited resources.[29]

Wenceslas was assassinated in 929[30]. The *Life* places all the odium on his brother Boleslas. Hence his supposed adherence to 'pagan reactions', in which there is probably no truth, though of course he may have had unbaptised among his followers. Dragomira had apparently been restored to favour by Wenceslas and no source suggests that she engineered this second coup against her own son.[31] Boleslas stands out as the natural person to be pushed into leadership of the anti-Saxon party. It is true that he did favour maintaining the Bavarian connection: he sent one of his sons to be educated at St Emmeram and remained a friend of Arnulf. Furthermore it was precisely in 929 that Wenceslas betrothed his infant son Boleslas to Emma, an Anglo-Saxon princess, closely connected with the Saxon house.[32] If this was the background to the *coup d'état* it still seems that no motives of high policy—above all religious—were involved. It has much more the aspect of a family quarrel allowed to go too far. Wenceslas was very pious and inclined to the ascetic life; Boleslas—worldy and ambitious to rule. Wenceslas had been persuaded to marry and produce an heir; this achieved, he renounced the married state.[33] Boleslas, with only the remote prospect of succession to his twenty-year-old brother, would be exceedingly put out by the advent of such an heir. The rest was the work of evil counsel and court factions. Needless to say, Boleslas also saw to the speedy removal of his infant nephew.

One might conclude from the legends that by 929 Wenceslas had so far identified himself with the Saxon connection that he was personally supporting Latin priests, whereas Boleslas still favoured the Slav church. For Boleslas inveigled Wenceslas to his own residence, Stará Boleslav (German *Altbunzlau*), to attend the consecration of a new church dedicated to SS Cosmas and Damian. At this ceremony two Slav priests, Paul and Krastěj, officiated. It was in this newly dedicated church that Wenceslas was murdered on 28 September 929, heedless of warnings of treachery and armed, in Christian's words, 'only with the weapons of faith'. But the contrast is surely artificial. It would be hazardous to suggest that Wenceslas's German priests were unpopular and that Boleslas had become the covert leader of a pro-Slav party. Rather Wenceslas was removed for being too much under the thumb of priests, too little attentive to government. Rulers of barbarian peoples, German and Slav, had been essentially military leaders and continued to be so when their peoples formally became Christian, since political needs as such had not changed. To be labelled 'pious' or the like (as Louis the Pious) was a reproach implying incapacity as a ruler, however saintly as a man. Such a man was Wenceslas. All stress in him those Christian virtues particularly laudable in princes: justice, care for the poor and needy, protection of widows and orphans, the building and endowment of churches and the provision of clergy. But he must have lacked the essential princely virtue of command. *Crescente fide* puts it baldly: 'qui princeps debebat esse perversus est a clericis et ut monachus'. Gumpold implies the same.[34] He further tells us that Wenceslas abhorred cruel punishments, especially the death penalty;[a] did much to evangelise the people; was strict in keeping fasts and vigils. During Lent he would arise secretly at night and, attended by one devoted page, make his way barefoot in bitter weather from one church to another through his domains, chanting the Psalter.[b] In the summer he would make the Communion wafers with his own hands. He laboured in person at the building of his church of St Vitus. Little wonder then if in the end, as Gumpold intimates, the disaster was touched off by the revolt of his military *comitatus*, which, as elsewhere under similar circumstances, is apt to be recalcitrant to a new religion of unwarlike virtues and to refuse to be led by a devotee of non-violence.[35] Wenceslas tried to create a Christian society at too fast a pace and in too uncompromising a spirit.

By his death, soon accounted a martyrdom, Wenceslas became a national saint. As heavenly protector he was more effective than as earthly ruler. Such veneration did he command that from the end of the tenth century the Czechs referred to Bohemia as *terra S. Wenceslai* and to themselves as *familia S. Wenceslai*. He was more than the patron saint of the state: the reigning duke or king was conceived as his representative, in much the same way as, on the highest level, the Byzantine emperor was the vicar of Christ.[c] As celestial patron St Wenceslas was the main device on the royal seals.[36] He was held to have speedily saved Bohemia from Polish occupation in 1003–4.[37] The hymn *Svatý Václave*,

---

[a] Cf. p. 266.

[b] The picturesque details of J. M. Neale's carol are taken from a later elaboration (first half of the thirteenth century) of the legend, known as *Ut annuncietur* (p. 91 above).

[c] Cf. St Olaf who was venerated as *perpetuus rex Norvegiae*. His relics were kept at St Clement's, Nidaros (see pp. 257–8).

vévodo české země, one of the four early popular religious texts in Czech, sums up this sentiment.

Boleslas succeeded to power, as was his ambition. There was nothing eccentric about him. He later repented of his complicity in his brother's murder and caused the martyr's relics, which had already begun to work miracles, to be brought to St Vitus in Prague (4 March 932). They have long vanished.

Boleslas had to accept Henry's overlordship as already imposed on his brother in 929. From this time the political status of the ruler of Prague, and later of all Bohemia, was similar to that of the Bavarian dukes before the province was fully incorporated in the Frankish Empire: the native dynasty was tolerated by the ruler of Germany but the latter will always interfere in the internal affairs of the country, including the succession, whenever high policy requires it. However, from Henry's death in 936 until 950 Bohemia was relatively independent.

For the next forty years there are few details to record of the progress of Christianity in Bohemia. The country grew rapidly more prosperous, partly no doubt with the increasing volume of international trade, especially of the slave trade for which Prague was a point of concentration.[a] Indeed Prague was, in the second half of the tenth century, one of the most important marts in Europe, the advanced post of economic penetration of the Western world into Central Europe and beyond.[38]

Churches built in the second half of the tenth century have been identified at Dobřichov, Malín, Plzeň (Pilsen) and elsewhere. Christianity spread at this time from castle to castle as each local count submitted to the radiation of Prague. The countryside, as always, could only be affected slowly. Boleslas II (?967–99) brought virtually all of Bohemia under the rule of Prague, supported the church and was instrumental in founding the first Benedictine house for nuns in Prague (St George's), where his sister Mlada (Maria) became abbess—a proper task for princesses. All his family promoted Christian institutions. The Western tithe was introduced. Though Prague remained the more important centre in most respects, it is certain that the Slavník house at Libice was no less Christian.[b] Into this house was born about the year 956 Vojtěch, later Adalbert, Bishop of Prague.

---

[a] Slaves were not kept in Bohemia (or Moravia) but collected for export to the Moslem world. See also pp. 144–5.

[b] It would appear that some of Wenceslas's devoted entourage, and also the priest Krastěj, fled to their territory after the murder. This is the most likely interpretation of the 'to the Croats' of the legends. The events of 995 (see below) suggest that Libice maintained the veneration of Wenceslas as much as or more than Prague.

The outstanding fact that strikes us about this first century of Bohemian Christianity is the peaceful—or at least apparently peaceful—coexistence of Latin and Slav in the church. The earliest churches were at princely residences and therefore in their rites presumably followed the preference of the prince. The Prague dynasty must have favoured the Slav church; had it not done so, it must surely have died out almost at once. The house of Slavník also probably patronised it. This duality is also characteristic of the eleventh century. The cultivation of the Cyrillo-methodian liturgical language, written in the Glagolitic alphabet, may not have been absolutely continuous since Methodios's time (if it in fact reached Bohemia so early) but it was reinforced at intervals—in 885/6, in 905/6, and perhaps in 955 when the Czechs occupied Moravia after playing their part in the great defeat of the Magyars on the Lechfeld.[a] Links with the Croat Glagolitic church, important at a later date,[b] may well have existed from early on. In this way Czech religious language absorbed side by side with Latinisms and Germanisms many elements of South Slav provenance. Some were in course of time eliminated. This cultivation of Church Slavonic in Bohemia was sufficiently intense to affect the nascent Polish Christian vocabulary.[c]

There is little to suggest that the Slav rite as introduced into Bohemia was not predominantly Western with Latin Mass formularies in Slav translation such as has already been posited for Moravia.[d] Those who do not accept the *Kiev Missal* as a translation of Constantine's must attribute it at least to the following generation. The consistent though incomplete West Slav cast of its language was preserved precisely because the text passed direct from Moravian to Bohemian use. The extant copy was probably made in Bohemia in the middle of the tenth century.[e] But the influence of the German-Latin church was too strong and persistent to allow pecularities to subsist for long in Bohemian practice. The church was in essence Western; only in language and literary tradition was there an adventitious Eastern element.

The conspicuous feature of early Bohemian religious texts is thus the

---

[a] The Bohemian contingent was the eighth of the eight 'legions' which composed Otto's army.

[b] See p. 112.　　　　　　　　　　　　[c] See pp. 122–3.

[d] See pp. 59 ff.

[e] Others prefer to attribute the copy to the Balkans (e.g. Macedonia still under the influence of Clement and Naum). This makes its recovery in Jerusalem (taken there no doubt by a pilgrim) rather less eccentric, but is hardly decisive. Both the retention of the dialect word *rěsnota* (apparently not Bohemian) and the regular if limited westernisation of the language (see p. 61 note b) point to an adoption of this and similar texts by Bohemia readymade from Moravia.

coexistence of Latin and Slav versions of the same subject, in many cases differing widely in detail, which lends colour to the supposition that the centres of cultivation of the two languages were often distinct. Christian, if indeed writing at the end of the tenth century, stands out as one who is equally at home in both. He was the first to make a single narrative out of the already divergent accounts of the Life and Passion of St Wenceslas. Side by side with veneration of the native saints that of SS Cyril and Methodios continued to hold an honourable place. The bias of later sources makes it impossible to assess the relative weight of Latin and Slav at any given date. At the time of the foundation of the see of Prague, a recognition of the maturity of the new church, Latin may well have had the upper hand but there is no record of open persecution on the part of the German-Latin clergy. The patronage of the Slav church by the dynasty was sufficient protection.

The bishopric of Prague was formally constituted in 967. This may be accounted the last achievement of Boleslas I before his death in that year.[a] He had no doubt hoped to make his new bishopric independent of the German church but political pressure was far too great. German interests insisted on Prague's subordination to Mainz, overriding the pretensions, if only on geographical grounds, of Salzburg through Regensburg.[b] The German Emperor reserved to himself the investiture of the bishop. Indeed such was the prestige of Otto I since his decisive victory over the heathen Magyars in 955 (in which Bohemian troops played their part), culminating in the proclamation of the German Empire in 962, that we may tend to exaggerate Bohemia's desire for independence, ecclesiastically and otherwise. It was not Boleslas himself who was likely to object to Prague's attachment to the great metropolis. Latin clergy certainly predominated, Slav clergy perhaps were only tolerated, in the new cathedral. Even the Pope, when he finally approved the erection of the bishopric (972/3), does not seem to have made any ruling on this matter. That he specifically forbade the Slav liturgy at this time is a later falsification which Cosmas of Prague, an adherent of the Latin party, understandably attributes to the foundation date.[39] Bavarian protests, led by Bishops Michael of Regensburg and Pilgrim of Passau, held up the

---

[a] This is the date given by Cosmas of Prague but it is possible that he did not die until as late as 972.

[b] The synod which met at Ravenna in April 967, in the presence of the Pope, discussed missions to Slavs in the North and the rights to be given to Magdeburg (see p. 118). Surely Prague must also have been discussed but there is nothing to suggest that either Pope or Emperor desired its subordination to Magdeburg.

implementation. The long negotiations bear witness to the great importance given to the new bishopric in contemporary politics. For no sooner had Papal approval of the imperial policy been given than Emperor Otto I died (May 973). Just before his death, at Easter 973, Otto had held a great council at Quedlinburg at which Boleslas II was present in person, as well as envoys of Poland, the Byzantine Empire, Bulgaria, Hungary, Russia (Kiev) and Denmark. Though the substance of the discussions is not known in any detail it is clear that Otto was acting, as he was of stature to do since 955, as the arbiter of European disputes and director of supreme policy. We may therefore suppose that the status of the bishopric of Prague and its territorial extent were finally determined at this moment.

The Emperor's death caused further delays. Neither Boleslas nor Duke Henry II of Bavaria was well disposed towards the new emperor, Otto II. In 973/4 Bavaria, Bohemia and Poland formed what amounted to an alliance against him. Henry took up arms against the Emperor and was obliged to take refuge in Bohemia; Bavarian loyalty to the Empire had always been precarious. This gave Otto the chance to put in his own nominee, Otto of Swabia, as Duke of Bavaria. Thus deprived of Bavarian support, Boleslas had to agree to the Imperial conditions and to the appointment of the Saxon Thietmar, known to be loyal to the Saxon house, as first bishop of Prague. Willigis, the Archbishop of Mainz, gave his approval to the appointment in January 975 and consecrated Thietmar later that year. Thietmar was finally able to take up his duties after Otto's military demonstrations against Bohemia in 976–7.

The subordination of Prague to Mainz, whose archbishop was *ex officio* Chancellor of the Empire, decided Bohemia's political future as a part of the Empire, formalised in 1002. Bavarian influences, however, remained strong. Bavarian clergy continued to come in numbers to Bohemia.[40] Typical of the continuing connection is the rotunda of St Peter at Starý Plzenec, built not long after 973, at an important point on the main route between Regensburg and Prague.

Thietmar (Dĕtmar), however, was no narrow-minded German cleric. He was in all probability from Corvey, the most cultured Saxon abbey closely in touch with the Slav world, a Slav speaker and as such evidently acceptable to both the Premyslids and the Slavniks. It is even possible that at his installation parts of the service were held in Slav in addition to Latin and German. The end of the long diplomatic manoeuvres did not come till 978 when Boleslas renewed his submission to Otto at Quedlinburg and it is surmised that the Emperor ordered that the Slavník Vojtěch should be appointed to Thietmar's staff at the cathedral with a view to succeeding to the see in due course. This was a political safeguard of the loyalty of the Bohemian church as a whole and of the Slavník principality in particular; for relations between Prague and the Slavníks were worsening.[41] Thietmar died soon after—on 2 January 982—and Vojtěch was duly elected to the see, under the name of Adalbert.

The view that Adalbert, as Bishop of Prague, was opposed to the Slav church need no longer be entertained. Many falsifications were introduced, more or less consciously, into later texts, from the middle of the eleventh century, when Latin animosity against the Slav language began to gather strength. Thus in a text of Bohemian provenance known in late Russian versions he appears as a rabid Latinist.[42] On the contrary, the end of the tenth century saw an intensive cultivation of Slav letters in Bohemia. This literature in Glagolitic was a part of the church's life and could not have existed independently of it. It was probably Adalbert who formally canonised Wenceslas and therefore stimulated the composition of the necessary texts. Králík[43] justly remarks that Christian, who dedicated his Latin *Legend of St Wenceslas* to the Bishop, is thereby the best evidence of the latter's own approval; for his Latin works are a qualified defence of the Slav language church. Moreover, Christian may have been the presumptive successor to Thietmar before Adalbert was imposed by Otto.[a] The point unfortunately does not come out clearly in the contemporary sources for Vojtěch-Adalbert's life, which are generally of high value. The three most important are:

1. the *Life* by John Canaparius[b] (*Vita antiquior* or *prior*), written in 999 at the command of Otto III, leading to divergent Italian and North European versions;[44]

2. the *Life* by St Bruno of Querfurt (*Vita posterior*), written in 1004;[45]

3. *Versus de passione*, of which there are no early manuscripts. Some consider that the work was used in the writing of 1 and 2; others relegate it to a much later date, perhaps the end of the thirteenth century.

Adalbert became willy-nilly a factor in the political rivalry between Premyslids and Slavníks. The rise in political importance of the Slavník

---

[a] The connection of Christian and Vojtěch falls to the ground, of course, if Christian's *Legend* is held to be a forgery of the early fourteenth century (see note 12 to this chapter)—a point of view which, it must be admitted, is now gathering strength again.

[b] Third abbot of the monastery of SS Boniface and Alexius on the Aventine. See p. 103.

principality at Libice in the tenth century was rapid. It controlled a large part of eastern and southern Bohemia—quite as large an area as Prague ruled—including the easiest routes into Poland. Dynastic ties with the Bavarian house, profitable to both sides *vis-à-vis* Saxony and Prague, were contracted. Both the palace and large basilica at Libice appear to date from the time of the greatest prosperity—about the middle of the tenth century.[46]

Despite the Bavarian connection, by the time of Vojtěch's birth (*c.* 956) the Slavniks were far from hostile to the Saxons. The boy was sent about 972 to the episcopal school at Magdeburg, already famous through its learned rector Otrik (Ohtrich). Further, he had received the baptismal name Adalbert at his confirmation at Libice by Bishop Adalbert of Trier in 961.[a] He was intended for an ecclesiastical career. The years spent in Magdeburg, itself a centre of missionary work to Slavs,[b] did not give him a strong German-Latin bias. The outstanding conviction of his education was the urgent need for further missionary activity in North Europe. Whether he received his first orders from Adalbert, now Archbishop of Magdeburg, or from Bishop Thietmar is not clear. But he served under Thietmar at Prague cathedral. He was still under the canonical age of thirty when Thietmar died suddenly in January 982; special dispensation had to be obtained to allow his succession as agreed in 978. He was invested by Otto II and consecrated by the Archbishop of Mainz in Verona in June 983.

Adalbert did not, however, prove the political prelate that the situation called for. He disliked the role and may well have accepted the charge unwillingly. In this he was at one with his biographer, St Bruno of Querfurt, who did not approve of the typical German bishop of his time and therefore conceived his *Life* in a more hagiographical style. Adalbert had been impressed by Cluniac ideas while still at Magdeburg and his ascetic bent was strengthened by a journey to Italy in 983. For the next few years he faced the difficult work of his large, undeveloped and politically disunited diocese. Early in 989 he abandoned Prague for Italy, accompanied by his half-brother Radim (Gaudentius) and a few others. The reasons, apart from personal inclination, can only be surmised: disapproval of Boleslas's alliance with the still pagan Veletians[c] and increasing estrangement between Boleslas and the Slavniks. His

---

[a] Adalbert was sent to Kiev by Otto at the request of Olga (see p. 251) as bishop for the Russians and appears to have performed the confirmation on the way back.

[b] See also pp. 146–7.

[c] See p. 121.

ultimate intention was a pilgrimage to the Holy Land. In the event the life of the Italian monasteries held him, first Monte Cassino,[a] then Valleluce, where the ascetic principles of the Greek St Nilus (Neilos) were more congenial to him. He made his profession on 17 April 990 at the monastery of SS Boniface and Alexius in Rome—a house where Eastern and Western practices coexisted and whose abbot, Leo, was a friend of St Nilus and influential at the Curia. This harmony between Greeks and Latins in Italy was not merely a factor favourable to Adalbert's personal development but on a wider front to ecclesiastical reform generally in the Ottonian period.[47]

Adalbert's position was still irregular. Boleslas II desired him to return to Prague since concessions to the Slavniks were still vital for internal unity; moreover he needed his knowledge and advice in view of deteriorating relations with Poland and Mieszko's increasingly close contacts with Rome in 990–2.[b] In 992 he was persuaded to return to his episcopal duties.[c] For a short time Adalbert was able to work amicably with Boleslas. Together they founded in 993 the abbey of Břevnov (German *Breunau*), near Prague, with twelve monks from his Roman monastery—the first such house in Bohemia. It was placed under the patronage of SS Benedict, Boniface and Alexius. As the monastery of SS Boniface and Alexius was a house of mixed observance,[d] a similar rule may well have been carried to Břevnov. However it has not been possible to prove that the Greek language or the Byzantine liturgy were used there nor even that it was a notable centre of the Slav liturgical language.[48]

Adalbert left for Rome again in 995. The presence of a prominent Slavnik in Prague had evidently become impossible. Boleslas could no longer tolerate Slavnik separatism and intrigues with Poland. In the same year 995 he took the common tyrant's step of eliminating his rivals by a general massacre, even ignoring the right of sanctuary. The blow fell, by accident or design, on the anniversary of Wenceslas's murder. Of the Slavnik house only Adalbert's elder brother Soběslav (or Soběbor) escaped,[49] being absent from Libice at the time. Bohemia was thenceforward under the single rule of the Premyslids of Prague.

In 995 must be placed Adalbert's visit to Hungary. We can accept the

---

[a] Hence we presume that Adalbert supplied the monk Laurence with all or most of the material for his *Life of St Wenceslas* (p. 90).

[b] See p. 121.

[c] Strictly speaking his monastic vows cancelled his episcopal status but the Pope could grant dispensation.   [d] On the Greek houses in Italy see also p. 337 note 182.

statement of the *Vita Sancti Stephani regis* (*Legenda maior*), written *c.* 1077–83, that Adalbert baptised Géza and his son Stephen (Vajk), then about twenty years old, though Bruno of Querfurt makes no mention of it. Adalbert may have been intermediary in Stephen's marriage to the Bavarian princess Gisela in 996.[50] He did not stay long in Hungary himself but sent a small party of missionaries led by his former tutor Radla, who was to become the first Hungarian archbishop with his see at Esztergom.[a]

Adalbert's entry into the Hungarian mission field came at a critical moment. Passau, in the person of its unscrupulous bishop, Pilgrim, had been attempting to gather the evangelisation of all Magyar lands into its own hands from 955 onwards, including even Moravia.[51] The longstanding rights of Salzburg in Pannonia were however upheld by Rome. Despite Passau's hold on the Danube artery, Adalbert and his missionaries were responsible for the decisive act of baptising the most powerful chieftain. It was in Stephen's hands that the entry of a united Hungary into Christendom lay.[52] The Bohemian intervention thus consolidated the influence of the see of Prague in Moravia and extended it into Slovakia at least as far as the old capital of Nitra. Dedications of early churches in Hungary to SS Wenceslas and Vitus on the one hand and to St Clement and Adalbert himself on the other, are well authenticated.

By 996 Adalbert was already prior of a Benedictine monastery in Rome. But the Archbishop of Mainz insisted, as he was entitled to do, on his return. Obediently Adalbert went to Mainz. Here he met and renewed his friendship with the Emperor Otto III (September 996) and went on to visit several of the great French abbeys, including St Denis and Fleury. The aims of the leading French monastic reformers confirmed the convictions which he had acquired in Italy.[b] His return to Prague after the massacre was out of the question.[53] He finally obtained leave of his ecclesiastical superiors to devote himself to missionary work and went with Radim to Poland where his brother had taken refuge. This strengthened Bolesław's hand against Bohemia; his close collaboration with Otto III bears witness to Adalbert's mediacy. But Adalbert did not remain to work in Poland; he preferred to attempt the conversion of the Prussians, a Baltic people who were causing Bolesław trouble on his eastern frontier. There he met a martyr's death in April 997. Radim and another companion Benedict were unharmed and returned to Gniezno with the news. His remains, redeemed for their weight in gold by

---

[a] Czech *Ostřihom*, Ger. *Gran*.

[b] He had met the great abbot of Cluny, Maïeul (954–94), in passing in Pavia as early as 983.

Bolesław, were brought to Gniezno, after temporary deposition at Trzemeszno, and richly enshrined. Part of his relics was immediately offered to Otto III, who the same year dedicated a church to him in Aix. He pressed for his immediate canonisation and commissioned the necessary accounts of his life and martyrdom in support of the claim. The canonisation took place in Rome on 29 June 999. In the following years Otto dedicated three further churches to him in Italy—at Ravenna, Subiaco, and on an island in the Tiber at Rome. In the last he deposited the arm of the saint given to him by Bolesław at Gniezno in 1000.[54]

Though Adalbert's frustrated life is lacking in obvious achievements he was with SS Romuald and Nilus one of the three chief spiritual influences on Otto III and a great Slav prelate venerated by the people. The centre of his cult was the shrine at Gniezno. But when Bohemia had Poland at her mercy in 1038–9, his relics together with those of Gaudentius were removed thence by Břetislav to Prague, as important a possession to the Czechs as those of Wenceslas and Ljudmila. Wenceslas was a national saint; Adalbert of international stature. St Adalbert figures, sometimes with St Wenceslas, on a number of twelfth-century Bohemian coins, and on a few Polish ones. Nevertheless no new life of Adalbert was written in Bohemia. His most remarkable monument is the great bronze doors of the Cathedral of Gniezno, designed and executed about 1175, with eighteen scenes from the life of the saint. This splendid work shows the influence or cooperation of artists of the Liège school, one of the main cultural influences on Poland in the eleventh–twelfth centuries.[55]

After Adalbert another monk of Corvey, Thiddag, was appointed Bishop of Prague (*fungebatur* 998–1017), to be followed by two more Germans, Ekkehard (1017–23) and Izzo (1023–30). The cathedral school was reorganised and no doubt became a purely Latin centre. These thirty years were a time of political impotence when Prague was alternately under German or Polish control. There is little to show how the Slav ministry fared. The weak Boleslas III was scarcely a patron; his one known foundation, the monastery of St John the Baptist 'na ostrově u Davle' (999), drew its monks from Niederaltaich.[56] Only at the end of the reign of Oldřich (Ulrich, d. 1034) did another prominent centre of Slav letters arise in the monastery of SS Mary and John the Baptist at Sázava. This house was founded by Oldřich and Procopius, his confessor, about 1032. It was a Benedictine house of predominantly, if not exclusively, Slav language. The Cyrillomethodian tradition was maintained here in its essentials.[57] It is therefore clear that Oldřich, though politically well disposed towards Germany, personally favoured the Slav language and succeeded in promoting its use through his native nominee to the see of Prague, Severus (Czech Šebíř, *fungebatur* 1031–67). Procopius himself appears in earlier life to have been a Latin priest.

From the time of Procopius's death (1053) difficulties assailed the monastery. In the following year the rift between Pope and Patriarch began to take on a more permanent complexion. Eastern traits in Western practice were more and more frowned upon. The continued use of the Slav liturgical language came to depend largely on the patronage of the ruler of Bohemia, clearly at Sázava and presumably also in the rest of the country. High policy, not merely personal predilection, now played a more conspicuous part. Břetislav (1034–55) continued to support Severus and Procopius, whom he made abbot of Sázava. He founded several monasteries, including that of Rajhrad in Moravia with Benedictines from Břevnov (1048). He abstracted St Adalbert's relics from Gniezno to Prague,[a] and may have applied unsuccessfully to the Pope at this time (1039) for the elevation of Prague to an archbishopric. Under him the cult of St Wenceslas began to take shape: he is credited with the foundation of the first two churches dedicated to the national saint— Brůdek and Stará Boleslav, the scene of his martyrdom.[b]

Spytigněv II (1055–61) did not favour the Slav language and had the *glagoljaši* of Sázava turned out (*c.* 1056). They retired under their abbot Vit, Procopius's nephew, to the monastery of Višegrad in Slovakia, then a part of Hungary.[c] His brother and successor Vratislav II (1061–92) brought them back about 1063. For the rest of his reign they continued undisturbed at Sázava. Abbot Vit was succeded by Procopius's son Emmeram. Vratislav also built a great new Cathedral of St Vitus in Prague with a worthy shrine for the relics of St Wenceslas.[d] With the election of his brother Gebhard-Jaromír to the see of Prague in 1068 on

---

[a] See p. 105.

[b] Brůdek commemorates a victory near that place in August 1040. The Stará Boleslav church may have been a guilt-offering for his disgraceful acts in Poland in 1038/9 (see also p. 132 below) and was consecrated, according to Cosmas of Prague, in 1046. Three churches dedicated to St Adalbert at Nimptsch, Breslau (Wrocław) and Militsch—all on a main route from Prague to Poznán and Gniezno—are also perhaps foundations of Břetislav, the appropriator of the saint's relics.

[c] Hungarian *Visehrád*. This monastery dedicated to St Andrew, a typically Eastern saint at this period, was founded by Endre (Andrew) I (1046–60), who had been baptised in Kiev and maintained close links with the Greek and Slav world.

[d] This building was burnt down in 1091. A new edifice, for the first time all of stone, was consecrated under Bishop Cosmas in 1096.

the death of Severus, a lengthy quarrel started which fatally involved the Bohemian church in international politics. On the one hand Vratislav wished to be rid of Jaromír. Though the bishop was suspended for a short time (1073–4) Rome would not countenance his removal.[58] On the other hand Pope Gregory VII made prolonged efforts to woo Vratislav away from his support of Henry IV. Failing in this, he broke off relations with Prague in 1075 and made sure of Polish cooperation against both Bohemia and the Empire. When the political crisis had blown over and Vratislav ventured again to approach Rome in 1079 for a formal and permanent recognition of the Slav liturgical language in Bohemia, the Pope categorically refused (January 1080).[59] As Jaromír opposed all Vratislav's ecclesiastical policy, in particular the establishment of a Moravian bishopric, he must be accounted an opponent of the Slav language and no doubt advocated its suppression to the Pope. Politics apart, Rome was intent now on eliminating from the Western church peculiarities which smacked of Eastern customs and estimated that Bohemian Christianity was sufficiently mature no longer to need the concessions sometimes made to missionary areas; the use of the Slav language could now be abandoned without prejudicial effects. This was the death-knell. That Vratislav had himself crowned a second time (if tradition is correct) in 1091 according to the Slav rite by Božetěch, last abbot of a Slav Sázava, after a coronation according to the Latin rite in 1085, proved a vain gesture.

The end came in 1096–7, when Břetislav II (1092–1100), a pious prince but a Latinist and loyal to the Papacy, finally expelled the Sázava monks and installed a German abbot, Dethard of Břevnov. Cosmas, the then Bishop of Prague (*fungebatur* 1091–8) was of like mind. From that date the Slav tradition in the Bohemian church came to a rapid end. Slav service-books were destroyed.

The triumph of the Latinists, perhaps inevitable in a country more and more firmly attached to the Western world, in whose capital a large German colony by now dominated trade and politics, is symbolised in the work of Cosmas of Prague who died in 1125 aged at least eighty: his *Chronicle*, written at the end of his long life, makes no mention whatever of the existence of a Slav language church in Bohemia at any time. Such was the distance travelled in the hundred years since the Slav legends of Wenceslas. Weingart has called the hymn *Hospodine pomiluj ny* (Kyrie eleison), with its mixture of Church Slavonic and colloquial Czech traits (the latter notably in the metre and initial accentuation of the words) the swan-song of Bohemian Slav culture, forced out of existence by 1100 by Latin and German.[60]

Of course, a 'mature' Christian country is a relative term. The suppression of openly pagan practices certainly continued down to the end of the eleventh century. Břetislav I's edict issued at Gniezno in 1039[61] shows how much remained to be done, whether in Poland or Bohemia; Břetislav II still faced the same problems in the 1090s.[62]

Prague remained the only Bohemian bishopric for a considerable time.[a] The ecclesiastical status of Moravia when part of the Bohemian state is somewhat obscure. Bohemian reoccupation can only have become slowly effective after 955. There is some evidence of a separate Moravian bishopric during the decade 975–85, notably an apparently authentic letter addressed by Archbishop Willigis of Mainz to the bishops of Speyer, Worms, Prague and Moravia under the date 28 April 976. This suggests that the decisions of 973 envisaged such a separation. Towards the end of the century, with increasing Bohemian interest in Hungary, Moravia must have been under efficient Bohemian administration but nothing more is said of a separate bishopric. There followed a short period of Polish occupation. Moravia returned from Polish hands to Bohemia about 1021. A Bohemian bishop, Vracen, is then recorded as active there. But from 1030 to 1063 Moravia was directly administered by Prague. In 1063 came another change: the bishopric of Olomouc (German *Olmütz*) was established. Vratislav II had to agree to its suppression in 1085 on the death of Bishop John, a former monk of Břevnov, but was able to restore it in 1090.[63] The recreation of a Moravian bishopric, though in itself not an attempt to renew an ancient tradition, may well have been a factor in stimulating the revival of Cyrillomethodian literature at this time at Sázava. Its expelled monks who returned in 1063 from Slovakia would be apt to take a special interest in the Moravian past: Cyrillomethodian survivals at Nitra and elsewhere are conceivable.[b] The *Privilegium moraviensis ecclesiae* mentioned by Cosmas might thus conceivably date as a formal document (if there ever was such) from 1063 or not long after.[64]

The limits of the diocese of Prague in other directions are also doubtful. At the time of its establishment Bohemia is thought to have held, apart from Moravia, the Cracow area of South Poland,[c] Silesia (till *c.* 990) and

---

[a] It became an archbishopric only in 1344 when Charles IV succeeded in detaching it from Mainz.　　　　[b] See p. 84.

[c] The Cracow area seems to have been Czech from *c.* 960 till the mid-80s, then Polish for a few years, Czech from about 990 to 999, and thereafter Polish again

parts of Slovakia; but very improbably parts of Galicia with the strategically important 'Red Towns', occupied by Russia in 981.[65] It is likely that the diocese as originally defined did not include any lands outside Bohemia proper. Not till the end of the eleventh century are other pretensions put forward in writing. The details given by Cosmas,[66] purporting to reflect the foundation deed, are highly suspicious, the 'facts' placed before the Diet of Mainz in 1085 equally so.[67] The latter document was no doubt occasioned by the fact that in 1085 Henry IV created Vratislav II King of Poland. It was therefore advisable that ecclesiastical boundaries should be reconsidered. Jaromír hoped to bolster up his pretensions to a much larger diocese by an appeal to history, namely that the original diocese had included Moravia, South Poland and Silesia, either in its own right or in virtue of its being the heir to the Moravian metropolis. Whether he knew this to be a falsification or not, is not certain, but as he had not (as far as is known) used these arguments in the long quarrel over the Moravian bishopric they appear highly artificial in 1085/6. At most some such enlargement may have been projected by Boleslas and Adalbert, presumably in 993–4, in support of the elevation of Prague to an archbishopric with missionary interests in all these eastern lands—a project, as we know, dear to Adalbert's heart. His success in Western Hungary in the following year, leading to the establishment of a missionary bishopric there, strengthened Prague's case but was not decisive. Jaromír assumed that the paper scheme in the episcopal archives was actually put into effect.

By 1100 the promising Slav church of Bohemia had been forced out of existence. Nearly fifty Slav texts have survived from its two centuries of life. This alone, considering the chances of survival, is enough to show that it was no restricted local form of worship unknown to the country at large. However, the triumph of Latin and the German church was such that scarcely any Slav Glagolitic manuscripts survived in Bohemia itself. The Latin church affected to ignore the very existence of an earlier colleague.[a] The preservation of the Slav texts is largely due to their having passed to Russia in the eleventh century and, we must suppose, above all from Sázava.[b] *The 2nd OCS Legend* is a typical case. To this we may add *Vita Methodii* and the *Encomium of SS Cyril and Methodios*,[c] both of which reached Kiev from Bohemia and chanced to survive in Russia alone. The case of *Vita Methodii* is especially instructive. While *Vita Constantini* was widely copied in the Balkans and

[a] Cf. p. 135.　　[b] See p. 349 n. 57.　　[c] See p. 31 no. 4.

certainly reached Russia and Serbia from Bulgaria, no early copies of *Vita Methodii* of obviously Balkan provenance have survived and it may have been little known there in its original form. The twelfth-century version preserved in Russia points directly to Bohemia. This favours the view that Methodios's *Life* was composed almost immediately after his death for local Moravian use. In the ensuing *débâcle* it was preserved by refugees to Bohemia but perhaps not by those who fled to the Balkans. The account of SS Cyril and Methodios, inserted arbitrarily in the *Russian Primary Chronicle* under the year 898, also bears witness in all probability to an active link between Sázava and the Cave Monastery in Kiev, where the *Chronicle* was being compiled. The text, parts of which the Russian editor found obscure, is clearly a Western tract in defence of Methodios preserved in Bohemia, with a number of quotations from the *Lives* of the two saints.[68]

Among other manifestly Western texts which reached Kiev at an early date, for which a Balkan route is improbable, may be mentioned: the *Homilies* of Pope Gregory the Great, the apocryphal *Gospel of Nicodemus*, and the *Life of St Vitus*, patron of Prague Cathedral. Most unexpected in Russia, yet evidently widely used at the time since a number of copies survive, is a prayer to the Holy Trinity followed by invocations to a long list of Western saints quite foreign to the Eastern tradition. Among them are St Alban (associated with Mainz, the metropolis of Prague), St Botolph of East Anglia, St Martin of Tours, the Scandinavian royal saints Canute of Denmark and Olaf of Norway; SS Christina, Lucia and Victoria. Not only are the saintly popes Clement and Sylvester commemorated but also the whole company of the Popes,[69] ranking after the Evangelists and before the Martyrs. SS Cyril and Methodios, St Wenceslas and St Adalbert underline the Bohemian origin of the whole prayer.[70] Nor is this the only example of its kind.

The sources of these texts cannot be precisely determined. Břevnov is a possibility. As Cosmas makes no mention of either Ostrov or its daughter house, Veliš (1003), the conclusion might be drawn that the Slav language was cultivated in them also. It should also be noted that after 999, when Cracow became Polish, the route to Russia via Hungary (including Slovakia) was likely to be the easier, for there were considerable Byzantine elements in the young Hungarian church of the later tenth and eleventh centuries and it is known that there were Russians at Višegrad. The monastery of St Hippolytus at Nitra, for which some scholars claim a long Cyrillomethodian tradition, is another possible middle term.[a]

The closeness of the connection must not be exaggerated. To judge by the mutilations of most Bohemian personal and place names there was little real knowledge of the country in Russia. Indeed the name of Sázava does not appear in any Russian source.

While Sázava was the purveyor of Cyrillomethodian and other Western texts to Kiev in its earlier years (1032–57)—a time when the rapidly expanding Russian church had much need of such reinforcement[71]—the commerce would seem to have been more balanced in the post-exilic period (1063–97). By this time Russia too had something to give. It may suffice to mention that the Cave Monastery at Kiev sent Sázava relics of the new Russian princely saints, Boris and Gleb, canonised in 1072;[72] an altar was dedicated to them there in 1093. The story of St Olga must also have reached Bohemia, where this specifically Varangian–Russian name was in use in the twelfth and thirteenth centuries. It is obvious that her legend was shaped after that of St Ljudmila. It is notable that the *Life of St Procopius* of Sázava apparently failed to be transmitted to Russia, nor is he commemorated in any Russian *Prolog*, no doubt because this text is not as old as often assumed but dates rather from the time of his canonisation (1204). By then its passage to Russia (it did not reach Croatia either) would have been more difficult and its adoption there less probable. The cult of St Wenceslas in Russia remained perhaps as local as the cult of Boris and Gleb in Bohemia, hardly reaching beyond Kiev and the Court. The name Wenceslas (Russian Вячеслав) was used sparingly in the princely family, probably for the first time in 1036 when a son was born to Jaroslav. The dynastic connections between the ruling houses of Kiev, Poland and Bohemia (and also Hungary) were constant and close in the eleventh and twelfth centuries. Thus Vratislav II (d. 1092), the patron of Bohemian Slav letters, was connected with the Kiev house through his wife Svjatoslava, a daughter of Casimir (Kazimierz) I of Poland, himself a grandson of the great Vladimir.

Bohemia in the eleventh century was an active source of Christian culture, for the first time in literary rather than missionary form, for other Slav lands. Some connection with Bulgaria is possible but unlikely. Bohemia's part in the formation of the Polish church will be discussed below.[b]

The link with Kiev was active but only for a relatively short period—

[a] See p. 84. [b] See pp. 115 ff.

not after 1097. The link with the Glagolitic church of Croatia,[a] the only other area apart from Macedonia where this alphabet was in normal use, holds a special place in Bohemian history. Croat Glagolitic breviaries of the fourteenth–fifteenth centuries are alone in the Balkans in perpetuating the cult of St Wenceslas, which clearly reached Croatia at an early date. The texts show signs of having been made from very archaic originals since they contain not only Cyrillomethodian words but also Czechisms.[b] *The Office of SS Cyril and Methodios* also reached Croatia in a Bohemian form.

The existence of a Cyrillomethodian church in Bohemia was not wholly forgotten. The contacts with Croatia were renewed some two centuries later at the time of the political ascendancy of the Bohemian kingdom and the revival of Slav letters. Charles IV, the founder of the new Cathedral of St Vitus and of Prague University, also founded the Emmaus monastery in Prague for Slav Benedictines (1346–7).[73] To re-create the old Glagolitic tradition he was obliged to summon monks from the Croatian monasteries, where alone by this time the alphabet was still in use. The monastery was formally consecrated by the Archbishop of Prague in 1372 in the presence of the Papal Legate; for Pope Clement VI had given permission for this special use in 1347.[c] During these years the Slav liturgy was occasionally sung in the church of SS Cosmas and Damian in Prague. This was of course an artificial revival, restricted to the liturgical field. No new compositions in Church Slavonic were made in Bohemia, though unexpectedly we find the occasional use of the Glagolitic alphabet to record Czech: an inscription of the Ten Commandments in this form has recently been found at the Emmaus monastery.[74] Charles and the Pope may also have envisaged Emmaus as a school for training missionaries capable of bringing Orthodox Slav countries into union with Rome; Serbia was particularly in mind.[75]

This revival of the Slav liturgical language was shortlived and had no important consequences. The Czech language was never considered for

[a] See pp. 204 ff.

[b] Cyrillomethodian are *miša, iskrĭnii, rěsnota*; Czech are *milovati* (*amare*) and probably *kostel* (church).

[c] The Pope's liberal attitude is to be explained as a conciliatory move towards several Slav states at this time, in particular Bohemia and Serbia, with a view to persuading them to a combined crusade against the Turks in the Balkans. The Pope further gave Charles IV the privilege of having the Mass said in Slav in his presence in any Bohemian church.

liturgical use until the Reformation. Even the Hussites for the most part kept to Latin, though it is claimed that John of Želiv was the first to say Mass in Czech.[76]

POLAND

The dynasty of Piast ruled, according to tradition, over the tribe of the Polanie, whose centre was at Gniezno (German *Gnesen*).[a] By the first half of the tenth century the Piasts had extended their rule over parts of Cujavia (Kujawy) and Mazovia (Mazowsze) to the east, and of Mało-polska[b] and Silesia to the south. The first Piast whose deeds were re-corded by the outside world, Mieszko,[c] must have been born about 922 and came to power at the latest by about 960. The earliest reference to him is found in *Widukind*[77]—*Misacam regem*—which refers to the year 963 approximately and suggests an already powerful ruler: Mieszko was attempting to conquer Western Pomerania with the invaluable outlet to the Baltic offered by the Oder estuary. Wolin, commanding the eastern outlet of the Oder delta, credibly identified with the Jómsburg of the Scandinavian saga, was already and remained an important commercial transit point: Adam of Bremen notes that in his day (a hundred years later) the journey from Hamburg to Wolin (Iumne) was reckoned at a week and from Wolin to Russian Novgorod at two weeks more.[78] The growing prosperity of Mieszko's lands, visible from the late ninth cen-tury, was mainly dependent still on these Baltic communications. By 965, the first dateable event, the rising Polish state had an important common frontier with Bohemia in Upper Silesia and with Germany as the result of Count Gero's recent conquest of considerable Slav lands up to the line of the middle Oder.[d] A new phase is now visible in Poland's commercial relations: the Central European trade-route linking Prague and Kiev now began to bring Islamic and Byzantine coins into Poland from the East[79] and an increasing volume of German issues from the West, especially those of Cologne and Regensburg, while Anglo-Saxon ones still entered via Hedeby and Wolin. Mieszko and his

[a] Archaeological investigation suggests that Gniezno had no importance before the end of the eighth and not much before the middle of the ninth century.

[b] The names Wielkopolska (the original Polanie area) and Małopolska are of later creation but will be used for convenience. They are founded on medieval Latin *Polonia maior* and *minor*.

[c] Mieszko is the conventional Polish spelling, a hypocoristic later interpreted in various Romantic ways (e.g. Miecław, Mieczysław). Forms in German-Latin sources vary between dissyllables (Mysco) and trisyllables (Misaka etc.); Ibrāhīm ibn Ya'qūb has M[i]šq[a]. [d] See p. 146.

state were about to become a factor in north and central European politics.

Of pagan religious practices in Poland there is little record.[80] Most Christian chroniclers purposely forbore to describe the cults which missionaries were at such pains to eradicate.[81] The Slavs of Poland had to all appearances been little disturbed by migration, but the rule of the Piasts, or perhaps even that of an earlier dynasty, had already succeeded in effectively sweeping away political and religious organisation on a tribal and clan basis over a considerable area. Hence the marked contrast with the history of the closely related Wendish tribes further west.[a]

There is little to record either of Christian influences before the 960s. It has been suggested that Irish missionaries may have reached some of the Slavs between Elbe and Oder (an area totally eccentric to their known routes)[82] and some Polish tribes even further east, but this is no better than speculation. Nor is good evidence to be found of the penetration of German missionaries so far east at any time before the foundation of the see of Magdeburg. The description of the Slavs of North Europe collected, partly for commercial and partly for missionary purposes, in the *Geographus Bavarensis* makes it plain that the Polish region was still very imperfectly known in the middle of the ninth century, for no important current of trade as yet attached it to its neighbours, except towards the north.[b] It is permissible to suggest that the story told by the *Gallus anonymus* at the beginning of his Chronicle[83] refers to 'missionaries' reaching Wielkopolska, presumably from the south. Two strangers (*hospites*) who were ill-received by the chieftain Popiel found better reception in the home of a peasant who invited them to take part in the ceremony of cutting his son's hair (*postrzyżyny*).[c] This peasant became Piast, the founder of the new dynasty. Mieszko was the great-grandson of the boy Ziemowit who had received their blessing. It is a further temptation to suggest that these men were missionaries sent by Methodios from Moravia, who had penetrated into lands to the north of the Vistulanians.[d] Such occasional journeys are not in themselves unlikely but there is no trace of durable results.[84]

The apparent suddenness of the beginnings in the time of Mieszko must be put down to an illusion of our ignorance. In him arose a ruler of talent, illiterate no doubt but no uncouth barbarian. He had a clear con-

[a] See pp. 142 ff., esp. p. 145.
[b] See p. 352 n. 79. Virtually no Carolingian coins have been recovered from Poland.
[c] See p. 93.   [d] See pp. 135–6.

ception of the politics of his time. By the 960s German religious policy in the north was no secret. He perceived the implications of becoming a Christian and of declaring his realm Christian. There were enemies on every side: the Germans in the west, his rivals for the possession of Lusatia, which covered the upper Oder frontier, and for the Oder delta, which decided the fate of Pomerania and Poland's outlet to the Baltic; Bohemia and Hungary to the south, between whom Moravia was disputed territory; and the rising power of the Princes of Kiev in the east. Moreover, the related Veletians beyond the Oder were always liable to be a nuisance. Of these the Germans were the most dangerous. Mieszko's relations with the Empire might become an urgent problem at any moment; for the Bohemians, now Christians for over half a century, had found it advisable, if unavoidable, to put themselves under the wing of the Empire. To become Christian was the only way to be accepted as civilised; to become a German Christian seemed a sure way of losing one's independence. Mieszko would have well understood the words which, according to the *Life of Methodios*, the prelate himself had spoken to a certain chieftain of the Slavs on the Upper Vistula (Wiślanie) nearly a century earlier: 'Better to embrace Christianity voluntarily and retain your independence than to be forcibly baptised in foreign captivity.'[85]

German pressure on Mieszko's western frontier was mounting rapidly in the 960s. He decided therefore to receive his Christianity in the first place from the Bohemians. He could scarcely have failed to know the story of St Wenceslas. The step was to be combined with a political and dynastic alliance. Dobrava,[a] the daughter of Boleslas I, became his wife and in 964 arrived in Poland with priests and Christian books. This implies that Mieszko had already signified a firm intention of embracing her religion. His baptism followed in 966.

The delay of two years is often ignored in the sources.[86] But the epitaph of Mieszko's firstborn son Bolesław, probably composed about 1075, preserves the tradition that Mieszko's formal conversion was not immediate:

Perfido patre natus es, sed credula matre.[87]

Bolesław's birth should fall in 965. Who performed Mieszko's baptism, who stood sponsor and where it took place remains unknown. To look further afield than Prague would be eccentric.[88] The simplest solution is probably the correct one: that it was performed at his own residence

---

[a] The form Dąbrówka is a later fancy, though defended by some. Others use *Dobrowa, Dubravka.*

either by a cleric in Dobrava's suite or by one summoned from Prague. His son, baptised at birth, was given the name of his Christian grandfather, the Bohemian ruler Boleslas I. This may be accounted one of several instances in early Slav history of Pope Boniface's remark: 'The unbelieving husband shall be saved through the believing wife'.[89] Thietmar of Merseburg stresses her part and naturally draws attention to the symbolism of her name: 'Quae, sicut sonuit in nomine, apparuit veraciter in re. Dobrawa enim sclavonice dicebatur quod teutonico sermone Bona interpretatur'.[90]

Dobrava's merits may well have been somewhat enlarged. But with her arrival a permanent ecclesiastical organisation became feasible. In this way Mieszko hoped to remain outside the clutches of the German church while free to combine with the Germans no less than with the Bohemians against the pagan Slavs whose lands they all coveted. Indeed he appears to have been on the best of terms with Otto in these decisive years.

There was also a territorial settlement. By the mid-tenth century the possession of Cracow, an essential link in the East–West trade-route across northern Europe (the alternative route via Hungary being closed by the barbarous Magyars), was a matter of great moment. The question, who had control of Cracow and Małopolska generally at any given date, remains undecided; not even approximate dates are wholly convincing before the extreme end of the tenth century.[a] We must of course allow for these lands being not fully incorporated in either the Polish or the Bohemian state, but a semi-independent Vistulanian principality. However this may be, it appears probable that Prague dominated the area for some twenty years after these important negotiations between the two states; and as Ibrāhīm ibn Ya'qūb considered Cracow Bohemian in 966, it may be that it was Mieszko's *Morgengabe* to Boleslas of Prague for a Christian wife.[91]

Mieszko's decision, it must be repeated, was surely not as sudden as it appears from the meagre sources. He may have known of the approach made by Olga of Kiev to Otto I in 959, which resulted in the sending of Adalbert to Kiev and his ignominious return in 961.[b] That the rulers of Kiev were likely to become Christians, if not already generally considered such, was also a factor to be taken into account. More important, there were in all probability a number of Christians within his dominions or close by at Cracow and other places in the south. These, it is

widely believed, were Christians of the Cyrillomethodian Slav church
established there by refugees from Moravia.[a]

But whatever he learnt of Christianity from the southern fringes of
his lands and despite the bilingual character of current practices in
Prague, there is no reliable evidence that Mieszko accepted Christianity
from Prague in other than Latin form—that is, Latin rites and Latin
alphabet. The personal predilections of Dobrava are unknown. The
likelihood is that she brought some Bavarian clergy with her.[b]

The first stone or partly stone buildings at Gniezno clearly belong to
these early Christian years—a new residence with a court chapel dedicated to St George, said to have been built on the site of a pagan temple.
In this dedication we may see the choice of Dobrava, whose sister Mlada
was abbess of St George's at Prague. Mieszko also built here another
church, a rotunda, dedicated to the Virgin Mary, possibly on the occasion of Dobrava's death. This architecture, as that of other very early
Christian edifices in Poland,[c] points directly to Prague, where the
rotunda of St Vitus (925–9) provided a widely admired model. There is
at least no trace left in Poland of the typical Saxon architecture of that
period, best exemplified today in St Cyriac, Gernrode.[92] Similarly, it has
been possible to trace the passage of reliquaries and crosses of certain
types from ninth-century Moravia to tenth-century Bohemia and thence
to Poland.[93]

Thus the conversion of Poland is conventionally dated 966. How far
Mieszko was personally zealous in the new faith cannot be judged. At
least he was wiser than Wenceslas. A newly converted ruler over pagans
cannot afford to shed his martial virtues in favour of incompatible
Christian ones if he wishes to retain the exercise of power and the loyalty
of his men.[d] Moreover Mieszko was immediately faced with ecclesiastical politics both delicate and intricate. These bore on the founding of
the first Polish bishopric in 968 at Poznań (German *Posen*)—still within
the original heartlands of the Polanie and probably Mieszko's main

---

[a] See pp. 135 ff. below.

[b] The Bavarian contribution does not seem to have been considerable since it is not
mentioned in any Bavarian source. The same applies to a hypothetical Saxon contribution (Corvey, Fulda?); such a tradition is unknown to the pro-Saxon Thietmar.

[c] See also p. 138, § 4.

[d] In view of the delay between the arrival of Dobrava and his own baptism we might
hazard the guess that his attitude was at first similar to that of Ethelbert of Kent who
embraced Christianity partly under the influence of his Christian wife but was cautious
of accepting all that St Augustine demanded and apparently found it too dangerous to
enforce Christianity generally among his people even after his baptism.

residence after his baptism.[94] Once again pious chroniclers seized on the name as symbolic of the new dispensation, connecting Poznań with *poznać*, to acknowledge, or, by extension, to embrace the Christian faith.[95]

Otto I's intention was that any new bishopric among the Slavs should come under his new metropolis of Magdeburg, whose eastern limits were for this reason not precisely defined.[96] This had been approved by Pope John XII in 962. But John XIII, elected in 965, showed some caution in giving the Emperor *carte blanche* in the matter of future Slav dioceses.[97] The Pope intended to reserve Poland—a missionary area—as an area of Papal interest. Thus Jordan, the first bishop of Poznań— surely a missionary bishop—was probably directly subordinate to Rome. Many see this as a deliberate act of policy on the part of Mieszko himself, and this is reasonable. Poland was not a part of the Empire: the Emperor was not Mieszko's overlord—at most he received a 'tribute' from him for a part of his lands.[98] It followed that the Emperor had no right to settle the status of Poznań without reference to the Holy See. No authentic documents of the see of Magdeburg mention Poznań, nor does Benedict VII's Bull of 981 include it as a subordinate bishopric. We do not know who appointed and consecrated the first two bishops of Poznań— Jordan and Unger. Both were foreigners; neither has any known connection with Magdeburg. Jordan was certainly not from Saxony, where the name was not used; he may have come from Prague, Italy or Lorraine.[a] He died probably in 984. Unger was bishop by 992. He is identified by some as Abbot Vunniger of Memleben in Saxony, a centre of Slav missionary work under the patronage of Henry I and Otto I. Thus the choice of Unger may have come from the Imperial government, especially if a diploma of 4 October 991 relates to this appointment.[99] The subordination to Magdeburg would only be a reasonable hypothesis if Poznań had been from the first a territorial bishopric. The title *episcopus posnaniensis* is in fact used.[100] But if it was primarily a missionary bishopric the Pope's interest may have prevailed. If Thietmar's description of Unger as *posnaniensis cenobii pastor*[101] is exact, Poznań started in the normal way as a monastic community of missionaries.[102] Probably Otto and Mieszko made at first no precise agreement about the status of Poznań. Magdeburg did not voice pretensions to Poznań nor manufacture the necessary evidence until after the creation of the archdiocese of Gniezno in 1000.

---

a In the tenth–eleventh centuries Lower Lorraine may be equated with the archdiocese of Cologne (hence including Liège), Upper Lorraine with that of Trier.

The situation between Elbe and Oder, the great Slav revolts from 983, in fact gave Magdeburg very little opportunity of developing control over Polish Christianity. With Saxony engaged to the full nearer home, Poland drew its inspiration from further south. The frequent use of the name Lambert in the dynasty from this time may point to a particularly close link with Liège, of which city St Lambert was patron. The development of Christianity from Poznań was surely also very slow. Not only were the labourers few but Mieszko may have been obliged to proceed very cautiously in view of these very revolts.[a] Was the native religion after all going to triumph over the Frankish God? We have no way of estimating the appeal of the new religion to his magnates but it is likely that the soldiers of his *comitatus*—the essential instrument of his power— were, as elsewhere, slow to give up their traditional beliefs. As there was apparently no bishop of Poznań between 984 and 992 approximately, precisely when the revolts in the West were at their height, one must conclude that the work of Poznań had a very limited radiation down to the time of Mieszko's death.

It would be wrong however to conceive Otto I's policy towards Poland and its nascent church as narrow-mindedly German. From the time of Charlemagne the King (or Emperor) of Germany had exercised very close control over the church in his dominions. It was through the educated clergy that a medieval monarch ruled. He would have close relatives among the prelacy; for example Archbishop Bruno of Cologne was Otto I's brother. The church provided not only his 'civil service' but also indirectly his army. The German church, as we have seen, had long favoured the system of proprietary churches (*Eigenkirchen*), whereby the incumbent was the life tenant of the secular landlord.[b] Similarly, royal monastic foundations were treated as part of the royal domains. The majority of bishoprics and abbacies were royal appointments. Otto's practice was wholly in the German tradition. His court chapel and its school were the training-ground for a loyal episcopacy. When he appointed Adalbert as first Archbishop of Magdeburg he was virtually appointing a warden of the Slav marches. But Otto was a man of profound piety with a sense of imperial mission little inferior to that of his grandson Otto III. He had himself crowned *imperator romanorum* on 2 February 962 by the Pope in Rome, symbolising above all that he had deserved well of Christendom by his decisive defeat of the pagan Magyars in 955. Widukind states that he could speak 'Romance' and

[a] See p. 148.   [b] See p. 48.

Slav but 'seldom deigned to do so'—that is, he understood the languages.[103] He appears to have had in fact some Slav blood in his veins on
his mother's side. Magdeburg had started in 937 as his personal pious
foundation, dedicated to his own patron saint, St Maurice, after successful campaigns against the Slavs to the west of the Oder in 928–34.
Monks were brought from St Maximin at Trier to ensure that the new
foundation should be in the forefront of the reform movement. Now, as
an archbishopric (968), it was not intended in his eyes to be a mere tool of
German ambitions. He saw clearly that the taming of the Magyars, permanently established in the heart of Europe, must be followed up by an
active policy of civilisation and evangelisation.[a] Bohemia could be considered safe; the see of Prague, planned at the same time as Magdeburg
but longer in the making, was his southern outpost. The rich endowment of Magdeburg, with twelve priests and lesser clergy in proportion,
the importance attached to its school, and the appointment of Adalbert,
former Abbot of Weissenburg and Russian missionary,[b] as first archbishop all point to Otto's conceiving Magdeburg as a cultural centre
rather than as a military camp. The northern outpost, completing the
front line of civilisation against the recalcitrant Slavs was Hamburg–
Bremen. Poland now arose as a country in a similar position to Hungary—
not yet easily accessible but vital to the great work of extending and
securing the frontiers of Christendom. It is therefore probable that Otto
did not attempt to force Mieszko into the arms of the German church to
the degree that the latter had anticipated.

Otto I died on 7 May 973. During the reign of Otto II (973–83) and
the minority of Otto III the internal progress of Polish Christianity is
only feebly illuminated in the sources. Poznań continued to be the sole
ecclesiastical centre. There was however no question of any closer
ecclesiastical relationship between Bohemia and Poland. The bishopric
of Prague, finally established in the 970s,[c] was in fact junior to Poznań.
The friendship and alliance between the two countries which had begun
in 964 was weakened though not broken by Dobrava's death in 977, had
little reality after 984, and disappeared altogether by 990. Rivalry for the
possession of Cracow, which could easily be made to supplant Prague as
the main economic centre on the trans-European trade-route, was now

---

[a] Their permanent establishment was clear to all by 907, when their territories
reached to the River Enns. Their first considerable defeat by a Western army came in
933.
[b] See p. 251 and p. 394 n. 61.
[c] See pp. 99–100.

acute.[a] The increasing wealth of the West, which brought about in the later tenth century a reversal of the economic flow, made Cracow even more important to Poland and caused her to cast covetous eyes on Prague also. The three political marriages to which Mieszko's eldest son Bolesław was subjected in rapid succession in the 980s illustrate the instability of the situation.

It was above all the great Wendish revolt of 983 which was responsible for the Polish realignment. As early as 979 or 980 Mieszko had made a second diplomatic marriage of friendship with Germany in the person of the former nun Oda. This may have provided some new links with the German church to make good the waning influence of Prague. Mieszko became to all intents and purposes an ally of the Empire in 986, ready to act in concert against their common enemy the Veletians (Ljutici). Conversely the Bohemians were prepared to support these pagans, if only passively, coveted Meissen in rivalry with Poland, and thus inevitably incurred Polish hostility. Mieszko was all the more in need of Imperial friendship in that the Wendish revolt might touch off similar revolts at home.[104]

The death of Bishop Jordan at this critical moment (984?) brought progress to a standstill. Mieszko could only confirm his policy of avoiding entanglement with territorial churches by giving final effect to his attachment to the Pope. He sent an embassy to Rome in 990 or 991 and made the so-called 'Donation of Poland' to the Holy See shortly before his death on 25 April 992. This effectively blocked all further pretensions of the Germans to control of the Polish church. Yet it is difficult to suppose that this was done in the face of Imperial opposition. The moment was of course favourable for Poland since the Empire was under a regency and much occupied with internal troubles. Nor must the dependence on Rome be exaggerated. In the troubles of the eleventh century this special relationship was completely lost sight of and not taken up again until its last decade. In all probability *Peter's Pence* were not paid as a matter of course by all Poland before the middle of the twelfth century, by which time the Holy See had been demanding its payment as of right from other countries also. But the policy of close relations with the Papacy clearly goes back to 972, when Mieszko caused his son's hair to be cut at the age of seven and sent the lock to the Pope. The recipient thereby became a kind of godfather to the child.[105] In all

[a] On the doubtful dates relating to the possession of Cracow see p. 108 note c. The dependence of Silesia at different dates is also very uncertain and cannot be entered into here.

probability direct relations go back to 967–8 with the appointment of Jordan as missionary bishop, or even to 963–4 when the marriage to Dobrava was being negotiated.[106]

The Donation is recorded in a document known, by its alleged first two words, as *Dagome iudex*.[107] It is unfortunately only an inefficient résumé made by a Cardinal Deusdedit about 1087. Neither the name *Dagome* (in some copies *Dagone*) nor the geographical names can be interpreted with confidence: the Cardinal did not realise that it was about Poland. The former may be a misreading of the expected introductory formula: ✠ *Ego Mesco dux*... though it is a little surprising that Mieszko does not use his baptismal name.[108] The use of the title [*Oda*] *senatrix* immediately following, if not corrupt, is known from Curial practice and guarantees that the donation was drawn up in Rome.[109] The document is by no one held to be a Papal forgery; but we can build little on it as it stands.

The early decades of Polish Christianity had thus seen contributions from Bohemia (leading to Regensburg), Germany (at least on the Imperial level)[a] and Rome itself. Of these we believe Bohemia to have been the most important. There is no evidence for the cultivation of the Glagolitic alphabet and the use of the Slav liturgical language in the diocese of Poznań. But it is abundantly clear that Polish religious language was largely beholden to Bohemia and by this mediacy absorbed a certain proportion of the Cyrillomethodian vocabulary as used in Moravia. These words were naturally more or less current in spoken Czech and could have passed to Polish as much by oral as by literary transmission. Here belong, for example, (in their modern forms) Polish *msza, chrzest, papież, kazanie* (sermon), *zakonnik* (monk), *krzyż, kościół, cerkiew*.[b] Other Polish terms come from the Latin or German vocabulary adopted in Bohemia in its early Christian period, but here it is difficult or impossible to tie the loan down to a specific moment before about 1100. Such are: ofiara (German *opfar* > Czech ofěra), bierzmowanie (German

---

[a] The commemoration of Mieszko's death at Fulda, at the height of its eminence in the tenth–eleventh centuries, may be held to suggest that he had patronised the monastery and therefore that it had sent missionaries to Poland in his reign.

[b] See further pp. 25 and 58 above. To these may be added two interesting words which show an exclusively Czech deformation: błogosławić < OCz. blagoslaviti < OCS blagosloviti (attracted by *slava*); rozgrzeszyć < OCz. rozgrešiti < OCS raz[d]rěšiti (attracted by *grěch*). Polish further often confused *błogosławić* (εὐλογεῖν) with *bogosławić* (θεολογεῖν). The influence of the Czech *literary* language on Polish can hardly have begun before 1200 and is easily separated from the above. The influence was strong enough, however, to affect Polish religious vocabulary a second time: there are Czechisms in the early fourteenth-century *Kazania świętokrzyskie*.

firmôn < Latin *fermare*), pacierz (*Paternoster*; Czech páteř), żegnać (German *seganôn* < Latin *signare*), and klasztor (apparently direct from German since it disagrees with Czech klášteř). Polish *ksiądz* (priest) is descended from Czech *kněz* and must be reckoned with the relatively early loans, although not recorded before the fourteenth century. The transplantation of this vocabulary to Poland must have been the work of Bohemian missionaries (possible sources in the Cracow area apart), and, although exact dating is out of the question, for the most part not later than *c.* 1025.

To this early period, and especially to the active period of Slav literary culture in Bohemia in the latter part of the tenth century, has often been attributed the famous Polish hymn *Bogurodzica*.[110] Some go so far as to name St Adalbert of Prague as the most probable author. The language of the existing manuscripts, none of which is older than the fifteenth century, exhibits both Czech and Church Slavonic features. The first words, *Bogurodzica dziewica*, manifestly did not come from a Latin source. The word *Bogurodzica* is as rare in Polish as in Czech.[a] Some of the Czechisms, however, can be shown to belong to the later period of literary influence in the fourteenth–fifteenth centuries.[111] It has been pointed out[112] that the poem is in form a typical Byzantine *triodion*, which would strongly support its composition before the end of the eleventh century, even if verses, as is certain, were later added and earlier ones remodelled.

The Easter hymn *Chrystus z martwych wstał je* is a similar case. The text seems to require both a Church Slavonic model (ultimately based on the *troparion* Χριστὸς ἀνέστη ἐκ νεκρῶν) and a Latin model for the Czech original of the Polish version.[113] But this text is much nearer to the Latin tradition, especially in its metrical form. We have already seen that such duality was a commonplace in Bohemia in the tenth–eleventh centuries. The hymn could therefore have passed into Polish use at an early date though the earliest text to survive is found only in the *Graduale* of Płock (1365).

Meagre though these indications are, they point beyond doubt to the work of missionaries from Bohemia in the early stages of Polish Christianity. Poland can surely not have expected the Roman link to be much more than formal. Bolesław's recovery of Cracow and the Upper Vistula

---

[a] OCS *Bogoródica* is a calque of Greek Θεοτόκος. The only other examples are late: Czech *bohorodicě* (fourteenth century); Pol. *bogorodzica, bogarodzica*—in the *Modlitwa Wacława* (later fifteenth century). They are probably due to Charles IV's revival of Slav letters in the Emmaus monastery (see p. 112).

region in 999, followed by his shortlived conquest of Bohemia, Moravia and Slovakia,[114] were clearly apt to maintain or even increase the Bohemian element.

The beginning of the personal rule of the young Emperor Otto III on attaining his majority in 995, confirmed by his imperial coronation in April 996, marks a new stage in Polish affairs. Bolesław, known as the Brave (Chrobry), who seized the succession to his father Mieszko,[a] had the qualities of a great ruler. This *rex christianissimus*[115] was able to build rapidly on Mieszko's foundations. He found in Otto III a no less exceptional man in whom the man of vision combined with the man of action. Born in 980 of the marriage of Otto II with the Greek princess Theophano,[116] he is held by his opponents to have brought unwonted Byzantine ideas into Western politics. As the tenth century marks the high tide of Byzantine influences on West European life, especially art, it would be strange indeed if politics had remained quite untouched, above all through the persons of a Byzantine princess, regent of the Empire from 983 to 991, and of her young and devoted son, who had a Greek monk from South Italy, John Philagathos, as godfather and tutor.

A single universal empire coterminous with a universal church had always been the Byzantine conception and was still the Byzantine fiction. That Otto embraced this idea may be conceded as a Byzantine element in his thought. His new seal of 999 linked the effigies of Charlemagne and Rome by the inscription *Renovatio imperii romanorum*. To such universalism neither Charlemagne himself nor Otto I the Saxon, nor any lesser ruler in between, could aspire.[117] Otto III was the first to attempt to establish with the Pope that closer relationship which the Byzantine Emperor, always the dominant partner, had with the Patriarch of Constantinople. A Gospel Book made for him about the year 1000 shows him in this Byzantine role.[118] Such a *renovatio imperii romanorum* required that the secular power and the spiritual authority of the Empire should come together again in Rome itself. Hence Otto's preoccupation with Rome, to the disgust of the Germans whose country, language and manners he openly despised, contrasting *saxonica rusticitas* with *graecisca nostra subtilitas*.[119] On his first visit to Rome in May 996 he installed a cousin as Pope (Gregory V), at whose hands he received sacred coronation as protector of the Church universal. On his second visit (December 997 – December 999) he secured the election to the Papacy of his tutor

---

[a] It seems to have taken him three years (992–5) to consolidate his sole rule, Mieszko having in the traditional way attempted to divide his realm among his sons.

and friend Gerbert. Gerbert chose the name Sylvester II, symbolising that his relationship to Otto should be like that supposed between Sylvester I and the first Christian universal emperor Constantine, Otto's supreme exemplar.[120] The essence of Otto's imperial conception lay not so much in the imposition of central rule (for the Ottonian Empire proper was in fact smaller than that of Charlemagne) as in a federation of all Christendom under Imperial direction. Poland thus stood out, with Hungary, as an important new state requiring integration into this Christendom.

Sublime though this conception of imperial office was, Otto was a man torn between two worlds: he greatly desired the life of a monk. All his closest spiritual advisers turned his mind in this direction: St Romuald of Ravenna, one of the leaders of the monastic revival in his generation;[121] St Bruno of Querfurt and St Odilo, the great abbot of Cluny; but above all St Nilus, the Greek ascetic from South Italy, and the Slav St Adalbert of Prague.[122] On his second Roman visit he appears to have disclosed to St Romuald a definite intention to abdicate and embrace the monastic life.[123] On his third visit (October 1000) St Bruno was present at his solemn reaffirmation of his intention to take monastic vows as soon as political cares made abdication possible.[a] His premature death on 24 January 1002—in his twenty-second year—naturally resulted in the abrupt collapse of all his great plans, which appealed to few outside his circle of friends. Moreover he evidently underestimated the Papacy's own conception of universalism, which had been maturing for two centuries and was now set on a path which made both the relinquishment of territorial sovereignty and exclusive attachment to any one secular power virtually impossible.[124] Christopher Brooke has written with justice that 'it is hard for a historian writing in the 1960s not to feel that Otto III's dream was a great deal more sensible than the national monarchy which most historians have belaboured him for not creating'.[125]

Only in the new countries—Poland and Hungary—did Otto's way of thinking have any real chance of bringing an immediate and lasting benefit. Otto had first met Bolesław on a joint campaign against the Veletians in 995. There is no question but that he was greatly impressed by the Polish ruler's capacity.

It is with this in mind that we must consider the events at Gniezno in

---

[a] It is only fair to add that his determination to leave the world does not appear to have been as firm as he led others to believe: a marriage was arranged between him and the Emperor Basil's niece, Zoe (probably Otto's cousin), and she arrived at Bari only to learn that he had died. Perhaps he saw in this step the hope of a more universal *renovatio*, embracing East and West, in the person of a son of this marriage.

March 1000. The year before Otto determined on the creation of a
Polish archbishopric in the old capital. Now he made a solemn pilgrimage
there to worship at the shrine of his friend and spiritual counsellor
Adalbert.[126] The Papal Legate Robert and many other notables took
part. The first archbishop—*archiepiscopus S. Adalberti martyris*—was
Gaudentius, Adalbert's half-brother and companion in Italy, who was so
consecrated in Rome in December 999. This implies that the whole Act
of Gniezno was a great act of statesmanship concerted between the three
parties—Pope, Emperor and Polish ruler—in conformity with Otto's
imperial conception. Bolesław was the custodian of St Adalbert's shrine
at Gniezno, potentially a great centre of European pilgrimage; the
Papacy's interest was secured through Mieszko's *Donation*; but the
guiding hand was manifestly the Imperium, Otto himself.

The ceremony at Gniezno of which Bolesław himself was then the
object is sometimes, surely wrongly, described as a 'coronation', for
example by Thietmar and Gallus.[127] Bolesław surely expected to be
made King of Poland; it would be natural to assume that Emperor and
Pope would not withhold this dignity once an archbishopric had been
approved. Why he was not immediately so acknowledged remains
obscure. His merits were no less than those of Stephen of Hungary who
received archbishopric and crown together a year later; his personal
favour with Otto and potential political importance were much higher.
Mieszko's *Donation* of Poland to the Holy See might have been expected
to be favourable now to Bolesław's aspirations.[128]

Uncertain titles were conferred on Bolesław at Gniezno. They have
been held—with little probability—to suggest something greater than
royal status, namely his designation as successor to the Empire, when
Otto abdicated, as he may still have hoped, in the near future—as Caesar
in the Byzantine manner.[129] Thus the *Anonymus Gallus* describes Otto's
action in these words: 'eum constituit fratrem et cooperatorem imperii
et...appellavit populi romani amicum et socium'.[130] Bolesław's epitaph,
less reliable, appears even more explicit, styling him *Caesar precellens*.[131]
At most Bolesław became *patricius*, a title conferred from time to
time on rulers, imparting the theoretical right to be considered guardians
of Rome and the Holy See and also the more practical one of deputizing for the Emperor in his absence.[a] However this may be, Bolesław
emerged from these ceremonies as head of his own church with authority

[a] *Patricius* was the title of the former governors of Rome and tended at this time to
revert to this narrower usage. It had first been conferred in the wider sense by Pope
Stephen on Pippin in 754.

to appoint bishops; that is, Otto surrendered the pretensions of the German *Reichskirche*, through Magdeburg, to control of the Polish church. Archbishop Gisilher of Magdeburg, who was in Otto's suite but unresponsive to his ideas, did not bow to the Imperial will without a protest.[132] Poland, in conformity with the principle of *Renovatio imperii*, was now *Sclavinia*, a Christian state of equal status with all other Christian states, not a lesser dependency of the German Kingdom. 'Sclavinia' is the fourth of the women, all sensibly alike in rank and importance, who are shown doing homage before the imperially enthroned Otto in a Gospel book made for him about the year 1000. Her companions are Roma, Gallia and Germania.[133]

Nobody at the time seems to have been very clear about the significance of the ceremonies. It may be that some intentions of Otto remained *in petto*, though transparent to Bolesław himself. In short, *cooperator imperii* was perhaps intended as a synonym of *adiutor*, part of the title of a *patricius*: Otto was doing no more than extend the principle of imperial deputies, just as he had exceptionally created his aunt, Abbess Matilda of Quedlinburg, *matricia* in 997, to act for him during his absence in Italy.[134] Yet even this might be held to imply that Bolesław was recognising Poland as within the Empire—which is more than doubtful—or at least as not fully independent.

Bolesław accompanied Otto from Gniezno to Magdeburg with great pomp. From there Otto went on to Aix. Later legend has it that he opened the tomb of Charlemagne and sent thence to Bolesław Charlemagne's golden throne—the last symbolic act in declaring the ruler of Poland his Caesar.[135] The two had already exchanged valuable relics during the ceremonies at Gniezno.[136]

Bolesław now built a fine new stone cathedral at Gniezno worthy of the martyr Adalbert's relics.[137] Gniezno was now the political capital again. Bolesław struck money here, no doubt in or immediately after 1000, with the inscription GNEZDUN CIVITAS. It is on these rare coins, perhaps a 'commemorative issue' never intended for general circulation, that the name of Poland first appears: PRINCES POLONIE. The title PRINCE[P]S is itself suggestive: it was then only usual in Italy and therefore appears here as part of the Imperial conception fostered by Otto and represented also by the new archbishop Gaudentius, the companion of his half-brother Adalbert in Italy and consecrated there.[138] Otto for his part carried the veneration of Adalbert to Aix, where he dedicated a new church to the saint.

In the years following 1000 began a vigorous new evangelising campaign in Poland. Otto III arranged for missionaries to be sent from St Romuald's training centre near Ravenna, the Pereum. It is stated that one of Bolesław's sons became a monk there.[139] Two monks arrived in Poland about the end of 1001 or early 1002 and were settled at Międzyrzecz (*Germanice* Meseritz). Here they were joined by three Poles.[140] All were soon after massacred by brigands. But the cell was later restarted. Bruno of Querfurt, who had intended to join them was delayed in Rome until 1005 and there consecrated as an independent missionary archbishop for Poland. Too little is known to assess what was accomplished in Poland before his death in 1009.[a]

Otto's premature death (24 January 1002) produced the expected reaction. If Bolesław had been encouraged to hope for the Empire he had no adequate means to enforce Otto's intention. The average German ignored the equality of the four parts of Empire and wanted the Kingdom of Germany to be paramount; in his eyes Otto had shown an inexplicable favouritism towards Poland. Henry IV of Bavaria was elected as Henry II, being indeed Otto's most natural successor. An attempt was even made to get rid of Bolesław by assassination, after Henry had refused at a conference in Merseburg (July 1002) to hand over to him the vital strategic point of Meissen in addition to Lusatia (the districts of Lużyce and Milsko), which Bolesław had occupied during the interregnum.[141] Similarly, when Bolesław was momentarily triumphant in Bohemia and Moravia (1003–4), he was expectedly not prepared to accept them from Henry as fiefs of the Empire; for Bohemia had recognised herself as such in November 1002. Further approaches to the Pope for a Polish crown—which we may suppose that Otto had approved in 1000 but left to the Pope to confer—were again blocked by Henry. There followed a long and sterile war between Germany and Poland (1005–18), to decide the ultimate fate of Bohemia. In anticipation Henry had taken the unpopular step of an alliance with the still pagan Ljutici against Poland. Bolesław's conquests were gradually whittled away until, by the Peace of Merseburg in 1013 and the Peace of Bautzen (Budziszyn) in 1018, he retained only Lusatia. For Thietmar the Saxon apologist even this was too much: Germany had had to make a peace 'non ut decuit sed sicut tunc fieri potuit'.[142] Polish hopes of pulling Bohemia at the eleventh hour out of a German into a Slav orbit had come to nothing. At least in salvaging Lusatia Bolesław safeguarded his natural frontier against Germany.

a For St Bruno see also pp. 274–5.

Nevertheless Henry did not deny all Otto's ideas. There is no doubt that he admired him and for similar reasons had himself crowned with the Imperial crown by the Pope in 1014. The state of Germany, after Otto's neglect, required his full attention. His piety was exercised nearer home: the foundation of the bishopric of Bamberg (1007) as a missionary centre for still unconverted Slavs within the Empire, and the resuscitation in 1004 of the see of Merseburg which had been dormant since 981. The Act of Gniezno, the spirit of which was now repudiated in Germany, had been an attempt to extend and reinterpret the ideal of the Christian commonwealth of peoples. It was no fault of the main actors in it if the moment was lost never to recur. The last pagans in Europe—the Baltic peoples from Prussia to Latvia—were thereby doomed to a darker history in the coming centuries.

Not till Henry's death and that of his Pope, Benedict VIII, in 1024 did Bolesław's fortunes take a better turn. He assumed a royal crown at Easter 1025, a few months before his death. Henry had seen to it that none was offered while he was alive.[143] Bolesław had made peace with Germany in 1018: Poland had refused to become a part of the Empire. Since 1018—indeed since the beginning of the century—he had been attempting to create a new northern Christian empire, predominantly Slav and closely linked to the Papacy. Though he occupied Kiev for a short time (1018), ostensibly to put Svjatopolk his son-in-law in power, internal difficulties, especially in the period 1018–25, were too great to bear such a structure.[144] His one more permanent success was the control of Galicia (the Red Towns),[a] which remained Polish till 1031. As Poland had refused to be part of the German Empire, so Bohemia had refused to be part of the projected Polish Empire. That Bolesław was *capax imperii* need not be doubted; but Western Europe was not yet ready to accept a Slav overlord.

The archbishopric of Gniezno remained the primatial see of Poland. At the time of its creation bishoprics were set up also in Cracow, Wrocław (Breslau) for Silesia, and Kołobrzeg (Kolberg) for Pomerania. Bohemia and Germany were thus to have no further claims in Poland. The Pomeranian see soon collapsed: Bishop Reinbern abandoned his mission as early as 1004 or 1005 in face of violent opposition. No bishopric was yet created for Mazovia (Mazowsze), which accordingly must be

[a] The name 'Red Towns' is taken from the *Russian Primary Chronicle*, s.a. 1018 and 1031, by a misconceived interpretation of the place name Červen (=red). The site of Červen is now securely identified at Czermno near Tyszowiec.

assumed still largely pagan. Thietmar reflects the Magdeburg outlook by his sour comment on the creation of Gniezno: *ut spero legitime*.[145] Magdeburg might still claim rights over the Polish church through Poznań. It is also noticeable that Bruno of Querfurt glosses over Gniezno and mentions by name only Unger of Poznań. This need not imply that he knew or thought that Poznań was subject to Magdeburg but simply that he was himself still an ardent admirer of Otto I, his creation and his policy, and was deeply grateful to Magdeburg for his own education. He preferred the older policy to that of attaching new provinces—missionary or otherwise—to the Holy See. In fact he disapproved of all Otto III's ideas, in particular the possible transference of the centre of imperial affairs to Rome.

The status of Poznań after 1000 is indeed somewhat obscure. In all probability the see was not immediately integrated into the archdiocese of Gniezno; Unger continued to administer it as a separate missionary bishopric. Only on his death in 1012 was it brought under Gniezno. Unger had protested in 1000, perhaps because Gaudentius was appointed over his head, certainly at the curtailment of his rights. A missionary bishop was deemed to have an indefinitely extensible range of activity; moreover at least during part of Mieszko's reign Poznań had been the capital.[146] The protest was serious enough for him to take the matter to Rome in person. On the way, however, he was kidnapped by German agents (1003/4). It may be that he was then persuaded under duress to admit that his see came under Magdeburg and that it was on the basis of this declaration that false documents of Magdeburg's claims were then elaborated. He probably never returned to his see, which remained vacant. Magdeburg's claims were produced in due course when political conditions were favourable, for example during the troubles of 1034–8. They continued to be pressed and found favour with Pope Innocent II who 'restored' its rights over the whole Polish church in 1133.[147] But this was a flash in the pan; they were cancelled again in 1136 as soon as Germany and Poland reached an agreement on Pomerania and the troublesome Norbert of Magdeburg was dead.[148] Magdeburg finally abandoned its pretensions. Ecclesiastically its influence had amounted to nothing. It triumphed in a different sphere—in implanting in Poland from the early thirteenth century the German institution of the free municipality with its written constitution based on the 'Magdeburg law'.

With the death of Bolesław in June 1025 Polish power declined rapidly. Mieszko II (1025–34) was harried by his brothers. The peripheral conquests (Galicia, Lusatia) proved too difficult to keep. Moravia had already been virtually lost to Bohemia and Slovakia to Hungary in 1017–18; certainly Poland had no longer any control over them by 1031.[149] The Danes occupied much of Pomerania in that year. From 1034 to 1039 Poland fell a prey to internal dissension. Břetislav of Bohemia invaded the country in summer 1039,[a] occupied Silesia and the south, thrust northwards as far as Gniezno, destroyed the cathedral and removed thence to Prague all its treasures, including a gold cross that 'twelve priests could scarcely carry' and the relics of St Adalbert.[150] For nearly a century Gniezno lost all its importance to Cracow.

The years following 1034 are supposed to be, with a proper irony, the reign of Bolesław Zapomniany—Bolesław the Forgotten, in the opinion of many Bolesław the Imaginary.[151] It is at the beginning of this collapse that we begin to hear of 'pagan revolts'. Bolesław Chrobry's territories were far from being securely Christian by 1025 and there was no doubt much back-sliding in the ensuing troubles. Mieszko II's wife, Rycheza (Rixa) of Lorraine, considered the Poles very imperfect Christians: she was glad to leave Poland for good when the troubles started. It is clear that she thought the state of Christianity in Poland parlous and that a stronger hand than Mieszko's was needed to save the situation.[152] It has even been noted that there are more burials of pagan type in a cemetery at Sandomierz in the second half of the eleventh century than earlier.[153]

The first such revolt is noted in Cosmas of Prague's *Chronicle* under the year 1022: 'In Polonia facta est persecutio Christianorum.[154] Another followed immediately on the death of Bolesław;[155] the greatest in summer 1034: 'Misacho Polianorum dux immatura morte interiit et christianitas ibidem a suis prioribus bene inchoata et a se melius roborata flebiliter—proh dolor!—disperiit'.[156]

The causes of these revolts can only be guessed at. Few are likely to have been exclusively 'pagan': religious unrest will have been exacerbated by local political and economic troubles. There is enough in the meagre reports to accept that some at least involved a pagan element. Clergy, especially in Wielkopolska, were murdered. The successes of the Veletians[b] against the might of Germany were liable also to strengthen Polish paganism when it was sufficiently supported by other considerations.

The situation was not retrieved until 1039, when Kazimierz, son of

---

[a] Some authorities believe that the campaign started in autumn 1038. See also p. 105.   [b] See p. 151.

Mieszko and Rycheza, who had fled the dangers in 1034, returned to Poland with adequate German military support and Russian backing to re-establish order.[157] He is known therefore as Kazimierz Odnowiciel— Casimir the Restorer—but also as Kazimierz Mnich, the Monk, for his piety.[158] A complete reorganisation of the church had to be undertaken. Little reference is made to the previous hierarchy, as if it had conspicuously failed in its duty at a time of crisis. The life of the church had come to a standstill except in a few favoured places, such as Cracow, where Bishop Rachelin appears to have weathered the storm. Not all the destruction was due to the Polish 'pagans', that is, warring bands of any kind: the Czechs in their lightning raid of 1038–9 had deliberately wrecked even the most sacred edifices. For this impious conduct the Archbishop of Mainz took Bishop Severus of Prague severely to task.[159]

Kazimierz treated Poland as still essentially a mission-field. Benedictines flooded in, for whom new monasteries were founded or old ones refounded, as centres of training for missionary work.[160] Foreign prelates and abbots were everywhere appointed. Kazimierz's main ecclesiastical adviser was, from about 1044, his new Bishop of Cracow, Aaron of Cologne. The Pope allowed Aaron the personal rank of archbishop until such time as Gniezno could be rebuilt.[161] The greatest contribution in men came from Lorraine and the Rhineland generally, then the most active intellectual centres in the Church. Tyniec, Mogilno and Lubiń drew a high proportion of their monks from the region of Liège. The connection with Cologne was particularly strong at this time since Archbishop Hermann of Cologne was Kazimierz's uncle through his mother, an Ezzonid of Lorraine. Though the Saxons (and the Czechs too) naturally also looked to such leading cultural central centres as Liège and Cologne, Poland maintained even closer relations. This continued into the twelfth century, when, for example, two eminent Walloon brothers, Alexander and Wauthier of Malonne, became respectively bishops of Płock (1129–56) and Wrocław (1149–69).

Cracow became Kazimierz's capital since it had suffered less in the wars than the old towns of Wielkopolska; Gniezno and Poznań cathedrals were both in ruins. A new cathedral was started at Cracow in the style then current in the Rhineland and probably with craftsmen from those parts. This replaced Bolesław's much smaller building, begun about 1018 in a more Saxon style.[162]

By the time of his death in 1058 Kazimierz had reimposed central control on all those peripheral provinces that could then properly be called Polish—Mazovia, Silesia, Pomerania—though local princelings continued to rule with a greater or less degree of independence. Kazimierz seems to have attached special importance to the evangelisation of Mazovia, which under the rule of Masław was particularly prominent in the 'pagan revolts' and had not yet acquired more than a veneer of Christianity. To the danger of Masław's combining with the heathen Baltic tribes to harry the civilised lands may be ascribed the Polish–Russian alliance of *c.* 1039, cemented by two dynastic marriages.[a]

The work of reorganisation was continued after Kazimierz's death by Bolesław II the Bold (1058–79), who is remembered in a Cracow cathedral calendar, under the date 3 April, as the prince who 'set up the sees in Poland'.[163] His new foundation was the see of Płock for Mazovia (1075–6). While the later years of his reign were a time of great Papal interest in Poland (Gregory VII was elected in 1073),[b] he was no tool of Papal policy. There was no thought of renewing Mieszko's 'Donation'. Even Bolesław's crown (1076) was not a reward for services to the Pope, since Lambert of Hersfeld writes: 'Dux Polonorum...regiam dignitatem regiumque nomen sibi usurpavit, diadema imposuit.[164] Bolesław finished restoration of the cathedrals of Gniezno and Poznań.[165] As late as 1075 Pope Gregory wrote to him in terms suggesting that Gniezno was not yet functioning properly again as the metropolitan see.[166] The Bull of 1136 finally defined its rights and privileges.[167]

For all his great work in rebuilding Polish Christianity Bolesław's reign ended ignominiously. The promotion of a native to high ecclesiastical office was no longer exceptional; Bishop Stanisław of Cracow was perhaps the most outstanding. Yet Bolesław treated him with incomprehensible cruelty and was obliged to flee Poland in 1079 for this one misdeed. The cause of the quarrel remains obscure.[168]

The final and definite reorganisation of the church was carried through by the Papal Legate, Aegidius (Idzi) of Tusculum, in 1123, in concert with Bolesław III Krzywousty. Even so, throughout the first half of the twelfth century remnants of paganism in Poland were still a commonplace. Shrines had been everywhere destroyed and open cults suppressed; but real conversion was a slower process. The gradual collapse of Wendish paganism in this century may have contributed to its final decline in Poland also. While the ancient sanctuary on Mount Sobótka in Silesia had been replaced by a Christian church about 1100, Silesia as a whole was far from fully evangelised. The influx of Cistertian monks in this century, who made a point of setting up their houses in wild places to be tamed for agricultural colonisation, gradually exercised a civilising effect at many scattered points. Silesia and Mazovia remained at a comparatively low level of Christian culture throughout the thirteenth century too.[169]

Given the instability of Polish Christianity in the eleventh and twelfth centuries, no important missionary activity on her part could be expected. While, for political reasons, Polish rulers had supported missions to the Pomeranians and Prussians, notably those of St Adalbert and St Bruno, they were scarcely her own. A more active policy only appears under Bolesław II. The abbeys of Lubiń and Mogilno were intended for work in West and East Pomerania respectively. The see of Belgard on the River Persanta was to be the bishopric of the newly converted Pomeranians, replacing the abortive see of Kołobrzeg. But it seems likely that the bishop rarely found it politic to reside there and was known more vaguely as *poloniensis episcopus*;[170] for the Danes were paramount in Pomerania during much of the eleventh century. In the event the decisive missions were carried out not by Poles but by the German Otto of Bamberg,[171] though with the support of Bolesław Krzywousty and the approval of the Pope.[172]

Otto's first journey (April 1124 to February 1125) concentrated on important towns near the Oder delta, following Krzywousty's occupation of them in 1121. For it was still as important to Poland as in Mieszko's time to keep open access to suitable Baltic harbours. Pagan shrines and their idols were destroyed and mass baptisms carried out at Stettin, Wolin and Belgard. Both at Stettin and Wolin new churches were dedicated to St Adalbert.

Otto's second journey in 1128, motivated by massive relapses,[173] was less successful though backed by threats of harsh military measures. Nevertheless by 1140 it was possible to appoint Otto to a viable see of Wolin. But his methods were superficial. Preparation for baptism was inadequate. Quantity prevailed over quality. As neither Otto nor the German clergy who accompanied him knew the vernacular the Pomeranian Slavs treated these approaches with suspicion: they appeared no different from those which their Western neighbours had been resisting for so long, except that Otto did eschew forced conversion as a matter of principle.[a]

---

[a] See pp. 142 ff. Compare the thorough preparation which Otto III and St Romuald had deemed necessary for their missionaries to Poland: 'Hii...ut predicare postmodum possent, sclavonicam linguam laboriose discere studuerunt. Septimo vero anno, cum jam loquelam terre plene cognoscerent...' (*Vita beati Romualdi*, cap. 28).

The chieftain Vratislav (*dux Wortizlaus*) is pictured, we hope justly, in the *Lives* of Otto as an enlightened ruler who recognised not only the evils of force but also the duty of the native rulers to take the lead in the adoption of the new religion.[174] Yet even he found difficulties in coming to terms with the Christian message. The Pomeranians would listen to an Otto who came to them clothed in magnificent vestments and accompanied by a train of assistants, symbols of his importance and power. Wealth and power were for the pagans the outward signs of Divine favour. The simple and poor missionaries who had appealed directly to them in Christ's name before Otto's arrival had made no impression. Unadorned Christianity could only hope to establish itself through gaining the ear of an intelligent and already semi-civilised ruler.

The Pope subordinated the new see of Wolin to Gniezno. Magdeburg's pretensions to control over the Pomeranian church were at first successfully countered. But here her claims were in fact the better. West Pomerania passed permanently out of Polish hands. It became a Saxon fief in 1181 and Magdeburg's ecclesiastical position was finally confirmed in 1216.

It remains to examine the view that Cyrillomethodian usages did gain a certain footing in Poland, to be precise, in those southern areas which were part of the Polish state intermittently in the tenth century and solidly incorporated during the reign of Bolesław Chrobry. The evidence is all circumstantial since it is held that the Catholic church deliberately attempted to obliterate all trace of them from the moment of its triumph in 1039; thus what loosely passed in some contemporary notices for 'pagan revolts' were in fact incidents in what amounted to a religious war between adherents of the Latin and Slav liturgical languages. The matter turns primarily on language: that is to say, it is claimed that there coexisted in Poland as in Bohemia two forms of Western Christianity— one using Latin and the Latin alphabet, the other Church Slavonic and the Glagolitic alphabet. Eastern liturgical practice is not in question. But there follows the larger question: did the partisans of the two languages form at any time two separate churches, each with its own hierarchy?

Though to interpret all the 'pagan revolts' in this sense is certainly to go a great deal too far, the view merits serious consideration.[175] The various lines of enquiry may be summarised as follows:

1. *The Life of Methodios*, chapter xi, mentions a mission to the Vistulanians during Methodios's lifetime. Svatopluk conquered the region

in 877–8. A fort of possibly Moravian type recently uncovered at Boni-kowo near Kościan may perhaps mark the northern limit of Moravian conquest at this time—that is to say, some thirty miles south of Poznań.[176] Methodios's prophecy[a] was presumably so far fulfilled in that the Vistu-lanian chieftain was baptised as a Moravian vassal or captive.[177] Recent excavations at Wiślica,[178] which was apparently till quite a late date known as *civitas Visly*[179] and therefore may well be the *vŭ Vislě[hŭ]* of the *Life*, have revealed Christian objects provisionally dated to the ninth and tenth centuries. The penetration of Christianity into the Upper Vistula valley about the time alleged is therefore confirmed. Thus Cyrillomethodian beginnings are more than probable in South Poland; but there is still too little evidence to judge of its permanence; moreover any work of Wiching[b] was sure to be in the Latin language.

2. A number of passages relating to the period of 'pagan revolts' seem rather to indicate a struggle between two Christian groupings: *Anonymus Gallus* speaks of rebels who 'a fide catholica deviantes...ad-versus episcopos et sacerdotes Dei seditionem inceperunt',[180] and again of *falsi christicolae* in Mazovia. No Catholic would have used such words of pagans whether before or after 1054. This is perhaps the clearest pointer to the presence of Cyrillomethodian Christians in Poland, per-petuating the tradition of the Slav liturgical language. But the step from this to the assumption of a separate ecclesiastical organisation for them, which could not have derived from Bohemia where Latin and Slav co-existed in one church, is a large one.

3. *Anonymus Gallus* states that after the Gniezno settlement (1000) Poland 'duos metropolitanos cum suis suffraganeis continebat'.[181] The words used by him on the death of Bolesław (1025) do not conflict with this: 'archiepiscopi, episcopi, abbates...cum suis precibus Domino com[m]endabant', and again: 'latinorum et slauorum quotquot estis incole'.[182] Neither of the last two, however, carries much weight since the death of Bolesław could be held to interest a wider world than Poland alone. As for the first, the Cracow area was in Bohemian hands on and off between the fall of Moravia (906) and 999, when Bolesław evidently took advantage of the death of the Bohemian ruler (February 999) to redeem the lost territory. If these territories received any formal ecclesiastical organisation in the tenth century, they would naturally have been attached to the diocese of Prague; Mainz would now be the second metropolitan see in question. The phrase might express this fact

---

[a] See p. 115 and n. 85 (p. 352).   [b] On Wiching, see pp. 81–2.

very loosely.[183] But after 1000 this could hardly appear relevant. Some other metropolitan see—inside Bolesław's Poland—should be meant. The most obvious choice is Cracow itself. That there were bishops at Cracow before the year 1000 can be seriously entertained. This was no unnatural place of refuge for some of the Cyrillomethodian disciples leaving Moravia or alternatively Slovakia (Nitra), whether about 885 or 906.[a] Two names of bishops are mentioned before 1000—Prokhor and Proculf; and sometimes a third—Lambert. A number of explicit lists place the consecration of Prohorius (or a variant of this name) as 'first' bishop of Cracow in one of the years 968–71 and that of Proculphus as second bishop in 985 or 986. Where Lambert's name does not appear,[184] Proculphus is alleged to have exercised his functions for twenty-seven years, that is, till long after the new arrangements made at Gniezno in 1000. The name Prokhor certainly does not suggest a western churchman but we cannot on this score alone ascribe him to a Cyrillomethodian 'church'. Both the names Prokhor and Proculf were in use in North Italy. Quite a number of Polish bishops in the following centuries came from Italy—probably more than can now be identified purely by their names; such were Hieronymus of Wrocław (from 1051) and Maurus of Cracow (from 1110), both known to be Romans.[185] Prokhor and Proculf may have been members of some recent Italian (even Papal) mission.[186]

Again, the *Rocznik kapitulny Krakowski* for 1027[187] records the death of 'Archbishop' Hippolytus, to whom succeeded Bossuta—ostensibly a Greek name followed by a Slav one (Bożęta?), neither held to be at all probable in a Latin see. But the Polish records are in so chaotic a state, as a result of the great eleventh-century *débâcle*, that it is unwise to trust them. In some lists these two prelates are ascribed to Gniezno,[188] and this is the most likely reason for the introduction of the title of archbishop. If we ascribe all these bishops to Cracow the lists are mutually contradictory. Nor is Hippolytus exclusively Greek. The saint is also Bavarian (Sankt Pölten) and from Bavaria reached Nitra in Slovakia. A link from Poland to St Hippolytus's monastery at Nitra is well authenticated for this period in the story of St Andrew-Zoeradus (Świerad?), who fled there from an unspecified part of Poland about the year 1022.[b] The name Hippolytus does not point unambiguously towards either language. Polish links with the Rhineland, Bavaria and Italy have been given too little weight in this discussion of names.

If Cracow was ever an archbishopric, when and through whom did it

---

[a] See pp. 82 ff.   [b] See p. 84.

acquire this status? One possible answer would be that Gorazd, properly consecrated as Methodios's successor in the archbishopric of Moravia,[a] established himself at Cracow after the fall of Moravia and developed a sufficiently stable hierarchy in South Poland to make the perpetuation of an archbishopric possible.[189] This is no more than an unsupported hypothesis. We have already noted[b] that Cracow may have been constituted a bishopric of Great Moravia under Mojmir II about 898, since the lands of the Vistulanians were apparently still a part of his state. The continuity of a bishopric from that time is much more probable than that of an archbishopric. Perhaps Gallus's two metropolitans should be explained as a misconception of the chronicler who knew of the long period when Aaron had had the personal status of Archbishop of Cracow (*c.* 1044–59)—Gniezno being in ruins—but was writing when the earlier situation had been restored. Aaron's status gave Cracow pretensions not only to be superior to Gniezno but also to Prague. This led to many falsifications, perhaps even to the invention of such worthies as Prokhor and Proculf, in order to bolster up the antiquity of Cracow's foundation date.[190] Gniezno and Cracow were thus two metropolitan sees but in fact (whatever the theoretical rights of the matter) at no time existed simultaneously.

The pretensions of Magdeburg may also have confused some minds. Those who believed that the see of Poznań had originally been subordinate to that metropolis—as Otto may conceivably have intended had not Rome disallowed it—would have concluded that its exclusion from the new archdiocese of Gniezno in 1000 confirmed this and consequently that there was part of a second metropolitan province in Poland. This is, of course, another approximation, since the metropolis itself was outside Poland.

4. The dedications of churches and monasteries sometimes provide reliable pointers. Several early churches on the Wawel (citadel) at Cracow were dedicated to saints more frequently, or exclusively, honoured in the Eastern church—St George the Martyr, St Mary the Egyptian and St Michael Archangel. This could be claimed as a Cyrillomethodian inheritance. Of two very ancient rotundas at Cracow St Saviour's may well go back to the ninth century and provide a further indication of the penetration of Methodian missionaries into South Poland. The rotunda of SS Felix and Adauctus[191] (originally dedicated to the Virgin Mary) is probably derived from the first St Vitus at Prague[c] but can scarcely be

---

[a] See pp. 81 and 84.   [b] See p. 84.   [c] See p. 94.

older than the second half of the tenth century. These affiliations support the early establishment of Christianity at Cracow but cannot tell us anything certain about language and hierarchy.

Several south Polish churches dedicated to St Clement of Rome and the Holy Wisdom (Santa Sofia) are also known. The veneration of St Clement of Ohrid and St Wenceslas is well authenticated in Małopolska; the latter is to be expected in either tradition, the former rather among Cyrillomethodians. Nevertheless the use and distribution of the name Clement in Poland has not been found to support the widespread presence of a Cyrillomethodian church. In place names it is not confined to the South but fairly equally distributed. About two-thirds of them have the Greek form Klim- (including many founded on diminutives); those founded on Klemens (the Latin form) are demonstrably a later stratum. It is difficult to avoid the conclusion that the names in Klim- are one of the quite general Czech loans to Polish.[192]

Kazimierz Odnowiciel and his successors, particularly Bolesław III (1102–38), concerned themselves with the rededication of many churches to typically Catholic saints, including that of the abbey of Tyniec near Cracow, which became under Kazimierz the head Benedictine house in all Poland.[193] A narrower Catholic outlook would naturally follow 1054.

It should be observed that Bolesław the Great's sobriquet was Old Polish *chabry*, not Church Slavonic *chrabry*, and is therefore no pointer to the use of the latter language either in his lifetime or later.[a]

5. Incontrovertible proof of the existence of monastic communities (*a fortiori* churches) in Poland using the Slav language at an early date is likewise not forthcoming. The Slav language may have been used here and there in Silesia.[194] It is clear that Cyrillomethodian usages could have been brought there from Bohemia, which controlled Silesia west of the River Oder from at least 973 until it became Polish again and certainly introduced the cults of St Clement and St Wenceslas into those parts. It would indeed be surprising if in all these disputed territories between Bohemia and Central Poland there were no traces at all of Bohemian missionary enterprise.

Though the monastery of Tyniec and several others[195] are supposed to have had relations with Sázava, any Cyrillomethodian current from the latter could only start in 1032[b] and therefore be relevant to the very last years of the alleged Slav church in Poland. Accepting this as possible—

---

[a] *Chrobry* (brave) is the modern normalisation. It is not certain how early the Poles applied this epithet to him.   [b] See p. 105.

even probable—we have an explanation for certain expulsions of monks mentioned in the years of Restoration, and particularly after 1054, reminiscent of the expulsion of the Sázava monks themselves in 1056. The exactness of the parallel is completed by a notice of the expulsion of Slav monks from Tyniec in 1096, the very year in which the Slav use came to an end at Sázava.[a] But reliable earlier evidence is again lacking. There is nothing against the assumption that monks came to South Poland— therefore the diocese of Cracow—from Moravia and Slovakia at various times, nor can possible devotees of the Slav language from such Bohemian houses as Břevnov (founded 993) be excluded. But the state of the Moravian and Slovakian monasteries after 906 is very imperfectly known.[b] A wholly or even partly Slav monastery in Poland remains an assumption. The possibility that Bolesław was persecuting certain monks in 1022—the date, it will be recalled, of Cosmas's *persecutio christianorum*— which appears faintly in the background of the story of St Zoeradus (Świerad),[196] cannot be interpreted safely as a change in policy towards a hitherto tolerated Slav use; nor could Cosmas have understood it so.

6. The linguistic evidence is lamentably weak. There is no question that Old Church Slavonic made some contribution to Polish religious vocabulary.[c] But no Polish religious term of Church Slavonic type can be proved to be independent of Czech mediacy. If we could establish a linguistic link from Cyrillomethodian Moravia or Slovakia to Cracow we should be on much firmer ground in positing an established and perhaps separate Cyrillomethodian church there. The only possibility so far advanced is Old Polish *cyrki*, which cannot be referred to a recorded Czech form but is clearly an element of the Cyrillomethodian vocabulary. But this variant might have come from Kiev.[197] Kiev was almost certainly also responsible for the unexpected Cyrillic inscriptions on certain of Bolesław Chrobry's coins—a gold issue obviously modelled on eastern, not western, prototypes, namely Vladimir of Kiev's first issue, which should be dated *c.* 1018 when Bolesław was closely involved in Russian affairs. These coins have been dated too early and are no evidence of an episcopal mint at Cracow with Cyrillomethodian implications. The Cyrillomethodian church in Central Europe never used the Cyrillic alphabet for the simple reason that it did not exist before 893.[d] A Glagolitic inscription under these circumstances would have been very strong evidence indeed of Cyrillomethodian tradition; but this alphabet was not used on any Bohemian coin either.

a See p. 107.   b See p. 84.   c See pp. 122–3.   d See p. 41.

Finally it must be remembered that no manuscripts at all have survived in any Slav script from the early Polish period. This might be hardly surprising given a forcible suppression of the use of the Slav language in the eleventh century. But it suggests rather that the Glagolitic tradition was never so deep-rooted in Poland as in Bohemia: there too the Latinists made a purge of Glagolitic manuscripts but enough survived, chiefly in Russian copies, to prove its former vitality. There was surely an equal chance that Polish manuscripts would have survived in the same fashion and in proportionate measure.

7. The ecclesiastical dispositions made at Gniezno in 1000 are not entirely clear. Thietmar states: 'eidemque [Gaudentius] subiciens Reinbernum, Salsae Cholbergensis ecclesiae episcopum, Popponem Cracuaensem, Iohannem Wrotizlaensem, Vungero Posnaniensi excepto'.[198] Are John and Poppo the first bishops of new Latin dioceses or the first incumbents of reformed ones? Or did Slav and Latin sees exist side by side for a time? No unequivocal answer can yet be given. Not only Bolesław but also Otto III and the Pope must have been fully aware of a Slav language church in South Poland, if such existed, in their deliberations of 999–1000. Nothing whatever is said on this score. One would not expect either Otto or Gaudentius, disciples of St Adalbert, to object to its continuation. To Bolesław it might have seemed an advantage to be preserved, both providing a *point d'appui* for dissidents in Bohemia and favouring his expansionist plans to the East. Nor was the Pope at this time attacking the use of Church Slavonic in Bohemia or Dalmatia. Furthermore, the silence of Thietmar of Merseburg on this matter must give pause: describing as he does the dispositions of Gniezno in some detail, would this Saxon, who lost few opportunities of denigrating the Slavs, have made no reference to a flourishing Cyrillomethodian church in Poland even more unorthodox than the new Latin organisation of Gniezno of which he so obviously disapproved?

To sum up: both Queen Rycheza and her German advisers and Kazimierz Odnowiciel (under Papal pressure) initiated a campaign of Latin uniformity throughout Poland. The Slav language, if it flourished in certain areas, seems to have been tolerated by Bolesław Chrobry and Mieszko II.[199] Altogether so little can be said with confidence about Cyrillomethodian survivals in Central Europe between the coming of the Magyars and their own entry into Christendom—indeed until well into the eleventh century—that to build on this foundation is to build a house on sand. Bohemia appears, and surely was, the most vigorous centre of the Cyrillomethodian tradition in the tenth century. We cannot exclude the possibility that this might have come to an end earlier than it did but for the support of co-religionists in Małopolska and elsewhere. In the light of the above arguments we must admit the likelihood of some extension of the Slav ecclesiastical language to South Poland but the strength and derivation of it are not yet sufficiently clarified. An early double influence of Bohemia, more Latin in Central Poland, more Slav in the South, seems a great deal more probable than the hypothesis of a widespread and independent Cyrillomethodian church of long standing on the Upper Vistula. Given that separate Latin and Slav churches (that is, hierarchies) never existed either in Moravia, Bohemia or Dalmatia, such an assumption must be held gratuitous in Poland in default of positive evidence. Polish sources of the fourteenth century and later, on which supporters of a separate Slav church in Poland have willy-nilly to base much of their argument, must all be treated with the greatest reserve as likely to have been coloured by the Slav revival in Bohemia under Charles IV.[a]

THE WENDS OF NORTH GERMANY

The line of the rivers Elbe and Saale was the approximate limit of Slav migration westwards.[b] In the triangle between Elbe and Saale were settled the northern Serbs or Sorbs,[c] who may have been incorporated in the Great Moravian state for a short period by Svatopluk. In the ninth century the Wends were still, generally speaking, organised in loose federations above a strong tribal and clan structure. The most conspicuous federations were those of the Obodrites in Holstein and Mecklenburg and the Veletians to their east and south-east.[200] While speaking closely related dialects, the Wends had no conception of themselves as a single people any more than their enemies the Saxons thought of themselves as Germans rather than Saxons. The fact that no supra-tribal sovereignty existed at the time of the first important Christian impact upon them answers for much in their subsequent history.

Owing to the great difficulties which Charlemagne met in subduing

---

a See also p. 360, note 189.

b Considerable Slav settlements west of the river were only to be found in the region bounded by the Elbe and the line Lüneburg–Magdeburg. It was in this area, particularly the Drawehn (*Slavice* Drěvěne), that Slav speech lingered on into the eighteenth century.

c German-Latin *Sorabi*. The two enclaves of 'Lusatian Sorbs', centred on Cottbus and Bautzen on the upper Spree, which have managed to retain their Slav language down to the present day, are of closely allied stock and dialect.

and christianising the Saxons the Slav world beyond them remained sealed off from serious Frankish penetration till well into the ninth century. Einhard refers to the Obodrites as *foederati* in the Roman style but the title has rather too grand a sound.[201] Nevertheless Charlemagne did make some allegedly sucessful attempts to extend Frankish control east of the River Elbe, when the situation among the Saxons was favourable, sketchily over some Veletians, more solidly over the Obodrites.[202] Louis the Pious and Louis the German maintained a precarious interest in the internal politics of this Slav world and took hostages from many ruling families. But in all this time only isolated conversions are recorded, as that of an Obodrite chieftain Slavomir in 821. Only on the frontier were such conversions probable, even there doubtfully durable.[203] The focal point of all evangelical work among the northern barbarians in the ninth century was Hamburg, temporarily replaced by Bremen from 845 when Hamburg was destroyed by a Danish raid. It was from Hamburg that St Ansgar (d. 865), true follower in the footsteps of the unpolitical Irish missionaries, began his pioneer work among the Scandinavians about the year 829. The importance of missionary development in these parts was fully recognised in 834 when the Pope appointed Ansgar first archbishop of Hamburg and his Legate to all Swedes, Danes, Slavs and other northern peoples.[204] During the next ten years Ansgar followed the expedient policy of educating as Christians young Danes and Slavs.[205] The setback of 845 shows that little headway could yet be made among the chieftains. But Ansgar was able to resume his work among the Danes and Swedes in the 850s, rightly judging that the most promising centres were the commercial entrepots such as Hedeby and Birka.[a] The following decades coincided with the peak of Viking expansion and aggressiveness. It is not surprising therefore that the Scandinavians proved to be a very slow and laborious missionary harvest.[206] Uniting the sees of Hamburg and Bremen, Pope Nicholas I reaffirmed in 864 the right of this missionary centre to work among the accessible Slavs,[207] but of success among them little is said and probably little was achieved, despite increasing volume of trade along the whole frontier in the second half of the ninth century.[208] Helmold records one temporary and local success which may point to others unrecorded: monks of Corvey established a chapel of St Vitus on the island of Rügen in the time of Louis II (855–75) but the Slavs soon fell away.[209]

By the early years of the tenth century the Saxons, under Henry the

[a] See p. 247 note a.

Fowler, were in a position to inaugurate a new advance. In 928 Henry reduced to obedience and tribute the Stodorane or Hobolane (along the River Havel), establishing a Saxon fortress at Brandenburg, the key-point for communications in this difficult country. In the following year he began to impose German overlordship on many of the Obodrites and Veletians, and strengthened his control of the Lusatian Sorbs by setting up a new fortress at Meissen.[a] The northern flank was strengthened by the occupation of Hedeby, the vital commercial transit point on the Danish isthmus, in 934. The intervention in Bohemia in 929 had consolidated his position to the south. The German world was now poised for expansion across the North European plain. The early successes of this 'crusade' culminated in the founding of the see of Brandenburg in 948, whose first bishop was the eminent Saxon Thietmar. At least by the date of his death (968) the tribe of the Hobolane must have provided a fairly stable Christian nucleus for the activities of a bishopric.[b]

The word 'crusade' is used advisedly, if not in its purest sense, since a difference in method is involved. We have been concerned up to now with what were essentially missionary enterprises. But here German policy envisaged on principle conquest first and conversion, forcible or not, second. The Saxons were about to subject the pagan Slavs to the treatment which Charlemagne had meted out to them as pagans. The recent converts became, as often, more rabid and extreme in their turn. The best men of the time had deplored Charlemagne's policy in Saxony.[c] Henry's policy did not yet amount to a systematic 'baptism or death' but this soon became a commonplace Saxon attitude.[d] There could be little doubt in the minds of these Slavs that German domination meant loss of independence and, in many parts, eviction by German colonists. The Germans openly coveted the best Slav lands, especially in the coastal regions. The Slav ports were busy and prosperous and very tempting.[210] To this must be added the certainty that prisoners of war, indeed all captives—men, women and children—would be sold as slaves. This trade was highly lucrative to those favourably placed on the confines of the civilised world, Franks and Scandinavians alike. Not merely wars, but raids specifically for this purpose into the territories of the pagan

a The incorporation of the Sorbs had started as early as 805–6 but control of the whole Saale–Elbe area had proceeded slowly.

b It does not seem likely that their conversion goes back as early as the first decade of the tenth century, when Dragomira of this tribe was married to the Christian ruler of Prague; see p. 93. The theory that there had been Irish missions in this area and that Brandenburg is called after St Brendan is not acceptable. See p. 352 n. 82.

c See pp. 18–19.   d See pp. 152–3.

Slavs, provided a constant supply from the early ninth until well into the eleventh century. The Islamic countries, to which the majority were sent, particularly valued young eunuchs—so much so that in the eastern emporia, for example Baghdad, the word *slav* (saqlab) took on this connotation. The majority of such captives from North Europe probably did not go further than Moslem Spain.[211] Lucrative though this trade was, the German advance had also a local economic motive in a desire to gain control of the northern, Baltic trade-route at a time when its yield was high compared with what intermittently reached North-west Europe from the Mediterranean. Both Slavs and Danes had therefore to be brought under control. This motive ceased to be decisive after 962, when the new German Empire opened up the routes debouching in Italy, and still less after 1000 when Hungary became Christian. Nevertheless it did not entirely disappear even when outweighed by that of permanent agricultural colonisation of the Slav lands.

It is not unfair to say that the deep-rooted and prolonged hostility of the Wends to Christianity was due as much to what they expected at the hands of the Germans as to the vigour of their own religion or to innate fierceness of temperament. They had hitherto lived according to their own traditions, with their clan structure intact and relatively unaffected by outside influences. There was consequently greater resistance to change, which found no answering native impulses to work on. Moreover the priestly office had apparently reached full development among them— a situation which we cannot clearly see in any other Slav area.[212] This meant that the priesthood could organise resistance even if the tribal chieftain was prepared to submit.

The sources for our knowledge of these events are chronicles written by German clerics.[213] Yet they not infrequently allude to the cruelty and rapacity of their countrymen. Thus it came about that it took a great deal longer to convert these Slavs by the wrong methods and those who were not callously wiped out in the German advance were assimilated and lost their identity and language.

It is not a part of the present purpose to describe their pagan religion in detail, even if this were possible. Much of the evidence is unreliable by the very nature of the sources. The German bookmen were apt to describe any pagan practices, in so far as they could bring themselves to do so at all,[214] in terms of the Old Testament. The Slavs were assumed to be 'idolaters' just as the Moslem enemies of Charlemagne were without reflection described as idolaters in the *Chanson de Roland*. It was long ago pointed out that the description of the idols at Kiev under Vladimir[a] hardly requires more than a knowledge of Psalm 115. The most striking feature of the German accounts is the allusion to many-headed idols. The truth of this has been altogether denied, probably wrongly.[215] The best attested deity among the Wends is a sky-god, of whom Svantevit (Svętovit, in Saxo's spelling *Zvanthevith*) at Arkona on Rügen island was one aspect.[216] Polycephaly, implying omnivision, is not an uncommon attribute of sky-gods. The sacred black or white horse associated with the cult at Stettin and Arkona respectively is also consistent with the shrine of a sky-god.[217] Saxo may have been an eyewitness of the destruction of Arkona in 1168 and therefore at least capable of giving an accurate report. He claims that he saw such an idol.[218] If there were any outside influences on this Slav religion, which appears more elaborate than that of which we have any knowledge among other Slav peoples, they should perhaps be sought not among the contiguous Germanic peoples but among the Swedes with whom the Slav Baltic ports principally traded. The great Swedish sanctuary at Uppsala was famous throughout North Europe.[219] However, polycephalic statues are not characteristic of Swedish religion. The Wendish predilection for them may have come from much earlier Slav contacts with the Thracians and Iranians in Eastern Europe.[220]

The initial military advance by Henry was developed on the missionary plane by his son Otto I (936–73). One of his outstanding lieutenants was Count Gero, the *comes marchio orientalium*. Based on the Lusatian area (Meissen), he pushed forward German conquest and pacification eastwards to the Oder until his death in 965. Thereby he initiated contact with the Polish tribes beyond the river.[b] In the north, up against Denmark, it was Hermann Billung who organised the Saxon advance.

Otto's decisive defeat of the Magyars on the Lechfeld (10 August 955) and his following campaigns against the Veletians for which the removal of the Magyar menace had freed his hands, ushered in a period of relative stability which enabled him to plan a general strategy for the future in North Europe, combining both colonisation and conversion. His ecclesiastical plan was on a grand scale. Magdeburg on the middle Elbe was to be a great missionary see with jurisdiction over all the Slavs of the north. The monastery of St Maurice (a favourite saint of Lower Lorraine) had been founded here by him in 936–7, the kernel of the future

a See pp. 254, 270.   b See p. 113.

archbishopric. Magdeburg had been since Carolingian times one of the main points of contact between Germans and Slavs, being the largest trading post on the northern section of the frontier and a key-point in north–south communications, from the Baltic to Prague and beyond. Though there were frequent local revolts in the conquered lands, notably that of 955, which Otto came straight from the glorious Lechfeld to suppress, it was possible to proceed to the organisation of the church. The see of Brandenburg had received its charter in October 948; those of Oldenburg (*slavice* Stargard) in Holstein[221] and Havelberg[222] date from the same time. Further north the Christian network was being extended by the erection of three new Danish bishoprics under Hamburg—Schleswig, Rupen (Ribe) and Aarhus.[223] Pope John XII approved the bishopric of Magdeburg in 962 at the time of Otto's imperial coronation.[224] At a synod held in Ravenna in April and October 967, at which both Emperor and Pope were present, the status of archbishopric was accorded and the first incumbent appointed—Adalbert, a monk of St Maximin in Trier, who had a wide knowledge of the Slav world.[a]

Between 932 and 963 the remainder of the Lusatian Sorbs lost their independence and were rapidly Germanised. The bishoprics of Meissen, Zeitz[b] and Merseburg, organised in 968 under Magdeburg, covered their territories. The first bishop of Merseburg was Boso of St Emmeram (968–70), a Slav speaker as were most of his successors, including Thietmar the chronicler (*fungebatur* 1009–18).[225] At the same time Brandenburg and Havelberg were transferred from Mainz to the new metropolis. The organisation of the Merseburg diocese had been considerably delayed since Otto had vowed on the Lechfeld to create a bishopric there if he were victorious against the Hungarians, to be dedicated to St Laurence on whose day the battle was fought.[226] But the jealousy of his own son, Archbishop William of Mainz, who saw his archdiocese being gradually eroded by his father's new policy, had postponed the fulfilment of the vow. The eastern limit of the see of Meissen in its early years was held to be the River Bober. Eastwards to the Oder, Silesia was to be long disputed between Bohemia, Poland and the Saxons owing to the increasing economic importance of its mines.

The Obodrites, more civilised than the Veletians, seemed at first more amenable to Christianity. Ibrāhīm ibn Ya'qūb, the Jewish merchant from Andalūs, estimated Nakon, ruler of the Obodrites, as one of the

---

[a] See p. 102 and p. 251.   [b] Transferred *c.* 1028 to Naumburg.

four most powerful Slav monarchs of the time (the 960s).[a] There is no evidence that Nakon became a Christian but there must have been more than a few in his territories, for the bishopric which had been founded for them at Stargard (Oldenburg) was certainly active by 968.[227] But evangelisation was very slow and the Germans were far less in command of the situation than they supposed. We learn most about this diocese from Helmold of Bosau, himself a native of Wagria (the Slav name of the province), particularly the devoted work of Bishop Wicelin and his successor Gerold, Helmold's own patron (*fungebatur* 1149–63). The dates themselves are eloquent of the extreme slowness of the work.

In 983 a great rebellion broke out against the German oppression of taxes and tithe. The Veletians took advantage of Otto II's absence in Italy and sacked Havelberg and Brandenburg. The Obodrites at first held aloof but joined in at an advantageous moment (990). Hamburg was razed again. Germany lost control of Denmark and of virtually all her establishments beyond the Elbe. The bishops fled their sees. Magdeburg was threatened but relieved. Only the Lusatians in the Elbe–Saale triangle were too firmly under German rule to dare to join in. This rebellion was evidently in sympathy with the general recrudescence of terror (especially in England) towards the end of the tenth century, when the Scandinavian North made its last forlorn effort to save its native pagan civilisation from extinction. The success of the Slav rebellion suggests that German adventurers in Italy, with prospects of much richer booty and more flattering perquisites, had momentarily diverted German interest from the Slavs and that there had been a consequent weakening of vigilance and military defences.[228]

The rebellion marks an important divide. We can properly speak here of a reversion to paganism, more complete among the Veletians than the Obodrites, among whom ecclesiastical organisation was not entirely wiped out. Only in such cases did enlightened clerical opinion countenance strong military counter-measures. Bruno of Querfurt, for example, disallowed the use of force in new missionary fields and considered war *à l'outrance* permissible only against apostates, heretics and schismatics.[229] This doctrine absolved all German action against the Slavs in advance. Many Germans concluded from this backsliding that the Slavs were incapable of civilisation. Evangelisation thenceforward took second place to conquest. From 991 Otto III, with Bohemian and Polish help, waged

---

[a] With Boleslas of Prague, Mieszko of Poland and Peter, Tsar of Bulgaria (d. 969). Nakon died in 965 or 966.

a series of campaigns with varying success. By 996 the Obodrites made peace; hostilities against the Veletians ceased about 998. But it was only many years later that the bishops appointed to the lost sees could in fact reoccupy them. The name Ljutici began to be used by the remnants of the Veletian confederacy about this time—the Wild or Fierce men.[230] Certainly they appeared to the Germans the more formidable opponents. Their most important sanctuary was at Radogost,[231] the religious centre and oracle of the paramount tribe. The Germans by now understood that to destroy the sanctuary was to destroy the tribe. Resistance would then collapse since its god had been conquered by a stronger god and could never be rehabilitated. Thus, even if the Wends all worshipped a sky-god, he was not in any real sense a supreme god. Each of his hypostases was limited to its tribal territory and had no power outside that. Helmold's description of Svantovit at Arkona as *deus deorum* is only very relatively true; the Dane Saxo was more accurate in stressing Svantovit's strictly tribal authority—an internal but not an external intolerance.[232] The Wendish gods' opponent was the 'German god' and the crucifix was his idol. If the Christian god prevailed in war his rival was discredited once and for all. Niklot, a chieftain of the Obodrites, exemplifies this belief: the essence of the matter for him and his like was still, which god is the stronger? He horrified the bishop who, as a zealous missionary, had personally directed the destruction of the pagan shrine, by announcing: 'Sit Deus qui in celis est deus tuus; esto tu deus noster et sufficis nobis'.[233] For it was the holy man himself who had brought Niklot's god low. The strictly monotheistic principle and universal message of Christianity was still beyond the comprehension of most Wends.[234]

Henceforward, therefore, German strategy aimed not only at the valuable ports but also at the vital centres of tribal religion. The alternating pulse in the tenth century of German advances, usually marked by the establishment of bishoprics, and reverses was to continue, to the dismay of German expectations, far into the future. We cannot follow all the peripeties in detail. For the Obodrites the great revolt had less permanent consequences. Pribignev-Udo, of the house of Nakon, seems to have been a Christian of sorts.[235] His son emerges as the first considerable Christian ruler. He took the German name of Gottschalk, under which we alone know him, after Bishop Gottschalk of Lüneburg, having been educated there at the monastic school of St Michael. The inevitable German cultural pressure was at work irrespective of politics and war. Despite his Christian education his reaction to the murder of his father in 1028/9 by the Saxons was still that of a clan chieftain: he declared vendetta on the assassins. Soon after he appears to have repented of this impulse and went into exile in Denmark. Restored to his lands in 1043 by Danish arms he attempted to organise them as a Christian state with the encouragement of Adalbert of Bremen, whose missions did not support the policy of force.[236]

The aim of Adalbert's policy was a great 'northern patriarchate' at Hamburg embracing all these new lands, a conception to which the average crude Saxon military leader was impervious. For men of vision the great German defeat and the destruction of Hamburg had been a sign from God that their method was wrong. Even the King of Denmark remarked that the Slavs might have been easily converted but for Saxon covetousness.[237] An attempt such as Gottschalk's (who did not even control all the Obodrites) was only likely to succeed if he had the active support of Hamburg, no interference from Saxon barons and a friendly Denmark—a situation which was only intermittently true. It seems that he felt strong enough about 1066 to attack the obstinately pagan Ljutici on his own account but did not succeed in destroying their main sanctuary at Radogost. He was known as a builder of churches.[238] He reinstated the see of Oldenburg and founded those of Mecklenburg and Ratzeburg. But his power was only apparent: he could not carry his subjects with him. In their eyes to be educated at Lüneburg and to become a Christian was tantamount to becoming a Saxon.[a] They felt that they were now being ruled by a foreigner. This is an inevitable transitional phase: one cannot belong at the same time to two mutually exclusive worlds. The result, as with Gottschalk and certain other Wend princes, is apt to be that the alienated ruler is tolerated but exercises no power of attraction over his subjects. This stage is very evident in the career of Gottschalk's son, the half-Danish Henry, who reigned a full thirty years (1093–1127) under Saxon and Danish patronage but in all that time apparently made no significant advance in the Christianity of his realm. He was obliged to tolerate the continuation of the traditional cults, while his subjects tolerated his chapel and chaplain at Lübeck.[239] The Christian zeal attributed to such rulers by the chroniclers is scarcely borne out by the facts.

By the beginning of the eleventh century a cleavage was developing

---

[a] The reverse situation probably occurred. For example, in 955 rebellious Saxon barons went over to the Slavs and led or helped to lead resistance. Whether they identified themselves completely enough with the Wends to shed their Christianity is not known.

between the two main Slav groups. After the Peace of Bautzen (January 1018) the two never made common cause against the Saxons, which was bound to be fatal to them in the long run. In 1018 the Ljutici turned their ferocity against the Obodrites as traitors to traditional Slav religion: a Christian Obodrite province would inevitably be too much under Saxon domination. They systematically destroyed Christian establishments in the Obodrite lands. Sixty priests were slaughtered;[240] no doubt only absence saved Bishop Bernard of Oldenburg from martyrdom. The Emperor Henry II broke his *alliance de convenance* with the Ljutici, which had been made in 1002 and had given them the opportunity, during Henry's preoccupation with the protracted Polish war, to turn on their own cousins. He did his best to repair the damage done in the Obodrite lands.

It was not until 1036 that the Germans regained sufficient control over the obdurate Ljutici to reimpose the payment of tribute—the symbol of a conquered barbarian country. Towards the middle of the eleventh century German rule seemed once again fairly secure. But Adalbert of Bremen's influence had been undermined; his more far-seeing policy was over-ridden.[a] In 1066 began another widespread revolt of the Slavs. In the case of the Obodrites this was perhaps more of an internal revolt against Gottschalk and his Christian and pro-Saxon policy. Gottschalk was assassinated; priests were martyred, including Bishop John of Mecklenburg. Hamburg and Danish Hedeby were again devastated. The resurgence of paganism continued; the Obodrite sees ceased to function. But no one Slav ruler commanded sufficient authority in the following years to make adequate resistance to the Germans and the Danes. The Ljutici were finally broken after the revolt of 1066. In 1067/8 the sanctuary at Radogost ('Rethra') was at last destroyed by Bishop Burchard of Halberstadt, who took the sacred white horse for his personal use. Thereafter the expected decline in Slav resistance took place.[b] The main aim of German policy then became the recapture of Havelberg and Brandenburg and the resuscitation of those sees. It was still to take a long time.

In the early years of the twelfth century Danish seaborne assaults on

---

[a] Adalbert and Anno of Cologne were joint regents for the minor Henry IV (1050–1116) from 1062, but soon fell out through the machinations of their respective partisans. Adalbert was banished in 1065 and not restored to a measure of favour till 1069, when Henry took over personal rule. The Saxons in any case hated Henry and Adalbert.

[b] Apparently attempts were made to rehabilitate the shrine but it never recovered its authority and was finally destroyed *c.* 1126.

the Slav ports increased in intensity, the Germans and Poles aiding and abetting as occasion offered. In 1108 the Saxons mounted another formidable attack. A first large-scale attempt to take the island of Rügen and destroy the sanctuary of Arkona failed in 1124–5. From that time Germans, Danes and Poles converged simultaneously, but not always in concert, against the Slavs, whose resistance was still fierce but uncoordinated. Albert the Bear became the military leader of the Saxons from 1134. Colonisation was now their unconcealed aim; it was a matter for shame that so little had been achieved since the time of Charlemagne. In 1143 Count Adolf of Holstein was able to take and rebuild the port of Lübeck.[a] According to Helmold these lands (Wagria) were then wholly devastated by the wars and the Count appealed for settlers from all over West Germany (Flanders to Friesland), where land-hunger was becoming acute with the general rise in the population of Western Europe from about the year 1000. As it was conquered territory, he said, they were entitled to live there and enjoy it—'the best of it is your due since you took it from the hand of the enemy'.[241] And since land lay to hand, thus obviating the need for dubious foreign ventures to which the French had had recourse, why not take it from the inferior Slavs? The appeal which launched the campaign of 1108, in the name of the Archbishop of Magdeburg and other Saxon bishops and leaders, had been couched in similar rhetorical expressions scarcely masking the plain cupidity of their intentions.[242] The German immigration set in train that *Drang nach Osten* which eventually embraced nearly the whole South Baltic coast.[243]

In 1147 another 'crusade' was launched, more consciously modelled on those of the Mediterranean, in which Saxony had but a small share, and with little of the *gesta Dei per Francos* in its objectives. For it was preached, in terms of 'convert or extirpate' by St Bernard of Clairvaux. No further concessions to the heathen were to be made, especially to the relapsed.[b] The distinction between heathen and heretic was more and more obscured. The dominical injunction 'Go out into the highways and hedges and compel them to come in' (Luke 14, 23) was used to support a policy of forcible conversion not merely by the crude Saxon military but now even by leaders of the church.[244] And the compulsion had led to a lowering of standards. A more and more superficial initiation into Christi-

[a] The see of Oldenburg (Stargard), resuscitated in 1149, was transferred to Lübeck in 1160. The Hanseatic city was founded on a new site upriver.

[b] In all fairness to St Bernard it must be admitted that he was not as intolerant as many of those who followed his lead. Persuasion and education were part of his programme: nor did he advocate harsh measures against the Jews.

anity was proffered and accepted as conversion in order that the material safety of baptism might be obtained. Baptism symbolised obedience to German rule in all things, in effect the status of a colonial serf. The bewildered and disheartened Slav could not decide whether the sanctions for staying outside the Church or for being an imperfect Christian within it (uninstructed as he remained) were likely to be the more unpleasant. German military and colonial policy in North Europe went ahead with this ecclesiastical backing, agreeing as it did with the inclinations of all but the few who were actively engaged in missionary work. German leaders took all into their own hands, quarrelled among themselves, like the Crusader knights, for territorial advantages, even attacking towns such as Stettin which were already partly or wholly Christian. As contemporaries bear witness, conscience no longer spoke against the extirpation of the Slavs for the creation of a new Saxon colonial empire. Vincent of Prague voices the minority opinion: 'ubi etenim dominus non fuit in causa, bono fine terminari difficillimum fuit'.[245] Small wonder that a Slav chieftain, Wirykind of the Brežane, had told Otto of Bamberg on his Pomeranian mission that they would all rather die than become the 'archbishop's slaves': the German church had made the work of its own missionaries intolerably difficult. Among many plagues was the immediate exaction of the tithe, about which the mercenary Saxons were particularly strict. Helmold, who is by no means pro-Slav, adversely criticises this.[246]

It was not till the early twelfth century that Brandenburg became again safe for Germans through a client Christian prince Pribislav-Heinrich (1127–50); not till 1184 that the bishopric of Havelberg was reinstated. In both cases a period of uneasy coexistence preceded the final imposition of German rule. Pribislav had found it politic to tolerate a shrine of Triglav (that is, the god with three heads) on the Harlungerberg in full view of his own castle and chapel on an island in the River Havel. This was destroyed by the Germans who usurped his lands on his death in 1150; they renamed the hill Marienberg. Similarly a German bishop was able to establish himself precariously at Havelberg from about the same date.

But the pagan spirit was now broken; its last strongholds were on the Baltic coast, particularly the island of Rügen. In 1160 Henry the Lion made alliance with Waldemar of Denmark to deal with these and to gain permanent control of the Oder ports. Numerous combined Danish–Saxon campaigns were still required (1160–85) to achieve this object.

And it took Waldemar as long as the Trojan war finally to reduce Rügen, bitterly defended to the last (1168). The shrine of Arkona was razed to the ground.[247] The island became for the time being Danish and was attached to the see of Roskilde. But Germany had reaped the lion's share of the harvest in territory and proceeded to exploit her long desired Baltic outlet by the development of the Hanseatic network of ports centred on a new German Lübeck.[a] From this time the Slav language rapidly declined in all North Germany.

For the Slavs this is a sad story. Though it is true that the Empire had no wish to bring large pagan populations within its frontiers, evangelisation was virtually from the start subordinated to other impulses. The Wends saw no great cultural advantage in becoming Christians, which was a conspicuous factor in the history of Bulgaria or Russia; the Saxons did not feel any compulsive need to convert them. Moreover, the embryonic city-state organisation of the Wends, most pronounced in the Baltic ports, meant the absence of a high kingship and of a monarch able to lead them decisively for or against Christianity. They were encircled by a ring of enemies. The enemies Bohemia, Poland and Denmark all produced such monarchs in the course of the tenth century and thus escaped dissolution themselves. But despite the unreal accommodations between Christian ruler and pagan priesthood, doomed to failure, we must resist the specious contention that the Germans had no other way out but to conquer and destroy if they were to fulfil their 'civilising mission' to the Wendish people. In Central Europe German eastward expansion, which made Austria into a German-speaking land and planted islands of German speech still further east, was eminently a colonisation by infiltration which did a minimum of violence to the existing Slav and other populations.[248]

By the time of these last campaigns in the North the slave-trade had at last petered out, there being no pagans left in Europe except the remote Baltic Prussians and Lithuanians—the next target for German 'crusades'. Official condemnations of the slave-trade, from as early as the Council of Meaux (845), had gone unregarded but the church stamped as forcibly as it could on trade in Christians and therefore contributed in the long run to its extinction.[b]

[a] The treaty with Gotland of 1161 is usually taken as the beginning of the Hanseatic system though it did not reach its full development till the fourteenth century.

[b] Cf. p. 349 n. 55 (St Adalbert of Prague inveighing against the slave-trade at a moment when Prague, now safely Christian itself, had become one of the main collecting-points).

4

THE BALKAN SLAVS

BULGARIA

The Bulgars—whose name is interpreted as 'mixed people—mixture'—part of a vast semi-nomadic horde speaking a Turkic language which ranged the steppes round the Sea of Azov in the fifth–seventh centuries, migrated under Khazar pressure from this 'Great Bulgaria' (as the Greeks called it) and reached the lower Danube about the year 660. The Byzantine government allowed, since it could not prevent, their leader Asparuch (Isperich) to bring them over the river and settle in the Dobrudja about the year 679. The next two centuries saw the gradual Slavisation of the Bulgars,[1] the firm foundation of a state and its increasing penetration by the irresistably attractive culture of the Greeks.

Byzantine interest in this people and all its cousins on the steppes was of long standing: they were a possible menace to the security of the Empire, especially to its Crimean and Caucasian outposts. As early as 619, according to tradition, a Bulgar chieftain Kubrat (or Kovrat), who attempted to create a single Bulgar Empire of the steppes, was converted to Christianity as a friend and ally of the Emperor Heraklios. But this seems to have been a personal act without consequences for his subjects.[2] Certainly none of his five sons, of whom Asparuch was one, was a Christian.

The conversion of Asparuch's successor Terbel (Tervel, 702–16?) is to be assumed. He was deeply involved in Byzantine politics in 704/5, helping the exiled Justinian II to regain his throne. For this he was rewarded with the high rank of Caesar and a daughter of Justinian's to wife; this surely implies baptism as a prerequisite. Again in 717/18 the Bulgarian ruler was of great service in defeating the last and most formidable Arab siege of the Imperial City. The full statehood of Bulgaria may be dated from 716 when a political and commercial treaty was made with the Empire.[3] Strictly supervised trading by Bulgars in Constantinople and Saloniki was permitted from this time.[a] Byzantine policy entered a new stage: to civilise and Christianise this power on her

[a] The old channels of trade had not wholly ceased to function via Byzantine ports on the Black Sea coast and less certainly on the right bank of the lower Danube. Towns far in the interior, such as Singidunum (Belgrade), Naissa (Niš) and Serdica (Sofia), which appear to a greater or lesser degree to have survived the disasters of the sixth century, may still have had some commercial importance.

northern doorstep, which was absorbing more and more of the *Sclaviniae* (nominally Byzantine territories settled by Slavs) in the North Balkans.

The sedentary Slavs in the regions closest to the Bulgar settlements, who now looked to the Bulgars for military protection and gradually became their subjects, were perhaps more amenable than the Bulgars to these new influences which closer relations with the Empire were to bring. These were the 'Seven Tribes' (a conventional number, not to be taken literally), evidently a Slav political unit in the making. In the early eighth century no Bulgar leader could afford, it would seem, to opt for Christianity in the face of the uncompromising attitude of the Bulgar military aristocracy which for the most part was stoutly maintaining its pagan traditions and steppe culture. Not till the *apartheid* between Bulgar and Slav at the higher social levels had been broken down—a process which remained slow down to 800—did Bulgar exclusiveness lose its force. Up to that time it was only the occasional Bulgar in especially close relations with Constantinople who ventured on the decisive step of baptism. So Telerig (*regnabat c.* 772–7), who was converted when he fled into exile and, like Terbel, was graciously allotted a Greek wife by the Emperor Leo the Khazar. But altogether little is recorded of Bulgaria in the eighth century: the iconoclast troubles within the Empire were not favourable to missionary work outside and the second half of the century was filled with inconclusive hostilities. We may note in passing that this necessity for a constant watch on Bulgaria diverted Byzantine attention from Italy and contributed to the loss of Ravenna (751) and thus to a complete revision of Papal policy both towards the East and the West.

A new line of exceptionally able Bulgar rulers started with Krum (*regnabat c.* 803–14) whose assumption of the title *khagan* announced him as heir to the Avar power recently broken by Charlemagne.[a] His sweeping conquests brought a considerable Christian population in the North Balkans for the first time under Bulgarian rule. He removed many Christian craftsmen into the interior of Bulgaria. Even quite high-ranking Byzantine officials and army officers appear to have remained, more or less voluntarily, in Bulgarian employ.[4] Further, some Bulgarian prisoners-of-war, exchanged in the peace negotiations of 812, had been baptised in captivity.[5]

[a] See pp. 18–20. Krum came of the Kutrigur Bulgars of Pannonia who had entered Europe in Justinian's reign and became more or less subject to the Avars from 567.

As the military advantage now tended to lie with Bulgaria, so the penetration of Greek culture was the self-perpetuating Byzantine answer. Greek as the cultural language made considerable headway in Bulgaria from the beginning of the ninth century. Two now fragmentary Greek inscriptions recording Krum's crushing defeat of the Emperor Nikephóros (811) have survived; these must have been done to the orders of Krum himself.[6] In his reign Bulgar and Slav reached approximate social and legal equality. The highest offices were now open to Slavs, witness Dragomir, his ambassador to Constantinople. There is reason to believe that Krum introduced a new code of laws for Bulgaria, more suitable for a now sedentary people than the tribal law of steppe nomads; this code may have been recorded in Greek. But in religious matters Krum was scarcely disposed to listen to the Greeks: he offered all Christian prisoners-of-war the alternatives of apostasy or death. No Greek was likely at this time to contemplate evangelisation of Bulgarians; the great barbarian war-leader who had brought Byzantine arms so low was an object of execration throughout the Empire.[7]

Omurtag (c. 814–c. 831) had the wisdom to conclude a peace of thirty years on his accession.[a] The new southern frontier with the Empire was heavily fortified—the 'Great Fence'. Persecutions of Christians continued. Several bishops were martyred, including Manuel, Bishop of Adrianople, who had been deported to Bulgaria when Krum took that city.[8]

Prisoners were forced to eat meat in Lent or suffer for their faith.[9] The Byzantine authorities hastened to redeem as many as possible. These, it is curious to note, included the parents of the future Emperor Basil I (867–86); Basil himself was apparently born in Bulgaria.[10] But it is permissible to suppose that the little we know of the treatment of Christians in Bulgaria under Krum and Omurtag is coloured by Byzantine hysteria. Both rulers may have been personally as tolerant as circumstances permitted.

In the generation of Omurtag's sons the Bulgar element was rapidly losing its identity in the Slav though the process was scarcely complete before the end of the ninth century. Two of Omurtag's sons adopted Christianity,[11] of whom one lost his life in a persecution on the accession

[a] Among Omurtag's surviving Greek inscriptions are two on columns, the one later incorporated in the Church of the Forty Martyrs at Tŭrnovo (built by John Asen II in 1230), telling of his glorious martial exploits and his new palace by the Danube; the other, now in the Sofia Archaeological Museum, recording the provisions of the treaty with the Empire.

of a third son, Malamir, in 831 or 832. This may have been, however, the normal Turkish elimination of rival claimants; Malamir appears as relatively tolerant throughout his reign, though not himself a Christian.

The 830s were thus still a period of very tentative adoption of Byzantine ways and a reserved attitude towards the Byzantine religion—more so on the part of the Bulgars than of the Slavs. An inscription found near Philippi in Greek Macedonia, dating from the reign of Presjan,[12] still uses the words *Bulgar* and *Christian* as opposites: a *Christian* meant a Greek.[a] The adoption of Christianity must not be politically and socially disadvantageous. This was the problem before the exceptionally capable ruler who succeeded in 852—Boris.[b] He saw that it was time to bring Bulgaria into the comity of Christendom; a proportion of his subjects, Greek and Slav, was already Christian. The Bulgar language was now virtually extinct; Bulgaria was a Slav state. In comparison with Rastislav of Moravia contiguity with the Byzantine Empire and the persistent infiltration of Greeks and Greek ways inevitably gave Boris's religious policy a far greater political content. Was it possible to make Bulgaria a Christian state without sacrificing its power and independence? He learnt that the polarity of secular power and spiritual authority invested in king and bishop, and at the highest level in emperor and patriarch, was the correct and only model of a Christian state. Given this, Bulgaria would take its place as a civilised country. But he also knew that all Orthodox dioceses had to belong to one of the Patriarchates, in his case manifestly to that of Constantinople, and that the Emperor of Byzantium was held to be the supreme *fidei defensor* of all Orthodox peoples. He was prepared to bargain his entry into the Christian world against some measure of independence for a Bulgarian church. The precise form of Christianity to be adopted was indifferent. There was still also a portion of the Bulgar aristocracy to be reckoned with, opposed to Greek and Christian ways.

His first overtures appear to have been made to Louis the German in 862. The two rulers met at Tulln on the Danube. Louis sought Bulgarian military help against his rebellious son Carloman and his Moravian supporters. Bulgaria had had a common frontier with Moravia since about 825 and contacts with the Franks for some years before that.[13]

---

[a] Cf. p. 246: a century later a similar situation between the Russians of Kiev and Constantinople produced the same usage.

[b] Bulgar *Bogor(is)*, thought to be cognate with Mongolian *bogori* = small. Boris is variously given as the nephew of Malamir (831–6?) or as Presjan's son. Some consider, probably rightly, that Presjan and Malamir are one and the same person, ruling 831–52.

The Franks were likely to remain conveniently distant allies rather than exacting neighbours. Byzantine reaction was swift and sharp. No extension of Frankish influence into Bulgaria could be tolerated; the spheres of influence agreed in 811 must stand. In this ecclesiastical and political needs were at one. The war which ensued in 863/4 ended in Boris's discomfiture. The peace terms imposed the rejection of the Frankish alliance and baptism into the Eastern church, which would undertake the further evangelisation of Bulgaria.[14]

Boris was baptised forthwith by the Patriarch of Constantinople; the Emperor as godfather gave him his own name Michael. This took place in 864 or 865, though there is some disagreement in the sources.[15] Boris's sister Maria may also have played a part: she had spent the greater part of her life in Constantinople and was completely hellenized. Later tradition that Methodios had some part in Boris's baptism can be ruled out: it is not supported by the biographies of Constantine or Methodios. There was also a territorial settlement which finally recognised Bulgaria's foothold south of the Balkan range (therefore called by them Zagorje, in Greek form Ζαγόρα)—a situation going back to Terbel over a century before. Though a concession of weakness on the Byzantine side, with grave consequences for the future, it was no doubt the unavoidable *quid pro quo* for Bulgarian adherence to the Eastern church—the overriding necessity for Constantinople at this difficult moment.[16] Boris had to crush a serious revolt of the remaining conservative Bulgar magnates at home, which nearly cost him his life and throne. But he steadfastly followed the principle of many later Slav rulers in seeing his duty in promoting what he believed to be right for his people.[17] As a Pomeranian chieftain, Vratislav, said: 'nos qui primi et maiores dicimur ac sumus, nostrae dignitati consulamus, tam dignissimae ac sanctissimae rei consentientes, ut populus qui nobis subiectus est nostro possit erudiri exemplo'.[18]

But no sooner had Byzantine clergy gained a foothold in Bulgaria than it became plain to Boris that Constantinople contemplated nothing less than a stranglehold on the new Bulgarian church. A letter sent by Patriarch Photios in 865 made clear what Boris was well aware of—that Bulgarian bishops, all necessarily Greeks, would come under the Patriarch of Constantinople with all the political implications thereof. There was no promise of ecclesiastical autonomy; naturally Bulgaria was still eminently a missionary area. There was no likelihood that Bulgaria would be handled in similar fashion to Moravia; Boris was to be a subservient Byzantine vassal. Consequently, in August 866 Boris made an approach to Pope Nicholas and perhaps again to Regensburg.

Nicholas wanted nothing better than to gain the obedience of Bulgaria. In 860 he had made another unheeded demand to the Emperor for the return of the former *Illyricum occidentale* and Sicily to his jurisdiction. His attention was shortly to be drawn to possibilities in Moravia. The tension between Rome and Constantinople was increased by the proffered prize of Bulgaria. It must be repeated that Boris, like Rastislav, was no doubt personally indifferent to the precise form of Christianity which he adopted. Even the most sincere and intelligent barbarian convert, among whom Boris can be numbered, could have no personal judgment in matters of theology and liturgy. But he is at once confronted with a multitude of practical difficulties in changing over his way of life to that of a Christian. He is unable to distinguish the essential from the inessential in the mass of prescriptions and rules thrust at him. He wants to know, in short, how little of existing customs need be changed; for enforcing change is the dangerous part. In answer to Boris's immediate difficulties of this kind Photios had sent him in 865[19] a long and elaborate disquisition in difficult Greek on the fundamentals of the Christian faith under the title 'On the duties of a prince' (τi $\dot{\epsilon}\sigma\tau i\nu$ $\ddot{\epsilon}\rho\gamma o\nu$ $\ddot{\alpha}\rho\chi o\nu\tau os$). Photios perhaps judged that it was the task of humbler men to deal with the 'trivialities'. Pope Nicholas did not so judge. He was aware of Boris's dissatisfaction. In a detailed reply to a long list of questions from Boris (November 866) the Pope gave his rulings on these things so important to a neophyte.[20] These hundred odd answers, based partly on the instructions of Pope Gregory the Great to St Augustine for his mission to the English, are yet in no sense propaganda in favour of Rome. Greek practices which differ from Roman are not condemned as such, and none of them bear upon doctrine.[21] Nicholas even corrects Boris's misunderstanding of certain Byzantine teachings. Conversely, Photios had not directly attacked Rome at any point in his recondite essay: to eradicate pagan practices and to know the duties and authority of a Christian prince was the burden of his message.[22] Further, the Pope did not attempt to deny existing Byzantine rights: he merely pointed out that if Bulgaria was to come under Roman obedience the appointment of prelates would rest with the Holy See (answer to question no. 73). The granting of a Patriarch is put in its right perspective: all must be done in due order—first bishops, then a prelate of higher rank.[23] Naturally the Roman view is adopted that the order of precedence of the

Patriarchates is Rome, Alexandria, Antioch, Constantinople, Jerusalem (nos. 92 and 93). In the last reply (no. 106) the Pope exhorts Boris to do nothing until he receives a bishop from him. Nicholas sent his replies by the hand of two bishops, Paul of Populonia and Formosus of Porto, with a mission for the conversion of Bulgaria. Louis had meanwhile sent his own mission under Bishop Hermanrich of Passau. The Pope delivered a direct snub to the Frankish church by causing Louis' mission to be expelled from Bulgaria (867).[24] Hermanrich never forgave this slight.[a] The Pope did not envisage the appointment of a Patriarch for Bulgaria; he could not even accede to Boris's wish to retain Formosus as bishop since such translations were not readily granted. It is clear that Boris was convinced that the best policy for his country's future was to extract the maximum of ecclesiastical independence from the offers made to him.

Constantinople had been greatly incensed by all Nicholas's actions, above all by his treatment of Photios and his interference (as it seemed to them) in Bulgaria. A Papal mission sent to Constantinople in spring 867 via Bulgaria was refused further conduct at the Imperial frontier unless the legates unreservedly acknowledged Photios, which of course they could not do. Relations were further exacerbated by the unavoidable raising of a dogmatic disagreement. As long as the addition of *filioque* to the Creed had been a local aberration of the Far West, not formally approved by the Papacy, Constantinople had been content to ignore it. But now Frankish missionaries had imported it into Bulgaria and Pope Nicholas supported it. To preserve an Orthodox Bulgaria Constantinople took the most serious possible step: Pope Nicholas was excommunicated (summer 867).[25] At the same time Louis was conceded the Imperial title in the hope that he could thereby be detached from cooperation with the Pope.

In the last months of 867 all the main actors changed: Basil ousted his protector Michael and at once (3 November) replaced Photios by Ignatios; on 13 November Nicholas I died. One of Pope Hadrian II's early acts was to secure some control of the Moravian mission.[b] But he evidently thought that Papal influence in Bulgaria was secure enough without hastening to implement the appointment of an archbishop.[26] In the early days of his pontificate he was much occupied with scandals in the church in Rome itself. He continued to temporise. Boris became impatient at the tardiness of Rome in dealing with his demands and

---

[a] See p. 69.   [b] See pp. 54 ff.

particularly by the refusal of both Nicholas and Hadrian to countenance the appointment of Formosus, to whom Boris had become greatly attached.[27] The Byzantine authorities took full advantage of this and intimated that a suitable prelate would be granted by them without delay. In 869 Bulgaria swung back again into the Byzantine orbit. A council which sat in Constantinople from October 869 to February 870—the VIIIth Œcumenical Council in Western reckoning—formally placed Bulgaria under the Patriarchate of Constantinople in an extraordinary session on 4 March 870, which the Papal legates refused to accept as valid.[28]

The Pope was able to complain that he had been tricked. Boris requested all Latin missionaries to leave Bulgaria. Ignatios at once appointed Bulgaria's first archbishop[29] with several other bishops and numerous clergy.

It is possible to argue that all Boris's approaches to the West were purely diplomatic—intended to frighten Constantinople into making him this very concession out of fear of losing Bulgaria altogether. This he achieved, and the matter appeared settled, though throughout the 870s Rome tried to regain the lost ground. The rivalry for the obedience of Bulgaria was throughout complicated by the Photian–Ignatian quarrel within the Eastern church in which the Holy See had become deeply involved.[30] The Pope expected Ignatios to abide by the stipulation that his recognition as Patriarch was dependent on his keeping his hands off Bulgaria. Thus after the death of Ignatios (23 October 877) the Pope again tried to make his approval of the reappointment of Photios dependent on Byzantine abandonment of Bulgaria and railed against the perfidy of the Greeks.[31] Indeed a further council held in Constantinople from November 879 to March 880 did concede the return of Bulgaria to Rome and thus end one aspect of the twenty-year-old quarrel. Pope John VIII for his part recognised Photios: Byzantine goodwill was now much needed in order to obtain help against the Moslems in South Italy.[a] The Pope would in future consecrate the Bulgarian archbishop but the Greek clergy were to remain and continue their work.[32] In the

---

[a] See p. 76 note a. It was at this council that Photios ensured that the canons made clear the Eastern rejection of the addition of *filioque* to the Creed (there were to be no further changes whatever in the Creed). John VIII by implication accepted even this, though Rome had not yet made any dogmatic pronouncement on the matter. It was evidently Imperial policy to prevent this new and potentially serious bone of contention interfering with political needs. In S. Italy too the extension of Byzantine power (especially 876–915) was not accompanied by interference with the existing Latin sees subordinate to Rome.

event the arrangement was a dead letter, as the Emperor must have calculated. Boris adhered to the decrees of 870 and the Pope could do nothing. Theodosius of Nin,[a] as special legate from the Pope to Boris in 880, met with a refusal to entertain dependence on Rome. As late as the pontificate of Stephen V (885–91) Rome was still adjuring Boris to respect its rights but was consistently ignored. By then Boris had embraced the idea of a church using the Slav language and was strong enough to pursue his own policy. Most remarkable of all, Formosus, the bishop on whom Boris had placed such hopes in the 60s, occupied the Papal throne from 891 to 896 but apparently now gave up these ineffectual appeals, for no approach by him to Bulgaria is known. The Papacy itself was too weak to maintain the aggressive policy of Nicholas I.

The status accorded to the head of the Bulgarian church in 870 is not made unequivocally clear in Byzantine sources. In 871 Pope Hadrian II used the ambiguous term *antistes*.[33] Byzantine references are to an archbishop and indicate a precedence for the Bulgarian Primate above metropolitans and autocephalous archbishops. This anomaly can be explained by supposing that he was not an autocephalous archbishop but one whose consecration, if not also nomination, was reserved to Constantinople, whereas an autocephalous archbishop was normally elected and installed by his own clergy. The political implications of this are obvious.[34]

Boris's policy must be contrasted with that of Svatopluk in Moravia. The latter was too much under the spell of Latin prestige and too wedded to the economic advantages of the Frankish ecclesiastical system to support Methodios wholeheartedly; he rejected the degree of independence guaranteed by a Slav church directly subordinate to Rome. Boris's tergiversations were designed mainly to protect his independence. He knew that Greek culture was already entrenched in his country. As a matter of course he sent his son Symeon to be educated in Constantinople. In 870 he had won half his battle. Learning of events in Moravia, he began to see the advantage to Bulgaria of a church using the Slav language; it would make for further independence from Constantinople. For since 870 Greek had been the language of the Bulgarian church and of the clergy sent from Constantinople. No wonder then that he received with enthusiasm in 885/6 the Moravian exiles who unexpectedly arrived on the borders of his dominions at Belgrade.[35] It is

[a] See also pp. 76–7, 194

clear that Boris was aware of, less probably in touch with, the Moravian mission and that the Governor of Belgrade was cognisant of Boris's wishes.[36] It is not so clear what the Byzantine reaction to this development was. If Methodios, as seems certain, left competent Slav teachers behind in Constantinople in 882, it would appear that the Byzantine authorities were not by then wholly unfavourable to the use of the Slav liturgical language.[37] But as long as the allegiance of Bulgaria had been at all doubtful they countered Latin with Greek and showed no readiness to ingratiate themselves with the Bulgarians by a concession over language. Photios nowhere suggests that he was in favour of such a thing for Bulgaria (as opposed to Moravia), which in Constantinopolitan eyes was a treacherous country where enemies of the Empire were wont to take refuge. Nor is it surprising that Photios should omit to mention to Boris in his letter of 865[a] the interesting experiment then going on in Moravia: Moravia had been since 863 the Empire's vital ally (formally or not) in keeping Bulgaria and the Franks apart and in reducing the danger of a westward-looking Bulgarian policy in general. Throughout the 870s Bulgarians went to Constantinople to be trained and the Greek missionaries in Bulgaria are not known to have paid serious attention to the Slav language. Only after 880, and particularly after Methodios's visit to the Capital, are there signs of a more liberal attitude in Byzantine ecclesiastical policy. It was now clear that Greek influence was assured and that the educated Bulgarian would automatically learn Greek. The church could be allowed to be bilingual. However there were still strong reasons for neither Constantinople nor Bulgaria embracing wholeheartedly the Glagolitic alphabet as the medium for the Slav texts. Each would prefer an alphabet as like the Greek as possible. Thus if Constantinople was now prepared to acquiesce in the use of the Slav language in the Bulgarian church, it might still refuse to sanction this 'Western' alphabet.[b] Therefore Methodios's pupils and books were probably not put to active use. Moreover Basil died in 886 and his son Leo adopted a more intransigeant policy in Bulgarian affairs, which led to a long period of estrangement and war. Any reluctance on the Byzantine side to permit the Bulgarian church to decide its own path was brushed aside.

Of the traditional 'Seven Teachers' of the Slavs, fathers of the Slav Orthodox church—the *sedmichislennitsi*—four now found acceptance for their ministry in Bulgaria. Cyril and Methodios were dead; of Gorazd we have already collected together the little that can be surmised.[c]

[a] See p. 160. [b] See pp. 38 ff. [c] See pp. 81 ff., 137–8.

Clement, Naum, Laurence (also called Sava) and Angelar were left. Angelar, and probably Laurence also, died shortly after coming to Bulgaria.[38] The tradition now lay in the hands of Clement and Naum. Without this new field of activity in Bulgaria the Slav language church might have been doomed to early extinction.

The sources

1. The *Life of St Clement* in OCS is lost but certainly existed. There are two *Lives* in Greek:

(*a*) The longer *Life* attributed to Archbishop Theophylakt of Ohrid (*fungebatur c.* 1085–*c.* 1109), sometimes known as the *Bulgarian Legend* (*Legenda bulgarica*) and usually dated *c.* 1100, a learned and rhetorical work partly based on the lost *Life*.[39] Most scholars accept Theophylakt's authorship but Snegárov has recently put forward some arguments for doubting this.[40] He prefers to date it to after 1200, perhaps *c.* 1235 when the Patriarchate of Tŭrnovo was created and Ohrid saw itself losing all its glory.[a] Certain passages of the *Life* may be read as a defence of Ohrid and its privileges; others bear upon the polemics between Greeks and Latins. Theophylakt was a prolific writer and many works were loosely attributed to him. But none of them are noticeably Bulgarophile, as the *Life of Clement* is, so the real author may be rather Archbishop Demetrios Khomatianós (*fungebatur c.* 1216–*c.* 1235), who is known to have been a devotee of St Clement and conversant with OCS. The value of the *Life* is variable, containing as it does obvious misconceptions, such as the statement that Methodios personally baptised Boris.[b]

(*b*) The *Short Life*, generally attributed to Demetrios Khomatianós (see p. 183)—also known as the *Ohrid Legend*—of little value, and if Snegarov is right, in fact a still later work.[41] The manuscript is thirteenth or fourteenth century.

2. Two *Offices* of St Clement, one OCS and one Greek.[42] The Greek one was composed at Ohrid probably over a considerable period (eleventh–fourteenth century). The OCS *Office*, of which there is only one manuscript of 1435, couples him with St Panteleimon, the patron of the monastery founded by St Clement at Ohrid, so there is a presumption that it was composed there not long after his death (916), together with the lost *Life*.

3. The *Life of St Naum* (commemorated on 23 December)[43] in OCS shows signs of being a companion to the lost *Life of Clement* by the same author, a disciple of the two saints still working in the area of their ministry. There is a tradition that Bishop Marko[c] commissioned these two *Lives*. The late medieval manuscript was found in the Zográphou monastery on Mt Athos. There is also a Greek *Life* (sometimes referred to as the *Macedonian Legend*) of unknown date and authorship, and another still unpublished.

[a] Thus the venerated relics of St John of Rila were transferred from Ohrid to Tŭrnovo at this time.   [b] See p. 159.   [c] Second Successor of Naum.

Boris was now within sight of his goal. It remained to train a hierarchy for a Bulgarian Slav church. All the early episcopal appointments naturally fell to Greeks; whether the changeover could be effected without further disagreement with the Byzantine authorities remained to be seen. Boris retained Naum at Court. Clement was sent to work in Macedonia. This is not to be interpreted as a disgrace: he was sent with a new civil governor for the province, a Slav Dometa, evidently to ensure proper conditions for his work.[44] He was given property—'three houses in Devol'—and other privileges. Clement was probably a Macedonian by birth and preferred to devote himself to missionary and teaching work among the Macedonian Slavs (the area was almost wholly Slav) rather than to remain attached to the Court, for him too political and too Greek. At most Boris may have felt that it was better to keep the Greek and Slav missionaries somewhat apart and not to risk too strong a reaction on the part of his Greek advisers until the Slav work was well established. The only potential stumbling-block was the use of the Glagolitic alphabet to which Clement loyally adhered.[a]

Boris was a great builder. Among his earliest foundations is to be reckoned the Court Chapel at Pliska. Tradition records that he built seven cathedrals for his new bishoprics.[45] The number seven must, as always, not be taken too literally. Among these can be identified, with variable certainty: the basilica on an island in Lake Prespa;[46] one of the churches at Ohrid,[b] and one at Nesébŭr (Mesembria); the church at Vodocha (near Strumitsa), which would seem therefore to be the cathedral of the see of Bregalnitsa (dateable to c. 886–9); and the church at Cherven, south of Rusé on the Danube.[47] Bulgarian were now, in greater or less degree, such Greek sees as Belgrade or Morava,[c] Dorostol (Drŭstŭr), Serdica (modern Sofia), whose church of the Holy Wisdom still survives,[48] Philippopolis (Plovdiv) and Develt (a short way south of Burgas). The seven bishops from Bulgaria who attended the Council of 879-80 in Constantinople therefore represented the majority, if not the totality, of the episcopacy. Boris's most important monastic foundation was St Panteleimon (Patlejna), on a steep hillside on the opposite bank of the River Ticha from the new royal residence at Preslâv.[d] A fragmentary inscription in Latin from Preslav, which appears to relate to

a See pp. 168 ff.

b A Bishop of Ohrid signed the acts of the Council of Constantinople of 879–80.

c Probably a Byzantine foundation of c. 879–80 and the see of Ἀγάθων Μοράβων, for whom cf. p. 342 n. 243

d See also pp. 170–2

the dedication of a church, is the only witness left to the activities of the Papal mission of the 860s in the sphere of architecture.[49]

The remains of Pliska give rise to many difficulties of interpretation. The small basilica within the palace area can in all probability be ascribed to Boris's reign.[50] The date of the huge basilica outside—some 320 by 96 feet, of which half is a vast *atrium*—is still in dispute.[51] Early excavation reports of Bulgarian savants, followed by several later scholars, too readily assumed that all the monuments belonged to the first creative period of Bulgarian culture in the ninth–tenth centuries. But it has become increasingly clear that old sites destroyed and abandoned in the invasion period were later reoccupied by squatters, eventually to become in some cases important new settlements. Nearby Mádara is a case in point. Originally an Imperial fortress watching the steppes (fifth–sixth centuries), it became a Bulgarian centre in the eighth–ninth centuries, and not merely a fortress but one of the main cult centres, as the famous cliff sculpture—the 'Madara rider'—and the remains of a pagan shrine side by side with Christian edifices bear witness.[52] An inscription on the rock-face which mentions Khan Omurtag and the goddess Tängri suggests that in the first half of the ninth century Madara was the religious and Pliska the political capital. The layout and mere size of Pliska leave little room for doubt that it too was originally a Roman military camp with outer *vallum* and inner stone defences. The drainage and heating systems in the palace area are likewise typically Roman. The place was reoccupied by the Bulgars in the seventh–eighth centuries. Understandably the new inhabitants often used old materials to hand: several stone blocks with Latin inscriptions can be seen in the palace walls. The plan, size and construction of the great basilica are strongly against its being a new foundation of Boris. A basilica of this type would normally be dated not later than the sixth century and this is surely its true age.[53] How far Boris restored it to use is problematical. Within the palace complex itself, the Court Chapel stands not far from what is believed to be a pagan shrine. Somewhat later a small basilica was built to the west of the palace, this time overlying a pagan religious edifice. This basilica is of the dimensions which we should expect for the time and place, in contrast to the great basilica standing isolated some distance away.

By 889 Boris was sufficiently satisfied that Christianity was well and truly established in his realm to take the decision to abdicate and retire to the monastery of his own foundation at Preslav. This proved too sanguine. His eldest son Vladímir aligned himself with that faction in the Bulgarian ruling class which still embraced the lost cause of rejecting everything Greek. Though Vladimir was nominally a Christian there may still have been some diehard anti-Christians among his supporters. He entered into relations with Arnulf of Bavaria who encouraged his anti-Greek policy. Though the crisis was essentially political the Greek hierarchy was inevitably involved. Vladimir imprisoned Archbishop Stephen and allowed other persecutions. Boris still commanded enough authority to come out of his retirement in 893 and depose his son. It was now a question of proving the political ability of Symeon, his younger son, whose devotion to Greek Christian culture was beyond all doubt.

, The year 893 marks the coming of age of the Bulgarian Slav church. At a council summoned by Boris in the autumn of that year he installed Symeon as the new ruler and decreed the official adoption of the Slav language in the church. The capital was now formally transferred from Pliska (near the modern village of Pliskov-Aboba) to Preslav, a better strategic point and less linked with Bulgaria's pagan past.[a] Boris then again withdrew to the contemplative life. He died on 2 May 907.[54]

The work of St Clement in Macedonia continued to be based on the tradition of his masters. Born about 840, he became a pupil of Methodios in his Olympian monastery, and remained one of his closest collaborators. Perhaps Methodios brought him from the Slav province which he governed. It is permissible to suppose that he received the name Clement when accompanying Cyril and Methodios on their mission to Khazaria, at the time of the invention of St Clement's relics at Kherson.[b] One of the Office hymns compares him to Timothy, the closest companion of St Paul. Clement transplanted the Glagolitic alphabet to Macedonia. According to the *Life* some 3,500 pupils passed through his hands in seven years; these gradually extended the area of missionary and pastoral labours. Clement's work remained essentially educational, earning for him, as for his revered masters, the title of 'teacher'. As little knowledge of Greek could be expected in the remoter parts of Macedonia he wrote for his flock many homilies in Slav; also hymns and prayers.[55] Clement was therefore, if traditional ascriptions are correct, the first prolific author of original compositions in Church Slavonic; to him must go a share in the glory of its development as a written language extending beyond close translation of Greek sacred texts. The area of

---

[a] Original form *Prějęslavǔ* (inheritor of glory), corresponding to Russian Пере-
яслав(ль) (cf. p. 280).   [b] See pp. 34–6

Clement's ministry can only be defined approximately. His first centre is given as Devol (Děvol, Greek Διάβολις), south-west of Lake Ohrid, which lay in the region then known as Kutmichevitsa, commonly taken to be roughly the triangle Saloniki–Skopje–Valona. The highway from Durazzo to Saloniki and on to the Imperial City—the *Via Egnatia*—skirted the lake, at that time frequently called Lake Devol.[56]

Symeon elevated Clement to a bishopric soon after his accession in 893. He thus became the first Slav bishop of the Bulgarian church, a matter of great pride to later Bulgarian writers.[57] The precise location of his see remains enigmatic. Its name only appears in an ambiguous adjectival form in the Slav texts, suggesting a place *Velika*, which agrees with some but not all Greek transcriptions.[58] *Velika* occurs nowadays several times in the toponymy of the upper Vardar valley and it would seem that the local Slavs so named the river itself (the 'Great River'). The see is surely to be sought on one of the main lines of communication of Macedonia, plausibly on the River Vardar itself. As Tunicki pointed out, Theophylakt's *Life* implies that the new see was not too far distant from Ohrid, which Clement continued to visit frequently, but that the diocese did not include, or at least was not identical with, the region of his educational labours.[59] A conceivable identification is therefore modern Veles on the Vardar. This would have been a strategic centre suitable for Clement's talents in organising the Slav Bulgarian church against Greek encroachments from Saloniki. Boris had appreciated this fact in creating the see of Bregalnitsa, not far east of Veles. Velika is obviously in Macedonia. The view still occasionally advanced that it is not to be sought in the Balkans but represents an inaccurate reminiscence of Great Moravia[a] or its alleged capital Velegrad (Velihrad) may be dismissed. That Clement was promoted bishop by Methodios himself rests on a passage in the unreliable *Short Life*[60] and finds no confirmation elsewhere. Indeed it agrees neither with what we know of Methodios's later years nor with the established fact that Symeon made Clement a bishop; he would not have ignored an earlier Methodian consecration.

Clement died on 27 July 916 and was buried in his own monastic foundation of St Panteleimon at Ohrid. A fresco in the church of the Holy Wisdom at Ohrid shows him standing next to St Cyril. The work belongs to Archbishop Leo's improvements in the middle of the eleventh century and can lay no claim to being a likeness.[61] It is now beyond reasonable doubt that Clement was the builder of the original

[a] See p. 326 n. 49

church of the Holy Virgin (Bogoróditsa) at Ohrid, now known as St Clement's. This church probably enshrined his relics for a time. The extant inscription recording Clement's death is however not contemporary.[62] Clement's St Panteleimon can scarcely be other than the church now revealed under the Imaret Mosque.[63] Theophylakt's *Life* notes that he founded two churches at Ohrid 'much smaller than the cathedral'. The inspiration of these 'round' churches—frequently of trefoil (triconchal) plan—in the Ohrid region and elsewhere in the Balkans is to be found in the numerous fourth–sixth century Byzantine baptisteries and martyria.[64]

On Clement's elevation to a bishopric, with power to ordain the priests whom he had trained for the Slav church, Naum took over his educational work in Macedonia. He had remained in the capital during the years 886–93, engaged perhaps more in learned work in the circle of Boris's son Symeon than in evangelisation. Little has been handed down of his activities and no extant writings are ascribed to him.[a] He founded a monastery at Devol and another on Lake Prespa. He retired into monastic life in 900 and died on 23 December 910. The monastery of St Naum, at the south end of Lake Ohrid, was dedicated to him and his relics were transferred there at an early date.[65] It became a notable centre of spiritual healing—and remained such for a millenium until within living memory.

Invaluable though the contribution of the Macedonians was, from 893 Preslav became not merely the civil capital but also the main centre of Bulgarian culture. Yet Symeon was not the man of vision that his father had been. Born about the time of Boris's baptism, he was educated in Constantinople and knew Byzantine strength and weakness from the inside. Indeed he was sometimes sarcastically called the 'half-Greek' ($\dot{\eta}\mu\acute{\iota}\alpha\rho\gamma os$):[66] ability to speak Greek, not blood, made one a Greek. Such was the influx of things Greek into Bulgaria from 864 that he must have gone to the City (*c.* 878) already proficient in the language. He attended the academy in the Magnaura Palace. Liutprand of Cremona confirms that Symeon studied Aristotle and other classical authors, therefore profane learning ($\dot{\eta}$ ἔξω σοφία).[67] But his father appears to have destined this younger son for an ecclesiastical career, that is, as a future Archbishop or Patriarch of Bulgaria. In Constantinople Symeon underwent the novitiate. His subsequent career does not suggest that he had a vocation for the Church; his association with the Patlejna monastery at

[a] See also pp. 76 ff.

Preslav, where he probably lived until he was called to the throne, suggests rather a patron of letters and the other arts.

Though Boris's court at Pliska was already on the way to adopting Byzantine manners, from 893 Symeon completed this Byzantinisation on an even greater scale at Preslav, now laid out as a great new walled city.[68] The place had been of some importance since the early ninth century when Omurtag made a military camp there but the fine buildings all date from after 893—churches, monasteries, hospitals. Recent investigation has shown that this Bulgarian town was, unlike Pliska, on a new site. The palace with its associated church thus raises no problems. It is not absolutely certain whether we can identify the edifice known as the 'Round Church' with the 'Golden Church' mentioned in Old Bulgarian texts as a splendid foundation of Symeon's.[69] As with the great basilica at Pliska, the plan of the Round Church suggests a Byzantine building of not later than Justinian's reign. Would Symeon have ordered the erection of such an archaic structure, recalling the church of SS Sergius and Bacchus in Constantinople or San Vitale at Ravenna? It is however a fact that no single early Slav church in the Balkans was built in the contemporary style of the Imperial capital until after the Byzantine reconquest begun in the 970s. Resources evidently did not as a rule stretch to summoning master-craftsmen from the capital. Local craftsmen therefore copied what was still to be seen, more or less in ruins, about them—that is, churches built before about 500.[70] Armenian, Cappadocian, perhaps Georgian and other monks, to be found in many parts of the Balkans, may have contributed to the adoption of 'provincial' styles. While this is an adequate explanation of this widespread tendency to archaism in the Slav Balkans, we might have expected differently of the Constantinople-educated Symeon. New edifices were so often raised on the ruins of old, more or less mechanically following the original ground-plan that we cannot accept the whole design of the Round Church as certainly the work of Symeon—new in 906/7.[a] Whatever may be the truth about the foundations, the decoration of the church was certainly due to him, in particular the marble facings and ceramic tiles. Such tiles were very unusual in contemporary Byzantine architecture. Together with the carved figures of animals and some other decorative features, they suggest a specifically Bulgar taste connected

[a] According to a note in an OCS translation of St Athanasius's *Sermons against the Arians* made by the monk Theodore (Todor Doksov—see p. 300), preserved however only in a very late Russian copy.

with the art of the steppes and thence with Persia and Central Asia.[71] The *graffiti*, mainly on the walls of the narthex, are of the greatest importance.[a] Their wording and a few legible dates allow no room for doubt that they were made between 893 and 927. One of these inscriptions[72] is part of a text recording, in all probability, Boris's installation of his son Symeon as ruler in 893. But they are naturally not incontrovertible evidence of the date of the walls themselves, whether made on old or fresh plaster—a point on which the experts are still in disagreement. The atrium at the west end is likely to have been an addition of Symeon's. A large atrium is characteristic of many early Christian churches and for the same reason of churches built many centuries later in newly Christianised lands. It was in the atrium that the unbaptised and those undergoing penance or excommunicate, not admitted to the church proper, and the catechumens, not permitted to be present throughout the whole liturgy,[b] could participate at a distance in the mysteries of the faith. Structures recently brought to light to the south of the church may also prove to be monastic buildings associated with it. The style of the Patlejna monastery (St Panteleimon), about a mile to the east beyond the river, is more typically Byzantine.[73]

John the Exarch gives a lyrical description of the glories of this Bulgarian capital.[74] Bulgaria reached under Symeon a never to be recaptured peak of wealth and power. Symeon was the first but far from the last Slav ruler to imagine himself on the throne of the Emperor—the only true emperor appointed by God—in Constantinople.

From the time of his accession war with the Empire became the normal state of affairs and warlike operations tended almost uniformly to Bulgaria's advantage. His southern frontier soon reached within striking distance of Saloniki.[c] For the political unification of all the Balkan Slavs under Bulgaria was the obvious first step in his ambition to attain Imperial power. After the extraction of favourable peace terms in 897 and again in 913 (following a dangerous attack on the City itself when the Byzantine authorities refused to pay the yearly blackmail for Symeon's quiescence), success seemed within his grasp. The Patriarch Nicholas Mystikós, Regent for Constantine VII, whose legitimacy and

[a] See also p. 41

[b] The catechumens (or learners) are dismissed by the deacon at the end of the Liturgy of the Word (Synaxis) and before the commencement of the Eucharist proper.

[c] A frontier marker of 904, only some 20 kilometres north of Saloniki, has been found with the inscription ὅρος Βουλγάρων καὶ Ῥωμαίων ἐπὶ Συμεὼν ἐκ Θεοῦ ἄρχοντος Βουλγάρων.

therefore claim to Imperial status was debatable even in many Byzantine eyes, acceded to the betrothal of Symeon's daughter to the young Emperor. Symeon might not rule in person but he would at least expect to dominate his son-in-law. But the Empress Zoe soon imposed her veto on the proposal. Though Symeon won another imposing victory in 917, Romanós Lecapenós put new heart into Byzantine resistance, made himself co-emperor and married his own daughter Helen to Constantine (919–20).[a] The negotiations of 913 had brought Symeon the style of Emperor and Autocrat of the Bulgars ($\beta\alpha\sigma\iota\lambda\epsilon\grave{\upsilon}\varsigma$ $\kappa\alpha\grave{\iota}$ $\alpha\grave{\upsilon}\tau\circ\kappa\rho\acute{\alpha}\tau\omega\rho$ $\tau\hat{\omega}\nu$ $Bo\upsilon\lambda\gamma\acute{\alpha}\rho\omega\nu$), recognised at a coronation ceremony performed by the Patriarch of Constantinople.[75]

By 920 his hopes of accession to the Imperial throne were slipping away. Further campaigns, which did not spare Christian churches and monasteries, gave him control of most of the Balkans and brought him to the gates of Constantinople in 922 and again in 924.[76] The Emperor continued to recognise him as basileus—in Slav, *tsar*—and therefore as a brother but nothing more.

The status of the head of the Bulgarian church thus remained equivocal. Symeon needed a Patriarch to match his assumed Imperial status, in due Byzantine form. It is probable that he made a unilateral declaration to this effect in 917 or 919, but Constantinople could not be expected to recognise this elevation, nor indeed that of succeeding patriarchs during the remainder of Symeon's reign.[b] After 924 he even styled himself Emperor of the Bulgars and Greeks ($\beta\alpha\sigma\iota\lambda\epsilon\grave{\upsilon}\varsigma$ $\tau\hat{\omega}\nu$ $Bo\upsilon\lambda\gamma\acute{\alpha}\rho\omega\nu$ $\kappa\alpha\grave{\iota}$ $`P\omega\mu\alpha\acute{\iota}\omega\nu$), as the realisation of his ambition receded. Symeon died suddenly on 27 May 927.[77] Recognition of the Bulgarian Patriarchate was only conceded by Constantinople in the general settlement on the accession of Peter when he also received the title of *basileus* (927), or at the time of his marriage to a granddaughter of Lecapenos, Maria, which took place shortly after (not later than 932). He was recognised as a 'son' in Byzantine diplomatic hierarchy.[c]

Thus Byzantine pride was saved. Peter, still a minor, came under the Imperial wing (the reverse of the situation attempted by Symeon) and

[a] A side-effect of the running sore of the Bulgarian menace was thus the strengthening of Imperial autocracy in the person of a succession of soldier emperors, from Romanos to John Tzimiskes, nipping in the bud the possibility of a greater political role for the Patriarchate, which Nicholas had momentarily achieved.

[b] As many as five are quoted—John, Leontij, Dimitrij, Sergij, Grigorij—but the list is unsubstantiated in reliable sources. It is quite probable that the first patriarch did not assume office until 926, a mere year before Symeon's death.

[c] See p. 373 n. 78.

could be granted a patriarch whose independence was not likely to be troublesome. At the same time the Bulgarian ambassador to Constantinople was given precedence over all others.[78] With Bulgaria at its greatest extension, the patriarchate included many Greek sees, especially in Thrace and the west Balkans.[79]

Meanwhile the mustard-seed of the Slav church which Boris had sown grew into a great tree. The council held in autumn 893, it is believed, not only decreed the general use of the Slav language in the church but also made the perfected Cyrillic alphabet official. The adaptations would have been decided during the previous half-dozen years after the arrival of Clement and Naum. The prime mover was surely Symeon himself, with his fresh Greek learning, to whom the Glagolitic alphabet must have been unattractive. If Constantinople had any further thoughts of preventing the use of the Slav language in the Bulgarian church, she had now to abandon them; forced hellenization now ceased until the collapse of Bulgarian independence at the end of the tenth century. The official declaration on alphabets is deduced indirectly from the statement in several Russian annals that the *prěloženije knigŭ* took place thirty years after the conversion of Bulgaria, taken as 863;[80] the phrase is perhaps best translated 'transliteration of the texts'. East Bulgaria with the two capitals, which politically and intellectually had so far taken the lead over the wilder West, was more penetrated by Greek culture and had long been in the habit of using the Greek alphabet; it did not take kindly to the Glagolitic script brought by Clement and his companions. It was of course learnt and used there but the decision of 893, which also took into account the need for the hellenized Cyrillic alphabet as the normal secular and administrative script, thus making as little change in existing habits as possible, created a division between East Bulgaria and Macedonia which was not entirely effaced for several centuries thereafter. Clement out of devotion to his masters developed his educational and literary activities in Macedonia on the basis of the Glagolitic alphabet and the language of the translations of Constantine and Methodios. In his hands Church Slavonic reached a relatively stable artificial norm returning to or confirming its original Macedonian character. But the dialects of East and West Bulgaria (including Macedonia) were certainly no more identical then than they are today.[a] Preslav set about imposing its own East Bulgarian

[a] The modern Macedonian language (lately elevated to separate written and literary status) is a later development, born of the overlay of Serbian dialect on Bulgarian.

norm on the ecclesiastical language. The sacred texts were all transcribed into Cyrillic and at the same time revised in language, removing words and forms which were too Macedonian or too Moravian to be readily acceptable in the East. Without being in any sense condemned or proscribed, Glagolitic gradually came to be felt as a provincial survival. The position of the priest Constantine is in all this difficult to define. As almost certainly a disciple of Methodios,[81] though not numbered among the Seven, he must have been an important voice at the council of 893. By 906 at latest he had been promoted Bishop of Preslav, that is, court bishop; perhaps this took place in 893 at the same time as the promotion of Clement. His attitude to the schism of the alphabets is not clear. His own training was of course Glagolitic, as the *Acrostic Prayer* (*Azbuchnaja molitva*), attributed to him with a high degree of probability, bears witness.[a] While admitting the excellence, indeed the Divine inspiration, of St Cyril's alphabet, the *literati* of Preslav could not but feel that it would be a barrier to the further assimilation of Greek culture.

It must also be clearly recognised that the Bulgarian church was from 893 Orthodox in all respects, using exclusively Greek liturgies and other services. If Clement used a liturgy of St Peter in Macedonia, in deference to Moravian practice, no evidence thereof survives. The preservation of such a text on Athos[b] is at best a very indirect pointer. It is much more probable, as we have seen, that the *Kiev missal* (and no doubt other Western texts now lost) indicates not so much a general as a rather special and local usage which SS Cyril and Methodios freely conceded to some Central European Slavs, whereas they themselves translated and normally used Byzantine liturgies and other services from the very beginning of their Moravian mission. Clement's work may be safely assumed to have followed in the main the usages of the Eastern church. Moreover the work of translation had still be to completed. According to Theophylakt's *Life of Clement* the saint finished the translation of the *Triodion* shortly before his death (916).[82] The *Triodion* contains the Byzantine offices for the period Lent–Pentecost, during which the Canons—or hymns—on Lenten weekdays consist of only three odes instead of the normal nine. Whether the translation of the *Triodion* was entirely Clement's work—either because it had never been done or because the first translation was lost in Moravia—or was merely completed by him, cannot be established. A reference in the *Russian Primary Chronicle* suggests that the *Oktoikh*, the complementary service-book

[a] See pp. 177–8   [b] See pp. 61–2

for the rest of the year, had already been translated in Moravia.[a] And the use of the *Oktoikh* and *Triodion* implies of course the use of the Orthodox Liturgy. Only the Glagolitic alphabet was linked with the West and this was rejected in 893 for official Bulgarian use.

The work of the 'Preslav School', under Symeon's personal patronage, not only set the character of the Bulgarian church once and for all as an Orthodox church of Slav language: it further enlarged Old Church Slavonic as a literary language. While Clement, as far as we know, composed original works of strictly religious content only, the capital could embrace new genres of Christian literature. Many new sacred texts were translated,[b] but now also Greek works of learning, particularly history. What Bulgaria needed was still typically the 'world chronicle' which carried on the history of the Bible into modern times, thereby showing the continuity of God's operation in the world down to and including the Byzantine Empire. Such was the *Chronicle* ($X\rho o\nu o\gamma\rho\alpha\phi\iota\alpha$) of John Malálas, which goes down to the reign of Justin II, translated in the tenth, possibly only in the eleventh century. And there are other similar compilations.[83] Here too we may note Symeon's *Encyclopaedia* (*Izbornik*), a choice of extracts from Greek theological, historical and other learned works covering the essentials of Christian education and life. Made about the year 900, this only survives in a Russian copy made for Svjatoslav in 1073.[c] It was prefaced by an encomium of Symeon in verse.

The main work of this group of authors no doubt falls after 893. How far it already existed in Boris's later years is difficult to answer. Symeon's return to Bulgaria in the 880s is a likely enough moment for new departures. But it may be that little was achieved during the disturbed years of Vladimir's rule (889–93) and before the dispute over alphabets had been settled.

The following authors (with works confidently ascribed to them) are known by name:

1. John the Exarch.[84] Assumed to be a Bulgarian, since his command of Greek is by no means perfect, he may have been born as late as

---

[a] See also p. 79. The reference is in the material of Western provenance s.a. 898.

[b] The treatment of existing texts in some cases went far beyond revision: the East Bulgarian Psalter is virtually a new translation, mainly following Theodoret in the Commentary. At least parts of the O.T. were newly done by order of Symeon (after the loss of Methodios's version), who not unnaturally favoured the texts current in Constantinople when he studied there.

[c] See p. 293. Byzantine models were such works as the Emperor Constantine's *Excerpta de legationibus* and Patriarch Photios's *Myriobiblon*.

890.[a] His notable translations are two treatises and many sermons of St John Damascene. His version of St Basil the Great's *Hexaemeron*[85] is rather an adaptation with additional matter, probably made *c.* 915. Both the *Hexaemeron* and the treatises of St John have adulatory addresses to Symeon in their Prefaces. The Preface to the *Nebesá*, that is St John's *Exposition of the True Faith*,[86] resumes what was then known about the early Cyrillomethodian translations.

2. The monk (*chernorizets*) Hrabr. His *Essay on the Slav alphabet*, variously entitled in different copies,[87] is vital for an understanding of the position at the end of the ninth century. He shows acquaintance with Greek grammatical and literary scholarship and demonstrates that the Slav alphabet is as well designed for the Slav language as the Greek is for Greek. The arguments are aimed at Greek pride: Greek is not such an ancient language as Syriac, which was Adam's tongue; the Greeks did not invent their own alphabet but adapted the Phoenician. Hrabr magnifies St Cyril's achievement in designing a wholly new alphabet (therefore the Glagolitic)[b] for the Slavs, who, as the saint consistently maintained, have a right to a sacred tongue and script of their own. 'For it is easier,' says Hrabr, 'to build on others' work than to create from scratch.'[88] Such arguments are evidently addressed to Bulgarians conversant with Greek who found the Glagolitic too troublesome and obscure. That the author, whose pseudonym is no genuine monastic name, was either one of the early companions of Cyril and Methodios or prompted by one of them is sufficiently clear.[89] Naum has been suggested and, with less probability, Boris's brother Doks.[c] The work must date from about 893 when the question of alphabets was being actively discussed. The author knows the *Vita Constantini* and writes of the 'chief disciple', that is Clement, as still alive.

3. Constantine the Priest, later Bishop of Preslav. He was the compiler and translator of a Gospel commentary based on St Chrysostom, St Cyril of Alexandria and St Isidore, written about 893/4. Three manuscripts of the thirteenth–fourteenth centuries are extant.[90] The *Acrostic*

[a] So little is known about John that there are widely different estimates of his dates. Another view maintains that he was born nearer the middle of the ninth century and spent some time in Constantinople in the 870s. The ostensible reference to Methodios as still alive in the Preface to his *Nebesa* is scarcely conclusive.

[b] The alphabet is not named but the argument surely requires the Glagolitic in all other respects. The work may have been revised when Glagolitic went out of use in East Bulgaria. See pp. 38ff.

[c] It has been suggested that Doks represents δόξα, which might be loosely rendered *hrabrŭ* in Slav.

Prayer[a] would appear to be his Preface to this work, following fairly closely the matter and manner of St Cyril's verse Preface to his translation of the Gospels.[b] It may therefore also be dated *c.* 894. There are at least eight Cyrillic manuscripts of the poem, dating from the twelfth–thirteenth centuries onwards, and showing clear signs of adaptation from a Glagolitic original.[c] Two of the manuscripts of the Gospel commentary also contain a description of the hierarchical organisation and services of the church—a free adaptation of a Greek original—which is likely to be Constantine's work too; there was need for such an essay in the still only imperfectly Christian Bulgaria of the 890s.

Constantine's *Outline of History* (*Istorikii vŭkratŭcě*), based on the Χρονογραφία σύντομος of Patriarch Nikephoros, also dates from the 890s.[91]

In 906/7 Constantine made a translation at Symeon's command of St Athanasius's *Tracts against the Arians*, of which only later Russian copies are extant. Though the Arian heresy was a thing of the past other heresies were becoming troublesome in Bulgaria against which these polemics could be useful, as witness the work of

4. Cosmas the Priest, whose *Treatise against the Bogomils*[d] is to be dated *c.* 969–72.[92]

5. Gregory the Priest, alleged translator of parts of the Old Testament and of John Malálas's *Chronicle*.[e]

To the above must be added Tsar Symeon himself who appears to have made or helped to make the *Zlatostruj*, being the Slav translation of selected sermons of St John Chrysostom. There are two manuscript traditions of this very popular compilation;[93] we cannot say which is closer to Symeon's version.

Many remain anonymous to us. Other valued devotional works translated at an early date were: the *Ladder to Paradise* (Κλῖμαξ θείας ἀνόδου) of St John Climacus—a fundamental treatise on the monastic life, the *Spiritual Meadow* of John Moschos (the *Sinai Paterik*) and works of St Ephraim the Syrian. More secular were the *Physiologos* (though it contains much moral symbolism) and the geographical work of Cosmas Indicopleustes.[94] It should be noted, however, that despite Symeon's alleged enthusiasm as a young man for the pagan Classics, there is no sign of their translation side by side with Christian literature. They could fulfil no spiritual need in a country of such young civilisation.

---

[a] See p. 335 n. 65　　　　　　　　　[b] See p. 57 no. 5
[c] E.g. ll. 12 and 26 represent Glagolitic letters unknown to the Cyrillic alphabet.
[d] See below, pp. 227ff.　　　　　　　[e] See p. 176.

The Classical Renaissance so conspicuous in Byzantine culture during the century from Photios to the scholar-emperor Constantine Porphyrogennetos left practically no mark on the emergent Slav peoples.[a] This humanism was the preserve of an exclusive Byzantine administrative class (and thus somewhat parallel to our Classical education of the eighteenth–nineteenth centuries), into which barbarians did not easily gain admission. The Slavs were adopting Christianity in the only proper way—in all its aspects simultaneously: as theology, as ritual, in all its associated arts. But since they now had their own liturgical language, Greek was primarily a source of Christian knowledge, far less a medium of knowledge in general. Moreover the Christian works of doctrine and spirituality which urgently demanded translation were the fundamental expositions written by the Fathers of the fourth–sixth centuries. More recent elaborations were of less immediate value: even the works of St John Damascene were for them relatively modern.

The decline of Bulgaria was as rapid as its rise. With the accession of the unwarlike Peter (927), high in dignity as an acknowledged *basileus* but without Symeon's authority, Constantinople regained the initiative and henceforward never made any secret of her determination to destroy Bulgarian power. A tame province, not a rival, was the most she could tolerate in the North Balkans. This thorn in her flesh, which had been her undoing, had been there long enough. As early as 931 Serbia and parts of Macedonia passed under Byzantine suzerainty. A few years later Bulgaria was subjected to severe attacks by the Magyars, who had already shorn the state of all its dependencies north of the Danube when they settled in Transylvania and the Alföld. Nikephoros Phokas was unwise enough in 965, when Peter's Byzantine empress Maria-Irene died, to refuse Bulgaria its annual 'tribute' and thereby reawaken quiescent hostility. Byzantine diplomacy then brought the Prince of Kiev's Russians into play. In 966/7 Svjatosláv of Kiev, receiving an inducement of 1,800 pounds of gold, started an invasion of Bulgaria from the north and took Preslav. What little cohesion the Bulgarian state still had disappeared on the death of Tsar Peter on 29 January 969. The general who ascended the Imperial throne in December of the same year, John Tzimiskés, embarked on the conquest of Bulgaria from the south. He also found it necessary to put an end to Russian conquests from the north which were proving far too successful for what Constantinople had envisaged as the contribution of a useful but minor ally.[95]

[a] Cf. pp. 293–4.

Preslav was snatched from the Russians and their forces finally defeated before Dorystolon (Dorostol) in July 971. By the end of the year Peter's successor, Boris II, had abdicated and all East Bulgaria was in Byzantine hands. The Byzantine authorities formally abolished the Bulgarian patriarchate and reunited the conquered territories to the Patriarchate of Constantinople. A Greek Metropolitan was installed at Dorostol, where the Bulgarian Patriarch had apparently resided for most of Peter's reign.[a] Patriarch Damian (*fungebatur ab* 945) now migrated with the centre of political resistance by stages into Macedonia.

Resistance to incorporation in the Byzantine Empire was organised by the sons of a renegade Armenian officer, Nicholas. Hence they are known as the Komitópouloi.[b] Tzimiskes had had to withdraw his troops hurriedly from Bulgaria without completing the conquest of the whole country in order to meet an Arab menace in the East. On his death in January 976 Byzantine hold on East Bulgaria further relaxed. By summer of that year Samuel, the most vigorous of the brothers, had regained nominal control of a considerable area. The Byzantine conquest had to be started all over again by Basil II.[96]

Basil's first important campaign took place in 986. His main opponent was Samuel who managed to eliminate his brothers in the years 986/7.[c] The civil war in Asia Minor which required Basil's full personal attention and Russian help,[d] again put a temporary halt to campaigns in Bulgaria until 991. Samuel was thus able to consolidate his position in Macedonia, take Dyrrachium, and embark on conquests in Thessaly on his own account.

The Komitopouloi had taken the expelled head of the church under their wing. The wandering 'patriarchate' moved from the Danube via Sofia into remoter Macedonia, reaching Lake Prespa about 976. The lake island of St Achilles became Samuel's capital for the next twenty years. The existing basilica was rededicated to this saint when his relics

[a] Perhaps from the time of its recognition by Constantinople about 927. See p. 173 above.

[b] The names of the brothers are given as Moses, Aaron, David and Samuel, very rarely used by those who considered themselves Greeks but current in the Transcaucasian Christian states; that of their mother was Ripsime (Armenian Hṛip'simē), a famous Armenian martyr of the third century, and is recorded on a monumental inscription dated 993.

[c] Moses and Aaron should perhaps be discounted as brothers; Yaḥyā of Antioch, more interested in these events than the Greek historians, only mentions two in all. They may have been cousins of the Bulgarian Tsar Roman, whose legitimate position Samuel never defied, only proclaiming himself Tsar on the latter's death.

[d] See p. 258

were deposited there in 983. The patriarchal title appears to have been unofficially readopted about this time.[97] In the 990s Samuel and the Patriarchate moved on to Ohrid, where the most impressive remains of his reign are still to be seen. Samuel proclaimed himself Tsar and his primate Patriarch in 998. But the war of attrition finally went against Samuel. Basil occupied Preslav and Pliska in 1002, Skopje in 1004. By 1018 all Bulgaria was at Basil's mercy and he had earned himself the title of 'the Bulgar-slayer' (*Voulgaroktónos*). Samuel had died soon after his decisive defeat on 29 June 1014; the final collapse came under his nephew John Vladislav.

Byzantine relief was profound.[98] Among other celebrations Basil held a service of thanksgiving in the Parthenon, then an Orthodox cathedral. As soon as the conquest was complete the Patriarchate of Ohrid was demoted to an archbishopric.[a] The Emperor reserved the right to appoint to the see. This was tantamount to restoring the original situation of 870, when Bulgaria received its first autocephalous archbishop; the title also remained unchanged—ἀρχιεπίσκοπος Βουλγαρίας. Autocephaly under Imperial patronage was to blot out the memories of the intervening patriarchate which Constantinople had never loved. At its most extensive the proscribed Bulgarian Patriarchate had embraced not only most of Bulgaria proper but also Serbia, Bosnia, Montenegro, Albania, Epirus and parts of Thessaly—some two dozen sees. The eparchy was thus for a short time at the height of Samuel's power wider than the recognised Bulgarian state had been.[99]

The Byzantine authorities dealt lightly with the Bulgarian church;[100] it was an important factor in their peaceful control of the country in the future. The autocephaly granted to Ohrid meant that the Archbishop could appoint his own bishops; the Patriarch of Constantinople did not interfere in this or indeed in any internal affairs. Greek became the administrative language of Bulgaria. But though the Archbishop and many of the bishops were thenceforward Greeks, the lower hierarchy of the church remained, as far as can be told, predominantly Slav. It would be misleading to say that the Slav church was persecuted. Yet there was certainly as time went on considerable destruction of Slav service-books and much local and unofficial hellenization. Ohrid itself is a typical case: no Slav manuscripts have survived there of earlier date than Tsar Dušan

---

[a] Ohrid was besieged by Basil in 1015 but probably only taken in 1018. The administrative capital of Byzantine Macedonia was however fixed at Skopje, where the Governor (ὁ κατεπάνω Βουλγαρίας) resided.

(mid-fourteenth century) whereas there are many Greek ones of all ages. Some deliberate destruction by the Greeks, whether in war or peace, is beyond doubt.[101] Perhaps their intensified attack on the Bogomil heresy[a] was partly responsible: all Slav manuscripts looked alike to them; it is less trouble to destroy everything than to pick out the heretical works. The earliest extant Balkan manuscripts in Church Slavonic date however from the period of troubles. Of those written in the Macedonian region the *Codices Zographensis, Marianus* and *Assemanianus* probably date from before the complete conquest of Samuel's state.[b] All three must owe their preservation to having been taken to Athos, with which Macedonia was always in close touch. Two others preserved in St Catharine's Monastery on Mount Sinai (no doubt reaching there via Athos)— the *Sinai Psalter* and *Euchologium*—also date from the eleventh century but a more precise date and provenance cannot be given. The Cyrillic *Savvina Kniga* is an East Bulgarian manuscript of the eleventh century, no doubt of Preslav, which continued to thrive under a Greek governor. But the production of Slav texts could not be expected to revive until the period of new Bulgarian and Serbian independence in the 1180s.

There is no sign of the removal of bishops by the Greek authorities even in the period immediately following the conquest. Though a new archbishop, John of Debar, was appointed to Ohrid in 1018, he was a Slav and occupied the see until his death in 1036/7. Indeed Basil, when ordering church affairs in 1018/19, retained under Ohrid some of the wholly non-Bulgarian dioceses which might more naturally have been re-attached to Saloniki or some other Greek metropolis. In 1020 Ohrid in fact received an addition of ten sees and three more a few years later.[102]

Among the outstanding incumbents of the see of Ohrid may be mentioned:

1. Leo (*fungebatur* 1037–56), appointed from the Church of the Holy Wisdom in Constantinople on the death of John of Debar—an outstanding patron to whom are due the exquisite frescoes in the Church of the Holy Wisdom at Ohrid.[103] In humbler form the church had probably been Samuel's cathedral. The eleventh century frescoes were only the first of many splendid works painted by Byzantine artists (with or with-

[a] See pp. 229–30.

[b] For the manuscripts see p. 64. *Ass.* is particularly clearly a product of the Ohrid area since the appended Menology is rich in Macedonian saints—Clement, Naum and various saints of Saloniki specially honoured in those parts.

out local Slav assistants) in Macedonia, now that it was reincorporated in the Empire.[a]

2. Theophylakt (*fungebatur c.* 1085–*c.* 1109),[104] reputed author of the important Greek *Life of St Clement*.[b] Ohrid became a natural mixing-place of Greek and Slav in the Church, just as Macedonia as a whole was notorious for its mixed population. Greek prelates of Ohrid defended their autocephaly by championing—up to a point—the Slav element in the archdiocese. To promote the cult of St Clement was part of this policy. Theophylakt, pupil of the great humanist Psellos, who felt himself, like Ovid at Tomi, an exile among barbarians, is typical of this attitude of condescending approval.

3. Demetrios Khomatianós (*fungebatur c.* 1217–35), a noted canonist and further promoter of the cult of St Clement.[c]

The Byzantinisation of Bulgaria and Macedonia went deep in the eleventh and twelfth centuries. Several Athonite monasteries became considerable landowners in Macedonia. This helped to establish the important cultural link between Athos and the later Serbian state.[d] Influences from the shores of the Adriatic, however, also penetrated without difficulty into the interior. There is a clear Western element in the decoration of most of the great Macedonian Glagolitic codices of the late tenth or early eleventh centuries, especially of *Codex Assemanianus*.[105] On the other hand Ohrid as the centre of Clement's Macedonian ministry based on the Glagolitic alphabet had never given up this use. Under Samuel there may well have been a certain tendency for this Macedonian element to increase in the church. But even if Glagolitic still predominated for sacred texts, Cyrillic was certainly the administrative alphabet, as a commemorative inscription of Samuel himself shows.[106] Knowledge of Glagolitic was propagated, side by side with Cyrillic, to the Orthodox Slavs of Serbia. It is difficult to say when Glagolitic ceased to be actively used in Macedonia, perhaps not till the end of the fourteenth century. It was still read by a few on Athos in that century, especially in the Bulgarian Zográphou monastery.[107] But its use became more and more restricted. The *Bitolj Triodion* of the twelfth century may serve as the type of hybrid text in alternating Glagolitic and Cyrillic; the scribe was evidently equally practised in both alphabets.

[a] It will also be recalled that it was the actions of Leo of Ohrid and the Patriarch Michael Kerularios in banning all Latin rites that precipitated the act of the Papal legates on 16 July 1054, when they laid the Papal excommunication on the altar of the Church of the Holy Wisdom in Constantinople. On the Great Schism see further pp. p. 287   [b] See p. 165.   [c] See also p. 220.   [d] See pp. 218 ff.

During the period 1018 to 1186 the archdiocese of Ohrid was gradually whittled away (Bosnia and Montenegro being lost first) until it became purely the diocese of Macedonia. Macedonia no longer commanded any special prestige. The 'Bulgarian theory' was more and more introduced into texts: St Cyril was a Bulgarian; he had translated the Scriptures 'into Bulgarian'; his first mission had been to the Bulgarians; Boris had been baptised by Methodios.[108] Nobody knew or wished to remember the curious episode of the Moravian mission.

The second half of the eleventh century saw Bulgaria proper at her lowest ebb, with Constantinople itself hard hit by the new Turkish menace in the East and able to do little more than hang on to possession of the country. The Danubian frontier could no longer be held against repeated incursions of Pechenegs, Uz and other barbarians.[109] The economic balance of the Empire was lost: the profits of commerce were passing rapidly into Venetian hands;[a] the value of the Byzantine gold *solidus* (later known as *hyperpyron* and *bezant*) as an international standard fell rapidly after a remarkable stability of over 500 years. By the second half of the twelfth century the Empire was manifestly succumbing to a fatal combination of maladies—loss of Asia Minor to the Seldjuk Turks (especially from 1176) and economic strangulation by the Latins. The Westernising policy of Manuel Komnenós (*regnabat* 1143–80), who twice took a Latin princess to wife, was the outward sign of impotence thinly disguised as far-sighted policy. With his death in September 1180 the Balkan peoples fell to exploiting the defencelessness of the Empire.[b] The leaders of the Third Crusade (1189) were already giving a thought to its dismemberment.

By 1186 it was possible to proclaim the Second Bulgarian Empire in the Church of St Demetrios (Dimitŭr) at Tŭrnovo, which became the capital and primatial see. Bishop Basil adopted the title of autocephalous archbishop, as in the time of Boris.

The creation of a new Bulgarian patriarchate for a new Bulgarian Empire was however not straight-forward. Byzantine political intrigue might support one aspirant to the Bulgarian throne rather than another but this was little more than playing a traditional game which had now passed beyond Byzantine control. Kalojan (1197–1207) saw the best way

---

[a] The concessions made to Venice in 1082 gave her a virtual stranglehold on Byzantine trade except in the Black Sea and certain reserved areas such as Cyprus and Crete. The Doge assumed the style 'Dalmatiae sive Chroatiae dux et imperialis protosevastos', since his fleet alone could ensure free navigation of the Adriatic.

[b] See also pp. 214–15.

of being duly recognised as Emperor of Bulgaria in soliciting a crown from the Holy See: his patriarch would then also be a Roman consecration.[110] The Pope appears to have been under the erroneous impression, based perhaps on a diplomatic embassy to Symeon from Pope John X in 924/5, that previous Bulgarian emperors, particularly Peter, had received that dignity from the Holy See. Kalojan despatched Archbishop Basil of Tŭrnovo to Italy in 1200 to put these matters in train. Faced by the deviation of the Fourth Crusade to Constantinople in early 1203, the usurping Byzantine Emperor Alexios III immediately sought help wherever it might be found and offered Kalojan the desired recognition of his own imperial and his primate's patriarchal titles. But Kalojan continued his negotiations with Rome, convinced no doubt that the Latins had come to stay. He was justified and immediately after the capture of the City in April 1204 proceeded to appropriate such Imperial territories in the North Balkans as he could lay hands on. The Pope's legate finally reached Bulgaria in November 1204. Cardinal-Legate Leo brought Kalojan a royal but not an imperial crown, and invested the archbishop of Tŭrnovo with the title of Primate only. Kalojan ignored the distinctions, called himself *Tsar* and assumed that Primate was the equivalent of Patriarch. Thus Bulgaria came under the protection of Rome.[111] But the weakness of the Latin Emperor Baldwin was as tempting as that of Alexios. In 1205 Kalojan defeated Baldwin and took him prisoner. Perhaps only his own death in October 1207 prevented him from establishing himself in Constantinople. Bulgarian arms thus contributed much to the downfall of the Latins and, though Bulgaria was at times a formidable rival, to putting heart and hope into Greek recovery. For the Greek government at Nicaea revived the Imperial and Patriarchal titles in 1208 and thereafter took its part, with Epirus, as a focus of resistance to the Latin Empire.

But the approach of the Bulgarian church to the Papacy lacked all serious intention. Kalojan's successors did no more than flirt with Rome whenever this was expedient. Nor did expediency counsel a policy of ecclesiastical dependence on Nicaea or Ohrid. The Byzantine rump at Nicaea together with its insecurely based patriarchate never looked likely, until the last moment of its success, to recapture Constantinople.

Kalojan had brought Ohrid under Bulgarian rule again in 1204 but it was lost to Theodore, the Despot of Epirus, in 1217;[112] to Theodore the archbishopric was of great value as the best counterpoise to the Patriarchate at Nicaea.[113] Ivan Asen II (1218–41) repudiated the Roman link in

1232. So great was Asen's part in breaking Theodore's ambitions[a] (though, like Kalojan, Asen himself might well aspire to a restored Imperial throne) that John Vatatzes of Nicaea was not slow to ally his family to that of Asen by marriage and to recognise in 1235 Asen's long-standing assumption of the independence of the Bulgarian Orthodox Church headed by the Archbishop of Tŭrnovo. The still weak Patriarch of Nicaea continued to temporise but a synod held at Gallipoli (Kallipolis), at which the Emperor John Vatatzes and Asen were present, at last approved the re-establishment of the Bulgarian patriarchate. Both the Emperor and the representatives of the Athonite republic insisted at the synod on the independence of Athos from Bulgarian political and ecclesiastical control. That St Sava of Serbia had any part in persuading the Greeks to recognise a Bulgarian patriarchate, as sometimes asserted, is highly improbable.[b] The patriarchal church at Tŭrnovo was built, together with the Imperial palace, on the summit of Tsarevéts Hill, in a great loop of the river gorge, defended by precipices on three sides and a strong wall on the fourth. All was destroyed by the Turks in 1393–6.[114]

The theoretical union of Bulgaria with Rome had lasted some thirty years. Throughout Bulgarian policy had been purely political; the formal union with the Latins counted for virtually nothing. Submission to Rome was all that was required of Greek clergy in the Latin Empire; this made, Orthodox bishops were to remain in office just as before 1204. In theory all the traditional customs of the East were to be left inviolate; in practice there was considerable persecution on the part of the Latins. Greek bishops and other clergy who for conscience' sake would not serve under the Latin hierarchy after 1204 betook themselves not only to the centres of Greek resistance but also to Bulgaria. Asen made a point of being gracious to all Greeks in the Balkans and especially sought the favour of the Athonite monasteries with grants of land and other endowments.[c] Neither Rome nor the Latin Patriarchate at Constantinople could offer him any tangible advantages, even though the Lateran Council of 1215, which re-defined Papal primacy, had purposely made its acceptance as easy as possible.

The political manœuvres of Michael VIII Palaeologos again brought

---

a Theodore proclaimed himself Emperor at Saloniki in 1224 and was crowned by the Archbishop of Ohrid. But his decisive defeat by Asen at the Battle of Klokotnitsa (1230) nullified this. The threat of a peninsular Empire was not wholly removed till 1259, long after Asen's death in 1241.

b See also p. 224.

c Vatopédi, for example, received important gifts immediately after Asen's victory at Klokotnitsa in 1230.

about an uneasy union with Rome for all territories over which he had some ecclesiastical control during the decade 1272–82. But the Orthodoxy of the Bulgarians was staunch enough to reject the kind of compromise later exemplified in the Uniate churches.

After the Turkish conquest of the Balkans the Bulgarian church reverted, with Serbia and Ohrid, to that status which the Empire from the beginning had tried to impose on it—subordination to the Patriarchate of Constantinople. But by then there was no Christian Empire and the Œcumenical Patriarch was head of the Orthodox communities throughout the Ottoman Empire—the *Rūm milleti*—and consequently of far greater authority than at any time when Constantinople was a Christian capital.

CROATIA AND DALMATIA

The movement of the Slavs into the Balkans seriously threatened the Dalmatian coast by about the year 600.[a] In July of that year Pope Gregory I wrote to the Archbishop of Salona: 'de Sclavorum gente quae vobis valde imminet et affligor vehementer et conturbor'.[115] Further attempts to hold the Danube–Sava frontier became futile from the reign of the incapable semi-barbarian Emperor Phocas (602–10). By the accession of Heraklios (614) the situation of Salona and even some of the Dalmatian islands was already desperate; indeed Spalato owed its future importance to refugees from Salona, abandoned in the course of his reign. Further down the coast the inhabitants of Epidauros fled to the more defensible islet of Ragusa.

There is a tradition, better authenticated of the Serbs than the Croats, that these two peoples carried out a migration separate from the general Balkan invasion, invited by Heraklios himself who needed help against the Avars. The centre of dispersion of the Croats was a 'White Croatia' north of the Carpathians—a geographical expression only recorded by Constantine Porphyrogennetos.[116] In course of time both Croats and Serbs became the political nuclei of larger areas in the Balkans, dissolving into the mass of Slav tribes already settled in those parts but imposing their own names.[117]

In these early centuries Croatia may be considered to include the northern half of the Adriatic coast and thence eastwards at least to the River Vrbas and northwards to the River Sava, which was an artery rather than a frontier. The Mesopotamia up to the River Drava was

[a] See pp. 3–6.

known as Pannonian Croatia; most of this was lost to the Magyars in the tenth century.[118]

All these Slavs arrived in the Balkans as pagans. Their descent on Dalmatia is reflected in some Roman churches: Pope John IV (640–2) had a mosaic executed in the chapel of St Venantius (baptistery of St John Lateran) recording the persecution of Christians in Dalmatia. He was himself a Dalmatian and sent agents to redeem Christian captives from the inflowing pagans and to save relics. The latter he deposited in the new chapel.[119] The looting of Dalmatian churches by the Slavs is noted in several sources. By this time they were firmly established along the greater part of the coast; those who settled in the region of the River Néretva (Narentans) were already strong enough in 642 to mount an expedition across the Adriatic to attack the territories of Benevento. The Narentans were peculiar in taking early to the sea and piracy.

The incoming Slavs (often mixed with Avars) were not disposed to destroy, even if they could, the civilised coastal towns. It was to their advantage that they should continue as markets and ports.[120] Many of the towns paid protection money to the new barbarians for immunity from their depredations. Nevertheless such was the disorganisation of the church in Dalmatia, and *a fortiori* in the hinterland, by the seventh century that probably little sustained evangelical work could be then undertaken. The leading ecclesiastical centres on the coast were now Spalato (replacing Salona) and Dyrrachium[a] in the extreme south, the main point of communication with South Italy. The Emperor Constantine was informed that the conversion of the Croats was attempted soon after their arrival in the seventh century: Heraklios had requested the Pope to organise missions, since the whole Dalmatian coast was still in the Papal diocese of Illyricum.[121] No record remains of any such large-scale attempt at their conversion, though the Imperial author alludes to a bishop and even an archbishop sent from Rome. But some sort of work in those parts went on, as would appear from a reference in a Papal letter of 680.[122] As in Greece, this is eminently the case of a gradual process—the slow effect of contact between the various centres of civilisation and Slav tribes, whose political organisation remained for long at a primitive stage. It is noticeable that those Croats who settled within the immediate radiation of the coastal towns, particularly Zadar, Trogir and Split,[b] were civilised and converted comparatively quickly,

---

[a] Italian *Durazzo*, Slav *Drač*, Albanian *Durrës*.   [b] Italian *Zara*, *Traù*, *Spalato*.

whereas the Narentans, who had no large town or bishopric on their coast (between the Rivers Cétina and Neretva), were among the last, perhaps not fully till after 900. The earliest new purely Slav ports probably date from the mid-tenth century, notably Biograd (sometimes referred to as Zara Vecchia), and were in that favourable part of Dalmatian Croatia which the Romance-speaking population had evacuated in the seventh century, taking refuge on the Quarnero islands.[a]

The eighth century remains a dark age. There is an occasional allusion to some individual missionary enterprise, such as the work of a certain Ursus on the Dalmatian coast towards the end of the century.[123] With the loss of Ravenna (751) and Emperor Leo's transference of Sicily, South Italy and the Western parts of the Balkan peninsula to the ecclesiastical jurisdiction of the Patriarchate of Constantinople[b] the whole Dalmatian coast became for a short time a Byzantine responsibility. But Ursus must have come from North Italy or from even farther afield in the Frankish dominions. It was not till the early years of the ninth century that the political scene became sufficiently reshaped for conversion of the barbarians to become a matter of urgency in the policy of all the interested states. The Franks had by then succeeded in extending their political control round the head of the Adriatic after breaking the power of the Avars in the 790s. They had occupied Istria as early as 788 and made their first attack on the Avars from this direction, that is, probably with Croat help. Byzantine interests extended all up and down the Dalmatian coast and embraced Venice. Constantinople attempted also to maintain what control she could over the inland Slavs; in this she was now more and more to find a rival in Bulgaria.[c]

Frankish suzerainty over Pannonian Croatia dates from c. 795, when the Croat chieftain Vojnomir accepted it (being baptised not long after), and over Dalmatian Croatia from c. 803. The Frankish secular authority was the Markgraf of Friuli (*Forum Julii*); the ecclesiastical authority was Aquileia (Cividale).[d] By 811 it had become necessary for the Byzantine

[a] The Dalmatian islands (some 50 large and 500 small) remained for the most part outside Slav settlement until c. 950. On the Croatian coast settlement probably started with Pag. Further south, Hvar, Kórčula, Mljet and Brač (*italice* Lesina, Curzola, Meleda, Brazza) were among the earliest to become Slav, some as Narentan lairs. In particular Hvar was probably, with Brač, ruled by a Slav chieftain as early as the first half of the ninth century. Slav colonies (Narentan?) are even known from the Gargano region across the Adriatic in the tenth–eleventh centuries but they must have rapidly lost their language and identity.

[b] See pp. 54–5.   [c] See pp. 207 ff.

[d] The name Aquileia can be ambiguous. As a result of the Lombard invasion of 568 North-east Italy became ecclesiastically divided between the Byzantine and the Lom-

and Frankish Empires to make a general settlement defining their respective spheres of interest in the North-west Balkans (Treaty of Aix). The dividing-line was drawn at the River Cetina, a short way south of Split. But Constantinople retained a theoretical suzerainty over all the offshore islands and over the coastal settlements from Grado to Venice. Thus both the Pannonian and Dalmatian Croats came more and more under Frankish influence in the ninth century. Borna of the Dalmatian and Ljudevit of the Pannonian Croats (with residence at Sisak) reaffirmed their loyalty to Louis the Pious in 814. Less directly affected by Frankish pressure, Borna remained loyal and even paid homage to Louis in person at Aix in 820. Ljudevit was more troublesome. After his removal about 823, Pannonian Croatia became for many years a bone of contention between the Franks and Bulgars. Its importance as a geographical link between Moravia and Pannonia on the one hand and the North Balkans on the other is clear enough despite lack of information for the rest of the ninth century.[124]

Venice, though scarcely yet ranking as a separate power, was already vitally interested in the free navigation of the Adriatic and paid 'tribute' to the coastal Slavs, particularly the Narentans, to safeguard this.[125] It was paid occasionally till as late as 996. Venice herself continued to be for a long time a Latin–Byzantine hybrid. The same duality was imposed on the life of the Dalmatian ports, especially Zadar and Split, and thence came to affect many coastal Slavs as well. A curious example is afforded

bard (later Frankish) churches. Paulinus of Aquileia took refuge from the Lombards on the lagoon island of Grado (*Aquilegia nova*). A large part of Northern Italy had broken off relations with Rome in the middle of the sixth century (the Schism of the Three Chapters). Grado, still Byzantine throughout the seventh century, ended this schism in 607; the Lombard see of Aquileia (finally located at Cividale) did not. Further, the schism had emboldened Aquileia, supposedly founded and evangelised by St Mark, to call itself a Patriarchate in rivalry to Rome. After the split both Aquileias—Grado and Cividale—used this title. The coastal province of Grado remained of importance to Constantinople; Heraklios presented the see with St Mark's reputed episcopal throne. The bringing of this and other relics to Venice in 829 started the process by which the patronage of St Mark and the patriarchal title (still in use) were transferred to the increasingly important political centre of Venice, finally and permanently in 1156. Meanwhile Cividale (Old Aquileia) became Frankish with the extinction of the Lombard kingdom in 774 and detached Istria, with its leading sees of Trieste, Parenzo and Pola, from Byzantine Grado. When the peninsula passed into Frankish hands (788–98), Grado, and then Venice, continued to dispute this loss but never regained Istria for long. In view of all these fluctuations it is impossible to be certain whether 'Aquileian' clergy working in Istria and Croatian Dalmatia in the ninth century are from Cividale or Grado. But generally speaking Grado was of minor importance and wealth compared with the Frankish see and with Venice, which developed its own bishoprics from the later ninth century. In default of precision Aquileia will be taken to mean Old Aquileia (cf. also pp. 49ff; Dold and Gamber, *Das Sakramentar von Salzburg* (*Texte und Arbeiten* 1/4, Beuron, 1960), pp. 12 ff.).

by the *Evangeliarium spalatense*, written in Dalmatia—almost certainly at Split—at the end of the eighth century, three pages of which are the Greek text of the opening of St John's Gospel transcribed in the Latin alphabet.[126] Again, the earliest Croat forms of the popular names John, Joseph, Stephen and others are clearly based on spoken Greek forms and were only later reformed on Latin models.[127]

The gradual advance southwards of the Frankish sphere of influence as far as the River Cetina brought in its train an increasing interest on the part of the Patriarchate of Aquileia. Until the fall of Ravenna in July 751 Dalmatia had been a part of the Exarchate and her ecclesiastical affairs came within the competence of Rome. Thereafter Zadar, local administrative centre since the abandonment of Salona, stepped into Ravenna's shoes but the Bishop of Split had long been the highest ecclesiastical authority.[a] Split was now the custodian of Salona's relics of SS Domnius and Anastasius.

Thus on the one hand the transference of Illyricum to the Patriarchate of Constantinople introduced a theoretical rather than a practical change: the Greek language and Byzantine religious practices found little extension outside the Greek population of the ports; Latin was the main liturgical and Dalmatian the main vernacular language.[b] On the other hand Aquileia's entry on to the scene, beginning in the last decades of the eighth century, was as much at the expense of Rome as Constantinople: for example, as early as 817 Split had to submit to a curtailment of its interests in the now Frankish territories to its north.

The first successful work of considerable scale among the Dalmatian Croats appears to be due principally to missions from Frankish Aquileia, whose control of Istria gave access alike to Carniola and to Croatia. Her initiative was confirmed by the general agreement on spheres of influence between Charlemagne and Constantinople made in 811/12.[c] Aquileia was better placed than Salona (and then Split) to gather up the *disjecta membra* of barbarised Illyricum. Borna (*c.* 810–*c.* 821) and his successor Vládislav (*c.* 821–*c.* 835) were at least nominal Christians.

[a] It is not known when Split became a Metropolitan archbishopric—perhaps as early as 615. The tradition that John of Ravenna, as Papal legate in Croatia, became its first archbishop in 640, is probably without foundation in fact.

[b] The interpenetration of all these languages is reflected in the local Slav religious vocabulary. Thus, *kaluđer* or *kalujer* (monk), from Greek καλόγηρος, is still widely used even in Catholic Croatia, while *križ* (cross), current in Orthodox parts, demands a prototype *croge[m] from Dalmatian or North Italian (Aquileian?) Romance, parallel to Venetian *doge* < duce[m]. In early times both *manastir* from Greek and *kloštar* from the Latin world were in general use.

[c] See p. 17.

Indeed we should probably put the date of a Christian dynasty back to Gódeslav and his successor Višeslav to judge by the edifices at their capital of Nin (Latin *Nona*). These include a baptistery and a funerary chapel dedicated to the Holy Cross. On the lintel of the chapel door is preserved the inscription GODES[L]AV IUPPANO [...] ISTO DOMO CŌSTRUXIT.[128] Neither palaeographical nor other considerations preclude a date between 788, when the Franks occupied Istria, and 800, which is the probable date of the slightly later baptistery with its font bearing a Latin inscription of Višeslav.[129] Such unsophisticated and diminutive buildings were presumably the work of local craftsmen copying what was to hand in Zadar, the environs of Salona and elsewhere. The closest extant parallels to the two buildings at Nin are however to be found at Grado and Pola.[130] It is not safe to conclude the establishment of a bishopric for the Dalmatian Croats as early as the beginning of the ninth century, though the presence of a missionary bishop at the prince's court would be (as we have seen elsewhere) a likely first step. The fact that from about 835 the Croatian princes more often than not resided at other places than Nin—in particular Klis above Split and Bihać on the route to Trogir—would not preclude a missionary bishopric with Nin as its working centre. The acts of the Synod of Split (928),[a] though biassed, may well have described the earliest cleric appointed to Nin correctly as *archipresbyter sub ditione episcopi*.[131] Whether the cleric, whatever his rank, was attached directly to Rome as is widely believed, or to Aquileia, cannot yet be certainly resolved. According to one local legend Nin and its environs were evangelised 'in apostolic times' by a Bishop Anselm and his deacon Ambrose, who brought relics of St Marcella from Francia. Such a legend might well grow up about the first missionary bishop actually appointed from Aquileia—by his name patently a Frank. The cult of St Marcella is also authenticated in North-east Italy.[132]

It is of course improbable that Aquileia was solely responsible for the evangelical work which led to the new bishopric. We should look also to Byzantine Zadar and to Split.[133] But when the Curia finally took a hand in the affairs of Nin it was only to connections with Aquileia to which it objected.

Throughout much of the ninth century Nin looked alternately more towards Frankish Aquileia or towards Byzantine Split as politics determined. Višeslav, Borna and Vladislav belonged to one house; Mislav

[a] See p. 198.

was of a different line. He and his powerful successor Trpimir (*c.* 845–64) now resided at Klis and understandably favoured closer relations with Split and through Split with Constantinople. These were close enough for Archbishop Peter of Split to stand godfather to Trpimir's son. But a transference of jurisdiction is improbable: both Trpimir and Mislav are known to have accepted the Frankish obligation to pay the tithe. Trpimir also founded the first Benedictine monastery in these parts, at Rižinice near his castle of Klis.[134]

Trpimir's death only intensified the dynastic rivalry. Domagoj, of the line of Vladislav and pro-Frankish, seized power and held it between about 864 and 876. Then Trpimir's sons Zdeslav, who had fled to Constantinople, and Mutimir regained the ascendancy with Byzantine help.[135] Zdeslav sent for Greek priests from Constantinople. Finally Branimir, Domagoj's son or nephew, succeeded in evicting them (879) and returned to Frankish allegiance with virtual independence. Rome was quick to take advantage of this by entering into close relations with Branimir: the re-establishment of Eastern ecclesiastical influence in Northern Dalmatia would have undermined the whole policy of the 870s designed to secure to the Papacy the various provinces of former Illyricum. A trial of strength with the Frankish church here took second place.

It was Domagoj, *sclavorum pessimus dux* to the Venetians, who made the first move to change the status of Nin. Either it was a matter of disengaging himself ecclesiastically from Split and Aquileia and achieving a relative independence directly under the Holy See, or (more probably) the see still needed formal establishment and this again had now better be taken to Rome. For there had almost certainly been a Bishop of Nin in the reign of Trpimir. The shadowy archpriests or bishops of Nin up to this time cannot even be given names. Pope Nicholas I, however, took no steps. We could judge the situation better if we knew exactly in what year during the period 864–7 Domagoj's request reached him, for these were the years of Nicholas's preoccupation with events in Bulgaria[a] and of awakening interest in the work of SS Cyril and Methodios in Moravia.[b] Perhaps Nicholas or his successor felt unable to take the matter up since the years 867–71 saw unusually close cooperation of the Franks and Greeks to the advantage of the Papacy against the Saracens in South Italy and on the Dalmatian coast.[c] Thus Byzantine prestige

---

[a] See pp. 160 ff.   [b] See pp. 52 ff.

[c] The Byzantine fleet raised the siege of Ragusa by a Saracen fleet in late 867. Bari was invested and finally recaptured from the Saracens in early 871. Byzantine administration then remained in South Dalmatia (now reorganised as a *Theme* to meet the

was exceptionally high along the coast and the Slavs were taking employment in the Byzantine as well as in the Frankish forces.

Domagoj nevertheless caused a new bishop of Nin to be elected, to which irregular act approval was only obtained from Hadrian II about 870. This date may therefore be taken as the final establishment of the see.[136] The bishop of Nin was recognised as *episcopus nonensis* or *episcopus chroatorum*. The first bishop known by name is Theodosius, consecrated in 879 on the advice of the Papal legate John, who returned from his mission to Moravia[137] by way of Dalmatia and is thought to have visited Nin. It is clear that Pope John VIII now desired that the Bishop of Nin should be consecrated by himself, so as to counter any further Byzantine influence by subordinating what was virtually still a missionary bishopric directly to Rome. Nevertheless it is not certain whether Theodosius was consecrated in Rome or Aquileia. Since a later Pope, probably Stephen V (885–91), reprimanded the Patriarch of Aquileia, Walpert (*fungebatur* 874–900), for consecrating a bishop at Split *ultra vires*, it may well be that Theodosius's consecration was also Aquileian.[138] Precisely in the years 879–80—the climax of the battle over Bulgaria[a]—Patriarch Photios saw to the strengthening of the ecclesiastical organisation of Split but at the same time recognised and even agreed to an extension of the powers of Frankish Aquileia on the coast: Rome was still the interloper. Yet on 7 June 879 the Pope wrote to the new ruler Branimir in terms implying that Croatia was now a Papal concern: 'Karissimum filium ad gremium sancte sedis apostolice matris tue... redeuntem suscepimus'.[139] The letter was perhaps hopeful rather than actual. On the same date he exhorted Theodosius to receive consecration nowhere but at Rome.[140] A few days later he appealed to the Byzantine hierarchs of Dalmatia, and once more to Boris of Bulgaria, to return to the Roman fold.[141] There was no reply in either case. In 881, after Theodosius had had consultations with him in Rome, the Pope again wrote to Branimir as if Croatia had accepted Roman jurisdiction.[142] Branimir presumably favoured this policy; it remains doubtful whether Theodosius did. Moreover, the Archbishop of Split considered that he had rights, to which he was not slow to give voice. The discussions in Rome evidently bore on this involved three-cornered problem. Even if

military situation) and was gradually reimposed in South Italy, partly as a protectorate of local Lombard princelings. Neither Constantinople nor Venice would tolerate a power (now the Saracens, later the Normans) which might control the exit of the Adriatic by holding at the same time both South Italy and the lower Dalmatian or Albanian coast.   [a] See p. 162.

some bishops of Nin had received Roman consecration, others had not. The tone of the Papal correspondence reveals a determination to drive a wedge between Aquileian and Byzantine establishments on the central part of the Dalmatian coast.

The election of Theodosius of Nin to succeed Archbishop Marinus of Split, who died in 885, was a setback to Papal policy. The Pope protested and exhorted him to come to Rome for his *pallium*.[143] The see of Nin was filled by one Adelfred, who by his name could well have been another Frank from Aquileia.[144] The next decades are however lost in obscurity; virtually nothing is known of the Bishop of Nin and his work, except the foundation of further churches. That of St Peter at Gorni Muć near Split is dated to 888 by an inscription set up by Branimir. Mutimir (*regnabat c.* 892–*c.* 910) built a church near Knin[145] and confirmed his father Trpimir's church endowments.[146] He remained on good terms with Split.[147]

Theodosius's episcopate however did not outlast the death of Branimir in 892. It was now becoming increasingly clear to all parties that some new regulation of Dalmatian affairs was needed at the highest level. For the see of Nin was no sooner well established than it began to develop pretensions on its own part. While the jurisdiction of the archbishop of Split was recognised in the coastal towns and islands, notably Krk (Veglia),[a] Zadar, Trogir, Ragusa and Kotor (Cattaro), it had none inland. The bishopric of Nin, being essentially a missionary see for the Croats, could now claim all territory under the rule of the Croat prince. This became a considerable pretension when Tómislav (*c.* 912–28?),[b] thought to be Mutimir's son and therefore of the house of Trpimir, was successful in welding the Dalmatian and Pannonian Croats into one state, with its northern frontier on the River Drava. The Magyars had all but extinguished Christianity on their side of the frontier. A Croatian church independent of both Aquileia and Split would now be no anomaly if Tomislav had pressed for it. But this was not necessary. In 924 Tomislav was recompensed for his military support of the Byzantine Empire against the Bulgarians and Serbs by recognition of his political control of the Dalmatian seaboard towns, including Split and Zadar, whose Prior (mayor) remained the representative of Byzantine interests.[148] At the same time the Patriarch of Constantinople surrendered

[a] Slav *Krk* from *Curicum*, no doubt an ancient Illyrian name; *Veglia* from Dalmatian *Vetula* [sc. *civitas*].

[b] The date of his death is quite uncertain; it has been put as late as 940.

13-2

his ecclesiastical jurisdiction over them to the Pope. Thus Tomislav's church (including Nin) was brought formally under Rome at this date, confirmed by his assumption of the title of King with Papal approval, most probably after his victory over the Bulgarians in 924.[149] At the Synods of Split in 925 and 928 an attempt was made to regulate all outstanding problems. For the question of ecclesiastical jurisdiction had been exacerbated by another equally grave matter: the orthodoxy and ecclesiastical language of the Croats now came under attack.

The Slav liturgical language had gained a firm foothold in the Croat church, at least in its Dalmatian portion. By 925 it is plain that native clergy, known as *glagoljáši*, were numerous, if not in the majority. The beginning of the connection with the Cyrillomethodian mission may reach back to 870, when Kotsel's Pannonia came under the thumb of the Franks. An immigration of Moravian exiles is very probable in 885, though none of the leaders known to us by name settled in Dalmatia. The *Life of Methodios* unfortunately does not state clearly whether the saint himself passed through Dalmatia either on his way back from Rome to Moravia in the earlier part of 880 or on his journey to Constantinople.[a] Nor do we know the substance of Theodosius's consultations with the Pope in 880. It remains therefore an open question whether Methodios and Theodosius knew one another and consequently whether a deliberate policy of introducing the Slav liturgical language and the Glagolitic alphabet was embraced by the latter.

The Slav liturgy was much in the mind of the Pope at this moment. It is at least conceivable that John VIII approved it for Theodosius's see of Nin at the same time as he confirmed it for Methodios in Moravia —and a formal or conditional approval at some date seems demanded. However that may be, it can scarcely be doubted that the Glagolitic alphabet and a Latin liturgy in Slav were transplanted to Dalmatia before the end of the ninth century.[b] The situation in Croatia was thus not very dissimilar to that in Moravia: the Slav books were brought to a people with nearly a century of Christianity behind them in other forms. Rome appreciated that Illyricum, including Bulgaria, might only be won back from Constantinople by concessions to local wishes. Thus John VIII underwrote in 873 Methodios's insistence on the continuation of the Slav church, especially as Methodios was himself a Greek still

---

a See pp. 74–7.

b There are no traces of a fully Byzantine liturgy in OCS in Croatia. The point is of importance: apparently only the more Westernised Cyrillomethodian texts were taken or accepted there. Cf. pp. 203 ff.

with potentially great influence at home. With the return of Photios to the Patriarchal throne in 877 there was even more reason to maintain the concession. In all that happened in those years (879–85), perhaps the most decisive in the whole history of the Slav church, Theodosius is a key figure. He knew what was going on in Bulgaria and Moravia; he knew about the use of the Slav liturgy up and down Dalmatia. Unfortunately his part is still elusive to us. It would have been shortsighted, we may judge, on the part of the Pope not to try and unify the policy of Methodios's archbishopric of Sirmium and the Croatian bishopric of Nin (or even the archbishopric of Split) on the basis of the free use of the Slav liturgical language and to dangle this before both Bulgaria and Serbia as no bar to dependence on Rome.

The success of the Slav clergy, at least among the people, must have been rapid. It is less certain that the Court and ruling class generally took much interest in a Slav church. The attraction of the predominantly Latin culture of the great coastal cities, politically so important to any Croat state, was too great. At all events the vigour of this transplantation is the best evidence that clergy from the north, with or without the formal approval of Aquileia or Rome, became an important element in Croat Christianity from the late ninth century. By 925 the position of the Latin church was greatly strengthened by the virtual withdrawal of the Byzantine administration. An attack on the anomaly could be undertaken.[a] For Split now became a Latin metropolis.

At the first Synod of Split (925) the Latin hierarchy gained most of its points. Split became the metropolis for the whole coast from Istria to Ragusa and Kotor; for Tomislav, at the height of his power, had some pretensions to rule the whole.[b] The see of Nin was placed under Split. The archbishop now styled himself *primas Dalmatiae totiusque Chroatiae* and boasted that his province extended *usque ad ripas Danubii*.[150] But the suppression of the Slav language was not pressed. The anomaly was, as we have seen, always a special concession on the part of the Holy See and a concession not readily forthcoming. It might be held now to have outlived its usefulness in Dalmatia to Papal policy. However Pope John X in approving the Canons may have decided that Croatia was not yet a 'mature' church[c] and that the abrupt prohibition of the Slav

[a] Greek as such was not under attack. The Greek liturgy continued to be used in the coastal towns after the withdrawal of the Byzantine church as long as there were enough Greek residents in the towns.

[b] The province of Hum was more or less independent under Michael of a different dynasty. See p. 209.　　　　　　　　　　[c] Cf. p. 107.

liturgy and removal of the *glagóljaš* priests was not practicable. Many of them knew no Latin. For the tone of his instructions to the Synod had been much less liberal: he treated the 'Methodian doctrine' as something strange and unacceptable.[151] At the same time (924/5) he wrote to Tomislav: 'Quis etenim specialis filius sanctae romanae ecclesiae, sicut vos estis, in barbara seu sclavinica lingua Deo sacrificium offerre delectatur?'[152]

Canon X of the Synod provided that the Slav language might continue to be used but only as a special concession—where there was a lack of Latin priests. The gradual suppression of the Slav parochial priesthood by preventing further exclusively *glagóljaš* recruits was envisaged as the best method.[153] The corollary was that the Slav liturgy should not be allowed to extend itself outside Croatia proper into any of the sees just recovered from the Eastern church. As far as possible all licensed *glagoljáši* should be proficient in Latin also. There is no sign at this time that the Latins went so far as to persecute the adherents of the Slav language; they were satisfied with limiting its use and putting an end to the autonomy of the see of Nin. The charge of heresy was not pressed either; it was not a serious issue. This was far from the liberal policy of John VIII some fifty years earlier. But the disappearance of Moravia and the loss of Bulgaria and its Serbian satellite made all the difference: the Papal Legate Madalbert, who attended the Synod on his way back from a mission to Bulgaria, would have been quite clear on this.

The Bishop of Nin, Grgur (Gregory) I, did not however accept the decrees without protest. The Pope too had second thoughts, not so much on language as on organisation. He summoned Grgur and the Archbishop of Split to Rome for further discussions. A second synod was convened at Split in 928 to reconsider the question of the bishopric of Nin. The new Pope, Leo VI (*fungebatur* 928), went further than his predecessor. He did not favour Croat separatism. The synod through his legate Madalbert now decreed the abolition of the see of Nin and Grgur was transferred to Scardona (Skradin).[154] By this decision all question of developing a Croat church with an independent hierarchy— whether Latin or Slav or mixed—was indefinitely postponed, which we may judge to have been a considerable disappointment to Tomislav the King, with his eye on the recognition of the Bulgarian Patriarchate.[a] From 928 the Archbishop of Split naturally consecrated the bishop

a See p. 173.

appointed for Croatia, but where he resided and with what title is uncertain. It is interesting to observe that Archdeacon Thomas of Split (1200–68), a rabid pro-Latin, ignores the decisions of 925–8, presumably because they did not debar the Slav liturgy. The two synods balanced the suppression of Nin by the creation of the see of Ston (Stagno) in Hum as a new centre of Latin influence further down the coast.

For over a hundred years the situation did not substantially change. The Slav language was tolerated within a probably gradually shrinking area, but supported by ties with Bohemia, as the literary evidence shows,[a] and perhaps also with Macedonia; for these were the two other preserves of the Glagolitic alphabet.

A new radical examination of the ecclesiastical position was not made until after the events of 1054 and the Lateran Council of 1059. By this time Venice had fully emerged as the dominant influence in the life of the Dalmatian cities, especially Ragusa, now virtually an independent city-state with a Latin archbishopric (1022). Croatia, still powerful under Stephen Držislav (969–97), acknowledged as King by Constantinople, then declined into anarchy and in the eleventh century began to look to the young Christian state of Hungary for support against Venice. Despite the episode of Samuel's Macedonian Empire[b] and the reimposition of Byzantine rule after 1018 and at various times throughout the eleventh century on varying portions of the Dalmatian coast, Byzantine civilisation was in constant retreat before Latin. Surviving Byzantine practices up and down the coast were more and more frowned upon. The Normans, self-styled protectors of the Papacy from 1059, had in mind to recover for the Pope all former Illyricum and therefore also stood behind the Papal policy of uniformity. They began to stamp out Greek customs in South Italy also. The synod held at Split in 1059–60, attended by all the Dalmatian bishops and the Papal legate Mainard, confirmed the Lateran canons in so far as they applied. The additions are significant: no clergy are henceforward to wear long hair or a beard (this aimed at remnants of Byzantine practice); no Slavs to be ordained to the priesthood who are incompetent in Latin (this above all to obviate possible heresy).[155] This still did not amount to a formal suppression of the Slav liturgical language but we should hardly be wrong in supposing a now much less tolerant spirit in the Dalmatian Latin church bent on uniformity; these were the greatest days of the archdiocese of Split under the reforming Archbishop Laurence (*fungebatur* 1060–99). The decrees

[a] See p. 112. [b] See pp. 180–1.

were at any rate interpreted as a suppression of the Slav liturgy and the Pope confirmed them.[156] The King of Croatia, Peter-Krésimir (*regnabat* 1058–74), who was half Venetian, apparently acquiesced. We can perhaps give credence to Thomas of Split's statement that the Croatian upper class was by and large pro-Latin. Most *glagoljaši* were parish priests still ignorant of or incompetent in Latin, and married as well; they ministered to the peasantry. Toleration would be extended only to those priests who were proficient in Latin and conformed in other respects. The argument that Methodios was a heretic and that the alphabet which he propagated (Glagolitic) was therefore to be eschewed was now aired.[157] This was countered on the Slav side by attributing it to St Jerome. For the first time we hear of some open persecution: churches using the Slav language were forcibly closed. The prohibition on its use was reaffirmed more clearly by Pope Alexander II in 1063.

The Croat clergy were not prepared to acquiesce in their own extinction. The Bishop for Croatia, Rainer, who had attended the synod, was evidently lukewarm towards the Slav language and did not fight the decision. His clergy took matters into their own hands. Thomas of Split tells an involved story of the appeal to Rome by clergy of Krk headed by a *glagoljaš* priest Cededa (or Zdeda).[158] On being falsely informed that the Pope supported their views, Cededa was despatched to Rome to be consecrated in place of the 'traitor' Rainer. This can only mean that the Croat *glagoljaši* hoped to secede from the Dalmatian Latin hierarchy. What took place in Rome is obscure but Cededa proceeded to act as bishop on the island of Krk. Alexander was obliged to send a legate, John of Porto, to declare him an impostor (*pseudoepiscopus*) and instruct the Croat authorities to recall the *glagoljaši* to obedience. This could be mostly *parti pris* on the part of Thomas, who calls Cededa *malesanus, fantasticus pontifex* and *fatuus senex*, but there is nothing to show that the Pope was inclined at this moment to grant Croatian autocephaly and did in fact consecrate Cededa. Cededa died in 1064 and was succeeded, properly or improperly, by another *pseudoepiscopus*. Troubles with the Latin clergy became more serious. Whatever the true status of these two bishops may have been, a compromise was reached: Bishop Rainer's authority was reimposed in 1066.

A general settlement of the affairs of the Dalmatian church was attempted by Pope Alexander II about 1066/7 through a synod held perhaps at Omiš (Almissa).[159] The whole coast was divided into two archbishoprics, that of Split northwards from Omiš, that of Duklja (Dioclea) southwards as far as Durazzo. Omiš is at the mouth of the River Cetina, the old dividing line of 812. Ragusa had some claims to be considered the natural ecclesiastical centre of South Dalmatia but those of Bar to this new metropolitan status were now vigorously pushed especially as the Pope intended Serbia, and perhaps Bosnia, to be attached to Dioclea. From this time rivalry between Ragusa and Bar comes to the fore and the claims of Durazzo to its former suffragan sees in Dioclea (where it must have been responsible for much of the missionary work) disappear. The archdiocese of Split was to contain the bishoprics of Trogir (established not later than 1000), Skradin near Šibenik (Sebenico), Biograd (Peter-Krešimir's new capital), Zadar, Nin, Rab (Arbe), Osor (Lussin) and Krk. Nin thus reappeared as an episcopal town. However, its importance after its resuscitation does not seem to have been great. Owing to Norman attacks on the Dalmatian seaboard (they were in full control of Apulia by 1071) the reorganisation was not fully achieved till 1075. In that year a synod at Split confirmed the status of Nin: *in hoc sinodo restauratus est episcopatus nonensis*, and in 1078 Archbishop Laurence held a local synod there.[a] There was no intention of tolerating the Slav language but it continued to be used more or less in secret in many outlying parts, particularly on the island of Krk. It must be borne in mind that most of the Dalmatian towns had accepted some measure of Venetian 'protection' since 1000, for in 998 they themselves called in the Venetian fleet to rid them of the Narentan pirates. The Doge then arrogated to himself the title of *dux dalmatiae*—recognised even by the Emperor Otto III. In 1000 the island of Krk, among others, had passed into Venetian hands and remained so with a Croat interlude (1058–1118) until the middle of the fourteenth century.[b] But neither Venetian doges nor harrassed Croat princes were concerned to suppress the use of the Slav liturgical language in such remote corners as Krk.

On the death of Peter-Krešimir in 1074 revolts broke out between rival political and ecclesiastical factions. Pope Gregory VII called in his Norman allies to restore order. At the ensuing synod of Split (1075/6) no concessions were made to the *glagoljaši*. In October 1076 Zvonimir-

[a] Nin, Skradin, Biograd and Knin were all royal residences in the eleventh century; it remains uncertain whether these sees were always formally distinct and where the *episcopus regius et palatinus* resided at any given time.

[b] Venice formally incorporated the diocese of Zadar with its dependent islands (Krk, Rab, Osor, Hvar) in 1154/5.

Demetrius, who had managed to gain control of all the Croat provinces, was crowned King of Croatia and Dalmatia in St Peter's church near Split,[160] receiving his crown from the Papal legate.[161] He forthwith built a new cathedral at Biskupija near his residence of Knin. He probably shared the hostile attitude of the Latin hierarchy towards the Slav liturgical language. With Guiscard holding the Byzantine fortress of Durazzo (1081) and a complaisant ruler of Dioclea,[a] the Pope was in a position to enforce uniformity of ecclesiastical practice, just as he was doing in Bohemia.[b] Yet his handling of Balkan affairs cannot be called narrow-minded. He expected Guiscard to introduce Roman rites and customs into territories conquered by him but placed no bar on the retention of the Greek rite for those who desired it. He may therefore have extended some tolerance to the use of the Slav language also. The end of the eleventh century nevertheless marks the low water mark of the fortunes of the Slav language.

The house of Trpimir was now extinct, for Zvonimir was an upstart. On his death in 1089 St Ladislas of Hungary (1077–95) claimed the succession through his sister Helen, the widow of Zvonimir. Hungary was becoming the leading power in Central Europe and now turned her protection of Croatia into domination. Inland Croatia was soon in Ladislas's hands; he proceeded to establish the see of Zagreb (Agram) in 1093/4, attached to his own primatial see of Esztergom (Gran).[162] Its first bishop was a Czech. From this time Croatia became a purely Latin Catholic domain.

The pacification of all Croatia was complete by 1097 when Koloman, Ladislas's nephew, was crowned in Biograd. The *Pacta conventa* of 1102 defined the status of all parts of Croatia in the Hungarian kingdom: while the Mesopotamia was fully integrated into Hungary, Croatia was to enjoy a personal union with Hungary under a single crown without derogation of her laws and customs. It does not seem that all the minor Croatian bishoprics under Split were immediately dissolved but they certainly lost importance. Krk, perhaps a few other islands, and a handful of monasteries alone kept the use of the Slav language and Glagolitic alphabet alive.

The twelfth century continued to be a difficult time. The Emperor of Constantinople, Manuel, took advantage of the death of Géza of Hungary (1163) to reassert himself in the Balkans. The re-establishment of Byzantine power in much of Croatia, Dalmatia, Bosnia and Monte-

[a] See pp. 210–11.   [b] See p. 107.

negro[a] in the second half of his reign (1167–80), though short-lived, was marked by the same anti-Slav measures as had for a long time been prominent in Byzantine-dominated Bulgaria and Serbia.[b] Many Croatian Glagolitic books were destroyed. As usual, suppression and destruction were not methodical; it is even recorded that Pope Alexander attended a Slav liturgy in the church of St Anastasia at Zadar on his way to Venice in 1177.

Byzantine pressure relaxed after the death of Manuel; indeed this was the last flicker of a Byzantine Dalmatia. Henceforward Venice disputed it alone with Hungary. Both Bulgaria and Serbia now rapidly rose to independence. With the establishment of the Latin Empire of Constantinople by the Fourth Crusade (1204), the Nicaean Emperors had little option but to grant Bulgaria and Serbia autocephaly,[c] in an attempt to ensure their adherence to the Eastern church and to the principle of the Byzantine Empire. A similar complaisance is visible too in the Catholic attitude to Dalmatian Croatia though the ascendancy of the Western church was not in any doubt. The Fourth Lateran Council of 1215 relaxed the theoretical ban on the Slav liturgical language through the general provision of Canon IX.[163] From that time the Glagolitic use of Croatia began slowly to recover some of its lost ground. This was still toleration rather than approval. Qualified Papal permission given in 1248 marks the turning-point.[164] Benedictine monks on Krk thought it advisable to apply again to Pope Innocent IV in 1252 for specific permission to use the Slav language. The permission was given ('concedimus ut super hoc facias, quod videris expedire') insofar as concerned those incapable of learning Latin ('qui...discere latinas litteras non possunt').[165]

As far as the perpetuation of the Glagolitic alphabet is concerned, manifestly the main credit goes to those monasteries which most consistently cultivated the language. Foundation dates for the considerable number of Benedictine houses which came into being up and down Dalmatia are for the most part unknown. About 1059 a Benedictine house was founded exclusively for Slavs near Biograd—the monastery of St John the Evangelist at Rógovo. It is thought that the Benedictine Rule was translated into Croat at this time. Those houses which are most likely to have cultivated the Slav use before that date, and were certainly strong foci of it subsequently are: St Lucia near Baška[166] and

---

[a] This Venetian name for Zeta only came into common use from the fourteenth century.   [b] Cf. pp. 181 ff., 213.   [c] See pp. 186 and 219–20.

St Nicholas at Omišalj, both on the island of Krk; St John the Baptist at Povlja on the island of Brač; and St Nicholas at Otočac (Lika). Almost equally important were: two others on Krk—St Mary at Košljun and St Laurence; St Mary on the island of Žirje (off Šibenik); and St George (Juraj) Koprivski at Óbrovac.[167] The monastery of SS Cosmas and Damian at Tkon on the island of Pašman, to which the Rogovo monks fled in 1129 after the destruction of Biograd by the Venetians, was also an important later centre.[168] It is believed that Charles IV of Bohemia brought Glagolitic monks from here for his foundation of Emmaus in the middle of the fourteenth century.[a] These houses are concentrated on the coast and islands of Dalmatian Croatia. It cannot be assumed that they were all exclusively and continuously Glagolitic. No Glagolitic houses are reliably known from Istria, still less from inland.

In the days of its greatest flourishing the Glagolitic use was still confined to the eight Croatian coastal dioceses, to wit Pazin (Pedena in South Istria),[169] Rijéka (Fiume), Senj, Krk, Zadar, Šibenik (created 1298), Split and Hvar[b]—much less in some than in others. It was a relict phenomenon, tolerated but not encouraged by any high authority. In the days of its final decline it hardly extended outside the dioceses of Senj and Šibenik. More early Glagolitic material has however survived from Krk, the backwater which from 1133 was virtually independent under the Croat house of Frankopan (Frangipani), originally known under the name of Krčki. To the determined separatism of these Croats is due the curious historical chance that only in this one corner of Croatia survived the Western form of the Cyrillomethodian tradition— a church using the Roman rite in Slav translation and in the Glagolitic alphabet; moreover that it helped by its very conservatism to preserve texts in danger of extinction in Bohemia, such as the *First OCS Legend of St Wenceslas* as it is now to be found in the Breviary of Novi.[170]

Church Slavonic in course of time here took on a Croat cast and the ductus of the alphabet was also modified, partly under the influence of Cyrillic, partly under that of Latin script.[171] At a place such as Split the Latin, Glagolitic and Cyrillic alphabets were all in use concurrently at certain times, though for more or less different purposes. The sacred texts were generally brought into conformity with Roman practice,

[a] See p. 112.
[b] As defined in 1147, the *episcopus insularum* administered Hvar, Brač, Vis and other lesser islands.

especially from 1248 when Papal recognition of the Slav use was renewed.[a]

Glagolitic as a secular alphabet for Croat literature saw a considerable development in the fourteenth–fifteenth centuries, evolving for this purpose a special cursive variant. But it was gradually superseded by the Croatian form of the Latin alphabet. After about 1600 the ecclesiastical language and script had little currency outside the service-books of the church and even here continued to be used regularly only in the Mass. Latin became more and more general for all other offices; even the silent parts of the Mass might be said in Latin. In 1927 a Latin transcription of the whole Missal was permitted and made. The alphabet has been virtually extinct since that date.

No very early Glagolitic manuscripts of the Croatian church have survived.[172] The earliest of importance is the fragmentary *Baška Missal* of the twelfth century. The best are of the fourteenth century: the *Vrbnik Breviary* (c. 1300, from Krk); *Codex Vaticanus Illyricus 4*, a missal of between 1317 and 1323, probably from Krk; *Prince Novak's Missal* (1368); *Cod. Vat. Illyr. 5–6*, breviaries of the late fourteenth century. The first printed Glagolitic service-book was the 1483 Missal; it has not been definitely established where it was printed.

The Dalmatian coast provides an example of a gradual changeover from the Eastern to the Western world. For a considerable time after the Slavs first arrived there the world they saw wore a Byzantine aspect. Ravenna, Venice and Istria perpetuated a predominantly Byzantine style round the head of the Adriatic for long after Byzantine power had ebbed away from those parts. The splendid churches of Torcello and Poreč (Parenzo)[b] bear witness to this. The present St Mark's at Venice was built with the cooperation of Byzantine craftsmen over more than a century from the time of Pietro Orseolo I (976–8). The radiation of Aquileian Christianity to Istria and Dalmatian Croatia propagated a 'Lombard' style which itself contained Eastern elements. Decorative sculpture of interlace patterns, sometimes reminding us even of early Irish Christian work, is particularly characteristic, from Višeslav's font (end of the eighth century) to Peter-Krešimir's pulpit at Split (c. 1070), and immediately proclaims its affinity with Lombard work such as can

[a] The Psalter long retained a very archaic and conservative aspect, more so even than *Ps. Sin.* at some points. Traces of Cyrillomethodian usage, in the form of the liturgy of St Peter (see p. 61) appear to have survived into the seventeenth century.

[b] Parenzo basilica dates from about 550 or somewhat later and is now one of the least altered Byzantine monuments of that time.

be seen in the cathedral of Cividale (Frankish Aquileia). Thus the small, centrally organised churches, such as Holy Cross and St Nicholas at Nin, St Mary at Trogir and Sr Ursula at Zadar, which include the earliest inexpert buildings of the Croat princes, are Byzantine only by indirect transmission—in its far western provincial forms whether of North or South Italy.[173]

The Eastern saint Hermagoras, believed to be St Mark's successor at Aquileia, became in Slav mouths *Mogor*.[174] Further down the coast all the names of the Eastern saints of the important churches early received Slav forms: at Zadar, St Anastasia became *Stošija*, St Chrysogonus—*Krševan*; at Trogir St Laurence became *Lovrec*; at Split St Domnius (a Syrian from Nisibis, martyred in 304)[175] appears as *Dujam* or *Dojam*; St Tryphon of Kotor as *Tripun*.[a] St Demetrios of Saloniki,[b] SS Sergius and Bacchus, SS Cosmas and Damian were all popular saints. Little by little, with some rallies, Byzantine culture retreated southwards. But it had never been deep-rooted: it had been superficially imposed on an old Latin world. The whole of the Dalmatian coast was on the Latin side of the Latin–Greek language frontier, which started at about Durazzo and ended on the Black Sea coast a little south of the Danube, following a roughly north-easterly line. Greek was in Dalmatia only the language of the seaboard communities and their church.[c] For those portions of the coast and its hinterland which became parts of Orthodox states the Adriatic was a potent source of Latin influences.[d]

The Croatian church was from its very beginning Latin (Catholic), with the unusual local features brought by the Methodian disciples. We have followed it mainly from the Dalmatian point of view since the ecclesiastical history of inland Croatia before 1094 is largely surmise. There is nothing inherently improbable in some Pannonian followers of the Cyrillomethodian tradition remaining in the interior, at Sisak, Ptuj, and other places on the routes to the South. The lack of large towns and active bishoprics in this region would be apt to favour its survival. Evidence of mixed Western and Eastern practices can be deduced for

[a] The first church of St Tryphon was consecrated in 809, when his relics were brought there from Constantinople. Similarly, relics of St Anastasia were brought to Zadar in 811, and the cathedral of St Peter rededicated to her.

[b] This saint was in fact a Pannonian who had little or no historical connection with the city of his adoption. An early church dedicated to him (early sixth century) has been identified near Pola in Istria.

[c] The Dalmatian Romance language survived on some of the Quarnero islands into the eighteenth century. It died out at Ragusa-Dubrovnik *c.* 1500, despite official attempts to keep it alive in preference to Slav.

[d] See esp. pp. 183, 224–6.

Zagreb before 1094 from service books in the Cathedral library. Thus a Latin manuscript, probably of the eleventh century,[a] preserves such Eastern rites as the Blessing of the Waters (6 January). It is less likely that such aberrant features were recent importations from Hungary (after 1000), where Greek practices were also to be found in the eleventh century. Similar anomalies suggest the early circulation of Cyrillo-methodian liturgical books in this area, possibly influenced by, but not copied from, Glagolitic books of Dalmatian Croatia.[176]

Carniola (modern Slovenia) had remained the preserve of Frankish Aquileia, which owned extensive lands there. But the same would apply; some Cyrillomethodian usages at Emona (Ljubljana), are probable. But much in all these parts, as in Moravia, was destroyed by the Magyars; Emona, for example, was sacked by them about 919.

Though peculiarities of Bosnian history[b] somewhat complicate the picture, in its essentials the eastern frontier of Croatia has remained remarkably stable both as a frontier between the Catholic and Orthodox worlds and as a political frontier between Europe proper and the Balkans. Through Croatia passed the later military frontier between Austria-Hungary and the Turkish Empire. The narrow strip of Dalmatian coast and the islands were secured to the Western world and Catholicism by being absorbed into or becoming cultural dependencies of Catholic Hungary or the Venetian maritime Empire.[177]

SERBIA

The Serbian tribe brought by Heraklios to Macedonia,[c] probably from the region of the Upper Tisza (Theiss), eventually moved north and settled in the difficult country between the Rivers Drina and Ibar.[178] This was the Serbian heartland. Established far from the Adriatic coast and off the main routes of Balkan communications, the Serbs long remained unheeded by the chroniclers of the civilised world. Between the early seventh and the early ninth centuries we know of no serious attempt to evangelise them. But by the time of Vlástimir, who ruled over an embryonic Serbian state in the second quarter of the ninth century, what had been an unregarded backwater of the Balkans became an object of rivalry between the Byzantine Empire and Bulgaria, both now intent on extending their control over the interior. The first attempt of Bulgaria to incorporate Serbia dates from 839–42, though Omurtag

---

[a] MR 165. [b] See pp. 227 ff. [c] Cf. p. 187.

(*c.* 814–31) may have laid some claims to it. But the Serbs held their own until a Byzantine occupation followed about 871. During the reign of Tsar Symeon Serbia still theoretically recognised Byzantine suzerainty but in practice, especially after 897, was a Bulgarian dependency and inevitably under much more immediate Bulgarian cultural influence. The conversion of the Serbs was thus due partly to Byzantine and partly to subsequent Bulgarian enterprise.

If we were to believe the Emperor Constantine, the growing power of Serbia towards the middle of the ninth century was coupled with a massive reversion to paganism, to prevent which the Serbian rulers appealed to Constantinople in the time of the Emperors Michael III and Basil I.[179] But it seems improbable that there was a previous state of grace from which the Serbs had relapsed. It is more important to observe that at least during Kotsel's reign in Pannonia (*c.* 861–74)[a] communication must have been possible between Serbia and Great Moravia—a fact of which the Pope was presumably aware in planning Methodios's diocese—as well as with the Dalmatian coast, in Byzantine hands as far north as Split.[180] We must therefore not exclude the possibility of some Cyrillomethodian pupils reaching Serbia—perhaps even sent by Methodios himself—precisely in the 870s when the Byzantine thrust into these parts was developing from other directions. But if there were any such participation it cannot now be detected in such general indications as names: there is for example no sign of the early use of Clement in Serbia as baptismal name or church patron. No more can be said than that the Serbian state must be accounted Christian from about 870.

Vlastimir was probably a pagan. His sons only appear in the record with the Slav names Mútimir, Strójimir and Gojnik. In the next generation we find Stephen and Peter. This change agrees with the imprecise notices of strong Byzantine missions to Serbia, as well as to other Slavs nearer the Adriatic coast, in the 870s. Peter Gojniković (*c.* 892–917) was certainly a Christian prince, adroit enough to tack between client of Constantinople and ally of Tsar Symeon. He had spent long years as a hostage in Bulgaria, whence came the backing to evict his brothers. The first Serbian bishopric had already been founded at Ras (or Raška), near modern Novi Pazar on the River Ibar, the then political centre. Its affiliation is uncertain. Subordination to Split or Durazzo has been suggested, both then Byzantine. The ruins of a very early church of SS Peter and Paul exist at Ras but cannot be dated with any precision; the

[a] See pp. 50, 66 ff.

building follows the rotunda plan of early Christian baptisteries so often adopted of necessity in the ninth–tenth centuries for the first court chapels.[181] We cannot be far wide of the mark in supposing that the Serbian bishopric came into being shortly after 871 in the reign of Mutimir and was part of the general plan, confirmed by the Council of Constantinople in 879–80, which envisaged the creation of a number of bishoprics for the Slav-populated parts of the Empire, notably in Greece and for the Slavs on the River Mórava, lying just to the east of Serbia proper.[a]

The annexation of Serbia by Bulgaria in 924, perhaps as early as 917 on the fall of Peter Gojniković, was important for the future direction of the Serbian church. By now at latest Serbia must have received the Cyrillic alphabet and Slav religious texts, already familiar but perhaps not yet preferred to Greek.

Serbia regained some measure of independence on the death of Tsar Symeon (927). Časlav, who returned to rule Serbia about 931 under Byzantine auspices, was of the line of the exiles brought up at the court of Preslav in its great days. Časlav also enlarged the state, incorporating parts of Bosnia and Travunia.[182] In Travunia he took over or made closer contact with territories lately ruled by Michael of Hum, who controlled much of the southern half of the coast from about 910, except Ragusa (Dúbrovnik) which paid him 'tribute'. Michael was a sufficiently prominent Christian prince to be addressed by the Pope as *excellentissimus dux Chulmorum*.[183] As an ally of Bulgaria he was much concerned in Serbian affairs but disappears from the record after 925.

The conquest of Bulgaria begun by John Tzimiskes in 969 and completed by Basil the Bulgar-slayer in 1018 ushered in a long period of uncertainty for the Serbian interior, a period of over two centuries during which, although Serbia was mainly a preserve of the Eastern church, she was not wholly committed to it and for political reasons often looked West rather than East. From about the year 1000 the more southerly Dalmatian towns, especially Ragusa and Kotor, became gradually more Slav in population (though the process was scarcely complete before the end of the thirteenth century)[b] and the trade-routes into the interior increasingly active. From these ports the influence of the Latin church and the culture of the Adriatic coasts seeped into the hinterland. But the long alternation of Byzantine and Bulgarian domination over Serbia continued. After a short period of Byzantine suzerainty (*c.* 972–90)

[a] On Mutimir see also p. 377 n. 135. [b] See p. 376 n. 120.

Serbia reverted until 1018 to a Bulgarian province under Samuel.[a] The Serbian church consequently came under the Patriarchate of Ohrid, which introduced, we must suppose, Macedonian elements into its life. From this time at latest must date the knowledge and use—restricted, it is true—of the Glagolitic alphabet in Serbia.[b] Finally the full Byzantine conquest of Samuel's state did not change the attachment of Ras to the reconstituted archbishopric of Ohrid, through which Greek influences again made themselves actively felt. But the Byzantine Empire reincorporated thereby not only the South Dalmatian provinces but also Bosnia and thus contributed to those closer contacts of Serbia with the Adriatic and Latin Croatia which Samuel's expansion had already initiated.

Indeed before the medieval Serbian state was truly born in the second half of the twelfth century, the several attempts to create such a state all started from the coastal provinces. In the 1040s the weakness of the Empire enabled Stephen Vojislav, semi-independent ruler of Zeta from about 1018 and brought up in Ragusa, to unite Zeta (approximately later Montenegro) with Travunia and Hum (approximately later Hercegovina). The Serbs of the interior were drawn into this enlarged state under his successor Michael (1051–81). By now, though nominally Byzantine, the coastlands were becoming rapidly more Latin in culture, a process which had become noticeable in the tenth century and was only temporarily checked by transitory reimposition of Byzantine rule, especially after 1018. We may draw a conventional dividing-line at the year 1000. The towns felt themselves Byzantine only as long as the Byzantine navy controlled the Adriatic and could treat Venice, the heir of Ravenna, as a colonial market. After 1000 Venetian and other Italian cultural influences tend to outweigh the Byzantine. Stephen and his son Michael were both in a difficult position in that, instead of a single ecclesiastical authority in their realm, there were portions of three archdioceses—Split, Durazzo, Ohrid—but not the metropolis of any. The creation of the Latin metropolitan diocese of Dioclea (Duklja) in 1066/7,[c] with its ecclesiastical centre at Bar,[d] was thus an improvement from the point of

[a] See p. 181. It is possible that during the period of Byzantine control Ras was attached to the metropolis of Durazzo.

[b] No previous radiation from Macedonia can be detected, that is, dating from the ministry of St Clement after 885. It cannot of course be excluded though it cannot have been considerable. Glagolitic continued to be known and used sparingly in Serbia down to *c.* 1200, perhaps even later.　　　　　　　　　　[c] See pp. 200–1.

[d] Italian *Antivari* from Greek. The town was probably founded in the seventh century during the Slav inroads and became a bishopric at an unknown date.

view of the ruler of Zeta and of the ambitious Bishop Peter of Bar. It was to embrace all the coast south from the River Cetina, but the bishopric of Ragusa was in practice excepted.[a] Michael indeed preferred Ragusa's independence as a buffer against the encroachments of Split to which the see of Ragusa had been originally subordinate. The new metropolis was, according to the Pope, to include, besides sees formerly subordinate to Byzantine Durazzo and Latin Split, Travunia (Trebinje), Bosnia and Serbia.

All this amounted to an attachment of Zeta to Rome, though much of the earlier evangelical work in Dioclea must have been done by Byzantine Durazzo. Indeed Michael's relations with Gregory VII were so good that the Pope sent him a crown in 1077.[b] By this act he hoped to block Norman pretensions to rule any part of the East Adriatic coast; for the Normans had made themselves 'protectors' of the Papacy in 1059 and from 1071 became a naval power to be reckoned with. Zeta was now a mature state with king and archbishop.

But two things must be borne in mind. The Roman attachment did not imply the sweeping away of all Byzantine clergy and practices on the coast, *a fortiori* further inland. The overlapping of the Roman and Byzantine ecclesiastical organisations is characteristic of South Dalmatia and their relative weight at any moment difficult to assess. Thus Bar, like Dioclea, had formerly been a suffragan see of Durazzo but with Samuel of Bulgaria's conquest of that town, the terminal of the vital *Via Egnatia*, in 989, Bar preferred to throw in its fortunes with its northern neighbours. Its rise to importance in the middle of the eleventh century increased the Latin component without suppressing the Byzantine. Even after the 1050s the Papacy did not press a thoroughgoing policy of extirpation of Byzantine practice in these parts: recognition of her jurisdiction, and its extension inland, was the first priority.

Secondly, the precise status of the interior provinces is obscure. Serbia (Ras) and Bosnia were to be included in the archdiocese of Dioclea (Bar) in 1067. This was the Papal intention but scarcely the reality. There is nothing to show that Ras did not maintain its dependence on Ohrid. It is not to be supposed that Michael made any violent changes

[a] The status of archbishopric was accorded in 1022 (perhaps as early as 1000, according to a possible interpretation of Benedict VIII's Bull of 27 September 1022) but apparently lost again about 1050. During these years Ragusa claimed ecclesiastical jurisdiction over all the coastal sees from Ston (Stagno) in Hum to Ulcinj (Dulcigno), and possibly also over Serbia proper.

[b] A fresco in the new Cathedral of St Michael at Ston, founded by Michael, shows him so crowned.

which would weaken his authority. In any case inland Serbia was lost again before 1077. Moreover, Split was never wholly reconciled to the decisions of 1066/7 and Ragusa's ambitions were gaining substance and strength.[184] Michael's son, Constantine Bodin, second King of Zeta (1081–*c.* 1106) and still ruler of Serbia and parts of Bosnia,[a] attempted to regulate the situation with more precision: Bar must have a position in the church consonant with the political scene. In 1088/9 Bodin persuaded the Antipope Clement III (1084–1100)[b] to reaffirm the disputed metropolitan status of Bar and redefine the archdiocese. The list of sees virtually repeats that of 1066/7: those of Zeta, all those about Lake Scutari[c]—which Durazzo probably still claimed—and the sees of Travunia, Bosnia and Serbia (Rascia). The title of church and prelate thenceforward usually appears in the form *dioclensis atque antibarensis*. Once again all this proved partly a paper scheme.

Bodin's death saw the end of Zeta as the nucleus of a Serbian state. The Emperor Alexios Komnenos still held the upper hand in the Balkans and annexed this so-called Kingdom of Dioclea. Bosnia drew closer to Croatia in the course of the eleventh century and became part of the Hungarian state shortly after Croatia itself.[d] It seems unlikely that the religious complexion of the Serbian bishopric of Ras had been much changed by all these manœuvres; it had continued to look towards Ohrid. However, it was now clear that any future Serbian ruler would attempt to re-establish the vital link between Raška and the Coast and, conversely, that the culture and religion of the interior would remain to a greater or less degree under the influence of Bar, Kotor and Ragusa through their role as terminals of the trade-routes debouching on the Adriatic.

For the moment Ragusa was satisfied with having defeated the claims of Split and achieved full ecclesiastical independence. Though Pope Innocent II might still write to the Archbishop of Split in 1139 as 'sole metropolitan of all Dalmatia', this was merely to repeat his official title.[185]

---

[a] Bodin had proclaimed himself 'Emperor' at Prizren in 1072 as leader of the Balkan Slavs against the Greeks but this had no lasting significance.

[b] Clement III was made Pope in 1080 by the Emperor Henry IV after the humiliation which Gregory VII had imposed on him at Canossa in 1077. He was recognised as Pope in Rome in 1084 (Urban II being the new rival Pope), when he crowned Henry as Emperor. Both Hungary and Croatia belonged to the party of Clement.

[c] Principally Skadar (*italice* Scutari) itself, Ulcinj (Dulcigno), Svač, Polat (Pilot), Drivast.

[d] See p. 202. The part of Bosnia concerned was then known as *Rama*, of uncertain extent. From 1138 the Hungarian rulers used the title *Hungarie, Dalmacie, Chroacie Rameque rex*.

But Ragusa's ambitions continued to grow in the south. As a high proportion of her trade was with Albania and Epirus she was determined to get rid of the archbishopric of Bar which might in the future be the metropolis of an unfriendly state or too firmly under Byzantine administration. This policy was pressed vigorously in the twelfth century. Bar itself was in a weak position after the collapse of the Kingdom of Dioclea. Rome came down on the side of Ragusa from about 1120, when Calixtus II called on all the clergy of the southern sees to submit to Girardus of Ragusa, to whom at the same time he sent a *pallium*.[186] From then on the Pope generally tended to support Ragusa against Bar. At the same time Ragusa gave more colour to her pretensions to the 'Serbian lands' (ranging far into the interior) by a liberal falsification of alleged Papal rulings in her favour.

Late in 1154, after several bishops in the archdiocese of Bar had shown themselves once again recalcitrant to overtures from Ragusa, Pope Innocent II formally transferred the sees of Kotor,[187] Ulcinj and perhaps others to the obedience of Ragusa. Not long after Ragusa reached the high tide of her success. On 29 December 1167 Pope Alexander III extinguished the metropolis of Bar and placed all its sees under Ragusa.[188] The whole Adriatic seaboard became, at least theoretically, fully Roman. But neither Bar nor Split accepted this change passively.

From this date the political fortunes of inland Serbia again became a decisive factor in the fortunes of the coast. Byzantine ascendancy over Serbia and the latter's ecclesiastical dependence on Ohrid continued throughout the twelfth century. But both Bulgaria and Serbia were constantly on the watch for signs of Byzantine weakness of which they might take advantage. These were evident enough by 1167 when the Emperor Manuel was in such straits that he was obliged to offer the Pope ecclesiastical union in return for military aid. As the century drew to an end this weakness became more and more manifest. The Bulgarians achieved independence (the second Bulgarian Empire) in 1186.[a] Serbia had been under the thumb of Manuel since 1150 but on his death (1180) Stephen Némanja (Grand Župan *c.* 1168–95) rapidly brought about a new independence of the Serbian state and inaugurated the two centuries of its greatness.

Nemanja[b] once more faced the problem of reconciling Rome-facing

---

[a] See pp. 184 ff.

[b] The origins of the Némanja family are obscure. The first two known to have used the family name Uroš (believed to be Hungarian and derived from úr = lord, prince), and perhaps also the name Stephen, were local župans of Raška from *c.* 1113 to

Zeta with the Orthodox regions of the interior. He followed in the main the policy of the kings of Dioclea by keeping the see of Bar clear of a politically disadvantageous subordination to Ragusa or Split, whose ecclesiastical rivalry again became acute in the 1180s.[189] Nevertheless Gregory of Bar had to make some concessions to Split for his own security.[190] The deeds and opinions of the bishops of Ras during all this long period are quite unknown to us. Nemanja is supposed to have been baptised a Catholic in infancy; Serbian annals preserve the tradition of his baptism in the Church of SS Peter and Paul by Leontios, Bishop of Ras, at the age of thirty.[191] If these later annals—kept, it is true, by Orthodox Serbs—are to be trusted, they would appear to confirm the strongly Orthodox temper of Raška and Nemanja's recognition of the political wisdom of conversion to Orthodoxy in the 1160s, that is, at the moment when he finally established himself as Grand Župan.[a]

Nemanja remained an ally of Venice against Hungary and the Empire until the Emperor Manuel defeated and took him prisoner about 1172 and forced him to recognise his suzerainty; Manuel's successful campaigns since 1165 had given him temporary control of Croatia, Bosnia and most of the Adriatic coast. Hungary resumed her possession of Croatia and North Dalmatia.

Nemanja was soon released from Byzantine captivity. By 1186 he had regained a firm grip on Zeta. Its ports, particularly Bar, Budva and Kotor, were as always one of Serbia's main economic and cultural life-lines.[b] Indeed Zeta with its earlier kings and more precocious literature[192] could not but be an object of envy to the wilder interior. Nemanja's youngest brother Miroslav had for long been ruler of the province of Hum in his name. Together they attempted to reduce Ragusa. The attempt failed but the essential was gained by a treaty with this city-state[c] (September 1186) which gave the Ragusans commercial

c. 1163. The original Hungarian connection (not now discernable) presumably dates from Hungarian ascendancy in Croatia and Bosnia (see p. 202) and was maintained by intermarriage. Némanja himself was born at Ríbnica (near modern Titograd). It has not been satisfactorily proved whether he was the son of Uroš II or of his brother Desa. At any rate the family had no roots in Zeta, of which they were merely regaining control in the first half of the twelfth century.

a Cf. p. 219, note a below.

b The trade-route from the coast into the interior was known in Italy as the *via di Zenta* since it followed the course of the River Zeta—nowadays an oasis in the dry plain—upstream and penetrated the difficult country of the Tara and Lim gorges to arrive at Ras in Serbia.

c Ragusa then held only the coastal strip from the base of the Pelješac (Sabbioncello) peninsula in the north to the north point of the Bocche di Cattaro in the south. The expansion of its territory came mainly in the fourteenth–fifteenth centuries.

privileges in his dominions. A similar agreement was made with Split. Of the two, Ragusa handled the more valuable part of the commercial traffic: she was from the first the main outlet for Serbian, and later Bosnian, precious metals.[a] Commercially speaking she was also much better placed than Bar and the southern ports and soon overhauled them. But Ragusa received no ecclesiastical encouragement from Nemanja. Bar was now in his hands and Gregory of Bar naturally supported Nemanja's policy.

All the Balkans now turned against the tottering Byzantine Empire. It would seem that this first ruler of a great Serbia dreamed the common Balkan dream—of supplanting the Emperor in Constantinople. He attempted to influence Frederick Barbarossa in his favour at Niš in July 1189, when the Third Crusade was passing through the Balkans.[193] But when in 1203–4 the Fourth Crusade did basely occupy and ravage the Imperial City it was the Western European dynasts who installed themselves there—and Venice who reaped most of the commercial advantages —not a Slav ruler.

New churches sprang up in the environs of Ras during Nemanja's reign. The church of the Virgin and St Nicholas was probably built in 1165–8. St George's monastery—whose ruins are now known as *Djúrdjevi Stúpovi*—on an eminence some five miles to the north-west of Ras, probably belongs to the 1180s. The style of their architecture is a blend of East and West.[194] Important churches were now built all over the Serbian dominions from Kotor, taken by Nemanja in 1186, and Ston to Kuršúmlija on the vital strategic route to Niš.[195] Each of Nemanja's brothers was an active patron in the province which he administered. To Míroslav is ascribed the church of St Peter at Bijelopolje on the River Lim;[196] to Pŕvoslav—St George at Búdimlje; to Sraćimir— the church of the Mother of God at Gradac (Čačak) on the River Morava.[197] Nemanja's greatest foundation was the monastery of Studénica. Its church of the Mother of God was built about 1183–91. Though the monastery was in all respects Orthodox we find here, as almost everywhere, some architectural features of Dalmatian provenance, notably the use of marble facings.[198] Studenica was his *záduzbina*, that is, a personal foundation for the good of the patron's soul, where he expects

---

[a] Serbian mining (principally silver) developed rapidly from the early thirteenth century and provided a large part of the royal revenues. The technical skill was furnished largely by Germans ('Saxons') who emigrated from Transylvania at the time of the Mongol raids. Commercial treaties with Ragusa were renewed at frequent intervals after 1186 on similar terms.

to be buried and commemorated in perpetuity. Though in his later years his devotion was exclusively to the Orthodox Church he appears to have been perfectly tolerant of Catholics in his lands, as the arrangements with his son Vukan suggest. It is known that he sent princely gifts to St Peter's in Rome and St Nicholas in Bari.

It was only in the generation of Nemanja's sons that some stability in political and ecclesiastical affairs was at last reached. But not without a struggle. The contrast between interior and seaboard was in fact intensified. In 1190 Serbia had once more to bow before Byzantine arms. Isaac Angelos tried to bolster up his weakness and ensure future Serbian loyalty by arranging a marriage between his niece Evdokia and Nemanja's second son Stephen. The displacement of Isaac by his brother Alexios in 1195 led to a settlement whereby Nemanja abdicated —which was his own wish; Stephen, as son-in-law of the Emperor and *sevastokrator* since 1190, became ruler of Serbia, and the eldest son Vukan (Vlk) remained the local prince of Zeta, no doubt with increased autonomy as a palliative. To justify the succession of the younger son, Nemanja alluded to the precedent of Jacob.

Zeta had after all formerly been a kingdom. Vukan made another bid to restore this. His wife was a relative of Pope Innocent III (elected January 1198) and he himself was undoubtedly a Catholic.[199] By January 1199 he had persuaded the Pope to resuscitate for him the royal title—King of Dalmatia and Dioclea—and to confirm again the independence of his church with a *pallium* for his archbishop.[200] Ragusa thus lost her ecclesiastical hold on Zeta. The Pope soon had second thoughts about the justice of this and for some months held up the re-establishment of Bar's independence.[201] In 1199 two Papal legates convoked a synod at Bar which enforced again all the Latin regulations for the church and its clergy (tithe, celibacy, no beards).[202] But it prudently did not attempt to include the see of Ras among its suffragan sees. Ragusa, backed by Venice, continued to protest against Bar's position. But Vukan was too important to Papal policy. Andrew, brother of King Emerich (Imre) of Hungary, was at this moment poised to extend Hungarian suzerainty over the whole of the Western Balkans. Indeed Emerich, who even assumed the title of *rex Rasciae*, was surely instrumental in negotiating Vukan's royal promotion and submission to the Pope in return for recognition of Hungarian suzerainty over his kingdom. Papal jurisdiction would follow in the wake of Catholic arms.

Vukan's fortunes reached their zenith in 1202–3 when in concert with Hungary he conquered his brother Stephen's Serbian lands. Stephen soon succeeded in re-establishing himself with Bulgarian help. If Vukan attempted formally to introduce Catholicism in Serbia little came of it. A *modus vivendi* was agreed between the two brothers through the good offices of the youngest brother Rastko, who returned to Serbia from Athos in 1207: Vukan was as before to rule the coastal provinces in Stephen's name.

Yet the weakness of Stephen's own position, especially *vis-à-vis* Hungary, now at the height of its influence over Balkan affairs, and the impotence of the Byzantine Empire immediately after 1204, invited Serbian compromise with the Latin world. Stephen did not suppress Bar, though its authority was weak; it remained Vukan's ecclesiastical centre.[203] Stephen now even repudiated his Greek wife and married a Venetian. In the face of the disapproval of his younger brother and most Orthodox clergy in Serbia he continued in a pro-Roman policy, culminating in his coronation by a Papal legate in 1217 as King of Serbia.[a] Western pressure on all parts of the Balkans dictated this move. Stephen had even once gone so far as to assert that he would 'always obey the precepts of the Roman Church'.[204] Pope Clement III had acted on the assumption that the ruling dynasty of Serbia (Rascia) was loyal to Rome. Pope Honorius III now expected Stephen to acknowledge Papal supremacy and promote the establishment of the Catholic church in his realm through the see of Bar. The Bulgarian church accepted the protection of Rome in 1204[b] so that at the moment of Vukan's ascendancy the Curia may well have thought that the major part of the Balkans— that *Illyricum* abstracted from Rome in the eighth century—was at last within its grasp. It is not easy to gauge how far Stephen's complaisance went. But it seems clear that Serbian sentiment, attached to the Byzantine world at heart, at last made itself unequivocally felt. The Latin claim to Serbia was exposed as a fiction. The Bishopric of Ras had apparently not wavered; it looked as always towards Ohrid. From Ohrid or from Bulgaria had come the Slav service-books which the Serbian church had long been using. Three centuries of Orthodoxy in Greek and Slav form weighed more than passing political considerations.[205] It was Rastko who had consistently represented in his policy this popular sentiment, which now triumphed.

[a] Hence he is known as *Stevan prvovénčani*—the 'first-crowned'.
[b] See p. 185.

The entry of the Slavs into Christendom

The sources

1. The most important biography of St Sava (Rastko) is the *Life* by Domentian, probably completed about 1242/3 and considered reliable since Domentian was almost certainly his close companion during the last years of his life.[206]

2. The monk Theodosius's *Life of St Sava*, written not earlier than 1261.[207] Like Domentian, Theodosius (Teodosije) was a monk of Hilandar.

3. With these must be coupled the three *Lives* of St Symeon (Stephen Nemanja), viz. (*a*) by his son St Sava, written *c.* 1208, included in the *Studenica Typikon*, now only extant in a seventeenth-century copy; (*b*) by his son Stephen (Prvovenčani), written not later than 1216; (*c*) by the same Domentian, written in 1264, drawing freely on (*b*).[208] These display an interesting contrast in style and intention: the first is typical of the hagiographical genre; the second, by Nemanja's successor, is notably political—a dynastic tract. None is intended, naturally, to be a plain and sober historical biography.[209]

Rastko (Rastislav), the youngest brother, was the most remarkable of the three. He was born about 1174 and was destined for the normal career of a younger son, being made by his father Prince of Hum at an early age.[210] He had received a good education together with his brother Stephen and from boyhood showed a serious and ascetic bent. Within two years the young man abandoned uncongenial rule in Hum and fled to Athos, in the autumn of 1192 or shortly after, to embrace the monastic life. He first entered the Russian monastery of St Panteleimon; soon he moved to Vatopedi.[a] According to tradition a Russian monk was responsible for his spiritual direction.[211] He was professed at St Panteleimon under the name of Sava.[b]

His flight was not viewed with favour by his family. His father sent in vain to Athos to persuade him to return. Sava replied: You have accomplished all that a Christian sovereign should do; come now and join me in the true Christian life.[212] Athonite monks had already been frequent visitors at Nemanja's court. It was probably the admonitions of one such which had determined Sava to abandon the world. Nemanja took his son's advice to heart. He summoned his state assembly to Studenica and announced his own abdication and withdrawal into the monastic life (25 March 1195).[c] For the moment he remained at

[a] See p. 299.

[b] The imprecision in dates does not allow us to say whether Sava underwent a novitiate of three full years, as was usual but not obligatory. He must have come to Athos in his eighteenth year or thereabouts. The younger the postulant, the longer the novitiate imposed was likely to be.

[c] The year 1195 is now considered a better reckoning than the generally accepted 1196.

Studenica but on the further insistence of his son joined him on Athos in 1198. His eyes were now fully opened to the significance of the Holy Mountain. Here father and son together founded, with Imperial approval, the Serbian monastery of Hilándar (June 1199).[213] Stephen Nemanja, as the monk Symeon, died there on 13 February 1200.[a] The international life of the Athonite community comes out clearly at Symeon's funeral: the rites were performed in turn, presumably each in their own liturgical language, by Greeks, Iberians (Georgians), Russians, Bulgarians and finally Serbs.[214] Nemanja's relics were brought back to his *zadužbina* Studenica in 1207, where they soon began to work miracles.

By the time of Stephen's coronation in 1217 Nemanja was already looked upon as a national saint and the time was ripe for a decisive change. The status of Ohrid, to which the see of Ras was still subordinate, now became as equivocal as that of Bar had often been. With the dismemberment of the Byzantine Empire in 1204 Ohrid passed, precisely in 1217, into the hands of the Greek Despot of Epirus. It was not only less accessible but in a potentially hostile state. Theodore of Epirus (*regnabat* 1214–30), though resistant to the Latins, looked upon the 'Empire' of Nicaea as no more legitimate than his own realm.[215] Who could tell whether the City would be redeemed from the Latins and if so at whose hands? There was no love lost between Arta, the Epirote capital, and Nicaea. But in Serbian eyes there could be no question that the Patriarch at Nicaea had a better claim to the obedience of all the Orthodox than any prelate in the Despotate, despite some signs that Theodore Láskaris of Nicaea was prepared to discuss union with Rome.[216] Thus when the creation of an independent Serbian church became a political desideratum authority had to be sought in Nicaea. Theodore of Epirus himself, though uncompromisingly independent in politics,

---

[a] The tradition that Nemanja died at the age of eighty-six or thereabouts is strong but hardly bears examination. If he had been born about 1114 he would only have set about raising a family of sons at the age of fifty—exceedingly improbable in those times. The dates of birth of Vukan and Stephen are unknown but there is little doubt about Sava's. Further, Nemanja's younger brother Miroslav died in 1199—another octogenarian? If we accept the tradition of his second baptism in Orthodoxy at the age of thirty (no doubt an approximate figure) it would be reasonable to bring this into relation with his rise to power and with Manuel's conquests ending in Nemanja's defeat and capture about 1172. Vukan, the eldest son who remained a Catholic, could have been born before this baptism, Stephen and Rastko after. Thus if Nemanja was in fact born in, say, 1135, the chronology wolud make better sense, viz. (i) married *c.* 1160, (ii) Vukan born early 1160s, (iii) Orthodox baptism in late 1160s, (iv) Stephen born *c.* 1170 (his first marriage was in 1196, i.e. *aet. c.* 25, died in 1227), (v) Rastko born *c.* 1174, (vi) abdicated 1195 *aet.* 60. (vii) died 1200, *aet.* 65 approximately.

shrank from the irregular step of declaring his own church autocephalous. Demetrios Khomatianós, appointed to Ohrid in 1217, liked to think of himself and acted as a patriarch but stopped short of actually assuming the title.[a] For all his political concessions Stephen never committed himself to ecclesiastical subordination to Rome: he had had too much trouble with his brother Vukan's machinations. Long tradition and the immediate history of the dynasty were both against such a step. The Orthodox piety of his father Nemanja, whose venerated relics Sava had brought back to Serbia at his request,[217] and the advice of his brother Sava, the monk of Athos (with which through the royal foundation of Hilándar relations were now very close), were decisive. Though the Byzantine government, even in this time of weakness, was still chary of granting autocephaly, in the cases of Serbia and Bulgaria such a concession promised to be of no little advantage.[b] For it is the duty of all Orthodox states to support their suzerain the Emperor, and the Emperor ardently desired their aid against the Latin encroachers and usurpers.

Consequently Sava was sent to Nicaea to negotiate for autocephaly. This may well have been in his mind since his return to Serbia ten years earlier. Now Stephen at last wished it and wished him as head of his church. Sava was consecrated as first archbishop of Serbia by the Patriarch Manuel Sarantenós (*fungebatur* 1215–22) in 1219.[218] Sava had become *hieromonakh* (monk in priest's orders) about 1200 and Domentian states that he was commonly accorded the title of *archimandrite*, that is a monk, especially an abbot, deemed worthy of a bishopric.

The details of the negotiations with and in Nicaea are not known for certain in default of documents but all appears to have been settled amicably. The Patriarch did not even insist on his right personally to consecrate the head of the Serbian Church in perpetuity. The Papal Legate seems to have finally withdrawn from Serbia at this moment. Archbishop Demetrios of Ohrid's official title—Archbishop of Justiniana Prima and All Bulgaria—was now an empty formula. Bulgaria had been lost as long ago as 1186. Ohrid as the self-styled heir of Justiniana Prima[c] had now lost Serbia too. The archbishop protested, as he was bound to do, at the creation of a Serbian autocephalous church on the grounds that Nicaea had no canonical right to detach Serbia from Ohrid, itself autocephalous, without his agreement.[219] Rádoslav, who had

---

[a] He went as far as to crown Theodore 'Emperor of the Greeks' about 1228 after the capture of Saloniki in 1224.

[b] See pp. 184–7.

[c] See pp. 6 and 370 n. 34.

succeeded his father Stephen in September 1228, showed some signs of complaisance in this matter towards Theodore of Epirus, who was his father-in-law, but Sava was strong enough to nullify it.[220]

As Dvornik rightly says, the case of Serbia is 'of unique interest in the study of relations between East and West'.[221] In the long run the centuries-old Byzantine culture of both Serbia and Bulgaria and their possession of the Slav ecclesiastical language made them consciously or unconsciously strive for national churches in the Eastern manner and reject the universalism of the Papacy which had more than once come close to catching the Balkans in its net. Whereas to be politically independent of Byzantium was their constant ambition, alienation from her communion was not. And whereas the Latins were inevitably the sworn foes of the ousted Greeks, they were often politically and economically useful to the Balkan Slavs. Stephen's Roman crown and Nicaean archbishopric symbolise the relative weight of these factors.

The Latin organisation of Bar was not suppressed by Stephen after 1217 but left in being for the Catholics in his dominions. Tolerance prevailed: churches passed from Catholic to Orthodox and *vice versa*. Stephen's own *Life* of his father is quite without *parti pris*.[222] But the Eastern was henceforward the 'established' and the Western the 'disestablished' church in the Serbian state. The established church was now to use nothing but the Slav liturgical language with its Greek background: Latin played no further important part.

The quarrel between Ragusa and Bar continued but was finally more or less settled during the pontificate of Innocent IV (1243–54). Despite all, Bar felt itself strongly attached to Serbia. *Dominus noster rex Urosius est nobis papa* was its firm reply to the Pope in 1247; it was not prepared to accept subordination to Ragusa.[223] The Pope found it politic to permit the use of the Slav language in the province of Bar, as he did for Croatian Dalmatia.[a] In 1248/9 the Pope appointed John de Plano Carpini (of Mongolian fame) Archbishop of Bar, hoping that he might reconcile all parties. But he died in 1252 without effecting much. Ragusa finally threw up her claims in 1255/6.

Sava returned from Nicaea to Serbia after a further short stay at Hilándar and in the Philókalos monastery at Saloniki. There followed a thorough reorganisation of the new autocephalous church. He established his archiepiscopal see at the monastery of Žiča, founded by his brother King Stephen and built with the help of Greek masters in the

[a] See p. 203.

years 1208–15. This was to be the coronation church of the dynasty.[a] But Studenica, which may be called the cathedral of Ras though it remained a private dynastic foundation, was still the real centre of ecclesiastical and political life.

New bishoprics were founded to cover every province: at the monastery of the Archangel Michael on the island of Prevlak in the Gulf of Kotor, for Zeta; at Ston (church of the Mother of God, now disappeared) for Hum; and at Dabar (Banja on the River Lim) near the Bosnian border— the monastery of SS Nicholas and George—all these in the potentially more Catholic parts. Four others were erected in the interior: at Hvosno, north-east of Peć—the monastery church of the Mother of God; at Kuršumlija—Nemanja's St Nicholas, now known as the bishopric of Tóplica;[b] at Búdimlje (now Ivangrad, near Ándrijevitsa)—the monastery of St George;[c] at Árilje (that is, St Achilles), known as the bishopric of Móravica.[224] The unreliable lists of sees traditionally associated with St Sava sometimes include the doubtful Gráčanica and Bránicevo[225] and two others which strictly speaking were still outside Nemanja's and Stephen's dominions at their widest extension—Belgrade and Prizren, whose Greek bishop probably remained under Ohrid.[d]

Sava naturally drew upon Athonite monks for his bishops. The monasteries of Saloniki may perhaps have provided some too: they were by this time centres of Greco-Slav mixing second only to Athos itself. Sava had close ties of friendship with the Orthodox Metropolitan of Saloniki and with several monasteries in the province.[e] It will be noted that the Serbian sees were normally situated in monastic churches on the main routes of communications. In a country such as Serbia, which of all the Balkan Slav states was the most deficient in towns, such a disposition was inevitable. In the early stages of the conversion of a

---

[a] As Stephen's first wife Evdokia was not merely a Byzantine princess but a *porphyrogennete*, the church was, and still is, painted the Imperial colour—a kind of dark red commonly called 'purple'. Despite considerable rebuilding in the fourteenth century after devastating Cuman raids in 1290 its general appearance is believed to have been preserved. The plan betrays a strong Athonite influence (in particular that of the Monastery of Pantokrator) but there are also Italianate decorative features. Žiča did not long retain the primacy; Arsenije (*fungebatur* 1234–63) removed to Peć in 1253 for safety from such barbarian incursions.

[b] See p. 215. This took the place of Niš, once more in Bulgarian hands.

[c] See p. 215.

[d] The northern frontier ran from the confluence of the River Lepenica with the Morava to the course of the River Neretva, the southern from the headwaters of the Morava to the mouth of the Drim. Prizren probably changed hands several times: Demetrios of Ohrid complained to St Sava for replacing a bishop of Prizren by one of his own.

[e] The diocese was much disturbed at this time. There was a Latin archbishop also till 1224.

country without urban communities monasteries, apart from the Court, are the natural centres for evangelisation and for the training of native clergy. This stage was unusually prolonged in Serbia. Indeed the social structure of the Serbian (including Montenegrin) countryside remained remarkably conservative until very recent times. This is to be seen especially in the widespread retention of the *zádruga* or 'great family' and in the very high proportion of Slav (pagan) names used in preference to those of Christian saints. The Serbian *slava* is a good example of the reinterpretation of a pagan rite in Christian terms: the clan ancestor became a Christian saint, frequently St Nicholas.

Sava's remaining years were devoted to establishing the Byzantine principle—that the spiritual authority and temporal power should work hand in hand to guide the state—until 1227 in the person of two brothers and thereafter of uncle and nephew. The autocephaly of the Serbian church was affirmed in every way, not the least in a new manual of Christian law (Nomokanon) which Sava translated or had translated in Saloniki for Serbian use on his way back from Nicaea. This master copy was deposited at Žiča and was still being faithfully copied in the fourteenth century.[226] This code, a selection of both canon and secular law to suit Serbian conditions, remained influential in the Orthodox Balkans, and even in Russia, for centuries to come.[227]

Sava made two pilgrimages to the Holy Land. On the first he made a special study of Palestinian monasticism, staying at the famous house dedicated to his own patron saint near Jerusalem. In Jerusalem itself he set up a hospice for Serbian pilgrims and houses for Serbian monks, thus laying the foundation for the active relations which obtained particularly in the fourteenth century. Serbian monks kept up the link with the Monastery of St Sava. His experiences there were applied in the monastic reforms which he put in train in Serbia after his return (not later than early 1230). A rule based on that of St Sava's monastery—the 'Jerusalem Rule'— was more and more widely adopted in the fourteenth and fifteenth centuries to the exclusion of the Studite Rule which had been the model for Sava's charters for Studenica and Hilandar.[228] Legend has it that the monks of St Sava presented him with the icon of the Virgin with Three Hands (Trikherousa), reputed to have belonged to St John Damascene who had been a monk there. This Sava took back to Studenica. In 1371 however, to save it from the Turks, the icon was tied to an ass which was turned loose; God caused the animal to find its way to Hilandar, where the icon still is.

With the accession in 1234 of Radoslav's brother, Vladislav, who was married to a daughter of the Bulgarian Emperor Asen, Sava decided that the time had come for him to retire from active affairs. He caused Arsenije to be elected archbishop in his stead and set out in the same year on his second pilgrimage, perhaps with a view to permanent retirement into a Palestinian or Athonite monastery. This time, after revisiting Palestine, he went on to various Egyptian monasteries, including St Catharine's on Mount Sinai. Finally, via Nicaea, he arrived at the Bulgarian capital, Tŭrnovo.[a] Here he died on 14 January 1236.[229] His body was first laid in the new church of the Forty Martyrs at Tŭrnovo but soon brought back to the monastery church of the Ascension at Mileševo.[230] The Bulgarians' request to keep the holy relics was refused.

The Nemanjid dynasty, which had produced its saint and patriot in St Sava, displayed an enthusiasm for pious foundations which did not cease till the collapse of the state before the Turks at the Battle of Kósovo in 1389. Of the more important may be mentioned briefly the monasteries of Sópoćani, built and decorated by Stephen Uroš I (*regnabat* 1243–76), Gráčanica by Stephen Uroš II Milútin (*regnabat* 1282–1321)[b] and Déčani by Stephen Uroš III (*regnabat* 1322–31), which earned him the by-name *Déčanski*. The abbots of these royal foundations counted among the most important functionaries of the state. It is in the interior decoration of these churches, particularly those of the thirteenth century, that the best work of the time in the Byzantine tradition is to be found. For the exiled court of Nicaea and the restored Empire from 1264 were both too poor to devote their resources to splendid building, whereas Serbia was riding the crest of prosperity which her silver mines brought.

If Serbian church interiors, which are the immediate and necessary background of the Orthodox services, were wholly Byzantine in conception, generally Macedonian in style and always having the indispensable symbolic dome over the crossing, their exteriors, as we have noted earlier, often incorporated features of the Western architecture of the Adriatic coast. Craftsmen from Dalmatia were appreciated and often more readily available than Greeks. This continued to be true down to

---

a It seems improbable that any diplomatic mission had been attached to Sava's journey, as is sometimes suggested, specifically that he was to negotiate at Nicaea in favour of a Bulgarian patriarchate which Vladislav might now wish to promote for his father-in-law. The patriarchate was in fact agreed between John Vatatzes and Asen in spring 1235 (see Bulgaria, p. 186); but we do not know precisely when Sava was in Nicaea.

b The frescoes include a fine genealogical tree of the Nemanjid dynasty.

the end of Serbian independence. The porch added to the Church of the Holy Wisdom at Ohrid by Archbishop Gregory in 1314 is wholly Italian in style. Dečani, built about 1327–35, amazes by its contrast of an Italianate exterior and a Greek interior; its architect was a Franciscan from Kotor.[231]

Few Serbian rulers between the time of St Sava and the Turkish conquest were without some connections, often close, with the Catholic world. Stephen Uroš I was much under the influence of his Catholic wife Helen, whose open patronage of Catholics caused some misgivings among the Orthodox. Her son, Dragútin (*regnabat* 1276–82) became a Catholic after his deposition.[232] Milutin was obliged to go softly with the considerable number of Catholics in his enlarged state, who had their own bishop. Yet he was the son-in-law of the Emperor and *sevastokrator*, and recognised Byzantine suzerainty. The coast of old Dioclea remained, as always, largely Catholic. Latin had to be employed side by side with Slav and Greek in Macedonia, the meeting-place of all Balkan currents. No intolerance appears until Stephen Dušan, proclaimed 'Emperor of the Serbs and Greeks' and so crowned at Skopje on 16 April 1346, made clear in his Law Code (1349–54) that the Serbian Empire, with its new Patriarchate at Peć, was Orthodox. Yet he was not harsh on Catholics: they were no longer allowed to proselytise, and conversely converts to Catholicism were to be persuaded (but not forced) to return to Orthodoxy.[233] We may also note Milutin's veneration of St Nicholas of Bari, who had become a Catholic saint by the felonious transfer of his relics from Myra to Bari in 1087.[234] Again, the style of Serbian coinage was a hotch-potch of Byzantine, Venetian and even Hungarian motifs. While Vladislav's issues were predominantly Byzantine and had Cyrillic inscriptions those of Stephen Uroš I and his successors were more Venetian with Latin inscriptions (VROSIVS REX).[235]

Western traits are visible, though not so immediately, in the literary field also. An early example of this duality is Prince Miroslav's *Gospel Book*.[a] It was written about 1180–90 in an Athonite-Macedonian *ductus* of Cyrillic but not by ecclesiastical scribes accustomed to using it (one scribe at least normally used the Latin alphabet) and the ornamentation, except for the first miniature, is in the Benedictine style current in Dalmatia. That it was written in Miroslav's province of Hum is further underlined by certain Westernisms of language, clearly of Ragusan provenance.[236] Conversely the Cyrillic *ductus* current in Serbia from the

[a] See p. 231.

thirteenth century was strongly under the influence of that of Ragusan documents, itself considerably influenced by contemporary Latin minuscules. This interaction is hardly surprising in a Ragusan chancellery where Latin and Cyrillic documents were written indifferently by the same clerks. Even the principal *Lives* of the Serbian dynastic saints[a] are not innocent of certain Latin stylistic features.

Serbia remained near the frontier between Orthodox East and Catholic West. Whereas in the early years of the thirteenth century both Serbia and Bulgaria had seemed momentarily within Rome's grasp, by the time of the Council of Lyons (1274) the hastily botched up union engineered by Michael Palaeológos appealed to neither. The day of a restored Papal Illyricum was past. St Sava had decided the direction of the Serbian Church once and for all. Even a recent religious map of Yugoslavia[237] still shows roughly the balance of forces which prevailed in the days of the medieval Serbian Kingdom: a nearly solidly Catholic Croatia and coastline down to Kotor with an Orthodox hinterland except in Bosnia, a patchwork of all possible denominations.[b]

Symeon and his son Sava were early recognised as saints in Serbian piety. Symeon, like the early princes of other Slav countries—Wenceslas,[c] Vladimir and Boris and Gleb[d]—with whom may also be coupled St Stephen of Hungary,[238] remained exclusively a national saint. The Patriarchate of Constantinople was not as a rule eager to recognise such laymen as saints of the Œcumenical church. In their own countries they represented God's Grace manifested towards the legitimate dynasty. St Sava continues to be highly venerated on Athos. He is also recognised as a saint in the Catholic church. The cell which he built in 1199 at the administrative centre of Karyés (*Órahovica* in Serbian) and himself frequently used for retreat after his father's death, still stands and the Rule which he drew up for it is still followed.[239] For the Serbian church St Sava is not only the first native archbishop but also its Illuminator (prosvétitelj) and Teacher (účitelj), the proud title accorded to St Cyril, the Teacher of the Slavs.[240] His biographers Domentian and Theodosius reflect the temper of the time in stressing that Sava was sent by God to fulfil the unfinished work of his forebears and to integrate Serbia finally into the comity of Eastern Orthodox churches. He was of that small company who sacrifice their own immediate salvation to return to the world for the sake of the salvation of others—the whole Serbian people.

[a] See p. 218.
[c] See pp. 92 ff.
[b] See also pp. 227 ff.
[d] See pp. 260, 266–7.

So Sava saw it himself.[241] The close link with Athos proved the keystone of the arch. The saintly pair—Symeon and Sava—represent dynasty and church, the twin pillars of the Serbian state, the source of its remarkable strength. So the Serbians conceived it. All the succeeding members of the house of Nemanja were held to have the Divine *charisma* for their rule.

The state has need of the church, but the church has no need of the state. Here the church long outlived the state. In the dark days of Ottoman rule the Serbian monasteries were the main foci of Serbian culture. The Turks became so alarmed at the veneration accorded to Sava's relics, not only by their Serbian subjects but also by many Moslems, that they were publicly burnt by Sinan Pasha in 1594.

BOSNIA AND THE BOGOMIL HERESY

Ignoring as we may divers heresies which flourished here and there, a general survey of early Balkan Slav Christianity would yet be incomplete without some account of the Bogomils.[242] A full exposition of their beliefs and customs must be sought elsewhere.[243]

Briefly, Bogomilism was both dualist and 'puritan'. It was dualist in that it believed that Satan or Satanael, God's rebel elder son, was the creator of the universe. All matter therefore derives from an autonomous evil principle at war with God. Our bodies and their functions are unsanctified and cannot be sanctified.[244] Satan made the body of man; the soul only was from God. It was puritan in that it rejected most of the dogmas and rites of the church as a human superstructure without the authority of Christ—an illusion which Satan has foisted on us.[245] Thus typical Bogomil doctrine rejected all the Old Testament except the Psalms and retained of the New only Jesus's teachings in the Spirit. His whole human life, as partaking of matter, was necessarily mere appearance.[246] Atonement and Redemption become meaningless if man, created not by God but by Satan, never fell. The Mother of God and the Cross are hateful debasements; the sacraments, including marriage, valueless; the Doctors of the church—false teachers. The doctrine of the Trinity was interpreted in various unorthodox ways. Their practice therefore was deceptively simple: prayer to God and to his true emanation, Jesus—especially the Lord's Prayer; non-involvement as far as possible in all the toils of matter, including sexual abstinence; the avoidance of wine and all food of living origin.

There will necessarily be an order of more 'perfect' Bogomils able, unlike the majority of men, to follow the most strict interpretation of these abnegatory principles. Further, since the church goes hand in hand with government, there was a strong element of social protest in Bogomilism, a refusal to obey civil and military authority in any way which conflicted with this conception of 'primitive Christianity'. Naturally over a long period of time doctrine and custom varied from place to place. Some consider this social disobedience the mainspring of the movement's success.

The main ingredient in Bogomil belief was the Paulician heresy indigenous to the Byzantine Empire's troubled eastern frontier over against the Monophysite churches and Islam. Both the Byzantine authorities and the Armenians took repressive measures against the Paulicians in the eighth and ninth centuries. On several occasions Constantine V Coprónymos (*regnabat* 741–75) took the unwise step of forcibly transferring large bodies of Paulicians to Thrace, since, partly by virtue of their strict religious principles, they were a well-disciplined and martial people:[a] the defence of the western approaches to the Imperial City was a more and more insistent need against Bulgars and others. This Iconoclast Emperor considered Paulicians less dangerous in the religious sense than some of his more Orthodox subjects. For about a century the heresy continued quietly spreading in Thrace.

The expansion of the Bulgarian state southwards at the expense of the Empire and its entry into Christendom in the 860s marked a new phase. From the earliest years of their Christianity the Bulgarians were faced not only with rival Christian missions but also with the presence among them of this self-styled pure and primitive form of Christianity. Monophysite Armenians, Jews and even Moslems, resident in the country, added to the confusion. It is very likely that the Slav peasantry in parts of Bulgaria was from the first in closer contact with Bogomil beliefs than with the Orthodoxy which was then being laboriously imposed on it from above. Dualist doctrine had the same advantage of theological simplicity that Arianism had had for the semi-civilised Germanic peoples.

The young Bulgarian church was immediately made aware of the danger. The last of Pope Nicholas I's *Responsa* to Boris[b] warns of the danger of false teachings without being specific about heresy as such.[247] A few years later (about 872) the newly appointed Archbishop of

---

[a] The Paulicians themselves were no doubt of many races, but a considerable proportion must have been Armenians.   [b] See p. 160.

Bulgaria received from Peter of Sicily a tract on the dualist heresy which he had been commissioned to investigate by the Emperor Basil I.[248] John the Exarch attacks heretics, presumably of this persuasion, in his *Shestodnev*, written *c.* 915: he argues at length that there is no evil principle (*zŭla sila*) in the Creation.[249]

The Paulicians and similar sects could not be stamped out either in Thrace or in Asia Minor; in Bulgarian territory it was far beyond the means of scattered missions to oppose their spread.

The peculiarly Bulgarian form of the heresy, however, does not seem to have arisen before the reign of Peter (927–69); for it was in his time that the eponymous founder of it, Bogomil,[a] lived and propagated a personal variant, or selection, of these diverse doctrines. The region in which he worked is not known for certain but is likely to have been Macedonia. Theophylakt of Ohrid alludes to 'a beastly heresy', which can scarcely be other than Bogomilism, as developing thereabouts in the years following St Clement's death (916). Whether SS Clement and Naum themselves had to contend with it does not appear from the available sources.[250]

Bogomil's preaching met with marked success. From the middle of the tenth century the sect as a native heresy began to flourish. The Patriarch of Constantinople, Theophylakt (*fungebatur* 933–56), sent an official warning to Tsar Peter against this new heresy.[251] The Bulgarian church itself, after a century of development, was not above reproach and needed in some respects to set its own house in order. This is clear from Cosmas the Priest's *Tract against the Bogomils*, written about 972.[b] He points to many shortcomings in the Bulgarian church which helped to account for the vigour of this popular movement—in particular, worldliness and ignorance of the clergy. Cosmas's strictures certainly appear to indicate an element of social protest in the Bogomil movement; its adherents were still largely drawn from the lower classes. His account is also one of the best sources for its beliefs at that stage, though in the nature of things it cannot be taken as a complete and unbiassed account.

The havoc wrought by the laborious Byzantine reconquest of Bulgaria during the next half-century was largely responsible for the further

[a] Originally, as in some early texts, Bogumil, a calque of Greek θεοφίλης or θεόφιλος (dear to God), but the later and more normal form for a Slav binomial name is generally adopted. It is curious, however, that his followers are always referred to as 'Bogomils' and not, as would be expected, by a derivative from the heresiarch's name. This has led a few scholars to doubt his existence and put the name 'Bogomils' on a par with 'Cathars'—that is, *pure ones*—a name known from the early eleventh century in Languedoc and North Italy.   [b] See p. 178.

dispersion of the Bogomil doctrines. The Paulician sect had even been strengthened about Philippopolis (Plovdiv) by another large transference of its adherents from Asia Minor by John Tzimiskes about 975; they were left undisturbed in their beliefs provided that they kept the Bulgarians at bay. There is nothing to suggest that Tsar Samuel was not himself Orthodox but some members of his family are suspect of Bogomil leanings and he may have found himself, under pressure of political and military needs, obliged to be more or less tolerant to the sect in his dominions. It was at this time that Bogomilism spread into Serbia and Bosnia, both for a time under his rule, and probably beyond.

The Byzantine authorities fared no better in dealing with the heresy in conquered Bulgaria. There is by this time more reason to associate it with a movement of national resistance to Greek domination and the hellenization of the country, including the official Church. On top of this Bulgaria was devastated by nomad incursions, especially by the Pechenegs in 1048, and soon Constantinople was too occupied with new difficulties on her eastern frontier to give more than scant attention to Bulgaria. Bogomil religious leaders had no doubt always been recruited, if lapsed Orthodox, from the lower, parish clergy, of Slav race. Now that Greeks increasingly filled the higher ranks of the Bulgarian church, this dichotomy was rendered more acute and obvious. At the same time, insofar as the movement became anti-Greek, it tended also to invade the higher levels of Bulgarian society. It was, in short, becoming more respectable.

The twelfth and thirteenth centuries show the heresy at its most vigorous. From the Balkans it had spread westwards, by the agency of merchants and perhaps Crusaders, via North Italy to Southern France, where the so-called Albigensian Crusade had to be organised for its suppression.[252] By about 1100 Bulgarian Bogomilism had already penetrated into educated Byzantine circles. Alexios Komnenós (1081–1118) took the drastic step just before his death of having a prominent Bogomil leader, Basil, burnt as a heretic.[253] Evidently the movement had come out into the open even within the Byzantine Empire. Several bishops and even one Patriarch—Kosmas Attikós (1146–7)—were suspect of contamination by these doctrines. A synod held at Constantinople in 1140 called for the destruction of various pernicious Greek works which contained doctrines similar to those of the Massalians, 'otherwise called Bogomils'.[254] Notices of more or less solidly Bogomil districts within the Byzantine Empire reach to the end of the twelfth century. In the East

Balkans the movement was strong enough to require organisation on a territorial principle. The main 'churches' were called *Bulgaria* and *Dragovitia*.[a]

Further west Bosnia, centred on the valley of the River Bosna, had become the most infected area. For long disputed between its ring of more powerful neighbours, Bosnia was not yet firmly integrated into any ecclesiastical body. A Bosnian see is assumed by Pope Alexander III in 1066/7,[b] perhaps a Latin see recently founded by the Croat Peter-Krešimir IV in the archdiocese of Split. If it survived it must have been transferred to Ragusa about 1100. That Bar's writ ever ran in Bosnia is dubious;[c] Ragusa was always Bosnia's most important link with the outside world, as is clear from Ban Kulin's commercial treaty of 1189.[255] Bosnia became under its *bans* a refuge for persecuted heretics, supporting its resistance to political extinction. Kulin (*c.* 1180–1204) and his successors all appear to have been favourable to, or at least tolerant of, this popular movement.

A more stern persecution of heretics in general and Cathars in particular was set in motion by the Edict of Verona in 1184. About 1199 Vukan of Zeta denounced Kulin to the Pope as a heretic and the Pope encouraged Hungary, which then dominated most of the North Balkans, to take repressive measures in Bosnia.[256] Kulin hastened to submit to a Papal enquiry. He made formal abjuration to the Papal Legate John de Casamaris in April 1203 but the condemnation of the heresy by this Bosnian synod remained a dead letter. The Pope's plans for strengthening Bosnian Catholicism by three or four new bishoprics did not succeed.[257]

The Bogomils were also strong in the province of Hum (modern Hercegovina)[d] where a Papal Legate reported the heresy as rife in 1180. Some Bogomil influence has been claimed in the miniatures of Miroslav's *Gospel Book*.[258] Bogomils were also numerous in the cities of Split and Trogir; they took refuge in Bosnia when the Dalmatian coast became too dangerous for them under the purifying measures of Bernard of Split (1199–1200). Stephen Nemanja and his son attempted to stamp the heresy out in their dominions, with what success is difficult to estimate. These persecutions no doubt helped further to concentrate the sectarians in Bosnia.

[a] Bulgaria = Macedonia; Dragovitia = Thrace, with centre at Plovdiv, the former territories of the Slav tribe *Dragovitai* or *Druguvitai*. The latter may also have remained more strictly Paulician than Bogomil.   [b] See pp. 200–1.   [c] See pp. 211–12.
[d] This name dates from 1448 when Stephen Vukčić was created by Frederick III 'Duke (Herzog) of St Sava'.

Constant Hungarian pressure on Bosnia had only limited success.[a] The heresy was difficult to pin down. When in danger its adherents had always assumed the outward mask of Orthodox or Latin Christians.[259] They claimed after all to be the purest Christians of all. They now passed under various local names, of which the most usual was Patarenes.[b] Ban Kulin's son Stephen was nominally a Catholic but could do little to influence what may by now have been the predominant religion of his land. He was deposed by the convinced Bogomil Ninoslav (1232–c. 1250).[260] But Ninoslav (Matthew) also found it politic to be outwardly accommodating to a Papal Legate despatched in 1232. Pope Gregory IX, who harried the heresy in all the affected areas, succeeded in having a German Dominican appointed Bishop of Bosnia (1234), perhaps now directly subject to Rome.

In August 1247 the Bosnian see was transferred to the Hungarian archbishopric of Kalocsa.[261] But the Hungarian arm hardly reached so far. Until Ninoslav's death Bosnia was regarded by all as an heretical state of which Bogomilism was the official religion. The head of the 'church' (Did) and twelve elders acted as the supreme council, chancellery and court of the land. But owing to the secretiveness of the convinced Bogomils and the bias of all outside observers it is well-nigh impossible to arrive at the truth. The strength of the Bogomil church and the complaisance of Ninoslav are held by some scholars to have been greatly exaggerated. Catholic bishops of Bosnia, subject to a distant metropolis in Dalmatia or Hungary, admittedly failed to get to grips with the scattered and mobile heretics; but anything in the nature of a formal Bogomil church has been denied.[262] Even the 'elect'—the *Krščani*—have been considered not so much heretics as an archaic, perhaps gnostic, monastic sect.[263] It is true that the Bogomils did not generally go as far as the Cathars in their rejection of the church. Thirteenth-century Bosnia may represent their most successful attempt to be treated as an 'elect' order within it. But Orthodoxy does not accept such esoteric orders.

[a] Hungary claimed Bosnia again under the *Pacta Conventa* of 1202 (see p. 202), as formerly Croatian territory which Béla III had given to his son Ladislas in 1137, but it could not formally be brought under the Hungarian crown.

[b] *Patarene* is often supposed to be from *pater*, a mode of address between them, or from *paternoster*, in allusion to the one Christian prayer constantly on Bogomil lips. But the consistent spelling is against this. The name appears to have originated in the eleventh century for a Milanese sect practising poverty: the *Pataria* was the quarter of Milan where the rag-merchants congregated. The name was therefore only transferred to the Bogomils and certainly spread to Bosnia via Ragusa. Another name, *Babun*, is even more obscure (Sadnik and Aitzetmüller, *Handwörterbuch*, no. 145): it is apparently perpetuated in the Croat surname Babunić.

Bogomilism must be considered as much the cause of the spread of the Glagolitic alphabet to Bosnia as the province's links with Croatian Dalmatia. The Greek conquerors of Macedonia were apt to assume the heretical nature of the unreadable and now 'unofficial' Glagolitic writings and destroyed many.[a] Refugees took them to Bosnia, where the Cyrillic script was normal.[b] Thus local orthographic habits arose from a Glagolitic veneer over a Serbian Cyrillic cursive style.[264]

Meanwhile the movement was losing its impetus in Bulgaria and Serbia. Under the Second Bulgarian Empire (from 1186) the heresy was sometimes persecuted, sometimes tolerated. It was formally condemned by Tsar Boril at the Synod of Tǔrnovo (1211)[265] but later rulers appear to have still shown some tolerance whenever it was politically expedient. A similar condemnation was promulgated at the Serbian Synod of Žiča in 1221. From these and other sources we learn that the heresy was still strong about Plovdiv and Ohrid.

The Latin conquest of Constantinople in 1204 contributed to this decline. There was more persecution within the Latin-ruled lands. Indeed the excuse for the capture of the Dalmatian town of Zadar (Zara) in 1202 by the Crusaders at the instigation of Venice was that it was a stronghold of the heresy, no doubt the chief focus of its continued radiation to North Italy.[266] Venice had long wished to reduce this inconvenient fortress, now in Hungarian hands, and acquire permanent control of it. These persecutions led to some further emigration to the West and to greater concentration in the less accessible parts of Bosnia and Hercegovina. Concurrently persecution in the West may have brought refugees back to the Balkans.[c] As the Serbian state expanded in the fourteenth century it again absorbed Bogomil subjects, not only in Bosnia itself. The heresy was thus a running sore which Tsar Dušan found it necessary to condemn explicitly in his Law Code (Zákonik) of 1346.[267]

Throughout the fourteenth century Bosnia continued to harbour the heresy, while Catholic and Orthodox now competed more openly for its ecclesiastical allegiance. Bosnia was at its most powerful under Stephen Tvrtko I (1353–91), half Croat and half Serb, who assumed the title of King of Bosnia and Serbia in 1377 and had himself crowned at St Sava's

[a] See pp. 181–2.

[b] The Latin alphabet, normal in Hungary and most of Croatia, had limited currency there before the eighteenth century, though the coinage minted from the abundant native silver from the middle of the fourteenth century usually had Latin inscriptions.

[c] The main 'Albigensian Crusade' was over by 1215 but the Pyrenean fortress of Montségur was only destroyed in the 1240s. The movement declined rapidly in the south of France from the middle of the thirteenth century.

tomb at Mileševo. His predecessor Stephen II Kotromanić (1314–53), who had conquered Hercegovina,[268] had passed from Orthodoxy to Catholicism and received on two occasions Franciscan inquisitors and missionaries. Tvrtko also veered between the two. Bosnia's independence was for a short time less precarious; any national sentiment which may have centred on Bogomilism was now satisfied.

With the Turkish conquest of the Balkans the heresy finally lost its *raison d'être*. Bosnia and Hercegovina were occupied in 1463 and 1483 respectively. Orthodoxy or Catholicism was strengthened as the life-line of the conquered Slav peoples. The Bosnians, who had never firmly opted for the one or the other, and as Bogomils considered both equally erroneous, went over in large numbers to Islam. As Moslems the nobility were able to preserve their estates and position. Bosnia to this day remains the most obviously Moslem area of the Slav Balkans. Bogomilism rapidly vanished.[269]

There are few material traces of the heresy left. By its nature it was iconoclast and did not encourage the building of religious edifices.[a] It may suffice to note two things. At Árilje, south of Titovo Užice towards Bosnia, Stephen Dragútin, King of Serbia from 1276 to 1282, built St Achilles as a new episcopal church about 1295.[b] A well preserved contemporary fresco shows Dragutin and his brother Milutin (a great ecclesiastical builder) enthroned on either side of their grandfather Stephen the First-crowned. Below them a disputation is in progress between Orthodox bishops and Bogomil 'priests'. The latter are of course on the left side of Stephen, the side of the goats.[270] Secondly, the so-called Bogomil sepulchral monuments (*stećak*, pl. *stećci*), numerous in certain parts of Hercegovina, have in all probability no close connection with the Bogomil heresy.[271] There are no specifically Bogomil symbols by which they could be definitely identified as monuments of these heretics. Some are clearly Orthodox or Catholic. The best suggestion is that the majority, which belong to the late period of the fourteenth–fifteenth centuries, were erected by the local tribes of Vlachs, highland pastoralists speaking dialects akin to Romanian. They were then still a prominent element in the population and provided the

[a] The virtual absence of twelfth-century Serbian icons is sometimes ascribed to Bogomil influence. Cosmas felt the need in his Tract (see p. 178) to defend the use of icons once again against Bogomil disapproval.

[b] Dragutin inherited North Bosnia in 1282 through his wife, a daughter of the Hungarian King Stephen V. Stephen Kotroman of Bosnia (1272–98) married Dragutin's daughter. Dragutin himself was converted in 1291 to Catholicism. But the church is essentially Byzantine in style.

animal transport for the trade caravans which plied between the Dalmatian ports, especially Ragusa, and the interior. What the religious beliefs of these Vlachs were cannot be ascertained.[272]

The chief remaining record of the Bogomil movement is therefore in written form—its service-books and scriptures together with the polemics of those who sought to eradicate it. Dualist texts spread as far as the Pyrenees and Novgorod in North Russia.[273] The manuscripts that survive date mostly from the declining days of the heresy, the fourteenth and fifteenth centuries. Various copies of New Testament compilations —*Tetrevangels* and *Apostols*—have been held to be Bogomil copies, though this is often difficult to substantiate.[274] The thirteenth century Provençal *Cathar Missal* is unambiguously dualist and may well go back to a now lost Bulgarian original.[275] Above all there are the numerous apocrypha which, as is the general habit of sects and heresies, tend to take the place of the Orthodox canon. Some of these were already well-known works, grafted onto material of the Old Testament (for example, the *Book of Enoch*) or the New (the *Gospel of Nicodemus* and the *Gospel of St Thomas*, otherwise known as the *Childhood of Jesus*).[276] Others appear to have been original Bogomil compositions, more directly promulgating dualist doctrine. Among these we may note: the so-called *Interrogatio sancti Iohannis*, whose date and original language are however uncertain, Latin versions alone being known;[277] the *Vision of Isaiah*, the *Story of Adam and Eve* and the *Razumnik* (passing under many different titles).[278] They were the esoteric core of the heresy, concealed as far as possible from the light of day.

5

THE EASTERN SLAVS

RUSSIA

Khazars and Varangians

Kiev owed its early importance to its geographical position. Situated on an easily defensible bluff overlooking the River Dnepr, on the boundary between the forest upriver and the parkland and open steppe to the south, it was destined to become a centre of communications and commerce. Here the forest-dwellers could exchange their products for those of the civilised world, brought up from the Black Sea coast; here East and West could meet at an easy crossing of the great river.

It is probable that much of the West Ukraine, including the Kiev area, had been part of the region within which the Slav peoples originally developed. Products of the Roman Empire at the time of its widest economic radiation reached this country via the many rivers falling into the Black Sea. After the withdrawal of the Romans from Dacia in A.D. 271 the chief middlemen were the Goths—both Visigoths in modern Romania and those Ostrogoths who had established a loose empire in Southern Russia and dominated at least a part of the Eastern Slavs.[1] The time of the Gothic Empire also saw the beginning of a great northward movement of the eastern Slavs up the River Dnepr and most of its tributaries—a colonisation of the forest zone by absorption or eviction of the Baltic and Finnic tribes in their path—by which the Dnepr became the main artery of their world. From that time on the importance of a political and economic centre somewhere in the Kiev region was assured. Moreover the capital of the Roman Empire was moved in the 330s from Rome to Constantinople, with a consequent different perspective on the barbarian world.

Evidence of the earliest settlements on the hills of Kiev is still meagre but the whole region had for long supported a relatively dense population. From the time of Justinian, when the more southerly Slavs became a permanent factor in Byzantine politics,[a] the Greek ports of the Black Sea were in more or less constant commercial relations with these more remote Slavs too and knowledge of them trickled back to the Imperial City itself. Thus the suggestion that Kij, the eponymous founder of

[a] See pp. 3 ff.

Kiev, lived (if he existed at all) in the sixth century[2] is plausible enough. And later Kievan patriotism was at pains to point out that Kij was no mere 'ferryman', protecting the Dnepr crossing at this strategic point, but a chief of his tribe who was a sufficiently important pawn in Byzantine diplomacy to visit Constantinople in person in the reign of 'whichever emperor it was at the time'.[3]

But the prerequisites for closer contacts between the East Slavs and the Christian world did not yet exist. Kiev was a long way up the Dnepr and these Slavs were always shy of the open country between themselves and the sea, which they could never hold against more mobile peoples bred to the steppes nor cultivate with the tools at their disposal. The Byzantine Empire naturally had closer relations at first with those Slavs, known to them as Antes, who were either mixed with Iranians or had absorbed a considerable amount of Iranian blood and had learned the military art of the steppe peoples.[a] Not till the ninth century did a great change occur among the more sedentary and purer Slavs of the interior. This was partly due to two external factors—the Khazars and the Vikings.

From the seventh century the Khazars played an important part in Byzantine politics. This people of uncertain ethnic composition,[4] practising agriculture and fishing along the Caspian shores north of the Caucasus, rose to prominence in the first half of the seventh century and had built a strong state (khaganate), controlling many other tribes between the Caucasus and the Volga delta, by the middle of the century. Allies of Byzantium against the Persian Empire,[b] they automatically continued in this role against the rising power of Islam which replaced it. Friendly relations were closest in the first half of the eighth century when, to counter increasing Islamic pressure on Christian Trans-caucasia, alliance was cemented by a marriage between Leo the Isaurian's son Constantine and a close relative of the *khagan* (733).[c]

Khazaria was a loose empire of many peoples and tongues. With the drift of many Turkic tribes such as the Bulgars westwards towards the Danube it incorporated those who had remained on the steppes north of the Black Sea and extended its control to the most easterly Slav tribes. Its stability was dependent on a temporary decline in the disruptive

[a] See p. 4.

[b] Jibghu, the Khazar *khagan*, was present before Tbilisi with Heraklios's army in 626.

[c] Baptised as Irene. Their son was the Emperor Leo IV 'the Khazar' (*imperabat* 775–80).

pressure of nomad movements westwards from Central Asia, its prosperity on control of transit trade. Importation of silk and other luxuries of Asia to Constantinople had formerly followed more southerly routes. Though the secret of silk had been learnt in Justinian's time the Asian trade-route remained important and had to be deflected to more northerly terminals after the incorporation of Syria and Persia into the Islamic Empire in the first half of the seventh century. The prevention of an extension of Islamic power to the Black Sea shores was thenceforward of paramount importance in Byzantine policy; the Khazar alliance was thus economically and politically indispensable.

All the higher religions were represented among the subjects of this empire under a government which recognised them all as equal. The ruling class began to embrace Judaism towards the end of the eighth century, from which time all the *khagans* bore Jewish names.[5] This was no doubt due to repeated migrations of Jews into Khazaria to escape persecution elsewhere—from the Persian Empire after the Arab conquest, from the Byzantine Empire during the reign of Leo III (717–41).[a] Islam came to Khazaria mainly from the East (Khwārazm), where the chief commercial interests lay; it was the religion of merchants and of mercenaries, especially the royal bodyguard. Though Arab victories almost succeeded in reducing Khazaria to vassalage in the 730s, the Khalifate failed to impose its hegemony north of the Caucasus. As much Christianity as Islam came to the Khazars from the Caucasian region; it may have been locally predominant among some peoples in the south of the Empire.[6] In the capital, however, the importance, if not the numerical weight, of the three higher religions was considered sensibly equal, since two permanent judges were appointed alike for Jews, Moslems and Christians, and one for the 'Slavs, Rūs and other polytheists'. Such was the situation as recorded by the Moslem geographer Mas'ūdī, writing in the middle of the tenth century: 'There are in this town [the Khazar capital Itil][b] both Moslems, Christians, Jews and pagans...and of the latter there are various kinds, including Slavs [*ṣaqāliba*] and Rus [*Rūs*].'[7]

Though we cannot expect precision in distinguishing and naming barbarians, in this context at least (and in the accounts of certain other

[a] There were further exoduses of Jews from the Byzantine Empire to Khazaria in the reigns of Basil I (867–86) and Romanós I (919–44). Unlike in Islam, they could never hold public office in the Empire but, various legal and financial disabilities apart, they were usually tolerated.

[b] Near modern Astrakhan on the Volga delta. See also p. 35. Itil was the Turkic name for the Volga; the proper name of the city was Khamlīkh.

foreign observers) *Rus* appears to mean Vikings.[8] These eastern Vikings, whose activities in Russia and the Near East were generally similar to those on the coasts of Western Europe, were mainly adventurers from Sweden, best known in the following centuries under the name of Varangians.[a] The Scandinavians were avid for silver, for they had none of their own. The beginnings of their restlessness in the sixth century are due in part to the blocking of the earlier Central European trade-routes by the great Slav expansion. Their early incursions along the east Baltic coasts were scarcely more than plundering raids but in time they explored the rivers leading into the interior and established more or less permanent base-camps at their mouths, such as Grobin in Courland (Latvia) from *c.* 650. It was in this way that they discovered and opened up, certainly in the eighth, possibly in the seventh century, the Volga route from the Gulf of Finland to Khazaria, whence abundant Islamic silver could be had in exchange for slaves, furs and other products of the North. At first the Volga Bulgars, established on the middle Volga in the region of its confluence with the River Kama, were their inter-mediaries, but later they traded in Khazaria in person and even made the further journey to Baghdad. The Volga route did not in the eighth–tenth centuries pass through territories colonised by the Slavs except at its north end, on the southern coast of Lake Ládoga, where the town Stáraja Ladoga had a mixed population of Scandinavians, Slavs and Finno-Ugrians.[9] Here the Vikings would learn that there was another route to the rich civilised world in the south lying almost entirely within the Slav territories—up the River Vólkhov and by devious ways to the Dnepr in the region of Smolensk. This information was also acquired by other Varangian bands who pushed up the Baltic rivers, particularly the Dviná. Permanent Viking settlements were made at an early date on the upper Dvina, for example at Pólotsk, whence the more vulnerable middle section of the north–south route could be dominated. The Varangians would also have learnt in Itil that the Khazars were gradually extending their suzerainty further west over those Slavs who controlled the southern portion of the route—the Dnepr waterway. This extension of the Khazar Empire not only encouraged further eastward colonisation by the Slavs themselves—up to the line of the River Don[b]—

[a] Russian Варяги, Greek Βάραγγοι, from Old Swedish *väring-* = member of a company of merchant adventurers.

[b] During his great campaign against Khazaria in 737 the Moslem general Marwān took prisoner 20,000 'Slavs' in the region of the River Don (*nahr aṣ-Ṣaqāliba*, which cannot at this date, as later, mean the Volga).

and an increase in their numbers throughout Khazaria in general: it also led finally to the installation, at a date which cannot be determined, of a Khazar governor in Kiev itself.[10]

In the ninth century Christianity had made as yet very little headway in Sweden itself.[a] But the Varangians met Moslems and Christians in Khazaria and appear to have understood the situation to the extent of giving themselves out to be Christians in Baghdad, since pagan traders were not welcomed there.[11] But few Eastern Slavs can have become Christians in the ninth century; it was not from backward Sweden that Christianity would be brought to them.

The Varangians continued to exploit the Volga route as long as it was commercially profitable. In the first half of the ninth century Khazar power began to decline, first militarily under the impact of new waves of migration on the steppes, and then economically owing to a decrease in the flow of Islamic silver. The standard silver *dirhem* (drachma) was replaced by the gold *dīnār* from the reign of Hārūn-ar-Rashīd (about 800).[12] Although gold coins have been found in the north in small quantity they were of little use to the Scandinavians for general purposes of trade. Compositions of hoards, whether in Scandinavia or Russia, generally show a minimum for Islamic coins minted between about 820–40.[13] Thus both the Varangians and the Khazar-controlled Slavs in the south were affected by this slump. Moreover, while the eastern end of the trade-route began to lose its attraction about 840, the western terminal in the Carolingian Empire also declined in importance. Viking aggressiveness in Western Europe from 840 reflects this.

The Swedes, an essential link in the great North European trade-route, were stimulated into seeking some other point at which to tap the riches of the South. They set out to gain control of the Dnepr route which led ultimately to Constantinople, now entering on a period of economic prosperity. The first step was to secure Novgorod, the main Slav town in the north,[14] which controlled the navigation of the River Volkhov. The lengthy struggle for this can be deduced from the few confused statements of the *Primary Chronicle*.[15]

Meanwhile another band of Varangians had succeeded in occupying Kiev in the 850s, we do not know by what route—presumably a more direct one from the Scandinavian point of view, via the Dvina or Neman.[16] Their first chief known by name was Askold. The leadership of such a small, enterprising and militarily experienced band at Kiev

[a] See p. 143.

appears to have been easily accepted by the local Slavs since Askold was able as early as 860 to mount a large-scale raid against Constantinople itself, naturally not without the participation of his Slav subjects. Byzantine sources make it possible to date the raid exactly to 18 June 860.[17] The appearance of these *Rhōs*, 'unknown barbarians', before the city produced the utmost consternation. They ravaged the suburbs for several weeks, wantonly killing and destroying, and making their getaway with booty as rich and plentiful as they could have dreamed.[18]

That they were an unknown people is surely an exaggeration but the name *Rhos* or *Rus* was evidently not in common use among the Greeks before this turning-point in Byzantine–Russian relations.[a] Quite the contrary. The Byzantine chancellery was always well informed about all that concerned the coasts of the Black Sea and their hinterland. Byzantine commercial interests continued an unbroken tradition of over a thousand years since the original planting of the Greek colonies. Moreover where there were Greek cities, there were bishops and, under favourable circumstances, missionary activity.

The Crimea had been from early times an active centre of Christianity. The population of the busy ports was not only Greek; there were many Syrian Christians, especially from the seventh century. The Greek diocese of Khersónnesos (ὁ Χερσώνος)[b] was prominent; the see is several times mentioned in the fourth century and became an autocephalous archbishopric not later than 553. In the more mountainous parts there was also a considerable Gothic Christian church, established at the end of the third century—an Orthodox branch quite distinct from that of the Arian Balkan Goths evangelised by Ulfilas (Wulfila) in the 340s. A Crimean Gothic bishop Theophilos signed the acts of the Council of Nicaea (325). An active radiation of Byzantine influence becomes visible from the sixth century with the increasing importance of the North Caucasian lands to the Empire. Kerch (Greek *Bósporos*) became a Byzantine town in the reign of Justin (518–27), again with an autocephalous archbishopric. We hear of the baptism of an important local barbarian chieftain in 528—the 'Hun' Grod or Gord, probably a Kutrigur Turk, to whom Justinian himself stood godfather—without

---

[a] It is likely that the name was not familiar to the Byzantine government before 839 and was still not in general colloquial use in 860. It soon became a term for the political centre of Kiev but probably not normally until the time of Oleg's unification of North and South (see p. 245).

[a] Early Russian *Korsun*, close to modern Sevastópol. The Slav form of the name suggests transmission via some Turkic dialect of the steppes rather than direct contact.

however permanent effect among his people.[19] Kerch continued to be a Greek bishopric even under Khazar occupation;[a] an eighth-century church of St John the Baptist still stands.

Byzantine concern for Christians who had become subjects of the Khazar Empire led to a reorganisation of the local churches in the eighth century. The Gothic see Doros (Mangup) became a metropolis with seven suffragans. Of these the two towns Itil (ὁ Ἀστήλ) and Tamatarkha (ὁ Ταματάρχα)[20] evidently had a considerable resident Christian population; three are clearly missionary bishoprics, since they take their title from peoples—ὁ Χοτζίρων, perhaps at Phullae in the Crimea, for work among the local Khazars and similar peoples; ὁ Ὀνογούρων for the Onogur Turks and others living about the Sea of Azov; ὁ Οὐννων for Turkic peoples, principally the Sabir or Savir, in the North Caucasus.[b] The date of this reorganisation is not certain; estimates vary from the first half of the eighth century to its last two decades.[21] How much was achieved in these missionary areas must remain doubtful. In all probability it was in part an unfulfilled project designed to counter increasing Moslem and Jewish influence in Khazaria. The majority of the sees soon lapsed since they do not appear in the *Notitia* (episcopal list) of *c.* 806–15.

Not all evangelisation in the Caucasian region was Byzantine. The transcaucasian Christian states of Armenia and Georgia were also active. Both Georgian and Byzantine influences reached, for example, the Iranian Alans on the upper Kuban, who seem to have been superficially christianised in the later seventh, more thoroughly in the early tenth century.[22]

Though little of this activity can have impinged on the Slavs we cannot exclude their presence in various parts of the Khazar Empire and therefore an increasing acquaintance on their part with Christianity, and, of course, equally with Islam. There is however no good evidence that Tamatarkha became at an early date a base of Rus and Slav pirates and that it was from the Taman peninsula, and not from Kiev, that raids such as that of 860 were mounted.[23] There is so far no archaeological confirmation of this view and the geographical assumptions are also without foundation.[24]

a Kerch was occupied by the Khazars in 576, other parts of the Crimea during the next century. Khazar domination of the peninsula waxed and waned but was probably at its maximum *c.* 800.

b The other two—ὁ Χουάλης and ὁ Ρετέγ—are not identified for certain but both appear to relate to the North Caucasus, the former to the Caspian coasts, the latter perhaps to the region of the River Terek.

For Kiev itself the most important Christian place is likely to have been Kherson. The town appears to have had a Khazar governor during most of the eighth century after the restored Justinian II had punished the place of his exile by exterminating its citizens.[a] But the city did not wholly lose its Greek character and reverted to a Byzantine municipality in the early ninth century. Its unimportance in the eighth century does not suggest that it was then an active centre of missionary work. In the ninth century the situation slowly changed. While Kiev was gradually emerging as a new political centre of more than local importance, Kherson revived after the economic recession of the eighth century, in common with most Black Sea ports. The decline in Khazar power also caused the Byzantine government to take new measures for the defence of the Crimea as a whole against barbarians whom the Khazars could no longer be trusted to keep under control. Thus the Crimean *Theme* ($\tau\tilde{\omega}\nu$ $K\lambda\iota\mu\acute{\alpha}\tau\omega\nu$), with capital at Kherson, was created about 833/4 to strengthen the military and civil administration.[25] The town was rebuilt and extended. A closer watch was kept on the steppe peoples. Knowledge of the Slavs beyond accumulated. Though there may have been some Slavs in the Crimea, direct contact was still rare. Finally the events of 860 made it apparent to the Byzantine government that the 'Russians' might be useful allies in controlling the steppe peoples between themselves and the Crimea but also that they must not be allowed to become a potential danger to Byzantine maritime communications.

In sum there had been no strong external religious influence on the Slavs and Rus of the Dnepr valley before the middle of the ninth century but Moslems, Christians and Jews were familiar to them. Some adherents of each faith may well have been already resident in Kiev.

The new Varangian masters of the town were worshippers of Thor. They too, on their wide-ranging expeditions, were impressed by the religions which they met. Two stories, though not very trustworthy, may illustrate this. According to a *Life* of St Stephen of Súrozh,[b] who died about the year 790 after much missionary and pastoral activity in the diocese, a pagan chieftain, Bravlin of Novgorod[c] raided the

[a] He was exiled to the Crimea in 695 but escaped to Khazaria and there married a sister of the *khagan*. In 705 he regained his throne with Bulgar help: see p. 155.
[b] Sugdaia on the south coast of the Crimea.
[c] Neither Bravlin nor Novgorod can be explained for certain. Bravlin is plausibly a Scandinavian name and has been interpreted as 'one who fought at the Battle of Bråvalla' (Bravellir), an important milestone in the unification of Sweden—the survivors were greatly honoured. But the date of battle is quite uncertain; recent opinion favours the early eighth century rather than the late seventh or the late eighth

neighbourhood not long after the saint's death and laid sacrilegious hands on his tomb. He was instantly struck down by a miraculous illness. The saint then appeared to him in a vision and promised him recovery if he were baptised. This came to pass. Again, the *Life of St George of Amastris*[a] tells that raiders from across the sea were greatly impressed by the Christian life of the city. Such raids are quite plausible in the 830s. The authenticity of these specific incidents can easily be denied as fabrications of the tenth century or later, the raid on Amastris being modelled on a real incident of Igor's campaign against Constantinople in 941, that on Surozh on the Amastris story, and Bravlin's conversion on that of Vladimir.[b] But the motive for fabrication does not seem strong; moreover the creation of the *Theme* of Paphlagonia, in which Amastris lies, about the same time as that of the Crimea, together with the building of the Khazar fortress of Sarkel on the Don also in the 830s[26] and the arrival of a Rus embassy in Constantinople in 839 are likely to be causally connected.[27] Such raids did take place and the Byzantine government tried for the first time in 839 to remove the menace by diplomatic means. No further raids are mentioned until Askold's more serious descent on the capital in 860.

The repercussions of this raid were profound. First, an embassy, in which Constantine and Methodios took part, was immediately despatched from Constantinople to Khazaria.[c] Secondly, contact was maintained with Kiev in the hope of now establishing friendly relations and of bringing Askold and his subjects into the Christian fold. Whether Askold himself took the initiative in soliciting baptism is not clear but his personal conversion is a credible assumption and there is a weak tradition that his baptismal name was Nicholas.[28] These years were, as we have seen, precisely a time of far-ranging missionary activity directed by Patriarch Photios in support of Imperial diplomacy. He surely pressed home his advantage in Kiev, particularly in view of the situation in Bulgaria.[d] It is probable therefore that he sent, or tried to send, a missionary bishop to Kiev about 864. At all events in an Encyclical sent to the eastern patriarchs in 867 he claimed that the conversion of the *Rhos* had been achieved and a bishop received by them.[29]

century. As for Novgorod ('New town'), the one in North Russia, if already existing under that name, is scarcely likely in this context. No Viking sites are known from the Crimea.

[a] Bishop from *c.* 787–90, died between 802 and 811. The *Life* was written between 820 and 842.   [b] See pp. 249 and 259.

[c] See pp. 34 ff.   [d] See pp. 158–9.

In late 867 Photios was replaced by Ignatios on the accession of Basil. Policy towards Kiev did not change. A treaty, perhaps the first formal one, is ascribed to about the year 874.[30] The paucity and unreliability of the sources does not allow us to judge whether the bishop (or archbishop) allegedly sent to Kiev by Basil and Ignatios was a second prelate distinct from the Photian missionary.[31] The degree of success of these missions is unknown. But we are justified in calling this Byzantine enterprise, however modest its results, the First Conversion of Russia. The Emperor Constantine believed it so some eighty years later. Its duration is easier to assess: in 882, or more probably some ten years later,[32] Askold's successor Dir[33] was supplanted by a new Viking adventurer from the North—Olég of Novgorod, the first commander to have both Kiev and Novgorod in his hands and to attempt the unification of all the Russian tribes under one rule.[34] With him came a new influx of Varangians untouched by southern civilisation. Christianity was either wiped out or reduced to impotence. Thus the achievements of Askold and Dir faded from tradition and later patriotism and learning, concerned as it was exclusively with the House of Rjurik (of which Ígor was the first to reign in Kiev, from 924)[35] and with the conversion of Vladimir of that House, paid scant attention to Christian beginnings in the ninth century.

The treaty of the 870s may well suggest a certain degree of literacy in Kiev by that date. The adoption of Christianity implies at least clerical literacy as soon as natives have been trained for the church. It is unlikely that this stage was yet reached in Kiev. Some more close acquaintance with the Greek alphabet is the most that we can assume. Writing was already familiar to most Slavs.[a] But there is no evidence that any Slavs had reached before the ninth century that degree of social organisation when the recording of one's own language becomes imperative; and there is no evidence of any alphabet evolved by them before this time: that of St Cyril was the first.[b] The Eastern Slavs must also have had some acquaintance with the scripts used in the Khazar Empire, principally a form of the Syriac alphabet (Hebrew and Arabic were also current).[36] The Scandinavians also brought their runes to Russia but this was a purely monumental script. Scandinavian society had no books or other documents.[37] We must therefore reject the 'Russian' Gospel book and Psalter alleged to have been examined by St Cyril in Kherson in 861[38] as the earliest known Slav documents, whether curiosities of the

[a] See p. 329 n. 99. [b] See pp. 38 ff.

Photian and Ignatian missions or of any other origin. The passage is almost certainly a later interpolation.[39]

The last decade of the ninth century directs our attention in a much more hopeful direction. The apparent regression of Christian beginnings for which Olég was responsible was aggravated by a disruption of communications with the South, probably at its worst in the early 890s when the Magyars were being replaced on the Black Sea steppes by the Pechenegs.[a] But by 898 it was possible for the Russians to go to war against the Empire as allies of the Bulgarians.[b] Bulgaria had held loose sway over much territory north of the Danube—even as far as the Dnestr—but this is the first known instance of cooperation. About 900 therefore Bulgaria comes to the fore as a potential source of Russian literacy and Christianity, and that at a moment when a written Slav language in a simple Slav script—the Cyrillic—was at last available.

Both Oleg, whose origins are obscure, and his *druzhina* (comitatus) were certainly pagan. His policy was at first still that of the Vikings of Askold's time—raids on the rich civilised lands for plunder. He directed such raids not only at Constantinople but also at the Islamic towns of Transcaucasia.[40] His warlike operations against the Greeks led to the signing of a treaty in September 911 which is quoted at length in the *Primary Chronicle*.[41] The text transmitted to us by the chronicler some two centuries later shows strong evidence of South Slav participation. It is likely that the Slav version of the Greek original was made by a Bulgarian employed in the Imperial chancellery, who would naturally use Church Slavonic. At Kiev it could probably only be read by a Bulgarian clerk; this must be taken as some indication that such were now always available to Oleg for we can scarcely suppose that he had anything that can be dignified by the name of a chancellery of his own. The two contracting parties to the Treaty are 'the Christians' and 'the Rus'.[c] There is no allusion to Christians on the Russian side. The treaty

[a] The Magyar horde had drifted westwards throughout the ninth century. St Cyril met some Magyars in the Crimea in 861. They are known to have sold their Slav prisoners as slaves to the Greeks. Though they appeared wild and intractable to the Crimeans they were not without some tincture of civilisation, gained from Khazaria and perhaps from the missions of the seventh–eighth century bishops to the Onogurs in the area of the Sea of Azov and the Kuban, from whom comes the name 'Hungarian' (see p.242). They were even semi-literate. For the Pechenegs (or Patzinaks) see also p. 248.   [b] See p. 172.

[c] *meži hrestiany i Rusju* (the members of the delegation who negotiated it in Constantinople were without exception Scandinavians of Oleg's entourage, as their names betray). The 'friendly relations which have long existed between the Christians [Greeks] and the Russians' is little more than a diplomatic formula.

regulated the trading rights of the pagans within the Christian Empire on the lines of the treaty made with the Bulgars in 718, and prescribed how crimes and disputes should be dealt with. The new trade-route 'from the Varangians to the Greeks' was fully open at last. The later chronicler adds—a duty if also a fact—that the Byzantine authorities took the opportunity of impressing on the Russian envoys the joys which might be theirs by becoming Christian.[42] Imperial policy aimed at taming the Russians and making them into dependable allies. Provision is made for the engagement of 'Russians' as mercenaries in the Byzantine army, thus initiating a more or less permanent link with the Christian and civilised world.

Oleg remains enigmatic. Himself a pagan, he may have been tolerant of Christians at home even if he could not restrain his *druzhina* from atrocities against Christian edifices and clergy when raiding Constantinople.[43] They certainly burnt churches in the suburbs—but then churches and monasteries were the richest sources of plunder, as Western Europe knew from its own experience of the Vikings.

Igor to Jaropolk

When we examine the text of the next Greek–Russian treaty of 944 (Ígor the Rurikid now reigning in Kiev)—a mere generation later—it is evident that a profound change has taken place.[44] Christianity in Kiev has taken a great stride forward. On the one hand commercial relations with Constantinople were now much closer and more regular;[a] on the other hand the mounting influence of Bulgarian Christianity can no longer be in doubt. The annual Russian trading party to the City passed through Bulgaria or along its coast. The treaty shows that the Byzantine government now assumed a considerable proportion of Christians among the Russians, whether Varangians or Slavs. Christians and pagans take the oath to abide by the provisions of the treaty each according to their own customs. That the pagans take second place is inevitable in such a document and implies nothing as to relative numbers.[45] Further we have good evidence that there was by then a church of St Elias at Kiev.[46] It could have been served by Greeks, by Bulgarians using the

[a] Kiev was now a vital point in the north–south trade, linked to the northern maritime economic field via Sweden. From North Russia goods passed on to Birka (some 30 km. west of Stockholm) and thence to Hedeby (Haithabu) on the waist of Denmark (Birka was replaced in the third quarter of the tenth century by Sigtuna and finally by Visby on Gotland). See also p. 143.

Slav liturgical language, or by both. The Bulgarian factor is likely to have been the larger.

It is not known for certain whether Russian troops took part in further campaigns on the Bulgarian side against the Empire, for example in the attack on the capital in 922. But we can assume that there were constant relations between Preslav and Kiev and that Bulgarian literary culture had begun to establish itself on Russian soil. That writing was by 944 a normal component of Russian life is again evident from the treaty, the Slav copy of which may well have been drawn up this time by Igor's own clerks in a language much nearer spoken Russian than Church Slavonic.[a] But the translator's knowledge of Church Slavonic is also manifest: the Biblical quotations (assuming that they were not revised later) are close to the standard OCS wording[47] and again bear eloquent witness to the Bulgarian contribution at this time. Thus Russia began to use the Cyrillic alphabet soon after its official adoption in Bulgaria.[48] No Russian Cyrillic documents of the tenth century survive but a Cyrillic *graffito* found at Gnëzdovo, an important junction of routes near Smolensk, is estimated to date from *c.* 925 and is sufficient evidence (if not imported) that writing was becoming a familiar art.[49] In all likelihood, therefore, copies of Christian scriptures were reaching Kiev from Bulgaria in the first half of the tenth century.

There is no allusion to missionary activity in Russia on the part of the Greeks in these middle years of the tenth century. But Kiev had now become vitally important to Imperial policy: the Greeks could no longer ensure the defence of the Crimea single-handed against nomad incursions. Both the Empire and Khazaria were alarmed at the growing power of Rus. In the Emperor Constantine's survey of Byzantine foreign policy (*De administrando imperio*) the information on Russia (chapter 9) stands quite logically between Pecheneg (chapters 1–8) and Khazar affairs (chapters 10–13).[50] Yet it was Imperial manipulation of the Magyars and Pechenegs which had built up the barrier between the Empire and Kiev and thus helped to delay the conversion of the Russians. Their plundering raids had grown into highly organized military expeditions. This was brought home to the Imperial City by

---

[a] The linguistic evidence is not strong as we only have texts inserted into the *Primary Chronicle* at a later date and then repeatedly recopied. More significant is the statement in the *Preamble* that Russian representatives had been accustomed up to that time to carry seals—the ambassadors golden ones and the merchants silver ones—but that thenceforward negotiations would be carried out through the medium of written documents (*grámoty*, a specifically East Slav oral loanword from Greek γράμματα).

Igor's descent on it in 941 (the immediate cause of the new treaty)[a] and to the Khazars during his Caucasian campaign in 943/4. It is possible that Igor now had a base in the Crimea itself, taken from the Khazars, since the operations of 941 are thought to demand two bases.[51] Whereas the attack on Constantinople may have envisaged no more than the extraction of even more favourable trading concessions (though it required two naval battles and the use of Greek fire to defeat it), the eastern operations were perhaps a quest for further permanent strategic bases.[52] The Byzantine government went a long way to meet the Russians' demands in the treaty of 944, but its fear of them is evident and it did its best to ensure that, far from infiltrating into the Crimea, they would undertake to defend it for the Empire.[53] Thus opportunities for peaceful Christian persuasion were no doubt small until after 944. The merchants then came in increasing numbers to Constantinople to reside for some three months in the summer in the suburb of St Mamas,[54] where there were resident Bulgarians too, mingled more and more with the Greeks and admired, under strict supervision, the wonders of the Imperial City.[b] In the event, despite all the precautions of the treaty, interference with Byzantine colonial possessions merely passed out of Khazar into Russian hands, reaching a turning-point, as the sequel will show, at the moment of Russia's official entry into Christendom.

In 945 Igor was murdered by the Derevljáne, a tribe whose control was vital to the security of Kiev but which he had treated in a high-handed manner. He was succeeded by his wife Olga as regent for her young son Svjatosláv. This remarkable woman directed the Russian state till 962, when Svjatoslav relegated her.[c] Igor must have been tolerant of the Christian religion; more cannot be said. We gain the impression that these Varangian leaders, not yet fully assimilated to their Slav subjects, were cautious of adopting Christianity, however attractive and politically advantageous, because their power (as

[a] Another threatened attack in 944 was halted on the Danube by a wise Byzantine decision to negotiate. Igor's army contained a large contingent of Pecheneg mercenaries, a combination particularly alarming to the Greeks.

[b] Slav *Tsarigradŭ* 'the Imperial City'. The Varangians called it *Miklagard*—the Great City—and the Slav lands through which they passed to reach it Gardaríki—the Land of Forts—since fortified centres were still unusual in Scandinavia.

[c] The chronology of the *Primary Chronicle* is again manifestly absurd. She must have been born, not married, in 903, and bore Igor's son Svjatosláv in the early 930s since he was still a child in 946, if the entry in the *Primary Chronicle* is correctly dated to this year. It is tempting to suppose that Olga was closely related to Oleg; Igor's relationship to Rjurik (grandson?), the supposed ancestor of the Kievan dynasty in later tradition, is quite uncertain.

elsewhere) rested on their military retinue, composed of Varangians constantly recruited from the north and still devoted to their own war-god. We might draw the inference that in the second half of the tenth century the Slav element in the Kievan realm was more Christian than the ruling Varangian minority. This is the more probable in that Bulgarian influence would be apt to have made more rapid headway among the Slavs. Furthermore, though literacy was increasing, it would not be the military caste which most readily embraced it. The chronicler's comment on the treaty of 944—'for many Varangians and Khazars were [by then] Christians'—is manifestly a later and untrustworthy gloss.[55]

However that may be, Olga's acts were all but decisive. Of the central fact there is no doubt, but, as often, the details are far from clear. Olga was baptised a Christian and died as such in 969.[a] Byzantine sources are contradictory: against those which indicate that she was baptised in Constantinople in 954/5 (for example, Zonaras)[56] we have a detailed account of her reception at Court on 9 September and 18 October 957, by the Emperor himself. He makes no allusion to baptism which he could scarcely have failed to do if that had been the object of the reception.[57] In 957 Olga travelled with her personal chaplain Gregory. The embassy appears to be concerned with wider political and economic questions; Gregory received smaller Imperial largesse than the officials and interpreters. Yet Olga's baptismal name was Helen, that of the Empress, and she built the first church of the Holy Wisdom at Kiev.[b] Constantine refers to her, however, only as Elga.[c] It is a gratuitous complication to assume two journeys to Constantinople, the first for baptism, the second showing a pointed lack of recognition of that baptism. It is perhaps safer to adopt the view that Olga was baptised in Kiev in 954/5, a baptism prepared by the community of St Elias. If it was known in Constantinople that other clergy had performed the rite it is conceivable that Greek pride chose to ignore it in 957.

It must be judged improbable that Olga was beholden to the Cyrillo-methodian church of Bohemia or some other part of Central Europe for her baptism. There is nothing inherently improbable in its radiation as

---

[a] In course of time she was accorded, like other outstanding Christian figures in Slav dynasties, national sainthood. In her case the Russian church did not officially recognise it till about 1550. An *Office* and *Life* are not known before the fifteenth century.

[b] This may have survived until 1017: see p. 301.

[c] Ἔλγα = Scandinavian *Helga*, of which *Olĭga* is the specifically Russian form. The *Primary Chronicle* treats Olga's baptismal name as symbolic of St Helena, wife of the first Christian emperor, Constantine.

far as Kiev, given the active movement in both directions along the great East-West trade-route which linked in its middle stages Kiev, Cracow and Prague. The culture of Great Moravia had followed similar paths of expansion[58] and 'Russian' merchants are mentioned at Raffelstetten as early as 906.[59] But good evidence of such a connection, abundant for the eleventh century, is lacking for the tenth.[a]

Olga's conversion was to all appearances a personal one. She could not impose the new religion in face of the recalcitrance of her son Svjatoslav and the military caste which he led. It is unlikely, therefore, that her journey to Constantinople in 957 was principally concerned with the affiliation of the church in Kiev (we cannot yet speak of the Russian church). Whatever Byzantine reservations may have been, she was received by the Emperor in the manner prescribed for a Christian ruler. Should we rather suppose that she hoped to negotiate an Imperial bride for Svjatoslav?[60] Byzantine agreement would of course force her son to embrace Christianity. The marriage settlement would also necessarily cover ecclesiastical affairs. If this was her grand scheme nothing came of it. We might tentatively draw a parallel with newly converted Bulgaria.[b] Olga returned to Kiev and adopted a policy similar to that of Boris. In 959 she despatched an embassy to the German King Otto I requesting missionaries to develop Russian Christianity. Otto responded by sending in 961 (after the sudden death of his first choice) Adalbert, a monk of the Benedictine monastery of St Maximin at Trier, with the rank of missionary bishop. Otto could not but welcome the opportunity as a potentially great step forward in the implementation of his general policy towards the Slavs in Northern Europe.[c] Adalbert's mission to *Elena, regina Rugorum*, was short and unsuccessful. He returned to Germany in 962, to be entrusted in 968 with the archdiocese of Magdeburg—the centre of German missionary activities to the pagan Slavs in the West.[61]

Olga's policies clearly did not command universal support in Kiev. Svjatoslav continued obdurate: 'my *druzhina* will laugh at me', he said, and tradition kept the saying alive for the chronicler to record.[62] His reign (*c.* 962–72) was dominated by military expeditions in the old Viking manner. He did nothing to further Christianity though he appears to have refrained from persecution.[63] No doubt Adalbert's failure was due to the fact that Svjatoslav assumed power at that moment, a change which may have amounted to a 'pagan reaction' and which

---

[a] See pp. 109 ff and 291 ff.   [b] See pp. 159 ff.   [c] See pp. 118 ff.

would account for the greater prominence accorded to Perun as the Varangian god and Volos as that of the Slavs in the wording of the next treaty with the Greeks, made in 971. His policy was the aggrandisement of his realm at the expense of all its neighbours. The Khazar Empire was in rapid decline and ripe for dissolution. In the years 963–5 Svjatoslav detached a number of North Caucasian peoples from Khazaria, brought the Slav Vjátichi in the basin of the River Oká for the first time under full control of Kiev (they had up to then been paying tribute to the Khazars) and destroyed the capital of the Volga Bulgars, thus opening the whole Volga line to attack.[64] His purpose was surely to pursue his conquests in the East but at this moment he was drawn into Bulgarian affairs, with immediate and lasting effects on the future of Russia as a Christian state. The evident weakness of Bulgaria now suggested to him a permanent conquest of this country, the eventual removal of the capital of his projected empire to the lower Danube, perhaps an attempt on the Imperial throne itself.[65] It was, in effect, a question of who could conquer Bulgaria first—the Greeks or the Russians, though Svjatoslav first appeared on the Bulgarian frontier (autumn 966) as the ally of the Empire. Events already described[a] and the military prowess of John Tzimiskes, who usurped the Imperial throne in December 969, in the end excluded Russia from any territorial profit in the Bulgarian collapse. Refugees from East Bulgaria must now have made their way north to Kiev, probably in greater numbers than at any previous time in the tenth century. Though armies destroy and Svjatoslav was indifferent, Bulgarian manuscripts were no doubt taken to Kiev from pillaged Preslav.[b] Russian–Greek relations were redefined once more by a treaty in July 971, followed by a personal meeting between Tzimiskes and Svjatoslav on the Danube.[66] He had to renounce his Balkan dreams but could still act as Greek champion in the Crimea, where indeed the Empire now held little except the town of Kherson.

While Svjatoslav was occupied in Bulgaria he had sent his generals to complete the overthrow of Khazar power (968–9). The capital Itil was looted and the Khazar Empire ceased to exist.[c] Kiev did not take over Khazaria's eastern trade since this had ceased to be important; rather a

---

[a] See pp. 179 ff.

[b] Such may have been Symeon's *Encyclopaedia*, copied for Svjatoslav II in 1073, and the Gospel Book from which *Ostromir's Codex* was copied in 1056–7 (see p. 293). Similarly the Emperor Tzimiskes took a famous icon of the Virgin from the Palace Chapel back to Constantinople.

[c] From this time Islamic sources name the Volga and the Black Sea respectively *nahr ar-rūs* and *baḥr ar-rūs*, replacing earlier *nahr al-khazar, baḥr al-khazar*.

task was thereby set the Princes of Kiev which was beyond their powers —to control the new waves of steppe peoples who could now freely pass westwards towards Kiev. The Pechenegs had already established themselves in the Black Sea steppes; and it was at the hands of the Pechenegs, lying in wait at a dangerous point on the route to Kiev up the Dnepr, that Svjatoslav met his death in 972. Either the Greeks or the Bulgars had bought their help against the trouble-maker.

The dates of birth of Svjatoslav's sons are unknown. That of Vladímir can be put at about 954. In the absence of Svjatoslav on his constant campaigns their Christian grandmother Olga is likely to have been a strong influence on their upbringing. As Vladimir's mother Malusha was a lady of her household she must surely have been at least nominally Christian also. Thus Vladimir grew up in an atmosphere of mixed Christian and Scandinavian religion. During his adolescent years he was thrown more and more back into the Scandinavian tradition of his dynasty. He became prince of Novgorod about 969, with the Varangian Dobrýnja, his mother's uncle, as his mentor.[a] On Svjatoslav's premature death his brother Jaropólk succeeded to the throne of Kiev, the eldest son by a different mother. With the elimination of Olég, Jaropolk's full brother, in 975/6, Jaropolk's intentions became clear and Vladimir fled to Sweden, there to gather power for a trial of strength with his half-brother. It is important to observe that, so far as we can judge, Christianity had yet made little headway in Novgorod, whether from the direction of Kiev or Sweden.

Jaropolk was well disposed towards Christianity. He had a Christian wife, a Greek. Though there is no concrete evidence of his baptism (nor of Vladimir's as a child), it is not at all improbable; the fact would easily be glossed over later in order to magnify the merits of Vladimir.[67] Svjatoslav had been oblivious to the religious implications of his exploits; Jaropolk could not be. An embassy sent by him to Otto I at Quedlinburg in 973 is of unknown purport but might be viewed in the same light as Olga's approach to Otto in 959. For communications with Constantinople were now difficult: the Pechenegs, who had encompassed his father's death, made the normal route unsafe; moreover Jaropolk may have believed, or known, Constantinople to have been the instigator of that murder. There were envoys from all the Slav lands at this great

---

[a] It was typical of Scandinavian pagan culture for the sons of a chief to be put in the hands of his trusted followers for education and training in war. Western Christian feudalism reversed this: a vassal placed his sons as pages in the household of his lord.

Imperial deliberation, at which *inter alia* a Bohemian bishopric at Prague may have been discussed.[a] Jaropolk was thus fully informed on international affairs. A further influx of Bulgarian refugees to Russia is also likely from the time of the Byzantine occupation of all East Bulgaria in 971–2.[68] However, nothing is known to have resulted from the embassy to the West nor of any positive steps by Jaropolk.[69]

In contrast Vladimir had a Scandinavian wife and acquired another in Rogneda, daughter of the Varangian Prince of Pólotsk (*c.* 977). Thus the years of civil war (975/6–977/8) appear as a defence of semi-Christian Kiev by Jaropolk against a brother who had identified himself with Scandinavian paganism and the North. By 978 Vladimir had made himself sole ruler in Kiev with this backing. It is to this that we must attribute the elaboration of pagan cults there at this late date, which the Christian chronicler of his reign is at pains to emphasize, no doubt to exaggerate. Vladimir set up idols of Perun, Khors, Dazhbog, Stribog, Simargl and Mokosh, to some of which human sacrifice was made.[70] Of these deities all except the first and last belong in their attributes, and partly in their names, to Iranian religious conceptions which gained wide currency in South Russia not later than the Sarmatian domination of the steppes (*c.* 200 B.C.–A.D. 200).[71] The most important Slav deities were Perun and the Mother (Earth), the fertilising god of the weather and the fertile earth, typical of agricultural communities.[72] Since the Varangian domination of Kiev Perun had been conflated with the martial god of the Viking war-bands, Thor; it was in the name of Perun that the pagan representatives swore to abide by the terms of the treaties made with the Greeks in the tenth century.[73]

Thus at the moment of Vladimir's triumph Perun-Thor still held the allegiance, it would seem, of most Scandinavians and of an unknown proportion of Slavs. It is important to stress the devotion of the typical Scandinavian warrior to him since this was the stumbling-block which Vladimir had to surmount—one which had seemed too great to his father Svjatoslav.[b] Vladimir therefore appears to have consolidated his

[a] See p. 100.
[b] Thor was still the war-god of the Vikings at Dublin in the eleventh century—the 'principal adversary of Christ'. Other Viking customs reflected in the East Slav world may be briefly mentioned here (one cannot precisely say whether they remained exclusive to the intrusive Scandinavians or were adopted on occasion by Slavs too): ship-burials, attested particularly in Sweden from *c.* 600 and clearly unfamiliar to the uncouth Derevljane since they misunderstood the tenor of the Scandinavian Olga's vengeance (see *Primary Chronicle, s.a.* 945), but known from Gnëzdovo (see p. 248) and the Volga, e.g. the remarkable one witnessed by Ibn-Faḍlān in 922; the solemn oath

own position in Kiev and that of Kiev as the capital of what remained of his father's abortive empire by encouraging the cult there of various local deities under the supreme war-god Perun-Thor. It is precisely at this moment that Christian Varangians are first reported—evidently exceptions. The *Primary Chronicle* notes under the year 983 the martyr-dom of a Christian Varangian and his son on whom the lot had fallen to be sacrificed after a successful campaign against the Baltic tribe of the Jatvingians. The father had been converted in the Byzantine Empire, not in Kiev or the North.[74]

Saint Vladimir

The early years of Vladimir's reign were taken up with campaigns to improve his political control and economic advantage. Some of Svjato-slav's campaigns had to be repeated, notably against the Volga Bulgars. Islamic silver from Central Asia ceased to reach Scandinavia after the 960s; Kiev's eastern trade collapsed *pari passu*. The prosperous centres of the Islamic world were now further south—Syria and Egypt, since the Mediterranean routes were again viable. Henceforward the Volga route had little economic value. Vladimir therefore was concerned to maintain his southern and to improve his western connections by campaigns in Galicia[a] and towards the Baltic coast. He needed access to Prague: the greater economic weight of Bohemia and Poland was the new factor in European trade in the later decades of the tenth century.[75] It is interesting to observe that the monetary systems of Kiev and Novgorod had parted company about the middle of the tenth century: its eastern interests waning, Novgorod had then adopted the standards of Western Europe and Scandinavia whereas Kiev retained the current Islamic standards which still suited its flourishing trade with the Byzantine Empire.[76]

The insight which Vladimir gained into the best interests of his realm soon led to his repudiation of the pagan cults to the elaboration of which he had at first subscribed. It had been dictated by expediency: newly arrived Varangians tended to be trouble-makers compared with those long resident in Kiev—a common colonial situation. The link with

taken by the Kiev Varangians on their own weapons in their treaties with the Greeks, e.g. in 944; hurling a spear to symbolize the start of a battle, recorded of the boy Svjatoslav in 946.

[a] The campaign of 981, to control the 'Red Towns' (see also p. 129) was not, as the *Chronicle* states, against Poland: there were still unattached tribes in between. The first real Polish–Russian War took place in 1018–31; in the former year Bolesław took the 'Red Towns' after evacuating Kiev, in the latter Russia recovered them again.

Scandinavia was now less vital to Kiev's economy than that with the Byzantine Empire and Central Europe. His grandmother's policy, his own early Christian upbringing, increasing contacts with the other Slav states—all anciently or recently Christian—made it clear to him what he must do. Of his personal convictions it is difficult to judge. Later accounts set out to present his conversion as a miracle, a direct inspiration from on high. They therefore paint his paganism and polygamy in gaudy colours. But the political motive can never be disregarded. It was the same as for the other young Slav peoples: only a Christian state enjoyed international approval and confidence. The narrowness of the Varangian outlook now defeated its own ends.

One may question whether Vladimir really had any hesitation as to what form of higher religion to adopt. The churches then active in Kiev —probably two[a]—followed, we believe, the rites of the Eastern church, either in Greek or Slav. But the *Primary Chronicle* introduces under the years 986-7 a picturesque 'Examination of the Faiths' now undertaken by Vladimir. Spokesmen of the great religions known to the Russians came to Kiev and tried to persuade Vladimir to embrace their faith, first the Moslem Bulgars of the Volga,[b] then the Western (Latin) Christians, Jews[77] and Greeks. Unable to make up his mind on the basis of their eloquent pleadings (for, as his advisers wisely remarked, everyone puts their own case in the best light)[78] Vladimir then despatched a commission of ten to observe the rites of these religions in their respective countries. Moslem practice they found to be dour and nasty; those of the Latins without beauty.[c] The Jews are passed over in silence; they scarcely enter in as a serious alternative and in any case had already admitted to having been driven from the land of their fathers by the wrath of God. But in Constantinople the emissaries were convinced that God truly dwelt among mankind; the liturgy was so beautiful that they did not know whether they were in heaven or on earth.[79] They clinched Vladimir's decision to be baptised in the Orthodox church by the same argument that seems valid to us: 'If the Greek religion were bad, your grandmother Olga, that wisest of mortals, would not have embraced it.'[80]

a St Elias and Olga's Holy Wisdom. The existence of four others, sometimes quoted as dating from the time of Askold and Dir—St Michael, St Basil, St Nicholas and St Irene—is highly doubtful.

b Ibn-Faḍlān's account of his mission to the Volga Bulgars in 921-2 shows that they were then in process of embracing Islam. Svjatoslav's and Vladimir's campaigns had recently increased their contacts with Kiev.

c No location is given for their visit to the Western Christians (*němtsi*), but Scandinavia can surely be excluded.

Though by some accepted as historical fact the story had better be taken as symbolic of the possibilities which presented themselves to Vladimir's mind. The whole passage is not only a well-known Greek literary genre[a] but no doubt was inserted in the *Chronicle* by a later pro-Greek editor who, as Vladimir was warned, puts his own case in the best light—at a time when the first serious recriminations between Greeks and Latins were to be heard in Russia.[81] The 'Examination of the Faiths' praises Vladimir for making the right choice. But it shows by implication that the choice was inevitable, if only for reasons of state, and the truth of the matter may well have been that Vladimir needed no persuading: it was he who had to convince his advisers that this was the right decision and the right moment to take the decisive step. The religious affiliation of Russia was not in any real doubt. The new lines of force set up by the Varangian opening of the route from Scandinavia to the Greeks, while temporarily retarding Christian beginnings, had tended to withdraw the Eastern Slavs from the gravitational pull of Islam, which some at least must have been disposed to embrace. If Svjatoslav's imperial plans had been successful, the attraction of Islam might well have gained strength again. Vladimir correctly interpreted the significance of his father's defeat by the Byzantine Empire.

Legends have accumulated round Vladimir. Showing little interest in his religious acts, oral poetry celebrated him in heroic terms as warrior and monarch of a brilliant Arthurian court. Christian legends developed particularly from the thirteenth century. The precise course of his reception into the Christian church has, once again, been obscured. Among sources containing valuable facts may be put the following: the monk Jacob's 'Memorial' (*Pamjatĭ i pohvala Knjazju russkomu Volodiměru*);[82] Metropolitan Hilarion's *Sermon on the Law and Grace*;[b] Nestor's *Chtenije o zhitii i o pogublenii Borisa i Gleba*;[c] together with the *Primary Chronicle*. Of foreign historians Michael Psellós (covering the period 976–1077) and Yahyā of Antioch[83] deserve particular mention.

The venue of his baptism was in all probability either Kiev or a royal estate not far away, then renamed Vasíljevo. We do not know whether Greeks or Bulgarians prepared his conversion and performed the baptism. Personal influences should not be overlooked. He had at least one Christian consort—Jaropólk's widow, a Greek and former nun. His friend the great Norwegian adventurer Olaf Tryggvason had taken

---

[a] A similar story is told of the Khazar *Khagan* Bulan opting for Judaism.
[b] See also pp. 285–6.   [c] See also pp. 266–7.

service with the Greeks and had become an ardent Christian. As King of Norway from 995 he took some of the decisive steps in making it a Christian state, founding the first bishopric (Nidaros-Trondhjem) about 997.[a] He was a long-standing friend of Vladimir and may have been in Kiev just before his conversion. The story in his *Saga* is explicit but all the saga texts as later written down have been subjected to considerable embroidery. According to it he came to Kiev (in 987 or 988?) with a Byzantine Bishop Paul, of whom nothing more is known.[84]

After consideration of all the chronological possibilities it seems best to put Vladimir's baptism in the year 987. This brings into agreement the two statements that he lived twenty-eight years after baptism (*d.* 15 July 1015)—so Jacob the Monk in his *Memorial*—and that he took Kherson in the third year after his conversion. The figures must be interpreted, as usual, as inclusive. This fits the best interpretation of the sequence of Byzantine events. The revolt of Várdas Sklerós in Asia Minor started in late 986. In 987 the Emperor Basil called in his old enemy Vardas Phokás against him. In September 987 Phokas defeated Skleros but then declared himself Emperor. In this emergency Basil at once appealed to Vladimir for military help since he also had the Bulgar problem on his hands: Samuel was now at the height of his success.[b] The tradition of alliance in Crimean affairs apart, it was vital to the Empire to prevent collusion of the Russians with the Bulgarians. The appeal to Russia has been variously dated but late 987 would appear to be the logical moment. Vladimir's own ambassadors were certainly in Constantinople in September 987. Vladimir knew his worth; he would only barter his aid for an Imperial princess—a condescension not made to Western monarchs, still less to barbarians.[85] Such was the Emperor's extremity that he must have agreed at once; and Vladimir must also have agreed to be baptised, if this had not yet taken place.[86] Immediately after the conclusion of the treaty (early months of 988) 6,000 troops were despatched by Vladimir. He did not lead them himself. In April 989 the main revolt was crushed by a victory at Abydos but it continued sporadically till the end of the year. Some at least of the Russian auxiliaries remained thereafter in Byzantine service as the Imperial 'Varangian Guard'. Probably Vladimir was now glad to see the last of the more unruly and pagan elements in his army.

[a] The surprising dedication of this first episcopal church to St Clement of Rome is presumably due to these contacts with Kiev, where the cult arrived shortly after Vladimir's conversion, if not earlier (see p. 260).

[b] See p. 180.

Meanwhile Basil was trying to find excuses for not sending his sister Anna to Vladimir. We cannot suppose that she relished the prospect of being sacrificed on the altar of political expediency.[87] The Emperor and Anna herself would of course have also insisted on the relegation of all Vladimir's other wives and concubines and strict monogamy for the future. His uxoriousness, though no doubt a fact, has been greatly exaggerated for effect by the later Christian chroniclers.[88] Jacob the Monk's *Memorial* would seem to indicate that Vladimir was expecting the arrival of Anna 'at the rapids'—on the normal route to Kiev up the Dnepr—in 988, that is, at the earliest possible moment after he had fulfilled his part by sending off the troops.[89] She did not come. Incensed by Greek duplicity he invaded the Crimea in the autumn and laid siege to the northern outpost whose safety most exercised the Empire—Kherson. All the former treaties had included clauses to safeguard this city. He took it between April and July (probably May) 989. Only then did Basil bow to the inevitable: the Russian military alliance was still essential to his security. He sent off Anna, this time direct by sea to Kherson, with a great retinue including ecclesiastics. There, too, the marriage was solemnized. It was at the moment of their meeting, according to the *Chronicle* account, that Vladimir was suddenly afflicted with blindness, to be miraculously cured at his baptism. We may take this as a literary touch. The pro-Greek chronicler curtly dismisses the statements of ignoramuses who maintained that he had already been baptised in Kiev or Vasiljevo.[90] Evidently a century after the event no one was certain. But it must be accounted highly improbable that his baptism was in fact delayed until this moment. Conceivably some second ceremony, insisted on by the Greeks, if the first was Bulgarian, was performed. Yet, whatever the bias of the chronicler, Greek participation is assured by Vladimir's assumption of the baptismal name Basil, that of the Emperor his brother-in-law. If he had assumed it as early as 987 this would greatly increase the likelihood that the Bishop Paul supposedly brought to Kiev by Olaf was a real person and that he baptised Vladimir then in the Orthodox church.[a] The church of St Basil in Kherson, 'which stands there to this day in the market-place', is given, rightly or wrongly, by the chronicler as the venue of his baptism. The conferring of a high Byzantine rank may be assumed also.

Vladimir handed Kherson back to the Greeks and returned to Kiev

[a] Accepting this, we can then suppose with some probability that Olaf Tryggvason was in effect the Byzantine negotiator for the military alliance.

with Anna, a number of Crimean ecclesiastics and part of the relics of St Clement recovered by St Cyril. Christianity was now the established religion imposed by the prince. Some of his retinue were baptised in Kherson. We hear of no further opposition from the Varangian element. Baptism of the people of Kiev began in early 990. The idols were thrown down, the statue of Perun subjected to multiple indignities and cast into the River Dnepr. Churches of St Basil and St Clement were immediately built, St Basil on the spot where the idol of Perun had stood.[91]

Exactly what clerics Anna brought with her to prosecute the conversion of the Russian people, and what others were available already in Kiev, is unfortunately impossible to establish. Yahyā of Antioch, writing while Vladimir was still alive, states that the Emperor sent him 'metropolitans and bishops', who baptised the Prince and all the people.[92] The question of a metropolitan must be discussed later;[a] but both plurals are surely inadmissible. Under the circumstances of hurried preparations for Anna's departure—resisted till the last minute —one missionary bishop might be conceded. The agreement between Basil and Vladimir in 987 can scarcely have gone very far in settling the future organisation of the church in Russia. All that is certain is that in 990 Greek missionary activity began again in Kiev and that Greek language and books thenceforward played a more immediate part in Russian culture.

Russia was still essentially a missionary area. The huge task of evangelisation is ascribed to Vladimir himself; tradition has not preserved the names of any other outstanding figures. Expectedly the Russian church declared Vladimir a saint, the Russian Constantine, and salutes him by the more exalted title of 'ranking with the Apostles'.[b] Behind this lies a wholly Greek, indeed Constantinopolitan, idea. It seemed right that each of the five sees of the church which had been accorded pre-eminence as patriarchates should have been founded by one of the Apostles—Rome, Alexandria, Antioch, Jerusalem and

---

[a] See pp. 268 ff.

[b] *Ravnoapóstolny*. His canonisation was Russian only, dating officially from about 1250. Commemoration on 15 July. Constantinople resisted this recognition, as it did in the case of a number of other purely national Slav saints. Vladimir's official *Life* (*Zhitije blazhennago Volodiměra*) is therefore late and of no great value (see sixteenth-century text in Golubinski, vol. 1, part 1, pp. 224–37). The manifest lack of interest in Byzantine sources in Vladimir's conversion and subsequent achievements as a Christian ruler is no doubt compounded of many elements—political *froideur*, ecclesiastical friction, chagrin over the affair of Princess Anna, other preoccupations; but chiefly perhaps the general feeling that Russia had already been converted, despite subsequent ups and downs, and that Vladimir's act was therefore not the beginning of a new era.

Ephesus. When Constantinople (displacing Ephesus) became the Christian capital of the Empire—the New Rome—it was natural that the traditions of its see should be re-examined, especially when the pretensions of Old Rome to absolute primacy became more insistent, and its apostolic foundation also made credible. Legends about the missionary journeys of St Andrew, the brother of St Peter and in fact the first apostle to be chosen by Our Lord, were amenable to such an interpretation.[93] Moreover, Andrew's mission-field was stated to be 'Scythia', a vague geographical term in Greek usage which embraced all the northern coasts of the Black Sea from the Danube to the Don. Missionary journeys by St Andrew in the Caucasus also appear in Georgian and Armenian legends. It may be a fact that Andrew visited the Crimea (Khersonnesos), sailing (as was normal) from Sinope. On this basis Russian piety later claimed that he had then sailed up the Dnepr to Kiev and predicted its future glory as a Christian metropolis. Further elaborations of the legend go beyond the credible but this much could be believed by many in Russia.[94] The name Andrew does not seem to have become notably popular in Russia before the twelfth century; but churches were dedicated to him at Kiev in 1086 and at Perejáslavl in 1089, during the reign of Vsévolod whose patron saint he was. The spread of the legend via its Greek sources therefore probably belongs to the second half of the eleventh century. But however flattering the alleged presence of Andrew on Russian soil, the merits of Vladimir were not obscured thereby, for his personal decision to make Russia a Christian state was seen as a truly apostolic act.[a]

No precise chronology can be given of Vladimir's subsequent acts. Outside sources are silent, which suggests that the process was slow and unspectacular.[95] The picturesque mass baptisms in Kiev 'with joy and gladness' are no doubt a literary fiction. But though he brought Greek ecclesiastics (including perhaps a bishop) from Kherson, they could not suffice for long. There is here a parallel between Vladimir's policy and that of Rastislav of Moravia.[b] We have seen good reason to believe that those Russians (using the word in its wide sense), including Vladimir himself, who were already Christian are likely to have received Christianity in its Bulgarian form. They were already familiar with the Slav liturgical language. Vladimir, like Rastislav, wished to press on with the conversion of his people at the best pace possible. For this a church

---

[a] That ἰσαπόστολος was one of the Imperial Byzantine titles can scarcely be relevant to its application to St Vladimir.　　　[b] See pp. 26–8.

using the Slav language was better than one using Greek, and Slav-speaking missionaries better than Greeks. Thus the services of resident Bulgarians became particularly valuable. There were also strong political reasons in favour of promoting the new religion in Slav form. Vladimir surely knew the facts of Bulgarian history and the details of Olga's *démarches* (which we do not). He would assert his independence to the full. Given the precarious position of Kherson, which Vladimir might take again, and the remoteness of Russia from Constantinople compared with Bulgaria, the Byzantine authorities were in no position to insist on exclusive control of the development of the Russian church even if that was in their minds. It is not even likely that by this date they would protest against the use of the Slav language in the Russian church despite its Bulgarian overtones. This concession would be apt to make Russia more, not less, amenable to close and friendly relations with Constantinople. Vladimir may have accepted the affiliation of his church to Constantinople as right and proper (though this also has been often denied) but as Prince of Kiev neither he nor his successors were disposed to accept the Byzantine corollary—the suzerainty of the Emperor with all its political implications.[a] Vladimir's actions over Kherson are enough to show that he knew how far to go in asserting independence: he could have kept Kherson if he had thought it worthwhile. Similarly he would clearly be apt, the difficult missionary period once over, to make a bid for ecclesiastical autonomy. The adoption of the Slav language for his church would be a vital factor in negotiating such autonomy. For the immediate future, however, the building of churches and the training of clerics was the pressing need. The fact remains that, with or without Greek protests, Church Slavonic was adopted as the ecclesiastical language of Russia.

One of Vladimir's earliest acts was to found and endow his Tithe Church (*Desjatínnaja tserkov*) in Kiev, dedicated to the Mother of God (*Bogoróditsa*). This was a dynastic church rather than a cathedral, to which he affected one-tenth of certain revenues.[96] Its construction was finished about 996, following a normal Byzantine model, by specially summoned Greek craftsmen.[97] It was the first stone and brick church in Russia, the first to be sumptuously decorated with marble, mosaics and fresco. Bronze horses, spoil from Kherson, were put up in front of it. Clergy from Kherson, probably members of Anna's suite, served it.

Training of clergy on a large scale had to be put in train. Here the

Bulgarians were essential as teachers of the Slav ecclesiastical language. The *Primary Chronicle* notes that Vladimir started a school for children of good family, despite parental protests.[98] Though the passage is not specific, they were surely intended to be trained for the church. Vladimir then turned to the evangelisation of other parts of his extensive territories. Novgorod and the north had only been securely tied to Kiev from about 912; its obedience to Kiev was always precarious. The Slavs of the central forests had been brought under Kievan control by Vladimir himself and his father Svjatoslav. He now sent his numerous sons to the important towns as governors accompanied by priests. Later and far from trustworthy tradition credits Vladimir with the establishment of seven sees—a conventional number which can scarcely be made good. These were:

1. Novgorod, the town of the Slovéne. A bishop, Joachim (Akim) Korsunjanin,[a] was almost certainly functioning here from about 900. He died in 1030. The line of incumbents is fairly complete thenceforward, Luká Zhidjáta being the first native (*fungebatur c.* 1036– *c.* 1060);[b]

2. Bélgorod—a royal burgh not far from Kiev, where Vladimir founded a church of the Transfiguration in the 990s;

3. Chernígov on the River Desná for the territory of the Severjáne;

4. Túrov on the River Prípet for the territory of the Dregovichí;

5. Vladímir in Volhynia, for the extreme western territories;

6. Rostóv for the remoter north-eastern districts;

7. Pólotsk (for long the seat of an independent Varangian princedom and still semi-independent), perhaps for the Krivichí of the centre.

Only the first two sees can confidently be ascribed to him. Chernigov, though important to Mstislav,[c] may not have functioned fully before about 1066. Leontios, who was murdered by pagans in 1073, is the first known bishop of Rostov. Vladimir, Polotsk and Turov are only well authenticated even later—*c.* 1090, 1105 and 1120 respectively.[99] It will be noticed that the important town of Smolénsk was not chosen—the reason is not clear[d]—and that there is no mention of Tmutorokan.[e]

[a] *Korsunjánin*=a native of the Crimea in general, not necessarily of the town of Kherson in particular: cf. *korsuniskaja strana*=Byzantine Crimea in the tenth-century treaties with the Greeks.　　[b] Zhidjata is a familiar form of Zhidislav or similar.

[c] See p. 267.

[d] Perhaps it was a very strong pagan centre. The *Life of Abraham of Rostov* shows that there were idols still standing there in the earlier part of the eleventh century.

[e] The probable sequence of further sees down to *c.* 1200 is as follows: Júrjev, a suffragan of Kiev (a short distance to the S.W.)—eleventh century; Perejáslavl (see also

It was a long time before the Russian church could claim that all people within the limits circumscribed above, settled more or less solidly by Slavs, were even nominal Christians. The conversion of the Vjatichi hardly began before the twelfth century, when the active centre of Russian culture had already moved from Kiev to Súzdal and Vladimir.

That there was resistance to conversion was to be expected, especially in the more backward North. Even in the more accessible parts of the country conversion of the peasantry was so superficial that the church was for many centuries grieved at their 'double faith' (*dvojeverije*). Many pagan festivals and customs survived openly, others only thinly disguised under Christian substitutes.[100] That the North clung to its paganism may be due to a Scandinavian strengthening there, as the most common term used for their religious leaders was *volhvŭ*, adapted from Scandinavian *vǫlva*[a]—to the Christian chroniclers wizards possessed by the Devil. A lost chronicle quoted by the eighteenth-century historian Tatishchev recounts a mission sent to Novgorod by Vladimir which met with bloody insurrection;[101] any success that resulted was achieved by force. Other such incidents may be assumed. The extreme paucity of information for the later years of Vladimir's reign gives us no lead.[102] Throughout the eleventh century and even later there are occasional allusions to recalcitrant pagans. One serious incident of this kind took place in the Suzdal area in 1024. The revolt, probably due to famine and oppression, was led by a still active body of *volhvy*, whom Jaroslav, then in Novgorod, suppressed with severity. However, if we consider the first few centuries of Russian Christianity as a whole, the record is excellent. Some pressure was no doubt applied in these early stages but thereafter the work passed out of the hands of the secular ruler, indeed virtually out of the hands of the church too. There were few special missions, rather self-appointed missionaries, usually solitaries who set their hermitages on the fringe of the 'civilised' lands and gradually won over the local inhabitants. As the fame of the ascetic grew, other God-dedicated men would join him. A monastery thus arose with an ever-widening spiritual radiation. Then the more ascetic of the brothers would move off again into wilder country and the process would be

p. 280)—eleventh century; Múrom (on the River Oka) from Chernigov before 1100; Smolensk 1136/7 (confirmed by the foundation statutes—the earliest which have survived); Gálich (on the upper Dnestr) before 1165; Rjazán (on the upper Oka) before 1207. The bishop of Novgorod was accorded the title of archbishop in the 1150s.

a Cf. the work known as the *Vǫluspá* (*Prophecies of the Soothsayer*), the first poem in the *Poetic Edda*.

repeated. Limitless Russia peculiarly lent itself to this wholly peaceful method of evangelisation. Oppression was rare; on the contrary the monasteries and missionaries protected their new converts against the secular officials who in due course followed in their wake.

By the date of Vladimir's death (1015) Kiev had had Christian residents for at least a century and had been a Christian capital for a quarter of a century. Economically it was approaching the peak of its prosperity. Both the prince and the magnates had built lavishly to the glory of God. We can scarcely take Thietmar's figure of 400 churches in Kiev at the time of Vladimir's death as accurate (there were only some 350 in the Imperial City itself at this time), yet 700 are said to have been destroyed in a great fire in 1017.[103] Whatever the true figure, the majority would certainly be private chapels.

The immediate social task of Vladimir and his successors was to inculcate the Christian principles of family and public life. All missions necessarily allowed for a transitional period during which the pagan cults and associated social customs were already proscribed but the voluntary acceptance of baptism and the new ways only took slow root. One aspect of the Bulgarian Boris's difficulties in this immensely difficult situation has been noted in his correspondence with the Pope.[a] The gulf between Greek Christian law as brought to Russia in a Slavonic version of the *Nomokanon*[b] and missionary teaching on the one hand and Slav customary law on the other is easy to appreciate since we have an early record of the latter in *Russkaja Pravda*—the Russian Law Code.[104] There is little sign of Scandinavian influence on this Code but it is broadly comparable to the various Germanic codes written down in the early days of Germanic Christianity, since it reflects the life of a similar transitional society, specifically Novgorod conditions at the beginning of the eleventh century.[105] The first two articles of the Code are sufficient evidence of the rapid extinction of the old ways. Jaroslav, the son of Vladimir, still recognised the principle of private vendetta within prescribed limits; his sons, in the second half of the eleventh century, abolished it. The legal penalties for the majority of crimes, including murder, were to be fines, in the spirit of Byzantine law.

The confrontation of Slav custom with Christian law emerges also from Vladimir's *Church Statute*, revised and added to by his successors. It lays down that since the teaching of the Christian life is in the hands of the church departures from it must be dealt with by ecclesiastical

---

a See p. 160.   b See pp. 78 and 223.

courts. Their competence included all matters relating to marriage and divorce, illegitimacy, inheritance disputes, sexual offences and the like, as well as the obvious domains of heresy, sorcery, sacrilege and blasphemy.[106] In recognising the respective spheres of lay and ecclesiastical jurisdiction in particular, Vladimir was by implication recognising the proper relationship in a Christian state between the secular power and the spiritual authority in general: the church enunciates the principles which should govern our actions; the prince must embody them in the practice of his rule.[107] The Emperor in Constantinople himself was the eminent example. To be an autocrat is not to be an arbitrary monarch— a mere despot or tyrant.[108] As the earthly representative of Christ he embodied the all-embracing virtue of φιλανθρωπία—concern for his subject's welfare and spiritual health alike. The best expression of this in Russia in literary form is the *Testament* of Vladimir's great-grandson Vladimir II Monomákh (1053–1125).[109]

Nothing so much persuades us of Vladimir's sincerity in his personal conversion and his devotion to Christianity as a way of life, not merely as a political convenience, as the notice in the *Primary Chronicle* under the year 996 that he was reluctant to execute brigands. It was his bishops who persuaded him that a prince cannot carry the principle of charity to such lengths.

This early maturing devotion to both the spirit and the letter of Christian principles is already perfectly exemplified in Vladimir's sons Boris and Gleb. Not all those who contended for the succession to his throne showed the like. There were about eight adult sons by four different mothers. Svjatopólk was able to seize Kiev. He pursued an Ottoman policy in ridding himself of as many rival brothers as possible by overt assassination. The least accessible brothers survived—Jaroslav in Novgorod, Mstisláv in Tmutorokan. Boris and Gleb were, according to the *Chronicle*, Vladimir's sons by a Bulgarian, as the name Boris might suggest. Their youth at the time of this dynastic crisis is stressed.[a] It appears that Vladimir thought so highly of the young Boris that he contemplated making him his principal heir. When Boris, on the return journey from a campaign, was warned that Svjatopolk was sending henchmen to murder him he refused to take up arms against his elder brother already established in Kiev. He would not answer wrong by

---

[a] Strict chronology would demand that Boris and Gleb were born after *c.* 990, that is, that they were illegitimate since born after his Christian marriage to Anna. But their youth may have been somewhat exaggerated in the legends. Anna died childless in 1011, though some believe Gleb to have been her son.

wrong. Having made the decision not to resist evil, he spent a night in prayer, adding finally his own: 'Lord Jesus Christ, who didst appear on earth in human form and freely offered Thyself to be nailed to the Cross, accepting Thy Passion for the sake of our sins; give me also now strength to accept mine.' Then the hired assassins fell upon him (24 July 1015). Gleb met his death some six weeks later, knowing already the manner of his brother's end. He too, though even younger than Boris, overcame his natural desire for life and accepted an unjust death in the name of Christ. Boris and Gleb, innocent victims of dynastic ambitions, were not martyrs, though they bore witness to the Truth in their own way. Notwithstanding they became the first canonised Russian saints, beloved of the people for their perfect attachment to Christian duty. Their proper title is therefore not martyr but 'one who has suffered the Passion' (strastoterpets).[110] The imitation of Christ's humility and non-resistance became one of the strongest strands in Russian spirituality. It was for these and similar acts that Svjatopolk earned in popular tradition the by-name of 'accursed' (okajanny).[111]

Of the surviving brothers Jaroslav emerged as the strongest. After varying fortunes he established himself in Kiev, only to be challenged a few years later by Mstislav, who with contingents of Crimean and North Caucasian allies, was able to make Chernigov his forward base. Jaroslav was decisively defeated in 1024 but such was his skill in negotiation[a] that he held Mstislav to a compromise: they agreed to divide Russia along the line of the Dnepr, Kiev and Novgorod being retained by Jaroslav while Mstislav made Chernigov his permanent capital (1026). Jaroslav continued for some years to reside in Novgorod, whose rich merchants had from the start backed him with funds and probably even prevented him from fleeing to Scandinavia for good after early defeats by Svjatopolk. Not till Mstislav's death in 1036 did Kiev become again the undisputed capital of an undivided Russia.

Though several of Vladimir's successors still had recourse to their Scandinavian connections in political and military need we may judge that by now the relatively small permanent Varangian element had been absorbed into the Slav mass and was no longer seen or felt to be alien.[b] The process must have been broadly similar to that undergone by the Normans in England—indeed more complete in this respect that the

---

[a] It is perhaps to his diplomatic skill rather than to any philosophical or literary attainments that he owed his name 'the Wise' (*Mudry*).

[b] Contrast the more difficult assimilation of the Bulgars, pp. 156–8.

invaders' language never attained official currency, for instance in the sphere of law. Svjatoslav was the first ruler of the dynasty to bear a Slav name and thereafter Slav names prevailed almost exclusively.[a] The Slav vernacular in secular administration and Church Slavonic for ecclesiastical use did not have to contend with any serious rival.

The status of the Russian church

Intermittent civil war since Vladimir's death is largely responsible for our scanty knowledge of ecclesiastical affairs. The status of the church in Russia during the fifty years from Vladimir's conversion to the unquestionable installation of a Greek metropolitan, Theopemptos, in 1039, has been a matter for high debate. It does not follow that because Jaroslav, sole ruler from 1036, accepted a metropolitan appointed and consecrated by the Patriarch of Constantinople, Vladimir had at the outset settled the affiliation of the new church in this sense. There would be nothing unusual in the proposition that for fifty years missionary bishops fulfilled the needs of the developing church, and this view has respectable champions.[112] Poland, for example, had nothing but a missionary bishopric from 968 to 1000 and the creation of the Archbishopric of Gniezno at that date was due to an exceptionally favourable combination of events.[b] The case of Bulgaria might seem the most relevant: Boris was granted an archbishop some half dozen years after his baptism; but this again was an exceptional concession wrung from Constantinople as the result of a very delicate international situation heightened by Bulgaria's much greater striking power against the Byzantine Empire compared with Russia.[c] We must consider six possibilities:

1. that Russia had nothing superior to a missionary organisation until the right moment came for a more permanent one;

2. that Vladimir considered himself bound through his baptism to the Bulgarian church (a fact which we cannot prove) and maintained this affiliation for its manifest advantages in developing a Slav language church of his own. Alternatively ecclesiastical attachment to Bulgaria

---

[a] Igor, Oleg and Olga are Scandinavian. These remained popular among the Rurikids, as also Gleb (*Gudleif*; English surname *Goodliff*). Names of other origins are rare, notably Boris (from Bulgaria). Princes of course bore also a Christian baptismal name as well as the Slav name they normally used, e.g. Vladimir—Basil, Jaroslav—George, Izjaslav—Dmitri (Demetrios), Vsevolod—Andrew.

[b] See pp. 124–7. [c] See pp. 159 ff.

could be used as a bargaining counter in extracting autocephaly from Constantinople, seeing that to prevent a Russo-Bulgarian *military* alliance was for many years a vital Byzantine concern;

3. that Vladimir exploited fully the concessions made to him at Kherson and confided the organisation of his church initially to that archbishopric (as Constantinople may have intended);

4. that, in face of Greek pressure, Vladimir rated the need for immediate autocephaly so high that he more or less forcibly transferred an (allegedly Russian) archbishop from Tmutorokan to act as his head of church;

5. that, actuated by the same considerations as Boris,[a] Vladimir made overtures to some branch of the Western church and brought Russia under it, at least as a temporary measure; or finally

6. that he freely accepted from the beginning that the Russian church should be subordinate to the Patriarchate of Constantinople.

In assessing these alternatives we must particularly bear in mind the silence of Byzantine sources on the matter (which may or may not be significant) and also that the Russian evidence is all of later date than 1039, from which time the head of the Russian church was normally a Greek metropolitan. Later chroniclers would thus be all too apt to assume the presence of a metropolitan in Kiev from the time of Vladimir's conversion and Byzantine marriage.

There is no authentic list of the first hierarchs. The earliest chronicles are silent; the *Second Novgorod Chronicle* assumes that Vladimir received a metropolitan at once, who was responsible for the consecration of Joachim (Akim) of Kherson as Bishop of Novgorod.[113] A number of later compilations, such as the *Nikon Chronicle* of the later sixteenth century, using some now lost sources, imply the sequence: Michael–Leon(tios)–John.[114] The pastoral activities ascribed to Michael, a Syrian, are often highly circumstantial but this has no bearing on the authenticity of the name.[115] The unreliable text of Vladimir's *Church Statute* implies that the Patriarch of Constantinople appointed Leon as first metropolitan in Vladimir's lifetime. The two narratives of Boris and Gleb[b]—relatively early sources—give John as the prelate concerned in the translation of their relics to Výshgorod in 1020, but his title varies between Metropolitan and Archbishop.

Of these names we may with some confidence discount Michael. If he belongs with the anachronistic introduction of Patriarch Photios into

[a] See pp. 159–60. [b] See p. 398, n. 111.

Vladimir's history he is a misconstruction of the Emperor Michael III or, more probably, of the Greek author Michael Synkellos whose *Profession of Faith* (*Napisanije o pravoj věrě*) was inserted in the *Primary Chronicle* under the year 988; the name was then transferred to Vladimir's supposed Metropolitan. Conceivably Michael was a real missionary bishop of the ninth century.[116]

With this in mind we may examine the various theories.

1. The assumption can of course be made that the prelates named here and there as active in Russia between 989 and 1039 are missionary bishops to whom wrong titles were later ascribed in ignorance. But this is a *pis aller* against which there is too much circumstantial evidence.

2. Dependence on Bulgaria would be logical and has some substance at first sight. The influence of Bulgarian clergy on the early stages of Kievan Christianity, enough to determine its adoption of Church Slavonic as the liturgical language and other Bulgarian peculiarities,[a] is beyond all doubt. Cultural contacts did not cease altogether when the eastern provinces of Bulgaria were reintegrated into the Byzantine Empire. What more natural than for Vladimir to use Bulgarian refugees to promote the conversion of his subjects just as Boris welcomed the Moravian refugees? Vladimir is even supposed to have requested Tsar Samuel to send him learned men and books.[117] By this time Samuel had perforce withdrawn his capital into Macedonia, finally establishing it at Ohrid about 996.[b] It was therefore the Patriarch of Ohrid who could have assumed direction of the Russian church which would thereby have become part of an autocephalous Slav church. The contribution of Bulgarian Christian literature to Russia is, to all appearances, greater than the direct Greek contribution, at least till the middle of the eleventh century. The knowledge of the Glagolitic alphabet in Russia must also be given due weight.[c] Communications with Ohrid must have been difficult enough, the route via Hungary having little to recommend it before about 1020. Despite these small indications and the obvious suitability of Ohrid as the only Slav Patriarchate and a capital which had no adverse political implications, it is a far cry to posit a formal dependence of the Russian church during the disputed fifty years on the Macedonian metropolis. The theory was originally proposed[118] to account for the metropolitan Leo of Vladimir's time and for the Arch-

---

a The involved problem of Bulgarian liturgical chant cannot be treated here. It is greatly hampered by the complete absence of early Bulgarian manuscripts with musical notation.

b See p. 181.   c See p. 393 n. 48.

bishop John who officiated at the translation of the relics of Boris and Gleb in 1020: the only well-authenticated John at this date was alleged to be John of Ohrid.

Yet all points to a decrease in the importance of Bulgaria to Russia from about the year 1000. From then till the final collapse of the Macedonian state in 1018 Byzantine armies continually ravaged the country. From 1018 to 1039 East Bulgaria, the *Theme* of Paristrion, underwent constant natural or human disasters—so much so that the historian Attaleiates calls the region 'a medley of barbarians' (μιξοβάρ-βαρος) in the second half of the century.[119] The higher ranks of the Bulgarian church were filled by Greek appointees (though Archbishop John remained till 1037) and a deliberate destruction of Slav books took place. Mošin[120] has pointed out that, though Jaroslav used Bulgarian émigrés as translators after 1039, Bulgarian writings of the eleventh century apparently did not reach Russia.

More important still, the archdiocese of Ohrid was redefined after the Greek triumph, on its demotion from a patriarchate (not indeed recognised by the Greeks), during the years 1019–25. The archdiocese was maintained intact, even extended. Neither side makes any illusion to the dependence of Kiev on Ohrid, which might have been expected to interest Basil not a little.[121] In ceasing to be autocephalous Ohrid ceased to be valuable to Vladimir's alleged policy. A close relationship before 1018 is not convincing.

3. The see of Kherson as the fountainhead of Vladimir's church might easily so appear from the account given in the *Primary Chronicle*. Later pro-Greek bias is very evident here. If not baptised, Vladimir was certainly married by the autocephalous archbishop of Kherson. It would be strange if Kherson had then contributed nothing to the promotion of Russian Christianity. That its archbishop became the immediate head of the Russian church is less likely. Much depends on the interpretation of the enigmatic figure of Anastasios of Kherson who is stated to have accompanied Vladimir and Anna to Kiev, perhaps as bishop, since he is mentioned before the priests and relics.[122] But we hear no more of him till 1018 when he apparently threw in his lot with the Pole Bolesław during his temporary occupation of Kiev and disappeared with him towards the West.[123] There is nothing else to suggest a close hierarchical connection with Kherson. But of course such dependence could have been agreed as a temporary measure.

4. The Tmutorokan theory has its protagonist in G. Vernadsky.[124]

It is based on the assumption that this town had been an important Russian (Slav rather than Varangian) centre since the middle of the ninth century and that Tmutorokan, not Kiev, was the venue of the 'First Conversion'. We also have to assume that its shadowy missionary bishops of the eighth century were sufficiently successful to establish a permanent see, and what is more, to procure its elevation to an auto-cephalous archbishopric. But this is a misconception. Tmutorokan, as all other sees in Khazaria, was at first a suffragan see of Doros (ὁ Δώρου) in the Crimea,[a] itself a metropolitanate in the Patriarchate of Con-stantinople known as the ἐπαρχία Γοτθίας. The elevation of Tmutoro-kan to an archbishopric directly dependent on Constantinople can be fairly certainly dated between 934 and 976, most probably about 965, as a consequence of Svjatoslav's eastern campaigns. The *Notitia* dating from *c*. 972–6 entitles it ὁ Ματράχων ἤτοι [*otherwise* or *formerly known as*] Ζηκχίας.[b] It is placed last of forty-nine archbishoprics, that is, the most recent. It was a purely Byzantine see and not autocephalous, which removes all reasons for Vladimir's alleged special interest in it.[125]

The Slav character of Tmutorokan before the middle of the tenth century also becomes more and more doubtful. Recent archaeological investigation has so far only shown that, though there were some Slavs on the lower Don in the ninth century, the Taman area had populations of more or less Iranian culture until the second half of the tenth century.[126] Tmutorokan is first mentioned in the *Primary Chronicle* under the year 988. Vladimir sent his son Mstislav there *c*. 989–90. He did not attempt to hold Kherson; control of the Kerch straits giving access to the Sea of Azov and the River Don was strategically and economically much more valuable.[c] Indeed Kiev may have held Kerch on the west side of the straits earlier than Tmutorokan—from the early tenth century. Ac-cording to a later addition to the *Life of St Stephen of Surozh*,[d] Vladimir and Anna made an extensive tour of the eastern Crimea before setting

---

a See p. 242.

b The Zikhi were a tribe of the Kuban area probably equivalent to the modern Adygei.

c Seals of the eleventh century with inscriptions of the form ἄρχοντ[ι] Ματράχ[ων] Ζιχίας καὶ πάσης [X]αζαρί[ας] relate to the Tmutorokan realm at its widest. After Mstislav's death in 1036 Tmutorokan remained under the rule of the house of Chernigov perhaps till Oleg's death in 1115. The Russian bishops of whom we have certain knowledge were a monk of the Cave Monstery in Kiev who was there (with breaks) from 1061 to 1074, and after him a Bishop Nicholas, also from the Cave Monastery. Therefore Tmutorokan was transferred at some moment to the Russian church, most probably in 1039. The town may have been lost to Russia as early as 1094 when the Cumans attacked it. It became a Byzantine possession again in the reign of Manuel Komnenós.

d See p. 243.

out from Kherson for Kiev. If Kerch was already a Russian possession there is nothing very mysterious about it. Vernadsky has preferred to interpret it as the moment when Vladimir persuaded or forced the prelate of Tmutorokan to accompany him to Kiev as his head of church, an act which is held to explain the subsequent Byzantine silence of profound resentment, not merely at Vladimir's insult to Constantinople and to Anna personally (she was supposed to be with him at the time!) but at the loss of the Russian revenues which the Patriarchate of Constantinople would suffer through Russian autocephaly.

5. Only the special pleading of certain Catholic historians has produced the semblance of a case for Vladimir's attachment to the Western church, specifically to Rome.[127] That the Papacy was profoundly interested in the conversion of Russia goes without saying, but not so much directly (as in the case of Bulgaria) as indirectly through the general missionary fervour of the later tenth century, setting as its goal the incorporation of the remaining parts of Eastern Europe into Christendom. The year 1000 marked, as we have seen, the full acceptance of Poland and Hungary as Christian states. Olga's approach to Otto I in 959[a] was not forgotten in the West. But it seems improbable that any organized mission from the West, Roman or other, went as far as Kiev after 960–1. Well authenticated embassies, it is true, passed from Rome to Vladimir in 988/9, 991 (returned by Vladimir *c.* 994) and 1000 (returned by Vladimir in 1001). Of these the first is thought to have reached Vladimir in Kherson and may have been rather a courtesy to Anna, a cousin of the Empress Theophano, widow of Otto II, who was in Rome at the time. There is no justification for the view that it was requested and so timed by Vladimir to provide him with the strongest possible bargaining counter with the Byzantine authorities, following the tactics of Boris. We have to assume, of course, as in all these theories, that Vladimir was set on autocephaly.

All we know of the 991 embassy is that it was friendly. The embassy of 1000 included Bohemian and Hungarian representatives.[128] That it was an important approach at the highest level is evident, following directly on the events at Gniezno.[b] Quite possibly it was the same embassy which had just performed the coronation of Stephen of Hungary in the name of Pope and Emperor. It is highly unfortunate that Vladimir's reception and reply are unknown. His relations with the West remained cordial but as far as can be seen uncommitted.

[a] See p. 251.   [b] See p. 126.

These approaches were shortly followed up by the mission of Bruno of Querfurt. This was not a mission to Vladimir and his people but to the wild Pechenegs, the scourge of Kiev and of the Byzantine frontiers. Such an undertaking was entirely in the spirit of Otto III and his circle.

Born about 974, Bruno was educated at the famous Magdeburg episcopal school and became one of Otto III's intimate advisers in 995. In his dedication to missionary work Bruno followed the example of his master Adalbert of Prague, recently martyred by the Prussians.[a] In 1001 Otto and Bruno were together in Ravenna planning a great missionary enterprise on the Eastern fringes of Christendom from Sweden to the Black Sea. Their aim was the pacific enlargement of Christendom under Imperial, rather than Papal, patronage. Bruno was consecrated missionary archbishop at Magdeburg in 1004. The next few years were spent in Hungary and Poland, during which he wrote his *Passio S. Adalberti* (1004) and *Vita quinque fratrum* (1005–6).[b] His journey to the Pechenegs took place in 1008. Vladimir, *Senior Ruzorum*,[129] received him in Kiev and tried to dissuade him from the hazardous enterprise. Bruno describes the Pechenegs as *omnium paganorum crudelissimi*; this was Vladimir's opinion too. It is a great pity that Bruno did not enlarge on his experiences in Kiev.[130] It is safe to deduce that the Western church had no designs of 'converting' Russia and that Vladimir had no objections to a western mission on his borders. Bruno says nothing about the organisation of Vladimir's church. What seems to have been agreed between them was that Bruno should exercise his diplomatic skill to make peace between Kiev and the barbarians whose position astride the trade-route was a constant nuisance. Vladimir formally conducted Bruno to the limits of his dominions.[131] Bruno and his companions spent five months in great personal danger among the Pechenegs and claimed thirty converts. Further, the Pecheneg chieftains undertook to be baptised if Vladimir would promise not to wage war on them. Vladimir therefore sent one of his sons—probably Svjatopolk, whom he disliked—back to the Pechenegs as an earnest of his peaceful intentions, together with a hurriedly consecrated bishop from among Bruno's companions. There the matter rested. Svjatopolk soon returned; of the bishop nothing more is known. The Pechenegs did not show any enthusiasm for Christianity for a long time after this, though the peace was kept until 1015.[c] Bruno

[a] See pp. 101–5. [b] See p. 355 n. 122.
[c] The Pecheneg mercenaries in the Byzantine army at the Battle of Manzikert (1071) were still apparently pagans.

embodies the highest principle of the Ottonian circle in calling on Christian states to combine without jealousy in promoting the conversion of the remaining pagans; possibly the pagan Balts were discussed, since both Poland and Russia were now interested in these difficult neighbours. He applauds Vladimir's personal Christianity.[132] Soon after his return to the West Bruno followed in his master's footsteps: he was martyred by the Prussians in 1009.

The pleasant incident of Bruno's visit to Kiev may be contrasted with the story of Bishop Reinbern.

In 1009 Vladimir married Svjatopolk, now Prince of Turov, to a daughter of the Polish ruler Bolesław Chrobry.[133] She came to Turov with Reinbern, Bishop of Kołobrzeg (Kolberg) in Pomerania. Reinbern appears to have been a trouble-maker; Bolesław wished to be rid of him, as his see was untenable and he no longer resided there. According to Thietmar Reinbern did much to evangelise Svjatopolk's still largely pagan appanage.[134] Probably Vladimir had no bishop there at the time.

Nevertheless it was not Reinbern nor any Latin ways that he may have spread, but Svjatopolk who caused trouble. Svjatopolk attempted to make himself independent in his western lands—an act of rebellion against his father Vladimir which could be disastrous to the precarious peace between Poland and Russia. Bolesław was not averse to extending his sphere of influence eastwards. Vladimir imprisoned not only Svjatopolk but also his wife and Reinbern. The bishop died in prison (1012).

There is no evidence that Svjatopolk veered in religion towards the Latins nor of any far-reaching ecclesiastical policy on the side of Poland. But there followed, naturally enough, an estrangement between Russia and Poland (1013) which darkened Vladimir's last years. Svjatopolk escaped from prison in 1015 and with Polish support ruled for a short time in Kiev. His unpopularity in Russia cannot be put down to religious causes.[a]

It would be idle to assert that Russian–Latin links such as these had profound significance. A Western affiliation for Vladimir's church would have to be sought, if at all, with some body using the Slav liturgical language, in the first instance with Bohemia. It will be recalled that the Cyrillomethodian use (Western, or predominantly Western, services in Church Slavonic) was able to survive in Bohemia till the end of the eleventh century.[b] The extent and vigour of this use in South Poland, especially Cracow, is more debatable.[c] In view of the great importance

[a] See p. 399 n. 111.   [b] See pp. 86 ff.   [c] See pp. 135 ff.

of the Kiev–Cracow–Prague trade-route, leading on in the west to Regensburg, the Rhine and the Rhone, there is a *prima facie* case for investigating the possibility in the later tenth and early eleventh century of a 'Cyrillomethodian church' embracing Bohemia, South Poland, parts of Moravia and the more culturally advanced section of the East Slavs centred on Kiev.[a] Some scholars argue for the existence of such an international body from the end of the ninth century—the immediate consequence of Methodios's work. At that date only the tribe of the Poljáne about Kiev would have belonged (in any view Kiev was then the only Christian centre).[135] Even if we were, with Paszkiewicz, to admit that the chronicler's phrase *slověniskǔ jazykǔ*[136] had in all contexts an incontrovertible religious significance—and this does not carry conviction—this still leaves the alleged specifically Cyrillomethodian implications of the adjective unproven; the Russians already had Church Slavonic in its Bulgarian form.

Certain Western traits are not to be excluded from early Russian Christianity. The origin of Vladimir's tithe is doubtful,[b] a Western element in his *Church Statute* uncertain. But these too would again imply nothing specifically Cyrillomethodian. To accept Kiev as a Cyrillomethodian centre in the time of Vladimir, *a fortiori* from the time of Olga or even from the lifetime of St Methodios, we should need convincing evidence of the hierarchy of such a church and its relation to that of South Poland and Bohemia. None is available.

Russian knowledge of Bohemian Christianity in the first quarter of the eleventh century, if admissible on general grounds, is weakly supported. St Boris is supposed to have compared his fate to that of St Wenceslas, in his last hours[137]—only too probably a later literary embellishment. The clear preponderance in Russia of Cyrillic over Glagolitic (the necessary vehicle of texts used in any Cyrillomethodian church developed in Central Europe) and the fact that no traits of the distinctive style of Western Church Slavonic or of Latin liturgical practice are detectable in surviving early Russian texts further tends to show that this alleged Western influence was notably slight during the whole period of uncertainty which surrounds Russian Christianity down to 1039. The Bohemian connections which can be securely established, to be discussed below,[c] belong to the later eleventh century only, certainly after the foundation of Sázava Monastery in 1032.[d]

---

[a] Cf. pp. 250–1.
[c] See pp. 291–2.
[b] See p. 397 n. 96.
[d] See pp. 105 ff.

6. We come, therefore, finally, to examine the evidence for the most conventional view—that the situation before 1039 was not essentially different from that which obtained from that year onwards: the young Russian church was attached to Constantinople and received thence, *conditions permitting*, metropolitans before 1039. In that year, it will be recalled, Theopemptos arrived in Kiev duly consecrated by the Patriarch of Constantinople. This is confirmed not only in Russian annals[138] but also in the acts of a synod held in Constantinople in September 1039, in which the twelfth metropolitan who appended his signature was Θεόπεμπτος Ῥωσίας.

For reasons given above (p. 269) it will be better to disregard Michael.[139] The following positive evidence can now be adduced:

1. There are no extant lists (*Notitiae episcopatuum*) of the hierarchy of the Patriarchate of Constantinople between the reigns of John Tzimiskes (969–76) and Alexios Komnenos (1081–1118). In the Komnenian compilation (Diatyposis) the Metropolitanate of Russia (no. 60) stands next before that of Alania in the North Caucasus and after that of Pompeiopolis. Such lists are intended to be strictly in order of precedence of creation. A Metropolitan Nikólaos of Alania is known to have been appointed in or before the year 6506, that is, September 997–August 998. Pompeiopolis, a see in Paphlagonia, is thought to have been an autocephalous archbishopric in the ninth century, but its subsequent history is obscure.

2. Yaḥyā of Antioch, who gives such an accurate account of Vladimir's negotiations with the Emperor, implies that he received a hierarchy almost at once.[a] His work was written by *c.* 1014–15.

3. Several Russian sources suggest that Leon, or Leontios, arrived in Russia in 991 or 992.[140] He must have been consecrated before the death of Patriarch Nicholas Chrysoverges.

4. An ecclesiastical history by Nikephóros Kállistos notes that a certain Theophylakt was translated from the see of Sebasteia in Asia Minor to Russia in the reign of Basil II (976–1025).[141] Admittedly the author wrote in the early fourteenth century but he has been shown to be generally reliable. It is thought that his source for this statement was Metropolitan Theodore of Sebasteia who was certainly occupying the see in the year 997. Theophylakt must therefore have been appointed before that year.

5. The Patriarchal throne was itself vacant for an uncertain length of

[a] See p. 260.

time from the death of Nicholas Chrysoverges to the consecration of Sisinnios II in April 996.[142] Consequently, although the Emperor could of his own authority create new metropolitanates, there was no patriarch to consecrate. Thus Theophylakt's translation also may have been technically impossible between about December 992 and April 996; it most probably falls under Sisinnios (996–7).

However, no Russian source mentions Theophylakt.

6. A seal, now at Dumbarton Oaks, datable to the first half of the eleventh century, gives the name of Metropolitan John:[143]

$$\maltese \ \Theta\epsilon[o\tau\acute{o}]\kappa\epsilon$$
$$\beta[o\eta]\theta[\epsilon\iota] \ \text{'}I\omega[a\nu\nu\eta]$$
$$\mu\eta[\tau]\rho o\pi o[\lambda\iota\tau\eta] \ \text{'}P\omega\sigma\acute{\iota}as$$

The style of the seal excludes that John who was Metropolitan of Kiev in the 1080s.[144] The reconstruction clearly leaves no room for doubt. From other sources it would appear that the first John took office between 1004 and 1008. The narratives of Boris and Gleb lead us to suppose that this same John was still Metropolitan in 1020. The *archbishop* of Kiev mentioned (without name) by Thietmar in 1018 need not contradict this since the title Metropolitan was scarcely used in the Western church.[145]

7. While not placing too much weight on the text of Vladimir's *Church Statute* as we have it, it implies that Vladimir received Leon as his first Metropolitan from Constantinople.

8. The *argumentum a silentio* must be used with great caution. It may or may not be significant that Bruno of Querfurt made no allusion to a metropolitan or other prelate in Kiev at the time of his visit in 1008.[a] These isolated facts suggest the following sequence of Greek metropolitans:

1. Leon (Leontios): appointed before December 991 but may have arrived in Russia as late as 992. The date of his death is unknown but evidently in or before 996.

(Vacancy in the Patriarchate December 992–April 996.)

2. Theophylakt: appointed 996 or 997? Probably never took up his appointment.

(The creation of the Russian Metropolitanate cannot be later than 997–8.)

3. John: appointed between 1004 and 1008 (probably at the very end

---

[a] See p. 274. The fact that a bishop was then and there consecrated for the Pechenegs implies the presence of two (properly three) bishops to perform the ceremony. But none need be an archibishop or metropolitan.

of this period if we accept Bruno's silence as significant); functioned till at least 1020, possibly well into the 1030s.

4. Theopemptos: arrived in Kiev in 1039.

It would be rash to assume that the office was filled uninterruptedly in these first fifty years, whatever the intentions on both sides. The gaps are real gaps. Consideration of Russian internal affairs tends to confirm the pattern which has emerged. If the creation of a Metropolitanate was agreed between Kiev and Constantinople at the time of Vladimir's baptism (987–9), the delay in the arrival of the first incumbent is comparable with that between Jaroslav's assumption of sole rule (1036) and the arrival of Theopemptos in 1039. The reason for Theophylakt's non-arrival is unknown (if he has been correctly identified). There is an apparent vacancy from approximately 996 to 1008, admittedly difficult to account for from our scant knowledge of Russian affairs.[a] On 15 July 1015 Vladimir died. The next ten years were filled with civil wars between his sons.[b] John apparently continued in office. In 1024 came the final reckoning between Jaroslav and Mstislav, leading to the division of the realm in 1026. By this pact Jaroslav retained all the lands west of the Dnepr. As well as Kiev he therefore had the episcopal town of Novgorod, where he resided. Mstislav for his part had only Chernigov. If John died in the 1020s a difficult situation arose. What would be the Byzantine attitude to the appointment of a metropolitan to a Russia now divided in two? In later times Constantinople always insisted on a single Russian province, resisting in particular Novgorod's aspirations to autonomy. It would be gratuitous to suppose an exception at this moment. If no new metropolitan was in fact appointed there are clearly three simple possibilities:

1. There was a gap in the sequence of metropolitans from the date of John's death until 1039. It is unfortunate that we cannot be certain of the year of his death.

[a] Partisans of the Ohrid theory might argue that, if Leon died in 996 or a little before, while Constantinople was deliberating a new appointment, Vladimir took the opportunity of summoning a Slav-speaking prelate from Ohrid (996 being approximately the year in which the Bulgarian head of church finally settled in that town). When the convenience of this link rapidly declined, as we believe, in the early years of the new century, he reverted to Constantinople in 1008, the intrusive Bulgarian prelate having died or been dismissed. A pure speculation, but these are precisely the years of the maximum potential usefulness of Ohrid to Kiev.

[b] Jaroslav was probably in control till 1018, when he was defeated by a Polish army brought against Kiev by the rebel Svjatopolk. The latter and Bolesław entered Kiev. Bolesław soon withdrew, being content apparently with establishing his son-in-law and protégé. There appear to be no religious implications. Jaroslav fled to Novgorod but regained control in 1019.

2. That John remained as Metropolitan in Kiev for all or most of the period 1026–36 while Jaroslav remained in Novgorod.

3. That John remained as Metroplitan for his surviving years but not in Kiev. By agreement between the brothers or for other reasons he passed to Mstislav's sphere.[a]

In favour of giving serious consideration to the possibility that the Metropolitanate passed for a short time to Mstislav this much can be said. The account of Jaroslav's new order given in the *Primary Chronicle* under the years 1037 and 1039 does not to an unprejudiced reading suggest the creation of a new Metropolitanate or the transfer of an existing one from one patriarchate to another, or any such radical change. But it would be compatible with the transference of the Metropolitan see from one town to another. Always bearing in mind the tendentiousness of Jaroslav's annals, we should not be surprised if the year 1039 marked the return of the Metropolitanate to Kiev, as also of Jaroslav himself, after a period of 'exile' which Jaroslav was ashamed to acknowledge. Jaroslav laid the foundations of his new cathedral of the Holy Wisdom in Kiev in 1037, as soon as possible after Mstislav's death (1036) and the end of divided rule. In effect a new cathedral was being prepared for Theopemptos. It is under the year 1089 in the *Primary Chronicle* that we find the remark, 'for [the] Metropolitanate was formerly at Perejáslavl'.[146] Some attention is due to such an apparently eccentric assertion. Official attempts to suppress something perfectly well known to everyone are often defeated by a casual mention long after the matter has ceased to be of current importance. Several notable historians, including Golubinski, have accepted the statement at its face value.[147] Is the truth of the matter that John was induced to emigrate to Perejaslavl in 1026, thus becoming Mstislav's metropolitan? If so, why Perejaslavl, down-stream from Kiev and dangerously exposed to raids from the steppes, whereas Mstislav was currently engaged in building a splendid new church in his capital Chernigov? Where all is guess-work one might propose that the town of Perejaslavl was part of the original endowment of the Metropolitanate[b] and that the Metropolitan may have

---

[a] It should be observed that, if the question arose of elevating a Russian to the Metropolitanate, of the two Jaroslav was in a better position to do so, since only he disposed (probably) of three episcopal sees providing the requisite minimum of three bishops for consecrating others. It is certain, however, that he did not attempt to elevate the Bishop of Novgorod to archbishop or metropolitan.

[b] Jacob the Monk in his *Memorial* states that Vladimir founded Perejaslavl (*Perejaslavli založi*) in the fifth year after his baptism, i.e. *c.* 991—presumably the town but perhaps also a church, certainly not a bishopric.

been simply overtaken there by the hazards of war and more or less forcibly retained by Mstislav for political reasons. There would then never have been any intention on either side of moving the Metropolitanate. We might compare this with the case of Cracow which temporarily became the acting centre of the Polish church while Gniezno was out of commission.[a]

But the true solution is probably even simpler, positing the same sort of confusion which has crept into Polish annals. Bishop Efrem of Perejaslavl was elevated to the metropolitanate in 1089. There is some evidence that the bishops of both Perejaslavl and Chernigov called themselves Metropolitan in the 1070s during the confused period of the Triumvirate.[b] The metropolitan status of Perejaslavl had therefore some sort of shadowy existence and the chronicler misguidedly underlined it precisely in the year in which Efrem received the true status of metropolitan.[c]

In the light of all that has been said we may pose three questions:

1. Is it conceivable that Vladimir, who had been prepared to mount an elaborate campaign against Kherson in order to acquire a Greek Imperial bride and high Byzantine rank, would have turned his back on the natural solution of his ecclesiastical needs, always provided that he kept the use of the Slav liturgical language?

2. It was a general principle that a missionary area *ipso facto* came under the ecclesiastical authority responsible for the missions. What church other than Constantinople could have fulfilled this role? Surely not Bohemia or Tmutorokan.

3. Have any facts demonstrated that autocephaly was of paramount importance either to Vladimir or to his successors before 1039?

Jaroslav the Wise and his successors

Jaroslav was sole ruler of Russia from 1036 to 1054—one of the most famous sovereigns of the time. His portrait has undoubtedly been touched up, while Svjatopolk has been denigrated. Even if he considered himself Vladimir's legitimate successor, luck and tenacity rather than brilliance brought success, for three brothers had to die and three

---

[a] See pp. 132–3.   [b] See pp. 287 ff.

[c] A similar error has crept into the title of a tract against the Latins witten by 'Metropolitan Leo of Preslav in Russia' (Λέοντος μητροπολίτου τῆς ἐν Ῥωσίᾳ Πρεσθλάβας πρὸς...Λατίνους περὶ τῶν ἀζύμων); it is certainly to be ascribed to the well authenticated *Bishop* Leo of Perejaslavl (1074–8).

be murdered before he could attain supreme power. The epoch of Jaroslav Mudry ('the Wise') was marked, like that of Symeon of Bulgaria, by a rapid flowering of Russian spirituality and culture. Russian annalists have glorified him as Solomon to Vladimir's David—a not unjust if banal parallel, for, as the consolidator of Vladimir's work after the difficulties and interruptions of the previous decades, he was a man at the same time more ostentatious and more calculating. And he built the temple. In the apt metaphor of the *Primary Chronicle* Vladimir ploughed and broke up the soil; Jaroslav now sowed the seed.[148] No sooner did he return to Kiev in 1036 than he put in hand a great reconstruction of the capital. Neglected for long and ravaged in recent years by the Pechenegs, it needed both rebuilding and expansion.[149] Vladimir's Tithe Church, perhaps already dilapidated, was no longer considered worthy to be the mother church of Russia; it is nowhere mentioned in the annals of Jaroslav's reign. Jaroslav at once (1037) laid the foundations of a splendid new cathedral to receive the next Greek Metropolitan, Theopemptos, whose appointment must have been agreed with Constantinople about 1036. It was dedicated to the Holy Wisdom. Kiev thus became Russia's Constantinople.

The Church of the Holy Wisdom has been repeatedly altered since the eleventh century as to its details but the main structure is still substantially the same.[150] The best available Greek masters were brought to direct the work, to design and make the mosaics,[151] and to paint the greater part of the frescoes.[a] Certain galleries and stairs of access from the Palace were decorated in fresco with secular scenes of life in the Imperial City—musicians and entertainers. At the West end is a great frieze of the royal founder and his family.[b] The portrait of Jaroslav himself is unfortunately not preserved.[152] Holy Wisdom was sufficiently advanced to be used by the new Metropolitan in 1039 but it was not consecrated till 1046 and the decorations were not completed until after Jaroslav's death.

Jaroslav was also responsible for two more personal foundations, the

---

[a] *Fresco* is here (as in the Balkans) used in a wide sense. The technique employed is usually the less exacting *tempera* than strict *al fresco*.

[b] 'Royal' by courtesy. The normal title of the ruler of Kiev was *Veliki Knjaz*, or Great Prince—the *primus inter pares* of the ruling family of Rurikid Princes. It is probable however that Jaroslav assumed the title of *tsar* (a contraction of καίσαρ = emperor) shortly after 1036; it is used in an inscription in Holy Wisdom recording his death. Hilarion couples the Byzantine Imperial title of *autokrator* (Russian *jedinoderzhets*, later *samoderzhets*) with the Khazar title of *khagan*, with reference to Vladimir. The Greeks tended to go on referring to the ruler of Russia simply as ἄρχων. Thietmar's *regem Ruszorum* (vii, 65), *regis Ruscorum* (vii, 72), etc., is conventional.

monastery of St George, his own patron, and the monastery of St Irene, his wife's.[a] He further completed Mstislav's cathedral at Chernigov (*Spaso-Preobrazhénski sobor*) in the 1030s, a magnificent edifice still largely intact, and built the Golden Gate in Kiev with the Church of the Assumption above it.[153] The plans and style of all these buildings follow the best Byzantine models of the time. Both the Golden Gate and its Church of the Assumption (Dormition) had Constantinopolitan prototypes. In Russia there was naturally no impulse to follow other than contemporary models, since in contrast to the Balkans the country was not littered with relics of the basilicas and baptisteries of an earlier age.

Kiev's Church of the Holy Wisdom was followed by that of Novgorod (1045–52), founded by Jaroslav's son Vladimir, and by that of Polotsk at the end of the eleventh century. In all these cathedrals the gradual emergence of a specifically Russian style can be observed imposed on a conventional Byzantine model. Novgorod's *Sofia* is a simplified version of Kiev's, with three apses instead of five.[154] Since it was started in 1045, just as the main structure of the Kiev *Sofia* was completed, it seems probable that the same craftsmen were sent north to carry out this second task. But at Novgorod the main material had to be brick, and the decorations all in fresco since mosaic was very costly indeed.

All was not plain sailing in the life of the church after 1039. Jaroslav's *rapprochement* with Constantinople in 1036 was as much political as ecclesiastical: a close military alliance was needed by both sides to meet the menace of the Pechenegs. Indeed, unless we believe in the full autocephaly of Vladimir's church and in the corollary that Jaroslav 'climbed down' in 1036 in accepting a metropolitan from Constantinople, there had been no significant estrangement since 989. It is difficult to define how Greeks and Russians conceived their mutual relationship. While new Slav churches subscribed to the Eastern church's conception of Christendom as a brotherly diversity in unity the Slavs were understandably hesitant towards the complementary doctrine of the one universal Christian Empire under God's viceregent ruling in Constantinople. Even in Byzantine political thought this was naturally seen more as a theoretical truth than as a practical possibility. It was patently untrue from the time of Otto I's imperial coronation in 962, reluctantly

---

[a] She was Ingigard, daughter of Olof Sköttkonung of Sweden: see note 130. It will have been noted that, more often than not, as with the assumption of an angelic name on taking monastic vows ('second baptism'), a Christian name is chosen starting with the same sound as the secular name: Jaroslav—Juri, Russian colloquial form of George; Ingigard—Irina.

recognised by Constantinople. The neophyte Russians of the ninth century could be looked on by Photios as autonomous but subject barbarians, similar in status to the Danubian Goths in the time of Wulfila (*foederati* of the Roman Empire).[155] But the Russian Varangian dynasty did not, any more than other Normans, see their rule in this light.[a] Jaroslav was too great a monarch to consider himself a vassal of the Emperor. Though he and his successors always recognised a special but undefined relationship towards the Emperor, even down to 1453, they did not allow it to affect their independence of action.[156] Clovis and succeeding Franks in the sixth–seventh centuries had similarly been aware of a vague attachment to New Rome, which had no effect on their internal affairs, though Clovis had been flattered to accept the Byzantine title of *Patricius*. The pervasiveness of the Imperial idea may be gauged from the fact that Edward the Confessor (1042–66) styled himself *Anglorum basileus* on the first known Great Seal of England. He and other Saxon kings probably used the title as a learned equivalent of the native *bretwalda*, with the real *basileus* in Constantinople at the back of their minds.

If a Slav ruler thought he might be sinning in this reservation towards the universal suzerainty of the Emperor—the 'visible ikon of the invisible King',—the logical response was to try and make himself that Emperor—witness the rulers of Bulgaria and Serbia.[b] But the rulers of Russia were ill placed to emulate their Balkan cousins in this respect.

The ecclesiastical relationship was much more immediate. Greek metropolitans (and in the early years bishops) predominated in the Russian church. This was not an imposition. By Canon XXVIII of the Council of Chalcedon a daughter-church or a province had the right to elect its own head subject to the approval of the Patriarch of Constantinople. This right was occasionally exercised in Russia. But though

[a] In the Russian case principally because they were a ruling *family*, according to the ancient Germanic tradition which prevailed also among the Franks, while Byzantine political theory was always strictly monarchic. The Byzantine theory of kingship was familiar in Russia through many translated Greek works (e.g. St Chrysostom, St Basil the Great), yet power became more and more fragmented between members of the Rurikid dynasty, much to Russia's detriment, as leading minds recognised. Jaroslav attempted to impose something approaching primogeniture, just as Carolingian practice restricted Merovingian, but it had little success.

[b] See p. 173. In the case of Serbia the most serious attempt was made only in the fourteenth century by Stephen Dušan. Byzantine Imperial theory shows much similarity to Chinese and the barbarians on the fringes of the Chinese Empire—Mongols, Manchus—reacted in the same way as the Balkan Slavs, with incomparably greater success.

local election remained canonical, in practice the Patriarch's Standing Committee (σύνοδος ἐνδημοῦσα) in Constantinople had from the beginning of the tenth century more and more taken over the appointment of metropolitans throughout the Empire.[157] The practice was extended automatically to Russia. In any case Constantinople could apply pressure through the latitude of the Canon. But she rarely did so and the Greek metropolitans did not in general attempt to deflect the Russian church from its own natural development as a church using the Slav liturgical language. One might venture to assert that at certain times, not long after Jaroslav, the warring Russian princes were glad to have a foreign head of church—a man who stood above internal politics both by virtue of his office and his origins—to whom they could turn for impartial counsel.

In Jaroslav's reign the position was simpler. Until the wherewithal existed for perpetuating a wholly Russian hierarchy,[a] outside help was imperative. Jaroslav could not call on Bulgaria for bishops. He therefore accepted many Greeks, as Vladimir had done, and there are no good grounds for calling his acceptance unwilling. Nor are there good grounds for ascribing the deterioration of relations with the Byzantine Government in 1042 to intransigeance on the part of Metropolitan Theopemptos. The short Russo-Byzantine war of 1043, which Psellós is pleased to call a 'rebellion of the Russians',[158] may rather have had economic causes: the murder of Russian merchants in Constantinople is mentioned. Theopemptos's retirement from Kiev is no more than the natural consequence of the situation; the Emperor had similarly removed all Russian subjects from Constantinople when hostilities were imminent.

Peace was made in 1046. This was the last passage of arms between the two powers. The interrupted friendship was restored by the betrothal or marriage of Jaroslav's son Vsévolod to the Greek princess Maria, probably in 1047.[b] The peace negotiations presumably also touched on ecclesiastical affairs. To them we may reasonably attribute the elevation of the Russian Hilarion (Ilarion) to the Metropolitanate in 1051. The argument that Jaroslav had not only once (in 1036–9) but now again failed to extract from Constantinople autonomy for the Russian church has naturally led to Hilarion's election being viewed as a much more

---

[a] In Orthodox churches bishops are normally chosen from the regular clergy (see p. 297). Hence native bishops are not available until monastic foundations are sufficiently developed. Jaroslav took early steps in this direction.

[b] It was through Maria that her son Vladimir Monomákh assumed this Byzantine name. He was born in 1053. See p. 266 above on his *Testament*.

serious 'rebellion of the Russians'. In this view Jaroslav had him elected in face of the indignation of the Byzantine authorities, especially the Patriarch Michael Kerularios (*fungebatur* 1043–58), but sacrificed him again in 1052 to the greater triumph of a Byzantine marriage for his son.[a] This is improbable. There is nothing in the available accounts to suggest any departure from all due formalities.[159] It is true that Hilarion is not mentioned as Metropolitan after 1052 but nothing contradicts his continuance in office during Jaroslav's lifetime. Most probably he resigned on Jaroslav's death. By amicable agreement with Constantinople a certain Efrém (Ephraim), perhaps a Greek who had already been many years in Russia, was translated to the Metropolitan throne.[160] There is in fact every sign that Byzantine policy had lost some of the rigidity of which it is commonly accused. The elevation of Hilarion could well have been agreed in advance.[161] The reading of these events depends largely on the internal evidence of Hilarion's own *Sermon on the Law and Grace* with its encomium to the first Vladimir. The date of this sermon certainly falls in the 1040s. One of its purposes was to put Vladimir's merits in such a light as to promote his canonisation. It is 'nationalist' only in the sense that he glorifies Vladimir as the great preceptor (*nastavnik*)[162] who brought the Russian people to regeneration in Christendom—a personal achievement directly inspired by God. It is not nationalist in the sense of being propaganda directed against the Greeks and Byzantine ecclesiastical tyranny. A date of 1042–3 to bolster up its alleged purpose as a call to prosecute the war against the Greeks is much less likely than 1049, when friendly relations again prevailed.[163]

A much stronger and more direct influence of Constantinople on Jaroslav's church must not be held to imply a decline in already existing relations with other Christian bodies. The international economic importance of Kiev was now at its peak. Jaroslav extended the policy initiated by Vladimir of close political ties with the major European states. Dynastic marriages provided the framework. He married Ingigard of Sweden about 1019.[164] Of their numerous issue he married Vsevolod into the Greek Imperial house at the end of the 40s. In 1049 he negotiated the marriage of his daughter Anna to Philip, son of Henry I of France;[165] a French embassy, led by two bishops, Roger of Soissons and Gauthier of Meaux, came to Kiev to fetch the bride. Jaroslav had already married other daughters to Andrew of Hungary[b] and to Harold of Norway (*c.* 1044). His

---

[a] Thus it is also necessary to put as late a date as possible for Vsevolod's marriage.
[b] He was an exile in Kiev during the long period 1034–46 and was baptised there.

son Izjasláv took a Polish wife, Gertrude daughter of Mieszko II, in 1043;[a] his sons Vladimir and Svjatosláv married Germans. Economically the European connections were now quite as important as the Byzantine. This is the background of Hilarion's claim in his *Sermon* that Russia was 'famed in all the four quarters of the earth'.[166]

The so-called schism of 1054 did not alter the tolerant temper of Russian Christianity. Its juridical validity is questionable, its immediate impact exaggerated.[b] While the fissure between the Eastern and Western churches had been imperceptibly widening since the time of Charlemagne, the stumbling-blocks to unity even in the middle of the eleventh century were far more political and cultural than strictly theological. The sharpening of tempers on both sides and the subsequent polemical intransigeance scarcely antedates the fatal intervention of the First Crusade (1096) which bred jealousy and suspicion between Greeks and Latins coming as conquerors to the Near East.[167]

Kiev knew of the schism at once. For the Papal Legate Humbert made his way back to Rome via Kiev (August 1054). Whether this was part of his original instructions from the Pope is not known for certain. The long journey could scarcely have had any other purpose than to persuade Russia, now a great power, to sever its obedience to Constantinople. The appeal was disregarded.[c] Latins continued to enjoy full tolerance. There were many Latin residents in Kiev who had their own churches and continued to have them undisturbed down to the final overthrow of Kiev in 1240. Novgorod had an even larger proportion of Latin residents. Contacts with Bohemia did not cease till the very end of the century and then because of events in Bohemia.[d]

Another period of troubles followed Jaroslav's death. Izjaslav, Svjatoslav and Vsevolod, the three eldest surviving sons, at first formed a Triumvirate. Jaroslav had designated Izjaslav-Dmitri as his successor; he had no bias against his Polish Catholic wife Gertrude or in favour of

[a] The relationship was double since Jaroslav had cemented his alliance with Poland by marrying his sister Dobronega-Maria to Kazimierz (Casimir) the Restorer *c.* 1039. Gertrude was the sister of Kazimierz. The Russo-Polish alliance was urgently needed, as soon as Kazimierz was re-established in Poland, to deal with the various unruly pagans between the two states, especially the Mazovians who had been partly responsible for the collapse of Polish Christianity in the 1030s. See p. 133.

[b] The Papal Legate Humbert deposited the anathema against Patriarch Michael Kerularios on the altar of the Church of the Holy Wisdom on 16 July 1054—some three months after Pope Leo had died. The Pope's death had automatically cancelled the Legature. On his side the Patriarch promulgated no general anathema.

[c] It is not certain whether Jaroslav was still alive. The date of his death is usually considered to be 20 February 1054, but 1055 may be correct.

[d] See pp. 109–11.

Vsevolod's Byzantine connection, Vsevolod being in any case the junior. Gertrude came of exalted lineage: she was the great-granddaughter of the Emperor Otto II through her mother Rycheza.[a] None of these dynastic marriages appears to have involved a forced conversion of the bride to her husband's faith. Jaroslav's own wife Ingigard is believed to have been a Catholic; she was greatly loved in Kiev and was buried in the Church of the Holy Wisdom. Gertrude was a Catholic and died as such in Kiev in 1108. Thus the Princess in Kiev was often a Latin Christian with her own religious household.[168]

There is nothing to show that the decline of Izjaslav's power in Kiev was due to the unpopularity of the Princess. A popular revolt broke out in 1068 in favour of Vseslav of Polotsk who had kept up a running fight against the Triumvirate and was then a prisoner in Kiev. Though Bishop Stephen of Novgorod was accidentally killed and the rioters attacked the Cave Monastery, these were chance incidents.[b] Izjaslav and Gertrude fled from Kiev in September 1068. Izjaslav reinstated himself with Polish military help in May 1070.[c] In March 1073 they were again forced to seek refuge in Poland by the combination of Svjatoslav and Vsevolod against them. In these three years a certain anti-Latin temper did flare up in Kiev but directed surely more against Bolesław II and his Polish troops than against Izjaslav's Latin wife. Izjaslav displayed no Catholic leanings; he was more concerned with regaining his throne. Indeed he is said to have commissioned Theodosius, Abbot of the Cave Monastery,[d] who seems to have been one of the more intolerant spirits, to compose his anti-Latin tract *Slovo o věře krestjanskoj i latinskoj*.[169]

Bolesław did not care to help Izjaslav a second time. German and Bohemian affairs absorbed him. He had no designs, political or ecclesiastical, on Russia; in fact it was more advantageous to him to make a treaty of friendship with Svjatoslav soon after he became Grand Prince in 1073. Izjaslav and Gertrude next sought aid from Germany, appealing to the Emperor Henry IV at Mainz in January 1075. With them was their son Jaropolk-Peter. Henry did not make even a half-hearted attempt to help the exiles though he could not be happy about the Polish–Russian understanding. But Pope Gregory VII saw in them a possible tool for his

a See p. 131. The name is sometimes spelt Rixa.

b It is possible to see here some elements of a 'pagan reaction': Vseslav, in popular tradition, appears as a wizard or *volhv* of miraculous birth and powers. But it is doubtful whether he can be considered a pagan and leader of pagans at this date.

c These dates are sometimes given as 1067 and 1069 (or even 1068) respectively.

d See pp. 303–4.

absolutist policy.[170] He at once took up their cause. He flattered them with the titles of King and Queen and sent a mission to discuss ways and means for their restoration. This was bound to require the complaisance of Bolesław. But Gregory conceived that he had the authority to decide the rights of the situation. His principles emerge clearly from the *Dictatus Papae*, published about this time, in which he made the claim that the Pope has *plenitudo potestatis* in Christendom, the *Respublica christiana*, even to making and unmaking emperors, and that there is no appeal from his pronouncements.[171] He decided that Izjaslav's brother Svjatoslav was an usurper. It is only natural that this tentative agreement with the Pope should have envisaged union with Rome in the event of Izjaslav's successful restoration. The tenor of the Pope's letter to Izjaslav (17 April 1075) is an anticipation of union.[172]

Jaropolk pursued these negotiations in Rome itself. It seems certain that Izjaslav and Jaropolk recognised the supremacy of the Pope in 1075 and swore *fidelitas*.[173] Coerced by Gregory, Bolesław again provided the military aid necessary to reinstate Izjaslav, who re-entered Kiev on 15 July 1077. Yet Bolesław was no mere Papal tool. The Polish–Russian pact remained in vigour until the end of 1076. With Henry, the common enemy of the Pope and Bolesław, humbled at Canossa, and Svjatoslav dead (27 December 1076), Bolesław appears to have decided that Izjaslav, in whom he had little faith, was less objectionable on the throne of Kiev than Vsevolod. If his personal advantage had not at this moment supported the move he would not have lifted a finger to reinstate the Pope's protégé.[174]

Izjaslav's rule lasted only till October 1078, when he fell in battle in renewed family squabbles. Vsevolod now succeeded as senior Rurikid. Jaropolk, who had been associated with the Roman negotiations, was granted the Western appanages of Vladimir-Volynsk and Turov. Whether he remained a convinced Catholic is not clear but he is reputed the founder of a Church of St Peter in Kiev and was buried in it (1086). This is the only known dedication to St Peter in early Russia.

Gregory's hopes were Dead Sea fruit. Union with Rome might be said to have existed for the year 1077–8. But there is no sign that Izjaslav intended to honour his promises. Indeed he had his supporters among Russian churchmen. Nestor's *Life of St Theodosius*,[a] written within a decade of Izjaslav's death, has much to say in his favour compared with the eminently Orthodox Svjatoslav and Vsevolod: he is *hristoljubets*

[a] See p. 305.

Izjaslav. The authority of the Greek Metropolitan John was never in question. At no time did the Russian church depart from the usages of Constantinople.

The anti-Roman temper of Byzantine politics in the 70s and 80s, which went as far as the closure of all the Latin churches in the Empire by Alexios Komnenos, did not go unnoticed in Kiev. A letter of Metropolitan John to the Antipope Clement III makes clear the attitude of the more enlightened prelates of the Eastern church. While showing due deference to the admitted Supreme Pontiff, he remains convinced that Greek practices are correct where they differ from Roman. But none of them are treated as fundamental disagreements: even the *filioque* difficulty is held to be mainly due to Western incomprehension.[175] Similarly, in his *Canonical Replies to the Monk Jacob*, covering problems of practical Christian life and clerical conduct in particular, John's attitude to Latins—who were to be found in most Russian towns—may be called eminently tolerant.[176] Conversions from the one church to the other were apparently not forbidden by either. One instance is given in the *Paterik* of the Cave Monastery: Shimon, a Varangian, came over from Catholicism to Orthodoxy under the influence of Antony and Theodosius and endowed the monastery with a new church (1073).[177] At no time in the Kievan period was the Russian attitude to Latins as harsh as that of the Greeks.[a] Russia did not yet have to contend with the military aggression of the Latin world. That only began at the time of her prostration under the attacks of the Mongols in the early thirteenth century, when the German knights on the Baltic coast took advantage of this favourable moment to extend their power towards Pskov and Novgorod. The expected ecclesiastical polemics were not slow to appear.

While Russian theological literature of the late eleventh century begins to engage in disputation with the Latins, there was little heat in it throughout the twelfth century. The immediate effect of the First Crusade was rather an aversion to Jaroslav's policy of dynastic marriages with Western Europe, which noticeably decline from this time. Finally we may note that in the reign of the weak Vsevolod (1078–93), who was easily persuaded to give one of his daughters in marriage to Henry IV

[a] Byzantine attitudes showed of course considerable fluctuations. The Latin churches closed by Alexios were soon reopened and were not forbidden to use azymes in the Mass. We may further note that a church of SS Nicholas and Augustine was founded in Constantinople in the 1080s for refugees from England after 1066 and other 'Varangians'.

and thus tacitly to take sides in the scandal of the Papal schism, the Russian church had no hesitation in adopting the new Feast of St Nicholas (9 May), instituted by Pope Urban II in September 1089 but repudiated by the Greeks, since his relics had been stolen from Myra by merchants of Bari. The festival is first recorded in the time of Metropolitan Efrem (1089–97), so may be plausibly connected with a Papal embassy which brought relics to Kiev about 1091. The Russian office of St Nicholas was certainly made from a Latin text within the next few years.

The literature of the eleventh century reveals the one Western connection which Kiev truly valued—that with the Cyrillomethodian church in Bohemia. While the literature of the Eastern church and Empire came increasingly to Kiev in the original Greek and was there translated, Latin literature rarely reached Kiev without going through the metamorphosis of a Slav translation in Bohemia. The period of the activity of Sázava Monastery (1032–96)[a] roughly coincides with the main influx of Bohemian material into Russia. The Bohemian link is proved by the cult of SS Boris and Gleb at Sázava, whither relics of the two saints were sent in 1072. The contribution of Bohemia to Russia appears larger than the reverse, and this may well have been so. Practically all Slav texts were destroyed in Bohemia; it is to Russian copies that many owe their survival.[b] Whether transmission was direct or in part via the Balkans is often hard to tell. The earliest surviving text of the *Life of St Methodios*[c] is most likely to have reached Russia direct in a collection of Bohemian texts since it is immediately followed by the *Life of St Vitus*, patron of Prague Cathedral, and shows no South Slav revisions in its language.[178] The legends of SS Wenceslas and Ljudmila achieved a certain popularity in Russia, particularly the former, owing to its points of similarity with the tragedy of Boris and Gleb.[d] Indeed Nestor's *Chtenije* shows literary dependence on the stories of Wenceslas.[179] The cult of St Wenceslas did not, however, become widespread in Russia. His Office appears in the Novgorod *Minei* of 1095–7 but principally he remained a subject of devotional reading. There are no Russian frescoes or icons, as far as is known, representing St Wenceslas.

[a] See pp. 105 ff. [b] See pp. 109–10. [c] See p. 30.
[d] Though in part the history of Olga (commemorated as a saint on 11 July) and Vladimir is similar to that of Ljudmila and Wenceslas, the Russian stories did not travel abroad, chiefly no doubt because their recognition as saints was too late to interest Bohemia, just as the canonisation of St Procopius of Sázava (1204) was too late to allow his legend to reach Russia. Did the history of Ljudmila influence the account of Olga in the *Primary Chronicle*?

Nor did the name Vjacheslav ever become widely popular in Russia.[a] With St Wenceslas came also the impermanent cult of other saints associated with Bohemia—St Adalbert of Prague and St Vitus, patron of Prague Cathedral.

Among other Western works which shed their Latin form before transmission to Russia, for which there is no credible source other than Bohemia, should be mentioned: the *Life of St Benedict of Nursia*, the *Martyrdom of Pope Stephen*, the *Martyrdom of St Apollinarius of Ravenna*, sermons of Pope Gregory the Great, the *Life of St Conrad*, the *Life of St Julian of Le Mans*. None of these are doctrinal works; Russia did not seek such from Bohemia. The Latin Fathers were virtually unknown in early Russia. Certain passages of the *Primary Chronicle* are also referable to Bohemian traditions or annals.[b]

The Baltic trade of Novgorod maintained a large resident Latin colony there with its own churches, including one dedicated to St Olaf of Norway. Novgorod alone preserved the Scandinavian links which had faded out at Kiev with the death of Jaroslav. As a channel for the entry of religious literature, however, Novgorod was relatively unimportant.

The source of odd Westernisms is often difficult to divine. Why does the *Menology* in Ostromir's *Gospel Book*, whose ultimate source is an early Bulgarian manuscript, put St Sylvester on 31 December as in the Western calendar? The Macedonian *Codex Assemanianus* has it on the Eastern date of 2 January.[180]

This first flowering of Russian culture in the eleventh century drew gratefully on all sources. The Bohemian contribution was relatively modest and short-lived. Bulgaria's dominant role was now over. Her imperishable merit had been the transplantation of the Slav liturgical language to Kiev and the earliest provision of the necessary liturgical texts. This South Slav written language so permeated Russian culture that it was not only perpetuated in Russian use as a learned tongue outside the strictly ecclesiastical field but, through its cultivation by the educated class, exerted a variable influence throughout the centuries on spoken and written Russian in much the same way as Latin was to influence many Western European languages. Mixed styles arose which steered a path between the pure liturgical language and the vernacular according to the genre and matter of the writing. The early coinage

[a] Jaroslav named one son Vjacheslav *c.* 1036.
[b] Especially the so-called *Skazanije o preloženii knigŭ* in the *Primary Chronicle, s.a.* 898—probably put together and incorporated on the basis of Bohemian texts, including *VM*, at the time of the final redaction at the beginning of the twelfth century.

shows some inscriptions in Church Slavonic, as is to be expected in a field which partook of the sacred in most medieval states.[a]

New Bulgarian works were no longer available. Nothing written after 1018 reached Kiev. Russians merely continued to exploit those of an earlier generation. Allusion has already been made to the copy of the *Aprakos* made for Ostromir in 1056–7, evidently based on a much earlier manuscript. Similarly in 1073 a copy was made for Svjatoslav II (1073–6) of an *Encyclopaedia* originally compiled for Symeon of Bulgaria. Another similar compilation of 1076, copied by the same scribe, rests mainly on Bulgarian material but also contains some passages in all probability newly translated in Russia.[181] Taken together they show the range of Christian learning being then assimilated in Russia in the form of excerpts both dogmatic and moral from the Church Fathers,[b] and from Greek historical works illustrating the Byzantine conception of world history as God's purpose revealed through Jewish history, the Christian church and the Byzantine Empire. The Greek chroniclers George the Monk (Hamartolós)[182] and John Malálas were freely drawn upon. But translation of complete works is exceptional; Russia was still content with excerpts, especially those which afforded prescriptions for the leading of a truly Christian life. Russia by now possessed the whole corpus of liturgical texts in full in Slav translation. Everything else was secondary to this.

Direct translations from the Greek now come to the fore. Outstanding among these is Josephus's *Jewish Wars*,[183] probably translated in Jaroslav's reign. It shows not only a thorough command of the Greek text but also the development of a native style of historical writing which contributed much to that of Russian annals then in the making.[184] The involved process of the creation of the Russian historical records cannot here be entered into. It must suffice to note that the first methodical records may go back to Vladimir's reign and that the material was gradually organized throughout the course of the eleventh century, drawing on local oral tradition and outside written sources, and crystallized in the texts of the *Primary Chronicle* as preserved in recensions of the early twelfth century.

However, as with Bulgaria, the translation of contemporary Greek works, whether religious or historical, was rare. It was the great Classics

---

[a] E.g. Владимиръ на столѣ. The Old Russian form of the name is Volodiměrŭ.

[b] Among the Fathers represented are: St John Chrysostom, St John Damascene, St Gregory of Nazianzen, St Basil, St Cyril of Alexandria, St Gregory of Nyssa, St Anastasios of Sinai, St Ephraim the Syrian.

of Christian spirituality that were required, and excerpts already translated in Bulgaria often sufficed.[a] An intermediate stratum is represented especially in hagiography: translations were made of the popular *Lives* of SS Theodore of Studios, Demetrios of Saloniki, Stephen of Surozh, Andrew the Fool (juródivy) and many others. The homilies of St Theodore of Studios were also popular.

It is important to observe that it was only Greek Christian culture which was now being eagerly absorbed. Greek Classical learning met with little response in Russia. It is true that, since Russia from the first possessed the fundamental texts of Christianity in a Slav form, there was less impulse to master Greek and therefore to extend enquiry into pagan and secular Greek literature. The Scriptures were the pearl of great price. The pagan authors and the Byzantine humanism which studied them contradicted the original spirit of Russian piety in the making. Knowledge of Classical Greek literature remained fragmentary and unimportant. The word *Hellene* and its derivatives indicated suspicion and, in later centuries, positive disapproval. It was a synonym for *pagan, pre-Christian,* as in the usage of conservative Greek monks. Concurrently knowledge of the Greek language gradually declined and became exceptional after about 1200.[185] The only secular Greek literature which appealed to Russians was of more or less historical content, in which class may be included the legends of Alexander the Great,[b] of the fall of Troy (partly taken from Malalas) and the heroic epic *Digenís Akrítas*.[186] The last great Greek humanist, who was also an outstanding contemporary historian, Michael Psellos (1018–*c.* 1078), was quite unknown in Russia. He knew the *Iliad* by heart; for Russians Homer was a nebulous name.

The best products of original Russian literature in the heyday of Kiev bear witness to the creative stimulus of Greek models. Such were Hilarion's *Sermon,* the stories of SS Boris and Gleb, the collection of lives of saints and pious men which made up the *Paterik* of the Kiev Cave Monastery. Outstanding among the latter is the Life of St Theodosius, its great abbot.[c] Even taking into account some loss in subsequent centuries it would still appear that the proportion of original Russian to translated devotional literature, as in Bulgaria, remained quite small.[187] It was the great works of the past that mattered.

a See pp. 176 ff.
b The *Alexandreis* was popular everywhere: there were also early Bulgarian and Bohemian OCS versions.
c See p. 304.

If this conservative attitude towards what the Greeks had to offer is to be considered an intellectual limitation it is one inherent in St Cyril's own principle of liturgical translation. The converse principle, which maintained international Latin in the West, cannot be allowed to have been an unmixed blessing either. But no exact antithesis can be constructed. As far as the Orthodox Slavs were concerned, Church Slavonic became their international language and performed for them a vital service, very similar to that of Latin, in the dark days from the fourteenth century to within sight of modern times. No blame is to be attached to their ancestors for rejecting Hellenism, which was scarcely more than an intellectual game; they concentrated on the vastly more important Christian thought. One can only successfully borrow what fulfils a conscious or unconscious need. The West itself only became permeable to secular Hellenism in the fourteenth century. As late as 1204 the behaviour of the Latin conquerors of Constantinople stands out as a notorious example of incomprehension not only towards Hellenism but towards Eastern Christianity as well.

Russia was fortunate enough to receive her Orthodox Christianity still within the great period of Byzantine culture, which had begun in the lifetime of SS Cyril and Methodios and came to a close at the end of the eleventh century. The maturity of the Russian church may be fitly symbolized in Daniel, abbot of an unknown Russian monastery, one of the growing number of Russians who made the pilgrimage to the Holy Land.[188] Arriving in Jerusalem via Cyprus and the Jaffa–Jerusalem road, opened not long before by the First Crusade, he attended the Easter ceremonies (in Latin) at the Holy Sepulchre in the year 1105.[189] King Baldwin and other dignitaries received him with all the friendship and honour due to a fellow Christian. He was accorded the signal privilege of lighting with his own hands an Easter candle at the Saviour's tomb in the name of the whole Russian church.

6

THE BEGINNINGS OF
MONASTICISM AMONG THE
ORTHODOX SLAVS

An Orthodox church is unthinkable without monastic institutions. While the Church calls upon us to live the life of a Christian according to our capacities the mere fact of living in the world imposes limitations on our spiritual achievements. Even a secular priest is concerned mainly with the sacramental aspect of religion, much less with the contemplative. The Church therefore recognises and gives full value to the many layers of human society, each with a different and necessary function, complementary to one another. Laymen, intermediate degrees and contemplatives all together make up the church. This is one aspect of the principle of 'community' (Russian *sobornost*), of each playing a part in a greater whole and in communion with the Holy Spirit each according to his lights. Thus without Marthas there can be no Marys. Our Lord Himself pronounced clearly on this: the Active life, being only a means, is of itself ineffective unless referred to the Contemplative.[1] The life of Contemplation ($\theta\epsilon\omega\rho\acute{\iota}a$), which reunites the soul to God ($\acute{\epsilon}\nu\omega\sigma\iota s\ \Theta\epsilon o\hat{v}$), is a witness by virtue of its mere being, not through knowing or doing. But what it knows by direct intellection it transmits to the world to be applied to its life of Action and to be embodied in its traditional forms. Thus Contemplation realises to the full Christ's First Commandment, active Christian life in the world—the Second. Each requires the support of the other.[2]

The first great flowering of solitary contemplation came into being in the deserts of Egypt and Palestine where the path of asceticism was explored as far as it could lead. But man is prone to extremes: the 'logical conclusion' may be a deviation into excess. St Basil (*c.* 330–79) was among the first to outline a Rule whereby contemplatives could live together for mutual advantage and control.[a] Whereas prayer is always and everywhere possible, under a Rule praise is also assured and also such work ($\pi\rho\hat{a}\xi\iota s$) as is proper for contemplatives. Thus was developed

---

[a] No original text of the Basilian Rule survives, if indeed it was ever so exactly formulated, but there is one drawn up by his forerunner Pachomios (286–346).

the daily sequence of praise from sunset through Matins at dawn and the central liturgy to sunset again. While men worked and slept the great monasteries never ceased in their intercession for the world before God. This was not the function of the parish church. The stress laid in Eastern theology on the hard way of salvation and on the contemplative life as the main way thereto led not only to the multiplication of monasteries but also through them to the pre-eminence of the monastic type of liturgy, long and elaborate, which had no reason to make concessions to lay participation. The liturgical practice of the Studios monastery as developed by Abbot Theodore in the early ninth century gained wide currency throughout the Empire.

The Eastern church did not evolve different orders of monks affected to various special tasks, such as teaching, partly within the life of the world. All Orthodox monasteries are essentially Basilian. But St Basil left no complete Rule after the manner of St Benedict's (*c.* 529); each monastery could determine its own Rule to suit its particular circumstances. Variation remained possible between the more primitive type of the *Lavra*ᵃ—a loose association of contemplatives who lived in separate cells but met together in a common church (*Katholikón*) for the work of praise—and the fully coenobitic house where all was held in common and all duties performed as a community. Basil had particularly advocated a proper proportion between prayer, work and charitable offices. The strenuous and spare life of a monk, likened to that of the angels, could not be undertaken by more than a few; irrevocable monastic vows might not be taken except after a long and proving novitiate. But a coenobitic monastery did not *ipso facto* exclude more rigorous forms of solitary asceticism. The younger monks were expected to live the communal life. If they proved apt for a more exacting spiritual régime they might receive the abbot's permission to withdraw partly or wholly from the community. The wisest of these would later return and make their spiritual counsel available to monk and laymen alike.[3] Illumination in solitude is exemplified for the monk in the life of Christ Himself.

Many, indeed the majority, of monks in a monastery were dedicated laymen. The spiritual stature of the priesthood was accorded only to the most worthy (ἱερομόναχος). It was almost exclusively from these proven men that every Orthodox church came to draw its episcopate. The secular clergy serving the parishes formed a different and more or less

---

ᵃ Greek λαύρα = passage, alley-way (between the cells).

closed and self-perpetuating caste. For a monk, by virtue of his angelic habit, could not be married, whereas the functions and social status of the parish priest required that he should be.

Every new Orthodox church therefore from its inception took up the task of developing monastic institutions, not as a decorative addition to the church but as its highest manifestation as well as the source of its hierarchy. A prince was baptised and declared his country Christian. The men who in the period of transition helped to implement this declaration were drawn for the most part from monasteries. The missions of St Augustine to King Ethelbert of Kent and of the community of Iona to the northern parts of England follow this general pattern.

The Eastern Slav churches were coming into being at a time when two factors were especially favourable to the development of their monastic aspect. In the first place the final defeat of the Iconoclast movement in the Byzantine Empire (843) had greatly enhanced the prestige and influence of the great Byzantine monasteries. For the religious houses had been in the main the consistent and ardent champions of images and their spiritual value. Theodore, the great abbot of the Studios monastery in Constantinople (759–826), was a leader of the Orthodox cause in word and deed. He reclaimed the house from decadence; his new Studite Rule (again not a complete and strict system), combining the practices of Palestinian monasteries with the Basilian prescriptions, was widely adopted. In the second place the most original and important of all Orthodox monastic institutions was in process of formation in the ninth–tenth centuries, namely the monastic republic of Mount Athos.[4]

On Athos, the Holy Mountain, all the phases of monasticism were resumed in sequence. Solitaries began to settle on the peninsula in the ninth century, perhaps even earlier, as some are likely to have been refugees from Iconoclast persecution. The century from about 850 is the period of *lavras*. By the early tenth century the monastic population had so increased that there was need for a common centre of government under an elected head ($\pi\rho\hat{\omega}\tau\sigma$), fixed, as it still is today, at Karyés. This took permanent form with the recognition by the Emperors in the tenth century of the special status of the Holy Mountain. The first steps had been taken by Basil I in 883 and by Leo VI ten years later. The Athonite monasteries became self-governing under the Emperor,[a] subject to no

[a] Athos transferred itself to the control (nominal) of the Patriarch of Constantinople in the eleventh century. This proved an invaluable safeguard during times of Imperial weakness and after the Turkish conquest.

outside ecclesiastical control, except, in certain minor matters, to that of the Bishop of Yérissos (Hierissos) who administered the adjoining diocese on the mainland. The 'Constitution' of Athos has hardly changed since it was granted by the Emperor John Tzimiskes in 972.[5]

The first fully coenobitic house, with a Rule based on that of Theodore of Studios, was that which retained its old simple title of *Lavra*, founded by Athanasios 'the Athonite' about 961, under the patronage of the Emperor Nikephóros Phokas.[6] It was followed before the end of the century by the Monastery of the Georgians (Ivéron, probably 976) and by two more Greek ones, Vatopédi and Philothéou. The number of monasteries proper reached its maximum—about 180—towards the end of the eleventh century, when there were probably 3,000 monks on Athos all told, and thereafter slowly declined. Not all the religious were incorporated into monasteries. Many solitaries remained, and many monasteries maintained smaller houses or hermitages (*sketes*) in remoter spots, for more rigorous retreat or penance. Athos commanded: 'Write, study, chant, sigh, pray, be silent'. Its life was much closer to the total withdrawal from the world of such a remote monastery as St Catharine's on Mt Sinai (founded in the fourth century and richly endowed by Justinian) than to that of a suburban monastery such as Studios, embroiled in the ecclesiastical and political affairs of the capital.

Of the introduction of Orthodox monasticism to the Slavs of Moravia and Pannonia little is yet known. SS Cyril and Methodios had both embraced the monastic life, though Cyril probably never took vows.[a] They had come to lands whose evangelisation had already begun at the hands of Western monks: the great Bavarian monasteries stood near the frontiers of Pannonia and Moravia and established dependent cells as forward posts in the missionary areas.[b] The two saints and their companions probably lived as a monastic community as far as their work allowed. Certain churches are now identified as built in the Cyrillomethodian period; only in one case has a probable trace of associated monastic buildings yet been found—at Sady.[c] Whether the Zobor monastery at Nitra, for which there is some later information, came into being before 885 remains doubtful, but it was likely to have been a predominantly or wholly Latin community.[d]

Expelled from Moravia, the Cyrillomethodian disciples followed the normal practice of organising their missionary work round a monastic

[a] See p. 56.
[b] See p. 16, 22, 72.
[c] See p. 71.
[d] See p. 84.

centre. St Clement and, after 893, St Naum were both responsible for personal foundations in Macedonia.ᵃ Meanwhile in Eastern Bulgaria the dynasty itself was the first great patron of monasticism. The most important princely foundation was at Preslav.[7] While Symeon's life was deflected from the church to the world, Boris was able after 893 to spend his remaining years peacefully in his own monastery. Boris's nephew, Theodore (Todor Doksov) became a monk, a prominent member of Symeon's intellectual circle.

Outside the capital the most revered figure in early Bulgarian monasticism was John of Rila, the first Bulgarian saint, born about 876. He was a Bulgarian of modest family from the Sofia region. In Tsar Peter's reign (927–69) a considerable group of monasteries came into being in the hills overlooking Sofia, sometimes referred to as the 'lesser Holy Mountain'. Devoted to the extreme ascetic life John retired from their proximity into the wild mountains to the south and moved his hermitage further and further up into their recesses. In the end the afflux of disciples obliged him to found a permanent house at Rila (about 930). He spent the last six years of his life as a solitary in a nearby cave.[8] His Office must have been composed at Rila shortly after his death (18 August 946).[9] His relics were moved to Sofia about 980 to add lustre to this see under which his monastery no doubt came. They were stolen by Béla III of Hungary after a victorious campaign in 1183 but were returned in 1187, not being greatly valued by the Catholic primate of Gran (Esztergom). In 1195 they were again removed to the new Bulgarian capital of Tŭrnovo, for which Asen desired the thaumaturgic power of this native saint. They were finally conceded to his monastery in 1469 when its reputation stood higher. For after a long period of obscurity it rose to importance in the fourteenth century when Stephen Dušan incorporated this area in his Serbian Empire. The earliest part of the extant buildings dates from this time (1335); the greater part dates from the nineteenth century only.[10] John's *Testament*, a copy of which is still preserved in the monastery, is of doubtful authenticity.

Bulgarians must also have come early to Athos. Their centre was the monastery of St George, known as Zográphou. The date of its foundation is unknown. The legend that it was founded by three prominent men of Ohrid in the time of St Clement is, like many other foundation legends, certainly a fantasy; but there would be nothing improbable in Bulgarian monks settling on Athos in the reigns of Symeon and Peter. They would

ᵃ See pp. 168–70.

not necessarily have a separate establishment at first. The angelic life is not concerned with worldly origins: Greeks, Syrians, Georgians and others (including in due course Slavs) were all be to found together in great monasteries such as St Catharine's on Mt Sinai. Zographou appears to have arisen as a small mixed community for long dependent on one of the larger houses. It can scarcely have been exclusively Bulgarian before the middle of the eleventh century, perhaps even later, with the re-establishment of Bulgarian independence at the end of the twelfth century. Abbot Makari of Zographou signed a document in Cyrillic in 980; we may take this as the latest date by which the Slav liturgical language began to be cultivated on the Holy Mountain. While there is evidence of both Slav alphabets being used by the Bulgarian monks there about this time, the collapse of East Bulgaria and the closer connections of Athos with Macedonia via Saloniki may have given the pre-eminence to Glagolitic, especially in the eleventh century. One of the early Glagolitic manuscripts, *Codex Zographensis*, was found in the library of Zographou though it was not necessarily written there. The mixed character of the monastery and its importance as a centre of Greek influence on the Balkan Slavs can be gauged by the fact that for a long time the services were sung there on alternate days in Greek and Slav.

Bulgarian monasticism, initiated by Boris soon after his baptism, thus took shape rather before the Athonite Republic had attained its mature form. That of Russia and Serbia developed somewhat later. The time of the arrival of Russian ascetics on Athos is as uncertain as that of the creation of the first monasteries in Russia. Hilarion implies in his *Sermon* that the earliest Russian foundations date, as is to be expected, from the reign of Vladimir.[11] This has not yet been definitely confirmed by archaeology. In view of the attribution of many good works to Jaroslav (whose piety is beyond question), we need not take too literally the statement in the *Primary Chronicle* that it was only in his reign that 'monks began to multiply and monasteries to be established'.[12] Certainly his reign provides evidence of the first fruitful contacts with Athos and of the multiplication of religious in Kiev. Indeed there is nothing improbable in accepting some embryonic monastic houses from the time of Olga. In his notice that the first wooden Church of the Holy Wisdom at Kiev was burnt down in 1017 Thietmar implies that it was at least by then attached to a convent of nuns.[13]

The hypothesis that Vladimir had already endowed a Russian house on Athos finds some support in the signature of an abbot Gerasim on an

Athonite deed, dated February 1016, as ἡγούμενος μονῆς τοῦ ʻΡῶς.[14] This may be the same one that receives mention several times in the eleventh century under the name of Xylourgoié (τοῦ Ξυλουργοῦ).[a] It may be assumed that such a house came into being under high patronage: the same was true of the Greek foundations. But it is not till considerably later that the wholly Slav character of Xylourgou is definitely confirmed.[b] The ever increasing number of Russian monks necessitated a move to larger buildings, traditionally ascribed to the year 1169. After this the Russian monastery is always known by the name of the patron of the newly acquired house, St Pantéléimon, or simply as *Rossikó*. By the twelfth century the monastery was quite rich and prominent and it would seem that a person of high rank was usually sent as abbot, thus preserving a close connection with Court and church in Russia. That the Russian monastery on Athos played some part in the complicated political relations between the Russian princes and Constantinople in the second half of the twelfth century is very probable but impossible to define for lack of adequate sources.[c]

The personal foundations of the ruling house in Kiev—St George (1055) and St Irene—have already been noted.[d] These may well have been the first to be fully endowed by a ruler of Kiev.[e]

But the greatest of all was not a princely foundation. The Cave Monastery at Kiev (*Kievo-pechérskaja Lavra*)[15] owed its being, if tradition is correct, to the inspiration of a simple layman, Antony of Ljúbech.

The geology of the Kiev region is particularly favourable to the making of caves and catacombs. The idea of such retreats may have reached Kiev from the Crimea where the practice was widespread from early times and was revived especially in the eighth century when many refugee monks fled to the Crimea during the first bout of iconoclasm (726–80).[16]

---

[a] *Monastyrĭ drĕvodĕla.* This no more implies that the Russian monks followed the craft of wood-carving than that the Bulgarians of Zographou were principally engaged in icon-painting. Such appellations are usually the name or by-name of a founder; cf. Hilandar (p. 306, note c below). The legend which gave rise to the name Zographou is recounted by R. Liddell, *Mainland Greece* (1965), p. 191.

[b] A document of 1142 lists the fifty-two books in its library—all Slav, none Greek.

[c] The monastery was apparently burnt down in the fourteenth century and was in any case languishing for lack of recruits. It was patronised by the Serbian dynasty in the later fourteenth and fifteenth centuries but did not revive as a specifically Russian monastery until the beginning of the nineteenth century.

[d] See pp. 282–3. Both were destroyed by the Mongols in 1240.

[e] Monasteries founded and endowed by an individual (*ktitor*) remained in the majority until after 1240. The founder had the right of personally appointing the abbot. A typical charter (*typikón*) begins with the merits of the founder, then rehearses any obligations laid on the monastery and finally lists its endowments and property.

Antony began his spiritual development as a cave hermit at Bérestovo, a royal demesne outside the city of Kiev. This, according to the *Paterik* of the Cave Monastery, was before Vladimir's death in 1015. Feeling the need of further instruction in the contemplative life he made his way to the Balkans and finally came to Athos. Here he again inhabited a cave. His spiritual director, perhaps the abbot of the small monastery of Esphigménou,[a] exhorted him to develop monasticism on the Athonite model in Russia, and thither, after taking vows, Antony returned by Divine command. In the words of the *Primary Chronicle*, 'Antony came back to Kiev and considered where to settle. He tried the various monasteries but was not satisfied with them (God not desiring it so).' He began to wander about the vicinity waiting for a sign. 'And he came to the hill where Hilarion had made his cave and took a liking to the place and settled there.' He then prayed to God: 'Lord, establish me in this place and let the blessing of the Holy Mountain and of the abbot who professed me be upon this place.' So he lived there, eating nothing but dry bread every other day with a little water. His fame grew. He found himself obliged to accept disciples. When these reached the symbolic number of twelve, they excavated a much larger artificial cave to include a separate church and cells, 'the ones which to this day exist in the catacomb under the old monastery'. Among those who joined him were the Russians Nikon and Theodosius, both future abbots.[b] By temperament an extreme ascetic, Antony then retired from this enlarged community to a solitary cell. He remained a layman. Varlaam, a high-born personage, became abbot. While these beginnings were independent of Court patronage it is possible that Varlaam was now chosen in view of the growing need for endowment. The number of monks continued to increase slowly, but Varlaam was not a great personality. When the community numbered some two dozen, about 1062, the decisive phase was reached. Prince Izjaslav withdrew Varlaam, whom he desired as abbot of his new foundation, St Demetrios (*Dmitrievski monastyr*), but in return granted the monks the land above their caves for expansion. And at this moment Feodosi (Theodosius), greatest of its abbots, took over the direction of the community. He was still a very young man.

[a] Esphigménou, probably founded in the early years of the eleventh century and never prominent, retained certain relations with Russia through its reputed possession of the cave which St Antony used.

[b] Nikon went to Tmutorokan *c.* 1060 and founded there a house dedicated to the Holy Virgin but later returned to Kiev and was abbot of the Cave Monastery from 1078 till his death in 1088.

St Antony died in 1073, at the age of ninety, according to tradition.[a] The *Paterik* of the Cave Monastery, which preserves for us the stories of its most outstanding and holy members down to about 1200, includes an excellent *Life* of St Theodosius,[17] to be set on a par with the *Lives* of SS Cyril and Methodios in its biographical exactitude and literary merit. The *Life* of St Antony has unfortunately been lost. Theodosius, determined from boyhood to devote himself to God,[18] set the whole future path of Russian monasticism on the middle way. Antony had been ascetic after the manner of the first eremitical St Antony; the most rigorous asceticism was not absent from Russia in later times. The more world-attached monk who is primarily a social worker is also found. But Theodosius introduced the Studite Rule, probably for the first time in Kiev, and thereby assured the coenobitic principle in this head and chief of Russian monasteries. While Antony's inspiration had been Athos,[b] Theodosius sent direct to Constantinople for a copy of the Rule, in the evolved forms in which by then it was alone available.[c] As an institution electing its own abbot and not directly dependent on the ruling house or the Metropolitanate, the Cave Monastery under Theodosius and his successors was able to play a dispassionate and sometimes decisive part in internal politics: it advised and persuaded for what it judged to be the general good. It also developed a strong tradition of social service. Theodosius did not approve of complete severance from the world. He directed his practical abilities to developing new buildings above ground, which became more and more the 'normal' monastery. The subterranean portions were reserved as retreats for the more ascetic brothers and as burial catacombs. By the time of his death (3 May 1074) Theodosius was already concerned at the accumulation of pious gifts—land and valuable objects—which had been made to the monastery. But resources were constantly needed for building: a new stone church of the Dormition (*Uspenski sobor*), replacing the original wooden one, was built in the

[a] This date seems assured but the chronology of the rest of his life is muddled, as we only have excerpts from his lost *Life* in the *Chronicle* and *Paterik*. The forty years which he is alleged to have spent in the caves is of course a notorious Biblical convention. It must remain a matter for doubt whether he made two journeys to Athos and when he returned finally to Kiev. The story of Moses the Hungarian (*Paterik, Slovo* 30) suggests that the Cave Monastery was well established by about 1025.

[b] Some (e.g. Smolitsch) are inclined to doubt the truth of Antony's visit to Athos and regard it as a later legend by a more Grecophil monk, designed to add to the dignity of the Cave Monastery.

[c] Efrem, a former brother of the Cave Monastery, then in Constantinople, sent the Rule as revised by Patriarch Alexios (1025–43). He may also have sent the Studios *Menaia*, translated at an early date in Russia.

1070s by craftsmen brought from the Imperial City itself. It was consecrated in August 1089 in the reign of Vsevolod. A large part of the monastery was destroyed by a Cuman raid in 1096.[19] Rebuilding was largely complete by 1108, the year of Theodosius's canonization.[a] Gifts of land, made by several princes, brought the monastery the possession of serfs, which was contrary to the Studite Rule and created another difficult problem. The question of monastic possessions remained a burning one in Russian ecclesiastical history.

The Cave Monastery was scarcely a centre of profound theological scholarship. But it trained a large proportion of the Russian episcopate in the early centuries and was the first prominent centre of Russian historical annals. Nestor, reputed author, certainly editor of one of the main redactions of the *Primary Chronicle*, became a monk there not long before Theodosius's death. To him, the outstanding writer of the early period, are ascribed the *Primary Chronicle*, the *Life of Theodosius*, and the *Story of Boris and Gleb*.[20] Simon and Polycarp and other anonymous monks contributed to the great collection of the *Paterik*. Of Theodosius himself five homilies have come down to us. The Cave Monastery was also an early centre of the art of icon-painting. The first painter known by name, Olympios (Alimpii), learnt his craft from the Greeks who were decorating the monastery's new church.[21]

The two great founders of the Cave Monastery built its life securely on the best Byzantine practice of the time. Both Athos and Constantinople made their contribution; the latter was seemingly the more important but there can be little doubt that connections with Athos were maintained. There is also a noticeable Palestinian strain (the *Life of St Sabbas* was especially popular) which kept the ambition of pilgrimage to the Holy Land alive. Palestinian monasticism was congenial to the Russian temperament in that it took a middle road between the extremes of asceticism and worldliness.

It is estimated that there were some seventy considerable houses in Russia by the time of the Mongol conquest (1240)—all still in or near the larger towns, particularly Kiev and Novgorod.[b] The movement into the wilds north of the Volga started in the later twelfth century and gathered

---

[a] The *Uspenski Sobor* was much damaged at the time of the Mongol invasions (1230, 1240), frequently restored later and finally largely destroyed during the Second World War.

[b] Kiev and Novgorod each had about twenty. The great monasteries that ringed Novgorod and played such a prominent part in its life all date from the twelfth century, from St Antony's (1117) to Khutyn (1192).

strength about a century later.[a] We may liken them to the deserts into which Mediterranean ascetics made their retreat.

The fruitful connection brought about by St Sava and his father between the Serbian church and Athos need not be repeated here.[b] The Abbot of Hilándar[c] was not infrequently chosen to be head of the Serbian church; such were Joannikije I (1272–6), successively abbot of Hilandar and Studenica, and Danilo II (1324–38). That Nemanja, prince and saint, died on Athos was never forgotten.[d] His cenotaph is still at Hilandar. Legend has it that there sprang from the empty tomb a vine which became a noted specific against sterility. Three dried grapes from it are given to petitioners, one to the husband, two to the wife. Sons then born by favour of St Symeon will, it is believed, be drawn to Hilandar and end their lives there as monks.

Hilandar was not exclusively for Serbs any more than Zographou for Bulgarians; monks of various Slav nations collected to form its first community. Hilandar and Zographou stand quite close to one another at the north end of the peninsula. Thus all the Orthodox Slav churches were in close contact with one another from 1200 at latest through their houses on Athos, if not by other means, and through Athos with religious communities even further afield, for example with St Catharine's Monastery on Sinai.[e] It is further probable that some Slavs were to be found in all the greater monasteries of Athos, indeed that until quite recent times Greeks formed the minority of the whole Athonite population. The common use of Church Slavonic, not only as the liturgical language (retaining on Athos its contacts with Greek) but also as the vehicle of intellectual exchange, also maintained a vigorous international Orthodoxy which proved of inestimable benefit to the Slavs in their long times of foreign domination. For more than a century from

a See pp. 264–5.

b See pp. 218–19.

c Greek χιλανδάρης, if from χελάνδιον, signifies 'ship-owner'. The site was bought from the monastery of Vatopédi, whose Slav monks then moved to the new house. The connection between the two was maintained. Nemanja's church was greatly altered by Milútin c. 1303 and much of it (as well as the rest of the monastery) was destroyed by a disastrous fire in 1722. There remains the original marble floor, a notable example of *opus alexandrinum*, certain frescoes of Milutin's reconstruction now being revealed below later layers of painting, and Milutin's tower (see Deroko, fig. 272–82, pp. 168–73).

d Following the example of Constantinople, Slav Orthodox rulers, especially in Serbia and Russia, early embraced the custom of retiring into a monastery or, more usually, of donning the monastic habit (*skhema*) on their death-bed, thus compensating for the secular element in a life that partook of the sacred in its functions.

e Two important early Slav manuscripts owe their preservation to this link—the so-called *Euchologium sinaiticum* and *Psalterium sinaiticum*. See p. 182.

the beginning of the Ottoman conquest of the Balkans Serbian and Bulgarian monks and prelates gave heart to Russia under the Mongol yoke and contributed to one of the outstanding periods of its spiritual achievement. With the rise of Muscovy as the only free Slav Orthodox state at the end of the fifteenth century the tide began to flow in the opposite direction and the debt was repaid.

CONCLUSION

The Roman Empire was destined to give birth to two Christian civilisations, one Latin and one Greek. However trivial the differences might seem at first and however long it might take for East and West each to realise and admit it, ineluctable divergence in way of life, above all in intellectual style, was bound to lead in the long run to a point of mutual incomprehension and hostility. For it is unity of style which makes and maintains a civilisation.

Justinian's restored empire in the sixth century had been an artificial construction which had rapidly crumbled, not the least owing to the incursions of the Slavs, but also through the Lombard domination of the greater part of the Italian peninsula. Any further attempt at such a restoration from the Eastern side was finally put out of court in the seventh century by Moslem command of Mediterranean communications. The following hundred or so years during which the Iconoclast troubles preoccupied the remnants of the Byzantine Empire (730–843) was heavy with consequences for the whole future shape of Europe. During the previous century the Empire had succeeded in denying Islam a foothold on the European mainland at the price of an enormous loss of territory, with all its Christian population, and of grave exhaustion of its energies. Now it plunged into the further exhausting internal strife over images, incidentally providing the Papacy with a perpetual grievance by detaching Illyricum and South Italy from the jurisdiction of popes who refused to acquiesce in the Imperial iconoclast policy.

The pulses of East and West tended to be opposite. During the Iconoclast troubles an impotent East lost Ravenna (751) and was faced with the first gathering of strength towards a Western Empire, arising beyond its effective reach on new ground in North-western Europe, though proclaimed in Rome at the coronation of Charlemagne (800). The Slavs had already completed their expansion, driving a wedge between East and West when they reached the Dalmatian coast of the Adriatic in the seventh century.

In the early ninth century, when the divergence between East and West was beginning to be clearly perceptible, the vast lands inhabited by Slavs were still outside civilisation. It was within this 'soft centre' of Europe, the direct consequence of their expansion, that a new frontier between East and West had to be drawn. The frontier would reflect in its oscillations the relative vitality and power of East and West, expressed in their bids for the spiritual allegiance of the various Slav peoples.

The critical period during which this process began for most of the Slavs—the second half of the ninth century—was a phase when the Eastern pulse was again growing stronger, the Western feebler, as Charlemagne's personal Empire disintegrated. It is not surprising therefore that at this time Byzantine civilisation was able to exert an influence far to the West, reaching Moravia and all its more or less precarious cultural dependencies. The mission of SS Cyril and Methodios stands out as a remarkable manifestation of this influence. But this potential cultural frontier was at no time a practicable political frontier; nor would it seem that the East expected that it could become such when the Moravian mission was planned and sent. The settlement made between Constantinople and Rome in 880 was already the sign that Moravia (and therefore Bohemia) was virtually lost to the East and Bulgaria to the West, despite later hesitations. The First Conversion of Russia showed rather the direction in which the East could most profitably recoup its losses and build a new polity in its own image, though this work had to be redone a century later: the expansion of the Scandinavian pagans held up the entry of the Eastern Slavs into Christendom, whereas in Western Europe it affected the Slavs at most indirectly insofar as it contributed to the disruption of the Carolingian edifice.

Another decisive period falls in the first half of the eleventh century. The irruption of the Magyars into Central Europe had not merely annihilated Moravia but also created a barrier between the Northern and Southern Slavs. From that time any unity which the Slav world might have retained (and it is idle to speculate what might have resulted from such a unity) was broken. Western policy recognised the great strategic importance of building in Hungary a commanding Catholic bastion, supported by the germanisation of Austria, the connecting link through which its supply lines ran. The granting of a Papal crown to St Stephen in the year 1000 marks the first achievement of this policy; Hungary as a possible client state of the Byzantine Empire was transformed into its rival in the North Balkans. The date is the more significant in that it contributed to determining the form of Bohemian and Polish culture. Questions of political independence apart, neither country could thereafter hold out against the spirit of uniformity which more and more animated Western ecclesiastical policy from the eleventh century. By 1100 the Eastern elements in their civilisation, superficial though they may have been, had been more or less forcibly removed. The greater part of the Central European Slavs thus found themselves on the western side of the frontier.

The Western capture of Hungary and Poland was reinforced by the growing economic importance of Venice which set about building up a Mediterranean maritime empire. The pulse of Eastern civilisation was now weak; its hold on the Balkan Slavs might even seem precarious. The strength of the Byzantine Empire was once again seriously undermined by the long duel with Bulgaria. Basil's triumph in 1018 was only a Pyrrhic victory. The insidious tentacles of Venetian commercial diplomacy began to encircle the Empire from the south; in addition to this a Western power—the Normans—established itself in Sicily and South Italy. The Orthodox world passed permanently to the defensive in the face of the Hildebrandine magnification of the Papacy and the expansive vigour of Latin civilisation, now entering a great creative phase. The West had already made good its claims to the 'soft centre', from Croatia to Poland.

The last critical period with which the present survey is concerned covers the twelfth century. Having consolidated its hold on the centre of the line Latin civilisation now engaged in a vast pincer movement which aimed at outflanking the Orthodox world both in the Mediterranean south and in the Baltic north. This proceeded from the natural facts of European geography and does not imply any conscious coordination between the two arms.

In the south, stimulated by Venetian ambitions and relying on Venetian aid, the Crusading movement gained a foothold in the Near East, in those lands which had been a part of the Byzantine Christian Empire before the conquests of Islam. Thereby the long latent antagonism and incomprehension between the two halves of Christendom was finally brought to overt expression, despite the moderation of the best spirits on either side, whether lay or ecclesiastical. Though frustrated of permanent success in the Holy Land the Westerners set the seal on their adventure by the rape of Constantinople in 1204, from which the Orthodox Empire never recovered. A Latin patriarch lording it in the City made the incompatibility of the two worlds finally plain.

In the North Poland now became the bridgehead for German conquest of the East Baltic coasts, as soon as the inconvenient irritation of Wendish resistance had been broken in the rear. The German town and see of Riga was founded in 1201. This northern arm of the pincer movement contributed to the definition of the frontier between East and West, here curiously featureless in geographical terms but culturally strongly marked. The contemporaneous Mongol conquest of the greater part of Russia redrew the frontier but in the long run sharpened it further by denying Central Russia all those European links which had allowed Kievan Russia to have a stake in the Western, though essentially a part of the Eastern, world.

The twelfth and early thirteenth centuries were a confused period for the Balkan Slavs east of Croatia. The Latin Empire made credible the revival of Papal claims to Illyricum of which Rome had been deprived in the eighth century. The Slavs asserted their attachment to Orthodoxy. But by this time, encouraged by the hope of greater prizes which the outflanking movements might bring, the Papacy scarcely gave high priority to the Balkans: the Orthodox Slavs of those parts seemed destined to fall to the West given the final dissolution of the Byzantine Empire. This proved a false hope: Byzantine power was replaced by Ottoman power without fundamentally altering the nature of the Eastern Orthodox world. The frontier between East and West, with some fluctuations, remained substantially the same.

The Cyrillomethodian experiment had been borne on the crest of a strong Eastern pulse and had been offered at a moment especially favourable to all the Slavs whom it reached. The ensuing centuries of gradually increasing Western pressure and ascendancy, which forced the frontier back towards the East—dividing Poland from Russia, Hungary from Romania and Croatia from Serbia—thus brought it about that the use of the Slav liturgical language became almost coincident with Orthodoxy and membership of the Eastern world. Only at two points astride the frontier, where politics dictated compromise, could old anomalies persist or new ones arise. These points were the North Dalmatian coast of Croatia, where the Glagolitic alphabet of SS Cyril and Methodios continued down to modern times to render a more and more Croatian form of Church Slavonic in a Catholic church, thus preserving a state of affairs which recalls Bohemian Christianity in the tenth–eleventh centuries; and, at a later period, the Ukraine, where many of Poland's Orthodox subjects, using Church Slavonic in the Cyrillic script, were marshalled into a Uniate church, theoretically Orthodox in all respects except for acknowledging the supremacy of the Pope.

But in general the frontier was well defined. The modern usage of the name and idea of 'Europe' arose towards the end of the tenth century; there are early examples in the Saxon chronicler Widukind. Neither heathen nor non-Catholic lands could be considered a part of 'Europe', which was Western Christendom. The frontier as eventually stabilised was a religious frontier between the Catholic and Orthodox worlds. This did not cease to be true when a great part of the Orthodox world passed under the rule of Moslem masters. The Balkan Slavs never felt themselves a part of this 'Europe', however much a purely geographical use of the term might attempt to obscure the fact. Even today Greeks may be heard to speak of 'going to Europe'. Further, to all the Eastern world (including most Moslems) Westerners were for century after century commonly lumped together as 'Franks'—a witness to the fundamental importance of the Carolingian imperial experiment in shaping the evolution of Europe.[a]

From the outset, and more obviously as time went on, the divergent civilisations of East and West moulded the Slavs in their respective styles. It must suffice to indicate a few fundamental contrasts.

There was a different relation between *sacerdotium* and *regnum* in East and West. The two principles of spiritual authority and temporal rule resided together in Constantinople, as a result of the contraction of the Empire which had removed the effective equality of the other three eastern patriarchates. The Emperor combined in his single person the direction of church and state, though not possessing by virtue of his office the *sacerdotium* and its spiritual authority. The Byzantine Empire became the heir of the Roman Empire without any violent disruption of continuity.[b] Lay education and a secular civil service remained. The Emperor maintained his position as the acknowledged head of a Christian polity in which the church was not a body apart but continued to be felt as the sum of all individual persons of whatever rank, class or calling. The Emperor remained an autocrat, with the duty of implementing God's will through true doctrine as interpreted by the church. The church (in the narrow sense) was an egalitarian body. The Patriarch of Constantinople could not acquire the hierarchical pre-eminence of the Pope in Rome; all bishops, enjoying as they did the Apostolic succession through their consecration, were held in theory to be charismatically equal.

[a] This usage was kept alive by the presence of the Crusader states in the Levant and by the Latin domination of the Aegean after 1204, but was established long before.

[b] Throughout the life of the Byzantine Empire and beyond the Greeks called themselves 'Romans' ('Ρωμαῖοι) and their vernacular language 'Roman' ('Ρωμαϊκό).

Not so in the West. Here *regnum* virtually disappeared; it was the Roman church which survived the collapse and barbarisation of the Western Roman Empire as the sole repository of tradition, both in doctrine and law. Rome had the greatness of unique, if not always unquestioned, spiritual authority thrust upon her. Thus the Western clergy were for long virtually the sole literate class, enjoying an intellectual monopoly, and through them the church came to exercise a dangerously dominant part in more secular spheres of action, by which alone could be made good the disappearance of the Roman civil service. New forms of temporal rule emerged (including the temporal rule of the Papacy itself) but there could be only feeble attempts to bring the two principles together in one place, still less in one person. Lay *potestas* was as a rule much divided and leaned heavily on the church for the exercise of its proper functions. Thus the rise of a new imperial *potestas* in the West accentuated the separation of the two poles of authority, of varying relative strength and often having contradictory policies and modes of action, and established the premisses for rivalry between ecclesiastical and lay pretensions, which came to the fore, for example, in the great Investiture Quarrel. The contrast is well shown in that the Iconoclast Quarrel in the East (the last important quarrel of this kind) concerned principally doctrine and ritual, the Investiture Quarrel—lay powers over the hierarchy and ecclesiastical administration. *Imperium* and *sacerdotium* in the West were more often at variance than in harmony.

It is therefore more epigrammatic than accurate to speak of Caesaropapism in the East and Papocaesarism in the West.

Thus though newly Christianised peoples were in either case subjected to similar political pressures, the Western Slavs felt the imposition of a church armed with all the appurtenances of secular rule and of secular rule containing a strong ecclesiastical element. The Slavs of East Europe, in contrast, were aware of two more separate currents which could be and were on occasion kept apart, despite the fact that they both emanated from Constantinople. To take an extreme case, the Greek Metropolitan of Kiev, appointee though he might be of the Emperor and Patriarch in Constantinople, was never in a position to exercise in Russia the kind of power which was given as a matter of course to many a Western diocesan bishop. The difference is one of principle since it proceeds from a different conception of the church. But it could often appear as no more than a difference of emphasis. Nowhere in medieval thought are 'church' and 'state' wholly separated: one cannot properly speak of states—only of constituent parts of Christendom. Nevertheless becoming Christian in the West was, generally speaking, more bound up with immediate political implications than in the East.

Owing to the geographical separation of the two poles of authority in the West Christianity reached some Western Slavs more under the aegis of the one or of the other. For example, from the middle of the ninth century the Papacy tended to be dominant over the fragmented Carolingian Empire. It was to this that the Cyrillomethodian mission owed its modest success in its original mission field and arguably also the survival of its tradition through propagation to new fields. Conversely, as we proceed further into the tenth century the scale of the Papacy is more and more out-weighed by that of the renascent Western Empire. Yet whether lay ruler or Pope played the leading part may be considered a secondary factor in determining the spiritual affiliation of those Slavs who became a part of Catholic Europe.

A further contrast is worth noting. The Byzantine Orthodox Empire was, except in the case of Russia, by and large attempting to redeem lost Christian lands, whether in the Balkans or the Near East. The Balkans were redeemed; it was the Slavs themselves who had dechristianised them. Where redemption failed Constantinople came to look on itself as the protector of those Christians who remained *in partibus infidelium*. The earliest Crusades appeared in Byzantine eyes as an unavoidable if hazardous method of redemption from which it proved impossible to profit to the extent that equity demanded. The Western Empire, on the other hand, was breaking new ground (with the converse exception of the Iberian peninsula) and conscious of enlarging Christendom by its missionary enterprise. It is difficult, however, to see that this added any further complexity to the situation not inherent in the different conception of the church itself in East and West.

Everywhere the development of the Slav peoples, in particular the emergence of Slav states, did not proceed without strong outside pressures, applied either by the East or by the West and serving directly or indirectly the ends of those higher centres of civilisation upon which the Slav expansion had impinged. Each Slav people had to opt for or accept either Eastern or Western Christianity; only Russia perhaps was exposed to the remoter possibility of being drawn into the Islamic world. But the political pressures were in themselves by no means necessarily favourable. They were instrumental in hastening or impeding the formation of viable Slav states; and where they hastened it may be that they deformed. Successful military resistance, *a fortiori* a policy of empire-building, on the part of a Slav people required effective centralisation of power in the hands of a military leader—a Symeon or a Bolesław Chrobry. Both the acceptance of Christianity and new political needs demanded a profound and disturbing social transformation. What remained at the critical moment of earlier barbarian social and political structure rapidly disappeared. The exceptions were few but instructive. In some remote mountainous areas, such as Montenegro, the old social structure remained virtually intact (to the delight of ethnologists) down to recent times, in much the same way as that of the Highland Scots. In the North German plain the Wends likewise retained until late a relatively stable clan society (reminding us rather of early Ireland) and their long drawn out delaying action against absorption into the German world was based not on unitary command but on more or less successful guerrilla tactics. Conversely, Imperial ambitions which infected those Slavs most directly exposed to the imperialism of either East or West must be accounted injurious, if understandable, aberrations. Militarism ruined Bulgaria early in its development; both Poland and Serbia came to grief under the strains of political ambitions which exceeded their strength.

Evangelisation proceeded successfully, as we should expect, wherever the dissolution of pagan Slav society, under the influence of migration, new ecological factors imposed by geography, and of external pressures, was already well advanced. Clear contrary cases are lacking. Among the Wends military pressures got too far ahead of missionary enterprise for theirs to be considered a normal evolution, though the imperviousness of this clan society seems a reasonable inference from the sources. Almost everywhere Christianity made its successful appeal to the ruler and ruling class generally and thence worked downwards into the body of the people. While the personal qualities of the missionaries must always be a considerable factor in the ultimate success of a mission, to be seen in the pace of conversion and the stability of the achievement, they must count for relatively little where the ground to be sown is stony and unreceptive, that is, where the social conditions are too alien to those in which Christianity normally operates. For Christianity, preached in a great Empire, rested on the fundamental principle of the absolute equality of all men in the highest manifestation of human nature; family, clan, nation and language were all subordinate to this. St Ansgar was a great missionary but his achievements in Scandinavia were exceedingly modest: the time was not yet quite ripe. If, after reviewing every case, we still account the brothers Cyril and Methodios the greatest missionaries who promoted the entry of the Slavs into Christendom it is because their work embodied the highest principles of missionary endeavour, partaking of the disinterestedness of the Irish and eschewing both the imperialist and the linguistic jealousy of East and West. Nevertheless, though addressing themselves to peoples at a favourably receptive stage of evolution, even they came very near to failure. The survival of a church using a Slav liturgical language was made possible—to all appearances—largely by Papal support at a crucial moment and by relatively weak external pressures in the ensuing stage, Western in Bohemia, Eastern in the Balkans.

To assess what was in each individual instance favourable or unfavourable to the development of the Slavs under the dual impact of Christian evangelisation and political pressures cannot here be attempted. Christianity undeniably laid the spiritual and cultural foundations for original local development. It must suffice to note one last contrast. The Slavs in the Balkans and Russia were apparently more favourably placed in the early stages. In the ninth–tenth centuries Byzantine civilisation was far superior to that of Western Europe. Even in the eleventh century an Easterner was painfully aware that, though the balance of power might now lie with the Westerners, the latter were, as the ancient Romans to the Greeks, still crude provincials. Yet a very great difference in intellectual level can be a bar to comprehension and lead in the long run to a less thorough assimilation of what is offered and hence to much greater internal inequalities and strains. The lower intensity of Western cultural pressure during the period of Carolingian decline and slow Ottonian ascent can scarcely be considered a decisive disadvantage to the Western Slavs. Both Bohemia and Poland were able to benefit in full measure from the great advance of Western culture in the twelfth and following centuries. Conversely, the Balkan Slavs may well have been somewhat inhibited by the slackening of Byzantine culture: there was less impulse to develop for themselves what had already been given in apparently complete and fully developed form.

The eccentric geographical position of Russia makes its history a special case. The political life of the East Slavs was shaped not by the imposing proximity of an empire but by problems of internal cohesion and of a shifting frontier against constant pressure from non-Christian peoples of the Eurasian steppes. Once initial hesitations were past, the ecclesiastical relations between Constantinople and Russia may be said to have attained that *amicabilis concordia* which is the pattern of Orthodoxy: since Russia was as yet innocent of imperial ambitions there was little to promote the idea of a native patriarchate such as early characterised Bulgarian and Serbian thought. The Mongol conquest—the most successful of the steppe incursions—changed all. Russia emerged from the Tatar yoke not only as the imperial power of Muscovy but also, after 1453, as the sole great independent Orthodox power. Moscow made its claim to be the Third Rome, the political heir of Constantinople. A Russian patriarchate now logically followed the assumption of Imperial status, but equally logically it took rank as the fifth of the Orthodox patriarchates (Rome having long fallen away into schism), still looking to the Œcumenical Patriarch in Constantinople as *primus inter pares*. The Muscovite Empire proved to be a monstrous hybrid, as much the successor of Mongol as of Byzantine imperial conceptions. But the Russians' defence of their Christian heritage, and indirectly of European Christendom as a whole, is well symbolised in a new linguistic usage which asserted itself during the two and half centuries of Tatar domination: the word for 'peasant'—the overwhelming majority of Russians— became and remains to this day крестьянин, a Christian.

ABBREVIATIONS

AAH	*Acta archaeologica ac. sci. hungaricae* (Budapest).
AB	*Analecta bollandiana* (Paris–Brussels).
ANT	*Antemurale* (Rome).
ASR	*American Slavic Review* (Menasha).
BB	*Byzantinobulgarica* (Sofia).
BSL	*Byzantinoslavica* (Prague).
BYZ	*Byzantion* (Brussels).
BZ	*Byzantinische Zeitschrift* (Leipzig).
Cahiers	*Cahiers du monde russe et soviétique* (Paris).
CD	Smičiklas, *Codex diplomaticus* (see bibliography).
CDEM	*Codex diplomaticus et epistolaris Moraviae* (see bibliography).
CDMP	*Codex diplomaticus majoris Poloniae* (see bibliography).
CDS	*Codex diplomaticus...Silesiae* (see bibliography).
CEH	*Cambridge Economic History of Europe.*
CMH	*Cambridge Medieval History.*
DAI	Constantine Porphyrogennetos, *De administrando imperio.*
DO	Dumbarton Oaks.
DOP	*Dumbarton Oaks Papers.*
EB	*Etudes byzantines* (Bucharest); continued as *REB.*
FOG	*Forschungen zur osteuropäischen Geschichte* (Berlin).
FRB	*Fontes rerum bohemicarum.*
HIST	*Historica* (Prague).
HSS	*Harvard Slavic Studies* (Cambridge, Mass.).
IJS	*International Journal of Slavic linguistics and poetics* (Hague).
INBI	*Izevstija na Instituta za istorija* (Sofia).
JGO	*Jahrbücher für Geschichte Osteuropas* (Breslau).
KSIS	*Kratkije soobshchenija instituta slavjanovedenija* (Moscow).
LIF	*Listy filologické* (Prague).
LMLS	*Language Monographs of the Linguistic Society of America.*
MGH	*Monumenta Germaniae historica.*
MPH	*Monumenta Poloniae historica.*
MSM	*Monumenta spectantia historiam Slavorum meridionalium.*
NP	*Nasza przeszłość* (Cracow).
OC	*Orientalia christiana* (from 1935 *Orientalia christiana analecta*) (Rome).
OCA	*Actes du XIIe congrès international d'études byzantines, Ohrid,* 1961 (3 vols, Belgrade, 1963–4).
OCP	*Orientalia christiana periodica* (Rome).
OCS	Old Church Slavonic (The abbreviations conventionally used for various works in OCS will be found on p. 64).
OHG	Old High German.
OO	*Oesterreichische Osthefte* (Vienna).
OST	*Ostkirchliche Studien* (Würzburg).

Abbreviations

PG	Migne, *Patrologia graeca.*
PL	Migne, *Patrologia latina.*
PR	*Polish Review* (New York).
PRI	*Prilozi za književnost, jezik, istoriju i folklor* (Belgrade).
PRZ	*Przegląd zachodni* (Poznań).
PSL	*Pamiętnik słowiański* (Cracow).
PSRL	*Polnoje sobranije russkih letopisej.*
RAV	*Rozpravy československé akademie věd* (Prague).
REB	*Revue des études byzantines* (Paris–Bucharest).
RES	*Revue des études slaves* (Paris).
RISL	*Ricerche slavistiche* (Rome).
SA	*Slavia antiqua* (Poznań).
SAE	*Saeculum* (Freiburg–Munich).
SCSL	*Scandoslavica* (Copenhagen).
SDH	*Slavistische Drukken en Herdrukken* (Hague).
SF	*Südostforschungen* (Leipzig).
SK	*Seminarium Kondakovianum* (= *Annales de l'Institut Kondakov*) (Prague).
SL	*Slavia* (Prague).
SLF	*Slavistische Forschungen* (Köln–Graz).
SLO	*Slovo* (Zagreb).
SLOR	*Slavia orientalis* (Warsaw).
SOCC	*Slavia occidentalis* (Poznań).
SPM	*Sacrum Poloniae Millenium* (Rome).
SR	*Slavonic and East European Review* (London).
SRH	*Scriptores rerum hungaricarum.*
SZ	*Studia źródłoznawcze* (Warsaw).
TM	*Travaux et Mémoires, Centre de recherche d'histoire et civilisation byzantines* (Paris).
TODL	*Trudy otdela drevnerusskoj literatury* (Moscow).
VC	*Vita Constantini* (see p. 30).
VDI	*Vestnik drevnej istorii* (Moscow).
VM	*Vita Methodii* (see p. 30).
VSIS	*Voprosy slavjanskogo jazykoznanija* (Institut slavjanovedenija, Moscow).
VV	*Vizantijski vremennik* (Moscow).
WS	*Die Welt der Slaven* (Wiesbaden–Munich).
WSJ	*Wiener slavistisches Jahrbuch* (Vienna).
ZO	*Zeitschrift für Ostforschung* (Marburg).
ZRVI	*Zbornik radova vizantološkog instituta* (Belgrade).
ZSB	*Zeitschrift für Slavistik* (Berlin).
ZSP	*Zeitschrift für slavische Philologie* (Berlin).

NOTES

In the interests of brevity: 1. where a component part of a large collection of texts (e.g. *MGH*) is cited, reference is made to the appropriate volume (e.g. *MGH*, SS 1). However, a few special separate editions of such texts are listed in the bibliography below and reference is made to these in the usual way; 2. references are given by author's name alone when there is no ambiguity (e.g. Beckwith = J. Beckwith, *Early Medieval Art*—the only entry in the bibliography for this author); if an author has several works listed in the bibliography his name and a contracted form of the title are cited.

Introduction

1 *The Phenomenon of Man* (English version, 1959), p. 121.

2 Authorities differ on this point: compare B. Zástěrová in *Vznik a počátky slovanů* 6 (1966) and I. Popović in *ZRVI* 7 (1961).

3 The earliest mention comes in the first half of the fifth century. Σκλάβοι/ *Sclavi* alternates with Σκλαβηνοί/Sclavini. From Greek came the Arabic Ṣaqlab (plural Ṣaqāliba), in the seventh century. The semantic shift to 'slave' is a later West European development; for details, see H. and R. Kahane in *Studi...Lo Gatto* (1962). Cf. also pp. 144–5.

Chapter 1. The Slavs in the Byzantine Empire

1 For bibliographies see especially Bon. p. 30; Ostrogorsky, p. 85; *DAI*, Commentary to cap. 49 and 50.

2 Prokopios's Περὶ κτισμάτων (*De aedificiis*) is also informative on the earliest Slav place names south of the Danube, concentrated in *Dacia mediterranea* nd *Dardania* (roughly the triangle Niš–Sofia–Skopje). They have been interpreted by V. Georgiev in *Vŭprosi na bulgarskata etimologija* (Sofia, 1958) and *SR* 44 (July 1966).

3 *De Bello Goth.*, iii, 40.

4 *Ibid.*, i, 27; similarly under Belisarius in 539–40 (*ibid.*, ii, 18 ff.). Paul the Deacon (*Hist. Lomb.*, iv, 28) records the use of Slav mercenaries in the armies of Odoacer and other Gothic chieftains.

5 Agathias, *Histories*, iii, 21: Ὀυσιγάρ(ε)δος [καὶ] Σουαρούνας, σκλάβος ἀνήρ; Δαβραγέζας, Ἄντης ἀνήρ, ταξίαρχος. Cf. also *ibid.*, iii, 6–7; iv, 20. On these names see Levchenko in *VDI* 4 (5) (1938) and Brajchevski in *VV* 19 (1961). Further Slav names are recorded in Theophylakt Simocatta: Ἀρδάγαστος = Radogost (*Histories*, i, 7; vi, 7); Πειράγαστος = Pirogost (*ibid.*, vii, 4–5).

6 Agathias, *Histories*, iv, 18.

7 Greek Δαυρήτας, probably representing Dobręta. Menander (*apud* Constantine Porphyrogennetos, *Excerpta de legationibus*: Migne, *PG* 113, col.

605 ff.) estimated the number of invading Slavs in this or a similar raid at 100,000 (col. 835), but such figures are notoriously unreliable.

8   The first collection of *Miracles* was made *c.* 610–20 by Metropolitan John of Saloniki. The second collection, by an unknown hand, was probably made in the reign of Constantine IV (668–85). Thus the legends are contemporary with the period of maximum Slav pressure on the city. Texts in Migne, *PG* 116, cols. 1203–1384. John of Ephesus (*Historiae ecclesiasticae*, vi, 25) alludes to the Slavs' mastery of war.

9   Isidore of Seville (*c.* 560–636) was already made fully aware of this during his visit to various Jewish communities in the East: *Chronicon* 120 (Migne, *PL* 83, col. 1056): 'Sclavi Graeciam Romanis tulerunt'. About the year 580 a Balkan soldier had scribbled in bad Greek the heartfelt cry 'Lord, protect Romania!', for which the old English parallel was the Litany supplication 'From the fury of the Northmen, Good Lord, deliver us!'

10   Hoddinott, pp. 89 ff.

11   The whole historical record is rather thin for the seventh and eighth centuries, the only notable sources being Patriarch Nikephoros' Ἱστορία σύντομος (Migne, *PG* 100, cols. 875 ff.), covering the period 602–768, and Theophanes Confessor's Χρονογραφία (Migne, *PG* 108, *ad init.*), which extends another fifty years to the reign of the Bulgarian Krum (see pp. 156–7).

12   *De Thematibus*, ii, 6: ἐσθλαβώθη δὲ πᾶσα ἡ χώρα καὶ γέγονε βάρβαρος. Fallmerayer's notorious theory (*Geschichte der Halbinsel Morea während des Mittelalters* (Stuttgart, 1830–6)) that the modern Greeks are almost wholly Slav in blood can no longer be taken seriously. The very small number of Slav words in the modern language (rather more, as one would expect, in the northern dialects) is sufficient to show that, generally speaking, Greek remained the dominant language rapidly adopted by the Slavs, not slowly learnt by the later reimportation of Greek. Both emigration and the plague reduced the number of Greeks in Greece in the eighth century but there was certainly no general flight then or earlier.

13   There is no substantial account of the Slav way of life between Prokopios's scattered references and Leo VI's *Taktika* (Migne, *PG* 107), xviii, 79–108, but the latter's information is earlier than the compilation (early years of the tenth century). To the period of the Slav *Landnahme* must be ascribed also the specialisation of the surviving Albanians and Latin-speaking peasantry (later to be known as Vlachs, speaking dialects of the Romanian group) as pastoralists practising transhumance. High mountain pasture did not attract the predominantly agricultural Slav settlers. On the *zadruga* see E. Sicard, *La Zadruga sud-slave* (Paris, 1943).

14   See especially Vasmer, *Die Slaven in Griechenland* (*Abhandlungen der Preuss. Ak. der Wissenschaften*, Berlin, 1941). The figures of course reflect the proportions of *survival*. It is possible that their distribution was more even at the time of maximum Slav control and that Greek recolonisation has reduced them at a greater rate in the most desirable areas from the Greek point of view. Further discussion by P. Charanis in *BSL* 10 (1949), *DOP* 5 (1950), *BZ* 46

(1953). It should be noted that all these Slavs spoke dialects of the Bulgar-Macedonian, not the Serbo-Croat type.

15 Patriarch Nicholas III (*fungebatur* 1084–1111) reckoned it as the 218 years from 587 to 805. See also P. Lemerle in *REB* 21 (1963), discussing the *Chronicle of Monemvasia*.

16 Ostrogorsky (*DOP* 19 (1965)) puts its formation between 789 and 802. See also *id.* in *SR* 42 (December 1963).

17 Vasiljev, *History*, I, 320 ff.; Ostrogorsky, pp. 82 and 120. The kernel of the Law probably goes back to the end of the sixth century.

18 Patriarch Nikephoros, Ἱστορία σύντομος, *PG* 100, col. 989.

19 See P. Lemerle in *TM* 1 (1965).

20 *DAI*, cap. 49–50 deals with the Slavs in peninsular Greece. The Commentary (vol. 2, p. 183) discusses this and other dates. See also Ostrogorsky, pp. 171–2.

21 See P. Lemerle, *Philippes et la Macédoine orientale* (Paris, 1945), pp. 124 ff.

22 F. Dvornik, *La Vie de Saint Grégoire le Décapolite et les Slaves macédoniens au IXe siècle* (Paris, 1926), pp. 31 ff.

23 The *Notitia episcopatuum* of Leo VI (886–912) includes the following regions or peoples with Slav names (*Izvori* 8, pp. 158 ff.): under Saloniki— ὁ Δρουγουβιτίας, ὁ τῶν Σερβίων (west of Mt Olympos); under Larissa— ὁ Ἐζεροῦ; under Philippi—ὁ Βελικείας, ὁ [τῶν] Σμολαίνων. For Philip-popolis, see note 59 to chap. 4. See also Gelzer in *Abh. Bayr. Akad. Wiss.*, *Phil.* 21 (1901).

24 It is said that in the reign of Justinian the Germanic Heruli in Pannonia were bribed to become Christians; but military alliance was naturally the more immediate aim. See V. Tŭpkova-Zaimova in *INBI* 12 (1963) for similar situations.

25 Text in Teodorov-Balan, II, 110 (*Slovo Kirila filosofa kako uvěri Bulgare*).

26 See Hoddinott, pp. 168 ff.

27 Bon, pp. 68–9, 106.

28 Laurent in *EB* 1 (1943). A precise number of functioning dioceses cannot be given owing to the habit of conferring titular dioceses on non-resident bishops and including administrative centres in episcopal lists even if the see was in abeyance. See also Ostrogorsky in *DOP* 13 (1959).

29 Ἐζερῖται=lake-dwellers; Μελιγκοί (Μηλιγγοί, Μελεγγοί) is of uncertain etymology, perhaps representing Slav *mělnik*=inhabitant of the (dry) limestone hills, in contrast to the marshy plain (so H. Grégoire in *Nouvelle Clio* 4 (1952)). See map in Bon, pp. 40–1. On the Slav element in the Maniots, see also *ibid.*, pp. 71–4.

30 *DAI*, cap. 50.

31 *Chronicle of Morea* (ed. H. Lurier), ll. 2992–3031, 3038–40, 4531–3, 4587–92.

Chapter 2. The Slavs in Central Europe

BAVARIA, CARANTANIA AND AVARIA

1 Texts of the *Lex baiuvarorum* from the first half of the eighth century contain some Christian elements, e.g. the observation of Sunday (I, 14). See Bauerreiss, pp. 151–2.

2 *Vita vel passio sancti Haimhrammi episcopi et martyris ratisbonensis* by Arbeo of Freising (*c.* 772), ed. B. Bischoff (Munich, 1953), pp. 14–16.

3 Bauerreiss, p. 73.

4 Jonas of Bobbio's *Life of St Columban* (*MGH, SS rer. merov.*, IV, p. 104).

5 *Vita S. Amandi*, cap. 16 (*MGH, SS rer. merov.*, V, pp. 439–40); written *c.* 725.

6 St Rupert's work in Bavaria is summarised by Bauerreiss, pp. 48–9. His *Vita* (*MGH, SS rer. merov.*, VI) is not very informative.

7 In a letter of 745/6 (*MGH, Epp.* III, no. 73) he finds room to praise their matrimonial morals, though the Slavs in general (Winedi) are 'foedissimum et deterrimum genus hominum'.

8 *Vita S. Bonifacii*, x, §31: 'ecclesias in confiniis Francorum et Saxonum atque Sclavorum suo officio deputavit' (referring to the work of his new see of Würzburg, *c.* 746) (*MGH, SS* II, p. 348).

9 See W. H. Fritze in *ZSP* 31 (1963) for the verses of Martin of Bracara on this theme. The virtue of the Irish missions was the total absence of any political implications, since the missionaries did not seek to attach their converts to any existing ecclesiastical, and hence political, centre. The Irish conceived their work as a voluntary exile, usually for life—a pure *peregrinatio pro amore Dei*—leaving behind all that they held most dear as a supreme act of penance. In the long run this was also a weakness: others were bound to follow to introduce conventional organisation. On the Irish missionaries in general consult Gougaud and Reiffenstein.

10 See *Vita S. Virgilii* (*MGH, SS* IX), *passim.*

11 Carantania, as understood at the time, might include also the greater part of Noricum and Pannonia; see B. Grafenauer, p. 49 (map). The basis of the Latinised *Carantania* is the pre-Slav name of the fortress *Karanta* (German *Karnburg*). The Slovene provinces are: Carinthia (German Kärnten, Slovene Koróško), Styria (Steiermark, Stájersko) and Carniola (Krain, Kránjsko).

12 German *Chorbischof* (from Greek χώρα=countryside), i.e. a suffragan without specific see sent into the rural areas for missionary work. He also represented the bishop whenever the latter could not make a personal visitation for reasons of age or illness. *Chorbischöfe* are typical of the period *c.* 730–930. See T. Gottlob, *Das abendländische Chorepiskopat* (Bonn, 1928).

13 *Conversio* 5 (see p. 32 and note 88, p. 328).

14 '...ut omnis populus christianus fidem catholicam et dominicam orationem memoriter teneat...tam latine quam barbarice'. See I. Grafenauer, p. 146 (no. 7), p. 152 (no. 18), and p. 46. Eggers (p. 188) notes a peak of Germanic versions of such texts in the late eighth and early ninth centuries.

15 '...propter incredulam generationem slavorum ad tramitem veritatis adducendam' (Bauerreiss, p. 126).

16 For land-holdings of Bavarian monasteries in general, see Kuhar, *Slovene Medieval History*, pp. 89 ff. Carantania was governed by a German count or duke from the early ninth century. Germinisation was more rapid in the north so that the Slovene language frontier has retreated southwards towards the River Drava. But the province retained its Slav character and customs well into the eleventh century.

17 'Osbaldus episcopus sclavorum regebat gentem' (*Conversio* 9).

18 Brackmann, *Germania pontificia*, vol. 1, *archiepiscopatus salisburgensis*, no. 4.

19 Details of rights in the Drava region continued to be discussed till *c.* 830. For the disputed areas, especially about Villach, see Kuhar, *Conversion*, pp. 109–10, and Schmidinger.

20 The Diedenhof Capitulary of 805 (*MGH, Leges* 1, p. 133, §7: 'de negotiatoribus qui partibus sclavorum et avarorum pergunt') specified those points on the frontier at which trade with the Slavs was to be done (see map in Preidel, 1, p. 38). Cf. also p. 362 note 208.

21 See note 8 above, p. 323.

22 Erben, no. 26 (846).

23 See map in *Słownik*, s.v. *Bawaria*. Many Slavs in the remoter areas were scarcely touched till much later and cannot be considered fully Christianised till the eleventh century when intensive work was taken in hand by Henry II's new see of Bamberg (founded 1007). Similarly the *Fulda Annals* state that this great abbey, founded by St Boniface's disciple Sturm in 744 in a region partly populated by Slavs, had constant contacts with the Slavs within reach and on its extensive properties. But the *Annals* tell us little about the abbey's work of evangelisation; indeed missions are not mentioned before 948, and soon after this it took second place to Magdeburg.

24 *MGH, Epp.* IV, no. 93 (796). Alcuin several times touches on Charlemagne's duty to convert the heathen, e.g. *MGH, Epp.* IV, no. 171 (799). See also Ullmann, pp. 69 ff.

25 *MGH, Leges* III, *Conc.* II/1, pp. 172 ff.; *Conversio* 6; Dümmler and Wattenbach, *Monumenta alcuiniana* (Berlin, 1873), Letter 68, p. 312.

26 *MGH, Epp.* IV, no. 113 (796). Further: 'quomodo potest homo cogi ut credat quod non credit? Impelli potest homo ad baptismum sed non ad fidem'. Cf. nos. 99, 107 and 110–12.

27 Alcuin, Letter 111 (*MGH, Epp.* IV, p. 159), dated (late) 796.

28 See Schmitz, vol. 1, chap. 5, *passim*.

29 Illustrated in J. le Goff, *La Civilisation de l'occident médiéval* (1965), pp. 160–1. It is idle to discuss whether a frontier monastery first exerted a missionary or an economic effect: the two went hand in hand. Fulda is a typical case: it acquired vast lands by clearing. The clearing was done not by the monks but by the peasantry whom they were able to attract to settle the new lands. If these were pagan Slavs they were automatically drawn into the Christian life of the monastery.

30 Löwe, *Die karolingische Reichsgründung*, pp. 76 ff., estimates that the existence of a concerted plan centred on Salzburg has been somewhat exaggerated. It is true that the Papacy still played a subordinate role but Charlemagne went in person to Salzburg in 803 to confirm the arrangements (*Conversio*, cap. 6).

31 All cathedrals and monasteries were expected to maintain a school for training clergy, through which uniformity of liturgy and chant would also be furthered. For the text see I. Grafenauer, p. 141.

32 *Enhardi Fuldensis Annales*, s.a. 805 (Theodore); *Annales Ratisponenses*, s.a. 805 (*Abraham cagonus baptizatus*) (both in *MGH, SS* 1).

33 Friedrich, *Codex* 1, no. 3. The division was finally consummated at Verdun in 843. The impact of Charlemagne himself on the Slavs is reflected in the fact that the general Slav word for king is taken from his name (Czech král, Russian король, etc.). At first this meant specifically the king or emperor in the West; later, but not before the tenth or eleventh century, when Slav peoples began to have kings of their own, it was generalised to any king.

MORAVIA

34 *Descriptio civitatum et regionum ad septentrionalem plagam Danubii* (ed. Horák and Trávníček). Most probably put together at St Emmeram in Regensburg *c.* 845 but some of the earlier material may have come from Fulda.

35 Letter of Bavarian bishops to the Pope (900); see p. 344 n. 267.

36 Fredegar's *Chronicle*, IV, 48 and 68 (*MGH, SS rer. merov.*, II, p. 144). Samo may have been encouraged to act independently by the Emperor Heraklios who needed a power to attack the Avars in the rear.

37 See especially G. Labuda, *Pierwsze państwo słowiańskie*; Dittrich, pp. 8–9; H. Balín in *SOCC* 22 (1962); C. Verlinden in *Revue belge de philologie et d'histoire* 12 (1933); map in Havlík, opp. p. 176.

38 Preidel, p. 123. The mixture of burial customs is significant: besides Avar-type deep graves, there are tumulus-type burials (German *Hügelgräber*) and the normal Slav cremations of earlier periods. This mixture continues into the first half of the ninth century at Staré Město, Mikulčice and elsewhere in Moravia.

39 A ninth-century source quoted by al-Gardīzī alludes to the considerable trading activities of the Moravians (*Morawāt*); see T. Lewicki in *Settimane di studio del Centro italiano di studi sull'alto medioevo*, XII (Spoleto, 1965), p. 474. Moravia was accessible to the radiation of Byzantine commerce from two directions—up the Danube via Bulgaria and from Venice.

40 Hensel, *Die Slawen*, fig. 323.

41 Kuhar, *Conversion*, pp. 85–6. It has been calculated that as much as one-third of the soil of Western Europe belonged to the church (bishoprics and monasteries) by the end of the ninth century.

42 So Cibulká, a protagonist of the 'Irish' theory. For the location of Modrá and other Moravian sites, see *Atlas československých dějin*, map 3 c.

43 His colleague Dub-dá-chrích (Dobdagrecus; see J. F. Kenney, *The Sources for the early history of Ireland*, vol. I, nos. 329 and 330 and M. A. O'Brien, *Corpus genealogiarum Hiberniae*, vol. I (Dublin, 1962); for the name cf. Fe-dá-chrích = *man of two regions*), acted as bishop as long as he remained abbot. Virgil's Irish scholarship, well above the normal Frankish level—he certainly knew Greek—aroused suspicions of heresy in the more intellectually limited St Boniface. See Löwe, *Virgil von Salzburg*, esp. pp. 44 ff. and K. K. Klein, *Die Anfänge der deutschen Literatur* (1954), pp. 45 ff. That *VC* 15 (see p. 30 no. 1) mentions Virgil's known belief in a race of men beyond the Equator (held to be heretical as long as the tropics were believed impassable and consequently all men could not be descendants of Adam) is sometimes quoted to show that Irish ideas and ways were more tenacious than was superficially apparent and therefore not impossible in Moravia even well after 800. By the early ninth century most of the prominent Irishmen on the Continent (Sedulius, John Eriugena) were scholars rather than missionaries. On the Irish contribution to early Germanic religious vocabulary see Eggers, pp. 154 ff.

44 Dyggve, fig. VI, 34, illustrates the ground-plans of a number of small Dalmatian churches with square eastern apses as at Modrá, in particular Bihać and Otok near Split. Cf. also fig. VI, 8 and 24. None of these is as early as 830, in all probability, but they represent the continuance of a local style which can be traced to Salona before its destruction by Avars and Slavs in the early seventh century. There is every reason to suppose that such a model was fairly widespread wherever the 'Lombard' style prevailed (north-east Italy, Istria and northern half of the Dalmatian coast).

45 Vavřínek, p. 35; *Magna Moravia*, p. 182; *Slownik*, vol. 3, fig. 131 (p. 295). See also p. 71.

46 Vavřínek in *HIST* 7 (1963). 'Na Valách' illustrated in *Magna Moravia* (Richter), pl. IV, no. 15; Mikulčice no. 6—*ibid.*, pl. II, no. 6 and Vavřínek, pl. 8 (opp. p. 32). For Mikulčice nos. 6 and 7 see J. Poulík, *Dvě velkomoravské rotundy* (*Monumenta archaeologica* 12 (1963)). On early Irish architecture see M. and L. de Paor, *Early Christian Ireland* (London, 1964), pp. 58 ff.

47 It was *mirae magnitudinis* for the time; see H. Vetters in *SLF* 6 (1964). Bavaria's links with Lombardy had always been close, especially since the marriage of Tassilo to the daughter of the last Lombard King Desiderius.

48 Preidel (p. 135) shows that there can be little doubt that some of the early Moravian churches were consecrated by Passau.

49 The name Greater Moravia, or better Great Moravia (on the analogy of Great Britain—in contrast to the Moravia of the Southern Slavs) is taken from ‘Η μεγάλη Μοραβία in *DAI*, cap. 13, 38, 40. The frontiers of the Moravian 'state' under Mojmir are not precisely known. The expansion which made it 'great' had not yet started. For useful maps see Vavřínek, p. 21 and pp. 144–5; Havlík, opp. p. 88; *Slownik*, vol. 3, fig. 130 (p. 291); Hrubý, map 1. See also R. Dostálová in *BSL* 27 (1966).

50 Einhard's *Annals* (November 822): 'In quo conventu omnium orientalium sclavorum, id est Abodritorum, Soraborum, Wiltzorum, Beheimorum,

Marvanorum, Praedenecentorum et in Pannonia residentium Avarum legationes cum muneribus ad se directas audivit' (*MGH, SS* I, p. 209).

51   *MGH, SS* xxv, pp. 623 and 655.

52   *Conversio* 10. V. Richter (*Magna Moravia*, pp. 131–2) suggests that Pribina was baptised before his removal and that only a small emendation to the text of *Conversio* will produce this better sense. Very large tracts of land all round Traismauer belonged to Salzburg; see maps in Havlík, *Staří Slované v rakouském Podunají* (*RAV* 73/9, 1963). There is no good reason to suppose that Passau was involved in Pribina's baptism, as is sometimes stated.

53   It has not yet been identified. If *Conversio* is to be trusted the church was entirely Salzburg work: 'roganti Priuinae misit Liuprammus archiepiscopus magistros de Salzpurc, murarios et pictores, fabros et lignarios'. The church therefore followed the widespread type of a mission church in Central Europe—foundations and perhaps some walls in stone with timber roof. See also pp. 50 and 333 n. 138 (Kotsel's churches).

54   For further details see M. Kos, *Conversio*, pp. 78 ff.

55   *VC* 15 (see p. 30): 'běhǫ že se glagoljǫšte latinĭstii sǔpričęstĭnici, arǔhijerei, ijerei i učenici'.

56   For a general discussion of the *burg* see Preidel, pp. 56 ff.

57   *Ann. Fuld.*, s.a. 846. Rastiz is a familiar form of Rastislav.

58   *MGH, Dipl. regum Germaniae ex stirpe Karolinorum*, vol. I (1934), no. 46 (p. 62); *Conversio*, cap. 12: '...Concessit illi in proprium totum quod prius habuit in beneficium'. See Dittrich, pp. 85–6.

59   Brackmann, *Germania pontificia*, vol. I: *episcopatus pataviensis*, no. 11.

60   Kuhar, *Conversion*, pp. 73–5.

61   To be deduced from *VM* 8 (see p. 30 no. 2), quoting Hadrian's bull *Gloria in excelsis Deo*. See also p. 339 n. 200.

62   'In rudem adhuc christianitatem gentis Maraensium' (*MGH, Leges* I, p. 414). Cf. Adam of Bremen, II, 23: Aestimo...quod in rudi christianitate nulli episcoporum adhuc certa sedes designata est'.

63   'Christianitatem abhorrere...ceperunt adeo ut via episcopo et predica-toribus illo non esset' (Friedrich, *Codex* I, no. 30)—no doubt an exaggeration.

64   A Frankish–Bulgarian frontier is difficult to establish for the early ninth century. It seems to be a reality *c.* 825 when diplomatic relations between the two countries start and there are discussions 'de terminis ac finibus inter Bulgaros ac Francos constituendis'. See V. Gjuselev in *BB* 2 (1966), p. 27, quoting *Einhardi Annales* (*MGH, SS* I), s.a. 825.

65   *VM* 5: 'Božijejǫ milostijǫ sǔdravi jesm[y]'.

66   *VM* 5: 'Sǫtǔ vǔ ny vǔšĭli učitelje mǔnozi krĭstĭjani iz Vlahǔ i iz Grĭkǔ i iz Němĭčĭ učęšte ny različĭ...'. The plurals represent the country rather than the people (as still in West Slav usage). The 'Vlachs' would no doubt come from the province of Aquileia, the 'Greeks' from Dalmatia. It is very improbable that 'Greeks' means Irishmen, who were sometimes so called in Western Europe owing to their unusual proficiency in that language.

67   *VC* 14 ('učitelja ne imamǔ takogo iže ny bi vǔ svoj językǔ istǫjǫ věrǫ hristĭjanĭskǫ sŭkazalŭ') is not very precise and does not necessarily reproduce Rastislav's own words.

68 Rastislav is supposed to have known of Constantine's reputation but does not ask for him by name in the Slav sources. The *Legenda italica* (see p. 32 no. 10) may however be based on a good source: 'audiens...quod factum fuerat a philosopho [Constantine] in provincia Gazarorum...' and further, 'verum doctorem talem non habent' [in Moravia].

69 The best computation, but it is awkward not to be able to specify when. For suggested route see Cibulká in *BSL* 26 (1965), who also tries to prove that they cannot have arrived before spring 864.

70 *VC* 14: 'da sę bišę i iny strany togo zĭręštę podobily namŭ.'

71 *Les Légendes de Constantin et de Méthode, vues de Byzance* (1933); see also his *Les Slaves, Byzance et Rome au IX siècle* (1926). For summary of the history of their study see Duthilleul, pp. 13 ff.

72 Text in *Żywoty Konstantina i Metodego*, ed. T. Lehr-Spławiński; *Constantinus et Methodius Thessalonicenses: Fontes*, ed. F. Grivec and F. Tomšić; Lavrov, *ad init.*

73 See Meyvaert and Devos in *AB* 73 (1955). Gauderich had been an eye-witness of the arrival of St Clement's relics in Rome. His work is now lost but was reworked by Leo, Bishop of Ostia and Velletri, 1101–15 (see p. 32 no. 10).

74 *VC* 10: 'učitelĭ našī arŭhijepiskupī Mefodĭi...'. But this may be a later retouching.

75 *VC* 12: 'naricajǫšte i imenīmī Alexandrŭ'. See in particular I. Dujčev in *Studi...Lo Gatto* (1962).

76 Text as for *VC*; also *Apophoreta slavica* I (Hague, 1957), pp. 148 ff.

77 Cf. *Life of Clement*, §22 (p. 165 no. 1(a)): τοῦ γὰρ τούτου βίου ὡς οὐδεὶς ἄλλος ἐγίνωσκεν οἷα ἐκ νέου καὶ ἁπαλοῦ ἐκείνῳ παρηκολουθηκὼς καὶ ὀφθαλμοῖς πάντα τά τοῦ διδασκάλου παρειληφώς.

78 *BSL* 24 (1963).

79 On dates and genre see Vavřínek, 'Staroslověnské životy Konstantina a Metoděje', *RAV* 73/7 (1963); and Grivec and Tomšić, pp. 20 ff.

80 Text: Teodorov-Balan, I, 109.

81 Text: *ibid.*, 118; see also Vašica, pp. 260 ff.

82 I.e. short lives to be read on the day of their joint commemoration from the Synaxarion (Russian пролог). Text: Teodorov-Balan, II, 42; Lavrov, pp. 100–1.

83 Teodorov-Balan, II, 34; Lavrov, pp. 101–3.

84 Text: Teodorov-Balan, II, 53; Ivanov, *Bŭlgarski starini*, pp. 290 ff.; Lavrov, pp. 108–11.

85 Text: Teodorov-Balan, II, 66; Ivanov, *Bŭlgarski starini*, pp. 300 ff.; Lavrov, pp. 111–15.

86 Teodorov-Balan, II, 74.

87 *MGH, Epp.* VII, *Anastasii epistolae*, no. 15 (pp. 435–8).

88 Ed. M. Kos (*Razprave znanstvenega društva v Ljubljani* 11, Ljubljana, 1936). Also *MGH, SS* XI. See pp. 68–9.

89 A reassessment of Theoktistos will be found in *CMH*, IV/i, pp. 105 ff.

90 So Dvornik, *Légendes*, pp. 45 ff., taking βιβλιοφύλαξ (*VC* vivliotikarĭ) as χαρτοφύλαξ. The patriarchal library and archives in any case came under the μέγας χαρτοφύλαξ, the head of the patriarchal chancery.

91 The embassy is noted by Ṭabarī in his *Tārīḫ ar-rusul wa'l-mulūk* under A.H. 241, months *ša'bān* and *rajab* (= Nov.–Dec. 855). He states that the plenipotentiary George was accompanied by representatives of the Patriarch to the number of fifty. No further names are mentioned but this is the only recorded mission of suitable date. *VC* gives an erroneous age to Constantine, thus ascribing the mission to 851, a date still accepted by some authorities.

92 *VC* 6, quoting *Qu'rān* XIX, 17. See also J. Meyendorff in *DOP* 18 (1964).

93 *VC* 9–10.

94 *VC* 12. The location of this town is still disputed.

95 *Ocherki*, vol. 1, pp. 75–82, rejecting the veracity of the details in *VC* 8–9.

96 The more fantastic theories take the brothers to Kiev itself, where they presumably personally baptised Askold! See pp. 240–5. Typical of this school is I. Nagajevski, Кирило-Методіївське християнство в Русі-Україні in *Analecta OSBM, ser.* II/1, no. 5 (Rome, 1954).

97 *VM* 5: 'Va bo esta Solunjanina da Solunjane vĭsi čisto slověnĭsky besědujǫtŭ.'

98 The statements of some late texts that Constantine had worked in Macedonia (in Methodios's province?), specifically on the River Bregalnitsa, a left-bank affluent of the River Vardar, and had already invented a system of writing for the local Slavs, are to be rejected as later Bulgarian confusions. The *Solun* (*Saloniki*) *Legend* (Teodorov-Balan, II, 110–11; Ivanov, *Bŭlgarski starini*, p. 281) is typical and can be shown to refer to another Constantine—the seventh-century St Constantine of Crete.

99 The fact that *pisati*, *čitati* and *kŭniga* are in one form or another common to all Slav languages in their specialised sense of *write*, *read* and *written text* (later *book*) indicates an acquaintance with literacy not later than the mid-ninth century, surely a good deal earlier. They knew of writing but did not practise it. This is the usual first stage as between barbarians and the literate civilisations with which they are in contact. In early Slav usage *bukŭvi* (letters)—a fairly recent Germanic loan—was used as a synonym of *kŭniga*, a word of uncertain but apparently non-European origin. This is sufficient to show how various these contacts had been. According to *VC* 14 the Emperor believed that his father and grandfather and 'many others' had already sought for a Slav alphabet (for missionary purposes?) but had failed to find one. That is, neither Slavs nor Byzantines had succeeded in inventing one. This would take the search back to the beginning of the Amorian dynasty in 820. The truth of the assertion must remain an open question.

100 *VM* 5: 'na molitvǫ sę naložista i sŭ iněmi iže běahǫ togo že duha jegože i si' (the best text).

101 *VC* 14: 'sŭ radostĭjǫ idǫ tamo ašte imajǫtŭ bukŭvy vŭ językŭ svoj...'.

102 'Vŭ vremena Mihaila cěsarja grŭčĭska, i Borisa kŭnęza blŭgarĭska, i

Rastica kŭnęza moravĭska, i Kocelja kŭnęza blatĭska (Mosaburg) vŭ lěto že otŭ sŭzdanija vĭsego mira 6363...' (*O pismeneh*, see p. 177 no. 2). As Kotsel only succeeded some time between February 860 and March 861 some prefer to take the Alexandrian reckoning and make 6363–5000=A.D. 863. The argument that Hrabr would scarcely have mentioned the Empress Theodora in establishing a date 863, since she was disgraced in 857, is not valid: she was restored to favour in 861 or at latest in 863. See also Vaillant in *BSL* 9 (1947–8).

103 The question of languages and alphabets (especially in connection with translations of the Liturgy) was apparently debated in at least one Olympian monastery about this time by Georgian monks; see Dujčev in *SLF* 6, pp. 77–8.

104 Eggers, especially pp. 48–51, 198, 249, notes the difficulties in finding adequate equivalents for Christian words in Germanic.

105 See p. 56. The 'litteras denique sclaviniscas a Constantino quondam philosopho repertas' are mentioned in *Industriae tuae*; see p. 74.

106 Simplification of the forms and evolution in the direction of symmetry can be observed in the later Croatian developments. See Vajs, *Rukovět*, pp. 77 ff.

107 Details in Trubetzkoj, *Altkirchenslavische Grammatik*.

108 The first letter *a* (Ⱑ) is fairly clearly based on the *chrismon* or cross prefaced to a text. See, e.g. the Glagolitic alphabet from Preslav reproduced by Goshev, fig. 53 (p. 61). For the individual comparisons see Vajs, *Rukovět*, pp. 60 ff.

109 Lettenbauer in *SLO* 3 (1953).

110 On the significance of the name *Aethicus Ister* see Löwe, *Virgil von Salzburg*, esp. pp. 27 ff.

111 So E. F. Karski. A number of Glagolitic signs show identity with or similarity to Greek zodiacal, medical, chemical and perhaps shorthand signs current in the ninth century (♌ *Leo* = ♌d; ♀ *vinegar* = ♀s); see Granstrem in *TODL* 11 (1955). An alphabet from such sources must once again be accounted improbable unless it was conceived eminently as a secret one. In this as in some other similar theories the arbitrary attribution of the signs does not inspire confidence.

112 *VC* 8: 'Obrětŭ že tu jevangelije i psaltyří rosĭsky pismeny pisano i člověka obrětŭ glagoljǫšta tojǫ besědojǫ...' (the manuscripts differ in detail). See also pp. 245–6.

113 Constantine Porphyrogennetos (*DAI*, cap. 9) characterises the Varangian (Swedish) names for the Dnepr rapids as ῥωσιστί and the Slav ones as σκλαβηνιστί. For him 'Ρῶς were the Varangian rulers of Kiev who managed the long-distance trade to Constantinople. Swedish Runic inscriptions are found along this route as late as the eleventh century, no doubt by then made by newcomers from Scandinavia.

114 A rough and ready adaptation of the Greek alphabet for Slav could have arisen as the work of some early Byzantine mission to the Kiev region before 861; cf. p. 391 n. 29. The presence of such a Kiev convert in Kherson would not be unusual. Attempts to record Slav in a Semitic alphabet are quite conceivable within the Khazar Empire; cf. pp. 238 ff. We can surely reject the more fantastic notion that Constantine, his mind already occupied with the problem of a Slav alphabet, elaborated one during his stay in Kherson from the mysterious signs of local inscriptions—with which of course similarities can be found—that occur in abundance along most of the north Black Sea coast; see N. A. Konstantinov in *Uchënyje Zapiski leningradskogo universiteta* 197 (1957). These inscriptions are probably Sarmatian and doubtfully alphabetic.

115 Vaillant suggests the obvious emendation *surĭsk-* for *rusĭsk-* (a frequent mistake, made by some manuscripts in *VC* 16—*Rusi* for *Suri*, Syrians): Syrian merchants were still numerous in Greek ports though they had lost their hold on the western Mediterranean. The language and script would resemble other Semitic ones which Constantine certainly knew and his feat would be similar to the immediately preceding episode with the 'Samaritan' (a Karaite Jew?). This is still the most probable solution, accepting the text as it stands, though it puts a strain on the words *svojej besědě* (his [i.e. Constantine's] language). Another possibility, open to the same objection, is to read *usk-* (OCS *ǫzŭk-*), the *r* having been wrongly transferred from the previous word *psaltyrĭ*, in some such sense as 'abbreviated', 'full of contractions', 'unpointed'; see Goshev in *Ezik i literatura* 13 (1958). This would point to a Semitic script. Recent research on the strata of OCS vocabulary raises the gravest doubts whether *pismena* (characters, alphabet) in the present and other contexts (*VC* 8, 13, 14, 15; *VM* 5) can belong to the original texts. The whole passage is most probably a later gloss and misunderstanding. See A. S. Lvov in *Bŭlgarski Ezik* 10 (1960) and his *Ocherki*, s.v.

116 Cf. the misconceived statement in the Russian *Khronograf* of 1512 (Lavrov, p. 172; *Magnae Moraviae fontes historici*, I, p. 198), ascribing the *translation* of sacred texts from Greek to Slav by Constantine to a date thirty years after the conversion of Bulgaria, i.e. *c.* 893.

117 *Starobŭlgarski glagolicheski i kirilski nadpisi* (Sofia, 1961).

118 See also Goshev in *Hiliada i sto godini*, p. 284 and Trubetzkoj (Cyrillic alphabet). The argument of E. Georgiev and others (protagonists of a proto-Cyrillic at least as old as the eighth century, which guided Constantine in his invention of Glagolitic), that the Glagolitic order ABVG must be dependent on Cyrillic АББГ (in which Б is assumed to be an adaptation of Greek B, whereas the forms of Glagolitic B and V are independent of one another) is very weak, since both the Latin and Semitic alphabets start with AB—all familiar to Constantine.

119 On the significance of the name Hrabr and of the author's arguments see especially V. Tkadlčík in *BSL* 25 (1964).

120 See J. Vrana and V. Tkadlčík in *SL* 33 (1964), and F. V. Mareš, *Michigan Slavic Materials* 6 (1965).

121 In *Cyrillomethodiana* (*SLF* 6, 1964).

122 P. 31, no. 4: 'nova apostola ne na tuždemĭ osnovanii svoje dělo položiša nŭ iznova pismena vŭobražiša i sŭvrĭšista vŭ językŭ novŭ.'

123 On the Armenian alphabet see J. Marquart, *Ueber den Ursprung des* *armenischen Alphabets* (Vienna, 1917). It should be observed that the situation was different in that the Armenians had already been Christian for two centuries, during which the Greeks tried to impose the Greek language and script and the Persians the Persian language and script on those parts of Armenia which they each controlled.

124 Demetrios Khomatianos, Archbishop of Ohrid in the early thirteenth century, may already be crediting St Clement with the Cyrillic alphabet, when he wrote: ἐσοφίσατο δὲ καὶ χαρακτῆρας ἑτέρους γραμμάτων πρὸς τὸ σαφέστερον (i.e. simpler, clearer) ἢ οὓς ἐξεῦρεν ὁ σοφὸς Κύριλλος (*Life of St Clement*, §14; Teodorov-Balan, II, p. 177). More probably he meant simplifications of Glagolitic introduced by Clement in Macedonia, if he had any clear idea of the facts at all.

125 *VC* 15: *trĭję̂zyčĭnikŭ*. They were the three tongues of the inscription on the Cross. See also Dujčev in *SLF* 6 (*Note sulla VC*).

126 Even the Orthodox Georgian Hilarion (827–80) was criticised by Greek monks on the Bithynian Olympos for celebrating there in Georgian. See Kuev (Kujew) in *BB* 2 (1966).

127 Migne, *PG* 138, *Responsa ad interrogationes Marci*, Question 5. We may further note that the Eastern church always expected at least the Gospels to be translated. In Byzantine iconography the Descent of the Holy Spirit at Pentecost clearly indicates this (contrary to Western practice) by showing in a vault beneath the room where the Twelve Apostles are seated, an aged man holding twelve scrolls—the Scriptures in twelve languages, one for each apostle. See the 'Painter's Guide', Appendix II to A. N. Didron's *Christian Iconography* (Eng. ed., 1886–91).

128 Frankish suspicion of the Irish missionaries naturally bore upon this. It was again the natural reaction of the Papacy to Certain Cyrillomethodian translations: Vaillant has shown (*BSL* 24 (1963)) that the phrase *gadę kŭnigy języka vašego* in *VM* 8 refers to possibly inaccurate or tendencious Slav translations.

129 Dvornik has recently speculated (*ASR* 23 (1964)) whether Otfrid of Weissenburg was alluding to Constantine and Methodios under 'some other men', when defending his *Harmony to the Gospels*, written in his German dialect *c.* 863–71. See also Repp in *Vorträge auf der Berliner Slawistentagung* (Nov. 1954) (Berlin, 1956). On the Gothic translations of sacred texts, which may have included the liturgy (though none survives), and their importance to other Germanic peoples see K. Gamber in *OST* 10 (1961); further Eggers, pp. 138 ff.

130 Cap. 52 (*MGH, Leges*, sect. III, *Conc.* II/1, p. 171).

131 Isaiah 35,5 and 32,4 (approximately). See Dujčev in *BSL* 24 (1963).

132 It is interesting to note how King Alfred the Great develops similar arguments (without theological support) in his Preface to his translation of Gregory's *Pastoral Care* (see *English Historical Documents*, vol. I, ed. D. Whitelock, London, 1955, pp. 818–19): neither are sacred languages limited in number nor is a sacred language which cannot be understood by the people of much spiritual value to them.

133 In agreement with Dvornik (*Orbis scriptus*, Munich, 1966) we must accept that *VC* is accurate in ignoring his ordination. Certainly as professor and patriarchal secretary he could not have been more than a deacon. *VC* 4 ('nŭ postriguše i na popovĭstvo otŭdadimŭ jemu služĭbǫ') implies his ordination in Rome (see p. 56) but this gives rise to doubt since *VM* 6 similarly implies Methodios's ordination in Rome ('Nikola...svęti že na popovĭstvo blaženajego Methodija'). How could they have run a large mission for over three years if neither were a priest competent in the Slav language? It must have been difficult enough with only one (Methodios). Cf. note 156, p. 335.

134 Cf. *VM* 9: 'Sŭ grǫbojǫ čędĭjǫ prěhŭ'. Attainments in Latin were not necessarily higher than in the time of St Boniface who heard a priest baptise 'in nomine Patria et Filia et Spiritus Sancti' (Tangl, *Die Briefe des heiligen Bonifatius und Lullus*, Berlin, 1916, no. 68, p. 141). For the low standard of Frankish clergy in general see Fichtenau, pp. 156 ff. The *Admonitio Generalis* of 798 outlines the position at that time.

135 It is at least noteworthy that Photios nowhere mentions Moravia among his missionary successes (e.g. in the Encyclical of 867 which mentions Russia [Migne, *PG* 102, col. 736–7]). But even if Constantinople lost interest in the mission it would not lose interest in the missionaries.

136 Neither the wording of *VC* 15 nor of *VM* 5 goes against the conclusion that they were winding up their personal participation in the mission.

137 The East always honoured Rome as the *prima sedes* and respected this position as an historical fact but not as a Divine institution. By Canon XXVIII of the Council of Chalcedon (451), following the lead of the Second Council of 381, Constantinople had been raised, for obvious practical reasons, to precedence next after Rome. Rome resisted this change. Canon XVII reiterated the long-standing principle that the ecclesiastical rank of a see must correspond to the administrative status of the city. The implications were obvious, given the humble civil status of Rome in the fifth century. Yet no one in the East thought of trying to exalt Constantinople ecclesiastically *above* Rome. Definitions were made by Justinian in *Novels* 9 (535) and 13 (545). Photios himself had summed up the Eastern attitude as recently as 861; the extreme Papal view was elaborated by Nicholas I in a letter to the Emperor dated 28 September 865 (*MGH, Epp.* VI, no. 88). In any case disagreements such as that over Photios involved personal factors as well as matters of principle. For further details see *CMH*, IV/I, cap. 10 and Dvornik, *Primauté*, pp. 61 ff.

138 St John the Baptist (*c.* 840?), tentatively identified with the basilica at Récéskut (German *Entenbrunnen*) by Zalavár (see *Magna Moravia*, p. 355, fig. 477 and Th. von Bogyay in *SF* 14 (1955)); St Mary (*c.* 850); St Rupert and St Hadrian (both *c.* 853; not yet traced); St Peter.

139 *Conversio*, cap. 13. According to some, 865/6. None of the churches which he then consecrated have been identified for certain.

140 The apparent contrast between the three years' training required in Moravia and the maximum of six months in Pannonia is easily accounted for by the probability that the Salzburg mission school at Mosaburg was much better than those of Passau in Moravia; the pupils were already half-trained.

Add to this the many practical difficulties under which the Moravian mission had laboured. Illumination on the training given in mission schools can be derived (for a slightly later date) from the list of fifty odd books owned by Bishop Madalwin, a Passau missionary, who handed them on to a successor in 903. They include the basic Western liturgical and legal texts, Lives of saints and martyrs, and primers of the seven profane arts (Donatus, Isidore, etc.). For details see Zagiba in *WSJ* 10 (1963).

141   *VC* 16. The Preface to the translation of the Gospels (the 'Macedonian fragment'—see p. 57 no. 5), attributed to Constantine, uses the same chapter (vv. 18–19) to support the same argument. The other Biblical quotations used in *VC* 16 to refute the position of the trilinguists are given in Lehr-Spławiński's ed., pp. 74–83.

142   On Photios in general see Dvornik, *The Photian Schism*, and his summary in *Berichte zum XI Int. Byz. Kongress* (Munich, 1958). On Constantine and Photios see F. Grivec in *SF* 17 (1958).

143   As Dvornik has expressed it (*Slavs in European History*, p. 390), the ecclesiastical hierarchy of the German kingdoms had become 'excessively involved in the snares of the feudal system'. When the game of chess was introduced into Western Europe about this time, the Eastern vizier or minister became a bishop. On the 'feudalisation' of the Western hierarchy see Bloch, vol. 2, pp. 345 ff.

144   Active *c.* 830–50. See Rimbert's *Life of Ansgar*, written *c.* 865–75 (*MGH, SS* II); the 'long' version is the more reliable.

145   See E. S. Duckett, *Carolingian Portraits* (Ann Arbor, 1962), pp. 223 ff.; P. J. Alexander in *SR* 20 (1941). The Archbishops of Cologne and Trier circulated a protest about their deposition by the Pope which was widely known not only in the West but also in the East.

146   *MGH, Epp.* VI, no. 140 (uncertain date): 'Ecclesia...quomodo sine apostolicae sedis instituetur nutu quando iuxta sacra decreta nec ipsae debent absque praeceptione papae basilicae noviter construi...?'

147   *MGH, Epp.* VI, no. 82 (860).

148   So *VM* 6: 'apostolikŭ Nikola posŭla po nja'.

149   *VC* 17.

150   On Formosus see Anastasius's *Life of Pope Nicholas I*, §§608–10 (Migne, *PL* 128).

151   The date 732 is still under dispute since no direct documentary evidence survives. There are some good reasons for putting the transference as late as the 750s (after the loss of Ravenna in 751). See *CMH* IV/I, pp. 70–2 and Ostrogorsky in *DOP* 19 (1965).

152   See also Dvornik, *Primauté*, pp. 68–9.

153   The following events are recorded in fair detail in *VC* 17 and *VM* 6.

154   Greek φάτνη; so also in the Slav text (φΑΤΗИ). The words (*VC* 17) 'pěšę nadŭ nimi [Slav service-books] svętǫjǫ liturgiǫ' do not necessarily imply that this was a service in the Slav language.

155   *VC* 18; *VM* 7: 'ty ljubiši gorǫ velĭmi, to ne mozi gory radi ostaviti učenija svojego'.

156 Reasons have been given for assuming that Constantine remained a deacon throughout his life (see note 133, p. 333). For similar reasons it must be accepted that he never took monastic vows before his death-bed, as *VC* clearly states. It should be added that Constantine would only logically have sought or accepted ordination in Rome if he expected to return to Moravia, whether as priest or bishop. *VC* 4, therefore, may reflect the Pope's intention rather than what actually took place.

157 E.g. the *Prolog Life*, certain Croat Glagolitic breviaries and the *Vita S. Procopii* (see S. Sakač in *OCP* 22 (1956)).

158 In Cyril's case 'philosopher' does not of course mean one who follows the true Christian life, viz. a monk—a common sense at this time, e.g. *Vita quinque fratrum*, cap. 3 (*MGH, SS* xv/2): 'ad sanctam civitatem Ierusalem monachum velle fieri et in abdita heremo...velle philosophari'. Cf. also the title *philosophus* accorded to Theodore of Tarsus (Archbishop of Canterbury, d. 690) for his outstanding scholarship, and that of 'illuminator' given to St Gregory of the Armenians.

159 OCS version (*Slovo na prenesenije moštemŭ sv. Klimenta*) reproduced and discussed by J. Vašica in *Acta Acad. Velehradensis* 19 (1948) (reprinted in *Slavische Propyläen* 8). Text also in Teodorov-Balan, II, 123; Lavrov, pp. 148 ff. See also Duthilleul p. 17.

160 Georgiev, *Kiril i Metodi*, p. 86.

161 *Epistola Anastasii ad Gaudericum* (Grivec and Tomšić, pp. 64–5; Teodorov-Balan, II, 244).

162 *RES* 24 (1948). See also Vašica, pp. 101–2.

163 Ivanov, *Bŭlgarski starini*, pp. 338–44; Lavrov, pp. 196 ff. See also Vašica, pp. 25 ff. and 103–6; Radojčić, *Hilandarski rukopisi o postanku slovenske pismenosti* (Novi Sad, 1963), *ad init.*

164 *RES* 33 (1956).

165 *Kiril i Metodi*, chap. 15. If Georgiev were right in ascribing the other poem—the acrostic *Azbučnaja molitva* (see Vaillant, II, pp. 76–9 for text) to Cyril, in view of a model in St Gregory Nazianzen's Ἀρχὴν ἁπάντων καὶ τέλος ποιοῦ θεοῦ (see *op. cit.*, pp. 141 ff. and 191 ff.), Cyril's authorship of the verse Gospel Preface becomes much more likely. See also pp. 177–8. The theme is typical of St Cyril—the right of all peoples to possess the Scriptures in a language which they understand (*vŭ sŭmyslině glasě*), but this does not in itself prove his authorship.

166 *Kiril i Metodi*, pp. 222 ff. See also Dujčev in *Studi...Lo Gatto* (1962).

167 See V. Grumel in *Echos d'Orient* 28 (1929). Text in Lavrov, pp. 175 ff.

168 *VC* 14 merely states that he started writing down (not translating) St John's Gospel, or conceivably a homily on the text of John 1, 1 (for this is a common sense of *besěda*). We cannot from this conclude that he translated any considerable proportion of the New Testament lessons before leaving Constantinople. Moreover neither the Aprakos nor the Apostol appears to have been translated from the texts then standard in the capital, which may be held to be against considerable preliminary work there. Cf. pp. 64–5.

169 OCS also *crŭky/crĭky*, probably from Gothic, the basis of the Bulgarian form and of others dependent on it. The form *cirŭky* of the *Kiev folia* (and the *Freising texts*—see p. 72) is conspicuously more Western, becoming the basis of the Czech and Polish words. It must rest on OHG (not Gothic) **kirikō* (cf. *chirichun* in *Conversio*). Note also that OCS *krĭstiti* (baptise), retained in West Slav (Polish *chrzcić*, from Czech), appears to have acquired this technical sense under the influence of OHG *kristenen* (< Krist[us] = Christ). See also K. H. Menges in *Orbis scriptus* (Munich, 1966).

170 Lat. *oblata* = Gk. προσφορά. In the *Kiev folia* the Offertory prayer is indicated as *Nadŭ oplatŭmĭ*. R. Auty (*RES* 40, *Mélanges A. Vaillant*, 1964) posits, in view of the gender, an OHG (Bavarian) prototype **oplāt* for it.

171 On this word see Eggers, p. 246.

172 A. S. Lvov (*SL* 34 (1965)) has shown, by comparison of the text of the Lord's Prayer (Matt. vi and Luke xi) in the *Aprakos* (Ass.) and *Tetrevangels* (Zogr. and Mar.), that *iskušenije* (temptation) must be 'original' (South Slav) as against Moravian *napastĭ*, and *ostaviti* (forgive) as against *otpustiti*. For further examples see *art. cit.*

173 For a philological argument in this sense see Shevelov in *SR* 35 (June 1957). OCS was never *consistently* Moravian. The fact that even the East Bulgarian school never entirely eliminated Macedonianisms suggests that the Macedonian basis of Constantine's language was always recognised as traditional.

174 *Euchologium sinaiticum*, ed. Frček (*Patrologia orientalis* 24–5, Paris, 1933–9), pt. 2, pp. 602 ff. The ductus of the two is practically identical; see Vajs, *Rukovět*, p. 131.

175 'Činŭ nadŭ ispovědajǫštijimŭ sę' (*ibid.*, pt. 2, pp. 490 ff.).

176 The second text in the sequence. See also the *Freising texts* (p. 72 and notes 227–8 below). For some doubtful points see Vaillant in *BSL* 21 (1960).

177 Glagolitic text in Vajs, *Rukovět*, pp. 117–18; Cyrillic transcription with a Latin parallel *en face* in Weingart and Kurz, pp. 114 ff. The first folio (*recto*) was filled in by a later hand and is irrelevant. Folio 8 is blank.

178 *Atti della Pontificia Accademia romana di Archeologia*, ser. 3, vol. 2 (1928).

179 Ed. A. Dold and K. Gamber, *Das Sakramentar von Salzburg* (*Texte und Arbeiten*, 1 Abt., 4 Beiheft, Beuron, 1960).

180 It has been argued in favour of translation in Rome itself that, as the Canon of the Mass is missing, the brothers respected the fact that they had no authority to translate the *secreta* (there would have been no objection in an Eastern liturgy) and that this authority may still have been withheld by the Pope at the time of the acceptance of the 'Slav books'; see e.g. K. Gamber in *OST* 6 (1957), Hellmann in *JGO*, N.F. 2 (1954). Both *Cod. Pad. D*47 and the *Salzburg Fragments* have a seventh weekday mass which includes the Canon. Secondly, that a translation of the Office of St Felicity would have been pointless in Moravia. Against this: (1) Traces of Cyrillomethodian language have been detected in the Canon of *Cod. Vatic. Illyr.* 4, the oldest extant Croat missal. Translation of the *secreta* was therefore done, if not accepted by Rome, but at what date cannot be determined; (2) St Felicity was commemorated on the same day as St Clement; his Office was absolutely required in Slav translation by missionaries who had his relics.

181 Also known as *missa graeca*. See Smržík, with further bibliography; Vašica, pp. 37–47.

182 Of the many houses then wholly or partly following the Basilian rule and the Byzantine rite in Rome may be mentioned: St Caesarius on the Palatine—prominent Greek house in the ninth century and remained so until at least the twelfth century; St Silvester *in capite*, founded by Paul I in 761 for Greek monks fleeing from iconoclast persecution; SS Stephen and Cassian, founded by Leo IV (847–55); SS Boniface and Alexius—probably existed from the seventh century, refounded with the added patronage of St Alexius *c.* 977 by Sergius, Archbishop of Damascus (d. 981) during the pontificate of Benedict VII (a house of mixed observance; see also p. 103); St Praxedis, founded by Paschal I (817–24), probably the residence of Constantine and Methodios in Rome. Also, after this period, Grottaferrata (Κρυπτοφέρρη), near Frascati, founded by the Greek St Nilus (Νεῖλος) shortly before his death in 1004. In general their rule was nearer the Benedictine than the Basilian but through them a number of Eastern saints entered the Western calendar and offices. No persecution of Greek practices is known even in the eleventh century but their Greek character was gradually effaced. On the monasteries, see B. Hamilton in *OCP* 27 (1961) and McNulty and Hamilton in *Le Millénaire du Mont Athos* (no. 9). Papal protection of iconodule refugees was particularly prominent from the time of Paul I, who zealously collected relics etc., in danger of destruction. S. Maria Antiqua shows in its frescoes Western saints on the right of the enthroned Christ, Eastern ones (with inscriptions in Greek) on the left. Between 817 and 824 Paschal I built S. Maria *in Domnica*, S. Praxedis and S. Cecilia, the decorations of which (all well preserved) are of markedly Byzantine style. In S. Maria Paschal is shown in supplication before the Virgin to forgive the Eastern persecution. In S. Cecilia Christ gives the blessing according to the canon of Byzantine iconography.

183 *VM* 11: '...svętajego Petra miši približajǫsti sę rekŭše službě [Methodios] posŭla kŭ njemu [Svjatopluk] glagolję jako ašte mi sę obětaješi na svętŭi Petrovŭ dĭnĭ sŭ voi svoimi sŭtvoriti u mene, věrujǫ vŭ Bogǔ jako prědati ti imatŭ ję [his enemies] vŭskorě'. However, in favour of such liturgical hybrids, Vašica (*VSIS* 7 (1963)) points out that Arts 4 and 7 of the *Zakon Sudnyj* (see pp. 65–6) follow certain Western penitential regulations in providing that those doing public penance in church, if penitents of the 'third stage', may remain till the Credo, if only of the 'second stage' until after the Gospel. In Western mass formularies there would have been no distinction here, whereas in the *Liturgy of St Peter* certain prayers intervene.

184 The 'Prague fragments' (Vajs, *Rukovět*, pp. 119–22; Weingart and Kurz, pp. 146–9) are irrelevant here, being an eleventh-century Glagolitic manuscript of part of the Eastern Good Friday Liturgy. They are a Bohemian copy of a Russian Cyrillic original probably brought to Sázava in the later eleventh century via some Hungarian monastery of Eastern observance. Their importance lies in the fact that their *ductus* is very similar to that of the *Kiev* *folia*, pointing to a stable tradition in the Moravian–Bohemian lands. See p. 349 n. 57.

185 Gorazd, one of the new Moravian pupils, apparently learnt good Greek (Theophylakt's *Life of St Clement*, §35) but this is likely to have been exceptional.

186 *VM* 15.

187 *VM* 17.

188 Vaillant's bald statement (vol. 2, p. 65) that the *Kiev* text 'est de rite romain et traduit du latin, *donc* postérieur à la liturgie de Constantin et Méthode, de rite grec et traduit sur le grec' suggests an unacceptable certainty.

189 See J. Lepissier in *RES* 42 (1963), p. 146. The mistakes which thus crept in are against Constantine's having used both texts together but the revision cannot have been long after. Later Croat versions naturally show the influence of the Vulgate in course of time (see Vajs in *BSL* 8 (1939–46)). K. Onash (*Wissenschaftliche Zeitschrift der Martin Luther-Universität, Halle-Wittenberg*, 7 (1957–8)) thinks there are also signs that a Hebrew (Masoretic) text was consulted, which would point to Constantine himself having used both Latin and Hebrew versions. But would he have had a Hebrew Psalter in Moravia? The change from *istina* to the Moravian synonym *rěsnota* at Ps. 30 is plausibly held by A. S. Lvov (*Ocherki*, s.v.) to prove that the bulk of the Psalter was translated during the Moravian years (863–7).

190 *Sinajskaja Psaltyŕ*, ed. S. Severjanov (Petrograd, 1922; reprinted Graz, 1954).

191 See L. Zhukovskaja in *VSIS* 7 (1963).

192 *VC* 14: 'načętŭ pĭsati besědu jevangelĭsku: Iskoni bě slovo'. Cf. p. 37. This is the lesson for 1 September, the date on which several service books normally begin.

193 V. Ganev, Законъ соудныи людьмъ (Sofia, 1959). The later Russian manuscripts have been edited by M. N. Tikhomirov and L. V. Milov (1961). See also T. Saturník in *RAV* 1/64 (1922), pp. 33 ff., 129 ff. and 143 ff.; S. Troitski in *OCA*, vol. 2 (1964).

194 Several contexts, notably in Arts. IV and VII, seem to require the restoration of *vŭsǫdŭ* (see p. 58 above)—a word unknown and misunderstood outside the Moravian school; see *Slovník jazyka staroslověnského*, s.v. (Prague, 1958–   ). Ganev's argument (see note 193 above) that Arts. II and VIIa are so patently dependent on Pope Nicholas's *Responsa* (see p. 160) that the text must be a Bulgarian production of *c.* 866–8, does not convince.

195 See Vašica in *VSIS* 7 (1963) and *BSL* 12 (1951). The *Ecloga* is a short summary of general law, especially (Christian) social and family law, and therefore eminently suitable for a neophyte people.

196 On law-codes see also Ullmann, p. 82.

197 M. Hellmann in *Cyrillo-Methodiana* (*SLF* 6, 1964). Against this Troitski (see note 193 above) maintains that *ljudi* means *soldiers* and sees the whole as a military penal code.

198 The question whether the diacritical marks in the *Kiev folia* (appearing on about a third of the words) are merely an accentual system combining

Greek, OHG and original orthographical rules (see Trubetzkoj, pp. 43 ff., and G. L. Trager, *LMLS* 13 (1933)) or represent ecphonetic signs required for recitation (see, e.g. E. Koschmieder in *SLO* 4–5 (1955), who considers them closer to the type of the Western *lectio solemnis* than to the Greek) is not finally settled. If the latter is right, the obsolescence of their Latin prototype is confirmed by the provision of the musical indications for the Offertory and post-Communion prayers, as well as for the Prefaces: by the mid-ninth century the former were normally treated as *secreta* and said silently (μυσ-τικῶς). This Cyrillomethodian mass therefore could have reproduced the *missa cantata* practice of the seventh–eighth centuries found in the Salzburg prototype.

199 Dittrich (p. 170) supposes a reluctance on Methodios's part to entertain episcopal consecration since he had formerly been a married man. But monastic vows cancel one's whole secular past. Moreover in the ninth century the evolution which led by the fourteenth century to the selection of bishops exclusively from the celibate monastic clergy was only in its early stages.

200 *VM* 8, containing the substance of the Papal letter, usually referred to as *Gloria in excelsis*, the original of which has not been preserved.

201 Discussions in Dvornik, *Légendes*, pp. 268–9, and Grivec, pp. 86 ff.

202 Boniface was *archiepiscopus provinciae Germaniae* from 732 until 745, when he became Bishop of Mainz.

203 M. Kos in his edition (1936) preferred 871 but it is surely linked with Methodios's arrest and trial, which on the best reckoning took place before the end of 870. See note 88, p. 328.

204 *Conversio* provides much valuable detail on these achievements. It is aggravating that few of the place names can be reliably identified. Some thirty Pannonian churches are mentioned; see Th. von Bogyay in *SF* 14 (1955) and 19 (1960). We can only feel confident of *Bettobia*=Ptuj (Ger. *Pettau*), *ad 5 basilicas*=Pécs (Ger. *Fünfkirchen*), and Mosaburg; *ad Ortahu* may be Veszprém (Ger. *Wesprim*).

205 *VM* 9: 'jako na našej oblasti učiši'.

206 *Conversio* 14. The 85 is usually taken as an error for 75.

207 'na staryję prědĕly postǫpajete črěsŭ kanony' (*VM* 9).

208 See Ziegler in *JGO*, N.F. 1 (1953). Ellwangen had been Hermanrich of Passau's monastery before his elevation to the episcopate (865/6). Certain of Methodios's companions would appear to have shared his captivity.

209 *MGH, Epp.* VII, p. 286 (Pope to Bishop Anno): 'Audacia tua et presumptio non solum nubes sed et ipsos celos transcendit...fratrem tuum Methodium, pannonicum archiepiscopum legatione apostolice sedis ad gentes fungentem, tyrannice magis quam canonice tractans...'. This reminds one strongly of Pope Nicholas's severe words to Archbishop Hincmar of Rheims in the matter of Bishop Rothad of Soissons (*MGH, Epp.* VI, *Nicolai I epistolae*, no. 55, dated 863 [pp. 353–4]): 'cognovimus quod Rothadus frater et coepiscopus noster ecclesiae Suessonicae...a vostra sanctitate sit impetitus et adhuc...episcopatus etiam absens expoliatus honore et in exilium deportatus [h]actenus in monasterio retrusus existat. Unde gemimus valdeque dolimus...'.

210 *MGH, Epp.* VII, p. 285 (Pope to Bishop Hermanrich): 'fratrem et coepiscopum nostrum Methodium carceralibus penis afficiens...O episcopum episcopo talia inferentem et ad hoc apostolice sedis manu sacrato et latere destinato!' In the *Commonitorium* (aide-mémoire) given to Paul he wrote further: 'vos sine canonica sententia dampnastis episcopum [ab] apostolica sede missum' (*MGH, Epp.* VII, pp. 284–5).

211 *MGH, Epp.* VII, p. 281–2 (Pope to Carloman, 873): 'reddito ac restituto nobis pannoniensium episcopatu liceat predicato fratri nostro Methodio qui illic a sede apostolica ordinatus est, secundum priscam consuetudinem libere que sunt episcopi gerere'.

212 The original document is lost but a later Papal letter to Methodios (*MGH, Epp.* VII, *Iohannis VIII epistolae*, no. 201, *c.* June, 879) implies some kind of previous restrictions. It was a widespread custom to read the Epistle and Gospel first in Latin or Greek and then in the vernacular—a practice no doubt followed by Constantine and Methodios. The restriction may not have amounted to much more than formally prescribing this. Outside the liturgy it is clear that the Pope still encouraged the use of the Slav language.

213 Thus the threat of the Bavarian church to Kotsel after Methodios's release (*VM* 10: 'ašte sego imaši u sebe ne izbǫdeši nasŭ dobrě') was fulfilled.

214 Cf. Pope John's *Commonitorium* to Paul of Ancona: 'ne suscipias occasionem excusationis prohibentem te vel fratrem nostrum Methodium transire ad Pentepulcum, sive bella pretendant sive inimicicias congerant' (Friedrich, *Codex* I, no. 18).

215 'Archiepiscopus sanctae ecclesiae marabensis' first occurs in the Bull *Industriae tuae* (880) (Grivec and Tomšić, p. 72; *MGH, Epp.* VII, no. 255). But see note 217 below.

216 From 874; dates unreliable but perhaps Vislania 875–80, Silesia 876–9, Sorbs after 880, Pannonia 883–4, Bohemia 890–5 (effectively). See map 8 in *Magna Moravia*, opp. p. 416.

217 I. Boba has tried to prove (*ASR* 26 (1967)) that the diocese entrusted to Methodios embraced Pannonia but not Moravia, north of the Danube, which was outside the old territories of Sirmium. It would follow that all the titles used must refer to Srěm, i.e. *Morava* was then the Slav name for that place, and Methodios could even have been buried there ('ležitŭ že vŭ velicai crĭkvi Moravĭstěi'—*Prolog Combined Life*, Lavrov, p. 101); cf. *Life of Naum* (Lavrov, p. 183): 'Metodie...otide vŭ Panoniu vŭ gradŭ Moravu'. While there may be some substance in the interpretation of the title there seems no doubt that Methodios became *de facto* Archbishop of Moravia.

218 Svatopluk's expansionist policy was perhaps so successful because most of West Europe was at this time (879–86) in the grip of unusually savage and large-scale Viking raids. On South Poland see pp. 135 ff.; a contemporary reference to this area is found in King Alfred's version of Orosius (*MPH*, I, p. 13).

219 V. Hrubý, p. 179, dates *Na valách* and its associated cemetery to 850+ and characterises it as the standard small Byzantine missionary church of that period, known from as far afield as the Kuban. Others consider it primarily a mortuary chapel. The only reason for considering Mikulčice no. 3 is its size— the largest so far found; but it may be later than 885. See Richter in *Magna Moravia*, pl. I, no. 3; *Slownik*, vol. 3, fig. 131 (p. 295). For a full list of the Mikulčice churches see *Magna Moravia*, pp. 182–3 and figures pp. 225 ff. The exact location of Staré Město, Mikulčice and the other Moravian sites will also be found in *Atlas československých dějin*, map 3 c.

220 Few Byzantine coins of any period have so far been found in Moravia but their number is not a direct function of the real volume of trade. The Byzantine gold *solidus* was for centuries the standard of international trade (Charlemagne stabilised the *pound* at 8 *solidi*). Both the *Zakon sudnyj* (see p. 65), translated for Moravian use in the 860s and the Raffelstetten Customs Regulations (Friedrich, *Codex* I, no. 31) of just after 900 use or refer to Byzantine monetary standards. See also J. Pošvář in *BSL* 26 (1965).

221 *Magna Moravia*, pl. I, no. 4; pl. II, no. 8; pl. IV, no. 16.

222 See Vavřínek, p. 33, pls 12–13 and also pp. 137 ff.; Richter in *Magna Moravia*, pl. III, no. 14; Hrubý, figs. 45/1, 46/2.

223 Richter in *Magna Moravia*, pl. III, no. 13. The church probably dates from 875–900.

224 Vavřínek, pp. 136–7, following Pošmourný in *Architektura ČSSR* 20 (1961).

225 A number of different standards were widely used, viz. the Roman (Byzantine) foot of 0·295 m., the Carolingian of 0·34 m. and the Lombard of 0·425 m. In particular *Na valách* can be more accurately interpreted in terms of the Carolingian foot (see *Magna Moravia*, pp. 186 ff.).

226 Cosmas of Prague alludes in his *Chronicle* (bk. i, cap. 14) to a small hermitage there which Svatopluk had patronized ('ubi olim...eius ope et auxilio edificaverant ecclesiam'). That he became a monk there himself in 894 is a fantasy of the chronicler. See also p. 84.

227 *Cod. Lat. Monach.* 6426. See Auty, pp. 92–6; analyses by I. Grafenauer (*Karolinška Kateheza*), and by F. Ramovš and M. Kos (*Brižinski spomeniki*). See also Isačenko in *VSIS* 7 (1963).

228 The additions to the original Prayer can also be traced for the most part to Western formulae of the eighth–ninth centuries. See T. Repp in *ZSP* 22 (1954), with parallel texts. On no. 2 see also J. Pogačnik in *PSL* 14 (1964).

229 It has been suggested that Bishop Abraham was himself a Slav. For possible survival of the Glagolitic tradition in Slovenia see also Kuhar, *Slovene Medieval History*, pp. 132 ff. On Freising's estates in the Slav areas see A. Ammer in *Korbinian-Festgabe* (1924), with map.

230 'Nec scribendo nec cantando licet inserere'. See Dom B. Capelle in *L'Eglise et les églises* (see bibliography). This was in answer to a further attempt of Charlemagne to make the addition official.

231 A short exposition will be found in P. Sherrard, *The Greek East and the Latin West* (1959), pp. 61–72. See also O. Clément, pp. 12 ff. and pp. 70 ff. On Photios's tract (866) see p. 369 n. 25. Even as late as 1285 the Eastern church tried to redefine the Procession of the Holy Spirit in a way which would not exclude the Western formulation.

232 'Audimus etiam quod missas cantes in barbara hoc est in sclavina lingua, unde iam litteris nostris per Paulum episcopum Anconitanum tibi directis prohibuimus ne in ea lingua sacra missarum sollempnia celebrares sed vel in latina vel in greca lingua...' (*MGH, Epp.* VII, no. 201, June 879).

233 *MGH, Epp.* VII, no. 255: 'Ipsum quoque presbiterum nomine Uuichinus, quem nobis direxisti, electum episcopum consecravimus S. eccl. nitrensis, quem suo archiepiscopo in omnibus obedientem...esse iubemus et volumus...'. Even if this is taken as a normal formula there is little to commend the view (e.g. L. Havlík in *BSL* 26 (1965)) that Methodios went to Rome fully backed by Svatopluk who now, at the height of his power, saw a Papal crown for himself if Methodios continued as Papal archbishop with the requisite quorum of territorial bishops under him.

234 The sense of this phrase is not established for certain. It is taken from Cosmas, *Chronica Boemorum*, I, 15, and has been identified by some with the text known as *Beatus Cyrillus* (see p. 92). The privilege in question is supposed to be Papal licence for the use of the Slav liturgical language in Moravia.

235 *MGH, Epp.* VII, no. 276; Friedrich, *Codex* I, no. 25; Grivec and Tomšić, p. 74.

236 Dittrich, pp. 238 ff.

237 *VM* 13: 'velĭmi tebe želajǫ viděti, to dobro sŭtvori potrudi sę do nasŭ...'.

238 *Ibid.*: 'cĕsarĭ sę na nĭ [Methodios] gnĕvajetŭ da ašte i obrěštetŭ nĕstŭ jemu života imĕti'.

239 Mansi, XVII, 373–524 (not reflecting clearly the compromise arrived at).

240 The fact that his enemies did taunt him with Imperial displeasure goes to show (which is more important) that there was some communication with Constantinople. Methodios at least was aware that there were some unfavourable opinions of him there. He now felt that he must justify himself as seriously in Constantinople as in Rome. Vaillant (*BSL* 24 (1963)) attributes the inclusion of what amounts to a Profession of Faith in *VM* (see pp. 30–1 above) to continued Byzantine suspicion of Methodios's orthodoxy and policy.

241 Pope John to the Emperor Basil, about August 880: 'tertio vero vobis grates multas referimus quia Bulgarorum diocesin pro amore nostro gratanti animo sancto Petro, ut iustum erat, permiseritis habere', and other passages of this letter (Migne, *PL* 126, cols. 909–10).

242 Dittrich, p. 252.

243 The words *obilĭno obdarilŭ* (*VM* 13) imply this. Those who imagine an impenetrable barrier between East and West at this time are apt to think of Constantine and Methodios as Photios's 'failures', further that Constantinople had written Methodios off when he accepted Papal consecration. Thus Honigmann (*BYZ* 17 (1944–5)) suggested that the Bishop Agathon (Ἀγάθων Μοράβων) who attended the Council of 879-80 was a bishop appointed by Ignatios to replace Methodios when he disappeared into Frankish captivity. There is no evidence that Agathon ever worked in Moravia, though he led an embassy to Louis (*Basilii Graecorum imperatoris legatus*) in November 873.

This theory cannot be accepted and Dvornik is surely right in supposing the title to refer to the Morava south of the Danube (see p. 166).

244 He had the power of excommunc, iation as Papal Legate; cf. *VM* 12 and Stephen V's Bull of 885. Several Bohemian Latin texts include Svatopluk in the excommunication, which is improbable.

245 For the events at Tulln see *Ann. Fuld.* (*Contin. Ratisb.*), s.a. 884. *VM* 16 tells of Methodios's meeting with a 'Hungarian king' after his return from Constantinople. As there were as yet few Magyars in Europe and they had no king, and moreover the word *kraljĭ* still denoted exclusively the Emperor in the West, evidently Charles III is meant and the adjective is a later erroneous gloss. Methodios is clearly conversing with a Christian ruler. The word *kraljĭ* is correctly used of Louis the German in *VM* 9 and *VM* 10. On the title 'king' (*rex* etc.) see further G. Labuda, *Wykształcenie władzy królewskiej u Słowian* in *Z polskich studiów sławistycznych*, vol. 3 (V Congress of Slavists) (Warsaw, 1963), *id.* in *Wieki średnie* (*Festschrift* for T. Manteuffl, Warsaw, 1962) and p. 282 note b.

246 E.g. Such words as *komŭkanije* (see p. 59 note a), *katolikija cĭrky*, *mŭnichŭ, dogoniti, neračenije, sŭ istinoju* (= Greek μεθ' οὗ ἔλαβεν). Full philological analysis by H. F. Schmid, *Die Nomokanonübersetzung des Methodios* (Leipzig, 1922), who also correctly restores *mĭša* (mass) in the corrupt *mĭnĭša tvoriti* (= λειτουργεῖν) and other contexts. See also I. Žužek, *Kormčaja kniga* (*OC* 168, Rome, 1964).

247 See W. Lettenbauer in *OCP* 18 (1952). It shows every sign of having been done by a learned Greek canonist: the phrase γόνυ κλίνων is rendered correctly *ašte pokajetsja*. Later Greek editors themselves misunderstood this phrase which had become obsolete (see Vašica in *VSIS* 7 (1963)).

248 The attribution cannot be considered absolutely certain; see A. Dostál in *ZRVI* 8/1 (1963) and his edition of *Cloz.* (pp. 127 ff.). Vašica (*SL* 35 (1966)) considers Constantine's authorship more probable.

249 Theophylakt, §73: καὶ τὸ λεῖπον τῷ τριῳδίῳ προστίθησι τὸ γὰρ ἀπὸ τῆς καινῆς κυριακῆς ἄχρι τῆς πεντηκοστῆς ψαλλόμενον τότε δὴ συνετέλεσε. See also p. 168.

250 *Russian Primary Chronicle*, s.a. 898 (Acad. ed., p. 22). For the different types of Oktoikh see Wellesz, pp. 139–40.

251 R. Jakobson is inclined to date it to not long after 885 and ascribe it to Clement and his school; see 'The Slavic response to Byzantine poetry' (*OCA*, vol. 1, 1963).

252 In both *VC* and *VM* the Popes with whom they dealt are referred to with all the respect to which the senior Patriarch was entitled but without the fulsome adjectives usual in contemporary Latin sources (*venerabilis, gloriosissimus*, etc.). See also M. V. Anastos in *HSS* 2 (1954).

253 As a conspicuous example of direct imitation may be cited the missionary work of the Russian St Stephen of Perm, modelled closely on that of St Cyril. He evangelised the Finnic Zyrians (Komi) from about 1379 and invented an alphabet for their dialect quite independent of the Cyrillic. The literary influence of *VC* is equally visible on St Epiphani's *Life of St Stephen of Perm* (text in *Apophoreta slavica* 2 (1959)).

254 It was frequently kept before then on the date proper to Methodios alone (6 April). For further details see Kiselkov in *Hiliada i sto godini*.

255 There were exceptions to this in distant mission fields where a long vacancy might be disastrous; cf. M. Deanesly, *Augustine of Canterbury* (1964), pp. 115-16.

256 Dittrich (pp. 270 ff.) puts forward the suggestion that he could have been consecrated in Bulgaria in 885 before Wiching's return from Rome—this being the Byzantine policy already agreed on.

257 See parallel texts in Duthilleul, pp. 9-10.

258 *Quia te zelo* (*MGH, Epp.* VII, pp. 354-8; Friedrich, *Codex* I, no. 26; Grivec and Tomšić, p. 75): 'Divina autem officia et sacra misteria ac missarum solemnia, que idem Methodius Sclavorum lingua celebrare presumpsit, quod ne ulterius faceret supra sacratissimum beati Petri corpus iuramento firmaverat...sub anathematis vinculo interdicimus'. Its authenticity has been doubted since it is clearly based on *Industriae tuae*; but it was no doubt inspired by Wiching. See Duthilleul, p. 7 and pp. 166 ff.

259 *MGH, Epp.* VII, pp. 352-3; Friedrich, *Codex* I, no. 27, Grivec and Tomšić, pp. 74-5: 'successorem quem Methodius sibimet contra omnium sanctorum patrum statuta constituere presumpsit ne ministret...donec suam nobis presentiam exhibeat et causam viva voce exponat'. The *Commonitorium* and *Quia te zelo* are closely related and neither is precisely dated. Hence it is better to accept *Quia te zelo*.

260 The *Bulgarian Legend* (Theophylakt's *Life of St Clement*), §§24 ff., is the main source at this point but cannot of course be implicitly relied on. See p. 165, no. 1(*a*).

261 *Office of St Methodios* (Lavrov, p. 125), Canon, verse 19.

262 See Dittrich, p. 302. It is perhaps in favour of Gorazd's having in fact filled with distinction some important charge that he continued to be numbered among the Seven Teachers of the Slavs (see pp. 164-5). He may therefore have stood his ground as acting head of the church for at least part of the period 885-93. A later period of office, *c.* 900-7 (see pp. 83-4 and note 266), is much more dubious.

263 *Ann. Fuld.*, s.a. 894 (*MGH, SS* I).

264 The Magyars plagued Bavaria from *c.* 900, won a crushing victory over the Franks near Bratislava in 907, in which three bishops fell (including the Archbishop of Salzburg), and went on to destroy almost all the Bavarian monasteries by 926. They were effectively curbed only from 955 (Battle of the Lechfeld). A précis of their impact on European affairs is given by Bloch, vol. I, pp. 8-14.

265 Friedrich, *Codex* I, no. 33.

266 Dittrich, p. 306.

267 Letter to Pope John IX of about July 900 (Friedrich, *Codex* I, no. 30; *CDEM*, I, no. 91; Mansi, XVIII, cols. 205 ff.), following the Synod of Reisbach. The likelihood that at this moment Moravia would become a Frankish province again gave the protest more substance. The protest may be held sufficient evidence that the Pope's intentions were carried through at least in part. The protest is solely concerned with the violation of their 'historical rights' after the manner of *Conversio*.

268 Further views: Dittrich, pp. 308 ff.

269 E.g. in *Diffundente sole*, §1 *ad fin.* (see p. 92) and in Bishop Pilgrim of Passau's letter.

270 On Nitra generally see B. Chropovský in *HIST* 8 (1964).

271 Details in Milik, who tries to prove that St Hippolytus had preserved the Cyrillomethodian tradition. But the evidence would appear to be consistent with the considerable Byzantine influence on early Christian institutions in Hungary in general. The *Vita SS Andreae seu Zoeradi confessoris et Benedicti martyris* (*SRH*, vol. 2, no. 8) was written by Bishop Maurus of Pécs in 1064. It is unknown when St Hippolytus was founded but the saint is eminently Bavarian (see p. 137).

272 See A. Sós, 'Zalavár' [i.e. Mosaburg] (*Archaeologia Hungarica, Dissertationes*, S.N. 41, Budapest, 1963).

Chapter 3.   *The Western Slavs*

BOHEMIA

1 According to Einhard (*Life of Charlemagne*, cap. 15) Charlemagne waged a successful campaign against the Bohemians (in 805–6?) but the number of 'wild and barbarous' Slav tribes which he is reputed to have incorporated, even loosely, into his Empire has surely been exaggerated. See also pp. 142–3.

2 *Ann. Fuld.*, s.a. 845 (*MGH, SS* 1): 'Hludowicus 14 ex ducibus Boemanorum cum hominibus suis christianam religionem desiderantes suscepit et in octavis theophaniae [January 13] baptizari iussit.'

3 Six Bohemian leaders are mentioned in *Ann. Fuld.*, s.a. 872, of whom Goriwei might be our Borivoj (modern Czech Bořivoj).

4 Cosmas, *Chronica Boemorum*, 1, 14 and 1, 10. The tradition is carried on into Dalimil (early fourteenth century) (ed. Havránek and Daňhelka, Prague, 1948):

[sect. 23]   Prosi křsta [Bořivoj] ot Svatopluka, Krále moravského,
    A ot Metudie, arcibiskupa velehradského.
    Ten arcibiskup rusín bieše,
    Mši slovensky slúžieše.
    Ten u Velehradě křti Čecha prvého,
    Bořivoje, Kněže českého,
    Léta ot narozenie syna božieho
    Po osmi set po devietidcát čtvrtého.   [894]

5 See O. Králík, 'Kreščenije Bořivoja', in *TODL* 19 (1963). See also pp. 105 ff. below.

6 *Moravian Legend* (see p. 92), §14. If we judge the whole story of Borivoj to be apocryphal this incident was probably modelled on the passage about Ingo of Carantania in *Conversio* (for this text see p. 32 no. 11).

7 The original missionary chapel was no doubt of wood. Traces of the foundations of a stone rotunda similar to those of Moravia may represent the next stage. See Richter in *Magna Moravia*, pl. v, no. 1; *Słownik*, s.v. *Levý Hradec*. Levý Hradec has proved notably rich in Moravian objects during recent excavation.

8 See Richter in *Magna Moravia*, pls. v–vi and fig. 60 (p. 312). The partly extant rotunda, still in the same Moravian tradition as Levý Hradec, may not be the first building on this site but probably perpetuates the earliest ground-plan. For the location of Budeč, Levý Hradec and other small places near Prague see *Atlas československých dějin*, maps 3e and 4a.

9 *Ann. Fuld.*, s.a. 895: 'omnes duces Boemaniorum...quorum primores erant Spitignewo, Witizla'.

10 Turek, pl. 66; Hensel, *Archeologia*, p. 43, fig. 6. See also Borkovský in *Památky archeologické* 44 (1953).

11 General collections of the texts mentioned below: *Fontes rerum bohemicarum* (*FRB*), ed. J. Emler, vols. 1–3 (Prague, 1873–); Vajs, *Sborník staroslovanských literárních památek o sv. Václavu a sv. Lidmile* (Prague, 1929). Extensive bibliography in Králík, *Sázavské písemnictví XI století* (*RAV* 71/12 (1961), p. 82).

12 Pekař, *Die Wenzels- und Ludmilalegenden* (Prague, 1906). Older historians, such as Novotný, dated Christian to the twelfth century. There are still adherents of a late dating, even to the early fourteenth century, especially Urbánek, *Legenda t. zv. Kristiána ve vývoji předhusitských legend ludmilských i václavských a její autor* (Prague, 1947–8). Much depends on whether we accept that Christian quotes Cosmas of Prague or not. Apart from this, Urbánek's structure rests principally on the arguments that (1) *Diffundente sole* is older than Christian, and (2) the *Legenda bodecensis* (Böddecke manuscript) is a valuable text forming the essential link between *Crescente fide* and Christian. Consult also: Vašica, *Slovanská bohoslužba v českých zemích* (1940); Králík, *K počátkům literatury v přemyslovských Čechách* (Prague, 1960); *id.* in *SL* 34 (1965); Ludvíkovský in *LIF* 6 (1958) and *ibid.* 75 (1951). The relegation of Christian to the fourteenth century allows Urbánek to suggest Abbot Bavor of Břevnov, a known falsifier, as its probable author.

13 See p. 103. On this text see Králík in *RISL* 7 (1959).

14 The Wolfenbüttel MS is not later than 1006 (text in *MGH*, *SS* iv). Gumpold (Humbolt) was Bishop of Mantua.

15 On the 1st OCS Legend see Králík in *BSL* 27 (1966).

16 See Králík in *Sázavské písemnictví* (*RAV* 71/12 (1961)); Weingart in *Svatováclavský Sborník*, vol. 1; Mareš in *SL* 34 (1965). Cyrillic transliteration from Glagolitic originals is indicated by the misreading of the date (March 3 for March 4). The account of the *Translation* presumably started as separate Latin and OCS works soon after 932 (see p. [97] above), as in other similar cases.

17 See Mareš in *SL* 34 (1965).

18 Text in Teodorov-Balan, II, 202 (*Legenda sanctorum Cyrilli et Methodii patronorum Moraviae*). On this text see P. Devos in *AB* 81 (1963), with reproduction of two versions.

19 On its author, see Bartoš in *LIF* 7 (1959). For text see Havránek in Bibliography.

20 J. Emler, *Památky staré literatury české*, 1/2: *Spisové Karla IV* (Prague, 1878), pp. 111–18.

21 See P. Devos in *AB* 81 (1963), with text (pp. 352–5).

22 See J. Ludvíkovský in *Sborník prací filosofické fakulty brněnské university* 10 (*řada hist.*) (Brno, 1961); Králík, *Sázavské písemnictví* and *id.* in *BSL* 21 (1960).

23 The *Letopisy české* (*FRB* 2, 380) has merely: 921 *defuncto Vratizlao*, but some (less reliable) sources state that he was killed in action against the Magyars. That Wenceslas was aged eighteen in 921, as given in some texts, is universally rejected.

24 Christian 10, *Crescente* 1. If he learnt his Latin at Budeč, he may have learnt his Slav at St Mary's in Prague or at Tetín. But even Budeč with its Regensburg links might have taught both. Some texts even credit him with a knowledge of Greek. A literate prince was in any case unusual at the time; the legends doubtless tended to magnify his accomplishments so that even his knowledge of OCS cannot be considered beyond all doubt.

25 The text of such a *postřižiny* will be found in the *Euch. Sin.* (see p. 59): 'molitva na postriženije vlasomŭ otročęte' (ed. Frček, vol. 1, pp. 650–1). The significance of the ceremony has been examined by K. Potkański, *Postrzyżyny u Słowian i Germanów* (*Rozpr. Ak. Um., wydz. historyczno-filozoficzny*, 11/7, Cracow, 1895). In its developed form as a commendation to a (spiritual) protector it appears also in early Polish history: see p. 114. Cf. also V. A. Komarovich in *TODL* 16 (1960) for some Russian instances.

26 Seven or eight was a usual age for dedicating a boy to the service of God in a monastery. See Bede's account of his own dedication at this age in his *History of the English Church and People*, v, 24. That Wenceslas was intended for the church would appear much more probable if, as one or two sources suggest (e.g. Laurence and the Russian *Prolog*), he was in fact the younger brother. But then we are left with the enigma, why was Boleslas passed over for the succession?

27 Christian 5 (the dedication is not mentioned, merely 'basilicam que adhuc benediccione pontificali carebat').

28 Reconstruction in Turek, figs. 54–5; plan in *Svatováclavský sborník*, fig. 105 (p. 719), also pp. 383 and 566. See also Richter in *Magna Moravia*, pl. VI, no. 5; Grodecki, pp. 153 ff. and fig. 60 (p. 162).

29 See also p. 170. St Vitus was widely copied. Cibulká (*Svatováclavský Sborník*, pp. 230 ff.) counts over two dozen more modest rotundas in Bohemia which were simplified versions of it.

Wenceslas's church soon perished. The Romanesque St Vitus was the work of Spytigněv II and Vratislav II (from *c.* 1060). The present Gothic cathedral dates from Charles IV's reign, but was never finished.

30 A number of eminent historians (mainly German, but also B. Włodarski, *Chronologia polska*) still date this event 28 September 935. The reasons for rejecting this date cannot be here discussed in full; see Pekař in *Svatováclavský Sborník*, pp. 60–1.

31 We can disregard later tradition, e.g. Charles IV's *Life of St Wenceslas*, which treats Dragomira throughout as a more or less convinced pagan.

32 Her sister Edith was the wife of Otto I. See also Preidel in *WS* 5 (1960), pp. 77–8.

33 Gumpold, cap. xvi, retained in the *2nd OCS Legend*. The marriage may be fictitious as Christian's account ignores it. See also Devos in *AB* 81 (1963).

34 Cap. 12. He also states (cap. 16) that Wenceslas contemplated going to Rome to take monastic vows.

35 Gumpold, cap. 13. Compare the case of King Sigebert of Essex who was assassinated for treating his enemies in too Christian a spirit after his conversion (Bede, *History of the English Church*, bk. 3, ch. 22).

36 See F. Graus in *RES* 39 (1961). Václav II's seal is reproduced in *Češi a Poláci v minulosti*, vol. I, figs. 7–8.

37 *Cosmas*, I, 36: 'sancti Wencezlai intercessio; sancto Wencezlao suis auxiliante' (s.a. 1002, his date for the return of Oldřich to Prague).

38 For the north European trade-route to Kiev see also p. 113. Coins of German mints began to reach Poland, mainly via Bohemia, about 950 and constituted the majority within about a decade—a sign of the rapid expansion of the German economy at this time, supported by exploitation of new silver mines in the Harz. The Magdeburg–Prague route is also described by Ibrāhīm (Kowalski, p. 49).

39 '...veruntamen non secundum ritus aut sectam Bulgarie gentis vel Ruzie aut sclavonice lingue sed magis sequens instituta et decreta apostolica' (*Chron. boem.*, I, 22). The word *secta* and the mention of Russia betray the anachronism.

40 In 973 the energetic St Wolfgang became Abbot of St Emmeram, also with episcopal powers. His reforming and educational zeal no doubt reached to Prague but that he played a decisive part in the final arrangements at Prague is not very probable (cp. Schmitz, vol. I, pp. 228 ff.). Bishop Michael of Regensburg (*fungebatur* 942–72) had also been active and popular in Bohemia.

41 See M. Hellmann in *Syntagma friburgense...H. Aubin dargebracht* (1956). Slavník himself died in 981. By this date the two houses were surely related by intermarriage, without affecting their rivalry. Some consider that Slavník independence has been exaggerated for the tenth century as a whole.

42 *Skazanije o gramote russtej*, often referred to as *Skazanije o slavjanskoj pismennosti* (Mareš in *TODL* 19 (1963), pp. 174–6: 'prišed Vojtěh v Moravu, v Čehi i v Ljahi i razdruši věru prav(ověrn)uju, ruskuju gramotu otverže a latinskuju věru i gramotu postavi i pravověrnyja episkopy isslěče a drugija razgna...'. It is clearly worthless as a historical source.

43 Králík, 'Povest vremennyh let i Legenda Kristiana' in *TODL* 19 (1963).

44 This and the following two texts are printed in *MPH*, vol. I, nos. 8–10; *MGH*, *SS* IV; Polish versions in *Pisemnictwo czasów Bolesława Chrobrego*, ed. A. Gieysztor (Warsaw, 1966). Also *FRB*, vol. I.

45 Discussion of this and related texts by J. Karwasińska in *SZ* 2, 4, 9, 10 (1958–65). See also L. Nemec in *PR* 7 (1962) and H. G. Voigt, *Adalbert von Prag* (1898).

46 See Dąbrowski, fig. 1 (p. 43) and fig. 2 (p. 49); Richter in *Magna Moravia*, fig. 214 (p. 326); *Słownik*, vol. 3, fig. 16 (p. 53). The basilica is of Ottonian style, probably consecrated by Bishop Adalbert of Trier in 961 and burnt down in 995.

47 See Gay, pp. 381 ff.

48 For the further history of Břevnov and its daughter houses see Krásl and Ježek, pt. 2. Foundation deed in Friedrich, *Codex* I, no. 38 (possibly not authentic).

49 More probably Soběslav since coins exist with the inscriptions Z O B E Z L A V and L I V B V Z (= Libice). Their authenticity is not in doubt: minting started in Bohemia under Wenceslas (see G. Skalský in *Svatováclavský Sborník*, pl. 19, opp. p. 184.)

50 *SRH*, vol. 2, no. 9, §§5 ff. See Dvornik, *The Making*, pp. 152 ff. By the fourteenth century Adalbert was widely referred to as the *apostolus hungarorum*. St Stephen figured him on his royal seal. Adalbert's baptism of Géza is not quite certain; this has been put as early as 974.

51 Friedrich, Codex I, no. 33: Pilgrim solicits an archiepiscopal pallium from Pope Benedict VI in 973 for his work among the Magyars.

52 While some Christian words in Magyar are much older than this period, perhaps even older than their settlement in Hungary (e.g. *kereszt* = cross), there is a clear Bohemian origin for *érsek* = archbishop (OCz. *jaršík* < archi-[episcopus]). Other Slav elements in Magyar are of Bulgarian, Slovak and Slovene (Pannonian) type. Byzantine diplomatic and missionary activity had already made some headway among the Magyars in the 940s; two of their leaders at the Battle of the Lechfeld claimed to be Christians. See Gy. Moravcsik, *Die byzantinische Kultur und das mittelalterliche Ungarn* (*Sitzungsber. der Ak. Wiss. Berlin, Klasse für Phil.*, 1955, no. 4). Greek influence was stronger in the eastern parts, especially Transylvania, but Stephen had several documents drawn up in Greek.

53 Prague's own view was vehement: 'nolumus eum; quia si ueniet non uenit pro nostra salute sed pro puniendis malis et iniuriis que fratribus suis fecimus et fecisse iuvat'. (*Vita antiquior*, §26 (*MGH, SS* IV, p. 593)).

54 See p. 356 n. 136. The island is now known as *isola di San Bartolomeo*, to whom the church was later rededicated. The rotunda at St Romuald's Pereum near Ravenna is described in St Bruno of Querfurt's *Vita quinque fratrum*, cap. 5.

55 Walicki, *Drzwi gnieźnieńskie* (Wrocław, 1956–9). The scenes start with his birth at bottom left, proceed clockwise, and end with his enshrinement at bottom right. Scene 16 shows Bolesław weighing out gold to redeem the saint's body from the Prussians. Not all the scenes are taken from known literary sources, e.g. no. 8, in which the saint appeals to Boleslas of Bohemia to put an end to the slave-trade (Walicki, vol. 3, pl. 40).

56 Friedrich, *Codex* I, no. 40 (also nos. 52, 97, 98—later endowments). Davle is at the confluence of the rivers Vltava (Moldau) and Sázava.

57 It is somewhat hazardous to ascribe particular texts to this monastery. The most probable are:

1. New versions of *VC* and *VM* both in OCS and Latin.

2. The separate *Lives* of St Ljudmila, in OCS (surviving in excerpt in the Russian *Prolog*) and in Latin.

3. A *Life of St Vitus*. We may note that Procopius was succeeded as abbot by his nephew Vit.

4. Perhaps the *Prague Glagolitic Fragments*, which could be a relic of the destruction of Slav service-books after 1097, but one not specifically attributable to Sázava. Cf. also p. 337 n. 104.

To these must be added the *Life of St Procopius*: texts reprinted by Chaloupecký and Ryba (see Bibliography). Weingart (*Českosl. typ cirkevnej slovančiny, passim*) takes a properly cautious attitude to these ascriptions; see also Vondrák, *O původu*. The ductus of the *Prague Fragments* is clearly independent of Balkan (Macedonian or Croat) Glagolitic style but raises no palaeographic difficulties as a direct development of that of the *Kiev folia* (see pp. 60 ff.). We can therefore accept that it reflects the native graphic tradition. See also Mareš in *SL* 20 (1951).

The *Life of St Procopius* survives only in Latin but the earliest form is probably based on a lost OCS original written in the 1060s; see Králík in *SL* 33 (1964) and Jelinek, *ibid.* 34 (1965).

The *Sázava Chronicle* (*Mnich sázavský*, *FRB* 2, pp. 240 ff.) also supplies details about Procopius (section *De exordio Zazavensis monasterii*).

58 *Cosmas*, II, 29–33. Documents in Friedrich, *Codex* I, nos 62–75.

59 Friedrich, Codex I, no. 81: '…quod secundum sclavonicam linguam apud vos divinum celebrari annueremus officium, scias nos huic petitioni tue nequaquam posse favere.' He called the request *vana temeritas*.

60 Weingart, pp. 87 ff. See also Havránek and Hrabák, *Výbor z české literatury od počátku*… (Prague, 1957), p. 108. For the development of Bohemian religious poetry in Latin from this time on see Dvornik, *The Slavs in European History*, pp. 152 ff.

61 An incomplete copy of this edict is reprinted by V. Vaněček in *SA* 3 (1951–2). It is in effect a law-code for the improvement of Christian morality in social life.

62 *Cosmas*, III, 1.

63 See Odložilík in *HSS* 2 (1954). Jaromír considered this an unwarranted derogation of Prague's authority and appealed to the Pope.

64 *Cosmas*, I, 15: '…quedam in Privelegio moraviensis ecclesie, quedam in Epilogo eiusdem terre atque Boemie, quedam in Vita vel passione sanctissimi nostri patroni et martyris Wencezlai.' Chaloupecký's attempt to reconstruct this text has not been generally accepted. On the possible identity of this *Privilegium* with *Beatus Cyrillus* see also p. 92 above. Urbánek connects the *Privilegium* with the approach to the Pope in 1079 (see p. 107) and the *Epilogus* with this quarrel over the see of Olomouc in 1085–90.

65 The *Russian Primary Chronicle* (s.a. 6489=981) states that Vladimir conquered the towns from the Poles. Some scholars are of the opinion that they more probably belonged to Bohemia at the time. But it is even more probable that they were not yet formally incorporated in any state. It must also be borne in mind that the rivalry between the Premyslids and the Slavniks must have made it difficult for Prague to control lands to the north and east in any real sense. This was an immediate cause of the massacre of the Slavniks in 995. It remains to be determined when this rivalry became serious. The two houses appear to have been cooperating in military expeditions in the years following 955 and not improbably till as late as 981. After that the situation rapidly worsened. This runs parallel with the decline of the Bohemian–Polish alliance, which did not outlast the Czech occupation of Meissen in 984 and Bolesław's second marriage to a Magyar princess *c.* 986/7.

66 *Chronicle*, I, 22 and s.a. 1086 (II, 37–8). Cf. also *ibid.*, II, 21. Discussion by B. Krzemieńska and D. Třeštník in *SZ* 5 (1960).

67 Friedrich, *Codex* I, no. 86. The document was finally put into shape at Regensburg in 1086 (*CDS*, no. 8).

68 *VM* cap. 6, 8, 15; *VC* cap. 2 and 14.

69 *Svętyj likŭ papežŭ.*

70 For details, see Dvornik in *L'Église et les églises.* The prayer may be of late eleventh-century Sázava origin.

71 See pp. 281 ff. It can be seriously entertained that a few words of the Cyrillomethodian tradition better preserved in Bohemia, or new words made there on Czech models passed in this way into Russian usage. The most likely are коварство/коварный, внезапно, бренныи. See Shakhmatov and Shevelov, *Die kirchenslavischen Elemente in der modernen russischen Literatursprache* (Wiesbaden, 1960), pp. 65–6.

72 See p. 398 n. 111. Both the *Skazanije* and the *Chtenije* of SS Boris and Gleb posit acquaintance with the Czech legends of Wenceslas not only in their OCS but also their Latin forms; see Ingham in *WS* 10 (1965).

73 See plan of Prague in Knox, p. 20. The Emmaus monastery (Emauzy or 'Na Slovanech') was only one of a number of new houses for different orders, promoted by Charles in Prague. The Glagolitic Bible, of which the only completely preserved volume, the second, is dated 1416, is the outstanding text of this kind outside Croatia at this time and is surely a product of Emmaus. The language shows a number of OCS (south Slav) traits. The Glagolitic portion of the *Reims Gospel Book*, on which kings of France swore their coronation oath, was written in Bohemia *c.* 1395, probably at Emmaus.

74 See Mareš in *SL* 31 (1962).

75 See M. Paulová in *BSL* 11 (1950). The example of Emmaus was taken up in Poland without permanent success (see p. 360 n. 189).

76 Dvornik, *The Slavs in European history*, p. 287. But this may have been no more than the common practice of reading the Gospel and Epistle in the local language as well as in Latin. There have been attempts to prove that Czech was used for liturgical purposes at the Emmaus monastery, e.g. Z. Nejedlý, *Dějiny husitského zpěvu* (Prague, 1913), vol. 2, pp. 410 ff.

POLAND

77 Widukind, *Res gestae saxonicae*, iii, 66 (*MGH, SS* III, p. 463).

78 *Adam of Bremen*, ii, 19 (*MGH*, SS VII). Wolin (Wollin, Volyń) is a Slav name occurring elsewhere, especially the province of 'Volhynia', south of the Pripet marshes. On Jómsburg see L. M. Hollander, *The Saga of the Jóms-vikings* (1955).

79 The considerable quantity of Islamic coins which reached North and Central Poland in the period 880–960 arrived mainly via Scandinavia. See Kiersnowski, pp. 39 ff. and map p. 45.

80 Review of the evidence by S. Urbańczyk in *Początki państwa polskiego*, vol. 2.

81 E.g. 'sed istorum gesta, quorum memoriam oblivio vetustatis abolevit et quos error et idolatria defoedavit, memorare negligamus' (*Gallus anonymus*, i, 3).

82 The hypothesis that the name Brandenburg commemorates the great Irish missionary St Brendan is without foundation. The earliest written forms are without exception *Brenna* or the like, the *-burg* being a later German addition; *Brenna* is clearly cognate with place names such as the Moravian *Brno*, to be interpreted 'marsh'. See Sadnik and Aitzetmüller, *Vergleichendes Wörterbuch der slavischen Sprachen 141* (pp. 155–6).

83 *Gallus*, i, 1–2.

84 However the traditional genealogy makes the supposition difficult. On an average computation of the generations and accepting that Mieszko was born in the early 920s it is almost impossible for Ziemowit to have been aged seven —the normal age for *postrzyżyny*—in the second half of the 870s or early 880s: there would seem to be one generation too many. On the genealogy see H. Łowmiański in *Początki państwa polskiego*, vol. 1.

85 *VM* 11: 'Dobro ti sę krĭstiti...voljejǫ svojejǫ na svojeji zemli da ne plěněnŭ nǫdĭmi krĭstenŭ bǫdeši na štuždeji zemli.' These Slavs, living about Cracow, should in all probability be called White Croats. See p. 187 below.

86 E.g. *Rocznik małopolska*: '964 Mescho dux cum Polonis sacrum baptisma consecuntur.' Cp. *Annales cracovienses breves* (*MGH, SS* XIX, p. 664): '965 Dubrowka venit ad ducem Mesconem. 966 Meszco baptizatur et fides catholica in Polonia recipitur.'

87 *MPH*, I, no. 14 (p. 320). Some scholars ascribe the text to a much later date, perhaps even the fourteenth century; see P. David, *L'Epitaphe de Boleslas Chrobry* (Paris, 1928).

88 E.g. Dowiat, who suggests Regensburg.

89 As quoted by Bede, *History of the English church and people*, ii, 11. The legend, reported by Gallus (i, 4) and other sources, that Mieszko was blind up to the age of seven is no doubt an example of the common symbol of sudden Divine illumination at baptism which later Christian fantasy has grafted onto an account of his *postrzyżyny*: 'vere Polonia caeca prius erat quae nec cultu-ram veri Dei nec doctrinam fidei cognoscebat...'

90 Thietmar, iv, 55: cf. iv, 56: 'laboravit enim pro conversione coniugis sui'.

91 '...būyslāw [Boleslas] malak frāǧa wa būyma wa Kr[a]kū.' On the exact date of his facts see Widajewicz, *Studia (Rozprawy wydziału historyczno-filozoficznego, Polska Akademia umiejętności*, seria ii, t. xlvi, nr. 1, Cracow, 1946).

92 Begun 959. See Möbius, pls. 35–7; Schulze and Vorbrodt, *Das Stift Gernrode (Mitteldeutsche Forschungen* 38, 1965), p. 93 and plates *ad fin.* It is of course not improbable that the first cathedral of Cracow, and perhaps others, had stylistic relations to those of Merseburg and Magdeburg, which were essentially Saxon.

93 See Preidel in *WS* 5 (1960), especially map on p. 87.

94 See Z. Kaczmarczyk in *Początki państwa polskiego*, vol. 2.

95 'Alias sic dicitur, et legi in alia cronica, quod Polonia in Poznania primo fidem recepit, unde dicetur Poznan, quasi "se recognoscens fidelem".' (*Chronicon polono-silesiacum, MGH, SS* xix, p. 558).

96 The official Magdeburg view can be read in *Gesta archiepiscoporum magdeburgensium*, cap. 9 (*MGH, SS* xiv, pp. 381 ff.). See also Holtzmann, *Geschichte*, p. 85.

97 '...censemus, ut censum et decimationem omnium gentium, quas idem piissimus imperator baptizavit, vel per eum suumque filium aequivocum regem successoresque eorum Deo annuente baptizandae sunt, ipsi successoresque eorum potestatem habeant distribuendi, subdendi Magdeburgensi, Merseburgensi, vel cuique velint futurae sedi...Cum vero Deus omnipotens per praetaxatum servum suum invicissimum imperatorem suumque filium regem successoresque eorum vicinam Slavorum gentem ad cultum Christianae fidei perduxerit, per eos in convenientibus locis secundum oportunitatem episcopatus constitui...[et] ab archiepiscopo Magdaburgensi episcopos consecrari volumus suffraganeos.' (Migne, *PL* 133, *Joannis Papae XII Epistolae*, xii, col. 1029).

In the following years the phrasing differed but the sense remained substantially the same. See Migne, *PL* 135, *Joannis Papae XIII Epistolae*, nos. ii, ix, x. See also Dvornik, *The Making*, pp. 73–4.

98 This 'tribute', which, according to Thietmar (ii, 29) Mieszko was paying a few years later (972), is a difficult question. If genuine, it may have arisen as Mieszko's return for Otto's abandonment of claims to Western Pomerania and the Oder delta in the 960s, when he is described as *amicus imperatoris*, therefore no vassal (*Widukind*, s.a. 967). See Dvornik, *The Making*, pp. 54–9. The title *fidelis* used by Thietmar of Mieszko could imply some degree of dependence; the word is also used of the Bohemian rulers Wenceslas I and Boleslas I. It is better not to load it with any precise feudal connotation. Poland can be considered quite independent after the defeat of Otto II in 979 (see L. Koczy in *ANT* 4).

99 *MGH, Diplomatum* ii/2, no. 75. On the bishops of Poznań see Sappok, p. 141.

100 E.g. *Rocznik poznański* 1 (*MPH*, N.S. 6, p. 129). The *Kronika wielkopolska* (*MPH* ii, p. 483) has the designation *episcopu[s] (totius) Poloniae*, which might fit a general missionary responsibility. P. Bogdanowicz (*NP* 23,

1966) considers that Jordan might be described as a 'court bishop', that is to say, of similar status to the early Croat bishops of Nin (see p. 192).

101 Thietmar, vi, 65 [1012]. On all this question Thietmar cannot be relied on since he accepted various German falsifications of 1004–12.

102 The best refutation of the spurious Magdeburg theory is given by P. Kehr in *Abhandl. der preuss. Akad. der Wissenschaften, Phil.-hist. Klasse* (1920), no. 1. See also W. Abraham, *Gniezno i Magdeburg* (Cracow, 1926).

103 *Widukind*, ii, 36; 'Ingenium ei admodum mirandum; nam...litteras in tantum didicit ut pleniter libros legere et intellegere noverit. Praeterea romana lingua sclavonicaque loqui scit, sed rarum est quo earum uti dignetur.'

104 See also Koroljuk, pp. 110 ff.

105 Bolesław's epitaph records the fact in a mutilated passage .For further examples see P. David, *L'Epitaphe de Boleslas Chrobry*, p. 24. A rite of this kind was widespread among the pagan Germans and Slavs (see pp. 93 and 114), but we are here concerned with a Christian or christianised ceremony of which a Greek prototype and Slav version can be seen in the *Euchologium Sinaiticum* (ed. Frček, 1, pp. 650 ff.—τριχοκουρία).

106 Only one source (*Kronika węgiersko-polska, MPH* 1, p. 500) mentions Papal participation at this moment. Presumably the Leo is Leo VIII (963–5). If this is genuine and Jordan was a Papal appointment, he could have arrived in Poland about 965 and performed Mieszko's baptism, before the formal constitution of his missionary bishopric. See P. Bogdanowicz in *NP* 23 (1966), especially sect. 5 (pp. 51 ff.).

107 The critical literature is considerable, but see esp. G. Labuda in *PRZ* 7 (1951) and Dąbrowski, pp. 51 ff. There is very little room for doubt that this donation was actually executed by Mieszko and that the Pope in question was John XV (985–96). On the text itself see W. Leitsch in *Studien zur älteren Geschichte Osteuropas*, 2 Teil, ed. H. F. Schmid (Graz-Köln, 1959).

108 See *MPH*, 1, no. 6; *CDS* 1, no. 2. For the *incipit* cf. Otto III's signature reproduced in Holtzmann, *Geschichte*, 4 ed., fig. 33 (opposite p. 336), on a document of 998. Mieszko's baptismal name, on the basis of the document, has been assumed to be Dagobert but one can see no motivation for the strange choice. It could have been Lambert, frequently used thereafter by the dynasty. More ingenious than likely is the solution Dagome = Dago[bert] + Me[sco]. Only partisans of a Scandinavian origin for the Piast dynasty interpret it as Germanic *Dago* (cf. Holtzmann, *op. cit.*, pp. 186–7). Full discussion of the manuscripts and text by B. Kürbisówna in *Początki państwa polskiego*, vol. 1. See also K. Buczek in *SZ* 10 (1965).

109 *Senator* and *senatrix* were still used by the great Roman families in the tenth century, but *iudex* had apparently little currency except as a title of the seven senior Papal officials—quite inappropriate for Mieszko.

110 Ed. J. Woronczak, E. Ostrowska and H. Feicht (Wrocław, 1962). See also A. Steffen in *Studia z filologii polskiej i słowiańskiej* 6 (1967).

111 See Lehr-Spławiński in *Od piętnastu wieków* (1961); the article was originally published in 1936. Also Havránek in *SL* 25 (1956), Birnbaum in *Orbis scriptus* (see Bibliography).

112   Birnbaum in *SCSL* xi (1965); Stender-Petersen in *Cyrillo-Methodiana*, pp. 454 ff.; R. Jakobson, 'The Slavic response to Byzantine poetry' in *OCA*, I (1963). Adalbert himself had considerable knowledge of Greek ecclesiastical literature, learnt in Italy, especially from St Nilus.

113   Stender-Petersen in *SCSL* viii (1962); see also Birnbaum, *loc. cit.*

114   The exact dates of occupation of each province are disputed. His hold on Bohemia proper was no more than transitory in 1003–4. Slovakia was lost to Hungary about 1007. On the chronology see H. Bubín in *Slovanské historické studie*, iv (1961).

115   *Adam of Bremen, MGH, SS* VII, p. 318, *schol.* 25 (not precisely dateable).

116   Her exact lineage is disputable but she was reputed a daughter of the Emperor Romanós II; see Ostrogorski, p. 263, note I. In any case the arrangement of this marriage by Otto I for his son and Byzantine recognition of his Imperial title was a considerable diplomatic triumph.

117   Charlemagne had used the phrase *renovatio romani imperii*—in 803 and later—but his thought always centred on the Frankish Kingdom and even after 800 he claimed no more than to be in his person *imperium romanum gubernans* and co-emperor with his Eastern colleague. He did not want to be bound to Rome and to consider the City his capital, which may have been Leo's hope through the pseudo-Byzantine coronation of 800. Nor did Otto I, in whom the first stirrings of a greater *renovatio* are visible, interpret his own Imperial coronation in Rome in 962 as having such implications. See Schramm, *ad init.*; Folz, pp. 25 ff.; Ohnsorge in *SAE* 14 (1963).

118   Beckwith, fig. 87 (*Otto Christomimetes*).

119   Letters of Gerbert, ed. J. Havet (Paris 1886), no. 186 (p. 172), *c.* Dec. 997.

120   Gerbert put his conception of Empire before Otto in the tract *Libellus de rationali et ratione uti* (Migne, *PL* 139, cols 157 ff.). Alcuin had performed the same office for Charlemagne in 802, building on Pope Gelasius (492–6) and St Augustine.

121   *Vita beati Romualdi* by St Peter Damian (*c.* 1042) (*Fonti per la storia d'Italia* (*medievo*) 94, ed. G. Tabacco, Rome, 1957). Romuald embodied the eremitical—more Byzantine—aspect of the monastic revival which had begun, in its institutional aspect, in the early years of the tenth century at Cluny (909) and Gorzé (*c.* 933).

122   The *Vita quinque fratrum* by St Bruno of Querfurt (*MPH* 6; *MGH*, SS xv/2), written about 1006, provides the most evidence. John Canaparius stresses that the Emperor 'treated him [Adalbert] as an intimate friend, gladly taking heed of all that he said' (*MGH, SS* IV, *Vita S. Adalberti*, §22 (p. 591): 'crebro alloquitur sanctum Adalbertum et habebat eum sibi familiarem, audiens libenter, quaecumque sibi diceret'). Otto's paternal grandmother, Adelaide of Burgundy, and his aunt, Abbess Matilda of Quedlinburg, both later acclaimed saints, bear witness to the strong religious strain in his heredity. See St Adelaide's *Life* by Abbot Odilo of Cluny.

123   *Vita quinque fratrum, cap.* 3: '...ubi est relinquere regnum sapienti et, deposito regio honore, ad sanctam civitatem Ierusalem monachum velle fieri et in abdita heremo...velle philosophari [=live the life of a monk]?'

124 R. Folz, *ad init.* Cf. also Bloch's estimate of Otto (vol. 2, pp. 392–3).

125 P. 166. Cf. Schramm, pp. 126–7 and Southern, p. 186 (on Gerbert's part).

126 Accounts in *Gallus Anonymus, Chronicae Polonorum*, i, 6 (*MGH, SS* IX), using native traditions, and in Thietmar, iv, 44 ff., who is not reliable on the implications owing to his pro-Saxon bias.

127 Gallus, *loc. cit.*: 'et accipiens [Otto] imperiale diadema capitis sui, capiti Bolezlavi in amicitiae foedus imposuit...'.

128 Certain Polish annalists, while inaccurate in details, evidently felt the same surprise, e.g. *MGH, SS* XIX, p. 618 (s.a. 1001): 'Mescho [*sic*] miserat Lampertum episcopum coronam petere. Sed Papa, angelica monitus visione, coronam quam preparaverat Meschoni, Affrico nuncio regis Ungarie dedit.' The *Vita beati Romualdi* (cap. 28) also stresses how normal the request was: 'Busclavus [Bolesław] autem volens coronam sui regni ex romana auctoritate suscipere, predictos venerabiles viros cepit...deposcere ut...coronam sibi a sede apostolica reportarent.'

129 See W. Meysztowicz in *ANT* 4 (1958) and *SPM* 3 (1956), who proposed the theory of Bolesław's Caesarship.

130 *Gallus*, i, 6. The *Kronika wielkopolska* has: 'Boleslaum consortem imperii ordinavit' (*MPH*, 2, p. 483). It is impossible to decide what the writers meant by such words as *cooperator, consors*. Similar high-sounding modes of address occur in some later Byzantine documents, e.g. Dölger, *Regesten*, II, no. 1382 (address to Frederick I in 1151): 'frater et cognatus imperii'.

131 *MPH*, I, p. 320. See also P. David, *L'Epitaphe* [note 87 above].

132 See *Gesta archiepisc. magdeburg.* (*MGH, SS* XIV), cap. 14 (p. 390). The Pope's confirmation of Polish ecclesiastical independence from Germany is shown in *CDS*, i, no. 4.

133 Beckwith, p. 101, fig. 85. Cf. the similar book made for Henry II between 1002 and 1014 (*ibid.*, fig. 94). A date before 1000 seems improbable: Otto's several campaigns against the Veletians and others were not sufficiently decisive to warrant such symbolic representation. On the other hand 'Sclavinia' may not have been intended as strictly limited to the Slavs within the Polish dominions. Otto holds the orb of Christendom in his left hand.

134 Brackmann, *Kaiser Otto III*, pp. 16 ff.; Holtzmann, *Geschichte*, p. 351.

135 This elaboration does not appear till a century later—in Adémar de Chabanne's *Chronicle* (*Ademari Historiae, MGH, SS* IV, p. 130). Contemporary accounts date the opening of the tomb to 997 and state that Bolesław accompanied Otto all the way to Aix.

136 *Gallus*, i, 6: 'pro vexillo triumphali clavum ei de croce Domini cum lancea sancti Mauricii [a copy, of course] dono dedit, pro quibus illi Bolezlavus sancti Adalberti brachium redonavit'. The lance of St Maurice was the talisman of Otto I who had carried it to victory against the Magyars on the Lechfeld (955). He had received it from his father Henry I, who believed that it had belonged to the first Christian emperor Constantine. Otto's gifts of lance and a nail from the True Cross do indeed provide a striking parallel to the symbolism of Imperial coronation.

137   It had to be rebuilt twice within a short period—in 1018 and again in 1039–64—so that little of the first structure remains. Part of the original glazed tile pavement has recently been identified. See K. Żurowski in *Początki państwa polskiego*, vol. 2, pp. 72–5; Hensel, *Najdawniejsze stolice*, plate facing p. 32; *id., Archeologia*, p. 87, fig. 37. This pavement, together with the rare use of mosaic in Poland, suggests Byzantine influences reaching Poland via Kiev.

138   Reproduction of the coin in *Początki państwa polskiego*, vol. 1, p. 125 (fig. 11) and p. 121 (fig. 12); Kiersnowski, fig. 25 (opp. p. 128); see also *ibid.*, pp. 130 ff.

139   For Otto and Romuald's foundation of the Pereum see *Vita beati Romualdi*, cap. 30. The *filius Busclavi sclavonici regis* is mentioned in cap. 26.

140   *Vita quinque fratrum*, caps. 6, 10, 12 (*MPH* 6 (1893), pp. 383 ff.). It is improbable that this missionary cell has any connection with that founded by St Adalbert, referred to as *Mestris*, where he sent monks from Břevnov under Astrik.

141   *Thietmar*, v, 15–18.

142   *Ibid.*, viii, 1.

143   The German view on Bolesław's self-coronation is given in *Ann. Quedl.*, s.a. 1025 (*MGH, SS* III, p. 90): 'adeo ut uncto etiam sibi imponi coronam temere sit usurpatus'.

144   These ambitions no doubt explain why Bolesław apparently minted coins with the inscription REX BOLIZLAUS rather before 1025, replacing the title DUX (Kiersnowski, pp. 133 ff.; Gumowski, type 12). The occupation of Kiev was presumably also responsible for a few issues with inscriptions in Cyrillic, otherwise never used in Poland. On Kiev see also p. 275.

145   *Thietmar*, iv, 45; cf. *Annales magdeburgenses* (*MGH, SS* XVI), s.a. 996 (p. 159): 'archiepiscopatus in eodem loco [Gnesin] fundatione, sed non legitima, honoravit'.

146   Hensel, *Najdawniejsze stolice*, pp. 197 ff., estimates the period at *c.* 966–80. Mieszko particularly favoured the place and was buried in Poznań cathedral. Little now remains of the original edifice; for details see Hensel, *op. cit.*, p. 148 (and fig. 96); Z. Świechowski in *Początki państwa polskiego*, vol. 2, especially p. 265 (fig. 83).

147   *CDMP*, vol. 1, no. 6 (4 June 1133). Innocent did this largely as recompense to Norbert, founder of the Premonstratensian Order (*c.* 1119) with its strong missionary interests, who had helped the Pope to recover his position in Rome.

148   *CDMP*, vol. 1, no. 7 (7 July 1136), *ad init.*

149   These dates are very uncertain. Some estimate that these provinces were lost in 1019–21 (as given in *Cosmas*, I, 40). The maps in Natanson-Leski, pp. 40 and 64, are certainly unfair to Bohemia.

150   *Cosmas*, s.a. 1039 ('xii presbiteri vix sustentantes pondus aurei crucifixi').

151   Among the few sources which mention such a person is the *Kronika wielkopolska* (or *Boguchwała*), *MPH*, vol. 2, p. 484. Some identify him with Mieszko's brother Bezprym who usurped power for a short time in 1031–2.

152 *Gallus*, i, 18–19 describes the general situation. See also *Thietmar*, viii, 2 for attempts to deal with lapses from Christian discipline by harsh punishments.

153 Dziewulski, p. 143.

154 *Cosmas*, 1, 40. This agrees with the oblique references in the story of Moses the Hungarian in the Russian *Paterik* (see p. 304), cap. 30, where the persecution is ascribed to Bolesław himself.

155 *Russian Primary Chronicle*, s.a. 1030 (wrong date): 'V se že vremja umrě Boleslav velikyj v Ljasěh i bystj mjatež v zemli ljadskě; vstavše ljudje izbiša episkopy i popy.' I follow here the chronology suggested by D. Borawska, *Kryzys monarchii wczesnopiastowskiej*; it seems improbable that this event should be transferred to the time of Bolesław the Forgotten (1034–8). See also *Gallus*, i, 19.

156 *Annales Hildesheimenses*, s.a. 1034 (*MGH, SS* III). Mieszko II's Christian zeal is not to be doubted; his most important act was the erection of the new see of Kruszwica.

157 Once again no agreement yet seems possible on the chronology. There is some support for the view that Kazimierz did not flee Poland till about 1037 nor return before 1040/1. See Bieniak, pp. 107 ff.

158 That he actually became a monk at Cluny (his mother was closely connected with the leaders of the Reform movement) is now generally considered a legend despite the fact that some sources state that the Pope granted him a dispensation from his vows on condition that, as a lay ruler, he re-established the Polish church in full obedience to Rome. But he received part of his education in a Polish monastery school. See P. David, *Casimir le Moine* (Paris, 1932).

159 *Annalista Saxo*, s.a. 1042 (*MGH, SS* VI, p. 685).

160 The foundation dates of the earlier Polish monasteries are very imperfectly known. To the eleventh century (but in what order we cannot say for certain) belong: Tyniec (near Cracow), Mogilno and Trzemeszno (near Gniezno), Czerwińsk, Kruszwica, Lubiń and Łęczyca (first mentioned in 1136). A church at least at Trzemeszno is certain from the late tenth century since St Adalbert's relics were first deposited there (see p. 105). Holy Trinity on Łysa Góra (later rededicated as Holy Cross—Święty Krzyż) was certainly not founded by Mieszko I's wife Dobrava with monks from Bohemia, as later tradition asserted, but whether it is of the early twelfth or early thirteenth century is still a moot point (for further discussion see P. David, *Les Bénédictins*, pp. 63–7).

161 *MPH*, 1, no. 20 (p. 358). See also St. Kętrzyński in *Rozpr. ak. um., wydział hist.-fil.*, II/18 (Cracow, 1902).

162 The dedication of Bolesław's cathedral is unknown. When Kazimierz started his new edifice he rededicated the old one to St Gereon of Cologne: see *Słownik*, s.v. *Kraków*, fig. 165.

163 *MPH*, 2, p. 918: 'qui constituit episcopatus per Poloniam'. It is not clear how many sees Kazimierz had been able to restore effectively.

164 Lambert of Hersfeld, *Annales*, s.a. 1077 (*MGH, SS* V). Thereby Bolesław repudiated Poland's status of imperial fief, virtual since the 1030s. What

Mieszko and his son Bolesław Chrobry had used all their strength and wiles to avoid—Polish subservience to Germany after the manner of Bohemia—had come dangerously close to permanence and was only just shaken off.

165 The crypt of St Leonard (a saint much venerated at this time in the Rhineland and Low Countries) at Cracow cathedral is thought to be the work of Kazimierz Odnowiciel. Portions attributed to the first quarter of the eleventh century (before the destruction of 1038/9) are held to be somewhat Saxon in style. See Szydłowski, p. 17 (fig. 7).

166 *MPH*, 1, p. 367 (=*CDMP*, vol. 1, no. 4): 'illud nobis primo attendendum est, quod episcopi terrae vestrae non habentes certum metropolitanae sedis locum nec sub aliquo positi magisterio huc et illuc pro sua quisque ordinatione vagantes...'.

167 Text in W. Taszycki, *Najdawniejsze zabytki języka polskiego* (1951), pp. 59 ff. For an ecclesiastical map of Poland in the twelfth century see *Słownik*, vol. 3, fig. 234 (p. 509).

168 *Vita (minor) S. Stanislai cracoviensis episcopi*, *MPH* 4 (1884), §32 (pp. 279–80); cf. *Gallus*, i, 27 (*De exilio Bolezlavi*): 'non debuit Christus in Christum peccatum quodlibet corporaliter vindicare'. The *Kronika Boguchwała*, cap. 14 (*de saevitate Boleslai*), throws no more light on the cause of the quarrel. It has been suggested with little probability that Stanisław was a Cyrillomethodian who resisted the Latinisation of his see and diocese (see pp. 135 ff. below).

169 See Dziewulski, pp. 163–4, 170 ff.

170 P. David, *La Pologne et l'évangélisation de la Poméranie* (Paris, 1928). Kołobrzeg remained however an important place—*gloriosa Pomoranorum urbs et precipua* (*Gallus*, ii, 28).

171 Sources: *Lives* of Otto of Bamberg by Ebbo (*MGH, SS* xii, pp. 823 ff.), *c.* 1151–2; and by the monk of Prüfening (*ibid.*, pp. 883 ff.), dating from the 1140s. Herbord's accounts (*ibid.*, pp. 746 ff. and *SS* xx, pp. 706 ff.) are based on these and less reliable. See also Hofmeister in Bibliography, and K. Liman in *SZ* 3 (1958).

172 Ebbo, ii, 3; Herbord, *Life*, ii, 6. Thus Otto himself recognized still the general principle that Papal approval was necessary.

173 Ebbo, iii, 1; iii, 16.

174 Ebbo, iii, 6: 'non est meum ad hanc vos religionem cogere, quia...non vult Deus coacta servicia sed voluntaria'; *Herbordi Dialogus*, iii, 3: 'superest modo, ut nos, qui primi et maiores dicimur ac sumus, nostrae dignitati consulamus, tam dignissimae ac sanctissimae rei consentientes, ut populus qui nobis subiectus est nostro possit erudiri exemplo'.

175 A detailed exposition will be found in K. Lanckorońska, *Studies in the Roman-Slavonic rite in Poland* (*OC* 161, Rome, 1961), with full bibliography. Hers is the point of view of one convinced of a widespread Slav church. Short exposition by the same in *ANT* 1 (1954). See also Grabski, *Bolesław Chrobry*, pp. 277 ff.; A. Stender-Petersen in *Cyrillo-Methodiana* (*SLF* 6); P. Bogdanowicz in *NP* 23 (1966), especially pp. 28 ff.; *Słownik*, vol. 3, pp. 450–1 (bibliography).

176 Hensel, *La Naissance*, pp. 81–2.

177 It is questionable whether the letter of the Bavarian bishops to the Pope in 900 (see p. 84), speaking of 'quandam neophytam gentem quam ipse dux bello domuit et ex paganis christianos esse patravit' (Friedrich, *Codex* I, no. 30), refers to this. Further references: Lehr-Spławiński in *SL* 29 (1960).

178 See *Odkrycia w Wiślicy* (1963).

179 *MPH*, I, no. 10 (p. 118), quoting a document of 1445. King Alfred the Great was aware of *Visleland* (c. 890) as something more important than a geographical term.

180 *Gallus*, i, 19.

181 *Gallus*, i, 11. Gallus was probably an Italian cleric in the Polish chancellery, who wrote his Latin chronicle in the second decade of the twelfth century. About a century later Master Vincent also alludes to Bolesław's *gemina metropolis* but the phrase is unlikely to be independent of Gallus.

182 *De morte Bolezlaui carmina*, l. 20 (Maleczyński, pp. 38–9). We might interpret *latinorum et slauorum* as 'foreigners and natives' among the Polish clergy as a whole.

183 This argument has been elaborated by C. Backvis in *BYZ* 22 (1952), pp. 282 ff.

184 Lambert's consecration is ascribed to 995; see *MGH, SS* XIX, pp. 616–17. But this is probably a misplacement of Aaron's successor Lambert (c. 1061–71).

185 Ptaśnik, pp. 267–8.

186 Friedberg, p. 38.

187 *MPH*, 2, p. 794.

188 E.g. *MPH*, 3, p. 405.

189 The inclusion of St Gorazd in a Polish calendar from Wiślica (probably of the fourteenth century) under 17 July, which is the date of his commemoration as one of the Seven Apostles of the Slavs (see p. 164) is interesting but could be explained as a fortuitous importation by Croat *glagoljaši* at that time. Monasteries for Benedictines using the Slav language were founded by Conrad II at Oleśnica (near Wrocław) in 1380, by Ladislas Jagiełło and Jadwiga at Kleparz (near Cracow) in 1390. The monks of the former came directly from Croatia, of the latter from the Emmaus monastery in Prague (see p. 112). The monasteries did not survive for long as Slav centres.

190 See especially P. David, *Les Bénédictins*, pp. 22 ff. The placing of the second metropolis at Sandomierz (e.g. H. Paszkiewicz, following Kętrzyński) raises profound scepticism. See also Lanckorońska, pp. 43 ff.

191 Szydłowski, fig. 1 (p. 12); Macůrek, *Češi a Poláci*, pl. 1; *Slownik*, vol. 2, s.v. *Kraków*, figs. 163–4.

192 *Onomastica* (Wrocław–Cracow), iv (1958).

193 See *Slownik*, vol. 1, pp. 103–4 (maps).

194 Lanckorońska, p. 34, quoting Nicholas of Hennefeld's *Annales Silesiae*, s.a. 967: 'slavicae seu henetae [Wendish] linguae usum...in sacris ecclesiasticis...inhibuit ac latina lingua concipi liturgiam precesque jussit'. An interdiction should imply widespread use of the Slav tongue there. It is perhaps remotely possible that this refers (if taken at its face value) to the local vernacular and not to Church Slavonic. We can agree with Lanckorońska that Nicholas is a late source (Leipzig, 1772) but not that it is a 'weighty' one.

195 See note 160 above. Tyniec may have been founded about 1044, on Aaron of Cologne's arrival in Poland, or, as P. David (*Les Bénédictins*, pp. 31ff.) judges, not till after his death, when the monks whom he had brought with him to Cracow finally settled there (*c*. 1060/1). See also Lanckorońska, pp. 98 ff. The brief of appointment of Aaron from Benedict IX (1046) directs that to him 'subiicimus omnes omnium episcopatuum parochias quae in toto regno sunt sclavonicae'. The phrase is generally held to be a later mendacious insertion.

196 Milik, *Święty Świerad*, pp. 28 and 35. The saint came from the Wiślica region. That he assumed the typical Eastern name of Andrew on migrating to Nitra in Slovakia hardly calls for comment.

197 Old Czech has *cierkev*, rarely *crkev*. Later Polish *cerkiew*, which appears in a number of place names scattered over the country, should indicate the presence of an Eastern rite church; Western rite churches are always *kościół* (from Czech *kostel*—used indifferently of all denominations). The problem needs further investigation (but see Klich, pp. 88 ff. and W. Taszycki, *Rozprawy i studia polonistyczne*, I, pp. 269 ff. (1958)). Later Czech *církev* is mainly used of a church as an organized body (československá církev). This sense is also recorded in Old Polish and is clearly a Czechism (e.g. in the *Kazania świętokrzyskie*).

198 *Thietmar*, iv, 45. *Salsae Cholbergensis*=Kołobrzeg (Kolberg, an important source of salt); Cracuaensem=Cracow; Wrotizlaensem=Wrocław (Breslau).

199 Mieszko II is judged by some to have been a devotee of the Slav language on the basis of a letter sent to him by Matilda of Lorraine in 1027 or 1028, with a gift of the Latin *Ordo romanus*. She asks: 'Quis enim praedecessorum tuorum tantas erexit ecclesias? quis in laudem Dei totidem coadunavit linguas? cum in propria et in latina Deum digne venerari posses, in hoc tibi non satis, graecam superaddere maluisti...' Text in *MPH*, I, 323–4; discussed by J. Umiński in *Roczniki humanistyczne* 4 (1957). Does *propria* signify Polish (for his private devotions) or Church Slavonic (for public worship)? His knowledge and approval of Greek is certainly interesting.

THE WENDS OF NORTH GERMANY

200 Wends: German-Latin *Windi*, *Winedi*, etc., by some considered a native Slav name but more probably transferred at a much earlier period to the Slavs from the Veneti, once a central European people. Obodrite may derive from *ob-odr-*=along the River Oder. Veletians: German-Latin *Wilzi*, etc.; the *Geographus bavarensis* (see p. 90) has *Uuilzi...regiones iiii*—i.e. a confederation of four tribes. *Regio* corresponds to the German *Gau*. I have adopted the simplest possible conventional forms for all these names.

201 *Einhardi Vita Karoli*, 12: '…Abodritos, qui cum Francis olim foederati erant'. See Gąssowski, pp. 91–2 (maps). The Obodrites had been allies *c.* 800–4 in Charlemagne's campaigns against the Danes, which already aimed at control of the Western end of the Baltic trade-route.

202 E.g. *Enhardi Fuldensis Annales* (*MGH, SS* I), s.a. 789: 'Karolus per Saxones iter faciens venit ad Albim fluvium habens in exercitu suo Francos, Saxones, Sorabos et Abodritos…Sclavorum qui vocantur Wilzi terram ingressus, magnis eos proeliis domuit ac dicione suae subiugavit'.

203 *Enh. Fuld. Ann.*, s.a. 821: 'aegritudine decubuit, perceptoque baptismi sacramento, defunctus est'. Several sources note (e.g. *Egil's Saga* 50) that the Scandinavians abroad were prone to accept the *prima signatio* as a temporary convenience when associating with Christians, without committing themselves to the further stages requisite for baptism. The same is probably true on this Slav frontier.

204 *Vita Sancti Anskarii*, cap. 13: '…legatum in omnibus circumquaque gentibus Sueonum sive Danorum necnon etiam Slavorum aliarumque in aquilonis partibus gentium constitutarum…delegavit' (*MGH, SS* II; written between 865 and 876 by his successor Archbishop Rimbert). Cf. Jaffé, 2574 (vol. I, p. 324). He had been Bishop since 831.

205 *Ibid.*, cap. 15: 'coepit quoque ex gente Danorum atque Slavorum nonnullos emere pueros, aliquos etiam ex captivitate redimere, quos ad servitium Dei educaret'.

206 For a summary of Scandinavian developments, whose further course cannot be followed here, see Bloch, vol. I, pp. 31 ff. German control of the Danish mainland (the islands remained centres of pagan resistance) made it possible to establish three bishoprics in the 940s but Denmark only became a fully Christian state with the baptism of Harald Bluetooth and the Christian zeal of his grandson Knut (Canute).

207 'In omnibus circumquaque gentibus Sueonum sive Danorum necnon etiam slauorum, vel in ceteris, ubicunque illis in partibus constitutis divina pietas ostium aperuerit, publicam evangelizandi tribui[mus] auctoritatem…' (Jaffé 2759, vol. I, p. 353). The date may be 858 rather than 864. Cf. note 204 above.

208 On the *limes sorabicus*, at whose main frontier stations (Bardowiek, Magdeburg, Erfurt, Forchheim, Regensburg) commercial exchanges took place, see also p. 324 n. 20. These exchanges were defined and regulated by Charlemagne in a capitulary of December 805 (*MGH, Leg.* i, pp. 131 ff.—§7, p. 133). See also G. Labuda in *Początki państwa polskiego*, vol. I (map—fig. 7, p. 65). That these Slavs were wild and hostile is shown by the categorical prohibition on the sale to them of all warlike material, especially swords. For the same reason selling of arms and horses to Scandinavians was forbidden throughout the ninth century.

209 Helmold (see note 213 below), i, 6: 'pervenerunt ad eos qui dicuntur Rani sive Ruiani et habitant in corde maris…postquam autem…Rani a fide defecerunt'.

210 The Slav towns became in fact models for the future Hanse cities as developed by the Germans. On Slav towns and commerce see J. Brankačk in *Hansische Studien* (*Forschungen zur mittelalterlichen Geschichte* 8, Berlin, 1961); also W. Kowalenko in *PRZ* 10 (1954); L. Leciejewicz in *Z polskich studiów slawistycznych* 3 (1963). Uznoim (Usedom) and Wologoszcz (Wolgast) traded mainly westwards to Rügen and the Atlantic. Ibrāhīm ibn Yaʿqūb's 'strong city by the sea' is one of these two; cf. Ebbo, *Vita Ottonis*, iii, 7 (*MGH, SS* xii; see p. 359 n. 171): *opulentissimam civitatem Hologast*. Wolin, to their east, traded more with Sweden and the Baltic generally.

211 The traffic southwards from the Baltic via Mainz, Verdun and Lyon was largely in the hands of Jews, sometimes called Radanites (Ibn Khordādhbeh's *Rādhānīya*), probably because their route followed the Rhône valley. Jews were at this time virtually the only professional international traders. See Lopez and Raymond, *Medieval trade in the Mediterranean world* (London, 1955), pp. 29 ff.; L. I. Rabinowitz, *Jewish merchant adventurers* (London, 1948).

212 See Helmold, i, 36: 'maior flaminis quam regis veneratio apud ipsos est'; and Saxo Grammaticus, *Gesta Danorum*, cap. xiv, *passim*. Nevertheless, since Adam of Bremen speaks of *sacerdotes* at Uppsala, where we know that there was no professional priesthood, the distinction of priest and chieftain among the Slavs should also be treated with some reserve.

213 The main chronicles are: Widukind of Corvey, *Res gestae Saxonicae*, written in the 60s of the tenth century (later extended to include all Otto I's reign); Thietmar of Merseburg, *Chronicon* (*c.* 1012–18); Adam of Bremen, *Gesta hammenburgensis ecclesiae pontificum* (*c.* 1074–6); Helmold of Bosau, *Chronica Slavorum* (*c.* 1170); Saxo Grammaticus, *Gesta Danorum* (to 1185). Widukind took relatively little note of the Slav world: Thietmar disliked all that he saw of it and was more interested in German conquest than in missions.

214 Thietmar, vi, 23: 'quamvis autem de hiis aliquid dicere perhorrescam'; *Adam*, i, 63: 'inutile videtur eorum acta scrutari qui non crediderunt'.

215 Wienecke, *Untersuchung* (see Bibliography). They are not unknown among the Balkan Slavs: cf. Hensel, *Die Slawen*, fig. 201 (p. 247)—a three-headed idol (*triglav*) from Croatia.

216 Svantovit was taken by the Christians to be the deity's name but it is somewhat more likely that the word should be interpreted as 'holy place', 'sanctuary': Arkona was a great oracular shrine. Slav *svęt*- meant 'numinous' and became the natural translation of Christian *holy* (ἅγιος, *sanctus*). The second component -*vit* appears in two other local names of deities (or shrines) —Rujevit (*rugievithus*) and Jarovit (*gerovitus*) and is indeed not uncommon in the most ancient stratum of Slav personal names in all areas. See also V. Machek in *Orbis Scriptus* (see Bibliography).

217 On sacred horses see G. Dumézil, *Le problème des Centaures* (Paris, 1929), especially p. 34.

218 *Gesta Danorum*, xiv (*c.* 1168): 'ingens in aede simulacrum, omnem humani corporis habitum granditate transcendens, quatuor capitibus toti-demque cervicibus mirandum perstabat e quibus duo pectus totidemque ter-gum respicere videbantur...'. See also Helmold's account of the destruction of a shrine near Oldenburg in 1156 (i, 83—*Conversio Pribizlai*), and the events at Stettin in 1124/5 as described by the Prüfening monk (*Life of Otto*, ed. Hofmeister, ii, 11–12).

219 See *Adam of Bremen*, iv, 26. It is fairly clear that the cult of Thor as at Uppsala influenced that of the storm- and war-god Perun among the East Slavs (see p. 254).

220 The notorious 'idol of Zbrucz', a tetracephalous pillar ascribed to the tenth century—but not accepted as genuine by all scholars—is discussed by B. A. Rybakov in Grabar and Lazarev, *Istorija russkogo iskusstva*, i, pp. 75ff. and Hensel, *Die Slawen*, p. 250. Recent discoveries have made the prevalence of such polycephalic pillars and their connection with Eastern Europe more probable: three were found in 1950 near Kamieniec Podolski, all four-sided and one with three faces (*Słownik*, vol. 2, pp. 55–6). Probably only at the greatest shrines, such as Arkona, was there a true statue with all limbs complete. Most were evidently of wood; a wooden Obodrite idol of uncertain date has been found at Behren-Lübchen in Mecklenburg. For a view of their possible Celtic descent see J. Rosen-Przeworska, *Tradycje celtyckie w obrzędowości protosłowian* (Ossol., 1964). See also Dittrich in *JGO* 9 (1961).

221 Labuda (*Fragmenty*, vol. 1, pp. 275–6) and others consider that Oldenburg belongs to 968, not 948. It was subordinate to Hamburg. For the probable limits of the sees see *ibid.*, pp. 276–7.

222 See *MGH, Diplomata reg. et imp. Germaniae*, vol. 1: Otto I, nos. 105 (p. 187) and 76 (p. 155). On Havelberg see Z. Sułowski in *Roczniki historyczne* 19 (1950), with map of the development of the diocese.

223 *Adam of Bremen*, ii, 23; iv, 1 (*MGH, SS* vii).

224 Migne, *PL* 133: *Joannis papae* xii *epistolae et privilegia*, no. 12 (col. 1027). Original endowment of the church: *MGH, Diplomata reg. et imp. Germaniae*, vol. 1, Otto I, nos. 14–16. The rebuilding of the monastery and church on a lavish scale began as early as 955. Only the crypt now preserves portions of the first cathedral, destroyed in 1207: see Beckwith, p. 86.

225 For the limits and endowments of these sees see Schlesinger, pp. 41 ff., 65 and 71. Merseburg was suppressed in 981 owing to a long quarrel with Bishop Giselher who demanded and eventually received promotion to Magdeburg. It was reconstituted on his death in 1004.

226 The story of the Holy Lance, the instrument of victory, is given by Schlesinger, pp. 21 ff. and by E. S. Duckett, *Death and Life in the Tenth Century* (Ann Arbor, 1967), pp. 53 ff.

227 This Stargard is not to be confused with Stargard in Pomerania. See Skalová, map 2.

228 Holtzmann, *Geschichte*, p. 289.

229 He was profoundly shocked (as was Thietmar the chronicler) by Henry II's sudden change of front in 1002/3 when he allied himself with the 'apostate' Ljutici to prevent their possible incorporation into a Polish empire (see his letter to Henry, *c.* 1008, *MPH*, i, no. 11, p. 226). The Bohemians and Poles did not act on any high principle in this: they were liable to side on occasion with their Slav cousins, if it suited them, e.g. in 990, when the

Ljutici were allies of Bohemia against Poland. Similarly, the Hobolane of Brandenburg were welcome allies of Bolesław Chrobry in the first decade of the eleventh century behind the German forward positions.

230   *Ann. Qued.* (*MGH, SS* III), s.a. 789: 'Carolus gentem Vilzorum subegit qui Liutici vocantur', is of course an anachronism. The names are in fact equivalent since *ljut-* is a common taboo replacement of **wlk-*=wolf.

231   Several contemporary variants, including Thietmar's *Riedegost*. See his description in *Chronicon*, vi, 23–4 (ed. Trillmich, pp. 266–8). The toponym is a possessive form of the common name Radogost, found all over the Slav world and recorded in its earliest form in Theophylakt Simocatta—'Αρδά-γαστος (*Historiae*, i, 7 etc.). The location of the shrine is still uncertain but most probably at the south end of the Tollensesee; see Skalová, map 15.

232   *Saxo Grammaticus*, xiv, s.a. 1136 (*MGH, SS* XXIX, p. 85). It will be remembered that Naaman took back Israelite soil to Damascus in order that he might continue to worship Yahweh there (2 Kings, 5, 1–9); cf. 1 Samuel, 4–6 (where however the Philistines find the possession of the ark of Yahweh too much for them) and Judges 11 (especially verse 24). Cf. also the tribal religion of the Goths (E. A. Thompson, *The Visigoths in the time of Ulfila*, Oxford, 1966, pp. 55 ff.).

233   *Helmold*, i, 83 (1156). Cf. also Herbord, *Life of Otto of Bamberg*, §§30–1 (1124). *Helmold* (i, 6) gives a much earlier instance of the limited understanding of the Wends, worshipping the (visible) St Vitus instead of the invisible God.

234   On the Wendish difficulties in understanding Christianity see H. D. Kahl in *Archiv für Kulturgeschichte* 44 (1962). For similar considerations in Scandinavia and England see H. R. Ellis Davidson, *Gods and Myths of North Europe* (1964), pp. 219 ff.

235   According to *Adam* (ii, 66)—*male christianus* (*c.* 1020). For the genealogy see Schmeidler, pp. 318 ff.

236   The career of this great churchman, whose influence extended to most of Scandinavia, will be found in his admirer, Adam of Bremen. On Gottschalk's fervent Christianity see *Adam*, iii, 19.

237   *Adam*, iii, 23: 'populos sclavorum iamdudum procul dubio facile converti posse ad christianitatem nisi obstitisset avaricia Saxonum'. Cf. *Helmold*, §84 (1156), referring to Pribislav of the Obodrites at Lübeck: 'principes enim nostri tanta severitate grassantur [harry] in hos ut propter vectigalia [taxes] et servitutem durissimam melior sit nobis mors quam vita'. The Bishop in reply admits the arrogant 'colonial' outlook of the laymen (not of the Church): 'Quod principes nostri hactenus abusi sunt gente vestra non est mirandum: non enim multum se delinquere arbitrantur in ydolatris et in his qui sunt sine Deo'.

238   *Helmold*, i, 20: 'Igitur omnes slavorum populi qui ad Aldenburgensem pertinebant curam toto tempore quo Godescalcus supervixit Christianam fidem devote tenuerunt' (no doubt exaggerated).

239   *Helmold*, i, 41 (*Electio Liuderi*). See Kahl in *Archiv für Kulturgeschichte* 44 (1962), pp. 102 ff. Cf. the story that the already Christian King Steinkel refused to destroy the great pagan temple at Uppsala.

240 *Adam*, ii, 43 (41 in *MGH, SS* vii).

241 *Helmold*, i, 57 (1143): 'Nonne vos terram slavorum subegistis et mercati eam estis in mortibus fratrum et parentum vestrorum? Cur igitur novissimi venitis ad possidendam eam? Estote primi et transmigrate in terram desiderabilem et incolite eam et participamini deliciis eius, eo quod vobis debeantur optima eius, qui tulistis eam de manu inimicorum'. Professor R. Koebner (*CEH*, I, pp. 84 ff.) appears to be surprised that, given that the Germans 'combined conquest and missionary work with thorough colonising activity... the enterprise was not a complete success. The Slavs attacked while the work was in progress'. The Slavs happened to live in those parts. Such words as 'enterprise' and 'work' are good examples of modern cant. Many Germans, then as now, seem to have subscribed to the view:

> Cet animal est très méchant:
> Quand on l'attaque il se défend.

The chronicler Thietmar of Merseburg was among them: Slav resistence to German pressure could only be due to *perfidia innata*.

242 Kötzschke, *Quellen*, p. 9: 'multimodis paganorum oppressionibus et calamitatibus diutissime oppressi, ad vestram suspiramus misericordiam... Gentiles isti pessimi sunt sed terra eorum optima, carne, melle, farina, avibus...Quapropter...hic poteritis et animas vestras salvificare et si ita placet optimam terram ad inhabitandum acquirere'.

243 How far Slav princes *called in* German immigrants deliberately, to improve, as some think, their farming methods, is a moot point. It seems unlikely that this formed any considerable proportion of the German immigration until a late period of the whole process. But as long as Wend society was still basically organized on tribe and clan there could of course be no true peasantry in the West European sense. See also *CEH*, I, pp. 52–3, 62, 83–4.

244 On *compellere intrare* see especially H. D. Kahl in *ZO* 4 (1955) and in *Miscellanea historiae ecclesiasticae* (*Bibliothèque de la Revue d'histoire ecclésiastique* 38, Louvain, 1961). The standard Church Slavonic translation of these words—which is probably that of SS Cyril and Methodios since it appears in the earliest codices—is: *ubědi vŭniti*—much nearer to 'persuade' than 'compel' (though the primary sense of *běda* is necessity, ἀνάγκη).

245 *Chronicon Boemorum*, s.a. 1147 (*Fontes rerum austriacarum, SS* v; *MPH* 2). The same policy of force was carried over against the heathen Prussians from 1226 by the German knights, with the added excuse that, as direct missionary work had for so long proved a failure, there was now no other course open.

246 *Helmold*, i, 68: [Duke Henry] 'quotiens enim offendissent eum Sclavi, admovit eis martiam manum, dederuntque ei pro vita simul et patria quicquid exigere voluisset. In variis autem expeditionibus...nulla de christianitate fuit mentio sed tantum de pecunia'. Cf. the detrimental effect of the exaction of the tithe on Charlemagne's Saxon missions: *MGH, Epp.* iv, *Alcuini epistolae*, no. 107 (*Decimae...Saxonum subverterunt fidem*); no. 110 (*melius est eam amittere quam fidem perdere*). For the tithe rights of Magdeburg see *MGH, Diplomata reg. et imp. Germaniae*, vol. 1: Otto I, nos. 222 (pp. 304–6)—

decimam quam Sclavani ad eandem urbem Magadaburg pertinentes persolvere debent...; 231; 232; 295 (p. 411); *ibid.*, vol. 2/i: Otto II, no. 118 (p. 131). In short, Christianity was made too expensive for neophytes, as the hesitation of the Slav chieftain Niklot exemplifies (*Helmold*, i, 84).

247 Account in *Saxo Grammaticus* (*MGH, SS* xxix, pp. 121 ff.), xiv, s.a. 1168 (written *c.* 1188). Main excavation by Schuchhardt in the 1920s. Only part of the shrine now survives owing to the erosion of the soft cliffs. See *Słownik*, s.v. *Arkona*.

248 See also *CEH*, i, pp. 63–4 on colonial policy. Aspects of the Germanisation of Austria (Ostmark) are explored by L. Havlík, *Staří Slované v rakouském Podunají v době od 6 do 12 století* (*RAV* 73/9, 1963).

Chapter 4.   The Balkan Slavs

BULGARIA

1 Asparuch's horde has been estimated at *c.* 10,000 all told; even if it was several times as large it was quite small in comparison with the number of Slavs which it soon dominated. The dialects of the Bulgars (including the Volga Bulgars) and Khazars (see p. 389 n. 4) were similar (the type is best preserved in modern Chuvash), but of a different branch from Osmanli Turkish. As with many conquering minorities, especially of nomads ruling over sedentary peoples, the Bulgars rapidly gave up their own tongue for that of their subjects, in this case Slavs. All that remains of it is a few dozen words in Balkan Slav; see Boev in *Bŭlgarski Ezik* 15 (1965).

2 See Grégoire in *BYZ* 17 (1944–5), pp. 100 ff. Recently Artamonov (*Istorija Khazar*, pp. 158 ff.) has doubted that this Kubrat was the Bulgar leader.

3 Terbel is usually credited with helping to raise the siege of Constantinople in 717/18 but there are grounds for supposing that it was his successor Kormisosh who already concluded the 716 Treaty. See Tsankova-Petkova in *Izsledvanija v chest na M. S. Drinov* (Sofia, 1960), pp. 615 ff. The treaty is mentioned in one of the rock inscriptions at Mádara (see p. 167).

4 See Moravcsik in *DOP* 15 (1961). The Hambarli inscription, dated by Venedikov (*BB* 1, 1962) to 813/14, provides further evidence.

5 Perhaps the monk ἐκ σκυθικοῦ γένους at the Studios monastery at this time was a Bulgar; see Alexander, *The Patriarch Nicephorus*, p. 101, quoting Theodore of Studios. On the baptised prisoners, whom Constantinople was loth to return, see Theophanes, *Chronographia* s.a. 6305 (Migne, *PG* 108, cols. 997 ff.).

6 See Beševliev in *IJS* 4 (1961). Some fifty Greek inscriptions are now known from the ninth century and quite a number of inscriptions in the Bulgar language in Greek letters: see, e.g. Venedikov in *Izvestija na bŭlg. arheol. institut*, 15 (1946), figs. 53–4 (pp. 148–9).

7 A Greek ἀκολούθιον, published by Follieri and Dujčev in *BYZ* 33 (1963), shows how the Greeks at this time (811–13) reckoned those killed in action against the Bulgars as martyrs for the cause of Christendom. Krum had also acted according to custom in making himself a drinking-cup from the skull of the Byzantine Emperor whom he had defeated and slain. The potent magic involved is clear from Paul the Deacon's account (*History of the Lombards*, Bk. i, ch. 27) of the similar fate of the Gepid chief slain by Alboin.

8 The other named bishops are George of Develt, Leo of Nicaea. The notice in the *Menologium Grecorum* (Migne, *PG* 117, col. 276, §132) hesitates between implying that Manuel was martyred at once by Krum (811) or after Leo the Armenian's accession (813).

9 See Dujčev, pp. 193 ff., quoting St Theodore of Studios.

10 Moravcsik shows (*DOP* 15 (1961)) that he cannot have been born before 817 or thereabouts. The family's return to Constantinople would fall in the 830s. Some however put his birth as late as *c.* 836. His father was probably Armenian, his mother Slav.

11 According to Archbishop Theophylakt's *Martyrium SS. 15 illustrium martyrum* (Migne, *PG* 126, §§29–33, cols. 191 ff.) the conversion of the one was brought about by a Greek prisoner of war, Kinnamon, a slave in Omurtag's household. But Theophylakt's stories are not very reliable.

12 See P. Lemerle, *Philippes et la Macédoine orientale à l'époque chrétienne et byzantine* (Paris, 1945), p. 135, who dates the inscription *c.* 837. Presjan is the Slav form of Persian (ὁ Περσιάνος).

13 That Boris was on the point of accepting Christianity from his new ally Louis is supported by Papal documents of 864, e.g. *MGH, Epp.* vi, *Nicolai I papae epistolae*, no. 26, §9: 'quia vero dicis quod christianissimus rex speret quod ipse rex Vulgarorum ad fidem velit converti et iam multi ex ipsis Christiani facti sint, gratias agimus Deo...'. Cf. p. 327 n. 64.

14 For an interpretation of the details of the war see P. Petrov in *BB* 2 (1966).

15 Vaillant and Lascaris (*RES* 13 (1933)) favour 864, surely correctly. The campaign against Bulgaria, concerted with Serbian and Croatian contingents, must have been begun in late 863 after the great Byzantine victory over the Moslems on 3 September of that year in North Asia Minor. This released the necessary troops. The Balshi inscription (Vaillant and Lascaris, *loc. cit.*; Ivanov, *Bǔlgarski starini*, pp. 12–16) cannot be taken to prove that the date 6374 (=September 865–August 866) there given refers specifically to Boris's baptism; it only proves that he was already a Christian (ὁ ἄρχων Βουλγαρίας Βορὴς ὁ μετονομασθεὶς Μιχαήλ). The *Annales Bertiniani* are also on the late side, with the statement s.a. 866 (*MGH, SS* i, p. 473): 'Rex Bulgarorum qui praecedente anno, Deo inspirante et signis atque afflictionibus in populo regni sui monente, Christianus fieri meditatus fuerat, sacrum baptisma suscepit;' cf. *ibid.*, s.a. 864: 'qui christianum se fieri velle promiserat'. This may be explained as recording the moment when Boris's ecclesiastical allegiance had already become a prominent international question. The date 6366 in the *Russian Primary Chronicle* may also represent 865/6. Cf. also Patriarch Photios's *Encyclical Letter* to the Eastern patriarchs (Migne, *PG* 102, cols. 721 ff.).

16 The Pope had finally declared Photios improperly elected (863) and the ecclesiastical status of the greater part of the Balkans was at stake. See pp. 75 ff. On the frontiers of Bulgaria in general see G. Tsankova-Petrova in *VV* 17 (1960).

17 Cf. *Responsa Nicolai papae*, no. 17 (see note 20) and *Ann. Bert.*, s.a. 866 (*MGH, SS* 1, pp. 473–4: *Hincmari Remensis annales*).

18 *Herbordi Dialogus*, iii, 3 (cf. p. 359 n. 174).

19 At least not later than May 866 (*Izvori* 8, pp. 59 ff.; Migne, *PG* 102, *Photii Patriarchae Epistolae*, 8, cols. 628 ff.).

20 The *Responsa Nicolai I papae ad consulta Bulgarorum* will be found in Migne, *PL* 119, cols. 978–1016; *MGH, Epp.* vi, pp. 568 ff. and *Izvori* 7. Thus Boris wished to know if, as Christians, they could continue to wear the traditional Bulgar horseman's dress of trousers (no. 58). This was of vital importance since it is precisely a reform of this nature (those of Peter the Great in Russia and Kemel Atatürk in Turkey are conspicuous examples) which can have fatal consequences for the reformer. On the possible source of the questions see also Duthilleul, p. 83.

21 See Dujčev, pp. 125 ff. and Dennis in *OC* 24 (1958). Greek practices which differ from Roman are touched on in nos. 6, 54, 55, 57, 66 and 94.

22 See Dujčev, pp. 107 ff.

23 No. 72: 'eligendus est inter eos [bishops] unus qui, si non patriarcha, certe archiepiscopus appellandus sit'.

24 *Ann. Fuld.*, s.a. 867 (*MGH, SS* 1). It should also be noted that Boris's relative Peter, his envoy to Rome, was also evidently a convinced Christian, but we do not know for how long.

25 Photios's tract against *filioque*, Περὶ τῆς τοῦ Ἁγίου Πνεύματος μυσταγωγίας (Migne, *PG* 101), is one of his most important works.

26 The success of the Papal mission and the indignation of Constantinople can be judged from the following correspondence: *MGH, Epp.* vii, pp. 403–15; *Epp.* vi, no. 100 (23 October 867). It should however be noted that all the episcopal leaders of the Papal mission appear to have been in Rome at the time of Nicholas's death.

27 Further details in Dujčev, pp. 183 ff. It was made clear that neither Formosus nor the deacon Marinus, too important to the Pope, could be spared (*Marino atque Formoso exceptis*).

28 *Anastasii Bibliothecarii Historia de vitis romanorum pontificum* (Migne, *PL* 128, col 1391–5). See also his *Interpretatio Synodi viii generalis* (Migne, *PL* 129; *MGH, Epp.* vii, pp. 403 ff., esp. p. 411).

29 His name is not known for certain. Various sources suggest Nicholas, George, Joseph and Stephen. See V. Swoboda in *BB* 2 (1966).

30 Summary by Dvornik in *Berichte XI Int. Byz. Kongress* (Munich, 1958), pp. 32 ff. See also his fundamental work, *The Photian Schism* (1948).

31 *MGH, Epp.* vii, *Johannis VIII Epistolae*, no. 66: 'Noli ergo sequi Grecos, fili carissime, quia argumentis semper fallacibus student, semper dolosis intendunt versutiis...'. See further Papal letters to Boris (878–9) in *MGH, Epp.* vii, nos. 66, 182, 192, 198; to Boris's brother (April 878), no. 70; to Peter, a Bulgarian magnate (October 878), no. 67. The letters to Patriarch

Ignatios (no. 68) and the Greek hierarchy in Bulgaria (no. 71), both dated April 878 (Ignatios was already dead), are virtual ultimata giving Ignatios a month to recall his Greeks on pain of excommunication. Fragmentary earlier letters to Boris (872/3 and 874/5): *ibid.*, *App.*, pp. 277, 294. Most of these letters are also reprinted in *Izvori* 7.

32 Pope John's letters both to the Emperor and to Photios, presented to the *Pseudo-synodus photiana* (879), as Rome always called it, rehearse what the Holy See considered its rights: Mansi, xvii, especially col. 406 ('ne frater et comminister noster Photius sanctissimus, neque quiquam successorum ejus, posthac ordinationes faciat in Bulgaria...') and col. 487 (cap. i: 'Ne posthac in Bulgaria ordinet antistes constantinopolitanus, neque pallium eo mittat...').

33 'Ignatius in Vulgarum regione consecrare praesumpsit antistitem' (10 November 871: *Hadriani epistolae*, *MGH*, *Epp.* vi, no. 41, p. 760); cf. note 32 above. The term will be found in most areas, sometimes for archbishop, e.g. Smičiklas, *CD*, vol. 2, no. 2 (1102): 'Pascalis episcopus...Dominico Racusie [Ragusa] civitatis antistiti...'; cf. *ibid.*, no. 3 with *archiepiscopo*,—sometimes for bishop. No early seals of the Bulgarian primate have survived to prove his exact title.

34 Discussion by V. Swoboda in *BB* 2 (1966), who suggests that the Byzantine authorities were following their habitual penchant for archaism in designing the new Bulgarian situation on that of Justiniana Prima, the territories of which diocese were now largely in Bulgarian hands.

35 Belgrade (to use its modern name) had become Bulgarian in the 820s and apparently became one of the Greek bishoprics set up or maintained after 870; see Theophylakt's *Life of St Clement*, §§43–8 and Pope John VIII's letter to Boris dated 16 April 878 (*MGH*, *Epp.* vii, no. 66, *ad fin.*).

36 At an unknown date the names of Boris and his family were recorded in a Latin *Tetrevangel* used as a Visitor's Book in a prominent Istrian monastery (perhaps Devin-Duino near Trieste). The manuscript is now known as the *Cividale Gospels* (*MSM* 7, pp. 382–4). Here also appear the names of Svjatopluk, Kotsel and several Croat princes. Whether Boris's visit was in person or by proxy cannot be decided for certain. In either case the monastery is a likely source of information about the Moravian mission, the existence of Christian scriptures in Slav translation and the Papal attitude towards them. See also F. Kos, *Gradivo*, vol. 2, pp. 248–56.

37 *VM* 13: 'udriža otŭ učenikŭ jego popa i dijakona sŭ kŭnigami'. The Cyrillomethodian pupils who were redeemed in the Venice slave-market (885/6) and were considered important enough to send to the Capital at official expense were also available. See p. 82.

38 Theophylakt's *Life of St Clement*, §51. The Seven Teachers (ἅγιοι ἑπτάριθμοι) are commemorated on 17 July.

39 Text in Migne, *PG* 126; A. Milev, *Teofilakt Ohridski: Zhitie na Kliment ohridski* (Greek text with Bulgarian translation *en face*) (Sofia, 1955). See also Kiselkov, *Sveti Kliment ohridski* (Sofia, 1941).

40 *BB* 1 (1962); see also Kussef in *SR* 27 (1948) and Dujčev in *SF* 19 (1960). Milev accepts Theophylakt's authorship.

41 Text in Teodorov-Balan, II, 177–8; Ivanov, *Bŭlgarski starini*, no. 34 (pp. 314–21). Blg. tr. in Kiselkov, *Sveti Kliment ohridski*. See also Lavrov, pp. 193–5.

42 Texts in Ivanov, *op. cit.*, no. 35 (pp. 322–7). See *Clemens velicensis* in Martynov *sub* 27/7 and 23/11.

43 Lavrov, pp. 181–92; Ivanov, *op. cit.*, no. 32 (pp. 305–11). Blg. tr. in Kiselkov, *op. cit.* See also Kussef in *SR* 29 (1950). There is no good reason to accept a late Bulgarian tradition that Clement and Naum were brothers.

44 Theophylakt's *Life of St Clement*, §53.

45 Theophylakt's *Life of St Clement*, §67.

46 Plan in *Słownik*, s.v. *Macedonia*, fig. 71; Mavrodinov, pp. 99–102 (with figures). See also p. 180.

47 Mavrodinov, pp. 90 ff.

48 Mavrodinov, p. 31, fig. 24.

49 Dujčev, pp. 183 ff., dating it *c.* 867.

50 Mavrodinov, p. 44, fig. 38.

51 Plan of Pliska in Gąssowski, p. 152; Mavrodinov, pp. 92 ff. (with figures).

52 Mavrodinov, pp. 54 ff.

53 St. Stančev in *Antike und Mittelalter in Bulgarien*; D. Krandžalov in *OCA*, vol. 3, against Mavrodinov, pp. 92 ff.

54 Theophylakt (or the author of the *Life of St Clement*), §60, evidently thought that he died on Symeon's accession in 893. Boris is commemorated (without formal canonization) in the Slav churches on 2 May.

55 On his authorship of *VM* etc., see pp. 30–1. His original writings may have started in the later Moravian years: the second *Freising text* has an evident relation to one of his homilies; see p. 72. For a complete list of works attributed to Clement see E. Georgíev, *Raztsvetŭt*, pp. 132 ff.

56 See *Atlas po bŭlgarska istorija* (Sofia, 1963), map 10 and *Słownik*, s.v. *Macedonia*, fig. 69. The frontier town of Kutmichevitsa on the south was probably Glavinitsa (near Valona), mentioned in the *Life of St Clement*, which later became a suffragan see of Ohrid or Durazzo. The Balshi inscription (see note 15 above) was a frontier marker not far from Glavinitsa. The site of Stari Devol has not yet been archaeologically investigated. Kutmichevitsa was apparently part of a larger region known as Κοτόκιος or Κοτόκιον (Theophylakt's *Life of St Clement*, §53), an equally obscure term.

57 Βουλγάρῳ γλώσσῃ πρῶτος ἐπίσκοπος (Theophylakt's *Life of St Clement*, §20; Migne, *PG* 126, col. 1227).

58 OCS *Klimentŭ veličĭsky* (e.g. in *Cod. Ass.*); Greek ἐπίσκοπος Βελίκας, with which we may range the emendation *episkopŭ vŭ Likii* > *Velikii* in one text of the *Uspenije sv. Kirilla* (see Lavrov, p. 157) and ἐπίσκοπος Τιβεριουπόλεως ἤτοι Βελίκας in the 'Ducange List' of Bulgarian bishops, dating from the mid-twelfth century but compiled at Ohrid from the archiepiscopal archives and therefore perhaps as reliable evidence as any. In contrast the *Life* attributed to Theophylakt has ἐπίσκοπος Δρεβενίτζας (or Δρεμβίτζας) ἤτοι Βελίτζας (§§61–2; cf. also §70), which yields an equally reasonable Slav place name *Velitsa* (less probably *Bělitsa*).

59 Tunicki, *Sv. Kliment, episkop slovenski* (Sergiev Posad, 1913), referring to *Life*, §21. See also Snegarov in *INBI* 10 (1962) and in *OCA*, vol. 2. Tunicki's further suggestions that (1) the see was in the Rhodope mountains and (2) the name is a corruption of some Slav tribal name (as often the case with missionary bishoprics, e.g. ὁ τῶν Σερβίων), are both improbable. The suffragan sees of Philippopolis entitled ὁ Δραμίτζης and ὁ Βελικίας (cf. p. 322 n. 23) in the *Notitia* of Leo VI (886–912) are unlikely to be relevant. There may have been confusion in later texts.

60 'ὑπὸ Μεθοδίου ἐπίσκοπος κατάστας'. Cf. Lavrov, p. 194; *Sinodik* of Tsar Boril (1211), §90 (Drinov copy): *episkopu velikie moravi*, which is ambiguous.

61 *Slovenska pismenost* (Ohrid, 1966), Section 8, discusses the iconography of St Clement.

62 Georgiev, *Raztsvetŭt*, pp. 154–5.

63 See *Slovnik*, s.v. *Macedonia*, fig. 70.

64 See D. Bošković and K. Tomovski, *L'architecture médiévale d'Ohrid* in *Recueil de travaux, éd. spéciale publiée à l'occasion du Xe anniversaire de la fondation du Musée et dédiée au XIIe Congrès international des études byzantines* (Ohrid, 1961); Stričević in *OCA*, vol. 1 and in *ZRVI* 8 (1964); *Slovenska pismenost*, section 7; *CMH*, iv/2, pp. 311 ff. Martyrium = memorial chapel.

65 The present monastery church is not the earliest structure: his own church (*c.* 910) has now been identified underneath it. See Kussef in *SR* 29 (1950) and *Slovenska pismenost*, section 7 (plan opp. p. 93).

66 Liutprand of Cremona, *Antapodosis*, iii, 29 (*MGH*, *SS* III, p. 309): 'Hunc etenim Simeonem emiargon, id est semigrecum, esse aiebant.'

67 *Ibid.* The Academy was principally for the secular education of civil servants.

68 Plan in *Atlas po bŭlgarska istorija*, map 14a.

69 Plan in Goshev, p. 31, fig. 27; Mavrodinov, p. 150, fig. 144; A. Raschenov in *Izvestija na bŭlg. arheol. institut*, 10 (1936), figs. 140–1 (p. 219); V. Ivanova-Mavrodinova in *OCA*, vol. 3, pp. 144–5. 'Golden' no doubt from the gold background of the mosaics, quite new to Bulgarian eyes. See also Stričević in *OCA*, vol. 1 and D. Bošković, *ibid.*

70 Baptisteries of the fifth–sixth centuries at Stobi, Caričin Grad, Ohrid and its neighbourhood, etc., which would provide convenient models, are studied by I. Nikolaević in *ZRVI* 9 (1966). See also Stričević in *ZRVI* 8 (1964).

71 Ceramic tiles became a prominent feature of Persian Moslem art and thence of Ottoman art; their origin may be Central Asian. The Bulgars arrived in the Balkans with far from negligible Sassanid elements in their culture, superficially visible in the use of such Persian names as Asparuch (Isperich) and Persian (Presjam) (see p. 368 n 12). On tiles see D. Talbot Rice, *Byzantine Art*, p. 115 (fig. 114).

72 Goshev, pp. 51 ff. and plates 3a, 3b.

73 Mavrodinov, pp. 167 ff. Some half-dozen monasteries have been identified in and about the capital, all founded before the destruction of the city by John Tzimiskés in 972.

74 *Shestodnev*, Part 6 *ad init.* (see p. 177).

75 The authenticity of this is not universally accepted; see Dvornik, *The Slavs* (1956), p.130 (with references). Symeon's aspirations can be followed in the sequence of Patriarch Nicholas's letters (Migne, *PG* 111, letters 14–31, especially 18 (921) and 28 (925). Dölger points out (*Byzanz*, p. 152) that the correspondence was carried on by Nicholas as Symeon's confessor since the Emperor could not demean himself to parley with a rebel.

76 For a description of the meeting of Romanos and Symeon see Runciman, *The Emperor Romanus Lecapenus*, pp. 91–2.

77 So great was Greek hatred of Symeon that several historians record solemnly the tale that sympathetic magic was used to encompass his death. See Dujčev, pp. 207 ff.

78 See *Liutprandi legatio*, §19 (*MGH, SS* III, p. 351). On the Byzantine system of diplomatic hierarchy see Dölger, *Byzanz*, pp. 159 ff. The special precedence accorded at Court to the Bulgarians—often diplomatically referred to as οἱ φίλοι Βούλγαροι—can be seen in Constantine's *De cerimoniis*, e.g. cap. 33 (Vogt I/i, p. 129). On the titles used by Bulgarian rulers from Krum to Symeon see also V. Beševliev in *BZ* 55 (1962).

79 For a map of the Bulgarian church in the tenth century see *Słownik*, vol. 3, fig. 229 (p. 495).

80 See, e.g. the *Khronograf* (1512), §171.

81 'učeniků sy methodovŭ, arhiepiskopa Moravy' (see E. Georgiev in *Sbornik...Teodorov-Balan* (1955), p. 209).

82 The section Easter–Pentecost (τὸ γὰρ ἀπὸ τῆς καινῆς κυριακῆς ἄχρι τῆς πεντεκοστῆς ψαλλόμενον τοτὲ δὴ συνετέλεσε—§73).

83 It is not certain whether the *Chronicle* (Χρονικὸν σύντομον, Migne, *PG* 110) of George the Monk (Hamartolós), ending in 842, was first translated in Bulgaria or Russia, under the title *Vremennik*. It can scarcely be earlier than the middle of the eleventh century. Another later version, certainly made in Bulgaria, was current also in Serbia (*Letovnik*). On historical writing in general see Angelov in *BB* 2 (1966).

84 The title *exarch* is usually interpreted as legate of the Patriarch of Constantinople accredited to an autocephalous church. But it had other uses. Kuev is probably right (*INBI* 14–15 (1964)) in equating it here with περιοδευτής, which might be translated 'visitor'—an official responsible for Christian education and discipline within a large province.

85 OCS *Shestodnev*; ed. by R. Aitzetmüller (Graz, 1958–   ). The earliest extant manuscript is a Serbian one of 1263.

86 Ἔκδοσις ἀκριβὴς τῆς ὀρθοδόξου πίστεως, the third part of his Πηγὴ γνώσεως. It is not a complete translation. For the Preface see Teodorov-Balan, II, 142.

87 Texts: Lavrov, pp. 162 ff.; Ivanov, *Bŭlgarski Starini*, no. 53 (pp. 440–6); Teodorov-Balan, II, 143–5; Kuev in *INBI* 10 (1962), giving variants. See also Dostál in *BSL* 24 (1963); Tkadlčík in *BSL* 25 (1964), with full details of the manuscripts. Kuev (*BB* 2 (1966)) has pointed out a late tenth-century Georgian parallel—by the Georgian monk John Zosimos of Sinai.

88 'Udobĕe bo estĭ poslĕdi tvoriti neže prŭvoje sŭtvoriti'.

89 This is suggested by the use of Rastits for Rastislav (of Moravia) and of *blatenĭskŭ* in Kotsel's title, signifying Mosapurc (*urbs paludorum*; see p. 25), which was misunderstood in later copyings.

90 See Georgiev, *Raztsvetŭt*, p. 168.

91 Migne, *PG* 100, cols. 1001 ff. (patriarch 806–15). The same source is used for an historical entry in Symeon's *Encyclopaedia*; see Angelov in *BB* 2 (1966). On Constantine of Preslav's works see also *Istorija na bŭlgarskata literatura*, vol. 1, pp. 112 ff.

92 Vaillant and Puech, *Le Traité contre les Bogomiles de Cosmas le Prêtre* (Paris, 1945). See also Dujčev in *WS* 8 (1963).

93 Georgiev, *Raztsvetŭt*, p. 275.

94 The apocryphal *Book of Enoch*, a type of work especially popular among sectarians (see p. 235), was translated in Symeon's reign an dnow only survives in various OCS versions. On apocrypha in general see also Dvornik, *The Slavs* (1956), pp. 184–5; Ivanov, *Bogomilski knigi*, pp. 60 ff.

95 See Dölger, *Regesten*, nos. 729, 737, 739; *Russian Primary Chronicle*, s.a. 6479 (971). The Russians drove as far south as Plovdiv (Philippopolis), having switched from Byzantine to Bulgarian allies in 969/70.

96 The sources for the period are discussed by N. Adontz in *Mémoires de l'Académie royale de Belgique, classe des lettres...II Série*, vol. 39 (1938). It is far from certain whether the resistance movement was headed by the Komitopouloi before the accession of Basil (976), perhaps not before 980. See also J. Ferluga in *ZRVI* 9 (1966). The best literary account of the downfall of Bulgaria is still that of Schlumberger (*L'Epopée byzantine à la fin du X siècle*, vol. 2, cap. 6–7).

97 A. Grabar has shown (*ZRVI* 8 (1964)) that this church was used as an archiepiscopal cathedral before Samuel's move to Ohrid.

98 See Dölger, *Regesten* no. 806 (*c.* 1018): ' Πολλῶν ὄντων καὶ μεγάλων τῶν παρὰ τοῦ φιλανθρώπου Θεοῦ δεδωρημένων τῇ βασιλείᾳ ἡμῶν ἀγαθῶν κατὰ διαφόρους καιροὺς καὶ ἀριθμὸν ὑπερβαινόντων, τοῦτο ἐστὶ παρὰ ἐξαίρετον τὸ προσθήκην γενέσθαι τῇ ῥωμαϊκῇ ἀρχῇ καὶ τὴν τῶν Βουλγάρων γενέσθαι ὑπὸ ζυγόν ...'.

99 Map of Bulgarian expansion in *Slownik*, vol. 3, fig. 69 (p. 142), s.v. *Macedonia*. Cf. Snegarov, *Ohridskata patriarshija*, ch. 3.

100 See especially Kedrenos, Σύνοψις ἱστοριῶν (Migne, *PG* 122), §530. Imperial charters of the years 1019–25 show that the land and revenues of the church were left more or less intact 'as in the time of Peter and Samuel': Dölger, *Regesten*, nos. 806–8. See Litavrin, pp. 74 ff.; Snegarov, *Ohridskata patriarshija*, chs. 4–5; Ivanov, *Bŭlgarski starini*, pp. 555–9; B. Granić in *BYZ* 12 (1937).

101 V. Mošin in *TODL* XIX (1963). The acts of the Synod of Constantinople held in 1140 (Mansi, xxi, cols. 551 ff.) provided one of many convenient pretexts for the destruction of Slav books since the Synod had particularly attacked certain heterodox works in Greek, tainted, or thought to be tainted, with Bogomilism (see pp. 227 ff.), and decreed their destruction.

102 Litavrin, p. 265. See also *Slownik*, vol. 3, fig. 230 (p. 496); *Atlas po bŭlgarska istorija*, map 15. The maximum was about thirty sees.

103 V. J. Đurić, *Crkva Svete Sofije u Ohridu* (1963), pls. 10–19. Further alterations and additions were made in the early fourteenth century.

104 V. Laurent, *Le corpus des sceaux*, vol. v/2 (1965), no. 1493, estimating *c.* 1088/9–*c.* 1107/8, but the latter date is very uncertain since he did not die till *c.* 1126.

105 *Slovenska pismenost*, section 9.

106 Auty, pp. 72–3 (dated 993).

107 See, e.g. the colophon reproduced by Ivanov, *Bŭlgarski starini*, p. 237. See pp. 300–1.

108 See particularly the so-called *Short Life of St Cyril* or *Uspenije Kirillovo* (Teodorov-Balan, ii, 115). The *Life of Naum* has acquired a similar bias: '...iže togda prohoždahu vse strany bolgarskie podvizajuštee se obraštati jazycy' (Teodorov-Balan, ii, 136). The late Serbian text known as the *Solun Legend* (Teodorov-Balan, ii, 110; Ivanov, *Bŭlgarski starini*, no. 26, pp. 282–3) has nothing to do with Constantine–Cyril. The Metropolitan John mentioned therein is no doubt the late seventh-century Metropolitan of Saloniki, present at the VIth Council.

109 On the barbarians see E. Stanescu in *ZRVI* 9 (1966) and N. Bănescu, *Les Duchés byzantins*.

110 Migne, *PL* 214 cols. 1112 ff.: *Innocentii III papae epistolae*, no. 115 (Kalojan to the Pope), no. 116 (Pope to Kalojan), dated 1202. His portrait may be seen in the church at Bojana near Sofia, built and decorated from 1259.

111 On Innocent III's policy see Ullmann, p. 112. Cf. also Toynbee, *A Study of History*, vol. 4, pp. 592 ff.

112 Thus during the years 1204–17 Bulgaria contained two autocephalous archbishoprics—Tŭrnovo and Ohrid—an unusual situation. Map of the Balkans *c.* 1210 in Stadtmüller, p. 212.

113 The full history of Theodore's attempt to become the leader of the Greek world and heir presumptive to a restored Empire at Constantinople is given by D. M. Nicol, *The Despotate of Epirus* (Oxford, 1957). See also pp. 219 ff.

114 For a recent review of archaeological investigation see K. Mijatev in *AAH* 17 (1965).

CROATIA AND DALMATIA

115 Rački, *Documenta* (*MSM* 7), no. 163/53 (p. 258); Migne, *PL* 77, col. 1092. The Pope went on: 'Affligor in his quae iam in vobis patior; conturbor quia per Histriae aditum iam ad Italiam intrare coeperunt'.

116 *DAI*, cap. 30 (Βελοχρωβάτοι). Dvornik's commentary on chapters 29–31 of this work (ed. Moravcsik and Jenkins, vol. 2, pp. 94 ff.) is the most exhaustive. The information of chapter 30 (a later insertion) was clearly gathered by Byzantine officials on the Dalmatian coast.

117 On the much disputed etymology of the name HRVAT (Croat), which may be Iranian, see H. Łowmiański, *Początki Polski*, vol. 2, pp. 127 ff.; *Słownik*, vol. 3, p. 357.

118 Croats often try to claim the whole Adriatic coast as original Croat settlements, the northern half being known, especially in the tenth century, as *White Croatia*, the southern half as *Red Croatia* (*red*, in the terminology of various Asiatic peoples, especially the Turkic group, means 'south', *white*— 'west'—hence also *White Russia*). But these were purely political terms. The historical dialectology of Serbo-Croat does not give much support to the view that typical Croat dialects ever extended south of their present frontier on the River Néretva, plus various small strips and offshore islands later forming the Republic of Ragusa (consult P. Ivić, *Die serbocroatischen Dialekte*, vol. I (Hague, 1958); I. Popović, *Geschichte der serbocroatischen Sprache* (Wiesbaden, 1960)).

119 E. Mâle, *The early churches of Rome*, p. 74; Rački, *Documenta*, no. 166 (p. 277); Kehr P. F., *Italia pontificia*, vol. 7, pt. 2—*Histria*, no. 5 (p. 203).

120 On the infiltration of the Slavs into the coastal towns see Kowalenko in *PSL* 9 (1959). Dubrovnik-Ragusa is a typical case. Dubrovnik was at first the Slav *grad* on the mainland opposite Ragusa (the Italian *Rocca del rè Bodino*). Slav names appear in Ragusan documents from the early eleventh century but the two parts did not coalesce into one town until the thirteenth century. Ragusan documents gradually change from Latin to bilingual to Slav (by the fourteenth century) and finally to Italian.

121 *DAI*, cap. 31, *ad init.*

122 Migne, *PL* 87, col. 1226A (Pope Agatho to Emperor Constantine IV at the time of the VIth Œcumenical Council). The reference is only to *Slavs* but the sequence of peoples mentioned suggests the more accessible Slavs near the Adriatic.

123 Perojević, *Ninski Biskup* (1939), p. 19. Date uncertain; perhaps as late as the first decade of the ninth century.

124 The Frankish client prince Braslav occasionally figures in Western annals, e.g. in campaigns against Great Moravia (Rački, *Documenta*, no. 193, pp. 379–81) but church affairs are not illuminated.

125 An emissary of the Narentans is alleged to have been baptised in Venice in the time of Doge John Particiaco (829–36). Despite Venice's concern for their conversion as an inducement to their abandoning piracy, this act was apparently not decisive. The incident is recorded in the Venetian chronicle of Andrea Dandolo (book 8, ch. 3, s.a. 829).

126 *Fol.* 245ᵛ, 246, 246ᵛ. See V. Novak, *Najstariji dalmatinski rukopis* (Split, 1923), especially pp. 56 ff.

127 I. Popović in *ZRVI* 5 (1958).

128 Šišić, *Priručnik*, p. 118, no. 5; Jelić, *Dvorska kapela*, pl. xviii (fig. 34).

129 Šišić, *op. cit.*, p. 119, no. 6, Jelić, *op. cit.*, pl. viii (fig. 12).

130 Dyggve, cap. vi. The no longer extant St Vitus at Zadar is claimed as the model for Holy Cross at Nin. Other relevant churches at Zadar are St Donatus, St Peter and St Ursula.

131 See Perojević, *Ninski biskup* (1939), p. 28.

132 *Ibid.*, p. 30.

133 For a view favouring Zadar rather than Aquileia see *DAI*, vol. 2 (Commentary), pp. 125–7 (by F. Dvornik), and Dvornik in *Cyrillo-*

Methodiana (*SLF* 6). Slav names appear relatively early in the town of Zadar (tenth century), suggesting an even earlier absorption of Slav blood into its population. There can be little doubt that Zadar counted for much, being after all the nearest centre of civilisation to Nin.

134 Ostojić, vol. 2, pp. 299 ff.

135 Perojević, *Ninski biskup*, pp. 66 ff., would like to identify the Prince 'Montemer' of Pope John VIII's letter (Friedrich, *Codex* I, no. 16; *MGH*, *Epp.* VII, no. 18, p. 282) with the Croatian Mutimir and assign to it a date *c*. 878/9, on the grounds that the Pope could scarcely encourage the Serbian Mutimir (*regnabat c.* 850–91; see p. 208) to return to the ecclesiastical allegiance of his 'predecessors' (*progenitorum*), since he was the first Christian ruler of those parts. Moreover the supposed connection with Methodios's see of Sirmium (see p. 67) is held to be very improbable. It was the Croats Zdeslav and Mutimir who had switched their ecclesiastical allegiance to Byzantine Split. Date apart (the transmitted date of the letter is May 873), the only emendation required is *pannonensium > nonensium*. But it is quite clear that the date must be correct: the Pope sent off a considerable number of letters about the *pannonensis diocesis* (or *episcopatus*) precisely in 873 when the rehabilitation of Methodios required energetic measures (see p. 70). The Pope no doubt knew that the Serbian Mutimir had just received or was about to receive a bishop from Constantinople, who might even be made a suffragan of Byzantine Split. As he was engaged in trying to reduce the ecclesiastical interests of both Aquileia and Constantinople along the Dalmatian coast and to recover his influence in Bulgaria, he would naturally exhort the Serbian ruler not to tie himself to the Eastern church. Mutimir's Christian predecessors are admittedly fabulous; pre-invasion Latin sees are what the Pope had in mind, part of that *Illyricum* which Leo had filched from Rome in the eighth century.

136 Dvornik (*Mélanges Ch. Diehl* (Paris, 1930), vol. I, pp. 61 ff.) is inclined to date the erection of a Papal bishopric to 860, when the dispute with Constantinople over Illyricum as a whole started in earnest. Others have put it earlier or later. But continuity cannot be proved from Trpimir's reign.

137 Dvornik (*The Slavs* (1956), pp. 124–5) implies that Theodosius assumed office under Zdeslav and worked for the exclusion of Byzantine influence. This is uncertain.

138 *MGH, Epp.* VII, *Fragmenta registri Stephani V papae*, no. 24 (p. 346), date uncertain: '...tuo tamen incitamur exemplo, qui transgressis terminis tibi commissis in ecclesia Salonensi episcopum ordinare ad indecentiam apostolicae sedis praesumpsisti...'. Documents of John VIII (*c*. 881) and Stephen V (886) are not consistent on Theodosius's consecration. Stephen at least believed that he had been consecrated by Aquileia: 'Nam cum piae memoriae decessor tuus hominem excessisse dicitur, ad aquilegensem diceris convolasse ecclesiam et exinde consecrationem suscepisse, quam in sede beati Petri ab apostolicis debueras manibus petere in quo et te deviasse et eum excessisse luce patet clarius' (*ibid.*, no. 9, p. 338). If Walpert had consecrated

Theodosius as Bishop of Nin he may well also have carried out the formal acts of his elevation to Split. See also Ritig, p. 132.

139 *Dilecto filio (MGH, Epp.* VII, no. 190, p. 152); cf. *ibid.*, no. 206 to the clergy and people of Croatia.

140 *Ibid.*, no. 191 (p. 153): 'Ideo monemus sagacitatem tuam ne in quamlibet partem aliam declines...sed...ad gremium sedis apostolice, unde antecessores tui divine legis dogmata melliflua cum sacre institutionis forma summique sacerdotii honorem sumpserunt, redeas, quatenus et ipse ab apostolica sede...episcopalem consecrationem per nostre manus impositionem...percipias.'

141 *Ibid.*, no. 196 (pp. 156–7): '...hortamur ut ad gremium sancte Romane ecclesie matris vestre redire ovanter adtendatis, ut electus a vobis canonice archiepiscopus una cum vestro omnium consensu et voluntate ad nos veniens gratiam episcopalis consecrationis sacrumque pallium a nobis more pristino incunctanter percipiat.'

142 *Ibid.*, no. 295 (pp. 257–8). It is quite possible that Branimir put his dominions under the protectorship of the Holy See for reasons similar to those of Mieszko of Poland (see pp. 121–2).

143 *MGH, Epp.* VII, no. 30 (p. 351), dated 888. If, as some think, the Pope had already exercised the privilege of investing the archbishop of Split with the *pallium* by agreement with the Byzantine authorities, this of course would not call for remark. But the letter may refer to an Aquileian consecration of Theodosius; see note 138 above.

144 Perojević (*Teodozije*, p. 26) believes that Theodosius held Nin and Split in plurality until 892.

145 Šišić, *Priručnik*, p. 124, no. 13 (MVNCIMYR).

146 *Ibid.*, p. 195 (dated 892); cf. *ibid.*, p. 192 (date 852).

147 Rački, *Documenta*, no. 12 (p. 15): 'ut nullus deinceps de successoribus meis de potestate spalatensium ecclesiae subtrahere audeat...'. (Letter of 28 September 892.)

148 Map of his dominions in *Poviest hrvatskih zemalja*, p. 175.

149 Perojević (*Ninski biskup*, ch. 7) supposes that the formal attachment of Nin to Aquileia continued till this moment. Ferluga has some reservations about the transfer of power to Tomislav and is inclined to think that the Byzantine administration continued to exist, at least in theory, until 950 or even later.

150 For a map of ecclesiastical Dalmatia in the tenth–eleventh centuries see *Slownik*, vol. 3, fig. 231 (p. 501). The alleged transference by Aquileia to Split of the doubtfully existing see of Siscia (Sisak; see also p. 190) would come at this moment; it was surely never subordinate to Nin, *pace* Kuhar, *Conversion*, p. 114.

151 Rački, *Documenta*, no. 149 (pp. 188–9): 'et quia fama revelante cognovimus per confinia vestrae parochiae [diocese] aliam doctrinam pullulare quae in sacris voluminibus non reperitur, vobis tacentibus et consentientibus, valde doluimus...sed absit hoc a fidelibus qui Christum colunt...ut doctrinam evangelii atque canonum volumina apostolicaque etiam praecepta praetermittentes, ad Methodii doctrinam confugiant, quem in nullo volumine inter sacros auctores comperimus. Unde hortamur vos...ut...in sclavinorum terra ministerium sacrificii peragant in latina scilicet lingua non autem in extranea...'.

152 Rački, *Documenta*, p. 190. The tone of shocked surprise need not be taken too seriously. Even if we are wrong in supposing that the question had been examined already by the Pope *c.* 880, with or without laying down a guiding policy, it is scarcely conceivable that John X was as ignorant of the facts as his words suggest.

153 Rački, *Documenta*, p. 192: 'Ut nullum episcopus nostrae provinciae [Split] audeat in quolibet gradu sclavinica lingua promovere...nec in sua ecclesia sinat eum [Slav priest] missam facere, praeter si necessitatem sacerdotum haberet; per supplicationem a romano pontifice licentiam ei sacerdotalis ministerii tribuat.' The lower clerical orders and monasteries were not affected: '[poterit] tam[en] in clericatu et monachatu Deo deservire'. See Ostojić in *SLO* 9–10 (1960); Ritig, pp. 142–3; D. Gruber in *Zbornik Kralja Tomislava*.

154 Rački, *Documenta*, no. 150 (pp. 194–7). There are some doubts about the authenticity of the acts of both synods, especially as regards the canons dealing with the Slav language. They may have been touched up at a later date (after the 1060s). Dvornik (*The Slavs* (1956), pp. 175–6) prefers to treat these references as later interpolations, which reduces protests of Nin entirely to the question of its independence.

155 Canon II: 'Sclavos nisi litteras didicerint, ad sacros ordines promoveri et clericum, cujuscunque gradus sit, laicali servituti vel mundiali fisco amodo subiugari, sub excommunicationis vinculo omnimodo prohibemus.' Thomas of Split (of the Latin party) has preserved another canon which, if genuine, goes further: 'ut nullus de cetero in lingua sclavonica presumeret divina misteria celebrare nisi tantum in latina et greca, nec aliquis eiusdem lingue promoveretur ad sacros ordines.' (*Historia Salonitana*, ed. Rački, cap. 16 (*MSM* 26, p. 49); *Izvori* 7, pp. 370–1). The retention of Greek at this time is unexpected.

156 Šišić, *Priručnik*, pp. 236–8 (letter dated October 1061).

157 Thomas of Split, *Historia Salonitana*, cap. 16 (*MSM* 26, p. 49).

158 *Historia Salonitana*, cap. 16 (*ibid.*, pp. 50 ff.). The name perhaps represents a familiar form of Zdeslav (or Sedeslav). An Aquileian cleric Ulfus (or perhaps Ulfilas) is also mentioned as a supporter of the *glagoljaši*.

159 Rački, *Documenta*, no. 152/2 (pp. 201–2); Stanojević, *Borba*, p. 157. The authenticity of the document has been questioned as an anticipation of the events of 1088/9 (see pp. 210–12). Perojević (*Ninski biskup* (1939), pp. 112 ff.) interprets this synod as the much-discussed *Sabor na duvanjskom polju*, mentioned in an unreliable 'Croat Chronicle' without precise date or names, but perhaps best ascribed to the end of Tomislav's reign.

160 Dyggve, fig. vi, 16 and 17 (Šuplja Crkva) may be this church.

161 See Šišić, *Priručnik*, pp. 268–9 for Zvonimir's coronation oath. This was one of Gregory's three Slav crowns, a notable aspect of his universalism. It was followed by that of Bolesław Śmiały of Poland (Christmas 1076) and that of Michael of Zeta (see p. 211) in 1077.

162 Rački, *Documenta*, no. 130 (p. 158).

163 Jelić, *Fontes*, no. 1: 'precepimus ut pontifices...provideant viros idoneos qui secundum diversitatem rituum et linguarum illis officia celebrent et ecclesiastica sacramenta ministrent...'.

164 Klaić, *Izvori*, vol. 2, no. 18. Bishop Philip of Senj, who applied for permission, was himself a normal Latin bishop but found his diocese almost wholly Slav in practice. Pope Innocent IV wrote: 'Porrecta nobis tua petitio continebat, quod in Sclavonia est littera specialis, quam illius terre clerici se habere a beato Jeronimo asserentes, eam observant in divinis officiis celebrandis. Unde cum illis efficiaris conformis et in terre consuetudinem, in qua consistis episcopus, imiteris, celebrandi divina officia secundum dictam litteram a nobis suppliciter licentiam postulasti. Nos igitur...licentiam tibi in illis dumtaxat partibus, ubi de consuetudine observantur premissa, dummodo sententia ex ipsius varietate littere non ledatur, auctoritate presentium concedimus postulatam' (Jelić, *Fontes*, no. 3).

165 Jelić, *Fontes*, no. 5 (26 January 1252), addressed to Bishop Fructuosus of Krk (*Veglensis*) and the monastery of Omišalj (...*monasterii S. Nicolai de Castro Muscla*).

166 The earliest surviving Glagolitic inscription comes from here—the so-called *Baščanska ploča* (*c.* 1120); see Šišić, *Priručnik*, p. 135, no. 25; *Slovenska pismenost*, pl. 4. Discussed by B. Fučić in *SLO* 6–8 (1957) (*Vajsov Zbornik*).

167 See Ostojić in *SLO* 9–10 (1960), and for full details of their history *id.*, *Benediktinci*, vol. 2, pp. 104, 168, 180, 182, 185, 204, 254 and 390.

168 See Jelić, *Fontes*, no. 10; Ostojić, vol. 2, pp. 221 ff. New Benedictine foundations were at their height in the eleventh–twelfth centuries, the majority of course fully Latin. See Schmitz, vol. 1, pp. 240–2; Ostojić, vol. 1, p. 153; *Slownik*, s.v. *Benedyktyni* (fig. 34, p. 104) and V. Novak, *Scriptura beneventana* (Zagreb, 1920), pp. 3–13.

169 The wider use of Glagolitic in other parts of Istria (e.g. Trieste) and further north in Carniola (e.g. Ljubljana) in the fifteenth century was due to a great influx of Slavs into those parts from neighbouring Croatia as a result of the Turkish conquests. See Benussi in bibliography.

170 See p. 91. Cf. also Weingart in *Svatováclavaský Sborník*, vol. 1.

171 The 'angular' variant of Beneventan script clearly influenced the 'angular' variant of Glagolitic (see table in *Slovník jazyka staroslověnského*, *Úvod* (Prague, 1959), p. lxxix.) On the Beneventan script, current in Dalmatian Benedictine houses during the tenth–thirteenth centuries and introduced via their close connections with Monte Cassino and other Italian houses, see V. Novak, *Scriptura beneventana* (Zagreb, 1920).

172 The status of *Codex Clozianus* (see also pp. 78–9) is doubtful. This eleventh century manuscript was probably found on Krk but it is not known where it was written. The language has some Croat features; ed. by A. Dostál (Prague, 1959). The twelfth-century *Vienna fragments* (Weingart and Kurz, pp. 139–41) show that the angular Croat ductus of Glagolitic evolved relatively early.

173   See especially L. Karaman in *L'art byzantin chez les Slaves* (ed. G. Millet), vol. 2 (1932). The larger structures of the eleventh century onwards follow, like the script, current Italian Benedictine style.

174   Skok, p. 143. The name appears in one of the leading early Croatian families—Mogorović. St Hermagoras is no reliable guide to Croat connections with Grado rather than Cividale (see p. 189 n. d); though the saint was certainly more closely connected with Grado in the ninth–tenth centuries his relics were stolen by Cividale and enshrined in its new cathedral in 1031. See R. Egger, *Der heilige Hermagoras* (Klagenfurt, 1948).

175   For St Domnius see *DAI*, vol. 2 (commentary), pp. 108–9.

176   See F. Fancev in *Zbornik Kralja Tomislava*. Manuscripts that reached Zagreb after 1094 from Bohemia are easily identifiable, e.g. MR 126, perhaps the first Czech Bishop of Zagreb's own Sacramentary.

177   G. Stadtmüller, *Geschichte Südosteuropas*, provides some synoptic maps (especially pp. 264 and 358).

SERBIA

178   See *DAI*, vol. 2 (commentary), pp. 131–3 (by F. Dvornik). The ethnic SRB is found not only in Lusatia (see p. 144) but also in South and Central Poland. Nothing reliable can be said about the northern origins of different waves of Balkan Serbs. The first Serbian settlement area in Greek Macedonia can be fixed by a number of place names, e.g. Σέρβια, near Mt Olympus. Portions also pushed south, witness Σερβιανίκα (near Corinth), Σερβοῦ (Arcadia), Σέρβικα (Laconia), Σερβοτά (Messenia). The ethnic HRVAT is rare in Greece.

179   *Vita Basilii*, §§ 52–4 (Migne, *PG* 109, cols. 303 ff.). It is understandable that he should interpret loss of Byzantine hegemony over Serbia as due to 'pagan reactions'. The stories collected by the Priest of Dioclea (see note 192 below) in his early chapters are quite unreliable.

180   It is difficult to form any precise idea of the area effectively ruled by these early Serb princes. It is generally accepted that from about the middle of the ninth century 'Serbia' extended some sort of political control as far as the lower Dalmatian coast, at least assuring contact with the ports, especially Durazzo. Recent research (see J. Kosačević in *AAH* 17 (1965)) has begun to show that Kotor, perhaps under encouragement from Durazzo, was a considerable centre of Christian radiation from early in the ninth century, reaching northwards to Dúbrovnik and southwards to Ulcinj. How early and how profoundly this affected the local Slavs remains problematical.

181   Plan and view in Deroko, figs. 21–2 (p. 37). Cf. pp. 94–5 and 170–1.

182   *DAI*, cap. 32.

183   Letter of Pope John X to Michael, *c.* 925 (Rački, *Documenta*, no. 149 b, p. 189). Hum or Zachlumia (Zahumlje) included the coastline, with an indefinite hinterland, from the River Neretva to Ragusa approximately. According to the Emperor Constantine (*DAI*, cap. 33) Michael claimed to come from South Poland; on this 'Vistulanian' dynasty of Hum, which may have imposed itself *c.* 875–8, see T. Wasilewski in *PSL* 25 (1965).

184   *Gregorii Papae VII epistolae* (ed. E. Caspar), v, no. 12 (=Mansi, xx, col. 246) of January 1078 to Michael of Zeta, shows one stage in the long quarrel: '...Quapropter Petrum Antibarensem episcopum atque Ragusanum, sive alios idoneos nuntios, ad nos mittere oportet, per quos de lite quae inter Spalatanum archiepiscopum ac Ragusanum justitia posset inquiri...'. Cf. pp. 201–2.

185   Stanojević, *Borba*, p. 48 (23 May 1139).

186   Smičiklas, *CD*, vol. 2, no. 35 (28 September 1120); no. 34 (28 September 1120).

187   Kotor had been attached to Bari in Apulia not long after its conquest by the Normans (1071), but the attachment could not always be maintained in practice. It seems that Rome did not formally recognise this until 1172 and at various times in between tried to enforce other arrangements. Bari itself was a Greek town. Up to its conquest by Guiscard it had alternated between Byzantine and Beneventan rule, with a Saracen interlude in 841–70. It rose to an archbishopric in the 950s under Rome but was soon reattached to the Greek metropolitan see of Otranto. This does not imply profound changes as the Latin and Greek sees in this confused area lived together on the whole with considerable tolerance. See Gay, esp. pp. 350 ff., Leib, pp. 106 ff.

188   Smičiklas, *CD*, vol. 2, nos. 103 and 105.

189   In May 1185 Ragusa and sees subordinated to it refused to take part in a Synod at Split. In 1189 Pope Clement III (1187–91) attempted to bring about a pacification by recognising Ragusa's jurisdiction over all the then Serbian territories but throwing Bosnia to Split as a sop. See Stanojević, *Borba*, pp. 66 ff.

190   Smičiklas, *CD*, vol. 2, nos. 155 (1178/9), 159 (1179), 169 (*c.* 1180).

191   Cf. Stojanović, *Rodoslovi i letopisi*, pp. 16–19.

192   The *Letopis popa dukljanina* [*Chronicle of the Priest of Dioclea*] is certainly of the twelfth century and has been dated by V. Mošin to *c.* 1148/9 but may be a few decades later. See bibliography under Mošin and Šišić.

193   Runciman, *History of the Crusades*, III, pp. 12–13; cf. also Dvornik, *The Slavs in European History*, pp. 91–2.

194   Note especially the arcading inside the cupola of St George (illustrated and discussed by A. Deroko in G. Millet, *L'Art byzantin chez les Slaves*, vol. 1). The Eastern features of the 'Raška style' are as much Bulgarian as specifically Byzantine, the Western ones probably South Dalmatian; see the full discussion by G. Millet in the same volume. General maps of Serbian ecclesiastical architecture in Deroko, especially fig. 51 (p. 47). Consult also D. Stričević in *ZRVI* 8 (1964).

195   The so-called 'White Churches' (*Bele crkve*) at Kuršumlija are counted among Nemanja's earliest foundations but were not all strictly new. The church of the Mother of God (Bogoroditsa) is certainly a sixth-century Byzantine structure, probably, as in so many Balkan cases, restored with added monastic buildings by Nemanja. The same is probably true of nearby St

Nicholas (Deroko, fig. 56). See D. Stričević in *ZRVI* 2 (1953) and in *OCA*, vol. 1 (Belgrade, 1963).

196 Deroko, figs. 15 (p. 35) and 29 (p. 41); *Slovenska pismenost*, sect. 2, pl. vi, no. 2 (inscription on the tympanum).

197 Stojanović, *Rodoslovi i letopisi*, p. 20.

198 Stewart, p. 42; Deroko, figs. 57 ff.

199 Theiner, *Vetera monumenta Slav.*, vol. 1, nos. 8 and 9 (1198) show the Pope's impatience to ensure the correct Catholicism of Vukan's province.

200 Smičiklas, *CD*, vol. 2, nos. 294, 295 (January 1199).

201 *Ibid.*, no. 311. Bishop John then assumed the traditional title of Archbishop of Dioclea and Bar. The Pope only acceded to this after making quite certain that Bar had been a metropolis properly constituted by his predecessors and not subordinate to Ragusa.

202 Theiner, *Vetera monumenta Slav.*, vol. 1, no. 13; Smičiklas, *CD*, vol. 2, no. 312.

203 By the events of 1204 Venice gained a free hand throughout Dalmatia, including Ragusa, whose archbishops were thenceforward usually eminent Venetians. Ragusa immediately attempted to have Bar suppressed again but unsuccessfully, e.g. at the Lateran Council in 1215; see Stanojević, *Borba*, p. 94.

204 Theiner, *Vetera monumenta Slav.*, vol. 1, no. 11 (dated 1199): 'Nos autem [Stephen] semper consideramus in vestigia sancte Romane ecclesie, sicut bone memorie pater meus, et preceptum sancte Romane ecclesie semper custodire...'.

205 As far as it can be established the tradition of Serbian ecclesiastical texts is overwhelmingly Macedonian, that is, derived from Ohrid. It should also be noted that Serbia (and Bulgaria) received a far from negligible contribution from Russia in the early days of their independence: only Russian texts could make good the losses caused by the hellenization of the Balkans. There were two routes—via Athos, and via Hungary which had longstanding dynastic connections not only with Constantinople but also with Kiev (Ladislas I, 1077–95, married a daughter of Vladimir the Great; Géza II, 1141–61, a daughter of Mstislav I). The Hungarian route was not interrupted till the Mongol devastation of southern Russia and raids into Hungary in the early thirteenth century. See V. Mošin in *TODL* 19 (1963).

206 Text (abridged): *Vies des Saints apôtres serbes Syméon et Savva rédigées par Dométien*, ed. K. Živković with French translation by A. Chodźko (Paris, 1858); Serbian translation in Mirković and Ćorović, *Životi sv. Save i sv. Simeona* (Belgrade, 1938).

207 Serbian versions in Bašić, *Stare srpske biografie* and in *Stara srpska književnost*, vol. 1.

208 Serbian versions of (*a*) and (*b*) in Bašić, *op. cit.* and in *Stara srpska književnost*, vol. 1; of (*c*) in Mirković and Ćorović, (see note 206). The text of (*b*) will also be found, together with other matter, in *Svetosavski Zbornik*, vol. 2. German versions of (*a*) and (*b*) by S. Hafner in *Slavische Geschichtsschreiber*, vol. 2 (Graz, 1962).

209 See further S. Hafner, *Studien zur altserbischen dynastischen Historiographie*, especially ch. 3.

210 It has often been doubted whether he in fact ever so ruled but Mošin (*TODL* 19 (1963)) states that a Latin transcript of Nemanja's treaty with Split (pp. 214–15), recently discovered, mentions Rastko as Prince of Hum (Zachlumia). Nemanja removed his brother Miroslav from the province in 1190.

211 Stojanović, *Rodoslovi i letopisi*, p. 22: 'mnihu někoemu Rusinu voděštu jego'.

212 Mirković and Ćorović, pp. 39–41, 45–55; Bašić, pp. 112–15.

213 For the deed see Mošin, *Paleografski album*, no. 16; also *ibid.*, no. 22 (the oldest manuscript of the *Typikon* or charter). The Georgian monastery of Ivéron was also founded by a father and son—a fact surely well known to Sava.

214 '...po tomu paky my, jegovo stado sŭvŭkuplenoje' (St Sava's *Life*; Bašić, p. 23). All the Slavs would of course use the same OCS.

215 For full details see D. M. Nicol, *The Despotate of Epirus*. Ohrid did not remain permanently within the Despotate throughout the ensuing complicated events.

216 Especially in 1219 when Theodore Laskaris proposed a joint council at Nicaea to discuss union. Theodore of Epirus refused to countenance the suggestion. For the election of the first Patriarch resident in Nicaea (March 1208), see *CMH* iv/1, p. 295.

217 'Jako da isplĭneno blagoslovenije jego javit se na nasŭ' (St Sava's *Life*; Bašić, p. 25). The sarcophagi of Nemanja and his son Stephen are both still in the main church of Studenitsa.

218 Not by Germanós II (*fungebatur* 1222–40), as some later accounts state. The title is found in an inscription at Studenica (Stojanović, *Zapisi i natpisi*, no. 5065): 'Sveti Sava prěosveščenyj arhiepiskopŭ vse srĭbĭske zemlĭe i pomorske' [i.e. *Zeta*, which was never called *Serbia*]. Domentian has: '...svih srpskih i pomorskih zemalja', and there are other variants.

219 See: Ostrogorski in *Svetosavski Zbornik*, vol. 2 (letter to St Sava dated May 1220); H. Gelzer in *BZ* 2 (1893).

220 The *Answers* ascribed to Archbishop Demetrios (see Granić in *Svetosavski Zbornik*, vol. 2) are considered, though not with certainty, to meet questions submitted by Radoslav bearing on dogmatic and ritual differences between East and West. But no more intimate association is known between the correspondents and Sava would scarcely have left Serbia after Radoslav's accession (see p. 223) if his work were likely to be overthrown behind his back. Practical difficulties are the most interesting part of the *Questions*, e.g. whether temporary altars are permissible on a journey—evidently parish churches were still few and far between in Serbia.

221 *The Slavs in European History*, p. 100 (see the whole passage pp. 99 ff.).

222 If further evidence of the same nature were needed we may note that the Greek Metropolitan of Durazzo was still ordaining Latin priests in his archdiocese after 1200; see Every, pp. 189–90.

223 Stanojević, *Borba*, p. 121.

224 Deroko, fig. 96 (p. 75).

225 Stojanović, *Rodoslovi i letopisi*, pp. 24–6. Braničevo may be the descendant of the earlier bishopric 'of the Moravians' (see p. 166 note c). For a map of the Serbian sees consult *Słownik*, vol. 3, fig. 235 (p. 521).

226 Stojanović, *Zapisi i natpisi*, I, no. 38 (dated 1305): 'Sije bo knigy pisani byše izĭ arhiepiskoplihĭ knigĭ i samĭ azĭ...potrudihĭ se i is těhĭ knigĭ ispravihĭ sije knigy da ne sut ničtože krivo.' The copy was by then apparently on Athos (at Hilandar?).

227 Based on the Σύνταγμα of Patriarch Photios with additions from the Πρόχειρος νόμος of Basil I. From Serbia it passed into Bulgarian use and was taken to Russia in 1262. Dušan's *Zákonik* (1349–54) superseded it in Serbia. See Žužek, *Kormčaja kniga* (*OC* 168, 1964).

228 Serbian church music also appears to have been based more on 'Syrian' than Byzantine (i.e. Athonite and metropolitan) models but from how early a date cannot be established for lack of early sources. See Wellesz, p. 325.

229 Neither the year nor the day is absolutely certain; see Slijepčević, p. 127 and J. Matl, *Südslawische Studien* (*Südosteuropäische Arbeiten* 63), pp. 56–7. He is usually commemorated on 14 January but sometimes on the 12th.

230 Miloševo or Mileševa, near Prijepolje, founded by Vladislav in 1234–5, for long centuries in ruins but now carefully restored. See Deroko, fig. 85 (p. 68). Here can be seen the fresco portrait of St Sava, made, it is believed, from the body or a death-mask and with a clear recollection of his appearance in life (Ž. Stojković, *Mileševa*, 1963, pls. 13–14). There is another fresco of St Sava, with Nemanja as founder, in the main church of Studenitsa, but later and more conventional.

231 Deroko, figs. 103 ff. Dalmatian style was of course not uniform. But even the more 'Lombard' style, e.g. of Trogir cathedral (1206) and Zadar cathedral (1255), was propagated as far as Kotor (St Tryphon, 1166), and Norman influence, especially from Bari, crossed the Adriatic to Kotor and Bar. The Slav Radovan, who made the great portals of Trogir cathedral (1240), was trained in Apulia.

232 Theiner, *Vetera mon. historica*, vol. I, no. 605 (Pope Nicholas IV to Dragutin, 1291); no. 606 (to his mother Helen). See also p. 234.

233 *Zakonik*, §§ 6–8 (text ed. N. Radojčić, Belgrade, 1960).

234 Cf. Dvornik, *The Slavs in European History*, p. 110. The feast of the Translation of St Nicholas's relics, instituted directly by the Pope and naturally never accepted in the East, was however adopted in Russia in the 1090s and a special Office composed there in OCS; see p. 291.

235 See G. Čremošnik, *Razvoj srpskog novčarstva do Kralja Milutina* (Belgrade, 1933); A. Cutler in *BSL* 26 (1965) and D. Metcalf, especially pp. 68–9 and 197. The changeover is due to the rapid economic decline of Constantinople in the East Mediterranean after 1204.

236 J. Vrana, *L'Evangéliaire de Miroslav*, esp. pp. 162–3; Mošin, *Paleografski album*, nos. 14–15. The term *mĭša* = *Holy Week* is Ragusan. With

Miroslav's should be compared Vukan's Gospel Book, also showing interesting hybrid features (*Vukanovo Evanđelje*, ed. J. Vrana, Belgrade, 1967).

237 *Jugoslawien* (*Osteuropa-Handbuch*), ed. W. Markert (Köln-Graz, 1954), map 8 opposite p. 176 (statistics of 1931).

238 Also John Vladislav (d. 1016), for whom see S. Hafner, *Studien zur altserbischen dynastischen Historiographie*, pp. 42 ff.

239 Greek and OCS versions of the Rule are given in Ćorović, *Spisi sv. Save.* The *Hilandar Typikon* of the same date also alludes to it in §42. See also P. Meyer, *Die Haupturkunden für die Geschichte der Athosklöster* (Leipzig, 1894), pp. 184 ff. and Ž. Tatić in *L'Art byzantin chez les Slaves*, ed. G. Millet, vol. 1 (1930).

240 *Studenički Letopis* in Stojanović, *Rodoslovi i letopisi*, p. 67.

241 See also A. Schmaus in *Slawistische Studien zum V internationalen slawistischen Kongress* (Göttingen, 1963). For this re-entry into the world Sava was criticised by Demetrios Khomatianos of Ohrid who adhered to the strict principle that a monk had renounced the world for good; to become a political ambassador and ecclesiastical organiser was not in his eyes a proper task. There is no reason to suppose that Sava undertook his self-imposed role, which would not call for remark in a Western monk, under the influence of Western ideas.

BOSNIA AND THE BOGOMIL HERESY

242 Sources in D. Angelov, *Bogomilstvoto v Bŭlgarija* (2nd ed., Sofia, 1961), cap. 2; A. Schmaus in *SAE* 2 (1951).

243 Consult: Angelov, *op. cit.*, especially pp. 98 ff.; S. Runciman, *The Medieval Manichee*; D. Obolensky, *The Bogomils*; Vaillant and Puech, *Le Traité de Cosmas* (see bibliography).

244 According to Orthodox Christian doctrine 'nothing is bad of its own nature' (see St John Damascene, Ἔκδοσις... ὀρθοδόξου πίστεως, bk. 4, cap. 20 (Migne, *PG* 94, cols. 1193 ff.), stigmatising dualism as a Manichaean error). Further, Jesus's Incarnation was a sanctification of matter, all of which was thus brought within the work of redemption. The great Christological definitions proclaimed God's complete humanity in Jesus and thus specifically excluded any form of dualism. The Bogomil doctrine is condemned in Boril's *Sinodik* (n. 265 below) under *Anathemas* 50 and 51 (Drinov copy).

245 *Sinodik Borila, Anathema* 56 (Drinov copy).

246 *Ibid.*, p. 82 (*Anathema* 111 of the Palauzov copy): '...iže Hristovo vŭplŭštenije prividěnije byti bljadivši[h]...'.

247 Migne, *PL* 119, col, 1015: '...in patriam vestram multi ex diversis focis Christiani advenerint qui...multa et varia loquuntur, id est Graeci, Armeni, et ex caeteris locis...'.

248 *Historia Manichaeorum* (Migne, *PG* 104, cols. 1239 ff.).

249 Day 1, ff. 11 d ff. (Aitzetmüller, vol. 1, pp. 87 ff.). 'vŭ prŭvyi bo dĭnĭ stvori Bogŭ vešti vsego zdanija'; f. 29 d (*ibid.*, pp. 231 ff.): 'nita bo tĭma zŭla jestŭ sila'. See also p. 177. The *Encyclopaedia* (*Sbornik*) of 1073, copied for

Svjatoslav (see p. 293) from an original compilation made for Symeon, contains a list of forbidden books placed on the index of the Eastern church, some of which are characteristic of later Bogomil taste in religious literature.

250 An Ohrid icon which shows St Naum (d. 910) contending with Bogomils (διώκεται ὑπὸ τῶν Βογομήλον [*sic*]) is, as D. Angelov (*Bogomilstvoto*, p. 87) remarks, no doubt an anachronism.

251 Ἡ νεοφανὴς αἵρεσις (text in Dujčev, pp. 311 ff., with commentary; also *id.* in *Studi i Testi* 232 (*Mélanges Eugène Tisserant*), vol. 2 (1964).

252 The heretical movements in these regions certainly had other origins as well but the connection is clear enough from the epithet *bougre* (=Bulgar) applied to the Albigensians. See also Primov in *INBI* 14–15 (1964).

253 Anna Komnéna, *Alexiade*, xv, 8–10. Basil was tricked into explaining his doctrines privately before the Emperor while the Patriarch Nicholas heard and secretaries recorded everything from a place of concealment. Compare Alexios's disputes with the Paulicians of Plovdiv, *ibid.*, xiv, 9. Cf. also *Euthymii Zigabeni Panoplia Dogmatica, tit.* xxvii (Migne, *PG* 130, cols. 1289 ff.).

254 Mansi, xxi, cols. 551 ff.: οὕτω ῥητῶς ὑπὸ τῆς τῶν Μασσαλιανῶν, ἤτοι Βογομήλων, παμβεβήλου θρησκείας δογματιζόμενον εὕρηται. The Massalians were frequently lumped loosely with the Bogomils, who may have taken over a few of their beliefs.

255 See *Poviest hrvatskih zemalja*, pp. 706 ff. Text in Smičiklas, *CD*, vol. 2, no. 221.

256 Smičiklas, *CD*, vol. 2, no. 310 (1199?), Vukan's delation: 'heresis non modica in terra regis Ungarie, videlicet Bossina, pullulare videtur in tantum, quod...ipse Bacilinus [Ban Kulin] cum uxore sua et cum sorore sua...et cum pluribus consanguineis suis seductus plus quam decem milia christianorum in eandem heresim introduxit'; vol. 2, no. 324 (11 October 1200), Innocent III to Emerich of Hungary; vol. 3, no. 11 (21 November 1202), Innocent instructs Archbishop Bernard of Split to enquire into the heresy: '...de dampnata Catharorum heresi sunt vehementer suspecti et graviter infamati'. The Pope further enjoined Vukan to purify his own realm (Smičiklas, *CD*, vol. 2, no. 293). (Documents also in Theiner, *Vetera monumenta* I.)

257 Smičiklas, *CD*, vol. 3, nos. 19 (April 1203) *et seq.*

258 See Stričević in *ZRVI* 1 (1952) and p. 225 above.

259 Anna Komnéna, Alexiade, xv, 8,1: κέκρυπται δὲ τὸ κακὸν ὑπὸ τὸν μανδύαν καὶ τὸ κουκούλιον.

260 Theiner, *Vetera monumenta historica*, 1, no. 200 (p. 120).

261 Theiner, *Vetera monumenta historica*, 1, pp. 202–4. Various Papal exhortations to the Hungarian ruler and church to proceed against the Bosnian heretics are illustrated by Smičiklas, *CD*, vol. 3, nos. 174 (1221), 216 (1225), 359 (1234); and to the Bishop of Bosnia in nos. 361 and 363 (1234). Cf. further *ibid.*, vol. 4, nos. 58–60 (1238).

262 See Ćirković, pp. 58 ff., for a reserved estimate.

263 See M. Miletić in *OC* 149 (1957).

264 The main peculiarity is Cyrillic 'ђ=dj, j. See for details D. Prohaska, *Das kroatisch-serbische Schrifttum in Bosnien und Hercegowina* (Zagreb, 1911).

There would appear to be an Italian, no doubt Ragusan, influence in the rendering of lj, nj (Serbian љ, њ) by the sign ħ placed before *l, n* (cf. Ital. *gl,gn*). To call Bosnian conventions a special alphabet—the *bosančica*—is something of an exaggeration, at least at this period.

265 M. G. Popruzhenko, *Sinodik Tsarja Borila* (Sofia, 1928) (= *Bŭlgarski starini* 8), especially *Anathemas* 46–8 (Drinov copy). We learn from this some of the special Bogomil terms, all modelled on Greek, e.g. *dědets* = head of a 'church': *Anathema* 78 in the Palauzov copy alludes to the *dědets* or *elder* of the Sofia centre. In Bosnia the term was *Djed* or *Did*, according to dialect.

262 Thomas of Split, cap. 24 (Rački, *MSM* 26, pp. 82–3): 'Et cum pluribus essent vitiis depravati, hoc etiam ad nequitie sue cumulum addiderunt ut catholice fidei normam spernerent et heretica se permitterent tabe respergi. Nam pene omnes, qui nobiliores et maiores Jadere censebantur, libenter recipiebant hereticos et fovebant.' This is, however, not reported by Villehardouin, who on the contrary states that the Abbot of Vaux tried to forbid the attack in the name of the Pope: 'car ele est de crestiens et vos iestes pelerin' (ed. E. Faral (Paris, 1938), vol. I, p. 84).

267 *Zákonik*, §10 (heretics in general); §85 (*o babunĭskoj rěči*).

268 See maps in Ćirković, pp. 64 and 162.

269 The Turks had sufficient contact with the heresy still to refer to the 'perfect' Bogomils as *Kristian*; they were probably the most resistant to Islam. See M. Tayyib Okiç in *SF* 19 (1960).

270 Reproduced in Stewart, pl. 31.

271 *Ibid.*, pls. 64–9. Consult also *Poviest hrvatskih zemalja*, pp. 629 ff.; Stričević, *Stećci* (Belgrade, 1963).

272 See M. Wenzel in *SF* 21 (1962).

273 A few of the Russian manuscripts are noticed by Ivanov, *Bogomilski knigi i legendi*, under the individual works. See also Murko, pp. 82 ff.; Dvornik, *The Slavs*, pp. 183 ff. The *Hozhdenije Bogoroditsy po mukam* (*Virgin Mary's Journey through the Pains of Hell*), which became popular in Russia, may have had Bogomil origins.

274 See *Poviest hrvatskih zemalja*, pp. 807–9; Angelov, pp. 100 ff.; E. Turdeanu in *Revue de l'histoire des religions*, 138 (1950).

275 Ivanov, *Bogomilski knigi*, pp. 113–30, with text. It is a Ritual rather than a Missal and contains the service of initiation to the 'perfect' (Cathar) grade. See also Primov in *Etudes historiques à l'occasion du XIe Congrès international de sciences historiques*, Stockholm, 1960 (Sofia, 1960).

276 Ivanov, *op. cit.*, pp. 227 ff.

277 Ivanov, *op. cit.*, pp. 60–87. It is almost certainly a Bogomil work taken to Italy in the twelfth century.

278 Ivanov, *op. cit.*, pp. 131 ff., 207 ff., 257 ff.

Chapter 5.   The Eastern Slavs

1 For the trade-routes of Europe *c.* A.D. 300 see A. R. Lewis, *Northern Seas*, p. 33.

2 Rybakov, pp. 22 ff. Ericsson's attempt (*SR*, Jan. 1966 [=vol. 44, no. 102]) to put Kij at the beginning of the ninth century is impossible.

3 *Primary Chronicle, Introduction* (Acad. ed., p. 13).

4 The Khazars are usually stated to be predominantly Turkic and therefore not dissimilar to the Bulgars, but there are reasons to suppose a considerable Iranian element in them: see L. N. Gumilëv in *AAH* 19 (1967).

5 Artamonov, pp. 276 ff.; cf. Dunlop, cap. 5–6. The ruling house can scarcely have already formally adopted Judaism when the Byzantine house married into it, or even during the lifetime of Leo the Khazar; some put their Judaism a good deal later still.

6 Zakhoder, p. 162. Also in the East Crimea, when this territory came under Khazar rule.

7 Mas'ūdī, *Kitāb murūj al-dhahab*, ed. Barbier de Meynard and Pavet de Courteille, cap. 17 (vol. 2, pp. 8–9). For the judges see *ibid.*, p. 11.

8 The origin of the word *Rus*, with the Greek form 'Pῶs, whence *Russian*, is still controversial with a vast speculative literature. The problem cannot be discussed here. The clearest identification with Scandinavians (not necessarily Swedes) is to be found in al-Ya'qūbī, who in his *Kitāb al-buldān*, written *c.* 889, describes the Viking raid on Seville in 844 as carried out by '*al-majūs* called *ar-rūs*' (*Majūs*=Magians, hence pagans in general). With this may be compared the *Jabal Rūs* (Mountains of the Rus) in which, if the corrupt name of the river is correctly restored, the Dnepr rises according to al-Khorezmī in his *Kitāb sūrat al-'ard* (written *c.* 836–47; manuscript of the eleventh century only). See Melvinger, pp. 44–5; Pashuto, pp. 373–4.

9 The basic population was Finnic. The Scandinavians called it Aldeigjuborg. Scandinavian objects of the eighth–ninth centuries have been identified there, Slav ones not till the tenth century. See G. F. Korzhukhina in *Abstracts of Papers of the II conference on the history, economics, languages and literatures of the Scandinavian countries and Finland* (Moscow, 1965; in Russian).

10 *Primary Chronicle*, s.a. 6453=945 (Acad. ed., vol. 1, p. 39): *Konečí pasynǔčě besědy* is a reflection of this since the word *pašanog*, known also from the Balkan Bulgars, was a Khazar title equivalent to *lieutenant* or *governor*. The Khazar name for Kiev was Sambat(a), still known to Constantine Porphyrogennetos in the tenth century (τὸ Κιοάβα τὸ ἐπονομαζόμενον Σαμβατάς—*DAI*, cap. 9) and thought to be from Armenian *Smbat*.

11 Pashuto, *Drevnerusskoje gosudarstvo*, pp. 384–5 (from Ibn-Khordādhbeh, whose information goes back to a ninth-century source). On the Scandinavian habit of accepting provisional baptism (*prima signatio*) in foreign parts to ease relations with Christians, and perhaps also with Moslems, see p. 362 n. 203.

12 R. Levy, *The Social Structure of Islam* (Cambridge, 1962), p. 320.

13 See Sawyer cap. 5 and analysis of selected hoards, pp. 207 ff.

14 Present Novgorod was probably developed only from the beginning of

the tenth century, replacing some earlier centre in the same region, called by the Scandinavians *Holmgard*. The earliest excavation stratum (no. 28) determined during the extensive studies of the last two decades cannot be dated earlier than *c.* 950, but as yet unexplored parts of the town may of course prove to be earlier. Some guess the earlier centre as Beloózero, the seat of one of Rjurik's (probably legendary) brothers and conceivably also the Arabic *Artha* (Pashuto, *Drevnerusskoje gosudarstvo*, pp. 411–12).

15 No exact dates can be given but clearly *c.* 840–80, by which time Rjurik had imposed his rule. The interruption in the flow of eastern trade was due to this revolt of the northernmost Slavs against Swedish domination, involving a considerable expulsion of Varangians from the Novgorod region. Under precisely what conditions they were 'invited back', as the *Primary Chronicle* has it, cannot now be reconstructed. The *Rus* embassy which was in Constantinople in 839 (*Ann. Bert.* [*MGH, SS* I, p. 434]) was constrained to return home via Western Europe since the Slav revolt in N. Russia had cut its normal route to Sweden. The fact that the *Rus* called their ruler *khagan* (*rex illorum*, *Chacanus vocabulo*) connects them closely with Khazaria where alone they could have picked up its use (and passed it on also to the later rulers of Kiev). Ibn-Rusteh (Pashuto, *Drevnerusskoje gosudarstvo*, pp. 397 ff.) confirms their use of this title and makes clear that they came from the forest zone in N.W. Russia via the Volga Bulgars. The *Vita Anskarii* (*MGH, SS* II), cap. 30, may be evidence of a similar expulsion of Swedes from Courland (*c.* 839–40?).

16 There is some evidence of Scandinavians returning to Courland *c.* 852–4 and of their passage eastwards through Grodno on the River Neman *c.* 854–6. See also on the general situation Bernshtejn-Kogan in *Voprosy geografii* 20 (1950).

17 Wrongly entered in the *Primary Chronicle* s.a. 866: *Vŭ lěto 6374: ide Askoldŭ i Dirŭ na greki*. See A. A. Vasiljev, *The Russian attack on Constantinople in 860* (*Medieval Academy of America Publications* 46, Cambridge, Mass., 1946). It is interesting to note that this exploratory raid was contemporaneous with the great Viking raids in the West—into the Mediterranean (859–62) and East Anglia (850–65).

18 Rhetorically described by Patriarch Photios in two homilies of June–July 860 (C. Mango, *The Homilies of Photios*, nos. 3 and 4). The safety of the city was ascribed to the special intervention of the Mother of God who spread a protective veil over it. This ironically became a festival of the church much honoured later in Russia (*Pokróv*, 1 October) but ignored in Constantinople.

19 See Gy. Moravcsik, *Die byzantinische Kultur und das mittelalterliche Ungarn* (*Sitzungsberichte der deutschen Akademie der Wissenschaften zu Berlin, Klasse für Philosophie*...1955, no. 4 (Berlin, 1956)), p. 8.

20 Later Russian *Tmutorokanj*; on a possible etymology of this name see H. Grégoire in *La nouvelle Clio* 4 (1952). Originally Greek Φαναγορία, with a bishopric attested from 519. It was a cosmopolitan port, opposite Kerch on the lower Kuban, of considerable importance, with a large Jewish colony since it was known in Moslem lands as *Samkarsh al-yahūd* (see Pashuto, *Drevnerusskoje gosudarstvo*, pp. 384–5).

21 Dvornik, *Légendes*, pp. 166 ff.; Artamonov, p. 260. The list comes from the 'de Boor *Notitia episcopatuum*'.

22 Z. N. Vaneev, *Srednevekovaja Alanija* (Stalinir, 1959). The Alans occupied an especially important sector of the trade-route. See also Peeters in *AB* 52 (1934) on St Abo of Tiflis, martyred about 786.

23 E.g. Vernadski, *Ancient Russia*, pp. 278 ff.

24 See P. O. Karyshkovski in *VV* 17 (1960). It is true that a name similar to *Rus* is recorded by Zacharias Rhetor in the sixth century in connection with the North Caucasian Alans but nothing solid can be built on this. For these apparent early uses of the name *Rus* in Eastern sources see also Pashuto, *Drevnerusskoje gosudarstvo*, pp. 360 ff.

25 The Kherson mint was revived *c.* 866/7; see A. L. Jakobson, *Srednevekovy Krym*, p. 57.

26 Byzantine engineers helped to build Sarkel at a point controlling an important route no longer protected by the client Magyar horde. See G. Fehér in *Studia slavica acad. sci. hungaricae* 5 (1959).

27 Dvornik, *Légendes*, pp. 172–4.

28 *Theophanes Continuatus*, iv, 33 (Migne, *PG* 109, col. 212) alone specifically records a Russian embassy to Constantinople shortly after 860, requesting Christian instruction. The wording of the *Primary Chronicle* s.a. 6390 (882)—a badly distorted entry—does not allow the assumption that Askold himself founded a church of St Nicholas at Kiev.

29 Migne, *PG* 102, cols. 736–7, §35: ὥστε καὶ ἐπίσκοπον καὶ ποιμένα δέξασθαι. The view of K. Ericsson (*SR*, Jan. 1966 [vol. 44, no. 102]) that there had been a previous conversion of 'the Russians' in the second Iconoclast period (815–42), therefore ignored by Photios and Byzantine historians at this time, requires elaborate juggling with dates and does not convince. It should also be noted that Idrisī (see Pashuto, *Drevnerusskoje gosudarstvo*, p. 416), summing up the facts available to his predecessors about the Slav world in the later ninth century, states that the Moslem world drew its information from 'Armenian' merchants who travelled as far as Kiev on business. We may take this to mean Transcaucasian Christians in general. Some little influence on their part side by side with Byzantine should not be discounted.

30 *Theophanes cont.*, v, 97: καὶ σπονδὰς πρὸς αὐτοὺς σπεισάμενος εἰρηνικάς. Cf. *Primary Chronicle*, s.a. 6374, which may represent 874 (Alexandrian reckoning), not 866.

31 *Theophanes cont., ibid.*: …τοῦ σωτηριώδους βαπτίσματος ἔπεισε καὶ ἀρχιεπισκόπου παρὰ τοῦ πατριάρχου Ἰγνατίου τὴν χειροτονίαν δεξάμενον δέξασθαι παρεσκεύασεν. A very late Greek text (the manuscript is of the fifteenth century) entitled Διήγησις ἀκριβὴς ὅπως ἐβαπτίσθη τὸ τῶν Ῥωσῶν ἔθνος (the *Banduri Legend*), confusing these events with those of the tenth century, states that one of these alleged archbishops was accompanied by 'Cyril and Athanasios' and that they went armed with an alphabet. See W. Regel, *Analecta*, no. 2 and E. Georgiev in *Cyrillo-Methodiana* (*SF* 6). *Theophanes cont.* (*loc. cit.*) records that the archbishop adopted the spectacular course of

throwing a copy of the Gospels into a fire in which it remained unconsumed—
ὅπερ ἰδόντες οἱ βάρβαροι...ἀνενδοιάστως βαπτίζεσθαι ἤρξαντο.

32 M. Taube in *Istina* 4–5 (1957–8). Little of the chronology of the *Primary Chronicle* before Vladimir will do as it stands. A number of Taube's emendations can be accepted.

33 The *Primary Chronicle* makes Askold and Dir joint rulers, which is highly unlikely. It is proposed that Dir ruled after Askold, *c.* 882–93. Kiev was important enough at this time for the name Dir (but not Askold) to be known in the Islamic world (Mas'ūdī, *Kitāb murūj al-dhahab*, cap. 34 (ed. Barbier de Meynard and Pavet de Courteille, vol. 3, p. 64): *fa'l-awwal min mulūk aṣ-ṣaqālibah malik ad-dīr.*

34 *Primary Chronicle*, s.a. 882–5 (6390–3).

35 Rjurik represents Scandinavian Hrœrek (Roderick). He established a local domination over the Slověne of the Novgorod region about 862; see *Primary Chronicle*, s.a. 6370 (=862, or perhaps 870) and notes 14–15 above. The Scandinavian name for Kiev was Kœnugard—the *Chungard* of German-Latin writers such as Adam of Bremen and Helmold.

36 On Khazar alphabets see Artamonov, p. 269, and *id.* in *Sovetskaja Arheologija* 16 (1952).

37 There is only one long runic text, the so-called *Codex runicus*; see Gwyn Jones, p. 347. The view that some system of runes was developed from Roman and Greek letters by the Goths in Eastern Europe and taken thence to Scandinavia should be noted but generally they are held to have been developed by the Germanic tribes in contact with N. Italy from *c.* 200 B.C. and gradually transmitted northwards. The earliest Scandinavian examples are dated to *c.* A.D. 300. See S. B. F. Jansson, *The Runes of Sweden* (English ed., London, 1962) and E. A. Thompson, *The Visigoths in the time of Ulfila* (Oxford, 1966), pp. 31–2 and 57 (note 4).

38 *VC* 8: 'Obrětŭ že tu jevangelije i psaltyrĭ rosĭskymi [var. rusĭskymi] pismeny pisano...'. See p. 331 n. 115.

39 A. S. Lvov, *Ocherki*, pp. 153 ff., shows that *pismeny* belongs to a later stratum of OCS vocabulary than the original text of *VC*. E. Georgiev, *Kiril i Metody*, pp. 60–2, still accepts them as Slav texts (with further literature).

40 On these raids in general see V. Minorsky, *A History of Sharvān and Darband in the 10th–11th cenutries* (Cambridge, 1958), pp. 108 ff.

41 S.a. 912 (6420). Some earlier articles of agreement s.a. 907 (6415) may belong to the preliminary negotiations or be wrongly dated, being applicable to the conclusion of the war as a Bulgarian ally (*c.* 899–900). The raid circumstantially described in the *Primary Chronicle* s.a. 907, though doubted by some, is certainly genuine, as shown by Ostrogorsky in *SK* xi (1940) and A. A. Vasiljev in *DOP* 6 (1951). See also Sorlin in *Cahiers* 2 (1961); H. Grégoire in *La nouvelle Clio* 4 (1952) (against its authenticity).

42 *Primary Chronicle*, Acad. ed., vol. 1, p. 29: 'The Emperor Leo attached officials to them to show them the beauties of the churches...and the Instruments of Our Lord's Passion...and the relics of saints, making known to them the true religion.'

43   See Vaillant in *PRI* 26 (1960), showing the corruption and mistranslation of the Greek in the phrase 'i ina mnoga zla tvorjahu Rusĭ Grekomŭ eliko že ratnii tvorjatĭ'.

44   *Primary Chronicle*, s.a. 945 (6453).

45   *Primary Chronicle*, Acad. ed., vol. I, p. 35: 'eliko ih kreščenje prijali sutĭ...i eliko ih estĭ ne hreščeno. Similarly: ašče li že kto ot knjazĭ ili ot ljudii ruskih li hrestejan ili nehrestejan...' (*ibid.*, p. 39).

46   'Hrestejanuju rusĭ vodiša rotě v cĭrkvi svjatago Ilji.' (*ibid.*, p. 39).

47   See A. S. Lvov in *Issledovanija istochnikov po istorii russkogo jazyka i pismennosti* (Moscow, 1966), pp. 91 ff.

48   The Glagolitic alphabet was also known in Russia but never had any wide currency. A few eleventh-century inscriptions exist (see *Slovenska pismenost*, section I, pl. II, nos. 4–5) but no manuscripts. See also p. 44.

49   Gnězdovo was an extensive cemetery mainly in use in the tenth century. There are some Scandinavian burials (e.g. ship-graves) among a majority of Slav ones. See literature in *Słownik*, s.v. *Gniezdowo*.

50   The information was compiled in the 940s, presumably mainly in 944/5, when Byzantine emissaries visited Kiev. See Sorlin in *Cahiers* vi/2 (1965).

51   See N. Ya. Polovoj in *VV* 18 (1961). Vernadsky would have us believe that this was already Tmutorokan (Tamatarkha).

52   See N. Ya. Polovoj in *VV* 20 (1961).

53   Art. *O Korsunĭstěj straně* (Acad. ed., vol. I, p. 37).

54   This was a harbour suburb on the Western side of the Bosphorus above Galata, thought to be modern Beşiktaş (the monastery of St Mamas was within the city); see Pargoire in *Echos d'Orient* xi (1908); R. Janin, *Constantinople byzantin* (Paris, 1950), p. 227. The khans where foreign merchants had to reside were called μητᾶτον, probably from Latin *mutation[em]*, a post-station.

55   'Mnozi bo běša varjazi hrestejani i kozarě' (Acad. ed., vol. I, p. 39).

56   Zonaras, *Annales* (Migne, *PG* 135), xvi, 21; the following section 22 deals with the death of Patriarch Theophylakt in the twelfth year of Constantine's sole rule, which can only be 956. Similarly *Primary Chronicle*, s.a. 6463 (955), with circumstantial details of her baptism at the hands of Emperor and Patriarch (the Emperor is wrongly given as John Tzimiskes).

57   Const. Porph., *De Cer.* (Migne, *PG* 112, cols. 1108–12). The date is assured by the days of the week. Dvornik (*The Slavs*, p. 200) does not accept Constantine's silence as decisive against 957 and adduces also the account given by the 'Continuator' of Regino of Prühm (*MGH, SS* I, s.a. 959). Cf. note 61. A later miniature of the event will be found in the Radziwiłł manuscript (*Primary Chronicle*, Acad. ed., vol. I, opp. p. 56).

58   A map of the cultural radiation of Great Moravia (in terms of material objects) in the ninth century is given by Dostál in *Magna Moravia*, opp. p. 416.

59   Friedrich, *Codex*, vol. I, no. 31. Cf. p. 341 n. 220. Raffelstetten is near the confluence of Traun and Danube (*Atlas československých dějin*, map 3 b).

60   See e.g. Kartashëv, vol. I, pp. 99 ff.

61   Thietmar, ii, 22; *Ann. Quedl.* (*MGH, SS* I) s.a. 960, with the comment:

'illique [Russians] per omnia mentiti sunt, sicut postea rei probavit eventus, quia nec ille praedictus episcopus evasit lethale periculum ab insidiis eorum'. Cf. also *Reginon. Cont.* (*MGH, SS* 1) s.a. 962: 'Adalbertus, Rugis [Russians] ordinatus episcopus, nihil in his propter quae missus fuerat proficere valens et inaniter se fatigatum videns revertitur, et quibusdam ex suis in redeundo occisis ipse cum magno labore vix evasit. . .'. It is generally thought that this 'continuator' of Regino of Prühm was Adalbert himself, when Abbot of Weissenburg in 966/7.

62 *Primary Chronicle*, s.a. 6463 (955): 'a družina moja semu smějatisja načnutĭ'. The Scandinavian word for *družina* (comitatus) was hirð, which appears also in Old Russian as гридь.

63 Tolerant derision was the attitude of him and his entourage: 'ašče kto hotjaše krestitisja ne branjahu no rugahusja tomu' (*Primary Chronicle*, s.a. 955).

64 The corrections in the chronology are noted by Vernadski, *Kievan Russia*, pp. 43–4.

65 *Primary Chronicle*, s.a. 6477 (969) shows clearly the main articles of commerce which a capital on the Danube would command as well as or better than Kiev; a Central European route would there cross an overland Kiev–Constantinople route.

66 *Primary Chronicle*, s.a. 6479 (971). Leo Diaconus (*Historiae libri decem*, ix, 11—written in 992 and covering the period 959–75) gives an eye-witness impression of Svjatoslav's personal appearance and dress, which was not typically Scandinavian. See also V. Terras in *ASR* 24 (1965).

67 In 1044 Jaroslav reinterred his uncles Jaropolk and Oleg in the Tithe Church (*Primary Chronicle*, s.a. 6552), that is, added them to the dynastic mausoleum. Since the bones were then baptised (*krestiša kosti jeju*), they were then considered unbaptised.

68 The Byzantine conquest did not completely interrupt commercial relations between Constantinople and Kiev via the lower Danube at this time. See I. Barnea in *Nouvelles études d'histoire* (Papers of the Historical Congress) (Rome, 1955), vol. 1.

69 The late Russian *Nikon Chronicle* records (s.a. 6487=979) an embassy from Pope Benedict VII to Kiev, not confirmed by any other source. Evidently, if genuine, it could have been motivated by the embassy to Otto in 973. Its arrival in Kiev about the time of Vladimir's triumph over Jaropolk would be enough to explain its unimportance.

70 *Primary Chronicle*, s.a. 6488 (980) (Acad. ed., vol. 1, p. 56).

71 Khors, Dazhbog and Stribog may have been the three sons of Svarog (Iranian *Svarga*, a sky- and sun-god), hence known as the Svarozhichi. More is known of this cult among the Polabian Slavs (see pp. 145 ff.). To illustrate the Slav–Iranian religious links it will suffice to instance that Slav bogŭ (god), if not borrowed from Iranian *b(h)aga*, has followed the same semantic evolution—*riches, prosperity > the god who grants these > God in general*; and that the nearest congener of Slav svętŭ = *holy* is again Iranian (cf. Avestan spənta = *beneficent*). Further, *Khors* is plausibly connected with Iranian *xurš*-, the sun or *hvarzu-, good. The name *Perun* may be a very ancient Indo-european one since a possible Hittite parallel has been found; see V. V. Ivanov in *Voprosy slavjanskogo jazykoznanija* 3 (1958).

72   Cf. the analysis of the Zbrucz idol by Rybakov in *Istorija russkogo iskusstva*, vol. 1, pp. 75 ff. See also p. 364 n. 220.

73   Perun, like Thor, was in all probability (in Dumézil's formulation) 'dieu du conflit atmosphérique'. Veles or Volos, sufficiently important to be included beside Perun in the Russo–Greek treaties of 907 and 971 (but not 944) does not appear in Vladimir's list. His origin and attributes are obscure. On the conflation of Perun and Thor see V. P. Darkevich in *Sovetskaja arheologija* 5/iv (1961).

74   'Bě že varjagŭ toj prišelŭ izŭ Grekŭ' (Acad. ed., vol. 1, p. 58).

75   For the trade-routes of the late tenth century see Lewis, *Northern Seas*, p. 369 and compare Carolingian map on p. 205.

76   See V. L. Janin, *passim*.

77   Probably Jews from Khazaria, but there were always some resident in Kiev as traders, witness the *Paterik* of the Cave Monastery (*Slovo* 8, *Life of St Theodosius, Slavische Propyläen* 2, p. 65: 'se bo takovĭ obyčaj iměše blaženyi jako že mnogaždy vŭ nošči vŭstaa i otaj vsěh ishoždaše k židomĭ i těh ježe o Hristě prepiraja i ukorjaa že i dosaždaa těm i jako otmetniky i bezakonniky těh naricaa...').

78   S.a. 987 (6495): 'Svojego niktože ne hulitŭ no hvalitŭ' (Acad. ed., p. 74).

79   S.a. 987: 'ne svěmi na nebě li esmy byli li na zemli' (Acad. ed., p. 75). Emissaries of Vladimir certainly saw the Great Church in September 987 (see p. 258) but there must have been many previous occasions in the tenth century. According to the *Book of Skálholt*, twelfth-century Scandinavian pilgrims considered the Church of the Holy Wisdom in Constantinople (Aegisif) the most wonderful in the world; see Riant P., *Expéditions et pélérinages des Scandinaves en Terre sainte* (Paris, 1865), p. 68. Indeed how could it not seem so to any foreigner whatever?

80   S.a. 987: 'ašče by lihŭ zakonŭ grečĭskij to ne by baba tvoja prijala Olĭga jaže bě mudrějši vsěhŭ člověkŭ' (Acad. ed., p. 75).

81   Moreover Moslems did not proselytise as a rule; a delegation of Moslem doctors to Kiev smacks of literary artifice. A fiction in normal Moslem terms is to be found in a work of the Moslem geographer Marwazī, who died a very old man *c.* 1120, *Sharaf al-Zamān Tāhir Marvasī on China, the Turks and India* (ed. V. Minorsky, London, 1942), especially Section 15: 'The *Rūs* live in an island in the sea...they became Christians in the year 300 [=A.D. 912/13]...[later] they desired to become Moslems...they therefore sent envoys to the ruler of Khwārazm, four kinsmen of their ruler, for they had an independent ruler named W(a)lādmīr...The Shah of Khwārazm was delighted at their eagerness to embrace Islam and sent someone to teach them the doctrines of the Moslem religion. So they were converted [*fa-'aslamū*]'! The date is clearly mutilated; perhaps it should be 987, the time of Vladimir's enquiries.

82   Generally thought to have been written *c.* 1200. Text in Golubinski,

vol. 1, part 1, pp. 238–45. Recent ed. of earliest known text (1470s) by A. A. Zimin in *KSIS* 37 (1963).

83 *Histoire de Yaḥyā ibn-Saʿīd d'Antioche*, ed. Kratchkovsky and Vasiliev, *Patrologia orientalis*, vols. 18 (1924) and 23 (1932).

84 See N. de Baumgarten, *Olaf Tryggwison, roi de Norvège et ses relations avec S. Vladimir de Russie* (*OC* 24/1, no. 73, 1931).

85 Precisely in 986 Samuel of Bulgaria had proposed to the Emperor a similar way of composing their differences; he had been fobbed off with an inferior substitute. The concession to Tsar Peter, who married Maria Lecapéna (see p. 173) was less than that now asked, since Peter was an Orthodox Tsar and Maria not a *porphyrogenneta*. On Byzantine marriages to foreigners see also L. Bréhier, *Les institutions de l'empire byzantin*, pp. 38 ff.

86 Dölger, *Regesten*, nos. 776, 777 show two Greek approaches to Vladimir, one to make clear that baptism was the prerequisite for the marriage and to find out Vladimir's position in this respect, the second a formal consent to the marriage.

87 The author of the *Primary Chronicle* (Acad. ed., vol. 1, p. 76) imagines it thus: 'She did not want to go. "I should be like spoils of war" [i.e. a slave-girl], she said; "I would rather die here" [now than go]'. Her brothers stressed that it was 'for the good of the Empire', and a great honour to be the instrument of Russia's conversion. Anna had been born a few days before Romanos's death in 963 of a later marriage and was not an influential person in the councils of her half-brothers. It is possible that Anna had been denied the role of Empress in the West when Theophano was sent in 972 in response to Otto I's solicitation for an Imperial bride for his son (see p. 124).

88 *Primary Chronicle*, s.a. 980 (Acad. ed., vol. 1, pp. 56–7).

89 'Na drugoje lěto po kreščenїi kŭ porogomŭ hodi'.

90 'Se že ne svěduščе pravo glagoljutї jako krestilŭsja jestї v Kievě inii že rěša v Vasiljevě druzii že inako skažjutї (s.a. 6496=988). The arrival of Anna and Vladimir's baptism at Kherson are illustrated in the Radziwiłł manuscript (*Primary Chronicle*, Acad. ed., vol. 1, between pp. 80–1).

91 Little is known about St Clement's. Thietmar's statement (vii, 74) that Vladimir was buried there is not generally accepted against the *Primary Chronicle* which indicates the more probable Tithe Church (s.a. 6523=1015). Dvornik suggests that St Clement's relics were in a special chapel in the Tithe Church (*The Slavs* (1956), pp. 227–8).

92 *Histoire de Yaḥyā*, ed. Kratchkovsky and Vasiliev, *Patr. Orient.*, vol. 23, p. 423.

93 The development of these ideas in Constantinople belongs to the later ninth century: Photios ignores them in his differences with Pope Nicholas. See Dvornik, *The Idea of Apostolicity* (1958) for a full analysis; also F. Dölger, *Byzanz*, pp. 70 ff.

94 The Russian legend is recounted in the *Primary Chronicle, ad init.* (Acad. ed., vol. 1, p. 12), a passage probably inserted in 1116. Cf. also *Stepennaja kniga* (*PSRL* 21/i), St. 1, cap. 23.

95 The Saxon Thietmar knew nothing more than that Vladimir had been baptised, and that vaguely, since he ascribes it to the influence of his last wife, a cousin of the Emperor Otto III (*Chronicon*, vii, 72).

96 There is no real distinction at this time between personal and state revenue; nor was it at any time a tithe in the Western sense of falling on the population as a whole. The origin of this tithe is disputed. It is unlikely to have been inspired by Western, even Bohemian or Polish, practice. Tithes of various kinds (μορτή) and 10% duties were current in the Byzantine Empire, Khazaria and elsewhere. See *Słownik*, s.v. *Dziesięcina*; Pashuto, *Drevnerusskoje gosudarstvo*, pp. 297 ff.; and H. F. Schmid in *Jahrbuch der Oesterreichischen Byzantinischen Gesellschaft* 6 (1957). Other later princely foundations received a similar tithe, e.g. Jaroslav's new church at Vyshgorod (see n. 149), St John '*na opokah*' at Novgorod (*c.* 1130), as also bishoprics (Smolensk, 1136–7).

97 According to Jacob the Monk's *Memorial* he laid the foundations in the fourth year after his conversion, i.e. in 990 or 991. Cf. *Primary Chronicle*, s.a. 989 (6497) and 996 (6504). The church was destroyed by the Mongols in 1240 but its foundations have been identified.

98 *Primary Chronicle*, s.a. 988 = 6496 (Acad. ed., vol. 1, p. 81). The parallel to *VC* 15 should be noted.

99 The most explicit list is in the late *Nikon Chronicle* (*PSRL* 9), s.a. 6500, which names the bishops appointed by the new Metropolitan Leontios (in addition to Novgorod) as follows: Chernigov—Neofit; Rostov—Feodor; Vladimir (Volodimer)—Stefan; Belgorod (Bělgrad)—Nikita, and adds: 'he also appointed bishops to many other towns'. The authenticity of these appointments and names is extremely improbable. Most authorities ascribe Vladimir and Turov to *c.* 1078–88.

100 The worship of Svarozhich in remote parts is still recorded in the early twelfth century. Thus the references to the pagan gods in the *Slovo o polku Igoreve* (provided the portions concerned do date from the end of the twelfth century or shortly after) may not have been exceptional for the time in oral poetry. Even thirteenth-century Russian versions of the *Hozhdenije Bogoroditsy po mukam* imply that the cult of Perun, Volos, etc., was not wholly extinct then. There are attacks on paganism in the *Slovo nekojego hristolyubtsa* (text in N. K. Nikolski, *Materialy dlja istorii drevnerusskoj duhovnoj pismennosti*, no. 14 (*Sbornik otdelenija russkogo jazyka i slovesnosti imp. ak. nauk*, 82/4, 1907)) and in the *Slovo o tom, kako pogani sušče jazyci klanjalisja idolom*. See also Komarovich in *TODL* 16 (1960). In the matter of adaptations Volos/Veles was reinterpreted as St Vlas (Blaise), perhaps also the female Mokosh as St Paraskeví (Russian пятница). St George (23 April) was made to cover many aspects of the spring agricultural festival. The acts of the Church Council of 1551 (Stoglav) are still concerned about the suppression of widespread popular 'superstitions', more pagan than Christian (text ed. E. Duchesne, Paris, 1920). This is not in any way remarkable. Any illiterate peasantry comes to terms with Christianity in much the same way: its traditional religion of the 'cosmic rhythm' is fitted to and reinterpreted in the light of the Christian story. The intellectual and historical elements of Christianity are outside its comprehension and needs. See M. Eliade, *Myth and Reality* (London, 1964), pp. 172 ff.

101 *Istorija rossijskaja*, pt. 1, cap. iv (Acad. ed., vol. 1, p. 112). The *bylina* of Dobrynja and the Dragon clearly symbolises the triumph of Christianity over paganism in Novgorod; see Rybakov, pp. 68–9.

102 See *Primary Chronicle*, years 998–1013. A reason for this gap is suggested by Rybakov, pp. 187–8.

103 Thietmar, viii, 32; vii, 72–4. The figure 400 (a score of scores) is suspiciously of the order of the 'forty times forty' churches proverbially existing in Moscow in its heyday and, like 1001, means 'too many to count'.

104 The earliest manuscript is dated 1282 but preserves remarkably well the material and language of the eleventh century. Editions: *Pamjatniki russkogo prava*, ed. S. V. Jushkov, vol. 1 (1952), ed. A. A. Zimin; *Pravda russkaja*, ed. V. D. Grekov, 3 vols. (Moscow, 1940–63); partial English version by G. Vernadski in his *Medieval Russian Laws* New York, 1947).

105 See Pashuto, *Drevnerusskoje gosudarstvo*, pp. 131 ff. The nucleus of the Code presumably goes back much further but how far is difficult to establish where oral transmission is concerned: the Icelandic Law continued to be transmitted orally for over a century after the formal adoption of Christianity in 1000. The customary law on vendetta in the *Russian Law Code* resembles that of Ethelbert's Kent, written down at the time of St Augustine's mission; see M. Deanesly, *Augustine of Canterbury* (1964), pp. 90 ff.

106 Szeftel, pp. 229 ff.; *Pamjatniki russkogo prava*, vol. 1, ed. Zimin (1952); Pashuto, pp. 289 ff.; L. K. Goetz, *Kirchenrechtliche...Denkmäler, ad init.* No manuscript now exists older than the fourteenth century. The text has clearly been much altered and contains some obvious errors but the essence of it can be safely ascribed to Vladimir. The same may be said of Jaroslav's *Statute*, dating in all probability from 1039.

107 For a full analysis see R. Guénon, *Autorité spirituelle et pouvoir temporel* (Paris, 1929).

108 Βασιλέως μέν ἐστι τρόπος ὁ νόμος, τυράννου δὲ ὁ τρόπος νόμος (Synesios, Περὶ βασιλείας (Migne, *PG* 66, col. 1061, §6), quoted by Hunger, p. 117).

109 See Fedotov's analysis in *The Russian Religious Mind*, vol. 1, pp. 244 ff. and Hunger, pp. 143 ff. Vladimir's *Poučenije,* inserted in the *Primary Chronicle* s.a. 1096, is based on a well-known Greek genre already appearing in the *Izbornik Svjatoslava* 1076 *g.* See T. Čyževska in *WSJ* 2 (1952) and A. S. Orlov, *Vladimir Monomakh* (Moscow, 1946).

110 The Orthodox church rarely acceded to the canonization of laymen. For this reason (as with Vladimir himself and others; cf. p. 226) their canonization was purely Russian, formalised in 1072 as soon as the necessary miracles wrought by their relics had been attested. The Greek Metropolitan John, nevertheless, seems to have had no reservations and there is some evidence that their Office and at least one other associated text were first composed in Greek, perhaps by the Metropolitan himself. See L. Müller in *Slawistische Studien zum V internationalen Slawistenkongress* (Göttingen, 1963).

111 Sources: two literary works of the late eleventh century—*Čtenije o žitii* *i pogublenii blažennuju strastoterpcu Borisa i Glěba* by the monk Nestor, written *c.* 1079 (see A. Poppe in *SLOR* 14 (1965)) and *Skazanije strastĭ i pohvala svjatuju mučeniku Borisa i Glěba*, ascribed, probably wrongly, to the monk Jacob and written about the time of the Translation of their relics in 1020 (see p. 269); also the accounts in the *Primary Chronicle*. Texts in D. I. Abramovich, *Pamjatniki drevnerusskoj literatury*, vol. 2 (Petrograd, 1916). Their mutual affiliation has been studied by L. Müller in *ZSP* 25 (1956) and *loc. cit.* (see note 110) and by N. W. Ingham in *WS* 10 (1965). Though the date 1015 is generally accepted as correct for the murders there is some evidence that Svjatopolk did not at once occupy Kiev, being still a refugee in Poland. Koroljuk, pp. 234 ff., therefore suggests 1018–19 as more probable. It has also been suggested that it was really Jaroslav who was responsible for their deaths (see N. N. Iljin, *Letopisnaja statja 6523 g. i jejë istochnik*, Moscow, 1957). He was certainly no less unscrupulous and, as the eventual victor in the struggle for power, allowed his own misdeeds to be put to the account of Svjatopolk, his Richard III. But the theory cannot be put higher than a surmise.

112 For a general review of the problem see L. Müller in *Osteuropa und der deutsche Osten* iii/6 (Köln, 1956), who personally favours this view.

113 *PSRL* 30 (reprinted Moscow, 1965), p. 169, s.a. 6497 = 989: 'krestisja Volodimerŭ i vzja [u] Fotija patriarh[a] caregradskago perŭvago mitropolita Kieva Leona, a Novugorodu arhiepiskopa [sic] Akima korsunjanina...'.

114 *Nikon Chronicle*, s.a. 6496, 6500, 6516.

115 E.g. in the *Stepennaja kniga* (sixteenth century; *PSRL* 21/i), st. 1, cap. 33 and 48.

116 Art. 2 of Vladimir's *Church Statute* in one form introduces Photios and Michael, in another Photios and Leon (*Pamjatniki russkogo prava*, vol. 1, pp. 237 and 244.)

117 V. N. Tatishchev, *Istorija rossijskaja*, pt. 1, cap. iv (Acad. ed., vol. 1, p. 112), quoting a lost chronicle, with Symeon anachronistically for Samuel.

118 By M. D. Prisëlkov, *Ocherki po tserkovno-politicheskoj istorii kievskoj Rusi X–XII vv.* (St Petersburg, 1913). Adopted by Kartashëv; cf. also V. Nikolaev, *Slavjanobŭlgarskijat faktor* (Sofia, 1949).

119 Μιχαὴλ τοῦ 'Ατταλειάτου 'Ιστορία (ed. Bekker, Bonn, 1853), p. 204.

120 In *TODL* 19 (1963); see also *id.* in *SLO* 11–12 (1962).

121 The three charters of Basil II relating to the archdiocese of Ohrid are given in Ivanov, *Bŭlgarski starini*, pp. 547–62. The most northerly sees are on the Danube—Belgrade, Vidin, Silistria. Silistria (Dorostol) remained in Byzantine hands all through the difficult times after 971, with a Greek hierarch (as far as is ascertainable). A *Notitia episcopatuum* (*Diatyposis*) of *c.* 972–6 includes *Rus* but the entry is clearly a later, probably thirteenth century, interpolation (see *Słownik*, s.v. *Notitiae*).

122 *Primary Chronicle*, s.a. 988: 'Volodiměrŭ že posemŭ poemŭ caricju i Nastasa i popy korsunĭski s moščmi svjatago Klimenta...'. He then was affected to Vladimir's new church of the Holy Virgin, again with precedence over priests from Kherson (*ibid.*, s.a. 989: '[Vladimir] poruči ju Nastasu Korsunjaninu i popy korsunĭskyja pristavi služiti v nej'), but exactly in what capacity is not clear. He could have been an archpriest. It should be borne in mind that *Korsunjanin* and *Korsunskaja strana* in the tenth-century treaties embrace the whole of Byzantine Crimea, not exclusively the town of Kherson.

123   *Primary Chronicle*, s.a. 1018 (6526).

124   Short exposition of his views in *SR* 20 (1941). Cf. also Golubinski, vol. 1, pt. 1 (2nd ed. 1901), pp. 264–9.

125   See N. Adontz in *BYZ* 9 (1934) and Honigmann in *BYZ* 17 (1944–5).

126   See A. L. Mongait in *Problemy obshchestvenno-politicheskoj istorii Rossii i slavjanskih stran* (essays offered to M. N. Tikhomirov, Moscow, 1963).

127   See particularly N. de Baumgarten, *Saint Vladimir et la conversion de la Russie* (*OC* 27/1, no. 79, 1932).

128   *Nikon Chronicle* (*PSRL* 9), s.a. 6508: 'otŭ papy rimskago i otŭ korolej čežĭskihŭ i ugorskihŭ' [sic].

129   The details come from Bruno's own letter to Henry II, written *c.* 1008 in Poland (*MPH*, vol. 1, no. 11). See also B. Widera in *Jahrbuch für Geschichte der UdSSR* (Halle) 3 (1959). On some doubtful points the chronology of W. Meysztowicz (*SPM* 5 (1958)) seems preferable.

130   Especially as the letter (see note **129**) has been held to suggest that Bruno sent missionaries with a bishop from Kiev to Sweden, who may therefore have been responsible for the baptism of Olof Sköttkonung about 1008. Olof was himself half-Slav and married to a Slav, and gave his daughter Ingigard in marriage to Vladimir's son Jaroslav. See A. Ruprecht in *Palaestra* 224 (1958).

131   '...duos dies cum exercitu duxit me ipse usque ad regni sui terminum ultimum' (Letter to Henry II). This vividly shows the proximity of the unsafe lands to Kiev itself—scarcely fifty miles to the south. Bruno quotes Vladimir's words as: 'duxi te, ubi mea desinit terra, inimicorum incipit'.

132   Unlike Thietmar (vii, 72–3), always ungenerous to Slavs, who did not know Vladimir personally. Cf. his slighting reference to Bolesław Chrobry, the plague of Germany (iv, 45): 'Bolizlavus qui maior laus non merito sed more antiquo interpretatur' (Bolesław = greater glory).

133   Koroljuk, pp. 208 ff., connects this with the conclusion of the Russo-Polish treaty. See also Grabski in *SLOR* 6 (1957).

134   vii, 72. Thietmar is the main source for this period of difficult Polish–Russian relations. See Koroljuk, pp. 170 ff.

135   See e.g. Paszkiewicz, *The Making of the Russian Nation*, ch. 2 (especially p. 62), following the arguments of his earlier *The Origin of Russia*, chs. 1–2 (especially pp. 17–25).

136   See note **135**. The most important context is *Primary Chronicle, ad init.* (Acad. ed., p. 13): 'se bo tokmo slověnĭskŭ jazykŭ v Rusi'. But the whole passage is clearly about languages and peoples: the learned monk lists the non-Slav peoples surrounding the land of Rus, each of which has its own language and all of whom were of course still pagan. That he omitted a couple of Slav-speaking tribes is surely pure oversight. The word *jazyk* (tongue) has two established collective senses: (1) all the speakers of a language, hence 'people' or 'nation', as in Medieval French *langue d'oc* and *langue d'oïl*;

(2) the more special sense taken over from Church Slavonic where *językŭ* translates *ἔθνος* (Latin *gens*) and provides the derivative *języčĭnikŭ*=gentile, unconverted, pagan. Thus *slověnĭskŭ jazykŭ* can certainly bear a sense parallel to the frequent *latineski jazyk* in thirteenth-century treaties, signifying 'all those who profess the Latin faith, Catholics'.

137 *Skazanije Borisa i Gleba* (Abramovich, p. 33): 'pomyšljašetĭ že mučenije i strastĭ svjatago mučenika Nikity i svjatago Vjačeslava, podobno že semu byti ubjenu'.

138 *Primary Chronicle*, s.a. 6547 (1039) merely records him as already in office.

139 If one were to trust the *Nikon Chronicle*, which records Michael's death in 992 (s.a. 6500: 'togo že lěta prestavisja presvjaščennyj Mihailŭ mitropolitŭ kijevskij i vseja Rusi'), we should have to accept Michael as a metropolitan who was sent with Anna to Kherson. It is surely unlikely that the pro-Greek narrator of those events in the *Primary Chronicle* should not mention him. In any case the whole passage in the *Nikon Chronicle* is full of anachronisms, notably the title quoted and the introduction of Patriarch Photios. According to a lost source quoted by Tatishchev, the seventeenth-century *Joachim Chronicle* (*Istorija rossijskaja*, pt. 1, cap. iv), Metropolitan Michael was a Bulgarian but sent from Constantinople—a most improbable combination.

140 E.g. the *Stepennaja Kniga* (St. 1, cap. 49), noting his departure from Constantinople in 6499 = September 990–August 991.

141 Migne, *PG* 146, col. 1196: ἐπὶ δὲ τῆς αὐτῆς ἡγεμονίας Θεοφύλακτος ἐκ τῆς Σεβαστηνῶν εἰς Ῥωσίαν ἀνάγεται (*Ecclesiastica Historia*, Bk. xiv, cap. 39—περὶ μεταθέσεων); or in another version published by P. Laurent (see Devos, *Chronique d'hagiographie slave* in *AB* 73 (1955), p. 223): ἐπὶ τῆς βασιλείας Βασιλείου τοῦ πορφυρογεννήτου Θεοφύλακτος ὁ Σεβαστείας μετετέθη εἰς Ῥωσίαν. Translations were forbidden by Canon XV of the Council of Nicaea and subsequently, but in practice exceptions were made; see Honigmann in *BYZ* 17 (1944/5).

142 The vacancy was largely due to the Emperor's absence on campaigns. It was long thought to have started as early as 991, following Yahyā's statements and some Byzantine sources, but it now seems probable that Nicholas died on 16 December 992. See V. Grumel in *REB* 22 (1964), following Grégoire and Orgels in *BYZ* 24 (1954).

143 V. Laurent, *Le corpus des sceaux de l'empire byzantin*: vol. 5, *L'Eglise*, pt. 1, *L'Eglise de Constantinople*; A.—*La Hiérarchie* (*Publications de l'Institut français d'études byzantines*, 1963), no. 781. Laurent is prepared to date it as early as the end of the tenth century.

144 A seal of Metropolitan John II exists also: *ibid.*, vol. v/2 (1965), *Supplément* no. 1605.

145 Thietmar, viii, 32.

146 S.a. 6597: 'Bě bo preže vŭ Perejaslavli mitropolija'.

147 The problem has been worked over again recently by A. Stokes in *SR* 37 (1959).

148 *Primary Chronicle*, s.a. 6545 (1037): 'Otecĭ bo sego Volodimerŭ zemlju vzora i umjagči, rekše kreščenĭjemĭ prosvětivŭ. Sĭ že nasěja knižnymi slovesy serdca věrnyh ljudij'.

149 *Ibid.* Building had of course not ceased even in the most troubled years. The modest wooden church which Jaroslav built in 1020–6 at Vyshgorod (a short way upstream from Kiev) for the relics of SS Boris and Gleb, was no doubt typical of the resources available. It was built by a native architect Mironeg and decorated in fresco also by natives.

150 Plan in Lazarev, *Mozaiki Sofii kievskoj*, p. 39. For reconstructions of the original aspect see *Istorija Kieva*, vol. 1, p. 56; *Istorija russkogo iskusstva*, vol. 1 (1953), p. 132; O. Powstenko, *The Cathedral of St Sofia in Kiev*, pp. 48–55.

151 See Lazarev, *Mozaiki Sofii Kievskoj*, p. 155.

152 See Powstenko, *op. cit.*, pls. 155–6, pp. 138–9 (seventeenth-century drawing still showing Jaroslav holding the church in his hands—the act of dedication); pl. 176 (possible portrait of Jaroslav in the N.W. tower).

153 Chernigov Cathedral: *Istorija russkogo iskusstva*, vol. 1, p. 123; *Primary Chronicle*, Acad. ed., vol. 1, opp. p. 292. The Golden Gate: *Istorija Kieva*, vol. 1, p. 55 (reconstruction).

154 D. R. Buxton, pl. 1, no. 1 (Kiev), no. 2 (Novgorod) and pl. 11; *Primary Chronicle*, Acad. ed., vol. 1, opp. pp. 296, 141; O. Powstenko, pls. 4 and 9; *Słownik*, vol. 3, figs. 193, 199–201. Bishop Joachim's original church was probably also dedicated to the Holy Wisdom. It was destroyed by fire in 1049. Novgorodian municipal life centred so closely on the cathedral that the people proudly called themselves *Sofijane*.

155 Migne, *PG* 102, cols. 736–7.

156 Cf. short discussion by D. Obolensky in *OCA*, vol. 1. Patriarch Anthony still impressed the principle of Empire and Church on Basil of Moscow as late as the last decade of the fourteenth century. While Jaroslav may have used the Imperial title *tsar*, the Imperial conception could not gain ground again until the unification of Russia and the fall of Constantinople in the fifteenth century. On the Byzantine conceptions of political sonship and brotherhood see Dölger, *Byzanz* pp. 159 ff.

157 *CMH*, iv/2, pp. 109–10.

158 Psellos, *Chronographia*, vi, 90 (περὶ τῆς τῶν ʹΡώσων ἐπαναστάσεως).

159 Cf. *Primary Chronicle*, s.a. 6559 (1051); *Nikon Chronicle*, s.a. 6559; L. Müller, *Des Metr. Ilarion Lobrede*, pp. 5 ff. (cf. p. 143 *ad fin.*). The difficult point was not so much who should *elect* as who should *consecrate* the head of church. It is nowhere stated who consecrated Hilarion. In contrast to the case of Bulgaria (including Ohrid after 1018) Constantinople appears to have insisted, within the measure of the possible, on retaining the consecration of the Russian metropolitan in the hands of the Patriarch.

160 It would appear that Hilarion consecrated Jaroslav's church of St George as late as November 1055, the year in which this shadowy Efrem is mentioned (*First Novgorod Chronicle*, ed. A. N. Nasonov, 1950, s.a. 1055, pp. 182–3). The once popular theory that Hilarion retired to the Cave Monastery in 1052 as the monk Nikon and died there at an advanced age as its abbot in 1088 has no factual basis.

161 This is not to be taken as an early instance of the alternation of Greek and Russian metropolitans sometimes adopted in later times. See D. Obolensky's study of this question in *DOP* 11 (1957).

162 L. Müller, p. 100. Hilarion no doubt purposely does not stress the merits of Olga who was hailed as the 'originator' (*nachalnitsa*; *Primary Chronicle*, s.a. 969).

163 Rozov (*SL* 32 (1963), with text) thinks that it was delivered on 26 March 1049, but the anniversary of Vladimir's death (15 July) is also possible; see L. Müller, pp. 20–1.

164 On Jaroslav's links with Sweden see Bilinbakhov and Zhigalova in *Abstract of Papers of the 2nd Conference on the history, economics, languages and literatures of the Scandinavian countries and Finland* (Moscow, 1965).

165 Anna's signature appears on a French state document dated 1063, in Cyrillic characters (АНА РЪИНА=Anna Regina). She was for a time Regent of France. It is doubtful whether the fresco in the Church of the Holy Wisdom at Kiev can be taken as a portrait (*Primary Chronicle*, Acad. ed., vol. 1, between pp. 296–7; Powstenko, pls. 157–8).

166 'Vědoma i slyšima estĭ vsěmi (četyrĭmi) konĭci zemljě.' (Müller, p. 101). Cf. Thietmar, viii, 32 and Adam of Bremen, ii, 22. On Jaroslav's matrimonial policy see also M. Hellmann in *FOG* 8 (1962).

167 For a valuable essay on the development of the Schism see Dvornik in *L'Eglise et les églises* (see Bibliography). Cf. also Runciman, *A History of the Crusades*, vol. 2, pp. 47–8. Rome had officially adopted the addition of *filioque* to the Creed, under German pressure, in 1014. New departures in Western thought from about 1100, while the Eastern church maintained relative intellectual immobility, soon made the theological chasm unbridgeable. On the political plane the alliance of the Papacy with the hated Normans disinclined Constantinople to any composition after 1054. In fact the Norman kingdom in S. Italy, by expelling the Greeks for good from those parts, was a considerable factor in the estrangement between East and West in the later eleventh century. Toynbee (*A Study of History*, vol. 4, p. 614) rightly also stresses the internal factor in the events of 1054 by defining Kerularios's action as the Patriarchate's 'revenge upon the Imperial Government for three centuries of humiliation'.

168 One of Gertrude's devotional books, the *Codex Gertrudianus*, consists of a Latin Psalter and various additional prayers, including one *pro papa nostro*. Her Creed also contains *filioque*. We cannot be certain that she used the book in Russia, though this is likely if the five miniatures added to it *c.* 1078–87 are in fact Russian work. See W. Meysztowicz in *ANT* 2 (1955).

169 Pavlov, *Kriticheskije opyty*, pp. 45–6. Theodosius's hostility is evident from the title itself and from his disapproval of mixed marriages. Another typical anti-Latin tract of the period is *Stjazanije s latinoju* by Metr. George (*fungebatur* 1062–79); see Ramm, pp. 61–2.

170 He wrote (Caspar, ii, 49): 'Cumvallat enim me dolor immanis et tristitia universalis quia orientalis ecclesia instinctu diaboli a catholica fide deficit et per sua membra ipse antiquus hostis Christianos passim occidit' (January 1075).

26-2

171 Caspar, ii, 55 a. The *per me reges regnant*, inscribed on Otto I's Imperial crown (961/2), had passed to the Papacy.

172 *Monumenta Gregoriana* (ed. P. Jaffé), ii, 74 (pp. 198–9): 'et quod regnum illud dono sancti Petri *per manus nostras* vellet optinere, eidem beato Petro apostolorum principi debita fidelitate exhibita, devotis precibus postularit; indubitanter asseverans: illam suam petitionem vestro consensu ratam fore ac stabilem, si apostolicae auctoritatis gratia ac munimine donaretur. Cuius votis et petitionibus...assensum praebuimus et regni vestri gubernacula sibi ex parte beati Petri tradidimus, ea videlicet intentione atque desiderio caritatis: ut beatus Petrus vos et regnum vestrum omniaque vestra bona sua apud Deum intercessione custodiat...'. Cf. his letter to Bolesław, dated 20 April 1075 (*Mon. Greg.*, ii, 73).

173 On the general sequence of events consult *Studi gregoriani*, i, ed. G. B. Borino (Abbazia di San Paolo di Roma, 1947). Among the miniatures added to the *Codex Gertrudianus* (see note 168 above) are: (1) Jaropolk and his wife Irene standing before St Peter with Gertrude kneeling beside them; (2) Christ crowning Jaropolk and Irene.

174 See T. Grudziński, *Polityka papieża Grzegorza VII*, pp. 74 ff.

175 Leib, pp. 32 ff. As late as 1285 an œcumenical council of the Eastern church in the interests of unity redefined the Procession of the Holy Spirit in such a way as to include the Latin position. The purely political surrender of the Emperor Michael VIII at the Council of Lyons (1274) led to nothing but his excommunication by both churches.

176 Text in Goetz, *Kirchenrechtliche...Denkmäler*, pp. 115 ff. (see §§4–5).

177 *Paterik, Slovo* 1. But the account was not written before the early thirteenth century and was revised even later.

178 Philological examination by A. S. Lvov in *Problemy sovremennoj filologii* (*Festschrift* for V. V. Vinogradov, ed. M. V. Khrapchenko, Moscow, 1965).

179 Cf. Gumpold, cap. xviii–xix (the betrayal at Stará Boleslav).

180 Martynov, *Annus ecclesiasticus*, pp. 329–32 (*Kalendarium ostromiranum* and *assemanianum*).

181 *Izbornik* 1076 *goda*, ed. S. I. Kotkov (Moscow, 1965). While certainly copied in 1076 it is not stated by the scribe that it was done for Svjatoslav himself but only during his reign.

182 Edition of the Slav version by V. M. Istrin (Leningrad, 1920–30). The translation appears to have been made by a group of Russians, Czechs and Bulgarians at Kiev in the middle of the eleventh century.

183 Editions: Istrin, Vaillant and Pascal, *La Prise de Jérusalem* (Paris, 1934–8); N. A. Meshcherski, *Istorija iudejskoj vojny Iosifa Flavija v drevne-russkom perevode* (Ak. nauk., 1958).

184 A knowledge of Hebrew in Russia must also be posited since the *Josippon* was also translated before 1100 (it is quoted in the *Primary Chronicle*) and, it is believed, also the books of *Daniel* and *Esther*. Where these were done is not known. See Meshcherski, *ed. cit.* (note 183), Introduction, esp. pp. 137 ff. Jews continued to take refuge in Russia from further east in the eleventh–

twelfth centuries to escape the fury of nomad Pechenegs, Cumans and others.

185 Clement of Smolensk, Metropolitan from 1147 to 1155, is the only writer in whose extant works there is any considerable element of Greek Humanism. An eleventh-century anthology entitled Μέλισσα, which contained favourite Classical as well as Christian passages, was translated in Russia in the twelfth century as *Pchelá*. See Fedotov, *The Russian Religious Mind*, vol. 1, pp. 41 ff.

186 On this work see H. Grégoire, *Digenis Akritas* (New York, 1942), especially cap. 6, with further references; A. Dostál in *OCA*, vol. 2. The religious elements in the story were emphasised in the Russian version.

187 Fedotov (*Russian Religious Mind*, vol. 1, p. 41) puts it as low as 5%.

188 French translation of Daniel's *Pilgrimage* in B. de Khitrowo, *Itinéraires russes en Orient* (Geneva, 1889); English translation in *Palestine Pilgrims Text Society*, vol. 4 (London, 1895) from another French version.

189 Possibly 1106. The chronology of his pilgrimage is discussed by Ju. P. Glushakova in *Problemy obshchestvenno-politicheskoj istorii Rossii i slavjanskih stran* (essays offered to M. N. Tikhomirov, Moscow, 1963).

Chapter 6.   *The Beginnings of Monasticism among the Orthodox Slavs*

1 St Luke 10, 38–42.

2 Cf. Dante's dream in *Purgatorio* xxvii.

3 Such a γέρων, or *starets* in Russian, was a prominent feature in later Russian monasticism. See I. Smolitsch, *Leben und Lehre der Starzen* (2nd ed., Köln, 1952). It is very noticeable that Eastern monks remained theologians and spiritual advisers only, never being tempted to intrude into secular literature and the like. Conversely lay theologians were not frowned upon in the East.

4 For a recent bibliography of Athos see I. Doens in *Le Millénaire du Mont Athos*, pp. 351–483.

5 Text in P. Meyer, *Die Haupturkunden für die Geschichte der Athosklöster* (Leipzig, 1894), pp. 141 ff.

6 Dölger, *Regesten*, pt. 1, nos. 704 (*c.* 964), 706 (*c.* 964), 745 (972). Cf. also *id.*, *Aus den Schatzkammern des Heiligen Berges* (Munich, 1948), no. 108 (December 984).

7 A not very reliable list of Bulgarian monasteries in the tenth century is given by D. Tsuhlev, *Istorija na bŭlgarskata tsŭrkva* (Sofia, 1910), pp. 512 ff.

8 *Rilskijat manastir* (Sinodalno izdatelstvo, Sofia, 1960), sect. 4, pl. 2.

9 *Life* in Ivanov, *Bŭlgarski starini*, no. 42 (pp. 369–83); *Office, ibid.*, no. 40 (pp. 359–67). The anonymous *Life*, by a monk of Rila, is a much later work, probably *c.* 1500. Other native sources: the short 'Prolog' *Life* (late tenth century); an account by the last Bulgarian Patriarch Evtimi (Euthymios) (late fourteenth century); the so-called *Rilska povest* (fifteenth century). See also V. S. Kiselkov, *Sveti Ivan Rilski* (Sofia, 1940).

10   Plates in *Rilskijat manastir* (see note 8).

11   '...Monastyreve na gorah staša, černorizcy javišasja' (*Des Metr. Ilarion Lobrede*, ed. L. Müller, p. 106).

12   *Primary Chronicle*, s.a. 6545 (1037): 'černorizĭci počaša množitisja i manastyreve počinahu byti'.

13   Thietmar, viii, 32. See p. 250.

14   *Archives de l'Athos*: I—*Actes de Lavra* (ed. Rouillard and Collomp, Paris, 1937), no. 18. The date 1016 is not absolutely certain. The form of words may indicate that it was then a very recent foundation; see V. Mošin in *BSL* 9 (1947–8).

15   The main sources are the *Primary Chronicle*, s.a. 1051 and 1074, and the *Kievo-pecherski paterik* (ed. Chizhevski, *Slavische Propyläen* 2, 1964).

16   Certain 'catacombs' on the upper Don, dated to the eighth–ninth centuries, are thought to be Christian but it is not known who used them; see Stratonov in *Kyrios* I (1936). Some of the catacombs near Kerch are certainly of the fifth century.

17   *Paterik, Slovo* 8.

18   'Ješče i k dětem igrajuščim ne približašesja...roditelja svoja datisja veljaše na učenije božestvennyh knig...' (*Paterik*, ed. Chizhevski, p. 23).

19   *Primary Chronicle*, s.a. 6604 (1096). The chronicler-monk describes the raid as an eye-witness: 'i pridoša na manastyřі pečerskyj, namŭ suščimŭ po kěljamŭ počivajuščimŭ po zautreni...' (Acad. ed., pp. 151–2).

20   It is however far more probable that there were two Nestors, or even three—Nestor the chronicler, Nestor the hagiographer who wrote the *Life of Theodosius*, and Nestor the historian of the Cave Monastery, who was responsible for the entries in the *Primary Chronicle* on the beginnings of the Cave Monastery (s.a. 1051), on the death of Theodosius (s.a. 1074) and on the translation of his relics (s.a. 1091). The author of the *Life of Theodosius* certainly also wrote the *Chtenije* of Boris and Gleb (see p. 398n. 111). See A. Poppe in *SLOR* 14 (1965).

21   *Paterik, Slovo* 34.

BIBLIOGRAPHY

Abgarowicz, K. and Kürbisówna, B. (eds.). *Kronika wielkopolska*. Warsaw, 1965.

Abramovich D. I. (ed.). *Zhitija sv. muchenikov Borisa i Gleba i sluzhby im* (*Pamjatniki drevnerusskoj literatury*, vyp. 2). Petrograd, 1916.

Adam of Bremen: *see* Tschan, F. J.

Adrianova-Peretts *et al.* (eds.). *Povest vremennykh let* (*Primary Chronicle*) (Acad. ed., 2 vols.). Moscow, 1950.

Aitzetmüller, R. (ed.). *Das Hexaemeron des Exarchen Johannes* (in progress). Graz, 1958–.

Ammann, A. M. *Abriss der ostslawischen Kirchengeschichte*. Vienna, 1950.

Untersuchungen zur Geschichte der kirchlichen Kultur und des religiösen Lebens bei den Ostslawen (*Das Oestliche Christentum*, NF 13). Würzburg, 1955.

Angelov, D. *Bogomilstvoto v Bŭlgarija* (2nd ed.). Sofia, 1961.

Anichkov, E. V. *Jazychestvo i drevnjaja Rus*. St Petersburg, 1914.

Anonymus Gallus: *see* Maleczyński, K.

Arbman, H. *The Vikings*. London, 1961.

Artamonov, M. I. *Istorija Khazar*. Leningrad, 1962.

Atlas československých dějin. Prague, 1965.

Atlas of the Early Christian World. London, 1959.

Atlas po bŭlgarska istorija. Sofia, 1963.

Auty, R. *Handbook of Old Church Slavonic*: Part II—*Texts and Glossary*. London, 1960.

Bănescu, N. *Les duchés byzantins de Paristrion. . .* Bucharest, 1946.

Barats, G. M. *Kritiko-sravnitelny analiz dogovorov Rusi s Vizantijej*. Kiev, 1910.

Bašić, M. (ed.). *Stare srpske biografije* (2nd ed.). Belgrade, 1930.

Bauerreiss, R. *Kirchengeschichte Bayerns, vol. 1—von den Anfängen bis zu den Ungarneinfällen*. St Ottilien, 1949.

Baumgarten, N. A. von. *Généalogies et mariages occidentaux des Rurikides* (*OC* 35). Rome, 1927.

Beckwith, J. *Early Medieval Art*. London, 1964.

Belaev, V. *Drevnerusskaja muzykalnaja pismennost'*. Moscow, 1962.

Benussi, B. *La Liturgia slava nell'Istria*. Parenzo, 1893.

Beshevliev, V. and Irmscher, J. (eds.). *Antike und Mittelalter in Bulgarien* (*Berliner Byz. Arbeiten* 21). Berlin, 1960.

Bieniak, J. *Państwo Miecława*. Warsaw, 1963.

Bihalji-Merin, O. *Byzantine frescoes and icons in Yugoslavia* (English version). London, 1960.

Bloch, M. *Feudal Society* (Eng. tr. by L. A. Manyon) (2nd ed., 2 vols.). London, 1965.

Böhmer, J. F. *Regesta imperii*, vol. 1. Innsbruck, 1889.

Bokes, F. *Dejiny slovenska a slovákov*. Bratislava, 1946.

Bibliography

Bon, A. *Le Péloponnèse byzantin jusqu'en 1204*. Paris, 1951.

Borawska, D. *Kryzys monarchii wczesnopiastowskiej w latach trzydziestych XI wieku*. Warsaw, 1964.

Brackmann, A. *Germania pontificia*, vol. 1. Berlin, 1911.
Kaiser Otto III und die staatliche Umgestaltung Polens und Ungarns (Abh. der Preussischen Ak. der Wiss., phil.-hist. Klasse, Nr. 1). Berlin, 1939.

Bréhier, L. *Le monde byzantin* (3 vols.). Paris, 1947–50.

Bretholz, B. *Geschichte Böhmens und Mährens bis 1306*. Munich–Leipzig, 1912.
(ed.). *Cosmas of Prague: Chronica Boemorum*. Berlin, 1923.

Brooke, C. H. *Europe in the Central Middle Ages*. London, 1964.

Brückner, A. *Dzieje kultury polskiej*. Cracow, 1931–46.

Brüske, W. *Untersuchungen zur Geschichte des Lutizenbundes*. Münster, 1955.

Budovnits, I. U. *Obshchestvenno-politicheskaja mysl' drevnej Rusi*. Moscow, 1960.

Bujnoch, J. *Zwischen Rom und Byzanz* (Ger. trans. of *VC*, *VM*, etc.) Graz, 1958.

Bullough, D. *The Age of Charlemagne*. London, 1965.

Buxton, D. R. *Russian mediaeval architecture*. Cambridge, 1934.

Cambridge Economic History of Europe [*CEH*] (ed. M. M. Postan), vol. 1 (2nd ed.). Cambridge, 1966.

Cambridge History of Poland (ed. W. F. Reddaway). Cambridge, 1950.

Cambridge Medieval History, vol. 4, parts 1 and 2 (ed. J. M. Hussey). [*CMH*]. Cambridge, 1966–7.

Caspar, E. *Das Register Gregors VII*. Berlin, 1920–3.

Červinka, I. L. *Slované na Moravě a Říše velkomoravská*. Brno, 1928.

Češi a Poláci v minulosti, vol. 1 (ed. J. Macůrek). Prague, 1964.

Chalandon, F. *Les Comnène* (2 vols.). Paris, 1900–12.

Chaloupecký, V. and Ryba, B. (eds.). *Středověké legendy prokopské*. Prague, 1953.

Chizhevski, D. (Čiževskij). *History of Russian Literature from the eleventh century to the end of the Baroque*. Hague, 1960.

Chizhevski, D. (Tschižewskij) (ed.). *Sbornik moskovskogo uspenskogo sobora* (*Apophoreta slavica* 1). Hague, 1957.

Das Paterikon des Kiever Hohlenklosters. Munich, 1964.

Cibulká, J. *Velkomoravský kostel v Modré u Velehradu a začátky křesťanství na Moravě*. Prague, 1958.

Ćirković, S. *Istorija srednjevekovne bosanske države*. Belgrade, 1964.

Clémencet, Grat and Vieilliard (eds.). *Annales de Saint-Bertin*. Paris, 1964.

Clément, O. *L'essor du christianisme oriental*. Paris, 1964.

Codex diplomaticus et epistolaris Moraviae (ed. A. Boczek) [*CDEM*]. Olomouc, Brno, 1836–.

Codex diplomaticus et epistolaris regni Bohemiae: see Friedrich, G.

Codex diplomaticus majoris Poloniae: vol. 1—984–1287 (ed. Zakrzewski and Piekosiński) [*CDMP*]. Poznań, 1877.

Codex diplomaticus necnon epistolaris Silesiae: vol. 1—971–1204 (ed. K. Maleczyński) [*CDS*]. Wrocław, 1956.

Bibliography

Codrington, H. W. *The Liturgy of St Peter*. Münster, 1936.

Constantine Porphyrogennetos. *De Cerimoniis* (*Le Livre des cérémonies*) [*De Cer.*] (ed. A. Vogt). Paris, 1935–40.

De administrando imperio [*DAI*] (eds. Moravcsik and Jenkins). Vol. 1 Budapest, 1949; vol. 2 London, 1962.

Ćorović, V. *Istorija Jugoslavije*. Belgrade, 1933.

Historija Bosne. Belgrade, 1940.

(ed.) *Spisi sv. Save*. Belgrade, 1928.

Cosmas of Prague: *see* Bretholz, B.

Crnjanski, M. *Sveti Sava*. Belgrade, 1934.

Cvjetković, B. *Povijest dubrovačke Republike*. Dubrovnik, 1917.

Cyrillo-Methodiana: zur Frühgeschichte des Christentums bei den Slaven, 863–1963 (*SLF* 6). Köln–Graz, 1964.

Dąbrowski, J. *Studia nad początkami państwa polskiego*. Ossol., 1958.

Dalimil: *see* Havránek.

David, P. *Etudes historiques sur la Pologne médiévale*. Including: 1. *La Pologne et l'évangélisation de la Poméranie* (1928); 2. *L'Epitaphe de Boleslas Chrobry* (1928); 5. *Casimir le Moine* (1932). Paris, 1928–33.

Les Bénédictins et l'ordre de Cluny dans la Pologne médiévale. Paris, 1939.

Dawkins, R. M. *The Monks of Athos*. London, 1936.

Deanesly, M. *A History of Early Medieval Europe* (476–911) (2nd ed.). London, 1960.

A History of the Medieval Church (590–1500) (8th ed.). London, 1962.

Deér, J. *Heidnisches und Christliches in der altungarischen Monarchie*. Szeged, 1934.

Der Nersessian, S. *Armenia and the Byzantine Empire*. Cambridge, Mass., 1945.

Deroko, A. *Monumentalna i dekorativna arhitektura u srednjevekovnoj Srbiji*. (2nd ed.). Belgrade, 1962.

Derzhavin, N. S. *Istorija Bolgarii*. Moscow–Leningrad, 1946–7.

Dictionnaire d'histoire et de géographie ecclésiastiques (eds. Janin and Baudrillart) [in progress]. Paris, 1912–.

Dictionnaire de spiritualité ascétique et mystique, doctrine et histoire, ed. M. Viller *et al.* [in progress]. Paris, 1937–.

Diehl, C. H. and Marçais, G. *Le monde oriental*, 395–1081. Paris, 1936.

Diels, P. *Die slavischen Völker*. Wiesbaden, 1963.

Dinkov, K. *Istorija na bŭlgarskata tsŭrkva*. Sofia, 1954.

Istorija na slavjanskite i tem sŭsedni pravoslavni tsŭrkvi. Sofia, 1960.

Dittrich, Z. R. *Christianity in Great-Moravia*. Groningen, 1962.

Dold, A. and Gamber, K. *Das Sakramentar von Salzburg* (*Texte und Arbeiten* 1, 4). Beuron, 1960.

Dölger, F. *Regesten der Kaiserurkunden des Oströmischen Reiches* (1—565–1025; 2—1025–1204). Munich–Berlin, 1924–5.

Byzanz und die europäische Staatenwelt. Ettal, 1953. (2nd ed. 1964.)

Dostál, A. (ed.). *Glagolita Clozianus*. Prague, 1959.

Dowiat, J. *Metryka chrztu Mieszka I i jej geneza*. Warsaw, 1961.

Bibliography

Duchesne, L. (ed.). *Le Liber Pontificalis*. Paris, 1886–92.

Duckett, E. S. *Alcuin, Friend of Charlemagne*. New York. 1951.

Dujčev, I. *Medioevo bizantino-slavo*, vol. 1. Rome, 1965.

Dunlop, D. M. *The History of the Jewish Khazars*. Princeton, 1954.

Duthilleul, P. *L'Evangélisation des slaves* (*Bibliothèque de théologie, série 4: histoire de théologie*, vol. 5). Paris, 1963.

Dvornik, F. *La Vie de S. Grégoire le Décapolite*. Paris, 1926.

Les Slaves, Byzance et Rome au IX siècle. Paris, 1926.

St Wenceslas, Prince of Bohemia. Prague, 1929.

Les Légendes de Constantin et de Méthode, vues de Byzance. Prague, 1933.

The Photian Schism. Cambridge, 1948.

The Making of Central and Eastern Europe. London, 1949.

The Slavs: their Early History and Civilisation. Boston, 1956.

The idea of apostolicity in Byzantium and the legend of the Apostle Andrew (*DO Studies* 4). Cambridge, Mass., 1958.

The Slavs in European History and Civilisation. Rutgers, 1962.

Byzance et la primauté romaine (*Unam Sanctam* 49). Paris, 1964.

Dyggve, E. *History of Salonitan Christianity*. Oslo, 1951.

Dzięcioł, W. *Imperium i państwa narodowe około r. 1000*. London, 1963.

The Origins of Poland. London, 1966.

Dziewulski, W. *Postępy chrystianizacji i proces likwidacji pogaństwa w Polsce wczesnofeudalnej*. Ossol., 1964.

Eggers, H. *Deutsche Sprachgeschichte: I—Das Althochdeutsche*. Hamburg, 1963.

Eisner, J. *Rukověť slovanské archeologie*. Prague, 1966.

Emler, J.: *see Fontes*.

Erben, C. J. *Regesta diplomatica necnon epistolaria Bohemiae et Moraviae*: vol. 1—600–1253. Prague, 1855.

Eremin, I. P. *Literatura drevnej Rusi*. Moscow–Leningrad, 1966.

Eubel, C. (ed.). *Hierarchia catholica medii aevi* (2nd ed.). Münster, 1913–.

Every, G. *The Byzantine Patriarchate* (2nd. ed.). London, 1962.

Fedotov, G. P. *Svjatyje drevnej Rusi*. Paris, 1931.

The Russian religious mind: vol. 1 *Kievan Christianity*. Harvard, 1946; Vol. 2 *The Middle Ages*. Harvard, 1966.

Ferluga, J. *Vizantiska uprava u Dalmaciji*. Belgrade, 1957.

Fiala, Z. *Přemyslovské Čechy*. Prague, 1965.

Fichtenau, H. *The Carolingian Empire* (English version). Oxford, 1963.

Fliche, A. and Martin, V. *Histoire de l'église*... Paris, [in progress].

Florovski, A. V. *Chekhi i vostochnye slavjane*. Prague, 1935–47.

Folz, R. *L'Idée d'empire en occident*. Paris, 1953.

Fontes rerum bohemicarum, ed. J. Emler [*FRB*]. Prague, 1873–1932.

Frček, J. (ed.). *Euchologium sinaiticum* (*Patrologia orientalis* 24/5 and 25/3). Paris, 1933–9.

Friedberg, M. *Kultura polska a niemiecka*. Poznań, 1946.

Friedrich, G. *Codex diplomaticus et epistolaris regni Bohemiae*: vol. 1—to 1197. Prague, 1904–7.

Bibliography

Gallus anonymus: *see* Maleczyński.

Ganev, V. *Zakonŭ sudnyj ljudĭmŭ*. Sofia, 1959.

Gąssowski, J. *Dzieje i Kultura dawnych Słowian*. Warsaw, 1964.

Gay, J. *L'Italie méridionale et l'empire byzantin*. Paris, 1904.

Gelzer, H. *Der Patriarchat von Achrida* [*Abh. der Königl. Sächs. Akad.* (*Phil.-hist. Klasse*), 20]. Leipzig, 1902.

Geographus bavarensis: see Horák, B.

Georgiev, E. *Slavjanskaja pismennost' do Kirilla i Mefodija*. Sofia, 1952.
Kiril i Metodi osnovopolozhnitsi na slavjanskite literaturi. Sofia, 1956.
Raztsvetŭt na bŭlgarskata literatura v IX–X v. Sofia, 1962.

Gerland, E. *Corpus notitiarum episcopatuum ecclesiae orientalis graecae* (vol. 1). Constantinople, 1931.

Goeje, M. J. de (ed.). *Bibliotheca geographorum arabicorum* (repr. 1965) (Arabic texts only). Leiden, 1870–94.

Goetz, L. K. *Das Kiever Höhlenkloster*. Passau, 1904.
Kirchenrechtliche und Kulturgeschichtliche Denkmäler Altrusslands. Stuttgart, 1905.

Golubinski, E. *Istorija russkoj tserkvi* (2nd ed.). Moscow, 1901–10.

Golyshenko, V. S. (ed.). *Izbornik 1076 goda*. Moscow, 1965.

Goshev, I. *Starobŭlgarski glagolicheski i kirilski nadpisi ot IX i X v.* Sofia, 1961.

Gougaud, L. *Gaelic pioneers of Christianity*. Dublin, 1923.

Grabar, I. E., Lazarev, V. N. and Kemenov, V. S. (eds.). *Istorija russkogo iskusstva*, vol. 1. Moscow, 1953.

Grabski, A. F. *Bolesław Chrobry*. Warsaw, 1964.
Polska w opiniach obcych X–XIII w. Warsaw, 1964.

Grafenauer, B. *Zgodovina slovenskega naroda*. Ljubljana, 1954–62.

Grafenauer, I. *Karolinška Kateheza ter izvor brižinskih spomenikov...* (*Razprave ZD* 13). Ljubljana, 1936.

Grekov, B. D. *Kievskaja Rus'*. Moscow, 1949.

Grekov, B. D. and Artamonov, M. I. (eds.). *Istorija kultury drevnej Rusi*. (2 vols.) Moscow–Leningrad, 1951.

Grivec, F. *Konstantin und Method, Lehrer der Slaven*. Wiesbaden, 1960.

Grivec, F. and Tomšić, F. (eds.). *Constantinus et Methodius thessalonicenses: Fontes* (*Radovi staroslavenskog instituta* 4). Zagreb, 1960.

Grodecki, L. *L'architecture ottonienne*. Paris, 1958.

Grodecki, R. and Plezia, M. (eds.). *Anonim tzw. Gall: Kronika polska* (Translation and commentary). Ossol., 1965.

Grudziński, T. *Polityka papieża Grzegorza VII wobec państw Europy środkowej i wschodniej*. Toruń, 1959.

Grumel, V. *Les Régestes des actes du patriarchat de Constantinople*, vol. 1/2. Constantinople, 1936.
Traité d'études byzantines (ed. P. Lemerle), 1: *La Chronologie*. Paris, 1958.

Guldescu, S. *History of Medieval Croatia to 1526*. Hague, 1964.

Gumowski, M. *Handbuch der polnischen Numismatik*. Graz, 1960.

Hafner, S. *Studien zur altserbischen dynastischen Historiographie* (*Südosteuropäische Arbeiten* 62). Munich, 1964.

411

Bibliography

Hafner, S. (*cont.*)

(ed.). *Serbisches Mittelalter: Altserbische Herrscherbiographien*, vol. 1 (*Slavische Geschichtsschreiber* 2). Graz, 1962.

Hahn, J. *Kyrillomethodianische Bibliographie 1939–1955*. Hague, 1958.

Halphen, L. *Charlemagne et l'empire carolingien*. Paris, 1947.

Hampe, K. *Das Hochmittelalter: Geschichte des Abendlandes von 900 bis 1250* (4th ed.). Münster–Köln, 1953.

Hasluck, F. W. *Athos and its monasteries*. London, 1924.

Hauck, A. *Kirchengeschichte Deutschlands* (4th ed.). Leipzig, 1904–20.

Haussig, H. W. *Kulturgeschichte von Byzanz*. Stuttgart, 1959.

Havlík, L. *Velká Morava a středoevropskí Slované*. Prague, 1964.

Havránek, B. and Daňhelka, J. (eds.). *Nejstarší česká rýmovaná kronika t. řeč. Dalimila*. Prague, 1957.

Helmold: *see* Stoob, H., Tschan, F. J.

Hensel, W. *The Beginnings of the Polish State*. Warsaw, 1960.

Najdawniejsze stolice Polski. Warsaw, 1960.

Polska przed tysiącem lat. Wrocław, 1960.

Archeologia o początkach miast słowiańskich. Ossol., 1963.

Die Slawen im frühen Mittelalter (Ger. version of 2nd ed. of *Słowiańszczyzna wczesnośredniowieczna*). Berlin, 1965.

La Naissance de la Pologne. Ossol., 1966.

Hiljada i sto godini slavjanska pismenost. Sofia, 1963.

Hirsch, P. and Lohmann, H. E. (eds.). *Die Sachsengeschichte des Widukind* (5th ed.). Hanover, 1935.

Historia Polski (ed. T. Manteuffel), vol. 1, pt. 1. Pol. Ac. Sci., 1957.

Hoddinott, R. F. *Early Byzantine Churches in Macedonia and Southern Serbia*. London, 1963.

Hofmeister, A. (ed.). *Das Leben des Bischofs Otto von Bamberg* (the Prüfening *Life*). Leipzig, 1928.

Holtzmann, R. *Kaiser Otto der Grosse*. Berlin, 1936.

Geschichte der sächsischen Kaiserzeit (900–1024) (4th ed.). Munich, 1961.

Hóman, B. *Geschichte des ungarischen Mittelalters*. Berlin, 1940.

Horák, B. and Trávníček, D. (eds.). *Geographus bavarensis (Descriptio civitatum ad septentrionalem plagam Danubii)* (*Rozpr. ČAV*, řada spol. věd, 66/2). Prague, 1956.

Horálek, K. *Evangeliáře a čtveroevangelia*. Prague, 1954.

Hrejsa, F. *Dějiny křesťanství v československu*, vol. 1. Prague, 1947.

Hrubý, V. *Staré Město:velkomoravský Velehrad (Mon. Arch.* 14). Prague, 1965.

Hunger, H. *Prooimion (Wiener Byzantinistische Studien* 1). Vienna, 1964.

Hussey, J. *Church and Learning in the Byzantine Empire*. London, 1937.

Iljinski, G. *Opyt sistematicheskoj Kirillo-metodievskoj bibliografii*. Sofia, 1934.

Isačenko, A. V. *Jazyk a pôvod frizinských pamiatok*. Bratislava, 1943.

Istorija Kieva (var. auct.). Kiev, 1963.

Istorija na bŭlgarskata literatura: 1—starobŭlgarska literatura (ed. P. Dinekov et al.) Sofia, 1962.

Istorija russkogo iskusstva (var. auct.): *see* Grabar.

Bibliography

Istrin, V. A. *1100 let slavjanskoj azbuki*. Moscow, 1963.
Ivanov, J. *Bogomilski knigi i legendi*. Sofia, 1925.
   Bŭlgarski starini iz Makedonija (2nd ed.). Sofia, 1931.
   Izvori za bŭlgarskata istorija [in progress]. Sofia, 1954–.
Jaffé, P. and Wattenbach, G. *Regesta pontificum romanorum* (2 vols.). Leipzig, 1885–8.
Jagić, V. *Entstehungsgeschichte der kirchenslavischen Sprache*. Berlin, 1915.
Jaksch, A. *Geschichte Kärntens bis 1335*. Klagenfurt, 1928–9.
Jakobson, A. L. *Srednevekovy Krym*. Leningrad, 1964.
Janin, V. L. *Denezhno-vesovyje sistemy russkogo srednevekovja*. Moscow, 1956.
Janković, D. *Istorija države i prava feudalne Srbije* (2nd ed.). Belgrade, 1956.
Jażdżewski, K. *Poland* (*Ancient Peoples and Places* 45). London, 1965.
Jelić, L. *Fontes historici liturgiae glagolito-romanae*. Veglae, 1906.
   Dvorska Kapela sv. Križa u Ninu. Zagreb, 1911.
Jenkins, R. H. J. *Byzantium: the Imperial centuries* (A.D. 610–1071). London, 1966.
Jireček, K. J. *Geschichte der Serben*. Gotha, 1911–18. (Repr. 1963.)
Jones, Gwyn. *A History of the Vikings*. Oxford, 1968.
Kahl, H. D. *Slawen und Deutsche in der brandenburgischen Geschichte des 12 Jahrhunderts* (*Mitteldeutsche Forschungen* 30). Köln–Graz, 1964.
Karger, M. K. *Drevni Kiev*. Moscow, 1958–61.
Karski, E. F. *Ocherk slavjanskoj kirillovskoj paleografii*. Leningrad, 1928.
Kartashëv, A. V. *Ocherki po istorii russkoj tserkvi*. Paris, 1959.
Karwasińska, J. *Les trois rédactions de Vita I de S. Adalbert*. Rome, 1959.
Kawerau, P. *Arabische Quellen zur Christianisierung Russlands* (*Marburger Abhandlungen zur Geschichte und Kultur Osteuropas*, 7). Wiesbaden, 1967.
Kehr, P. *Italia pontificia*, vol. 7. Berlin, 1906–.
   Das Erzbistum Magdeburg und die erste Organisation der Kirche in Polen. Berlin, 1920.
Kętrzyński, S. *Polska X i XI wieku*. Warsaw, 1961.
Kiersnowski, R. *Początki pieniądza polskiego*. Warsaw, 1962.
Kiselkov, V. S. *Rilskijat manastir*. Sofia, 1937.
   Sv. Ivan Rilski. Sofia, 1940.
   Sveti Kliment Ohridski. Sofia, 1941.
Klaić, N. (ed.). *Izvori za hrvatsku povijest:* I—do g. 1107; II—do g. 1526. Zagreb, 1955–8.
Klaić, V. *Poviest Bosne do propasti Kraljevstva*. Zagreb, 1882.
Klich, E. *Polska terminologia chrześcijańska*. Poznań, 1927.
Knox, B. *The Architecture of Prague and Bohemia*. London, 1965.
Koroljuk, V. D. *Zapadnye slavjane i Kievskaja Rus' v X–XI vv*. Moscow, 1964.
Kos, F. *Gradivo za zgodovino Slovencev v srednjem veku*. Ljubljana, 1902–28.
Kos, M. *Zgodovina Slovencev do petnajstega stoletja*. Ljubljana, 1955.
   (ed.). *Conversio Bagoariorum et Carantanorum* (*Razprave ZD* 11). Ljubljana, 1936.

413

Bibliography

Kötzschke, R. *Quellen zur Geschichte der ostdeutschen Kolonisation im 12 bis 14 Jhdt.* (2nd ed.). Leipzig, 1931.

Kovačević, J. *Arheologia i istorija varvarske kolonizacije južnoslovenskih oblasti od IV do početka VII veka.* Novi Sad, 1960.

Kovalevski, A. P. *Kniga Ahmeda ibn-Fadlana.* Kharkov, 1956.

Kowalski, T. *Relacja Ibrāhīma ibn Jaʿḳūba...w przekazie al-Bekrīego [MPH, Seria II, vol. 1].* Cracow, 1946.

Králík, O. *K počátkům literatury v přemyslovských Čechách (RAV 70/6).* Prague, 1960.

Sázavské písemnictví XI století (RAV 71/12). Prague, 1961.

Krásl, F. and Ježek, J. *Sv. Vojtěch, druhý biskup pražský.* Prague, 1898.

Kratchkovsky, I. and Vasiliev, A. (eds.). *Histoire de Yahya-ibn-Saʾïd d'Antioche (Patrologia orientalia, vol. 18, 23).* Paris, 1924, 1932.

Krekić, B. *Dubrovnik et le Levant au Moyen Age.* Paris, 1961.

Kretschmayr, H. *Geschichte von Venedig.* Gotha, 1905.

Kuhar, A. L. *The Conversion of the Slovenes.* New York, 1959.

Slovene Medieval History. New York, 1962.

Kushelev-Bezborodko, G. G. (ed.). *Pamjatniki starinnoj russkoj literatury,* vyp. 3 (ed. Pypin). St Petersburg, 1862.

Labuda, G. *Pierwsze państwo słowiańskie: państwo Samona.* Poznań, 1949.

Fragmenty dziejów słowiańszczyzny zachodnej (2 vols.). Poznań, 1960–4.

Lanckorońska, K. *Studies in the Roman-Slavonic rite in Poland (Or. Chr. Analecta 161).* Rome, 1961.

Lassus, L. A. and Giabbani, D. (eds.). *S. Pierre Damien et S. Bruno de Querfurt* (translations of the *Life of St Romuald* and the *Life of the Five Brothers*). Namur, 1962.

Latourette, K. S. *A History of the expansion of Christianity.* London, 1938–45.

Laurent, V. *Le Corpus des sceaux de l'empire byzantin:* vol. 5, pts. 1 and 2. Paris, 1963–5.

Lavrov, P. A. *Materialy po istorii vozniknovenija drevnej slavjanskoj pismennosti (SDH 67).* Hague, 1966.

Lazarev, V. N. *Istorija vizantijskoj zhivopisi.* Moscow, 1947–8.

Old Russian Murals and Mosaics (tr. B. Roniger). London, 1966.

L'Eglise et les églises, 1054–1954 (Etudes et travaux...offerts à Dom L. Beaudouin). Chevetogne, 1954–5.

Lehr-Spławiński, T. *Rozprawy i szkice z dziejów kultury Słowian.* Warsaw, 1954.

Żywoty Konstantina i Metodego. Poznań, 1959.

Od piętnastu wieków. Warsaw, 1961.

Leib, B. *Rome, Kiev et Byzance à la fin du XIe siècle.* Paris, 1924.

Levchenko, M. V. *Ocherki po istorii russko-vizantijskih otnoshenij.* Moscow, 1956.

Levison, W. *England and the Continent in the eighth century.* Oxford, 1946.

Lewicki, T. *Źródła arabskie do dziejów Słowiańszczyzny* (vol. 1). Wrocław, 1956.

Lewis, A. R. *Naval power and trade in the Mediterranean, A.D. 500–1100.* Princeton, 1951.

Bibliography

Lewis A. R. (*cont.*)
The Northern Seas, *A.D. 300–1100*. Princeton, 1958.

Likhachëv, D. S. *Russkije letopisi i ih kulturno-istoricheskoje znachenije.* Moscow, 1947.

Vozniknovenije russkoj literatury. Moscow, 1952.

Novgorod veliki. Moscow, 1959.

Litavrin, G. G. *Bolgarija i Vizantija v XI–XII vv.* Moscow, 1960.

Löwe, H. *Die karolingische Reichsgründung und der Südosten.* Stuttgart, 1937.

Ein literarischer Widersacher des Bonifatius: Virgil von Salzburg (Akad. der Wissenschaften und der Literatur in Mainz, Abh. der geistes- und sozialwiss. Klasse, no. 11). Wiesbaden, 1951.

Łowmiański, H. *Podstawy gospodarcze formowania się państw słowiańskich.* Warsaw, 1955.

Początki Polski (2 vols.). Warsaw, 1963.

Ludat, H. (ed.). *Siedlung und Verfassung der Slawen zwischen Elbe, Saale und Oder.* Giessen, 1960.

Lurier, H. E. (ed.). *Crusaders as conquerors: the Chronicle of Morea.* New York, 1964.

Lvov, A. S. *Ocherki po leksike pamjatnikov staroslavjanskoj pismennosti.* Moscow, 1966.

Macartney, C. A. *The Magyars in the ninth century.* Cambridge, 1930.

Macůrek, J. *see Češi...*

Magna Moravia—sborník k 1100 výročí příchodu byzantské mise na Moravu. Prague, 1965.

Magnae Moraviae fontes historici, eds. D. Bartoňková, L. Havlík, Z. Masařík and R. Večerka (2 vols.). Prague-Brno, 1966–7.

Mal, J. *Probleme aus der Frühgeschichte der Slowenen.* Ljubljana, 1939.

Mâle, E. (tr. D. Buxton). *The Early Churches of Rome.* London, 1960.

Maleczyński, K. (ed.). *Anonima tzw. Galla Kronika (MPH*, seria II, vol. 2). Cracow, 1952.

Mana—introduction à l'histoire des religions, 2: *Les religions de l'Europe ancienne*, III: *La religion des anciens slaves* (B. O. Unbegaun). Paris, 1948.

Mango, C. (ed.). *The Homilies of Photius (DO Studies* 3). Cambridge, Mass., 1958.

Mansi, J. D. *Sacrorum Conciliorum nova et amplissima Collectio.* Florence etc., 1759–.

Mansikka, V. J. *Die Religion der Ostslaven.* Helsinki, 1922.

Martynov, I. (=Martinov, J.) *Annus ecclesiasticus graecoslavicus.* Brussels, 1863.

Mas'ūdī: *see* Meynard.

Mavrodin, V. V. *Obrazovanije drevnerusskogo gosudarstva.* Leningrad, 1945.

Ocherki istorii SSSR: drevnerusskoje gosudarstvo. Moscow, 1956.

Mavrodinov, N. *Starobŭlgarskoto izkustvo.* Sofia, 1959.

Mélanges Ch. Diehl (2 vols.). Paris, 1930.

Melvinger, A. *Les premières incursions des Vikings en Occident d'après les sources arabes.* Uppsala, 1955.

Bibliography

Metcalf, D. M. *Coinage in the Balkans, 820–1355*. Saloniki, 1965.

Meyer, K. H. *Fontes historiae religionis slavicae*. Berlin, 1931.

Meynard and Courteille. *Maçoudi: Les Prairies d'or* (=*Kitāb murūj al-dhahab wa maʿādin al-jawahr*). Paris, 1861–4.

Migne, J. P. *Patrologiae cursus completus: series latina (PL)*. Paris, 1844–.
Patrologiae cursus completus: series graeca (PG). Paris, 1857–.

Mihailov, G. *Inscriptiones graecae in Bulgaria repertae*, vol. 1. Sofia, 1956.

Milev, A. (ed.). *Teofilakt ohridski: Zhitie na Kliment ohridski*. Sofia, 1955.

Milik, J. T. *Święty Świerad*. Rome, 1966.

Millénaire du mont Athos, Le: 963–1963—Etudes et mélanges (2 vols.). Chevetogne, 1963.

Millet, G. *L'ancien art serbe: Les églises*. Paris, 1919.
(ed.). *L'art byzantin chez les Slaves* (2 vols., = *Orient et Byzance*, vols. 4–5). Paris, 1930–2.

Mirković, L. and Ćorović, V. (eds.). *Životi sv. Save i sv. Simeona*. Belgrade, 1938.

Möbius, H. and F. *Mediaeval churches in Germany* (English version). London, 1965.

Mohlberg, K. *Il messale glagolitico di Kiew* (*Atti della Pontificia Accademia Romana di archeologia*, ser. 3, *memorie* vol. 2, pp. 207–320). Rome, 1928.

Monumenta Germaniae historica [MGH]. Hanover etc., 1826–.

Monumenta musicae byzantinae. Copenhagen, 1935–.

Monumenta Poloniae historica [MPH] (=Pomniki dziejowe Polski). Lwów, 1864–; New Series: Cracow–Warsaw, 1946–.

Monumenta serbica spectantia historiam Serbiae, Bosniae, Ragusii, ed. F. Miklosich. Vienna, 1858.

Monumenta spectantia historiam slavorum meridionalium [MSM]. Zagreb, 1868–.

Moravcsik, Gy. *Byzantinoturcica* (2nd ed.) (*Berliner Byzantinische Arbeiten* 10). Berlin, 1958.

Mošin, V. A. *Varjago-russki vopros* (*Slavia* 10). Prague, 1931.
(ed.). *Ljetopis popa dukljanina*. Zagreb, 1950.
Paleografski album na južnoslovenskoto kirilsko pismo. Skopje, 1966.

Mošin, V. and Solovjëv, A. (eds.). *Grčke povelje srpskih vladara* (*Fontes rerum Slavorum meridionalium* 6/i). Belgrade, 1936.

Müller, L. *Des Metropoliten Ilarion Lobrede auf Vladimir den Heiligen*. Wiesbaden, 1962.

Murko, M. *Geschichte der älteren südslawischen Litteraturen*. Leipzig, 1908.

Musset, L. *Les invasions* (*Nouvelle Clio*, vols. 12 and 12 bis). Paris, 1965.

Nahtigal, R. *Starocerkvenoslovanske študije* (*Razprave znanstvenega društva* 15). Ljubljana, 1936.
(ed.). *Euchologium sinaiticum*. Ljubljana, 1941–2.

Nasonov, A. N. '*Russkaja zemlja' i obrazovanije territorii drevnerusskogo gosudarstva*. Moscow, 1951.
(ed.). *Novgorodskaja I letopis*. Moscow, 1950.

Bibliography

Natanson-Leski, J. *Rozwój terytorialny Polski od czasów najdawniejszych.* Warsaw, 1964.

Nicol, D. M. *The Despotate of Epirus.* Oxford, 1957.

Niederle, L. *Manuel de l'antiquité slave.* Paris, 1923–. (New Czech ed. *Rukověť' slovanských starožitností*, ed. J. Eisner. Prague, 1953).

Nikolaev, V. *Slavjanobŭlgarskijat faktor v hristijanizacijata na Kievska Rusija.* Sofia, 1949.

Novak, G. *Prošlost Dalmacije.* Zagreb, 1944.

Novotný, V. *České dějiny.* Prague, 1912–.

Obolensky, D. *The Bogomils.* Cambridge, 1948.

Odkrycia w Wiślicy (Rozprawy zespołu badań nad polskim średniowiezcem univ. warszawskiego, 1). Warsaw, 1963.

Oppermann, C. J. A. *The English Missionaries in Sweden and Finland.* London, 1937.

Orbis scriptus: D. Tschiževskij zum 70 Geburtstag (eds. D. Gerhardt *et al.*). Munich, 1966.

Ostojić, I. *Benediktinci u Hrvatskoj i ostalim našim krajevima* (2 vols.). Split, 1963–4.

Ostrogorsky, G. *History of the Byzantine State.* Oxford, 1956.

Palikarova Verdeil, R. *La musique byzantine chez les Bulgares et les Russes du IXe au XIVe siècle.* Copenhagen, 1953.

Palm, T. *Wendische Kultstätten.* Lund, 1937.

Pamjatniki russkogo prava, ed. S. V. Jushkov: see Zimin.

Pashuto, V. T. *et al. Drevnerusskoje gosudarstvo i ego mezhdunarodnoje znachenije.* Moscow, 1965.

Paszkiewicz, H. *The making of the Russian nation.* London, 1963.

Pauliny, E. *Slovesnosť a kultúrny jazyk Veľkej Moravy.* Bratislava, 1964.

Pavlov, A. *Kriticheskije opyty po istorii drevnejšej greko-russkoj polemiki protiv Latinjan.* St Petersburg, 1878.

Pekař, J. *Die Wenzels- und Ludmilalegenden und die Echtheit Christians.* Prague, 1906.

Perels, E. *Papst Nikolaus I und Anastasius Bibliothecarius.* Berlin, 1920.

Perojević, M. *Ninski biskup Teodozije.* Split, 1922.

Ninski biskup u povijesti hrvatskog naroda. Zagreb, 1939.

Początki państwa polskiego: księga tysiąclecia (ed. Labuda, Łowmiański and Tymieniecki), 2 vols. Poznań, 1962.

Polnoje sobranije russkih letopisej [PSRL]. St Petersburg, 1848–.

Popruzhenko, M. G. *Sinodik Tsarja Borila (Bŭlgarski Starini 8).* Sofia, 1928.

Popruzhenko and Romanski. *Kirilometodievska bibliografija za 1934–40.* Sofia, 1942.

Poulík, J. *Staroslovanská Morava.* Prague, 1948.

Staří Moravané budují svůj stát. Gottwaldov, 1960.

Veľkomoravské hradiště Mikulčice. Brno, 1962.

Dvě velkomoravské rotundy v Mikulčicích (Monumenta archaeologica 12). Prague, 1963.

417

Bibliography

Poviest hrvatskih zemalja Bosne i Hercegovine od najstarijih vremena do godine 1463 (var. auct.), vol. 1. Sarajevo, 1942.

Powstenko, O. *The Cathedral of St Sofia in Kiev (Annals of the Ukrainian Acad. of Sciences in the U.S.*, vols. 3–4). New York, 1954.

Preidel, H. *Slawische Altertumskunde des östlichen Mitteleuropas im 9 und 10 Jhdt.*, vol. 1. Munich, 1961.

Presnjakov, A. E. *Lektsii po russkoj istorii.* Moscow, 1938–9.

Primary Chronicle, Russian: see Adrianova-Peretts.

Prisëlkov, M. D. *Ocherki po tserkovno-politicheskoj istorii kievskoj Rusi.* St Petersburg, 1913.

Istorija russkogo letopisanija XI–XV vv. Leningrad, 1940.

Problemy obshchestvenno-politicheskoj istorii Rossii i slavjanskih stran (in honour of M. N. Tikhomirov). Moscow, 1963.

Prohaska, D. *Das kroatisch-serbische Schrifttum in Bosnien und der Herzegowina.* Zagreb, 1911.

Prokeš, J. *Dějiny Prahy.* Prague, 1948.

Promnitz, E. *Der heilige Herzog Wenzel.* Prague, 1929.

Psellos, M. *Chronographia* (ed. Sewter). London, 1953.

Ptaśnik, J. *Kultura włoska wieków średnich w Polsce.* Warsaw, 1959.

Puech, H. C. and Vaillant, A. *Le Traité contre les Bogomiles de Cosmas le Prêtre.* Paris, 1945.

Quirin, K. *Die deutsche Ostsiedlung im Mittelalter.* Göttingen, 1954.

Rački, F. *Borba južnih slovena za državnu neodvisnost* (2nd ed.). Belgrade, 1931.
    (ed.). *Documenta historiae chroaticae periodum antiquam illustrantia* (= *MSM* 7). Zagreb, 1877.
    (ed.). *Archdeacon Thomas of Split: Historia salonitana* (= *MSM* 26). Zagreb, 1894.

Radojčić, S. *Mileševa.* Belgrade, 1963.
    Staro srpsko slikarstvo. Belgrade, 1966.

Radonić, J. *Sveti Sava i njegovo doba.* Srem. Karlovci, 1935.

Ramm, B. Ya. *Papstvo i Rus' v X–XV vekah.* Moscow, 1959.

Ramovš, F. and Kos, M. *Brižinski spomeniki.* Ljubljana, 1937.

Ratkos, P. *Pramene k dejinám Vel'kej Moravy* (a selection of historical sources in translation). Bratislava, 1964.

Regel, W. *Analecta byzantinorussica.* St Petersburg, 1891–8. (Repr. 1964.)

Reiffenstein, I. *Das Althochdeutsche und die irische Mission im oberdeutschen Raum.* Innsbruck, 1958.

Rengjeo, I. *Corpus der mittelalterlichen Münzen von Kroatien, Slavonien, Dalmatien und Bosnien.* Graz, 1959.

Rhode, G. *Die Ostgrenze Polens: 1—bis zum Jahre 1401.* Köln–Graz, 1955.

Ritig, S. *Povijest i pravo slovenštine u crkvenom bogoslužu...* Zagreb, 1910.

Runciman, Sir J. C. S. *The Emperor Romanus Lecapenus.* Cambridge, 1929.
    A History of the First Bulgarian Empire. London, 1930.
    The Medieval Manichee. Cambridge, 1947.
    Byzantine Civilisation (4th ed.). London, 1954.

Ruprecht, A. *Die ausgehende Wikingerzeit (Palaestra 224).* Göttingen, 1958.

Bibliography

Russian Primary Chronicle: see Adrianova-Peretts.

Rybakov, B. A. *Drevnjaja Rus'*: *skazanija, byliny, letopisi*. Moscow, 1963.

Sadnik and Aitzetmüller, *Handwörterbuch zu den altkirchenslavischen Texten* [*SDH* 6]. Hague, 1955.

Sappok, G. *Die Anfänge des Bistums Posen* (*Deutschland und der Osten* 6). Leipzig, 1937.

Sas-Zaloziecky, W. *Die byzantinische Baukunst in den Balkanländern* (*Südosteuropäische Arbeiten* 46). Munich, 1955.

Saturník, Th. *Příspěvky k šíření byzantského práva u slovanů*. Prague, 1922.

Sawyer, P. H. *The Age of the Vikings*. London, 1962.

Schieffer, T. *Winfrid-Bonifatius und die christliche Grundlegung Europas*. Freiburg, 1954.

Schlesinger, W. *Kirchengeschichte Sachsens im Mittelalter*, vol. 1 (*Mitteldeutsche Forschungen* 27). Köln–Graz, 1962.

Schlumberger, G. *L'Epopée byzantine à la fin du dixième siècle*. Paris, 1896–1905.

Schmeidler, B. *Hamburg–Bremen und Nordost–Europa vom 9–11 Jahrhundert*. Leipzig, 1918.

Schmidinger, H. *Patriarch und Landesherr: die weltliche Herrschaft des Patriarchen von Aquileia*. Graz–Köln, 1954.

Schmidt, K. D. *Die Bekehrung der Germanen*. Göttingen, 1935–.

Schmidt, K. D. and Wolf, E. *Die Kirche in ihre Geschichte*. Göttingen, 1961–.

Schmitz, P. *Histoire de l'Ordre de S. Benoit*, vols. 1–2. Maredsous, 1942.

Schnürer, G. *Kirche und Kultur im Mittelalter*. Paderborn, 1924–9.

Schramm, P. E. *Kaiser, Rom und Renovatio: I. Teil–Studien*. Leipzig–Berlin, 1929.

Schreiber, G. *Stephan I der Heilige*. Paderborn, 1938.

Schubert, H. von. *Geschichte der christlichen Kirche im Frühmittelalter*. Tübingen, 1921; (2nd ed.) Hildesheim, 1962.

Schwartz, M. *Untersuchungen über das mährisch-slowakische Staatswesen des 9 Jhdts*. Munich, 1942.

Scriptores rerum hungaricarum, ed. E. Szentpétery (2 vols.) [*SRH*]. Budapest, 1937–8.

Sergheraert, G. *Syméon le Grand*. Paris, 1960.

Šetka, O. J. *Hrvatska kršćanska terminologia* (3 vols). Šibenik 1940, Makarska 1964–5.

Sherrard, P. *Constantinople: Iconography of a sacred city*. Oxford, 1965.

Šišić, F. *Priručnik izvora hrvatske historije*: *1/1—do god. 1107*. Zagreb, 1914. *Geschichte der Croaten*. Zagreb, 1917.

(ed.). *Letopis popa dukljanina*. Belgrade–Zagreb, 1928.

Skalová, H. *Topografická mapa území Obodriců a Veletů-Luticů ve světle místních jmen* (*Vznik a počátky Slovanů* 5). Prague, 1965.

Skok, P. *Dolazak Slovena na Mediteran*. Split, 1934.

Skrzypek, J. *Studia nad pierwotnym pograniczem polsko-ruskim w rejonie Wołynia i grodów czerwieńskich*. Warsaw, 1962.

Slijepčević, B. *Istorija srpske pravoslavne crkve*, vol. 1. Munich, 1962.

Bibliography

Slovenska Pismenost: 1050-godišnina na Kliment Ohridski. Ohrid, 1966.

Słownik starożytności słowiańskich [in progress]. Ossol., 1961–.

Smičiklas, T. (ed.). *Codex diplomaticus regni Croatiae, Dalmatiae et Slavoniae* [*CD*] (= *Diplomatički Zbornik Kraljevine Hrvatske, Dalmacije i Slavonije*). Zagreb, 1904–.

Smolitsch, I. *Russisches Mönchtum (Das östliche Christentum, N.F. 10/11).* Würzburg, 1953.

Smržík, S. *The Glagolitic or Roman-Slavonic Liturgy (Cyrillomethodiana 2).* Rome, 1959.

Snegarov, I. *Ohridskata patriarshija: nejnijat proizhod, granitsi i eparhii.* Sofia, 1919.

Sveti Kliment Ohridski. Sofia, 1927.

Duhovno-kulturni vrŭzki mezhdu Bŭlgarija i Rusija prez srednite vekove. Sofia, 1950.

Southern, R. W. *The Making of the Middle Ages.* London, 1953.

Spinka, M. *A History of Christianity in the Balkans.* Chicago, 1933.

Stadtmüller, G. *Geschichte Südosteuropas.* Munich, 1950.

Stanimirov, St. *Istorija na bŭlgarskata tsŭrkva* (3rd ed.). Sofia, 1925.

Stanislav, J. (ed.). *Ríša vel'komoravská* (2nd ed.). Prague, 1935.

Stankiewicz, E. and Worth, D. S. *A selected bibliography of Slavic linguistics (SPR 49).* Hague, 1966.

Stanojević, S. *Borba za samostalnost katoličke crkve u nemanjićskoj državi.* Belgrade, 1912.

Sveti Sava i nezavisimost srpske crkve. Belgrade, 1935.

Istorija srpskog naroda u srednjem veku: I—izvori i istoriografija; 1—o izvorima. Belgrade, 1937.

Stanojević, S. and Glumac, D. *Sv. Pismo u našim starim spomenicima.* Belgrade, 1932.

Stara srpska književnost: vol. 1 (ed. D. Pavlović). Novi Sad, 1966.

Starý, O. (ed.). *Československá architektura.* Prague, 1962.

Stender-Petersen, A. *Die Varägersage als Quelle der altrussischen Chronik.* Aarhus, 1934.

Varangica. Aarhus, 1953.

Stewart, C. *Serbian Legacy.* London, 1959.

Stojanović, L. *Stari srpski zapisi i natpisi.* Belgrade, 1902–5.

Stari srpski rodoslovi i letopisi. Sr. Karlovci, 1927.

Stare srpske povelje i pisma. Belgrade, 1929–34.

Stoob, H. (ed.). *Helmold von Bosau: Chronica Slavorum.* Berlin, 1963.

Strohal, R. *Hrvatska glagolska knjiga.* Zagreb, 1915.

Svatováclavský sborník. Prague, 1934–9.

Svetosavski Zbornik (2 vols.). Belgrade, 1936–9.

Szeftel, M. (ed.). *Documents de droit public relatifs à la Russie médiévale.* Brussels, 1963.

Szydłowski, T. *Pomniki architektury epoki piastowskiej we województwach krakowskiem i kieleckiem.* Cracow, 1928.

Szymański, W. *Kontakty handlowe wielkopolski w IX–XI wieku.* Poznńa. 1958,

Bibliography

Talbot Rice, D. *The Beginnings of Christian Art.* London, 1957.
The Art of the Byzantine era. London, 1963.
Taube, M. de. *Rome et la Russie avant l'invasion des Tatars.* Paris, 1947.
Teodorov-Balan, A. *Kiril i Metodi* (2 vols.). Sofia, 1920–34.
Theiner, A. (ed.). *Vetera monumenta historica Hungariam sacram illustrantia:*
    vol. 1—*1216–1352.* Rome, 1859–60.
Vetera monumenta Slavorum meridionalium historiam sacram illustrantia:
    vol. 1—*1198–1549.* Rome, 1863–.
Thietmar of Merseburg: *see* Trillmich, W.
Thomas of Split: *see* Rački, F.
Tikhomirov, M. *Krestjanskije i gorodskije vosstanija na Rusi XI–XIII vv.*
    Moscow, 1955.
Trillmich, W. (ed.). *Thietmar of Merseburg: Chronicle.* Berlin, n.d.
Trillmich, W. and Buchner, R. *Quellen des 9 und 11 Jahrhunderts zur Ge-*
    schichte der Hamburgischen Kirche und des Reiches. Darmstadt, 1961.
Trogrančić, F. *Letteratura medioevale degli Slavi meridionali.* Rome, 1950.
Trubetskoj, N. S. *Altkirchenslavische Grammatik.* Vienna, 1954.
Tschan, F. J. (ed.). *Helmold: Chronicle of the Slavs.* New York, 1935.
Adam of Bremen: History of the Archbishops of Hamburg-Bremen. New
    York, 1959.
Tunitski, N. L. *Svjaty Kliment.* Serg. Posad, 1913.
Tŭpkova-Zaimova, V. *Nashestvija i etnicheski promeni na Balkanite prez VI–*
    VII v. Sofia, 1966.
Turek, R. *Čechy na úsvitě dějin.* Prague, 1963.
Tymieniecki, K. *Polska w średniowieczu.* Warsaw, 1961.
Uhlirz, M. *Die älteste Lebensbeschreibung des heiligen Adalbert.* Göttingen, 1957.
Ullmann, W. *A History of Political Thought in the Middle Ages.* London, 1965.
Unbegaun, B. O.: *see Mana.*
Urbańczyk, S. *Religia pogańskich słowian.* Cracow, 1947.
Urbánek, R. *Legenda t. zv. Kristiána...a její autor.* Prague, 1947–8.
Vaillant, A. *Manuel du vieux-slave* (2 vols.). Paris, 1948.
Vajs, J. *Sborník staroslovanských literárních památek o sv. Václavu a sv.*
    Lidmile. Prague, 1929.
Rukověť hlaholské paleografie. Prague, 1932.
Valjavec, F. *Geschichte der deutschen Kulturbeziehungen zu Südosteuropa*
    (2nd ed.). Munich, 1953–8.
Vancsa, M. *Geschichte Nieder- und Oberösterreichs* (2 vols.). Gotha, 1905–27.
Vašica, J. *Literární památky epochy velkomoravské.* Prague, 1966.
Vasiljev, A. A. *Byzance et les Arabes* (French version of *Vizantija i araby,*
    SPb, 1900–2). Brussels, 1935–50.
History of the Byzantine Empire (2nd ed.) (Engl. tr.). Madison, 1958.
Vasmer, M. *Die Slaven in Griechenland.* Berlin, 1941.
Vavřínek, V. *Cirkevné misie v dějinách Velké Moravy.* Prague, 1963.
Vernadsky, G. *A History of Russia:* vol. 1—*Ancient Russia;* vol. 2—*Kievan*
    Russia. Yale, 1943–8.
The Origins of Russia. Oxford, 1959.

Bibliography

Vizantiski izvori za istoriju naroda Jugoslavije (ed. G. Ostrogorski): vol. 1—1955; vol. 2—1959; vol. 3—1966. Belgrade, 1955–.

Vladimirski Sbornik. Belgrade, 1938.

Vogt, A.: *see* Constantine Porphyrogennetos.

Voigt, H. G. *Adalbert von Prag.* Berlin, 1898.

Völker, K. *Kirchengeschichte Polens.* Berlin, 1930.

Vondrák, V. *O původu kijevských listů a pražských zlomků.* Prague, 1904.

Vrana, J. *L'Evangéliaire de Miroslav (SDH 25).* Hague, 1961.

Vries, J. de. *Altgermanische Religionsgeschichte* (2nd ed.). Berlin, 1956–7.

Vznik a počátky slovanů [in progress]. Prague, 1956–.

Walicki, M. (ed.). *Drzwi gnieźnieńskie* (3 vols.). Wrocław, 1956–9.

Warnke, C. *Die Anfänge des Fernhandels in Polen (Marburger Ostforschungen 22).* Würzburg, 1964.

Weingart, M. *Československý typ cirkevnej slovančiny.* Bratislava, 1949.

Weingart, M. and Kurz, J. *Texty ke studiu jazyka a písemnictví staroslověnského* (2nd ed.). Prague, 1949.

Wellesz, E. *A History of Byzantine Music and Hymnography* (2nd ed.). Oxford, 1961.

Wenskus, R. *Studien zur historisch-politischen Gedankenwelt Bruns von Querfurt.* Münster, 1956.

Widajewicz, J. *Studia nad relacją o Słowianach Ibrahima ibn Jakuba.* Cracow, 1946.

Państwo Wiślan. Cracow, 1947.

Polska i Niemcy w dobie panowania Mieszka I. Lublin, 1953.

Widmann, H. *Geschichte Salzburgs.* Gotha, 1907–14.

Widukind: *see* Hirsch, P.

Wienecke, E. *Untersuchungen zur Religion der Westslawen.* Leipzig, 1940.

Wijk, N. van. *Geschichte der altkirchenslavischen Sprache.* Berlin–Leipzig, 1931.

Winter, E. *Byzanz und Rom im Kampf um die Ukraine.* Leipzig, 1942.

Russland und das Papsttum, vol. 1. Berlin, 1960.

Wojciechowski, Z. *L'Etat polonais au Moyen-Age* (original Polish ed., 1945). Paris, 1949.

Woronczak, J., Ostrowska, E. and Feicht, H. *Bogurodzica.* Ossol., 1962.

Yanich and Hankey. *Lives of the Serbian saints.* London, 1921.

Yanin: *see* Janin.

Zakhoder, B. N. *Kaspijski svod svedenij o vostochnoj Evrope.* Moscow, 1962.

Zakythenos, D. A. Οἱ Σλάβοι ἐν Ἑλλάδι. Athens, 1945.

Ἡ βυζαντινὴ Ἑλλάς, 392–1204. Athens, 1965.

Zbornik kralja Tomislava. Zagreb, 1925.

Zernov, N. *Eastern Christendom.* London, 1961.

Zibermayr, I. *Noricum, Baiern und Oesterreich.* Horn, 1956.

Zimin, A. A. (ed.). *Russkaja pravda (Pamjatniki russkogo prava,* vol. 1). Moscow, 1952.

Zlatarski, V. N. *Istorija na bŭlgarskata dŭrzhava prez srednite vekove.* Sofia, 1918–40.

INDEX

Index

Index

Index

Index

Index

Index

Index